The Last Dance

The Last Dance

EIGHTH EDITION

Encountering Death and Dying

LYNNE ANN DeSPELDER

Cabrillo College

ALBERT LEE STRICKLAND

Higher Education

Boston   Burr Ridge, IL   Dubuque, IA   New York   San Francisco   St. Louis
Bangkok   Bogotá   Caracas   Kuala Lumpur   Lisbon   London   Madrid   Mexico City
Milan   Montreal   New Delhi   Santiago   Seoul   Singapore   Sydney   Taipei   Toronto

Higher Education

The Last Dance: Encountering Death and Dying, Eighth Edition

Published by McGraw-Hill, an imprint of The McGraw-Hill Companies, Inc., 1221 Avenue of the Americas, New York, NY 10020. Copyright © 2009, 2005, 2002, 1999, 1996, 1992, 1987, 1983 by Lynne Ann DeSpelder and Albert Lee Strickland. All rights reserved. No part of this publication may be reproduced or distributed in any form or by any means, or stored in a database or retrieval system, without the prior written consent of The McGraw-Hill Companies, Inc., including, but not limited to, in any network or other electronic storage or transmission, or broadcast for distance learning.

This book is printed on acid-free paper.

1 2 3 4 5 6 7 8 9 0 DOC/DOC 0 9 8

ISBN: 978-0-07-340546-9
MHID: 0-07-340546-9

Editor in Chief: *Michael Ryan*
Publisher: *Beth Mejia*
Executive Editor: *Michael Sugarman*
Executive Marketing Manager: *James Headley*
Editorial Coordinator: *Jillian Allison*
Production Editors: *April Wells-Hayes/Melissa Williams*
Cover Designer: *Ashley Bedell*
Interior Designer: *Jenny El-Shamy*
Media Project Manager: *Thomas Brierly*
Production Supervisor: *Randy Hurst*

This text was set in 10/12 New Baskerville by Thompson Type and printed on 45# New Era Matte Plus by R.R. Donnelley & Sons, Inc.

Cover art: Edvard Munch, *The Dance of Life.* 1889–1900. Oil on canvas. 49¼″ × 74¾″. National Gallery, Oslo.

Credits: The credits section for this book begins on page 627 and is considered an extension of the copyright page.

Library of Congress Cataloging-in-Publication Data
DeSpelder, Lynne Ann
   The last dance: encountering death and dying / Lynne Ann DeSpelder, Albert Lee Strickland—8th ed.
      p. cm.
   Includes bibliographical references and indexes.
   ISBN: 978-0-07-340546-9; ISBN: 0-07-340546-9 (alk. paper)
      1. Death—Psychological aspects. 2. Death—Social aspects. I. Strickland, Albert Lee. II. Title.
   BF789.D4 D53 2001
   155.9'37—dc21   2008344527

www.mhhe.com

Contents

CHAPTER 1

Attitudes Toward Death: A Climate of Change   5

CHAPTER 4

Death Systems: Mortality and Society　127

CHAPTER 5

Health Care: Patients, Staff, and Institutions   *167*

CHAPTER 6

End-of-Life Issues and Decisions

CHAPTER 7

Facing Death: Living with Life-Threatening Illness

CHAPTER 8

CHAPTER 9

Survivors: Understanding the Experience of Loss   *311*

CHAPTER 12

Suicide   *413*

CHAPTER 15

The Path Ahead: Personal and Social Choices   525

Preface

*T*he study of death—or thanatology, from the Greek *thanatos*, meaning "death"—is concerned with questions that are rooted at the core of our experience. Thus, the person who sets out to increase his or her knowledge of death and dying is embarking on an exploration that is partly a journey of personal discovery. In writing *The Last Dance: Encountering Death and Dying*, our goal is to offer a comprehensive and readable introduction to the study of death and dying, one that highlights the main issues and questions. This book embodies an approach to the study of death and dying that combines the intellectual and the emotional, the social and the psychological, the experiential and the scholarly.

The Last Dance provides a solid grounding in theory and research as well as in methods for applying what is learned to readers' own circumstances, personal and professional. It encourages readers to engage in a constructive process of self-discovery. The text is not an indoctrination to any one point of view, but an introduction to diverse points of view. It emphasizes the values of compassion, listening, and tolerance for the views of others. Readers may well form their own opinions, but, when they do, we hope it is only after considering other possibilities in a spirit of open-mindedness. Unbiased investigation leads to choices that might otherwise be neglected because of ignorance or prejudice.

While retaining all of the popular features of earlier editions, the eighth edition of *The Last Dance* reflects the ongoing evolution of death studies. Every chapter has been revised to enhance clarity of presentation and integrate the latest research, practices, and ideas. Accompanying this edition is a companion Web site of activities and resources to promote mastery of the material covered in the text itself.

The study of death is unavoidably multidisciplinary. Accordingly, contributions from medicine, the humanities, and the social sciences are all found here in their relevant contexts. Throughout the book, principles and concepts are made meaningful by use of examples and anecdotes. Boxed material, photographs, and other illustrative materials expand upon and provide counterpoint to the textual presentation. Specialized terms, when needed, are clearly defined. We urge readers to make use of these features.

For those who wish to pursue further study of particular topics, a list of recommended readings is provided at the end of each chapter, and citations given in the chapter notes provide guidance to additional sources and references, including pertinent selections in the companion reader to this text, *The Path Ahead: Readings in Death and Dying.* Thus, while the text serves as an introduction to a broad range of topics in death studies, readers are pointed to resources for investigating more deeply topics that evoke special interest.

In the book's first three chapters, we examine the influence of sociocultural forces on our understanding of death. We look at attitudes toward death, how we learn about death through processes of socialization, how historical and cultural factors shape our attitudes and practices relative to dying and death, what it means to live with an awareness of mortality, and death in a cosmopolitan society. These first three chapters provide a foundation for appreciating how specific issues in death, dying, and bereavement are dealt with in distinctive ways by different individuals, families, and social groups. In Chapter 3, we look not only at death in Western culture, but also in Native American, African, Mexican, Asian, and Celtic traditions. Throughout the text, attention is given to the importance of ethnic traditions in shaping our relationship with death in culturally diverse societies.

Chapter 4 focuses on "death systems," showing how matters of public policy affect our dealings with dying and death. Here you will find discussion of such topics as the response to disasters, medicolegal views of homicide and capital punishment, procedures for legally defining and making a determination of death, rules and customs regarding organ donation and transplantation, ways of classifying different modes of death into socially useful categories, how death notification is accomplished, the manner in which investigative duties are carried out by coroners and medical examiners, and the criteria that apply to performing autopsies. The chapter includes an instructive cross-cultural example describing how Japan has dealt with ethical, moral, and legal questions involving brain death and organ transplantation.

The changing nature of health care, especially care of the dying, is given detailed coverage in Chapter 5. Topics include the caregiver-patient relationship; care provided in hospices and palliative care, and at home; types of elder care; trauma and emergency care, as well as social support for dying patients and their families. Caregiver stress, as well as principles of "care for the caregiver," and a discussion of being with someone who is dying round out this chapter.

Issues and decisions pertaining to the end of life take the focus in Chapter 6. Some of these issues and decisions become important in the context of diagnosis and treatment—for example, informed consent. Other end-of-life issues and decisions tend to come to the fore when individuals face the more immediate prospect of dying. These include choices about withholding or withdrawing life-sustaining medical treatments, physician-assisted suicide, and euthanasia, as well as issues involving artificial nutrition and hydration.

Yet other issues involve matters that can be dealt with before the crisis of a life-limiting illness—for example, making a will, obtaining life insurance, and completing advance directives to express wishes about medical treatment in the event one becomes incapacitated. Some of these may be initiated early in life but not completed until after a person's death. These include the settling of an estate through the legal procedures of probate and the disbursement of proceeds from insurance and other death benefits to survivors.

Chapter 7 provides comprehensive coverage of how people live with a life-threatening illness. Attention is given to the psychological and social meanings associated with such illnesses and insights about the various ways individuals and families cope with "living/dying," from the time of initial diagnosis to the final stages of the dying trajectory. The chapter provides an overview of treatment options and issues, as well as complementary therapies and pain management.

The ceremonies and rites enacted by individuals and social groups after a death form the focus of Chapter 8. Such death rituals and customs create opportunities for expressing grief and integrating loss. The chapter examines the nature and function of "last rites," with particular attention paid to the history of mortuary services in the United States. Included is practical information about selecting among the available options for funeral services and body disposition.

Chapter 9 is devoted to an in-depth discussion of bereavement, grief, and mourning. Alternative models of grief are discussed and evaluated, with the recognition that "one size fits all" models are inadequate. A comprehensive understanding of the ways people experience and express grief, and of the variables that influence grief, results in an awareness that there are many methods for providing social support to the bereaved. Despite loss, bereavement can present opportunities for growth.

Making use of a life-span perspective, Chapters 10 and 11 deal with death-related issues associated with different stages of life, from childhood through old age. Chapter 10 includes discussion of situations involving children with life-threatening illness as well as children as survivors of a close death, such as the death of a parent or sibling. It provides guidelines for helping children cope with change and loss. Chapter 11 examines losses occurring in adulthood, such as the death of a child, parent, spouse, or close friend, as well as losses associated with aging.

Chapter 12 takes up the subject of suicide and examines various risk factors that have relevance at different stages of life. Additional topics discussed in this chapter include theories of suicide and suicidal behavior, types of suicide, suicide notes, the antecedents of suicidal behavior, and psychological autopsies. Suicide prevention, intervention, and postvention receives attention, and the chapter concludes with discussion about helping someone who is in a suicidal crisis.

Broadening the scope of death-related threats, Chapter 13 addresses a variety of topics crucial for gaining a comprehensive understanding of death and dying. These topics include risk-taking, accidents, violence, war, and emerging diseases, including AIDS, which continues to threaten the health of many people around the world. This chapter includes discussion of the threat of terrorism, including analysis of the attacks of September 11, 2001, and their aftermath.

Questions about the meaning of human mortality are at the forefront in the final two chapters of the book. Chapter 14 draws on a variety of religious and secular traditions, as well as accounts of near-death experiences, to present a wide-ranging survey of concepts and beliefs concerning immortality and the afterlife. Whether death is viewed as a "wall" or as a "door" can have important consequences for how we live our lives.

Chapter 15 emphasizes personal and social values that are enhanced through death education. Examples of new directions in thanatology are discussed, including bridging research and practice, clarifying the goals of death education, gaining an international perspective, and creating compassionate cities. Bringing together a host of topics covered in the text, the chapter presents food for thought about death in the future and stimulates readers to consider how a "good death" might be defined.

The Last Dance has been reviewed by professors in a broad range of academic disciplines. Their suggestions have helped to make this text an outstanding teaching tool. Formal reviews have been provided by

Susan Adams, University of Central Arkansas
Joel R. Ambelang, Concordia University, Wisconsin
Lisa Angermeier, Indiana University at Bloomington
Thomas Attig, Bowling Green State University
Ronald K. Barrett, Loyola Marymount University, Los Angeles
Michael Beechem, University of West Florida, Pensacola
Laura Billings, Southwestern Illinois College
John B. Bond, University of Manitoba
Sandor B. Brent, Wayne State University
Tom Bruce, Sacramento City College
Richard Cording, Sam Houston State University
Charles A. Corr, Southern Illinois University
Gerry R. Cox, Fort Hays State University
Steven A. Dennis, Utah State University
Kenneth J. Doka, College of New Rochelle
Stephen J. Fleming, York University, Toronto
Audrey K. Gordon, Oakton Community College
Judy Green, Walsh University, Ohio
Debra Bence Grow, Pennsylvania State University
John Harvey, Western Illinois University
Russell G. Henke, Towson State University
David D. Karnos, Eastern Montana College
Linda C. Kinrade, California State University, Hayward
Dennis Klass, Webster University
Anthony Lenzer, University of Hawaii at Manoa

Daniel Leviton, University of Maryland
Paul C. Luken, Arizona State University West, Phoenix
J. Davis Mannino, Santa Rosa Junior College
Coleman C. Markham, Barton College, North Carolina
Wendy Martyna, University of California, Santa Cruz
Samuel J. Marwit, University of Missouri
Debbie Mattison, University of Michigan School of Social Work
Marsha McGee, Northeast Louisiana University
Walter L. Moore, Florida State University, Tallahassee
Lachelle Norris, Tennessee Tech University
Vincent M. Rolletta, Erie Community College
Lee Ross, Frostburg State University, Maryland
Rita S. Santanello, Belleville Area Community College, Illinois
Thomas W. Satre, Sam Houston State University
Edwin S. Shneidman, University of California, Los Angeles
Judith M. Stillion, Western Carolina University
Gordon Thornton, Indiana University of Pennsylvania
Jeffrey S. Turner, Mitchell College
Mary Warner, Northern State University, South Dakota
Hannelore Wass, University of Florida, Gainesville
Jack Borden Watson, Stephen F. Austin State University,
Nacogdoches, Texas
John B. Williamson, Boston College
C. Ray Wingrove, University of Richmond
Robert Wrenn, University of Arizona, Tucson
Joseph M. Yonder, Villa Maria College of Buffalo
Margaret H. Young, Washington State University
Andrew Scott Ziner, University of North Dakota

In addition to those named, many other colleagues and students have generously shared ideas for enhancing and improving the text. We thank all who have offered helpful suggestions about the book through its successive incarnations.

We also thank our collaborators on various editions of the *Instructor's Guide*, including Barbara Jade Sironen, Patrick Vernon Dean, Robert James Baugher, and Carol Fern Berns. Our thanks to Matt and Kelley Strickland for their work on the test bank, as well as for help with the Online Learning Center at www.mhhe.com/despelder8. Alma Bell, of Thompson Type, deserves thanks for uncommonly error-free typesetting. In addition, we are grateful to staff members at many museums, libraries, and governmental institutions, who have assisted us in our research and in gathering both text and art resources over the years.

Over the course of eight editions of *The Last Dance,* we have had the great pleasure of working with many talented people who exemplify excellence in publishing. At McGraw-Hill, among the many individuals who helped bring this book to press, we want to thank Mike Sugarman, executive editor in psychology, and editorial coordinators Kate Russillo and Jillian Allison; Linda Toy, vice-president of editing, design, and production for humanities, social sciences, and languages, along with Melissa Williams and the other members of her exceptionally talented staff in San Francisco; and April Wells-Hayes of Fairplay Publishing Service, who managed the production of this book with good cheer and consummate professionalism.

To all whose help was instrumental in bringing this edition of *The Last Dance* to readers, our heartfelt thanks.

L. A. D.
A. L. S.

P R O L O G U E

I don't know how much time I have left. I've spent my life dispensing salves and purgatives, potions and incantations—miracles of nature (though I admit that some were pure medicine-show snake oil). Actually, half the time all I offered was just plain common sense. Over the years, every kind of suffering person has made his or her way here. Some had broken limbs or broken bodies . . . or hearts. Often their sorrow was an ailing son or daughter. It was always so hard when they'd lose a child. I never did get used to that. And then there were the young lovers. Obtaining their heart's desire was so important to them. I had to smile. I always made them sweat and beg for their handful of bark, and for those willful tortures I'll probably go to hell . . . if there is one. My God, how long has it been since I had those feelings myself? The fever, the lump in the throat, the yearning. I can't remember. A long time . . . maybe never. Well, there have been other passions for me. There's my dusty legion of jars. Each one holds its little secret. Barks, roots, soils, leaves, flowers, mushrooms, bugs—magic dust, every bit of it. There's my book—my "rudder," a ship's pilot would call it. That's a good name for it. Every salve, every purgative . . . they're all in there. (Everything, that is, except my stained beard, scraggly hair, and flowing robes—they'll have to figure those out on their own.) And then there's my walking stick (always faithful) . . . and the ballerina. And ten thousand mornings, ten thousand afternoons, ten thousand nights. And the stars, Oh, I have had my loves.

It hurts to move. My shelf and jars seem so far away, though I know that if I tried I could reach them. But no. It's enough and it's time . . . almost. I hope he makes it back in time. He burst through my door only two days ago. A young man, well spoken. Tears were streaming down his face. He looked so bent and beaten that I could not refuse him. He told me that his wife had died over a month ago and that he had been incon-solable since.

"Please help me," he pleaded, "or kill me." He covered his face with his hands. "Perhaps they're the same thing. I don't know anymore."

I let him cry a while so I could watch him, gauge him. When at last he looked up, with my good hand I motioned him to take a seat. Then, between coughing fits, I went to work. "Do you see that toy there?" I said. "The little ballerina . . . yes, that's it. Pick it up."

"Pick it up?"

"It won't bite. Pick it up." (He probably thought it was a trick—that's what they expect.) He grasped it carefully, with one hand, then wiped his eyes with the other. "That's better," I continued. "That's just a toy to you. You don't know what meaning to put to it yet. So I want you to look at that ballerina."

He was hesitant, but I waited, stubbornly, until he looked down and fixed his attention on the little toy dancer. I went on: "I knew a young man once who was very handsome—always had been. He not only turned every head, he was strong and smart, and his family was wealthy. His main concern each day was which girl he should court that evening. He had planned that after several seasons of playing at love he would marry a beautiful girl, have beautiful children, and settle down to spend the money his father had promised him. And he had plans for that money. He had already purchased the land he wanted to live on and was having built there the biggest house in the area. He was going to raise and race horses, I think. One morning he got on his favorite horse and went for a ride. He whipped that horse into a gallop; it stepped in a hole and threw him. The young man broke his neck, and died." I stared at my guest and waited.

"That's a tragedy," he finally croaked.

"For whom? For those he left behind, perhaps. But was it for him? When he opened his eyes that morning, he didn't know he would die that day. He had no intention of dying for another sixty years—if then. None of us does." The young man looked con-fused. "His mistake was that he forgot that he could die that day."

"That's a morbid thought," he replied, and he looked as though he had just smelled something putrid.

"Is it? A moment ago you asked me to end your grieving by ending your own life. Suppose I oblige?" I stared at him for a few moments with my most practiced penetrating glare. "Suppose I did agree to kill you. How would you spend your last few minutes?"

He was still a little wary of me, but relieved that I seemed to be suggesting a hypo-thetical situation, rather than a serious course of action. He considered the possibilities for a while, then straightened in his chair: "Well, I guess I would step outside and take a last, best look at the sky, the clouds, the trees."

"Suppose you lived that way all the time?" He stared at me, then looked down at his hands, searching them. "That young man I told you about . . . perhaps the tragedy for him was not that he died, but that he failed to use the eventual certainty of his death to make him live! Did he woo each of those ladies as though it might be his last romance? Did he build that house as though it might be his last creation? Did he ride that horse as though it would be his last ride? I don't know; I hope so." My young guest nodded, but he was still sad. I pointed to the toy ballerina he was holding. "That was given to me by a young lady who understood these things."

He looked at the figure closely. "Is she a dancer?"

"Yes, she is, and she is dead." The young man looked up, once again off balance. "She has been dead for, oh, a very long time." After all these years, a tear fell onto my cheek. I let it go. "She was many things. A child, a woman, a cook and a gardener, a friend, lover, daughter. . . . But what she really was—who she was—was a dancer. When she was dying, she gave that doll to me, smiled, and whispered, 'At the moment of my death, I will take all of my dancing and put it in here, so my dancing can live on.' "

Tears welled in my guest's eyes.

"I can help you," I said, "but first there is something that you must do." He became very attentive. "Go to town and knock on the door of the first house you come to. Ask the people inside if their family has ever been touched by death. If so, go to the next house. When you find a family that has not been touched by death, bring them to me. Do you understand?" He nodded, and I sighed: "I'm tired now."

He got up, set the ballerina back on the table, and started for the door. I stopped him. "Young man!" He faced me from the doorway. "Come back as soon as you can."

David Gordon

In a Spanish village, neighbors and relatives peer through the doorway upon the deathbed scene of a villager.

CHAPTER I

Attitudes Toward Death: A Climate of Change

Dead. Dead end. Dead center. Dead heat. Dead drunk. Deadwood. Deadbeat. Dead reckoning. Dead on. Dead against. Dead stop. Deadlock. Deadpan. Dead ahead.

Take a look at the connotations of the word "dead" in the English language. Are they positive or negative? There is no place to go when you get to a "dead end," and there are usually dire consequences when you miss a "deadline." In contrast, however, "dead reckoning" gives us direction to a place where we are going.

Perhaps this bit of linguistic exploration points up a paradox involved in the study of death and dying. How is our social world, our culture, set up to deal with death and the dead? Do we, consciously or unconsciously, relate to death as something to avoid? Or does death capture our attention as a defining moment in our lives, a place where we all end up?

Of all human experiences, none is more overwhelming in its implications than death. Yet, death often remains a shadowy figure whose presence is only vaguely acknowledged. We tend to relegate death to the periphery of our lives, as if it can be kept out of sight, out of mind.[1] Death may be like a mysterious stranger at a costume ball, whose mask conceals the face beneath. Perhaps the disguise is more terrifying than the reality, yet how can we know unless we risk uncovering the face hidden behind the mask? Learning about death and dying helps us lift the mask and encounter death in ways that are meaningful for our own lives. As

Mexican poet and social philosopher Octavio Paz says, "A civilization that denies death ends by denying life."[2]

A first step toward gaining new choices about death is to recognize that avoiding thinking about it estranges us from an integral aspect of human life. Where death is concerned, the adage "What you don't know won't hurt you" is false.

Expressions of Attitudes Toward Death

Direct, firsthand experience with death is rare for most people, yet death still has a significant place in our social and cultural worlds. Attitudes held by individuals in a given society are revealed through the manner in which death is portrayed by the mass media and in the language people use when talking about death, as well as in music, literature, the visual arts, and even in the jokes and other forms of humor people employ in response to matters involving death. As you read about some of the ways attitudes toward death are expressed, notice how these varied expressions reveal thoughts and feelings about death, both individually and culturally.

Mass Media

Modern communication technology makes us all instantaneous survivors as news of disaster, terrorism, war, and political assassination is flashed around the world. Stunned viewers watch in disbelief as the terrible event unfolds. When situations involve a perceived threat, people turn to the mass media as sources of information. Because the vicarious experiences filtered through the mass media significantly influence our attitudes, it is worth asking, What do these secondhand sources tell us about death and dying?

In the News

When you are reading the daily newspaper or an online news source, what kinds of encounters with death vie for your attention? Scanning the day's news, you are likely to find an assortment of accidents, murders, suicides, and disasters involving sudden, violent deaths. A jetliner crashes, and the news is announced with banner headlines. Here you see a story describing how a family perished when trapped inside their burning home; in another, a family's vacation comes to an untimely end due to a fatal collision on the interstate.

Then there are the deaths of the famous, which are likely to be announced on the front pages, as well as via feature-length *obituaries*.[3] Prefaced by headlines and set in the larger type used for feature stories, obituaries send a message about the newsworthiness that editors attribute to the deaths of famous people. In fact, news organizations maintain files of pending obituaries for individuals whose deaths will be newsworthy, and these obituaries are updated periodically so that they are ready for publication or broadcast when the occasion demands.

In contrast, the death of the average Joe or Jill is usually made known by *death notices*—brief, standardized statements, printed in small type and listed

Relative News Values

alphabetically in a column of vital statistics "as uniform as a row of tiny grave plots."[4] The death of a neighbor or colleague is not likely to be reported with the emphasis afforded the famous. Ordinary deaths—the kind most of us will experience—are usually ignored or mentioned only in routine fashion. The spectacular obscures the ordinary. Obituaries for "ordinary Joes" may be experiencing a revival among some newspapers, however, as "egalitarian obits" try to "nail down quickly what it is we're losing when a particular person dies."[5]

Whether routine or extraordinary, our encounters with death in the news media influence the way we think about and respond to death. News reports may have less to do with the *event* than with how that event is *perceived*. This point is illustrated by Jack Lule in his description of how black activist Huey Newton's death was reported in newspapers across the country.[6] As cofounder of the Black Panther Party, Newton had a public career spanning two decades, yet most reports focused on the violent nature of Newton's demise while ignoring other aspects of his life and, indeed, the tragic nature of his death. The implicit message seemed to be "He who lives by the sword dies by the sword."

A very different perception was communicated in reports of the explosion of the space shuttle *Challenger* shortly after launch and of the reentry failure of the shuttle *Columbia.* These events were portrayed as tragedies affecting the whole country, evoking a sense of shared grief. As in the aftermath of the terrorist attack of September 11, 2001, television was likened to a national hearth around which Americans symbolically gathered to collectively work through their shock and grief.

Whether television is best characterized as a national hearth or as simply another household appliance, people look to the media not only for information about events but also for clues about their meaning. This can present problems in determining what is appropriate to cover in stories that involve death and survivors' grief. The distinction between *public* event and *private* loss sometimes blurs.

When a Canadian newspaper published a photograph of a distraught mother as she learned of her daughter's fatal injuries in an accident, many readers expressed outrage, characterizing the photograph as "a blatant example of morbid ludicrousness" and "the highest order of poor taste and insensitivity."[7] The mother, interestingly enough, did not share these feelings. Seeing the published photo, she said, helped her comprehend what had happened. People who are bereaved by sudden, unexpected death typically want to obtain details to help them reconstruct the events surrounding the death, as an aid in coping with the reality of their loss. So, was the newspaper right to publish the photo? Or were outraged readers correctly defending the rights of a grief-stricken mother, who appeared to have been victimized by an intrusive press? Or, yet again, did such volatile emotion result from the readers' own uncomfortable feelings about death? As this example suggests, people sometimes ascribe emotions to the grief-stricken that are not actually present.

Even so, media coverage of horrific deaths sometimes leads to "revictimization" or "second trauma" after the initial trauma of the event itself. Reporters may capture the experience of a tragedy at the expense of victims. The journalistic stance, "If it bleeds, it leads," can set priorities. (To be fair, this stance is a journalistic response to the human tendency toward voyeurism—our desire to have a close-up view of what's going on in other people's lives, a trait apparently shared with our primate cousins.[8] Characterizing tragic events as "defining moments" plays to a human yearning to escape rather humdrum lives and feel that we are living in extraordinary times.)

In recent years, the Internet not only increases the speed at which the news is reported, it also allows one to follow along with online updates from international news agencies and comments from blogs giving further details and opinion.[9]

An important question is whether the media help us explore the meaning of death or merely seek to grab our attention with sensationalistic news flashes. Robert Fulton and Greg Owen comment that the media often "submerge the human meaning of death while depersonalizing the event further by sandwiching actual reports of loss of life between commercials or other mundane items."[10] News of a bus crash or mine disaster is interposed between reports about the stock market or factory layoffs. The grief experienced by survivors or the disruption of their lives is generally given little attention.

Deaths from car accidents, cancer, and heart disease don't seem to interest us as much as deaths from plane crashes, roller-coaster mishaps, or mountain lion attacks; only bizarre or dramatic exits grab our attention. Although
the odds of dying from a heart attack are about one in five, we seem more fascinated by death from bee stings (1 in 56,780), lightning (1 in 79,746), or
fireworks (1 in 340,733).[11] Think about your own experiences regarding
deaths reported in the media. How accurately do such reports resemble the
losses we experience in our own lives?

Media analyst George Gerbner observes that depictions of death in the
mass media are often embedded in a structure of violence that conveys "a
heightened sense of danger, insecurity, and mistrust."[12] Such depictions reflect what Gerbner and his colleagues have called a "mean world" syndrome,
in which the symbolic use of death contributes to an "irrational dread of dying
and thus to diminished vitality and self-direction in life." The suggestion that
we live in a "mean world" is reinforced "as news media seek to attract and
hold audiences [with] stories that depict worsening trends and threats."[13]
There is general agreement among media analysts that, in recent years, a "discourse of fear" has been increasingly evident in the mass media.[14]

Entertaining Death

With an average of 2.5 television sets in American households, television's
influence on our lives is well established.[15] Far from being ignored, death is a
central theme of much television programming. Besides its appearance in
movies of the week and on crime and adventure series, death is a staple of
newscasts (typically, several stories involving death are featured in each broadcast), nature programs (death in the animal kingdom), children's cartoons
(caricatures of death), soap operas (which seem always to have some character dying), sports (with descriptions such as "the ball is dead" and "the other
team is killing them"), and religious programs (with theological and anec-
dotal mention of death). Yet these diverse images seldom add to our understanding of death itself. Few programs deal with such real-life topics as how
people cope with a loved one's death or confront their own dying. This relative lack of stories that include themes dealing with death, dying, and bereavement in positive ways has been characterized by Frederic Tate as "an
impoverishment of death symbolism" in the entertainment media.[16]

Turning to programming directed toward children, recall Saturday morning cartoon depictions of death. Daffy Duck is pressed to a thin sheet by a
steamroller, only to pop up again a moment later. Elmer Fudd aims his shot-
gun at Bugs Bunny, pulls the trigger, bang! Bugs, unmarked by the rifle blast,
clutches his throat, spins around several times, and mutters, "It's all getting
dark now, Elmer . . . I'm going. . . ." Bugs falls to the ground, both feet still in
the air. As his eyes close, his feet finally hit the dirt. But wait! Now Bugs pops
up, good as new. Reversible death!

Consider the western, which mutes the reality of death by describing the
bad guy as "kicking the bucket"—relegated, no doubt, to Boot Hill at the edge
of town, where the deceased "pushes up daisies." The camera pans from the

dying person's face to a close-up of hands twitching—then all movement ceases as the person's breathing fades away in perfect harmony with the musical score. Or, more likely, the death is violent: the cowboy gunfight at the OK Corral, high noon. The gent with the slower draw is hit, reels, falls, his body convulsing into cold silence. (You may also recall similar scenes set in an imagined future in the *Terminator* films.)

People who have been present as a person dies describe a very different picture. Many recall the gurgling, gasping sounds as the last breath rattles through the throat; the changes in body color as flesh tones tinge blue; the feeling of a once warm and flexible body growing cold and flaccid. Surprised by the reality, they say, "Death is not at all what I thought it would be like; it doesn't look or sound or feel like anything I see on television or in movies!"

When told of his grandfather's death, one modern seven-year-old asked, "Who did it to him?" Death is generally portrayed on television or in movies as coming from outside, often violently, reinforcing the notion that dying is something that *happens to* us, rather than something we *do*. Death is an accidental rather than a natural process. As our firsthand *experiences* of death and violence have diminished, *representations* of death and violence in the media have increased in sensationalism.[17]

Thrillers featuring extreme violence are a profitable genre for moviemakers. The road to more "blood and gore" in popular films was paved in part by the success of classic "slasher" films like *Halloween* (1978), *Friday the 13th* (1980), and *Nightmare on Elm Street* (1984), which included point-of-view shots from the killer's perspective. In traditional horror films, the audience usually views the action through the eyes of the victim and thus identifies with his or her fate. In slasher films, however, viewers are asked to identify with the attacker. (A similar form of identification can be found in violent video games.) The apparently universal appeal of depictions of violence in movies and other media suggests that residual tendencies from our evolutionary background may attract human beings to "exhibitions of brutality and terror."[18]

Unrealistic portrayals of violent death fail to show the real harm to victims, their pain, or appropriate punishment for perpetrators. As a result, they may cause viewers to be less sensitive to both real violence and its victims, increase unwarranted fears of becoming a victim, and contribute to aggressive behavior.[19]

To be fair, films and television programs do at times focus more responsibly and realistically on important topics involving dying, death, and bereavement, as in the film *WIT,* which tells the story of a college professor who discovers she has advanced ovarian cancer and only a short time to live, or *World Trade Center* and *United 93*, which dealt with the catastrophe of September 11, 2001. Another example was the television series *On Our Own Terms,* hosted by Bill Moyers, which examined end-of-life care. Featuring experts in palliative medicine and hospice care, the series opened a window into the experiences of terminally ill patients and emphasized the importance of talking about issues related to dying and death. Moyers said, "I realized that each day of filming was one day closer to my own death," and "Looking at dying taught me about living."

Lessons about living with loss were also central to the story line of *The Son's Room [La Stanza del Figlio]*, a film written and directed by Italian filmmaker Nanni Moretti, which tells the story of a family's grief after the teenage son dies in a diving accident. In an affecting and accurate manner, the film depicts the varied emotions that can be present in coping with a senseless tragedy, with family members retreating into their own private corners of grief before eventually arriving at a shared recognition that life goes on despite loss. Moretti told an interviewer: "These characters cannot forget what happened, they don't want to forget what happened, but, in the end, something starts to change. Their lives will not be the same. But maybe they have found the means within themselves to turn grief into something else."[20] As one critic observed, the film stands as a reminder that, while loss is inevitable, it need not be ruinous.[21] Movies often engage our psychological faculties in profound and unique ways.[22] In thinking about the films and television programs you've watched recently, what are your observations about the ratio of positive and negative images of dying and death?

Language

Listen to the language people use when talking about dying or death, and you are likely to discover that it is often indirect. The words *dead* and *dying* tend to be avoided; instead, loved ones "pass away," embalming is "preparation," the deceased is "laid to rest," burial becomes "interment," the corpse is "remains," the tombstone is a "monument," and the undertaker is transformed into a "funeral director." Such euphemisms—substitutions of indirect or vague words and phrases for ones considered harsh or blunt—tend to suggest a well-choreographed production surrounding the dead and may be used to keep death at arm's length by masking its reality. Hannelore Wass, a pioneering death educator, notes that euphemisms substituting for plain-spoken "D" words even turn up in the language of death and dying experts as terminal care becomes "palliative care" and dying patients are described as "life-threatened."[23] Death may be described as "a negative patient-care outcome" and an airline crash as an "involuntary conversion of a 727."[24] Careful listeners will notice that euphemisms, metaphors, and slang comprise a large part of "death talk" (see Table 1-1).

Euphemisms devalue and depersonalize death when plain talk about death is subverted by a lexicon of substitutions—for example, when individuals killed in battle are described in terms of "body counts" or civilian deaths are termed "collateral damage." Used in this way, euphemisms mask accurate descriptions of the horror of death in war.

The use of euphemism and metaphor does not always imply an impulse to deny the reality of death or avoid talking about it, however. These linguistic devices also can be employed to communicate subtler or deeper meanings than those associated with plainer speech. For example, terms like "passing"

TABLE 1-1   *Death Talk: Metaphors, Euphemisms, and Slang*

Passed on	Gathered home
Croaked	Taking the dirt nap
Kicked the bucket	On the other side
Gone to heaven	God took him/her
Gone home	Asleep in Christ
Expired	Departed
Breathed the last	Transcended
Succumbed	Bought the farm
Left us	With the angels
Went to his/her eternal reward	Feeling no pain
Lost	Offed himself/herself
Met his/her Maker	His/her time was up
Wasted	Cashed in
Checked out	Crossed over Jordan
Eternal rest	Perished
Laid to rest	Ate it
Pushing up daisies	Was done in
Called home	Translated into glory
Was a goner	Returned to dust
Came to an end	Subject just fataled
Bit the dust	In the arms of the Father
Annihilated	Gave it up
Liquidated	It was curtains
Terminated	A long sleep
Gave up the ghost	On the heavenly shores
Didn't make it	Out of his/her misery
Rubbed out	Ended it all
Snuffed	Angels carried him/her away
Six feet under	Resting in peace
Passing	Changed form
Found everlasting peace	Dropped the body
Went to a new life	Returned to the source
In the great beyond	That was all she wrote
No longer with us	Passed away

or "passing on" may convey an understanding of death as a spiritual transition, especially among members of some religious and ethnic traditions.

Sympathy cards represent a way for people to express condolences to the bereaved without directly mentioning death.[25] Some cards refer to death metaphorically, as in sentiments like "What is death but a long sleep?" while others apparently deny it in verses like "He is not dead, he is just away." Images of sunsets and flowers are used to create an impression of peace, quiet, and perhaps a return to nature. The fact of bereavement, losing a loved one by death, is generally mentioned within the context of memories or the healing process of time. You may find it interesting to check the greeting-card rack to see if you can find a card that plainly uses the word "dead" or "death." By acknowledging loss in a gentle fashion, sympathy cards are intended to comfort the bereaved.

After someone dies, our conversations about that person usually move from present tense to past tense: "He *was* fond of music," "She *was* a leader in her field." Using this form of speech, which grammarians term the *indicative voice,* is a way of acknowledging the reality of the death, but it tends to distance us from the dead. One way to continue to include the "voice" of the deceased in present circumstances lies in the use of the *subjunctive,* which has been described as the mode of "as if," of what "might be" or "could have been." It is a "zone of possibility," rather than certainty.[26] We hear examples of this when people say things like, "He would have been proud of you" or "She would have enjoyed this gathering tonight."

Language usage can also tell us something about the intensity and immediacy of a person's close encounter with death in the form of "danger of death" narratives—stories about close calls with death. In such stories, a tense shift typically occurs when the narrator reaches the crucial point in his or her story, the point when death seems imminent and unavoidable. Consider the following example: A man who had experienced a frightening incident some years earlier while driving in a snowstorm began telling his story in the past tense as he described the circumstances. As he came to the point when his car went out of control on an icy curve and began to slide into the opposing lane of traffic, however, he abruptly switched to the present tense, as if he were *reliving* the experience of watching an oncoming car heading straight for him and believing in that moment that he was about to die.[27]

Word choices may also reflect changes in how a death event is experienced at different times. For example, after a disaster occurs, as the focus of rescue efforts changes, so does the language used to describe the work of emergency personnel and search-and-rescue teams. As hours stretch into days, *rescue* work becomes *recovery* work.

Look again at the words and phrases used in death talk (see Table 1-1). Notice how language offers clues about the manner of death and a speaker's attitude toward the death. Consider, for instance, the difference between "passed away" and "passed on." Subtle distinctions may reflect different attitudes, sometimes involving cultural frameworks. Paying attention to the metaphors, euphemisms, slang, and other linguistic devices people use when talking about death is a way to appreciate the variety and range of attitudes toward dying and death.

Music

Themes of loss and death are heard in all musical styles (see Table 1-2).[28] For example, the lyrics of Elvis Presley's early hit, "Heartbreak Hotel," reportedly were inspired by a suicide note that contained the phrase "I walk the lonely street." In fact, it has been suggested that death imagery in rock music helped break the taboo against public mention of death. Support for this thesis is found in surveys of Top 40 songs.[29] The branch of heavy metal music

TABLE 1-2 *Death Themes in Contemporary Popular Music*

Performer	Song	Theme
Tori Amos	Little Earthquakes	Multiple losses
Beatles	Eleanor Rigby	Aging and loss
Boyz II Men	Say Goodbye to Yesterday	Loss and grief
Garth Brooks	One Night a Day	Coping with grief
Jackson Browne	For a Dancer	Eulogy
Johnny Cash	The Man Comes Around	Death and Judgment Day
Eric Clapton	Tears in Heaven	Death of young son
Elvis Costello	Waiting for the End of the World	Threat of death
Joe Diffie	Almost Home	Anticipating father's death
Dion	Abraham, Martin, and John	Political assassination
Doors	The End	Murder
Bob Dylan	Knockin' on Heaven's Door	Last words / Death scene
Grateful Dead	Black Peter	Social support in dying
Jimi Hendrix	Mother Earth	Inevitability of death
Indigo Girls	Pushing the Needle Too Far	Drug-related death
Elton John	Candle in the Wind	Death of Marilyn Monroe
The Judds	Guardian Angels	Ancestors
Patty Loveless	How Can I Help You to Say Goodbye?	A mother's dying
Madonna	Promise to Try	Mother's death
Metallica	Fight Fire with Fire	Nuclear catastrophe
Mike and the Mechanics	The Living Years	Father's death
Morrissey	Angel, Angel, Down We Go	Suicide intervention
Holly Near	The Letter	Friend dying of AIDS
Sinead O'Connor	I Am Stretched on Your Grave	Mourning behavior
Oingo Boingo	No One Lives Forever	Facing death stoically
Pink Floyd	Dogs of War	War-related deaths
The Police	Murder by Numbers	Political killings
Elvis Presley	In the Ghetto	Violent death and grief
Queen	Another One Bites the Dust	Violent death
Lou Reed	Sword of Damocles	Coping with terminal illness
Henry Rollins	Drive-by Shooting	Satire on death by random violence
Carly Simon	Life Is Eternal	Desire for immortality
Snoop Doggy Dogg	Murder Was the Case	Urban homicide and justice system
Bruce Springsteen	Streets of Philadelphia	Dying of AIDS
James Taylor	Fire and Rain	Death of a friend
Stevie Wonder	My Love Is with You	Violent death of a child
Warren Zevon	My Ride's Here	Arrival of hearse and death

known as death metal is defined partly by its lyrics conveying striking images of homicide, catastrophic destruction, and suicide, performed by bands with names like Morbid Angel, Napalm Death, Carcass, and Entombed. Themes involving dying and death are also commonplace in rap and hip-hop, with examples like Coolio's description of a "Gangsta's Paradise" and Puff Daddy's grief over a close friend's death in "I'll be Missing You."

The tragedy of the September 11, 2001, terrorist attacks led musicians to respond with songs like Alan Jackson's "Where Were You (When the World Stopped Turning)" and Neil Young's "Let's Roll," inspired by the words of a passenger on Flight 93, which crashed in the Pennsylvania countryside, as well as Bruce Springsteen's "My City of Ruins," a song composed earlier about the artist's hometown but which poignantly related to the smoldering Twin Towers of the World Trade Center in New York City. Imagery of ash, rubble, and nightmare was common in religious hymns written after September 11, and many of these hymns began with the word "when," which grounded the text in a moment in time.[30]

Murder, mayhem, and misery have long been staples of American music. In folk music, for example, ballads describe premonitions of death, deathbed scenes, last wishes of the dying, the sorrow and grief of mourners, and expectations about the afterlife. Themes of suicide and murder are also common, especially when they combine tales of love and death. Consider the themes in such songs as "Where Have All the Flowers Gone?" (war), "Long Black Veil" (mourning), "Casey Jones" (accidental death), and "John Henry" (occupational hazards). Some songs glorify outlaws and other "bad guys," as in "The Ballad of Jesse James," a musical genre also found in Mexican popular culture in the form of "narcocorridos," narrative songs or *corridos* that describe the lives and careers of smugglers and drug lords.[31]

In American blues music, we find themes involving loss and longing, trials and tribulations, separations and death. In "See That My Grave Is Kept Clean," Blind Lemon Jefferson expresses the desire to be remembered after death. In "I Feel Like Going Home," Muddy Waters tells us that death sometimes brings relief. Other examples include Bessie Smith's "Nobody Knows You When You're Down and Out" (economic reversal), T-Bone Walker's "Call It Stormy Monday" (lost love), John Mayall's "The Death of J. B. Lenoir" (death of a friend in a car accident), and Otis Spann's "The Blues Never Die" (consolation in loss). As Edward Hirsch notes, the blues express "a deep stoic grief and despair, a dark mood of lamentation, but also a wry and ribald humor."[32]

Sometimes characterized as the flip side of the blues, gospel music expresses many images of loss and grief. Examples include "Will the Circle Be Unbroken" (death of family members), "Oh, Mary Don't You Weep" (mourning), "Known Only to Him" (facing one's own death), "When the Saints Go Marching In" (afterlife), "If I Could Hear My Mother Pray Again" (parent's death), and "Precious Memories" (adjustment to loss and sustaining bonds with the deceased).

Turning to classical music, death themes are heard in both religious and secular compositions. Leonard Bernstein's Symphony No. 3 (Kaddish) is based on the Jewish prayer for the dead. The Requiem Mass (Mass for the Dead) has attracted composers like Mozart, Berlioz, and Verdi, among others. One section of the Requiem Mass, the *Dies Irae* ("Day of Wrath"), is a musical symbol for death in works by many composers. In Berlioz's *Symphonie Fantastique* (1830), this theme is heard, first following an ominous tolling of bells and then, as the music reaches its climax, in counterpoint to the frenzied dancing of witches at a *sabbat*. Berlioz's *Symphonie* tells the story of a young musician who, spurned by his beloved, attempts suicide with an overdose of opium. In a narcotic coma, he experiences fantastic dreams that include a nightmarish march to the gallows. The *Dies Irae* is also heard in Saint-Saëns's *Danse Macabre* (1874) and Liszt's *Totentanz* (1849), two of the best-known musical renditions of the Dance of Death (discussed in its historical context in Chapter 3). Opera, which combines drama with music, commonly includes themes of murder and suicide.

The *dirge* is a musical form associated with funeral processions and burials. Beethoven, Schubert, Schumann, Strauss, Brahms, Mahler, and Stravinsky all wrote dirges. The jazz funeral of New Orleans is a famous example of a popular interpretation of the dirge. Related to dirges are *elegies*—musical settings for poems commemorating a person's death—and *laments*.

Laments are an expression of stylized or ritualized leave-taking found in many cultural settings, one example being Scottish clan funerals, where bagpipes are played. Vocally, the typical lament is an expression of mourning called "keening," an emotional expression of loss and longing that is reminiscent of crying. For the ancient Greeks, lamentation was intended to both "praise the deceased and provide emotional release for the bereaved."[33] Laments may help the bereaved identify their altered social status and seek sympathetic understanding from the community.[34] Italian philosopher Ernesto De Martino traced how the practice of lamentation—in word, gesture, and music—moderates the tendency toward collapse or breakdown that threatens persons in moments of extreme crisis, such as the aftermath of the death of a close relative.[35] In this way, laments promote the cultural reintegration of the mourner while simultaneously reestablishing bonds of alliance between the living and the dead.[36] In a well-known Greek lament, a mother says that she will take her pain to the goldsmith and have it made into an amulet so that she can wear it forever.[37]

In traditional Hawaiian culture, chants known as *mele kanikau* were the traditional lament for commemorating a person's death.[38] Some *kanikau* were carefully composed; others were chanted spontaneously during the funeral procession. Imagery of the natural world is called upon to portray the writer's experience of loss.[39] Memories of shared experiences amid natural surroundings are mentioned: "My companion in the chill of Manoa" or "My companion in the forest of Makiki." Such chants fondly recall the things that bind together the deceased and his or her survivors. The message of the Hawaiian lament was not "I am bereft without you" but, rather, "These are the things I cherish about you."

In reflecting on how music functions to provide solace in experiences of loss, a recent article stated:

> For the human heart and mind, music is a gift that brings hope and comfort through even the darkest times. As we cope with the losses that beset us throughout life, certain songs and musical works bring to mind poignant memories that refresh our grief. Whether Mozart's *Requiem* or a Top 40 tune, music has the capacity to cue the recall of happy moments shared with loved ones whose death has left us bereft. At other times, a lyric or melody sets us thinking about our own mortality.[40]

As you listen to various styles of music, notice the references to dying and death and ask yourself, What messages are being conveyed? What attitudes are being expressed? Whatever your musical taste, you will find a wealth of information about individual and cultural attitudes toward death.

Literature

From the epic poetry of Homer's *Iliad* and the classic drama of Sophocles' *Oedipus the King* and Shakespeare's *King Lear,* through modern classics like Leo Tolstoy's "The Death of Ivan Ilych," James Agee's *Death in the Family,* William Faulkner's *As I Lay Dying,* and Ernest J. Gaines's *A Lesson Before Dying,* death is treated as a significant human experience. Recall for a moment a favorite novel or short story. Was death an element of the plot? How did the author portray dying or death in the story?

In literature, the meaning of death is often explored as it relates to society as well as the individual. Novels about war, for example, depict how individuals and societies search for meaning in shattering experiences of trauma and loss. In *All Quiet on the Western Front,* a novel set in the time of the First World War, Erich Maria Remarque described the pointlessness of modern warfare by telling the story of a youthful combatant who quickly moves from innocence to disillusionment. The technological horror of the Second World

Buffalo Bill's
defunct
       who used to
       ride a watersmooth-silver
                  stallion
and break onetwothreefourfive pigeonsjustlikethat
                               Jesus
he was a handsome man
               and what i want to know is
how do you like your blueeyed boy
Mister Death
    e.e. cummings

War, particularly devastation caused by the atomic bomb, shaped the focus of John Hersey's *Hiroshima.* The surreal aspects of the Vietnam War received attention in books like Michael Herr's *Dispatches* and Tim O'Brien's *Going After Cacciacato,* and accounts of the recent war in Iraq formed the content of *What Was Asked of Us: An Oral History of the Iraq War by the Soldiers Who Fought It.*

In literature of the Holocaust, a revealing genre for students of death and dying, devastating experiences of horror and mass death are dealt with in victims' diaries, as well as in novels and psychological studies.[41] Examples include Chaim Kaplan's *Warsaw Diary,* Charlotte Delbo's *None of Us Will Return,* Elie Wiesel's *Night,* and Anne Frank's *Diary of a Young Girl.* Writings like these lead readers to contemplate human nature and spirit.

Modern literature often explores the meaning of death in situations that are seemingly incomprehensible. The fictional hero tries to come to terms with sudden and violent death in situations that allow no time or place for survivors to express their grief or mourn their dead.[42] Such literary themes may focus on a "landscape of violence."[43] In "vigilante" stories, such as detective novels and some westerns, the hero sets out to avenge evil but is often corrupted by a self-justifying morality that only perpetuates violence.[44] Finding meaning in death is problematic, as violence reduces persons to the status of *things.*

Uncertainty about death is also found in the *elegy.* Jahan Ramazani says, "The poetry of mourning for the dead assumes in the modern period an extraordinary diversity and range, incorporating more anger and skepticism, more conflict and anxiety than ever before."[45] Modern elegies include Wilfred Owen's poems of moral objection to the pain wrought by industrialized warfare; Allen Ginsberg's *Kaddish* after the death of his mother; Seamus Heaney's memorials to the suffering caused by political violence in Ireland; and the "parental elegies" in the poetry of Sylvia Plath, Anne Sexton, and Adrienne Rich. Ramazani observes that poetry is an important "cultural space for mourning the dead," as writers search for "credible responses to loss in the modern world."

Edward Hirsch says, "Implicit in poetry is the notion that we are deepened by heartbreaks, that we are not so much diminished as enlarged by grief, by our refusal to vanish—to let others vanish—without leaving a verbal record."[46] William Lamers points out that grief is a common theme in poetry and that poems can give us insight into the universality of loss in ways that can be consoling and therapeutic.[47] Ted Bowman observes that the language of bereavement and grief is enhanced by literary resources that help people give voice to their own stories of loss.[48] For caregivers, abstract clinical descriptions become more humanized by exploring the impact of frightening diseases and unsettling circumstances through stories and poems. Cadets at the United States Military Academy (West Point) are taught about the historical role of poetry in shaping culture, attitudes, and values, with the aim of "dispelling the illusion that prepackaged answers are always there for the taking in a world flush with ambiguities."[49] Among the insights communicated in the work of Emily Dickinson, one of America's foremost poets, is the recognition that it is impossible to affirm life without an examination of death.[50]

Visual Arts

Edvard Munch's *The Dance of Life*, which appears on the cover of this text, represents the artist's summing up of human fate: "Love and death, beginnings and endings, are fused in a roundel that joins private lives and lusts to the larger, inexorable cycle of ongoing generations."[51]

In the visual arts, death themes are revealed through symbols, signs, and images.[52] Cultural attitudes and beliefs influence the way in which such themes are expressed. On ancient Egyptian sarcophagi, scenes inscribed in relief attest to that culture's beliefs about death and the afterlife. Graphically portrayed on these limestone coffins is the expectation that, after death, a person will be judged according to his or her deeds during earthly life. Some themes in death-related art transcend cultural boundaries, such as those that draw upon natural processes of life, growth, decay, and death.

In some art, we find a whimsical attitude toward death, as in the engravings of Mexican artist José Guadalupe Posada, which contain skeletal figures from all walks of life engaged in daily routines, or in American sculptor Richard Shaw's *Walking Skeleton*, with the skeleton composed of twigs, bottles, playing cards, and similar found objects.

During the Middle Ages, there arose in Western Europe one of the most arresting expressions of dying and death ever to emerge in the graphic arts: the *Dance of Death*. Growing out of widespread fears about the spread of plague, the images associated with the Dance of Death display a concern with mortality and fears of sudden, unexpected death. A similar concern is evident in the work of artists more recently, as in Fritz Eichenberg's woodcuts depicting the fears of our era: annihilation caused by war, environmental catastrophe, and diseases such as AIDS.[53]

Francisco José de Goya's *Self-Portrait with Dr. Arrieta* exemplifies an artistic genre that depicts deathbed scenes and persons *in extremis*. Completed for the doctor who aided in Goya's recovery from a life-threatening illness, this painting shows the doctor holding medicine to Goya's lips while the figure of Death is depicted next to people who are thought to be Goya's priest and his housekeeper. Suicide is another theme dealt with by artists of virtually all eras and cultures. A well-known example is Rembrandt van Rijn's *The Suicide of Lucretia*, which portrays Lucretia with a tear in her eye, moments after she has stabbed herself with a dagger.

Art gives us a window into the customs and beliefs of other ages and places. For example, Charles Willson Peale's *Rachel Weeping* (1772 and 1776) depicts a deathbed scene from the American colonial period in which the artist's wife is shown mourning their dead child. The child's jaw is wrapped with a fabric strap to keep it closed. Her arms are bound with cord to keep them at her sides. Medicines, all of which have proved ineffective, sit on a bedside table. As the mother gazes heavenward, she holds a handkerchief to

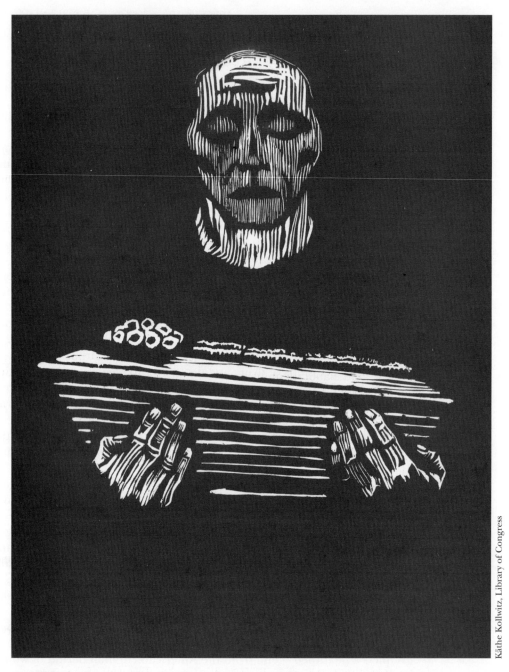

Of the modern artists who have expressed death themes in art, few have done so more frequently or more powerfully than German artist Käthe Kollwitz—as in this 1925 woodcut, Proletariat—Child's Coffin.

wipe away the tears streaming down her face, her grief in marked contrast to the dead child's peaceful countenance.

Art is often a vehicle for expressing the powerful impact of personal loss. When Pan Am flight 103 was brought down by a terrorist bomb, Suse Lowenstein's son was among those killed. As a sculptor, she found a way to express her grief, and the grief of other women bereaved by the crash, by making a series of female nude figures that compose an exhibit titled *Dark Elegy*. In earth tones, the larger-than-life figures are shown in the throes of grief. About creating the work, Lowenstein said:

> One by one, they come into my studio, step onto a posing platform, close their eyes, and go back to December 21, 1988, to that horrible moment when they learned that their loved one had died. . . . This is the moment I freeze in time. This is the pose that I shape into sculpture.[54]

Some figures look mute. Others are obviously screaming. Some look as though they were eviscerated. The artist expressed the hope that *Dark Elegy* will be "a reminder that life is fragile and that we can lose that which is most precious to us so easily and have to live with that loss for the remainder of our lives."

Within the context of nineteenth-century mourning customs, ordinary Americans incorporated both classical and Christian symbols of death to memorialize public figures as well as family members.[55] Embroidered memorials to the dead were hung in the parlor, the most important room of the house, and elaborate quilts were sewn into designs that celebrated the life of the deceased. Such mourning art provided not only a way to perpetuate memories of a loved one but also a focus for physically coping with grief, an opportunity to actively grieve by doing something.

Similar motives led more recently to the making of a massive quilt to commemorate persons who died from AIDS: The Names Project AIDS Memorial Quilt.[56]

> The quilt symbolized individuals sharing their grief by sharing their continuing bonds with friends and lovers, and in doing so the survivors became a community of mourners.[57]

In folk art, quilts represent family and community. As the largest ongoing community arts project in America, the AIDS Quilt affirms the value of creative expression as a means of coping with loss. Maxine Junge points out:

> Creativity in the face of death offers a spectrum of life-enhancing possibilities. These possibilities can ward off a meaningless conclusion to a life, give meaning and hope to a life lived and to a future in which the dead, through memory, still exist.[58]

Like the AIDS Memorial Quilt, the Vietnam Veterans Memorial Wall in Washington, D.C., designed by architect Maya Lin, is an example of contemporary mourning art that works to counter the anonymity of lives lost. It has been described as the "iconographic reversal of the Tomb of the Unknowns," with its "vast polished surface" serving as "the tombstone of the known."[59]

The making of a memorial quilt was among the elaborate personal and social mechanisms for dealing with grief widely practiced during the nineteenth century, as in this example memorializing a granddaughter who died in infancy. This traditional mourning custom was revived recently to commemorate and remember persons who died from AIDS; in the example shown here, words and symbols express beloved qualities of Joe's life. For survivors, the creation of such memorials provides not only a focus for physically working through grief, but also a means of perpetuating the memory of the loved one.

On the wall, names of the dead are listed chronologically by the date of their death, not alphabetically, presenting a chronicle that vividly depicts the scale of losses.

The urge to memorialize the dead and offer comfort to the bereaved through artistic means is also demonstrated by a variety of "homemade condolences" sent to relatives of military men and women killed in Afghanistan and Iraq.[60] For example, Operation Gold Star Flag, formed by a group of military wives, revived a tradition of flag-making that began during the First World War, when families with relatives in the military displayed in their windows small flags—white fields with red borders and, in the middle, a blue star, which was changed to gold if the serviceman was killed. Other groups, with names like Marine Comfort Quilts and Operation Homemade Quilts, fashioned quilts with center squares personalized in memory of each casualty.

A woman who had been given one of the Marine Comfort Quilts described how, when she finds herself missing her brother who was killed in Iraq, she wraps herself in the quilt and cries until the wee hours of the morning: "It's called a 'comfort quilt,'" she said, "and that's exactly what it is; it has so much love from so many different people who never even met my brother." Another woman, a mother whose son was killed by "friendly fire" (by his own comrades), said: "Your friends and family are there, but when you receive good deeds from people you don't even know, it makes you feel like you're not alone."[61]

Such sentiments reinforce the importance of the arts in a comprehensive understanding of how people cope with loss. In this regard, a statement published by the International Work Group on Death, Dying, and Bereavement is pertinent:

> The arts and humanities with their images, symbols, and sounds express themes of life, death, and transcendence. They are the language of the soul and can enable people to express and appreciate the universality as well as the particularity of each person's experience.[62]

In the visual arts, these themes and this language are evident in a broad range of works, from those formed out of the particulars of an individual's unique loss, as in the woodcuts shaped by Käthe Kollwitz and the sculptures of Suse Lowenstein, which depict the grief of a parent following the death of a child,[63] to those that function on a larger scale as *sites of memory* for losses that are both personal and communal, such as those commemorated by the AIDS Memorial Quilt, and the Vietnam Veterans Memorial Wall. Whatever the scale, as Sandra Bertman points out, one of the main functions of art is to engage our awareness and "bring us closer to what language cannot reach."[64]

Humor

Serious and somber matters can be easier to deal with when there is comedic relief. Humor defuses some of our anxiety about death. It helps put fearful possibilities into more manageable perspective. Death-related humor comes in many different forms, from funny epitaphs to so-called black or

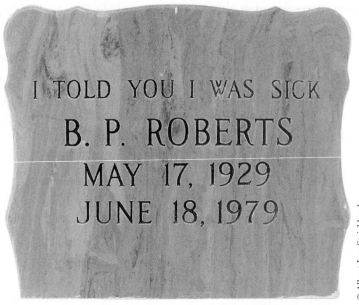

In place of the conventional sentiment usually engraved on tombstones, a touch of whimsy adorns this memorial to B. P. Roberts at a cemetery in Key West, Florida.

gallows humor.[65] On an interstate highway, motorists appear to be taken aback by a gleaming white hearse with the cryptic license plates, "Not Yett."

Mary Hall observes that "what is humorous to each of us depends on our particular cultural set, our own experience, and our personal inclination."[66] Humor often functions as a kind of comment on incongruity or inconsistency relative to social norms or perspectives, as when a young girl wrote a letter to God asking, "Instead of letting people die and having to make new ones, why don't you just keep the ones You have now?"[67]

Humor functions in several ways relative to death: First, it raises our consciousness about a taboo subject and gives us a way to talk about it. Second, it presents an opportunity to rise above sadness, providing a release from pain and promoting a sense of control over a traumatic situation, even if we cannot change it. Third, humor is a great leveler; it treats everyone alike and sends the message that there are no exemptions from the human predicament. Thus, it binds us together and encourages a sense of intimacy, which helps us face what is unknown or distressing. Humor can be a "social glue" that helps us empathize with others. After a death has occurred, humor can comfort survivors as they recall the funny as well as painful events of a loved one's life. A sense of humor can moderate the intensity of negative life events.

When things are bad, humor doesn't necessarily change the situation for the better, but it can serve a protective psychological function and help people maintain their equilibrium. In situations involving interactions between patients and health care providers, humor is "one of the great tools of reassurance on the hospital ward."[68] For people who are seriously ill, humor offers a way to cope with the effects of a shattering diagnosis. It provides another perspective on a painful situation, as in the jest "Halitosis is better than no breath at all."

Individuals who encounter death on their jobs, as emergency services personnel do, use humor to distance themselves from horror as well as to rebond as a team rather than feeling isolated in their individual grief after traumatic incidents. A firm that provides instructional materials for emergency medical technicians includes in its catalog a musical recording titled "You Respond to Everyone But Me." In another example, a group of doctors at a medical center avoided using the word "death" when a patient died because of concern that it might alarm other patients. One day, as a medical team was examining a patient, an intern came to the door with information about the death of a patient. Knowing that the word "death" was taboo and finding no ready substitute, she announced, "Guess who's not going to shop at Wal-Mart any more?" This phrase quickly became the standard way for staff members to convey the news of a patient's death among themselves. In the health care setting, humor serves to communicate important messages, promote social relations, diminish discomfort, and manage "delicate" situations; it has been called the "oil of society."[69]

The things we find funny about death can reveal a great deal about our attitudes. A joke that is shared gleefully by one group of people may be shocking to others; there are constraints on the kinds of humor that a particular person or group finds acceptable. Nevertheless, humor can help us cope with

---

 The Undertakers

Old Pops had been stone cold dead for two days. He was rigid, gruesome and had turned slightly green and now he lay on a slab at the undertakers, about to be embalmed by two lovable old morticians.

"At least he lived to a ripe age," said one.

"Yep," said the other. "Well, let's get to 'er."

Suddenly, Old Pops bolted upright and without opening his eyes, began to utter this story:

"In 1743, Captain Rice set sail from England with an unreliable and mutinous crew. After three days at sea, the mast of the mainsail splintered, and then broke completely in half. The ship tossed about at sea for two days; the men mutinied, and the ship tossed about for another two days. At the end of the third day, a ship appeared on the horizon and rescued them and good Captain Rice failed to mention to the admiral the incident of mutiny, and his crew became faithful and hardworking and devoted themselves to their captain."

Old Pops laid back down on the marble.

"Well," said one mortician, "there goes the old saying, 'dead men tell no tales'!"

Steve Martin, *Cruel Shoes*

adversity and painful situations. Individuals held as prisoners of war during the Vietnam War considered humor so important to coping that they would "risk torture to tell a joke through the walls to another prisoner who needed to be cheered up."[70] In short, humor is an important aid in confronting our fears and gaining a sense of mastery over the unknown. Finding humorous aspects to death, casting it in an unconventional light, relieves some of the anxiety that accompanies awareness of our mortality.

Studying Death and Dying

Take a death and dying course or read a book like this and someone will probably ask, "Why would you want to take a class about death?" or "Why are you reading about death?" Despite public interest in death-related issues, individuals exhibit varying degrees of avoidance and acceptance when it comes to discussing death openly. Our relationship with death seems to be in a period of transition.

Ambivalent attitudes toward death are evident when one educator applauds the study of death as the "last of the old taboos to fall," while another contends that death is "not a fit subject for the curriculum." In response to this state of affairs, Patrick Dean observes that, if death education is criticized by some as a "bastard child of the curriculum, hidden in the closet," then those who value death education can be grateful to such critics because they are creating opportunities for highlighting the importance of death education as preparation for living.[71] In fact, Dean says, death education could appropriately be renamed "life and loss education," because "only through awareness of our lifelong losses and appreciation of our mortality are we free to be in the present, to live fully."

The Rise of Death Education

Informal death education occurs in the context of "teachable moments" that arise out of events in daily life. Such an event may be the death of a gerbil in an elementary school classroom, or it may be an event experienced widely, such as the accidents involving the space shuttles *Challenger* and *Columbia*, the September 2001 terrorist attacks, an Asian tsunami, Hurricane Katrina, or the sudden death of a famous person, as in the deaths of John F. Kennedy Jr. and Princess Diana.

The first formal course in death education at an American university was initiated by Robert Fulton at the University of Minnesota in the spring of 1963.[72] The first conference on death education was held at Hamline University in Minnesota in 1970. From these beginnings, death education has embraced a wide range of issues and topics, from nuts-and-bolts issues such as selecting mortuary services or probating an estate to philosophical and ethical matters such as the definition of death and speculation about what happens after death.

Because death education addresses both objective facts and subjective concerns, it receives broad academic support, with courses offered in a variety of disciplines.[73] In most courses, mastery of facts is enhanced by personal narratives that describe the myriad ways human beings encounter and cope with death.[74] The arts and humanities serve to balance scientific and technical perspectives. Images, symbols, and sounds express themes of life, death, and transcendence that allow for other ways of knowing and learning.

In the broad picture, death education includes training for physicians, nurses, allied health personnel, funeral directors, and other professionals whose duties involve contact with dying and bereaved individuals.[75] This includes police officers, firefighters, and emergency medical technicians (EMTs). As witnesses to human tragedy in the line of duty, they are called upon to comfort victims and survivors. The stoic image of the police officer, EMT, or firefighter who "keeps it all in," instead of expressing natural emotions, is challenged by the recognition that such a strategy may be physically and psychologically harmful.

All of these avenues of death education benefit from opportunities for collegial interaction and communication offered by organizations such as the Association for Death Education and Counseling (ADEC).[76]

Pioneers in Death Studies

The modern scientific approach to the study of death is usually traced to a symposium organized by Herman Feifel at a 1956 meeting in Chicago of the American Psychological Association.[77] This symposium resulted in a book, *The Meaning of Death* (1959), edited by Feifel and published by McGraw-Hill. This landmark book brought together experts from different disciplines whose essays encompassed theoretical approaches, cultural studies, and clinical insights. Death was shown to be an important topic for public and scholarly consideration. Given the prevailing resistance at that time to discussing death, this was no easy feat. Of early efforts in death studies, Feifel says:

> The realization soon began to sink in that what I was up against were not idiosyncratic personal quirks, the usual administrative vicissitudes, pique, or nonacceptance of an inadequate research design. Rather, it was personal position, bolstered by cultural structuring, that death is a dark symbol not to be stirred—not even touched—an obscenity to be avoided.[78]

Feifel recalled that he was emphatically told that "the one thing you never do is to discuss death with a patient."

The same message was communicated to Elisabeth Kübler-Ross, whose book *On Death and Dying* (1969) helped create demand for a better way to care for dying patients. Hospice pioneer Cicely Saunders addressed similar issues in her work, *Care of the Dying* (1959). Barney G. Glaser and Anselm L. Strauss applied the tools of sociological analysis to conduct studies focusing on the way awareness of dying affected patients, hospital staff, and family members and on how the "timing" of death occurred in hospital settings. These studies, published as *Awareness of Dying* (1965) and *Time for Dying* (1968), showed that caregivers were reluctant to discuss death and avoided telling patients they were dying. Jeanne Quint Benoliel, who collaborated with Glaser and Strauss, published *The Nurse and the Dying Patient* (1967), calling for systematic death education for nurses.

Another influential work during this era was an essay by Geoffrey Gorer titled "The Pornography of Death" (1955; reprinted 1963).[79] It compared contemporary attitudes toward death with Victorian attitudes toward sex. The 1950s have been characterized by some commentators as a turning point or threshhold of a new era in which death and dying were "rediscovered." Lindsay Prior suggests that it may be more accurate to say that there was a new "object of interest" in which the question became "What does death mean to you?"[80]

The 1960s were a fruitful period for death studies. John Hinton's *Dying* (1967) shed light on contemporary practices and suggested how care of the dying could be improved. In "Death in American Society" (1963), sociologist Talcott Parsons looked at the impact of technological advances in health and medicine on dying. Philosopher Jacques Choron traced the history of ideas and attitudes about death and investigated the fear of death and its meaning for human beings in *Death and Western Thought* (1963) and *Death and Modern Man* (1964). Robert Fulton gathered a group of scholars and practitioners to address both theoretical and practical issues in his compilation, *Death and Identity* (1965). During the same era, literary works such as C. S. Lewis's *A Grief Observed* (1961) brought attention to issues involving bereavement and mourning.

The progress of death studies during the 1960s continued into the 1970s with works like Avery D. Weisman's *On Dying and Denying: A Psychiatric Study of Terminality* (1972), which astutely combined research skills and clinical experience with dying patients, and Ernest Becker's *The Denial of Death* (1973), which drew upon a broad range of psychological and theological insights in order to better understand the "terror" of death in human life. The early 1970s also witnessed the blossoming of the first peer-reviewed journal in the field of death studies, *Omega: Journal of Death and Dying*, which had begun its life as a newsletter in 1966 with an article in the first issue by Avery Weisman on the "Birth of the Death-People."[81] This was a decade of collaboration and connection, as individuals recognized a mutual interest manifested in organizations like Ars Moriendi (a forerunner of the International Work Group on Death, Dying, and Bereavement).[82]

In the decades since these pioneering contributions, *Omega* has been joined by other scholarly journals, including *Death Studies, Journal of Personal and Interpersonal Loss, Illness, Crisis, and Loss,* and *Mortality* (an international journal published in the U.K.). Books written for a general readership, such as *Tuesdays with Morrie* and *The Year of Magical Thinking,* have become best-sellers, and information about death and dying is now widely available on the Internet. The publication of several encyclopedic works covering death studies (including at least one on the Internet[83]) is another sign of the maturing of the field.[84] Clearly, the seeds planted a few decades ago by pioneers have ripened into a thriving interest in dying, death, and bereavement that is evident in both the academic setting and the larger public arena.[85]

Yet it is also true that this discipline is still a work in progress, an endeavor that welcomes ideas and visions of new contributors. In looking toward the future, Hannelore Wass observes that the study of death and dying has the potential to help individuals and societies "leap from a parochial to a global view," transcending self-interest in favor of concern for others.[86] The ultimate rationale for death studies, Wass says, "is about love, care, and compassion . . . about helping and healing."

Living with Awareness of Death

People living in the present "cosmopolitan era" have been described as *hibakusha,* a Japanese word meaning "explosion-affected." Used originally to describe survivors of the atomic bombings of Hiroshima and Nagasaki, the term connotes pervasive anxiety about the threat of annihilation. In this regard, the threats of war, nuclear catastrophe, environmental destruction, violence, and terrorism have been joined by the specter of emerging pandemics, such as AIDS.

The forces of globalization expose us to information about deaths far distant from the comfort of our homes. On a daily basis, the mass media contain scores of death-related stories, so many that an assignment to clip out all such articles from a newspaper can be frustrating. As the story on one side of the paper is cut, another relevant piece on the reverse side is obliterated. Confronted with so much death, do we find ourselves overwhelmed? Or does it stimulate our curiosity to learn more about and better understand the place of death in our lives?

The study of dying, death, and bereavement compels us to look at our own stories, as well as the stories of our neighbors, both locally and globally, with the aim of comprehending the diverse social and cultural influences not only on our understanding of death, but also on our personal mortality. The decision to embark on such a study is usually made out of a variety of personal or professional reasons. Some come to this study with no prior direct experience with death; others with what feels like too much.

Contemplating Mortality

Why is there death? Looking at the big picture, we see that death promotes variety through the evolution of species. The normal human life span is long enough for us to reproduce ourselves and ensure that the lineage of our species continues. Yet it is brief enough to allow for new genetic combinations that provide a means of adaptation to changing conditions in the environment. From the perspective of species survival, death makes sense. But this explanation offers little comfort when death touches our own lives.

At the heart of the story in Tolkien's *The Lord of the Rings* is the idea that death is both curse and blessing. All that is beautiful and beloved eventually dies, but "not all tears are evil." Mortality is ultimately viewed as a gift.[87] In an article titled "Human Existence as a Waltz of Eros and Thanatos," the authors suggest that the proper antidote for death is love, but until the ubiquitous and powerful role of death is accepted, until we learn to "dance with death," love will continue to be treated as something appropriate only for romance and Sunday School.[88]

To remedy this misapprehension and expand our understanding of the relationship between love and death, we need to step out of our fast-paced lives and take time to learn how to "waltz with death" by contemplating the basic questions of human existence.

Dimensions of Thanatology

In Greek mythology, *Thanatos* was the personification of death, the twin brother of *Hypnos* (sleep). Over time, the ancient Greeks came to use *thanatos* as a generic word for "death." Our word "thanatology," defined as the study of death, is a linguistic heir of the Greek term. Although this definition of thanatology is documented in English usage by the mid-1800s, the word *thanatos* became associated in the early twentieth century with Freudian psychoanalytic theory as a term describing the source of unconscious destructive urges, or the death instinct, in contrast to the constructive activities of *eros*, or life instinct. Freud postulated that all the variations of human behavior and activity were produced by interaction between eros and thanatos.

As pioneering Italian thanatologist Francesco Campione points out, death is not only a topic for reflection, study, and research; it is also an "existential problem," which touches every aspect of human existence and every field of knowledge.[89] Robert Kastenbaum says that, although the term *thanatology* is usually defined as the "study of death," it is perhaps better defined as "the study of life with death left in."[90]

Thus, as a field of study, thanatology encompasses a variety of disciplines and areas of concern (see Table 1-3). Other dimensions and examples can be added to this listing. For instance, "religious thanatology" has concerns similar to those of philosophical thanatology, but, specifically, as they occur in the context of devotion to a set of beliefs about the nature of ultimate reality (usually involving a deity); issues such as what happens to a person's "soul" or "spirit" after death and the nature of the "afterlife" are important within this domain of thanatology. We might also add the designation "practical thanatology" to account for a focus that gives rise to multiple concerns relating to the question "How, then, does one live with recognition of the fact of mortality (that is, one's own death and the deaths of others)?"

Acquiring a "core" knowledge of thanatology involves becoming familiar with all of these dimensions and their aspects. Together, they comprise what might be called "Thanatology" with a capital T.

Recently reviewing the scope and mission of death studies, Robert Kastenbaum suggested that "thanatologists still face the challenge of integrating all of death into our views of life."[91] He notes that mainstream thanatology has devoted its efforts to improving the care of people faced with life-threatening illness or bereavement, and it may be time to broaden the focus to include "large-scale death" and "death that occurs through complex and multi-domain processes." This perspective would include not only the "hor-

TABLE 1-3   *Dimensions of Thanatology*

Focus	Major Areas of Concern	Example Issues
Philosophical and ethical	The meaning of death in human life; questions of values and ethics	"Good" vs. "bad" death; concept of death; suicide and euthanasia.
Psychological	Mental and emotional effects of death on individuals	Grief; coping with terminal illness; death anxiety.
Sociological	How groups organize themselves to deal with social needs and problems related to dying and death	Response to disaster; disposal of the dead; socialization of children.
Anthropological	Role of culture and environment across time and space regarding how individuals and societies relate to death and dying	Funeral rites; ancestor worship; memorialization.
Clinical	Management of dying and death in medical settings; diagnosis and prognosis; relationships among patients, doctors, nurses, other caregivers	Treatment options; hospice and palliative care; pain and symptom control.
Political	Governmental actions and policies related to dying and death	Capital punishment; organ transfer rules; conduct of war.
Educational	Death education; increasing public awareness of death-related issues and concerns	Curricula for instruction in schools; community programs.

rendous deaths" that human beings inflict on each other in war and other forms of violence, but also human-caused activities that threaten or result in the extinction of other species.

Death Anxiety and Fear of Death

Our relationship with death has, as Herman Feifel observed, "a shaping power on thinking and behavior at all points in the life span."[92] The way in which we anticipate death, Feifel says, governs our "now" in an influential manner. This applies not only to people who are terminally ill, combatants in war, or people who fit other categories we tend to associate with an increased risk of death, such as those who are very old or suicidal. On the contrary, it is true for everyone and "for all seasons."

Death challenges the idea that human life has meaning and purpose.[93] The manner in which individuals respond to this challenge is "intertwined with the death ethos of the cultures in which they are embedded."[94] The distinctive stance toward death in a particular culture affects the behavior of its members as they go about their daily lives, influencing, for example, their willingness to engage in risky behaviors or their likelihood of taking out an

"*Carl! No!*"

Drawing by Pat Byrnes,
© 2005 The New Yorker Collection

insurance policy, as well as their attitudes toward such issues as organ dona-tion, the death penalty, euthanasia, or the possibility of an afterlife. In a vari-ety of ways, our culture helps us "deny, manipulate, distort, or camouflage death so that it is a less difficult threat with which to cope."[95] Consider, for example, the effect of a public health discourse that suggests death and mis-fortune can be avoided if people behave properly—eat the right things, exer-cise, stop smoking, and so on.[96]

Avery Weisman pointed out that *realization* is critical in our efforts to un-derstand death: "Most people concede that death is inevitable, a fact of na-ture. But they are not prepared to realize. We postpone, put aside, disavow, and deny its relevance to us."[97] Individuals and societies must, in fact, both accept and deny death. We must accept death if we wish to maintain a grasp on reality. Yet we must deny it if we are to go about our daily lives with a sense of commitment to a future that is inevitably limited by our mortality. Accord-ing to Talcott Parsons, the characteristic attitude toward death in modern so-cieties is less a matter of outright denial than it is "bringing to bear every possible resource to prolong active and healthful life" and accepting death only when "it is felt to be inevitable."[98]

The largest area of empirical research in thanatology is concerned with the measurement of attitudes toward death, and, more particularly, *death anx-iety*.[99] In posing the question "What do we fear when we fear death?" Robert Neimeyer and his colleagues suggest that the term *death anxiety* may be un-derstood as "a shorthand designation for a cluster of death attitudes charac-terized by fear, threat, unease, discomfort, and similar negative emotional reactions, as well as anxiety in the psychodynamic sense as a kind of diffuse fear that has no clear object."[100]

Generally speaking, the findings from this research indicate that death anxiety tends to be higher among females than among males, higher among blacks than among whites, and higher among youth and middle-aged adults than among older people. People who describe themselves as "religious" tend to report less death anxiety than those who do not characterize themselves this way. Individuals who report a greater degree of self-actualization and sense of internal control also report less death anxiety than their counterparts. This summary gives a very broad-brush understanding of the overall picture of death anxiety research.

Despite the accumulated data from numerous studies, there are significant questions, which Robert Neimeyer summarizes as follows:[101] First, what definition of death is implied by the various testing instruments? Second, what are the strengths and limitations of the various instruments that have been used in death anxiety research? Third, based on answers to the first two questions, what are the implications for future research? And, finally, reviewing the data gathered up to now, what do we really know?

Research into death anxiety has been characterized as "thanatology's own assembly line."[102] Part of the appeal of death anxiety research, Robert Kastenbaum says, lies in the fact that it "allows the researcher (and the readers, if they so choose) to enjoy the illusion that death has really been studied." How data from such research can be applied to practical issues is uncertain. If, for example, it were possible to reliably state that doctors with high death anxiety relate poorly to dying patients, then that finding might be applied constructively in health care settings. However, we are mostly unable to adequately gauge the effect of death anxiety on real-world issues. What shall we make of studies showing that women have higher death anxiety scores than men? Does this gender difference mean that women are *too anxious* about death, or that men are *not anxious enough*? Reviewing the research in this area, Herman Feifel said:

> Fear of death is not a unitary or monolithic variable. . . . In the face of personal death, the human mind ostensibly operates simultaneously on various levels of reality, or finite provinces of meaning, each of which can be somewhat autonomous. We, therefore, need to be circumspect in accepting at face value the degree of fear of death affirmed at the conscious level.[103]

Ernest Becker's insights regarding terror management theory help answer the question "How do people cope with an awareness of death?" In an interview days before his death, Becker addressed "four strands of emphasis" in terror management theory:[104]

1. The world is a terrifying place.
2. The basic motivation for human behavior is the need to control our basic anxiety, to deny the terror of death.
3. Because the terror of death is so overwhelming, we conspire to keep it unconscious.
4. Our heroic projects that are aimed at destroying evil have the paradoxical effect of bringing more evil into the world. . . . We are able to focus on almost any perceived threat, whether of people, political or economic ideology, race, religion, and blow it up psychologically into a life and death struggle against ultimate evil. . . . This is the dynamic of spiralizing violence that characterizes so much of human history.

Because death is always a possibility, fear of death is built into human life.[105] Studies show that "fear of death functions as a motivating force whether people are currently focused on this particular issue or not; it is the implicit knowledge of death rather than current focal awareness that is the motivating factor."[106] In a commencement address at Stanford University, Steve Jobs of Apple Computer pointed out the irony of this when he said, "Death is very likely the single best invention of life." He called it "life's change agent."[107] In this view, death is necessary to give existential meaning to life.[108]

Factors Affecting Familiarity with Death

The past hundred years have seen dramatic change in the size, shape, and distribution of the American population—that is, its *demographics*. These changes—the most notable of which involve increased life expectancy and lower mortality rates—affect our expectations about death. In the past, a typical household would include parents, uncles, aunts, and aged grandparents, as well as children of varying ages. Such extended families, with several generations living together under the same roof, are rare today. One consequence is that most of us have fewer opportunities to experience our relatives' deaths firsthand. Moreover, our greater geographic mobility makes it less likely that we will be present when relatives die.

Consider how experiences with dying and death have changed over the last hundred years or so.[109] During the nineteenth century, individuals typically died at home, often surrounded by an extended family that spanned several generations. As death drew near, relatives and friends gathered to maintain a vigil at the bedside. Afterward, they washed and prepared the body for burial. A home-built coffin was placed in the parlor of the house, where friends and relatives participated in a wake and shared in mourning the deceased. Death was a domestic experience.

In close-knit communities, a death bell tolled the age of the deceased, giving notification of the death so that others in the community could join in the rites and ceremonies marking the deceased's passing (see Figure 1-1). Children were included in activities surrounding the dead, staying with adults and sometimes sleeping in the same room as the corpse. Later, in a family plot at the homeplace or a nearby churchyard cemetery, the coffin was lowered into the grave, and those closest to the deceased shoveled dirt over the coffin to fill in the grave. Throughout this process, from caring for the dying person through burial, death remained within the realm of the family.

If you were a person of the nineteenth century suddenly transported to the present, you would likely experience culture shock as you walked into the "slumber room" of a typical mortuary. There, in place of a simple, wooden coffin, you view an elaborate casket. The corpse shows the mortician's skill in cosmetic restoration. At the funeral, you watch as relatives and friends eulogize the deceased. Ah, that's familiar, you say—but where is the dear departed? Off to the side a bit, the casket remains closed, death tastefully concealed. At the graveside, as the service concludes, you are amazed to see mourners leaving while the casket lies yet unburied; the cemetery crew will

❧ You can feel the silence pass over the community as all activity is stopped and the number of rings is counted. One, two, three—it must be the Myer's baby that has the fever. No, it's still tolling—four, five, six. There is another pause at twenty—could that be Molly Shields? Her baby is due at any time now—no, it's still tolling. Will it never stop? Thirty-eight, thirty-nine, another pause—who? It couldn't be Ben; he was here just yesterday; said he was feeling fit as a fiddle—no, it's starting again. Seventy, seventy-one, seventy-two. Silence. You listen, but there is no sound—only silence. Isaac Tipton. He has been ailing for two weeks now. It must be Isaac.

Figure *1-1* *Tolling the Bell*

complete the actual burial. As a nineteenth-century observer at a modern funeral, you may be most impressed by the fact that the deceased's family and friends are spectators rather than participants. The tasks of preparing the dead for burial and managing the rites of passage are carried out by hired professionals.

Our familiarity with death has also been powerfully influenced by sophisticated medical technologies, which have affected both the *place* where death most often occurs and the *manner* in which most people die. In contrast to earlier generations, who generally had major roles in care of their dying and dead, we usually rely on professionals—from the cardiologist to the coroner to the cremator—to act as our go-betweens. The net result is that, for most of us, death is unfamiliar.

Life Expectancy and Mortality Rates

Since 1900, average life expectancy in the United States has increased from forty-seven to seventy-eight years (see Figure 1-2).[110] These figures reflect what demographers call "cohort life expectancy," meaning the *average* number of years a specified group of infants would live if they were to experience throughout their lives the age-specific death rates prevailing in their birth year.[111] Thus, for 2004, the life expectancy at birth for the U.S. population as a whole was 77.9 years. When this overall U.S. cohort is broken out into the four race-sex groups, however, we find that white females continued to have the highest life expectancy (80.4 years), followed by black females (76.5 years), white males (75.7 years), and black males (69.8 years).[112] In addition to differences between birth cohorts, it should be recognized that such figures represent statistical life expectancies. The actual life span lived out by any particular individual may well be significantly shorter or longer than the average for his or her cohort.

Today, we tend to assume that a newborn child will live into his or her seventh or eighth decade, perhaps longer. This was not the case in 1900. Whereas over 99 percent of infants born in the United States now survive the first year of life, less than 88 percent survived beyond their first year in 1900.[113] Perhaps even more illustrative of such change is the observation that over half of the deaths in 1900 occurred among children age fourteen

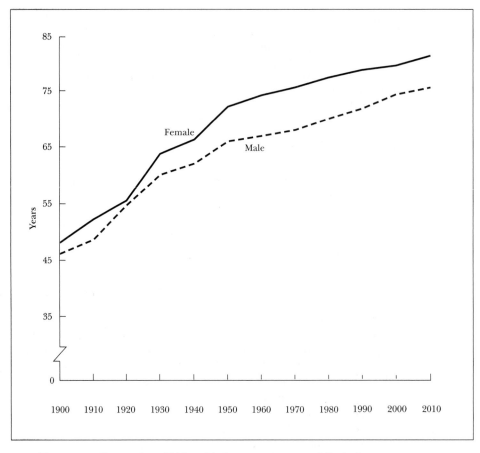

Figure *1-2* *Expectation of Life at Birth, 1900–2000, and Projections 2010*
Sources: U.S. Census Bureau, *Historical Statistics of the United States, Colonial Times to 1970*
(Washington, D.C.: Government Printing Office, 1975), p. 55; and *Statistical Abstract of the*
United States: 2006, p. 76.

and younger; now, less than 2 percent of deaths occur among this age
group.[114] This fact influences how we think (or don't think) about death.

Another way to appreciate the changing impact of death is to examine
death rates (which are typically stated as the number of individuals dying per
1000 population in a given year). In 1900, the death rate in America was
about 17 per 1000; today, it is about 8.2 per 1000 (see Figure 1-3).[115]

Imagine yourself in an environment where death at an early age is common. Consider how different experiences of dying and death were at a time
when the comparatively high percentage of infant deaths tended to be thought
of as a matter of "fate" that could not be changed. Both young and old were
familiar with death as a natural part of the human condition. Mothers died in
childbirth; babies were stillborn; one or both parents might die before their
children had grown to adolescence. Surviving siblings often had a postmortem

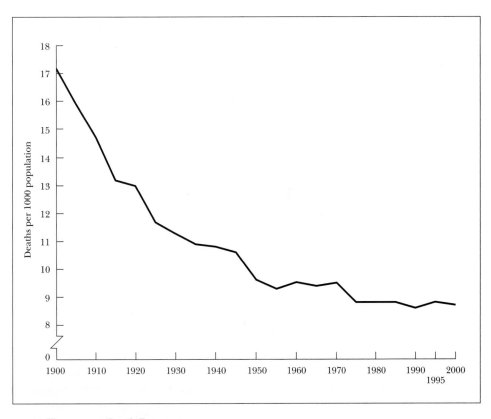

Figure *1-3* *Death Rates, 1900–2000*
Sources: U.S. Census Bureau, *Historical Statistics of the United States, Colonial Times to 1970* (Washington, D.C.: Government Printing Office, 1975), p. 59; and *Statistical Abstract of the United States: 2006*, p. 79.

photograph of a dead brother or sister displayed, a memorial to the deceased and testament to the integrity of the family.[116] Living with such a common-place awareness of mortality, our ancestors could not realistically avoid the fact of death as a more or less familiar event in their lives. Ultimately, of course, none of us is exempt. Despite the increases in life expectancy and lowered death rates, the statistical odds of dying still finally add up to 100 percent.

Causes of Death

Changes in life expectancy and mortality rates are due largely to changes in the most common causes of death. In the early 1900s, the leading causes of death were related to acute infectious diseases such as tuberculosis, typhoid fever, diphtheria, streptococcal septicemia, syphilis, or pneumonia. Most such diseases came on suddenly, and death soon followed. Today, most deaths result from a chronic illness, such as heart disease or cancer, and tend to follow a slow, progressive course that lasts weeks, months, or even years (see Table 1-4).

TABLE *1-4*   *Ten Leading Causes of Death: United States*

Cause of Death	Deaths	% of Total Deaths
All causes	2,448,288	100.0
Heart disease	685,089	28.0
Cancer	556,902	22.7
Stroke	157,689	6.4
Lung disease	126,382	5.2
Accidents	109,227	4.5
Diabetes	74,219	3.0
Influenza and pneumonia	65,163	2.7
Alzheimer's disease	63,457	2.6
Kidney disease	42,453	1.7
Septicemia (infection)	34,069	1.4

Source: D. L. Hoyert and others, "Deaths: Final Data for 2003," *National Vital Statistics Reports* 54, no. 13 (Hyattsville, Md.: National Center for Health Statistics, 2006), p. 5.

Statistics show that the ten leading causes of death account for about 75 percent of all deaths in the United States, with the top two causes, heart disease and cancer, accounting for just over half of all deaths.[117]

This historical shift in patterns of disease and causes of death—a shift that demographers call an *epidemiologic transition*—is characterized by a redistribution of deaths from the young to the old.[118] (Epidemiology is the study of the patterns of health and disease.) With a reduced risk of dying at a young age from infectious diseases, more people survive into older ages, where they tend to die from degenerative diseases. This results in a growing proportion of aged people in the population. In 1900, people sixty-five and older made up 4 percent of the population in the United States; now they comprise slightly over 13 percent.[119] In 1900 people sixty-five and older accounted for about 17 percent of deaths; today, about 74 percent of the 2.4 million deaths each year in the United States occur among people in this age group.[120] In short, people are living longer and dying at older ages. One result is that we tend to associate death with the elderly when, in fact, it is not confined to any particular segment of the life span.

Geographic Mobility and Intergenerational Contact

Nearly one-seventh of the American population is on the move each year as people pull up stakes and say goodbye to friends, neighbors, and relatives.[121] Historically, such relationships were closely tied to place and kinship; today, they depend more on one's present role or function than on a lifetime of shared experiences. Children, once grown, rarely live in the same house with parents or, even more rarely, with their brothers and sisters in an extended family setting. Few high school or college friendships continue through marriage and the childrearing years into retirement. Because of social and geographic mobility, people are less likely to be present at the deaths of relatives or friends, resulting in the loss of shared death rituals.

Of course, some families maintain close relations, even when they don't share the same dwelling or live in the same town. Patterns of mobility also vary among individuals and groups. Some ethnic and cultural groups continue to place a high value on maintaining strong family ties despite general trends in society. In some instances, reduced contact with kin may be partly compensated for by increased contact with friends and neighbors.[122]

Generally speaking, in modern societies, there is less intermingling of the generations, a normal part of daily life in earlier times. Consider the experience of two small children on a Halloween trek, going door to door. After knocking on several well-lighted doors in a seniors-only mobile-home park and receiving no response, their cries of "Trick or treat!" were answered by a woman who said, "You'll not get any Halloween treats in this place. Only old people live here, and they leave their lights on for security and safety, not to welcome children on Halloween!"

Life-Extending Technologies

Seriously ill or injured individuals are likely to find themselves surrounded by an astonishing array of machinery designed to monitor life until the last electrical impulse fades. Sophisticated machines monitor biological functions such as brain wave activity, heart rate, body temperature, respiration, blood pressure, pulse, and blood chemistry. Signaling changes in body function by light, sound, and computer printout, such devices can make a crucial difference in situations of life or death.

But advanced medical technology that seems to one person a godsend, extending life, may seem to another a curse that only prolongs dying. Dignity can be devalued amid technology focused solely on the biological organism. What are the trade-offs in applying medical technologies to the end stage of life? The conventional definition of death as "the cessation of life, the total and permanent cessation of all vital functions" may be superseded by a medicolegal definition, which acknowledges the fact that life can be sustained artificially. The modern definition of death is not always as straightforward as the simple statement "When you're dead, you're dead."

Thus, medical technology is yet another factor in lessening our familiarity with dying and death. The nature of modern medicine tends to distance family and friends from the patient who is dying. The commonplace attitude that "what can be done, should be done" increases the odds that technological fixes will be tried, even when success or cure is unlikely. When death does come, it may seem unexpected. Technological medicine sometimes seems to promote a view of death as an event that can be deferred indefinitely rather than as a normal, natural part of life.

All of these demographic and social variables can be understood as sociocultural forces that influence the way we learn about death through childhood and beyond.

Five generations of the Machado family form an extended family network rarely seen today. Firsthand experiences of death in such a family come through the closeness of multigenerational living.

Gordon Parks, FSA Collection, Library of Congress

Examining Assumptions

Death is unavoidably part of our lives. Not thinking or talking about death doesn't remove us from its power. Such ostrichlike behavior only limits our choices for coping with dying and death. As death educator Robert Kavanaugh said, "The unexamined death is not worth dying."[123]

Historian David Stannard tells us that in societies in which each person is unique, important, and irreplaceable, death is not ignored but is marked by a

I often wonder what it would be like to be born and raised and live one's whole life in the same zip code. I wonder what it would be like to be able to dial all of one's family and friends without an area code. What it would be like not to always be missing one person or the other, one place or the other. What it would be like to return to a family home in which one grew up and still had things stored in the attic.

My family is in area code 405 and my best friend's in 415 and I'm living in 212. The in-laws are in 203. And there are other friends in 213 and 202, in 412 and 214.

Beverly Stephen, "A Mobile Generation in Search of Roots"

"community-wide outpouring of grief for what is a genuine social loss."[124] Conversely, in societies where people feel that "little damage is done to the social fabric by the loss of an individual," death tends not to be acknowledged outside of that person's immediate circle.

Among communities where traditional beliefs, values, and practices are maintained, death is part of the natural rhythm of life. The act of dying, the most private act any person can experience, is a community event.[125] A person's death initiates an outpouring of social support for the bereaved family and for the wider community.[126] Our values and preferences play an unavoidable part in the quest to examine assumptions and think clearly about death.

Death in a Cosmopolitan Society

At the California Science Center in Los Angeles, a public exhibition of over 200 cadavers attracted more than 650,000 visitors (doubling the previous record set by an exhibit of *Titanic* artifacts).[127] Titled "Body Worlds: The Anatomical Exhibition of Real Human Bodies," previous exhibitions in Europe and Asia had spawned protests over displaying bodies that had been "plastinated" (a process that involves replacing body fluids with clear, pliable plastic, making it possible to position not only a whole cadaver, but also skeletal bones and internal systems such as blood vessels, into dynamic poses), thereby offering viewers an "insider's view of the effects of disease and ailments, such as lung disease, hardened arteries, tumors, and ulcers." German physician Gunther von Hagens, inventor of the plastination process, calls the result "anatomic artwork."

Some said the exhibit's popularity was due to the fact that "morbidity has always been a spectator sport," alluding to the exhibit's macabre aspects. Others praised it as an educational opportunity for both children and adults to appreciate firsthand the wonder of the human body, as well as its deterioration from the ravages of disease. What do these contrasting reactions tell us about attitudes toward death? Is the specter of death, positive or negative, in the eyes of the beholder? What do you imagine your own response might be?

The quest for meaningful answers to questions involving human mortality requires us to contemplate what it means to live in a society that scholars

*Grandmother,
When Your Child Died*

Grandmother, when your child died
hot beside you
in your narrow bed,
his labored breathing kept
you restless
and woke you when
it sighed,
and stopped.

You held him through the bitter dawn
and in the morning
dressed him, combed his hair,
your tears welled, but you didn't weep
until at last he lay
among the wild iris in the sod,
his soul gone inexplicably to God. Amen.

But grandmother, when my child died
sweet Jesus, he died hard.
A motor beside
his sterile cot
groaned, and hissed, and whirred
while he sang his pain—
low notes and high notes
in slow measures
slipping through the drug-cloud.
My tears, redundant,
dropped slow
like glucose or blood
from a bottle.
And when he died
my eyes were dry
and gods wearing white coats
turned away.

Joan Neet George

describe as "postmodern" and "cosmopolitan." This perspective encourages us to value diversity and pluralism by examining "taken-for-granted" beliefs and considering ideas and practices from other historical periods and cultures. It involves reappraisal of assumptions about culture, identity, history, and language. We are "surrounded by images and artifacts from all periods and of all geographical and cultural locations," which makes us "aware of the entire experience of the human race in ways that were not available to previous generations."[128]

According to Ulrich Beck, a German scholar and keen observer of the "cosmopolitan society," the human condition in the present century cannot be understood nationally or locally, but only globally.[129] British sociologist Anthony Giddens says:

> In a globalizing world, where information and images are routinely transmitted across the globe, we are all regularly in contact with others who think differently, and live differently, from ourselves.[130]

He adds that cosmopolitans welcome and embrace this cultural complexity. Global concerns are becoming part of local experiences for an increasing number of people.[131]

Your classmates may arrive at different conclusions as they seek appropriate responses to death. Some may prefer an option for swift and low-cost body disposal instead of the traditional funeral. Others might choose a conventional funeral because they feel it provides a necessary framework for meeting the social and psychological needs of survivors (see Figure 1-4). Or consider the likelihood of differing values and attitudes concerning such issues as medical care at the end of life and decisions about whether to withhold or withdraw life-sustaining treatment. Is it feasible to allow space for

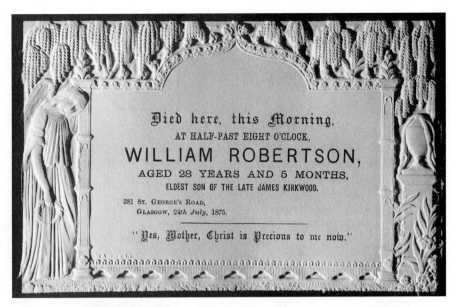

Figure 1-4 *Embossed Linen Death Notification, 1875*
This card exemplifies the formality of nineteenth-century mourning
customs. The etiquette books of the period often devoted considerable space
to the procedural details associated with the wearing of mourning clothes,
the issuance of funeral invitations, and other behaviors appropriate to
the survivors of a death.

only one point of view? Or do we need room for diversity of opinion and
practice?

Medical technology, demographic changes, shifting disease patterns, urbanization, and professionalization, among other factors, all influence how
we die, grieve, and care for our dead. Regarding grief, for example, Glennys
Howarth points out that, until relatively recently, "We have clung to models
that have reflected the dominant discourse of society," but in today's world,
"We cannot simply construct a 'new model' of grief, because society is increasingly diverse and fragmented."[132]

Marina Sozzi, an Italian thanatologist, observes that the wish to die a "natural" death, seen as an event that concludes a genetically determined life
cycle, has become a modern myth. By delegating our relationship with death
to professionals—doctors, nurses, undertakers, and so on—we try to avoid
thinking about mortality and "dream about someone who, equipped with the
necessary skills," will guarantee us a "sweet" death with no real loss of self.
"Our culture," she says," has lost the capacity of making the experience of
death fecund; thus, death becomes an impersonal deadline of the body, a fa-
tality inscribed inside it, pure biology."[133]

The latest chapter of the modern story of dying is perhaps best termed
"managed death." Even when a prognosis of death has been accepted by medical staff and families, and when further treatments intended to cure have

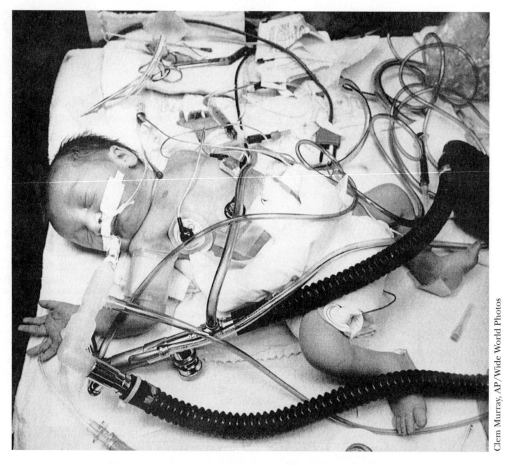

*Lifelines—tubes and wires monitoring heartbeat, breathing, and blood pressure—
increase this premature baby's chances of survival in the intensive care unit of
Philadelphia's Children's Hospital. The special-care nursery often becomes an
arena for many of the most difficult ethical decisions in medicine.*

been put aside, there may nevertheless be a strong desire to manage the situation so that it comes out "right." One expression of this involves the aim of ending treatment just at the proper moment so that the person is enabled to die a quiet or peaceful death. Another involves the attempt to control the timing of death even more completely through physician-assisted suicide or euthanasia. In light of such efforts, Daniel Callahan says it seems that death is becoming "just one more choice-and-efficiency issue, to be domesticated along with traffic jams and other excesses of modern life."[134]

Exploring Your Own Losses and Attitudes

Social scientists use the term *cultural lag* to describe the phenomenon of societies "falling behind" in dealing with new challenges resulting from rapid technological and social change. It may be that we are in a period of cultural lag with respect to dying and death.

Individual preferences and cultural perspectives both play important roles. Andrew Ziner says:

> Like nearly every other aspect of our lives, our understandings and feelings about dying and death are derived from our involvement in the myriad of groups, organizations, and institutions that represent our communities and, ultimately, constitute our society. As these religious, economic, legal, and familial structures change over time, we also change. This is because, as social beings, all of the meanings we attach to personal and cultural concerns—including dying and death—are inexorably tied to our social worlds. For example, how do you feel when you hear the word *death?* If you were born a century earlier, would you feel the same way? Is the difference due to individual or social factors?[135]

A perspective informed by values of connectedness and community, one that acknowledges and celebrates difference and diversity, can help us discover personally meaningful and socially appropriate choices for the times in which we live and die, giving us a "pluralistic way of understanding and being in the world."[136] Although death's finality appears harsh, for the ancient Greeks it was death that makes life significant. Mortality "compels humans to make some sense of their existence, here and now, each day to discover what it means 'to live well.'"[137]

Our attitudes toward death develop out of a lifetime of experiences with significant losses, beginning in childhood and continuing into old age. Exploring the meaning of these losses, and their influence on our attitudes and practices, is part of a comprehensive study of death and dying. It can be helpful to construct a "loss-ography," an account of the losses we have experienced, allowing time for investigation and reflection about the circumstances in which they occurred and the ways in which we, and significant others in our environment, responded to those losses.

Further Readings

Sandra L. Bertman, ed. *Grief and the Healing Arts: Creativity as Therapy.* Amityville, N.Y.: Baywood, 1999.

Glennys Howarth. *Death and Dying: A Sociological Introduction.* Malden, Mass.: Polity, 2007.

Marilyn Johnson. *The Dead Beat: Lost Souls, Lucky Stiffs, and the Perverse Pleasures of Obituaries.* New York: HarperCollins, 2006.

Gary Laderman. *The Sacred Remains: American Attitudes Toward Death, 1799–1883.* New Haven, Conn.: Yale University Press, 1996.

Jeff Malpas and Robert C. Solomon, eds. *Death and Philosophy.* New York: Routledge, 1998.

Dan Nimmo and James E. Combs. *Nightly Horrors: Crisis Coverage by Television Network News.* Knoxville: University of Tennessee Press, 1985.

Tony Walter, ed. *The Mourning for Diana.* New York: Berg, 1999.

Robert F. Weir, ed. *Death in Literature.* New York: Columbia University Press, 1980.

A father and son make an offering at the grave of their Chinese ancestors during village cremation ceremonies held in 1994 in Peliatan, Bali. In this way, religious and cultural traditions are passed along to successive generations through socializing processes that are important to the ongoing life of the community.

CHAPTER 2

Learning About Death: The Influence of Sociocultural Forces

*I*magine yourself as a child. Someone says, "Everybody's going to ziss one of these days. It happens to all of us. You, too, will ziss." Or, one day as you're playing, you are told, "Don't touch that, it's zissed!" Being an observant child, you notice that, when a person zisses, other people cry and appear to be sad. Over time, as you put together all your experiences of "zissing," you begin to develop some personal feelings and thoughts about what it means to ziss.

The understanding of death evolves like this. As a child grows older, incorporating various experiences of death, his or her concepts and emotional responses to death begin to resemble those of the adults in the culture. Just as a child's understanding of "money" changes over time—at first it is a matter of little or no concern; later it seems to come into the child's experience almost magically; and finally, it engages the child's attention and participation in many different ways—so, too, does the child develop new understandings about the meaning of death. Like other aspects of human development, the understanding of death evolves as experiences stimulate reevaluation of previously held knowledge, beliefs, and attitudes.

A Mature Concept of Death

Through observing and interacting with children at different ages, psychologists have described how children gain a mature understanding of death. In reviewing more than 100 such studies, Mark Speece and Sandor Brent conclude, "It is now generally accepted that the concept of death is not a single, unidimensional concept but is, rather, made up of several relatively distinct subconcepts."[1] A formal statement of the empirical, or observable, facts about death includes four components:[2]

1. *Universality.* All living things must eventually die. Death is all-inclusive, inevitable, and unavoidable (although unpredictable in its exact timing; that is, death may occur at any moment to any living thing).
2. *Irreversibility.* Death is irrevocable and final. Organisms that die cannot be made alive again. (This is separate from a belief in a spiritual afterlife.)
3. *Nonfunctionality.* Death involves the cessation of all physiological functioning. All life-defining bodily functions and capabilities cease at death.
4. *Causality.* There are biological reasons for the occurrence of death. This component includes a recognition of both internal (e.g., disease) and external (e.g., physical trauma) causes of death.

A fifth component, *personal mortality,* may be added to this list. Although it is a subcomponent of universality, it makes explicit the understanding not only that all living things die eventually, but also that each living thing will die ("I will die").

In addition, individuals with a mature understanding of death typically hold *nonempirical* ideas about it as well.[3] Such nonempirical ideas—that is, ideas not subject to scientific proof—deal mainly with the notion that human beings survive in some form beyond the death of the physical body. What happens to an individual's "personality" after he or she dies? Does the self or soul continue to exist after the death of the physical body? If so, what is the nature of this "afterlife"? Developing personally meaningful answers to such questions, which involve what Speece and Brent term "noncorporeal continuity," is, for many individuals, part of the process of acquiring a mature understanding of death.

A child's understanding of death evolves from infancy and toddlerhood, with the most dramatic changes normally occurring from about ages four to nine. Research suggests that most children understand that death is a changed state by about three or four years of age, that they grasp most components of a mature concept of death by about five to seven years of age (although the recognition of personal mortality as a subcomponent of universality may not emerge until somewhat later), and that they are likely to possess an understanding of all the components by about nine years of age. The component of causality—an understanding of biological causes of death—is acquired as part of this continuum. A major shift occurs between the ages of five and eight in how children think about biological phenomena and, specifically, how the human body functions to maintain life, which leads to the recognition that death involves the breakdown of bodily functioning.[4]

Children who experience the death of someone close may look to adults for models of appropriate behavior. Amid the regalia of high military and political office that characterized the funeral of President John F. Kennedy, young John F. Kennedy Jr. salutes the flag-draped coffin containing his father's body as it is transported from St. Matthew's Cathedral to Arlington National Cemetery. The day also marked John-John's third birthday.

The ever-expanding understanding of death during childhood is further refined during adolescence and young adulthood, as individuals consider the social and emotional impact of death on close relationships and contemplate the value of religious or philosophical answers to the meaning of death. Thus, a mature understanding of death goes beyond a biological focus to an appreciation for the life lost, the characteristics that make the loss of life a tragedy.[5]

What a person "knows" about death may change from time to time. We may hold conflicting or contradictory notions about death, especially our own. When facing a distressing situation, an understanding of the facts may give way to a more childlike attitude, such as the notion that we can bargain where death is concerned. A patient told that he or she has only six months to live may imagine that by some "magical" act, some bargain with God or the universe, the death sentence can be postponed. Thus, although the main evolution toward a mature understanding of death occurs during childhood, how a person understands death fluctuates among different ways of knowing throughout life.

Development of the Understanding of Death

The evolving understanding of death is a process of continuous adjustments and refinements. This process is often quite rapid; a child's understanding of death can change dramatically in a very brief time. By observing children's behavior, developmental psychologists devise models to describe the characteristic concerns and interests of children at various ages. These models are like maps that describe the main features of the territory of childhood at different stages of development. The models are useful for describing the characteristics of a typical child at, say, age two or age seven. They give a general picture of each stage of development.

Models of human development are abstractions, representations, interpretations of the actual territory. But the map should not be mistaken for the territory. Such maps are helpful in guiding one's way, locating certain landmarks, and sharing knowledge with others, but the particular features of the landscape possess qualities that aren't fully described by a map. Children vary in their individual rates of development—not only physically, but also emotionally, socially, and cognitively. Thus, with respect to a child's understanding of death, emphasizing developmental *sequence* is more reliable than correlating stages of understanding to *age*.

A child's understanding of death usually fits with his or her model of the world at each stage of development. Thus, an adult could give a young child a lengthy, detailed explanation of the concept of death as adults understand it, yet the child will grasp its components only as he or she is developmentally ready to understand. Experience plays an important role. A child who has had firsthand encounters with death may arrive at a more mature understanding of death than is typical of other children of the same age. Children's interactions are not "preparations for life" but, rather, both "life itself and preparations for future life."[6]

Children are active thinkers and learners. In recent decades, studies have shown infants and young children behaving in ways that imply an understanding of physical and perceptual phenomena at ages younger than previously thought possible.[7] They are seen as more competent, not as "pre" this or "pre" that as was once thought.[8] Very young children appear to make theory-like assumptions about the world, and they use basic reasoning systems to make causal explanations about physical, biological, and psychological events.[9]

In tracking the development of the understanding of death in children, it is useful to have a framework within which to place the distinctive attitudes and behaviors that pertain to various phases of childhood. The formal study of children's understanding of death can be traced to the pioneering work of Paul Schilder and David Wechsler (1934).[10] However, studies conducted in the early 1940s by Sylvia Anthony in England and Maria Nagy in Hungary have received greater attention. According to Anthony, children under the age of two have no understanding of "dead," by five they have a limited concept, and by nine they can give general explanations for death; in addition, young children engage in magical thinking (that is, the notion that, for example, angry thoughts or feelings can cause someone's death).[11] Nagy found three developmental stages in children's understanding of death between the ages of three and ten. In the first stage (ages three to five), children understood death as somehow being less alive; the dead "lived on" under changed circumstances and could return to normal life. In the second stage (ages five to nine), children understood death as final, but as avoidable and lacking inevitability (all die) and personal reference (I die). In the third stage (ages nine and older), children recognized death as the result of a biological process that is final, inevitable, universal, and personal.[12]

Although research generally has indicated that most children have acquired a mature concept of death around the age of nine, newer studies show that children begin to conceptualize death as a biological event around age five or six, at the same time they construct a "biological model" of how the human body functions.[13] By preschool age, a potent animate/inanimate distinction serves "as the center of a vast cluster of conceptual distinctions," including a naïve theory of biology.[14] Less attention has been given to the way children's *emotional* responses develop alongside these benchmarks in cognitive sophistication. It is also important to stress the role of culture. It is said that the single most important thing one can do to influence the development of an infant is to "decide where on earth—in what human community—that infant is going to grow up."[15]

In the discussion that follows, children's development is placed within the framework of two major theories or models of human development—namely, those devised by Erik Erikson and Jean Piaget.

The model of human development devised by Erikson focuses on the *stages of psychosocial development,* or psychosocial milestones, that occur successively

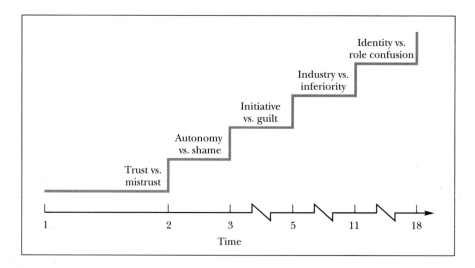

Figure *2-1 Five Stages of Preadult Psychosocial Development Proposed by Erikson*
Source: Based on Erik H. Erikson, *Childhood and Society,* 2nd ed. (New York: Norton, 1964), pp. 247–274.

throughout a person's life (see Figure 2-1).[16] In this model, psychosocial development depends significantly on the environment and is linked to the individual's *relationships* with others. Each stage of development involves a turning point, or crisis, that requires a response from the individual.

Piaget's focus was on the *cognitive transformations* that occur during childhood (see Table 2-1).[17] Accordingly, Piaget distinguished four different periods of cognitive, or intellectual, development based on the characteristic ways in which individuals organize their experience of the world: *sensorimotor, preoperational, concrete operational,* and *formal operational.* Although children move through these stages in the same sequence, each child's rate of development is unique.

Infancy and Toddlerhood

According to Erikson's model, infancy is characterized by developing a sense of *trust* toward the environment. If the infant's needs are not met, the result may be distrust. Thus, other people in the environment—typically, parents—play an important part in the infant's development as he or she acquires a sense of self and trust in others as reliable and nurturant. The death of a caregiver during infancy can disrupt the building of a foundation of trusting others. Similarly, a close death in the infant's environment, which puts other family members under stress, can adversely affect the infant's developing sense of predictability about the world.

During toddlerhood (roughly one to three years of age), the child grapples with issues of *autonomy* versus shame and doubt. As the toddler explores the environment and develops greater independence, there are clashes be-

T A B L E   *2-1*   *Piaget's Model of Cognitive Development*

Age (approximate)	Developmental Period	Characteristics
Birth–2 years	Sensorimotor	Focused on senses and motor abilities; learns object exists even when not observable (object permanence) and begins to remember and imagine ideas and experiences (mental representation).

2–7 years	Preoperational	Development of symbolic thinking and language to understand the world.
		    (2–4 years) *Preconceptual subperiod:* sense of magical omnipotence; self as center of world; egocentric thought; all natural objects have feelings and intention (will).
		    (4–6 years) *Prelogical subperiod:* beginning problem solving; seeing is believing; trial and error; understanding of other points of view; more socialized speech; gradual decentering of self and discovery of correct relationships.

7–12 years	Concrete operational	Applies logical abilities to understanding concrete ideas; organizes and classifies information; manipulates ideas and experiences symbolically; able to think backward and forward; notion of reversibility; can think logically about things experienced.
12+ years	Formal operational	Reasons logically about abstract ideas and experiences; can think hypothetically about things never experienced; deductive and inductive reasoning; complexity of knowledge; many answers to questions; interest in ethics, politics, social sciences.

tween what the child wants to do and what others want the child to do. Exercising independence is a hallmark of this stage. Toilet training typically occurs during this time. In both physical and psychosocial development, this is a period of "letting go" and "holding on." The death of a significant other, especially a parent, affects the child's task of pursuing independence and may cause a regression to earlier behaviors, such as clinging, crying, and being more demanding.

Turning to Piaget's model, we find that the first two years of life are characterized as the *sensorimotor* period, as a child develops and strengthens his or her sensory and motor, or physical, abilities. A parent who leaves the room has simply vanished; there is no thought, "My parent is in the other room." As the child accumulates experiences of the flow of events in the environment, he or she gradually begins to perceive patterns that become generalized into what Piaget terms "schemes," which tie together the common features of actions occurring at different times. During this period of development, Piaget says, "a Copernican revolution takes place," with the result that "at the end of this sensory-motor evolution, there are permanent objects, constituting a universe within which the child's own body exists also."[18]

Early Childhood

In Erikson's model, the preschool and kindergarten years (roughly three to five or six years of age) involve issues of *initiative* versus guilt. The child increasingly seeks his or her own purpose and direction, yet is concerned about how parents (and other significant adults) perceive these tentative efforts to express initiative and individuality. The egocentric orientation of the infant gives way to the socially integrated self of the older child. During this transitional period, situations arise that induce feelings of guilt. For instance, a child who has fantasies of doing away with a parent—expressed perhaps by the frustrated scream "I wish you were dead!"—may feel guilty about having such thoughts. Most children become fascinated with the idea of "gone" or "all gone." For the young child, being dead is a diminished form of life. A four-year-old girl told Robert Kastenbaum, "They have only dead people to talk to, and dead people don't listen, and they don't play, and they miss all the TV shows they liked."[19]

This period marks the beginning of the child's moral sense, the ability to function within socially sanctioned modes of behavior. Reflecting emerging communication skills, the child's concept of death expands quite rapidly during the preschool and kindergarten years.

The body becomes important to children's self-image as they race around on tricycles, learn to cut small pieces of paper precisely, and generally gain greater control over their bodies. During this period, bodily mutilation is one of the death-related fears that may manifest. This preoccupation with the body can be illustrated: A five-year-old witnessed the death of his younger brother, who was killed when the wheel of a truck rolled over his head. The parents, who were considering having a wake in their home, asked the surviving son how he might feel if his younger brother's body was brought into the house for a wake. His question was "Does he look hurt?" Concern about bodily disfigurement is characteristic of this stage of psychosocial development (see Figure 2-2).

In Piaget's model, early childhood is characterized as the *preoperational* period. A child's cognitive development centers on learning to use language and symbols to represent objects. Vocabulary develops at an astounding rate. During this period, the child's primary task is to appraise his or her situation in the world.

How does Piaget's model apply to children's concepts of death? A study conducted by Gerald Koocher supplies a partial answer. Children were asked four questions about death.[20] (You might want to answer each of these questions for yourself.) The first question was "What makes things die?" Children in the preoperational stage used fantasy reasoning, magical thinking, and realistic causes of death (sometimes expressed in egocentric terms). Here are sample responses:

Figure 2-2 *Accident Drawing by a Five-Year-Old*
In this drawing by a five-year-old who witnessed his younger brother's accidental death, the surviving child is depicted as riding a "big wheel" on the
left side of the truck that ran over his brother. The four wheels of the truck
are shown, and the younger brother's head is drawn next to the wheel far-
thest to the right. This drawing is similar to one drawn by the child on the
night of the fatal accident, when he told his parents, "I can't sleep because
I can't get the pictures out of my head." The act of externalizing these disturbing images by making a drawing had therapeutic value for this child in
coming to terms with the traumatic experience of his sibling's death.

- Nancy: "When they eat bad things, like if you went with a stranger and
  they gave you a candy bar with poison on it. [*The researcher asks, "Anything
  else?"*] Yes, you can die if you swallow a dirty bug."
- Carol: "They eat poison and stuff, pills. You'd better wait until your Mom
  gives them to you. [*Anything else?*] Drinking poison water and stuff like
  going swimming alone."
- David: "A bird might get real sick and die if you catch it. [*Anything else?*] They
  could eat the wrong foods like aluminum foil. That's all I can think of."

The understanding of death during the early childhood years is also illustrated in a study done by Helen Swain.[21] Most children in this study expressed
the notion that death is reversible, attributing the return of life to the good
effects of ambulances, hospitals, or doctors, whose help is often summoned
magically, as if a dead person could ring up the hospital and say, "Will you
send me an ambulance over here? I'm dead and I need you to fix me up."
About two-thirds of the children said that death is unlikely or avoidable or is
brought about only by unusual events such as an accident or a catastrophe.
About one-third expressed disbelief that death could happen to them or to
their families. Nearly half were uncertain about whether they would ever die
or else thought they would die only in the remote future.

The Dead Mouse

We had been out of town and the neighbors had been caring for our various pets. When we returned, we found that our cat had, as cats will, caught and killed a mouse and had laid it out ceremoniously in front of his bowl in the garage. I discovered that that had happened when I heard loud screams from the garage. "Pudley's killed a mouse. There's a dead mouse in the garage!" Loud screams, for the whole neighborhood to hear. I went downstairs. It was the first time that I had a chance to observe how my children dealt with death. I said, "Oh, there is?" "Right here," they said. "Look!" They began to tell me how they had determined it was dead. It was not moving. They had poked at it several times and it didn't move. Matthew, who was five years old, added that it didn't look like it was ever going to move again. That was his judgment that the mouse was dead.

I said to him, "Well, what are we going to do?" I could feel myself being slightly repulsed; my fingers went to my nose. It was obvious to me that the mouse was dead—it had started to decay. Matt said very matter-of-factly, "Well, we'll have to bury it." Heather, seven, climbed on a chair and announced, "Not me. I'm not going to touch it. Don't bring it around here. Aughhh, dead mouse!" At that time, she was intent on being what she thought was feminine, and part of the stereotype involved not getting herself dirty.

So Matt volunteered for the job. "I'm going to need a shovel," he said. I stood back and watched, interested to see what would happen. I noticed that he didn't touch the mouse. From somewhere he already had gotten the idea that it wasn't appropriate to touch dead things. He carefully lifted it with the shovel and took it into the backyard to dig a hole. Heather peered around and watched at a safe distance.

After the mouse was buried, Matt came back and said, "I'm going to need some wood, a hammer, and a nail." I thought, "Oh great! He's going to perform some kind of little ceremony and place a symbol of some kind on the grave." Matt went to the woodpile and carefully selected a piece of wood maybe two inches long and another piece a bit wider, perhaps three inches wide and about four or five inches long. I thought, "Tombstone?" He got the nail and put the pieces of wood together in the shape of a cross.

I thought, "Oh. A cross, religious symbol, burial, funeral—all the things I knew about what happens with a dead body." Matt picked up a marking pen and wrote on the front of the cross: "DEAD MOUSE, KEEP OUT!" And he pounded it into the ground in front of where the mouse was buried. I thought, "What's going on in this kid's mind?"

I asked him, "Does that mean that when I die there should be a sign saying, "Dead Mommie. Keep out"? He put his hand on his hip and looked at me with that disgust that five-year-olds can muster for somebody who is *so* dumb, and said, "Of course not. You're going to be buried in one of those places where they have bodies. This is a backyard. Kids could ride their bikes over it. Who would know that there is a mouse buried back here?" I was flabbergasted.

A few weeks later there was a long discussion about what the mouse would look like at that time. My first thoughts were "Don't do that! You can't dig it up. It's not nice. It's not good. The mouse has to rest his spirit." Then I realized that all those things were coming from that place in me that didn't want to see what a month-old dead mouse looked like.

So I kept quiet. They dug and dug, and I could feel the sweat dripping off me. They dug a huge hole, but could find no remnants of the mouse. I was a bit relieved. But that brought up all kinds of questions about what happened to the mouse. I made this elaborate picture of a compost pile, really a lengthy explanation. Finally I realized that they didn't understand at all and that what I was saying was of no interest to them.

I said, "Well, it's like if you buried an orange." Something safe, I thought, something I can deal with that can be dug up day by day by day to see how it goes back into the earth.

They buried an orange and dug it up and dug it up and dug it up. And it wasn't an orange anymore.

I came away from that experience thinking, "Where did they learn all that? Matt's behavior, particularly. . . . Where did he get that from?"

Middle Childhood or School-Age Period

In Erikson's model, the years from about six to eleven correspond to the stage of *industry* versus inferiority. This is a period when the child is busy in school, interacting with peers in a variety of ways. As a child's efforts begin to gain recognition and bring satisfaction, he or she may be anxious about those areas in which there is a sense of inadequacy or failing to measure up. The death of a parent at this stage is likely to deprive a child of an important source of recognition. During these years of development, as children learn new tasks, they are also comparing themselves with their peers. When one nine-year-old moved to a different school shortly after her mother's death, she didn't want her new acquaintances to know about her mother's death. When questioned about this, she replied, "Having a dead mother makes me too different from other kids."

In Piaget's framework, this period is denoted by the term *concrete operations*. The child begins to use logic to solve problems and to think logically about things without having to have their relationships demonstrated directly. The ability to do arithmetic, for instance, requires the recognition that numbers are symbols for quantities. Children at this stage are able to manipulate concepts in a logical fashion, although they typically do not engage in abstract thinking. In other words, the ability to think logically is applied to objects, but not yet to hypotheses, which require the ability to carry out "operations on operations." Thus, the characteristic mode of thought in this developmental period emphasizes concreteness and the logic of *things*.

During this period, children name both intentional and unintentional means by which a person may die, and they are familiar with a wide range of causes of death. Here are some responses from the children in Koocher's study when asked about causes of death:

- Todd: "Knife, arrow, guns, and lots of stuff. You want me to tell you all of them? [*As many as you want.*] Hatchets and animals, and fires and explosions, too."

- Kenny: "Cancer, heart attacks, poison, guns, bullets, or if someone drops a boulder on you."
- Deborah: "Accidents, cars, guns, or a knife. Old age, sickness, taking dope, or drowning."

Adolescence

In Erikson's model, adolescence is marked by the milestone of establishing an individual *identity*. A bridge is established between the past—the years of childhood and dependency—and the future—the years of adulthood and independence. Adolescence is a period of integration as well as separation. The central question is "Who am I as an emotional, thinking, physical, and sexual being?"

Remember what it's like being a teenager? Becoming more your own person? Striving to express your own ideas and beliefs? Sorting out the tangle of all that's happening to you? Deciding what you want for your life? Adolescence can be confusing and challenging. For adolescents, the achievement of goals and dreams seems nearly within their grasp; death threatens that achievement. Surviving a close death may result in a more rapid "growing up."

In Piaget's model, adolescence is characterized by the use of *formal operations*. The fourth and final phase in Piaget's theory, this period begins at about the age of eleven or twelve and extends into adulthood, although a person's fundamental way of seeing the world is thought to be fairly well established by about the age of fifteen. With the arrival of formal operational thinking, the individual is able to "think about thinking"—that is, to formulate concepts that are abstract or symbolic. Relations of correspondence or implication between complex sets of statements can be perceived, analogies recognized, and assumptions or deductions made. It becomes possible to predict outcomes without having to try them in the real world. In a chess game, for example, formal operations of thought allow players to consider a number of complicated strategies and to predict the likely result of each move, without having to touch a single piece on the board.

In Koocher's study, most of the children who used formal operations of thought were twelve or older, although some were as young as nine or ten. The children interviewed by Koocher reflected a mature understanding of death in their responses to the question "What makes things die?"

- Ed: "You mean death in a physical sense? [*Yes.*] Destruction of a vital organ or life force within us."
- George: "They get old and their body gets all worn out, and their organs don't work as well as they used to."
- Paula: "When the heart stops, blood stops circulating. You stop breathing, and that's it. [*Anything else?*] Well, there's lots of ways it can get started, but that's what really happens."

Although adolescents typically demonstrate a mature understanding of death, this does not necessarily mean that there are no differences in the ways

I was astonished to hear a highly intelligent boy of ten remark after the sudden death of his father: "I know father's dead, but what I can't understand is why he doesn't come home to supper."

Sigmund Freud, *The Interpretation of Dreams*

adolescents and adults understand and cope with death. For example, an adolescent's understanding of the universality of death may be influenced by a sense of invulnerability ("It can't happen to me"). The concept of personal death may not be easily accepted. In forging a sense of individual identity, the adolescent is confronted by the need to "reconcile that identity with ultimate disintegration and not being."[22]

Although "adolescence" generally is defined as ages eleven or twelve through eighteen or twenty, some psychologists propose a developmental category, "emerging adulthood," for the period from the late teens through the twenties, especially ages eighteen to twenty-five. Because a prolonged period of independent role exploration occurs during these years, this is a time of life when many possibilities and directions in work, love, and worldview can be imagined. People in this age group no longer view themselves as adolescents, but they also may not see themselves entirely as adults. "Emerging adults can pursue novel and intense experiences more freely than adolescents because they are less likely to be monitored by parents and can pursue them more freely than adults because they are less constrained by roles."[23] The prevalence of certain types of risk behavior—including unprotected sex, substance abuse, risky driving, and binge drinking—appears to peak during the years of emerging adulthood. Like adolescents in this regard, emerging adults may think they are "beyond death."

The Evolution of a Mature Concept of Death

Through successive periods of development, individuals progress toward a mature understanding of death and exhibit characteristic responses to loss. We looked at children's responses to the question "What makes things die?" Their answers to other questions posed by Koocher also corresponded to varied developmental stages. Asked "How do you make dead things come back to life?" children who thought of death as reversible gave answers like "You can help them; give them hot food and keep them healthy so it won't happen again." Another child said, "No one ever taught me about that, but maybe you could give them some kind of medicine and take them to the hospital to get better." Children in later developmental stages recognized death as permanent: "If it was a tree, you could water it. If it's a person, you could rush them to the emergency room, but it would do no good if they were dead already." Another child said, "Maybe some day we'll be able to do it, but not now. Scientists are working on that problem."

Asked "When will you die?" younger children gave answers ranging from "When I'm seven" (from a six-year-old) to "Three hundred years." In contrast, older children expected to live a statistically correct life span, or a bit more; the usual age at which death was expected was about eighty.

In answer to the researcher's question "What will happen when you die?" one nine-and-a-half-year-old said, "They'll help me come back alive." The researcher asked, "Who?" "My father, my mother, and my grandfather," the child responded. "They'll keep me in bed and feed me and keep me away from rat poison and stuff." According to some models, a child of nine would understand that none of those measures would work. Thus, this example illustrates the point that age-and-stage correlations provide, at best, a rule of thumb concerning how children develop.

In answer to the same question, an eight-and-a-half-year-old replied, "You go to heaven and all that will be left of you will be a skeleton. My friend has some fossils. A fossil is just a skeleton." Notice how this child used comparison to help interpret what happens when death occurs. An eleven-year-old said, "I'll feel dizzy and tired and pass out, and then they'll bury me and I'll rot away. You just disintegrate and only your bones will be left."

A twelve-year-old said, "I'll have a nice funeral and be buried and leave all my money to my son." One ten-year-old said, "If I tell you, you'll laugh." The researcher assured the child, "No, I won't. I want to know what you really think." Thus encouraged, the child continued, "I think I'm going to be reincarnated as a plant or animal, whatever they need at that particular time." The ability to imagine what things might be like in the future is seen in this child's response.

Sociocultural Influences on Our Understanding of Death

Acquiring a mature understanding of death is part of the developmental process known as *socialization*. This process involves learning and internalizing the norms, rules, and values of society. Through socialization, younger members of a society acquire knowledge, behavior, and ideals from older generations. Socialization does not stop with childhood's end, but continues throughout life as people develop new social roles and values. Nor is it a one-way process whereby individuals simply learn to fit into society. Society's norms and values are modified as its members redefine their social roles and obligations.

Society can be defined as "a group of people who share a common culture, a common territory, and a common identity; and who feel themselves to constitute a unified and distinct entity which involves interacting in socially structured relationships."[24] The social systems and institutions of a society give it a distinctive flavor and set it apart from other societies. This sense of distinctiveness is captured in the term *culture,* which is a kind of shorthand for referring to the lifeways—that is, the ways of thinking, feeling, and acting—of a given group of people. We often refer to societies in ways that highlight this

TABLE 2-2   *Nonmaterial Aspects of Culture*

Knowledge: Conclusions based on empirical evidence.

Beliefs: Conclusions for which there is not sufficient empirical evidence for them to be seen as necessarily true.

Values: Abstract ideas about what is good and desirable.

Norms: Social rules and guidelines that prescribe appropriate behavior in particular situations.

Signs and symbols: Representations that stand for something else; this category includes language and gestures.

Source: Adapted from Norman Goodman, *Introduction to Sociology* (New York: HarperCollins, 1992), pp. 31–34.

cultural distinctiveness—for example, Japanese culture, Western European culture, and so on.

Culture can be defined as "all that in human society which is socially rather than biologically transmitted."[25] This definition encompasses both material and nonmaterial components. Material culture consists of "things"— that is, manufactured objects (for example, buildings and consumer goods) or physical manifestations of the life of a people. Nonmaterial aspects of culture lie in the realm of ideas, beliefs, values, and customs (see Table 2-2). Culture is dynamic; that is, it changes as the members of a society reevaluate inherited beliefs, values, and customs in light of ongoing experiences. In this sense, culture operates as a framing device that channels, rather than determines, attitudes and behaviors.

Agents of Socialization

Socialization involves a variety of influences, beginning with the family and extending to the mass media and the global "transcultural" environment. Children today are exposed to a broader range of influences on their socialization than at any other time in history. As Hannelore Wass says, "Children adopt many values and beliefs from significant adults in their world [including] parents, teachers, public figures, sports heroes, and famous entertainers."[26]

Although the main phases of socialization occur during the years of childhood, the process continues lifelong. *Resocialization,* a term that refers to the "uprooting and restructuring of basic attitudes, values, or identities," occurs when adults take on new roles that require replacing their existing values and modes of behavior.[27] This occurs, for example, with religious conversion, starting a new job, getting married, having children, or surviving the death of a mate. Widowhood involves changes in many areas of life, as new roles and activities are taken on. Rapid social change also leads to resocialization, as when women began entering the workforce in large numbers.

People tend to acquire their learning about dying and death on an ad hoc basis—that is, in a disorganized and impromptu fashion. Formal education about death is offered through courses, seminars, and the like, but these avenues of socialization are not part of most people's experience. The term *tactical socialization* refers to strategies that hospice caregivers, for example, use to informally teach people about death and dying.[28] It involves an active effort to change other people's perceptions and behaviors about some aspect of their social world.

The way we learn about death tends to be less a result of systematic instruction than of happenstance. It is not always possible to pinpoint the genesis of ideas that an individual acquires about death. Consider the following incident, involving two siblings, ages eight and ten. When asked to draw a picture of a funeral (see Figure 2-3), they got out their colored pencils and immersed themselves in the task. After a while, Heather (ten) said to Matt (eight), "Hey, you've got smiles on those faces! This is supposed to be a funeral. What are they doing with smiles on their faces?" In her model of appropriate death-related behavior, people don't smile at funerals; to her younger brother, smiles were perfectly acceptable. One can only guess the influences that provoke such strong statements about what kind of behavior is appropriate at funerals. It is in interactions like this that attitudes about death are incorporated into a child's understanding of death.

Family

The family is the foundational social institution in all societies, although the definition of "family" varies from place to place and time to time. In the routines of daily life, the beliefs and values of parents are transmitted to their children. The family is the first source of death education in our lives, and its influence continues throughout our lives.[29]

Think back to your own childhood. What messages did you receive about death that remain to this day in the back of your mind? Possibly some messages were conveyed directly: "This is what death is" or "This is how we behave in relation to death." Perhaps some messages were indirect: "Let's not talk about it . . . ." How would the rest of that sentence go? Let's not talk about it . . . because it's not something that people talk about? When, as a child, one woman encountered a dead animal on the highway, she was told, "You shouldn't look at it." Her mother admonished, "Put your head down; children shouldn't see that." This is a parental message about appropriate behavior toward death.

Other parental messages about death are communicated unconsciously. Consider the notion of replaceability. A child's pet dies, and the parent says, "It's okay, dear, we'll get another one." Children differ in their emotional response to the death of a family pet; some grieve intensely when a beloved pet dies. Quickly replacing it may not allow time for acknowledging the loss. What lesson about death is taught? Imagine a situation in which a mother's grief over her mate's death is interrupted by her child's remark, "Don't worry, Mommy, we'll get you another one."

The lessons about death that are learned in the family are conveyed by actions as well as words. A woman now in her thirties tells the following story: "I remember a time when my mother ran over a cat. I wasn't with her in the car, but I recall my mother coming home and just totally falling apart. She ran into the bedroom and cried for hours. Since that time, I've been extremely conscientious about not killing anything. If there's an insect on me or in my house, I'll pick it up and carry it outside." Parental attitudes, and the attitudes of other family members, shape the values and behaviors not only of the child but also of the adult that the child will become, and they influence how that adult conveys attitudes toward death to his or her own children.

School and Peers

Schools teach more than "reading, 'riting, and 'rithmetic." The social world of a child is dramatically broadened during the school years. "The scraps of lore which children learn from each other are at once more real, more immediately serviceable, and more vastly entertaining to them than anything which they learn from grown-ups."[30] Even before school years, children enter the social world of their peer group as they play with other children of the same age and general social status. Recall how, in chasing games, a touch with the tip of a finger can have a noxious effect, as if the chaser were evil, magic, or diseased, and the touch was contagious.[31] Hobbies and sports also connect children to a community and a set of social norms. With the broadening of a child's social network, there is an increase in learning about death.

Mass Media and Children's Literature

Television, movies, radio, newspapers, magazines, books, videos, records, CDs, and the Internet—these media have a powerful socializing influence. Media messages communicate cultural attitudes toward death to children, even when the message is not purposely directed to them, as with news reports of disasters. When President John F. Kennedy was assassinated, a classic study found that children tended to select from the details presented by the media those aspects that were consistent with their developmental concerns.[32] Younger children worried about the appearance of the president's body and the effects of the death on his family; older children expressed concerns about the impact of Kennedy's death on the political system.

Many classic children's stories and fairy tales depict death, near deaths, or the threat of death.[33] There are "tales of children abandoned in woods; of daughters poisoned by their mothers' hands; of sons forced to betray their siblings; of men and women struck down by wolves, or imprisoned in windowless towers."[34] Death has often had a place in children's literature, and this is especially true of the earliest versions of familiar stories that parents and other adults share with children. Elizabeth Lamers says, "American children taught to read with textbooks such as *McGuffey's Eclectic Readers* found that death was presented as tragic, but inevitable, and many of the death-related stories conveyed a moral lesson."[35] In the nineteenth century, the violence in children's stories was usually graphic and gory so that it would make the desired moral impression.[36]

The manner in which death is presented in children's stories communicates cultural values. Consider, for example, the contrasts between different versions of the tale of Little Red Riding Hood.[37] In the traditional version of

Figure 2-3 *Children's Drawings of a Funeral*

Instructed to draw a picture of a funeral, a sister (age ten) and brother (eight) did so. The ten-year-old, whose drawing is at the left, emphasizes the emotional responses of the survivors. We see the picture as if we are looking in (and down) upon their grief. The figures in the first two pews have tears streaming down their faces and one woman shouts "No!" At ten, this child reflects on the sorrowful and unwelcome nature of death. When questioned about the empty pews, she said they were for anyone who came late.

The eight-year-old's drawing (above) is viewed from a similar perspective (looking in and down at the scene). Here we see the survivors grouped around a flag-draped and flower-bedecked coffin. The figures are portrayed with smiles on their faces. The focus in this drawing is on the symbols of death (for example, the casket) and the ceremony rather than emotions. During the drawing session, the older sister commented that her brother's picture was "too happy" for a funeral scene.

Little Red Riding-Hood

... "Dear me, Grandmamma, what great arms you have!"
The wolf replied:
"They are so much better to hug you with, my child."
"Why, Grandmamma, what great legs you have got!"
"That is to run the better, my child!"
"But, Grandmamma, what great ears you've got!"
"That is to hear the better, my child."
"But, Grandmamma, what great eyes you've got!"
"They are so much better to see you with, my child."
Then the little girl, who was now very much frightened, said:
"Oh, Grandmamma, what great teeth you have got!"
"THEY ARE THE BETTER TO EAT YOU UP!"
With these words the wicked wolf fell upon Little Red Riding-Hood and ate her up in a moment.

Journeys Through Bookland, Volume One

the story, the wolf eats Little Red Riding Hood, but she is saved by a woodsman who kills the wolf and slits its stomach, allowing Little Red Riding Hood to emerge unharmed. In more recent versions, Little Red Riding Hood's screams alert the woodsman, who chases the wolf and then returns to announce that she will be bothered no more (the killing of the wolf occurs offstage and is not mentioned).[38]

The Chinese tale of *Lon Po Po* (Granny Wolf) comes from an oral tradition thought to be over a thousand years old. In this version of the story, three young children are left by themselves while their mother goes away to visit their grandmother. The wolf, disguised as Po Po (Grandmother), persuades the children to open the locked door of their house. When they do, he quickly blows out the light. By making perceptive inquiries, however, the oldest child cleverly discovers the wolf's true identity and, with her younger siblings, escapes to the top of a ginkgo tree. Through trickery, the children convince the wolf to step into a basket so that they can haul him up to enjoy the ginkgo nuts. Joining together, the children start hauling up the basket. But, just as it nearly reaches the top of the tree, they let the basket drop to the ground. The story says, "Not only did the wolf bump his head, but he broke his heart to pieces."[39] Climbing down to the branches just above the wolf, the children discover that he is "truly dead." Unlike the Western version, which has a solitary child facing the threat of the wolf by herself and ultimately being saved by someone else, the Chinese folk tale emphasizes the value of being part of a group effort to do away with the wolf.

Some children's stories are written with the specific aim of answering their questions about dying and death. In many such books, especially those for young children, death is often presented as part of the natural cycle. These stories express the idea that, like the transition from one season to the

The Shroud

A mother once had a little seven-year-old boy with such a sweet, beautiful face that no one could look at him without loving him, and she loved him more than anything in the world. Suddenly, the child fell sick, and God took him. The mother was inconsolable and wept day and night. Soon after he was buried, the child began to appear in places where he had sat playing in his lifetime. When his mother wept, he too wept, and when morning came he vanished. Then when the mother could not stop crying, he appeared one night wrapped in the little white shroud he had been buried in and wearing a wreath of flowers on his head. He sat down at her feet and said: "Oh, mother, if you don't stop crying I won't be able to sleep in my coffin, for my shroud is wet with all the tears that fall on it." When she heard that, the mother was horrified, and from then on she shed no tears. The next night the child came again. He held a candle in his hand and said: "You see, my shroud is almost dry. Now I can rest in my grave." After that, the mother gave her grief into God's keeping and bore it silently and patiently. The child never came again, but slept in his little bed under the ground.

Grimm's Tales for Young and Old

next, each ending in life is followed by renewal. (A list of children's books about death is included in Chapter 10.)

Lullabies also contain themes of death and violence.[40] In every human culture and in every historical period, adults have sung to children. It is said that, with the first lullaby a mother sings to her child, death education begins.[41] Consider the message in this well-known lullaby:

Rockabye baby, in the treetops.
When the wind blows, the cradle will rock.
When the bough breaks, the cradle will fall.
Down will come baby, cradle and all.

Some lullabies are "mourning songs," which describe the death or funeral of a child; others are "threat" songs that warn of violence if a child does not go to sleep or perform some other action in the expected manner.

Of two hundred nursery rhymes examined in one study, about half described the wonder and beauty of life, whereas the other half dealt with the ways in which humans and animals die or are mistreated.[42] Death-related themes in these rhymes include accounts of murder, choking to death, torment and cruelty, maiming, misery and sorrow, as well as stories of lost or abandoned children and depictions of poverty and want.

Religion

As a key element of human culture, religion and, more broadly, spirituality have the potential to shape individual lives and personalities.[43] Contemplating one's place in the universe is a crucial aspect of human development. Religion is a basis for morality and human relationships, helping people live in harmony with the gods and giving meaning to life.[44] A significant theme in the work of W. E. B. Du Bois, a pioneering American sociologist of religion, is the insight that religious institutions do more than connect people with God, they connect people to one another.[45]

For children as well as adults, religion can offer pathways toward understanding and coping with dying and death. It provides an interpretative framework within which to find some constructive or positive meaning in an otherwise negative or tragic event by placing the event in a larger context. In difficult times, religion enhances coping resources by fostering self-esteem and a sense of control through, for example, trust and faith in God.[46]

The death awareness movement has gained much from its connection with religion and spirituality. Lucy Bregman says,

> Spiritual beliefs and practices provide an interpretation of the dying process, aid in the developmental task of transcendence, and afford comfort to dying individuals and their family members.[47]

For dying patients and their families, religion may offer solace, suggest some meaning in dying, and provide rituals that help ease the pangs of grief. Vernon Reynolds and Ralph Tanner note that religion is concerned with "ministering to the dying person, preparing him or her for the world to come, generally being involved with his physical needs and psychological feelings at this time, and likewise helping those who are especially close."[48]

It is useful to distinguish between two related concepts: *religiosity* and *spirituality*. Although a partial definition of spirituality is "to be concerned with religious values," it is understood more broadly as a search for ultimate meaning and purpose in life, which may or may not be directly related to a particular religious tradition. "It entails connection to self-chosen and/or religious beliefs, values, and practices that give meaning to life, thereby inspiring and motivating individuals to achieve their optimal being."[49] It emphasizes "a personal search for connection with a larger sacredness" and "a bonding with others that cannot be severed, not even by death."[50]

The consolations of a religious or spiritual orientation are likely to depend on the manner in which that person makes such an orientation part of his or her life. For instance, someone who attends religious services mainly because they create opportunities for social interaction is likely to have a different experience than someone who participates because he or she finds deep personal meaning in religious creeds and beliefs. In this sense, religiosity embraces several dimensions, including[51]

1. Experiential religiosity (emotional ties to a religion)
2. Ritualistic religiosity (participation in religious ceremonies)
3. Ideological religiosity (religious commitment)
4. Consequential religiosity (degree to which religion is integrated into the person's daily life)
5. Intellectual religiosity (knowledge about the religion's traditions, beliefs, and practices)

T A B L E   2-3   *Four Functions of Religion in Societies*

1. Religion provides a shared set of beliefs, values, and norms around which people can form a common identity. Thus, religion is a unifier, "the social glue that binds a group together by giving it a common set of values."
2. Religion provides answers to the "big questions" about human existence and purpose. It addresses issues of life and death, outlines the kind of life people are expected to lead, and explains what happens to them after they die.
3. Religion often provides a foundation for the norms and laws of a society. Laws acquire a moral as well as legal force when they are embedded in religious values.
4. Religion is a source of emotional and psychological support to people, especially at times of crisis.

Source: Adapted from Norman Goodman, *Introduction to Sociology* (New York: HarperCollins, 1992), pp. 205–206.

Any or all of these dimensions can have an impact on how a person faces death and copes with loss. For example, a young Filipino American man whose father had died talked about the comfort he felt in connection with a funeral mass held in the church where his family worshiped. Commenting on the language and other symbols present in the service, he said, "You know, I've never thought much about what those prayers are about, but the soothing rhythms of the chants and the pungent smell of the incense caused me to feel that my dad is somehow still being cared for, that he's really okay." This young man's experience includes aspects of experiential, ritualistic, and consequential religiosity.

Even in so-called secular societies, religion plays a significant role in shaping attitudes and behaviors toward death (see Table 2-3). In the United States, more than 90 percent of the population is affiliated with a religious tradition.[52] Such traditions are part of a child's socialization. Many concepts central to religious traditions "are not as opaque to young children as often thought."[53] A survey of teenagers in the U.S. indicates that 95 percent believe in God and about one-quarter consider religious faith more important to them than it is to their parents.[54]

Teachable Moments

In the course of their daily lives, opportunities abound for children to learn about dying and death.[55] Consider, for example, a mother who discovers her eleven-year-old son sitting at her new computer writing his will. Taken aback, she pauses for a moment as thoughts race through her head: Why is he writing a will? How did an eleven-year-old become interested in giving away his favorite treasures? Does he believe he is going to die soon? What should I do? What can I say? Gathering her courage, she cautiously adjusts her tone to suggest a neutral stance and asks, "What has made you think about writing a will?"

Turning to her, the joy of accomplishment lighting up his face, the boy says, "I was looking at the menu on your computer and found *Willmaker*. The program came up and all I have to do is fill in the blanks. It's easy, see? Then I can print out my very own will."

I recall with utter clarity the first great shock of my life. A scream came from the cottage next door. I rushed into the room, as familiar as my own home. The Larkin kids, Conor, Liam and Brigid, all hovered about the alcove in which a mattress of bog fir bedded old Kilty. They stood in gape-mouthed awe.

I stole up next to Conor. "Grandfar is dead," he said.

Their ma, Finola, who was eight months pregnant, knelt with her head pressed against the old man's heart. It was my very first sight of a dead person. He was a waxy, bony specimen lying there with his open mouth showing no teeth at all and his glazed eyes staring up at me and me staring back until I felt my own ready to pop out of their sockets.

Oh, it was a terrible moment of revelation for me. All of us kids thought old Kilty had the magic of the fairies and would live forever, a tale fortified by the fact that he was the oldest survivor of the great famine, to say nothing of being a hero of the Fenian Rising of '67 who had been jailed and fearfully tortured for his efforts.

I was eleven years old at that moment. Kilty had been daft as long as I could recall, always huddled near the fire mumbling incoherently. He was an ancient old dear, ancient beyond age, but nobody ever gave serious consideration to the fact he might die.

Leon Uris, *Trinity*

Thus we encounter the concept of a "teachable moment," a phrase used by educators to describe opportunities for learning that arise out of ordinary experiences. Because of their immediacy, such naturally occurring events are ideal for learning. The learner's questions, enthusiasm, and motivation guide the educational process. If we assume that learning always flows in a single direction, from adult to child, we miss the quintessential quality of education as an interactive process. In the example of the young boy filling in the blanks of a computerized will-making program, the mother appears to occupy most clearly the role of the learner. She learns something about her son's exploration of the new computer and, more important, she learns the crucial lesson of gathering information before reacting.

Suppose this mother, acting out of initial shock at her son's apparent interest in death, had hastily responded, "Stop that! Children shouldn't be thinking about wills or about dying!" A lesson about death would surely be taught, but it wouldn't promote a healthy understanding. It is useful to ask: *What* is being taught? Does the "teaching" result from a conscious design? Or is it unintentionally conveying unhealthy messages about death?

Let's return to our story of the mother and son. Having elicited information without acting on her initial anxiety, the mother can use this conversation as an opportunity to discuss death with her son. She might call attention to the entry for "Designated Guardian for Minor Children," informing her son about the steps she has taken to ensure his well-being ("Did I tell you that Aunt Martha and Uncle John are listed in my will as your guardians?") as well as to respond to his concerns ("No, I do not intend to die for a long time").

They might spend a few minutes talking about other aspects of death and how people prepare for it. An atmosphere of openness is promoted as information is exchanged between adult and child. Much learning can take place in a brief conversation.

Teachable moments are often defined in the context of unplanned or unexpected occurrences, but it is useful to recognize that parents, educators, and other adults can intentionally create situations that encourage such opportunities for learning about death.[56] There is no rule that we must wait until such events happen spontaneously. Indeed, in the example given earlier, the mother used her son's experience with the computer program as a way of introducing their subsequent discussion about death. Similarly, in films produced for children, death is frequently part of the plot, and this can lead to a natural discussion about how grief, for example, is portrayed among the various characters.[57] The key to making the most of such opportunities is adequate preparation by trusted adults in the child's environment.

Teachable moments take place not only between adults and children, but also between adults. While on an airplane trip, an executive for a large corporation engaged one of this book's authors in conversation. Upon learning the subject of this textbook, his tone changed a bit as he said, "Could I ask your opinion on a personal matter?" The question involved a family dispute about whether the man's five-year-old son should attend his grandfather's burial

Children experience the impact of war on their lives in a variety of ways. For the German child seen here, war brought a stark encounter with death. This child was one of many German citizens who, at the end of World War II, were ordered by the provisional military government of the U.S. Third Army to view the exhumed bodies of Russians, Poles, and Czechs killed while imprisoned in the concentration camp at Flossenberg. For Amanda Wille (facing page), the impact of war was felt in terms of the anticipated loss of her father, a Navy computer technician, as he prepared to board the USS John F. Kennedy for service during the Persian Gulf War. Understanding only that her father was going away, the three-year-old seemed anxious and bewildered until she found a piece of string on the Norfolk, Virginia, dock. After her father broke the string and tied one piece around his wrist and the other around hers, Amanda cried and hugged him goodbye.

ceremony at Arlington National Cemetery. He was concerned that the military ceremony—with uniforms, soldiers, and a twenty-one-gun salute—would frighten his son. After he shared additional information about his family and child, suggestions were offered about ways that parental support could be provided to the child during the funeral rites. Hearing these suggestions made it possible for the man to reconsider his earlier decision to exclude the child. With specific recommendations in hand, he decided that the child should be present at his grandfather's funeral. You do not have to be the author of a textbook to offer information that is helpful to people who are

© Robin Layton Kinsley

coping with death-related issues. In reading this book, you will gain information that can be appropriately offered.

Experiences with Death

When children are included in activities surrounding the death of a close family member or friend, they usually acquire an understanding of death that is associated with children at a later stage of development. One six-year-old who witnessed the accidental death of her sibling expressed a clear understanding that death is final, that people die, and that she herself could die.

She was concerned about how she could protect herself and her friends from the dangerous circumstances that had led to her brother's death. Her attitude was displayed in admonitions to schoolmates that they should try to prevent accidents.

Encounters with violent death can powerfully alter a child's understanding of death.[58] Drawings made by Cambodian children in refugee camps depict death as the predominant theme.[59] Having seen the deaths of parents and others from starvation, children responded to that traumatic experience in their drawings. One such picture shows a woman in the midst of six smaller bodies with the caption "Mother's Dead Children." James Garbarino says, "Few issues challenge our moral, intellectual, and political resources as does the topic of children and community violence—war, violent crime on the streets, and other forms of armed conflict."[60]

A diary written by a young girl in war-torn Sarajevo highlights the effects of violence on children. Zlata Filipovic's diary displays an evolution from the ordinary concerns of teenage life to a shattering preoccupation with destruction and death as warfare disrupts normal life. In one entry, Zlata writes: "War has crossed out the day and replaced it with horror, and now horrors are unfolding instead of days."[61] Many children and teenagers growing up in America's cities experience warlike disruptions due to drug-related violence and gang warfare, a situation that writer, actor, and musician Ice-T characterizes as "the killing fields" of America.[62]

Children who experience firsthand the reality of death through war or violence, or in connection with other forms of catastrophic death, often exhibit a fatalistic attitude that contrasts with the attitude of children whose experiences of death occur in benign circumstances. When questioned about the "ways people die," children in violent or death-saturated environments tend to answer quite differently from children whose lives are comparatively sheltered from such experiences (see Figures 2-4 and 2-5).

When children in an urban school in Germany were asked about the ways people die, violent deaths were described as being caused by "weapons" and "sharp knives." Conspicuously absent was any use of the word *gun*.[63] In Germany, handguns, being illegal, are not available to the general populace. The children's responses corresponded to their environment.

Take a moment to consider your own circumstances. Do you live in a rural, urban, or small-town environment? What region of the country do you live in? The North, East, South, or West? Was your school environment ethnically and religiously diverse, or was it not? Your response to death is likely to be influenced by such factors. Life experiences are powerful in shaping a person's attitudes and beliefs about death. When such experiences occur in early childhood, a person may become fully aware of their impact only in adulthood.

Chance encounters, or fortuitous happenings, may be beneficial or detrimental, depending on the nature and interplay of personal and social forces.[64] Children (and adults) who have a positive sense of self-esteem and are comfortable with themselves, who see themselves as active, vital, and interesting, and who have caring relationships with others tend to be less fearful about dying and death. Consider the responses to death that you have

Figure 2-4 *Ways People Die: Children's Images*
Above: A seven-year-old African American boy in a large Midwestern city draws a picture of murder by decapitation. (In separate incidents, two young girls in his city had recently been killed in this manner.)
Below: In contrast, the drawing created by a seven-year-old Caucasian boy attending Catholic school in a small California town portrays the child's concept that people die when "God calls you home." Notice the child's depiction of the voice of God and heavenly "pearly gates."

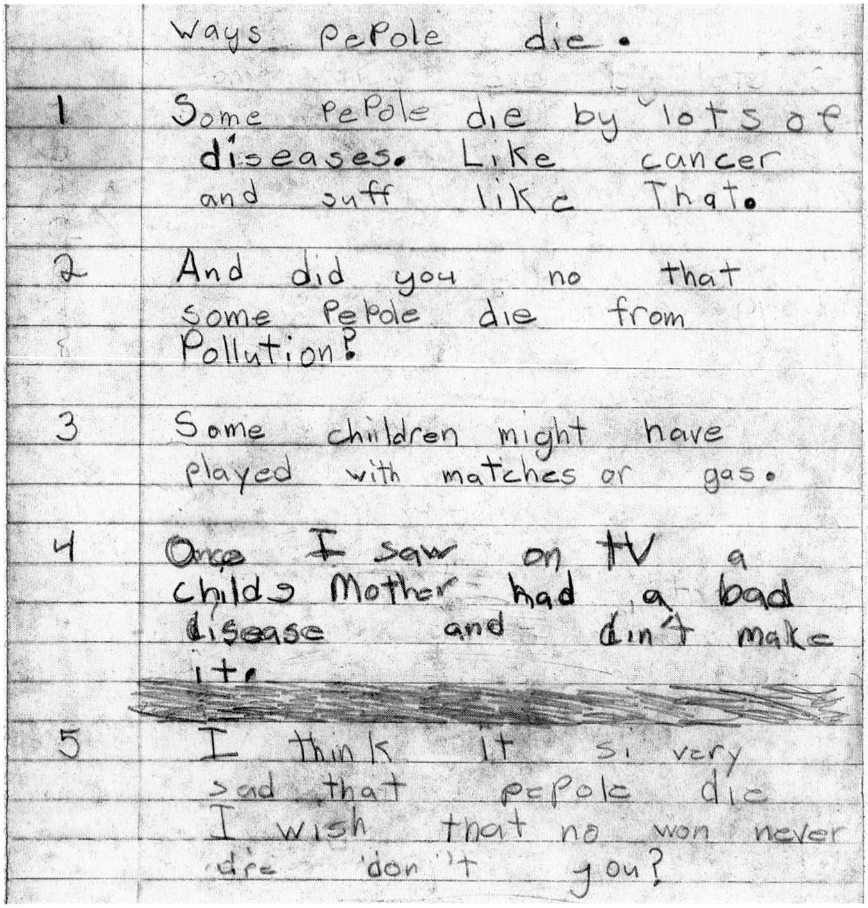

Figure 2-5 *Ways People Die: Children's Explanations*

Environment, including both time and place, influences a child's understanding of death. The impact of environment on children's views of death
can be evoked by asking them to make a list or draw a picture in response
to the question "What are the ways people die?" The list shown above was
written in 1978 by a seven-year-old Caucasian girl living in a small coastal
California town. It stands in sharp contrast to the thirteen-item response
(*facing page*) written in 1995 by a seven-year-old African American boy living
in a major Midwestern city. Although both lists were created by children of
the same age, the second list reflects both the passage of time (seventeen
years) and the circumstances of life in an inner-city metropolitan environment. Whereas the first child's list focuses on diseases and accidents, the
second child's explanation shows familiarity with a broad range of causes
of death, few of which relate to "natural" events. His illustration of item
number 11, "cut your head off," is shown in Figure 2-4.

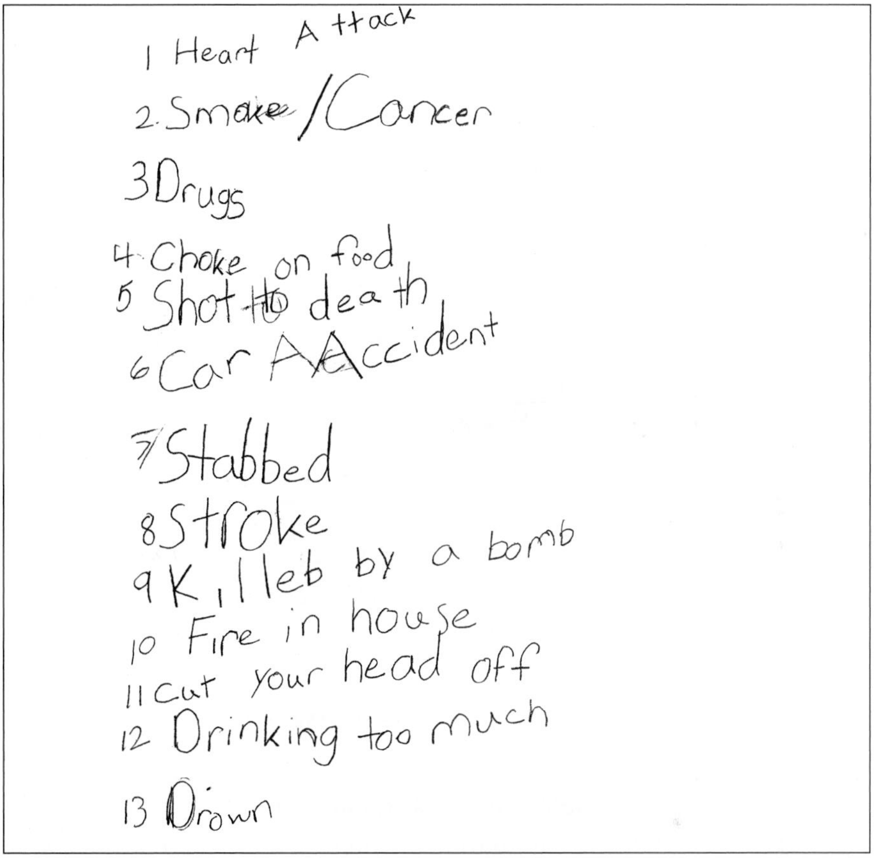

> 1 Heart Attack
> 2. Smoke /Cancer
> 3 Drugs
> 4. Choke on food
> 5 Shot to death
> 6 Car Accident
>
> 7 Stabbed
> 8 Stroke
> 9 Killed by a bomb
> 10 Fire in house
> 11 Cut your head off
> 12 Drinking too much
>
> 13 Drown

observed. A ten-year-old's agonized phrase, "It's sickening, don't talk about it!" can survive into adulthood.

Theoretical Perspectives on Society and Culture

Sociology provides useful tools for understanding how social and cultural factors affect people's attitudes and behaviors relative to death. The three theoretical perspectives discussed here represent different vantage points from which to observe how societies work. The first takes a broad view of social structures and institutions. It emphasizes the interrelationships among major elements of society, including the family, the economy, and the political system. The second focuses on social relations and interactions among members of a society. This theory calls attention to the way people shape and are shaped by the social world in which they live, as well as the ways in which social meaning is created and shared. The third explanation provides a model of how people become members of a society through the interplay of personality, behavior, and environment.

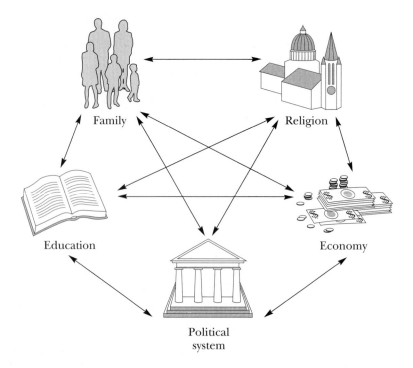

Figure 2-6 *Structural-Functionalist Approach*

The Structural-Functionalist Approach

Much as in studying the human body, where we look at the structure and function of various organs and their interrelationships, we can view society as an organic whole, with constituent parts working together to maintain each other and the whole society. The patterns of interaction among the members of a society are part of that society's *social structure.*

Sociologists usually delineate five major social institutions: (1) the economy, (2) the educational system, (3) the family, (4) the political system, and (5) religion. These institutions are related in such a way that a change in one leads to changes in others (see Figure 2-6). For example, in northeastern Brazil, a region where many people live in extreme poverty, political authorities do not bother to keep accurate statistics about infant mortality among the poor.[65] Looked at from the perspective of social structure, this example illustrates how economics has an impact on the political system, with consequences that, in turn, affect the social reality of poor Brazilian families.

The structural-functionalist view of society helps us appreciate the institutionalized bases of attitudes and behaviors toward death. In North America, cultural expectations about death reflect a social reality consistent with a technology-oriented and bureaucratic society. An appropriate death is one that occurs naturally and is correctly timed—that is, occurs in old age.[66] The bureaucratic aspect of death in modern societies is designed to prevent dis-

Recently my seven-year-old son hopped in my lap and we watched the evening news together. The concluding line of a report on environmental pollution was a quote from U.N. scientists predicting that in twenty years the world would be uninhabitable. As the TV switched to a Madison Avenue jingle designed to encourage us to purchase a non-greasy hair tonic, my son turned to me with a terribly small voice and asked: "Dad, how old will I be when we all die?"

Robert D. Barr, *The Social Studies Professional*

ruptions and preserve the equilibrium of social life.[67] In this structural framework, death tends to be moved to the periphery of social life.[68]

Symbolic Interactionism

The theoretical approach known as *symbolic interactionism* "seeks to explain human action and behavior as the result of the meanings which human beings attach to action and things."[69] Symbolic interactionism emphasizes "the freedom of individuals to construct their own reality as well as to potentially reconstruct that which has been inherited."[70] According to this theory, people are viewed as actively responsive to the social structures and processes in their lives. This theory highlights the fact that socialization is a two-way process; it is not simply "putting in" information at one end and "getting out" a finished product at the other.

After observing terminally ill children and their families in a leukemia ward, Myra Bluebond-Langner commented that our perspective is limited when we define children in terms of "what they will become" while viewing adults as the active "agents" of their socialization.[71] This insight applies not only to the socialization of children, but also to interactions between adults. In a study of dying Native Canadian patients and their grieving families in urban hospital settings, researchers found that Euro-Canadian caregivers and Native Canadian patients bring to their encounters differing interpretations of appropriate care.[72] Engaging one another in interactions to resolve the conflict between these differing views created beneficial changes in attitudes and behaviors of both caregivers and patients. As new "meanings" emerged, the hospital "culture" changed.

Social scientists refer to this process as the *social construction of reality:*

> Each society constructs its own version of the world, its "truths." In some societies the guiding forces of the world are seen as supernatural; in others they are the impersonal forces of nature. Some individuals structure their lives around their belief in a personal deity. . . . For others no such supreme being exists. Different versions of reality are not limited to weighty issues like religion. They also come into play in everyday events in people's lives.[73]

The social constructionist orientation, says Kenneth Gergen, focuses on "the processes by which people come to describe, explain, or otherwise account for the world (including themselves) in which they live.[74] According to this

George Willard became possessed of a madness to lift the sheet from the body of his mother and look at her face. The thought that had come into his mind gripped him terribly. He became convinced that not his mother but someone else lay in the bed before him. The conviction was so real that it was almost unbearable. The body under the sheets was long and in death looked young and graceful. To the boy, held by some strange fancy, it was unspeakably lovely. The feeling that the body before him was alive, that in another moment a lovely woman would spring out of the bed and confront him, became so overpowering that he could not bear the suspense. Again and again he put out his hand. Once he touched and half lifted the white sheet that covered her, but his courage failed and he, like Doctor Reefy, turned and went out of the room. In the hallway outside the door he stopped and trembled so that he had to put a hand against the wall to support himself. "That's not my mother. That's not my mother in there," he whispered to himself and again his body shook with fright and uncertainty. When Aunt Elizabeth Swift, who had come to watch over the body, came out of an adjoining room he put his hand into hers and began to sob, shaking his head from side to side, half blind with grief. "My mother is dead," he said. . . .

Sherwood Anderson, *Winesburg, Ohio*

theory, mind, thought, self, and reality are products of history, culture, and language. Individuals cannot stand above or outside society.[75] The "meaning" that death has for an individual can be seen as resulting from socially inherited ideas and assumptions formed over the lifetime of the society in which that person lives.[76] Thus, grief is expressed in ways that reflect the influence of cultural norms that prescribe certain emotions as appropriate for a given social situation.[77]

The question whether there are "universals" in grief—that is, whether people everywhere and in all cultures have essentially the same response to loss—has not been resolved. However, studies indicate that the human response to loss is culturally learned. In other words, people do not "naturally" grieve any more than they "naturally" laugh or cry.[78] Wolfgang and Margaret Stroebe point out:

> Grief is channeled in all cultures along specified lines [and] there are substantial differences in the rules laid down by cultures as to how long the deceased should be grieved over and how long mourning should last. . . . What is sanctioned or prohibited in one culture may differ dramatically from what is or is not permitted in another.[79]

Although death is fundamentally a biological fact, socially shaped ideas and assumptions create its meaning. This is borne out in the experiences of the Hmong who emigrated from Southeast Asia to North America.[80] In the mountains of northern Laos, their traditional funeral customs included firing mortars to alert the village that a death had occurred and slaughtering oxen and buffalo for the funeral ceremony. In the significantly different social setting of their new homeland, mostly urban settings in North America, the traditional elements of Hmong funeral ritual cannot be readily accommodated and have been dramatically changed.

Similarly, migrant Muslims in Germany are pressured to adapt their funeral ceremonies to European cultural norms and practices. Religious leaders "carry out a balancing act in order to adapt to the new situation without violating the ritual which holds their community together," a cultural dilemma that has been characterized as "the knife's edge."[81]

Hindus who live in England encounter similar cultural imperatives related to death rituals.[82] In India, where there are few undertakers or funeral directors, funeral arrangements are usually made by the deceased's family. Cremation is a public event, and a principal mourner lights the sacred flame of the funeral pyre; in Britain, the body is placed inside a coffin and concealed from view inside the cremator, which is operated by employees of the crematorium. "For the mourners there is neither the smoke to sting their eyes, nor the fire to singe their hair, nor the smell of burning flesh to bring the poignant immediacy and reality of the experience to their consciousness." Living in a very different cultural environment, some Hindus in England feel that they are socially constrained to give up a communal and spiritual ceremony and, in its stead, are left with an anonymous, individualistic, materialistic, and bureaucratic procedure.

The Hmong in North America, Muslims in Germany, and Hindus in Britain illustrate the multicultural nature of modern societies and the resulting challenges to traditional cultural identities. Such challenges apply not only to members of immigrant populations, but to people generally. Most people worldwide now develop a bicultural or "hybrid" identity that "combines their local cultural identity with an identity linked to elements of the global culture."[83]

This change in how people think about themselves in relation to their social environment is especially evident in the lives of children and young adults, as "where a child grows up now matters less than in the past in determining what the child knows and experiences."[84]

The Social Learning Approach

According to social learning theory, people learn through conditioning how to behave as members of a society. Behavior is shaped "by the stimuli that follow or are consequences of the behavior, and by imitation or modeling of others' behavior."[85] When we conform to social norms, our behavior is rewarded; when we fail to conform, our behavior is punished or goes unrewarded. This conditioning mechanism is obvious as parents discipline their children for certain behaviors and reward them for others, according to the norms and standards that the parents want the children to learn and emulate.

Much of our learning about social norms occurs through reinforcement, imitation, interaction, rationalization, and other such behavioral and cognitive processes. We may not even be aware that we are conforming to some social norms because they are embedded in our way of life. We accept them as natural, "the way things work." For instance, in modern societies, people are unlikely to consider disposing of a relative's corpse by placing it on a scaffold outdoors where it will gradually decompose; yet, to Native Americans living

Childhood activities such as "playing dead" can be a means of experimenting with various concepts, trying them on for size, and thus arriving at a more comprehensive and manageable sense of reality.

on the Great Plains in the nineteenth century, platform burial was a natural part of their social norms.

A person with a different cultural orientation may perceive as deviant the norms we accept uncritically. Ronald Akers says:

> Every society and group has a set of social norms, some applying to everyone in the system, some to almost everyone, and others only to persons in particular age, sex, class, ethnic, or religious categories. Some norms apply to a wide range of situations; others govern specific situations. In a heterogeneous society, different systems of normative standards exist side by side, and one may automatically violate the expectations of one group simply by conforming to those of another.[86]

In culturally diverse societies like the United States, we have ample opportunities to apply the insights of social learning theory to expand our understanding of customs and behaviors associated with dying, death, and bereavement. A young Hispanic American woman who had recently attended her first "Anglo" funeral said that she was "genuinely puzzled" at the absence of storytelling and gentle humor about the deceased's life. "Everyone was respectful of the family," she said, "but I was surprised that it was all so serious. I'm used to people talking and laughing at funerals." By recognizing that social norms function much like the rules of a game or the script of a drama, we can observe their influence in the ways people grieve and the ceremonies they enact to commemorate death.

The Mature Concept of Death Revisited

The process of socialization is complex and ongoing. As we experience loss in our lives, we modify previously held beliefs, exchanging them for new ones that provide a better fit with our current understanding of death and its meaning in our lives. A "mature" concept of death, acquired during childhood, becomes a foundation for further development in adulthood.[87] Sandor Brent and Mark Speece note that a basic understanding of death is "the stable nucleus, or core, of a connotational sphere that the child continues to enrich and elaborate throughout the remainder of life by the addition of all kinds of exceptions, conditions, questions, doubts, and so forth." Instead of the "neat, clean, sharply delineated concepts of formal scientific theories of reality," the end result of this process may be a kind of "fuzzy" concept that acknowledges the reality of death while leaving room for elaborations about its meaning. Thus, the binary "either/or" logic that young children use to grasp the core components of a mature concept of death is a precursor to the greater sophistication in understanding death that comes later in life.[88]

David Plath says:

> We are born alone and we die alone, each an organism genetically unique. But we mature or decline together: In the company of others we mutually domesticate the wild genetic pulse as we go about shaping ourselves into persons after the vision of our group's heritage. Perhaps the growth and aging of an organism can be described well enough in terms of stages and transitions within the individual as a monad entity. But in a social animal the life courses have to be described in terms of a collective fabricating of selves, a mutual building of biographies.[89]

Understanding ourselves as cultural beings, we are better able to understand others as cultural beings. Even though we identify (or are identified by others) with a particular group, we are also individuals who sometimes do things our own way. Psychologists tell us that every person is composed of "multiple identities" and that the ability to manage different identities is an important aspect of the self.[90] Culture does not determine behavior but, rather, gives us a "repertoire of ideas and possible actions" through which we understand ourselves, our environment, and our experiences.[91]

Further Readings

David Clark, ed. *The Sociology of Death: Theory, Culture, Practice.* Cambridge, Mass.: Blackwell, 1993.

Lynne Ann DeSpelder and Albert Lee Strickland. "Culture, Socialization, and Death Education." In *Handbook of Thanatology,* edited by David Balk, pp. 303–314. Northbrook, Ill.: Association for Death Education and Counseling, 2007.

Artin Göncü, ed. *Children's Engagement in the World: Sociocultural Perspectives.* New York: Cambridge University Press, 1999.

Clive F. Seale. *Constructing Death: The Sociology of Dying and Bereavement.* Cambridge: Cambridge University Press, 1998.

Robert S. Siegler. *Emerging Minds: The Process of Change in Children's Thinking.* New York: Oxford University Press, 1996.

In this celebration of el Día de los Muertos, *or* Day of the Dead, *held in a California community, a child enters into the festivities by drawing a skull, an activity that reinforces her identity as a participant in age-old traditions that mark her culture's particular attitudes and behaviors relative to death. In pluralistic societies, such celebrations both perpetuate cultural traditions and allow them to be shared with people from the wider community, who may choose to adopt elements of those traditions in their own lives, thereby creating a distinctive sense of local identity with respect to death-related customs and practices.*

CHAPTER 3

Perspectives on Death: Cultural and Historical

Death is a universal human experience, yet our response to it is shaped by our cultural environment. Learning how people in different cultures relate to death can shed light on our own attitudes and behaviors. Cultures can be thought of as occupying a continuum from "death-welcoming" to "death-denying."[1] As you read about the cultures described in this chapter, consider where you might place each of them on the welcoming-denying continuum. Consider, too, where your own "cultures"—the national, ethnic or subcultural, and family groups of which you are a member—might fit on such a continuum.

Broadening our perspective to include cultures other than our own increases the range of choices available in our encounters with death. People tend to view the world from a single perspective—their own. We counter this tendency by becoming aware of how we are prone to apply our own cultural criteria as benchmarks for judging the values of other communities.

In becoming culturally competent, we need to be aware of the fallacy of stereotyping others. Stereotypes are sometimes used as a learning strategy to organize and interpret information, but, in fact, there may be more differences within cultural groups than between cultural groups. It is important to keep in mind that culture is not defined simply by ethnicity. Especially within culturally diverse societies, we can expect to find great variation within each ethnic group.[2] Also, discrepancies may exist between *expressed* norms and *observed* behaviors within groups.[3] Identity is situational and adaptive, and it can serve multiple purposes. The meanings people attach to a particular cultural identity vary among cultural groups.[4]

Culture is dynamic, and attitudes toward death change over time. Engaging the ideas and customs of other cultures is an antidote to ethnocentrism—that is, the fallacy of making judgments about others in terms of one's own cultural assumptions and biases. Seeing others as they see themselves, sharing in some way their perceptions and customs, enriches individual as well as social life and, indeed, may be the essence of education.

Traditional Cultures

Traditional cultures typically view death not as an end but as a change of status, a transition from the land of the living to the world of the dead. The living are careful to help the dead in their journey to the other world. They take precautions to offset fears about the potential malevolence of the dead, who might harm the living if not shown respect.

Human concern for the dead predates written history. A cave excavated at Atapuerca in northern Spain is said to be the first evidence of human funerary behavior, dating to at least 300,000 years ago.[5] Many human remains recovered in Europe from the Upper Paleolithic period, about 40,000 to 10,000 years ago, are recognized as having been intentional burials, accompanied by manufactured objects, personal effects, and other grave goods.[6] In some burials, the corpse is stained with red ochre and placed in a fetal posture, suggesting revitalization of the body and rebirth (see Figure 3-1).[7] In Neanderthal burials, ornamental shells, stone implements, and food were sometimes buried with the dead, implying belief that such items would be useful in the journey from the land of the living to the land of the dead. In considering such evidence, we are reminded that "the dead do not bury themselves, but are treated and disposed of by the living."[8] The Italian philosopher Giambattista Vico classified burial of the dead as a basic social institution and pointed out that humanity received its name *humanitas* from the word *humare,* which means "to bury."[9] These early burials illustrate the long history of social groups bonding together and expressing shared emotion when death occurs.

Questions about the meaning of death and what happens when we die are central concerns to people in every culture and have been since time immemorial. An essential concern for living well—and dying well—is present in all human cultures.

Origin of Death

The foundations for human attitudes, values, and behaviors are generally found in myths—that is, stories that explain ideas or beliefs.[10] What do such stories tell us about how death became part of human experience?[11] In some stories, death becomes part of human experience because ancestral parents or an archetypal figure transgressed divine or natural law, through either poor judgment or disobedience (see Figure 3-2). The stories sometimes

Figure 3-1 *Neanderthal Burial*

When the first man, the father of the human race, was being buried, a god passed by the grave and inquired what it meant, for he had never seen a grave before. Upon receiving the information from those about the place of interment that they had just buried their father, he said: "Do not bury him, dig up the body again." "No," they replied, "we cannot do that. He has been dead for four days and smells." "Not so," entreated the god, "dig him up and I promise you that he will live again." But they refused to carry out the divine injunction. Then the god declared, "By disobeying me, you have sealed your own fate. Had you dug up your ancestor, you would have found him alive, and you yourselves when you passed from this world should have been buried as bananas are for four days, after which you shall have been dug up, not rotten, but ripe. But now, as a punishment for your disobedience, you shall die and rot." And whenever they hear this sad tale the Fijians say: "Oh, that those children had dug up that body!"

Figure 3-2 *Fijian Story (Traditional): The Origin of Death*

When Hare heard of Death, he started for his lodge & arrived there crying, shrieking, *My uncles & my aunts must not die!* And then the thought assailed him: *To all things death will come!* He cast his thoughts upon the precipices & they began to fall & crumble. Upon the rocks he cast his thoughts & they became shattered. Under the earth he cast his thoughts & all the things living there stopped moving & their limbs stiffened in death. Up above, toward the skies, he cast his thoughts & the birds flying there suddenly fell to the earth & were dead.

After he entered his lodge he took his blanket and, wrapping it around him, lay down crying. *Not the whole earth will suffice for all those who will die. Oh, there will not be enough earth for them in many places!* There he lay in his corner wrapped up in his blanket, silent.

Figure 3-3 *Winnebago Myth: When Hare Heard of Death*

involve a test of some person or group. When the test is failed, death becomes a reality. A story told by the Luba of Africa describes how God created a paradise for the first human beings and endowed it with everything needed for their sustenance; however, they were forbidden to eat of the bananas in the middle of the field. When humans ate the bananas, it was decreed that humankind would die after a lifetime of toil. This motif is akin to the biblical story of Adam and Eve's transgression in the Garden of Eden, an account of death's origin that persists in the religious traditions of Judaism, Christianity, and Islam.

In some myths, a crucial act that would have ensured immortality was not properly carried out; an *omission* rather than an *action* introduces death to humankind. Some stories tell of a messenger who was supposed to deliver the message of eternal life, but the message was garbled due to malice or forgetfulness, or it did not arrive on time. Among the Winnebago of North America, the trickster figure, Hare, is an example of this motif (see Figure 3-3). Momentarily forgetting his purpose, Hare failed to deliver the life-saving message. In a variant of this motif, two messengers were sent—one bringing immortality, the other bringing death—and the messenger bringing death arrived first.

In the "death in a bundle" motif, death is introduced into human experience when a bundle containing the mortal fate of all humankind is opened, either inadvertently or because of poor choice. A story from Greek mythology told by Aesop is a variant of this theme (see Figure 3-4). Another motif describes how a message of immortality was addressed to human beings, but people were not awake to receive it.

Although most myths portray death as unwelcome, some describe how it is actively pursued because of weariness with life or disgust with its misery. In these stories, people barter for or buy death from the gods so life does not go on interminably, or death is obtained as a remedy for overpopulation.

All of these myths echo a theme that is surprisingly familiar: Death comes from outside; it cuts short an existence that would otherwise be immortal.

It was a hot, sultry summer afternoon, and Eros, tired with play and faint from the heat, took shelter in a cool, dark cave. It happened to be the cave of Death himself.

Eros, wanting only to rest, threw himself down carelessly—so carelessly that all his arrows fell out of his quiver.

When he woke he found they had mingled with the arrows of Death, which lay scattered about the floor of the cave. They were so alike Eros could not tell the difference. He knew, however, how many had been in his quiver, and eventually he gathered up the right number.

Of course, Eros took some that belonged to Death and left some of his own behind.

And so it is today that we often see the hearts of the old and the dying struck by bolts of Love; and sometimes we see the hearts of the young captured by Death.

Figure 3-4   *Aesop: Eros and Death*

This notion still influences our attitudes. We understand the biological processes of disease and aging, yet still feel that, if only this defect could be repaired, we could remain alive. We find ourselves believing that death is foreign, not really part of us.

Ultimately, of course, we cannot avoid the recognition of our own mortality. The epic of Gilgamesh tells the story of a king who sets off on a journey to find the secret of immortality, a journey undertaken because of the death of his friend, Enkidu. After overcoming great perils while searching for the power to renew one's youth, Gilgamesh returns from his quest empty-handed. Finally, grieving the death of his beloved friend, Gilgamesh realizes that he too will die. Our mortality may be acknowledged most profoundly in grieving the death of a loved one.

Causes of Death

Even when we find a meaningful explanation about how death came into the world, there remains the question "What causes *individual* human beings to die?" The immediate cause of a death from accidental injuries or wounds sustained in battle is clear, but its ultimate cause is open to question: Why did this fatal event happen to this person at this particular time? Might it be due to some evil influence, possibly shaped by magic? An unexpected or untimely death is likely to be viewed as unnatural. When such deaths occur, an explanation may be sought in supernatural causes. Although such explanations are not subject to proof or disproof, they comfort the bereaved by helping make sense of what otherwise seems inexplicable.

Illness and death signal the fact that something is "out of balance." When a child dies among the Senufo people of Africa's Ivory Coast, for example, it disturbs the whole community. To restore a sense of security and proper order, animal sacrifices are offered to purify and protect the community from further calamity.[12]

In seeking the cause of a death, traditional societies typically embrace an ecological orientation.[13] They look at the possible role of such phenomena as the wind or moon, heredity, and behavioral excesses, such as staying out late and not getting enough sleep. A variety of socioeconomic and psychosocial, as well as natural and supernatural, factors are explored. The cause of death may be related to the person's social interactions. Was anger, anxiety, fright, or envy involved? The search for answers takes place within an environment that encompasses both the living and the dead. Did the person offend the ancestors or neglect to carry out the prescribed rites for the dead? The health of the whole community depends on maintaining a proper relationship with the environment, including its unseen aspects.

Power of the Dead

In cultures that maintain strong bonds between the living and the dead, "the land echoes with the voices of the ancestors."[14] Together, the living and the dead comprise the clan, the tribe, the people. The bond between living and dead is a sign that the community endures. In Balinese society, the village territory belongs to the ancestors, and the living members of the community maintain contact with them to ensure their livelihood and well-being.[15] The community is a partnership of living and dead. This understanding is implicit when people refer to the "founding fathers" of a nation or college, who are spoken of metaphorically as "being with us in spirit" as living members of the group celebrate their common purpose with those who preceded them.

In traditional societies, grief may be expressed with loud wails or with silent tears, but almost always there is deep respect for the still-powerful soul of the deceased. If the soul or spirit of the deceased is not treated properly, harm may result. Conducting the prescribed funeral rites ensures the successful journey of the soul into the realm of the dead, a journey that benefits the living. Of special concern are evil-intentioned spirits that wander about aimlessly, seeking to disrupt the well-being of the living. Such spirits are often associated with catastrophic deaths, such as deaths in childbirth.

In the rhythm and flow of communal life, the deceased—in death as in life—is part of the whole. As unseen members of an ongoing social order, the dead are often allies who can perform services for the living—as interpreters, intermediaries, and ambassadors in the realm beyond the reach of our physical senses. Such communication with the dead is often facilitated by a *shaman,* a visionary in the community who projects his or her consciousness to the other realm and acts as an intermediary between the worlds of living and dead.[16] Because the dead are not bound by human time, *necromancy* (from the Greek, meaning "corpse-prophecy") offers access to past and future events.[17] By entering into a trance, a shaman contacts the dead and reports back the prophetic message that will benefit the living.

Ancestors serve as role models and uphold standards of conduct. They form a crucial spiritual link between human beings and powerful—but distant and impersonal—gods. Keeping alive the memory of one's ancestors and calling upon them allow individuals to sustain family loyalties and maintain bonds beyond death.

Names of the Dead

If calling a person's name is a way of summoning the person, then refraining from using a name will presumably leave its bearer undisturbed. Hence, a common practice related to the dead is name avoidance: The deceased is never again mentioned or is referred to only obliquely, never by name. For example, the deceased might be referred to as "that one," or allusions may be made to particular traits or special qualities a person was known for during his or her lifetime. Thus, "Uncle Joe," who gained renown as an expert fisherman, might be referred to after his death as "that relative who caught many fish." A woman who had displayed extraordinary bravery might be referred to as "that one who showed courage." In some cultures, the deceased is referred to by his or her relationship to the speaker.

Customs like these involving name avoidance continue into the modern era among indigenous people who value traditional cultural practices. When a famous Aborigine painter died in 2002 at the age of seventy in the central Australian town of Alice Springs, family and friends asked the media not to publish his name out of respect for the Aborigine belief that the dead not be identified by name.[18] Although he had achieved international fame during his lifetime for the Dreamtime paintings depicting his homeland, he became anonymous in death because his people's beliefs forbid the mention of his name.

Name avoidance can be so complete that living people with the same name as the deceased must adopt new names. Among the Penan Geng of central Borneo, naming practices involving death are incorporated into all forms of social discourse.[19] When a person dies, "death names" are given to closest kin. Thus, as a person goes through life, he or she may take on a series of names and titles that refer to different categories of relationship to the deceased.

Some cultures, rather than avoiding the deceased's name, give it special emphasis. For example, the name may be conferred on a newborn child. Such naming takes place out of a desire to honor the memory of a loved one or to ensure that the soul of the dead person is reincarnated. In some cases, when a woman nears the time of giving birth, she has a dream that reveals which of her ancestors is to be reborn, thus determining the name her new baby receives.[20] Among Hawaiians, children may be named for ancestors or even named by the gods. Especially important are names bestowed by gods, which are communicated through dreams. Naming a child for a relative who has died allows the name to live again.[21]

Respect for the dead or anxiety about provoking spirits may prompt name avoidance in traditional cultures. In modern societies, however, people avoid mentioning the deceased's name to prevent conjuring up painful reminders of the loss. In both situations, name avoidance may be a way of managing grief. Similarly, when a child is named after a beloved grandparent or respected friend, aren't parents hoping that qualities valued in the namesake will be "reborn" in the child? Although cultural forms differ, common threads run through human experience.

Western Culture

Beginning in the early Middle Ages, about the year 400, and continuing for a thousand years, people in Western European culture shared a view of the universe as bound together by natural and divine law.[22] The teachings of the Church influenced the manner in which people died and offered hope for the afterlife. An acceptance of death associated with this outlook generally prevailed until the European cultural Renaissance, or rebirth, in the 1400s and 1500s.

During the early medieval period, people viewed death with the understanding that "we shall all die." This reflected a sense of death as the collective destiny of humankind. The end of life was not thought to be synonymous with physical death; rather, the dead were "asleep"—in the Church's keeping—with assurance of resurrection at the apocalyptic return of Christ. With this faith, people tended not to fear what awaited them after death.

This sense of a common, collective destiny began to change during the period of the High Middle Ages, about 1000–1450, transforming into an emphasis on the destiny of the individual. The collective idea that "everyone dies" was replaced by an individual acknowledgment, "I will die my own death." This change occurred over the course of several centuries and coincided with a general enrichment of life and culture. The achievements of this

 Death Knells

During many centuries one item of expense for survivors was the fee that must be paid for the ringing of the soul bell. Every cathedral and church of medieval Christendom had such a bell, almost always the largest one in the bell tower.

By the time John Donne wrote the immortal line "for whom the bell tolls," ringing of the soul bell—in a distinctive pattern, or knell—was popularly taken to be merely a public notice that a death had occurred. This use of the soul bell came into importance relatively late, however.

Not simply in Christian Europe but also among primitive tribes and highly developed non-Christian cultures of the Orient, bells have been linked with death. Notes from bells (rung in special fashion) served to help convince a spirit that there was no need to remain close to a useless dead body. At the same time, noise made by bells was considered to be especially effective in driving away the evil spirits who prowled about hoping to seize a newly released soul or to put obstacles in its path.

Ringing of the soul (or passing) bell was long considered so vital that bell ringers demanded, and got, big fees for using it. Still in general use by the British as late as the era of King Charles II in the seventeenth century, bell ringers then regulated the number of strokes of the passing bell so that the general public could determine the age, sex, and social status of the deceased.

Webb Garrison,
Strange Facts About Death

period include the building of the great cathedrals of Notre Dame and Chartres in France, Canterbury in England, and Cologne in Germany, as well as the creation of literary works such as Dante's *Divine Comedy* and Chaucer's *Canterbury Tales.*

Whereas, during the earlier period, the teachings of the Church had provided assurance of resurrection on the Last Day and entry into heaven, people now became personally anxious about Judgment Day, the cosmic event that would separate the just from the damned. An individual's good or bad deeds, not the community's faith, would determine his or her ultimate and eternal fate. The *liber vitae,* or Book of Life, which previously had been pictured as a sort of vast cosmic census, was now imagined to contain the biographies of individual lives, a kind of balance sheet by which each person's soul would be weighed.

The period of Renaissance and religious reformation, beginning about 1450, has aptly been called an "age of transition." Gutenberg's *Bible* went to press in 1456 and, in 1517, Luther nailed his Ninety-Five Theses to the door of the church at Wittenberg Castle, inaugurating the Protestant Reformation. The dominant culture became increasingly humanistic, secular, and individualistic. The living were distanced from the dead by the Protestant reformers' denial of Purgatory, an intermediate state "where the dead might be imagined as residing after the decease of their natural bodies" and where the living could have "a sense of contact with the dead through prayer."[23] Geographic boundaries fell away, with explorations such as Columbus's voyage to America in 1492, and a scientific revolution ensued with publication in 1543 of Copernicus's *On the Revolution of the Heavenly Spheres,* which posited the radical notion that the earth revolves around the sun.

Transformations in cultural and intellectual life were accompanied by changes in how people related to death. Conventional wisdom was challenged by competing ideas in the religious marketplace and by the revolutionary discoveries of scientists and explorers. As the reassuring notions of earlier centuries were questioned, people began to feel more ambivalent about death and the afterlife. The scientific revolution of the 1500s and 1600s challenged traditional notions of authority and ushered in an age of "enlightenment" in the 1700s, with an emphasis on reason and intellect. This era marked the birth of a modern worldview. Death was no longer something to be contemplated only in the realm of the sacred. It became an event that could be manipulated and shaped by human beings.

These modernizing trends accelerated with an industrial revolution, from about 1750 to 1900. This 150-year period was a time of rapid technological innovation, mechanization, and urbanization, accompanied by progress in public health and medicine. The attitude toward death during this period emphasized the death of the other, "thy death."

This emphasis occurred in connection with the Romantic movement in the arts and literature, which exhibited a fascination with acts of chivalry, as well as with mystery and the supernatural. Secular notions about death and the afterlife began to replace (or coexist with) religious concepts. Nature symbolism was increasingly present in death-related art and memorials, and there was widespread interest in spirits and spiritualism.

Within the context of an emphasis on "thy death," the meaning of death focused on separation from the beloved, giving rise to impassioned expressions of grief and desires to memorialize the dead. Hence was born the ideal of the "beautiful death," in which the sad beauty of a loved one's death elicits feelings of melancholy, tinged with optimism for eventual reunion with the beloved in a heavenly home. With the death of her prince consort, Albert, in 1861, Queen Victoria of Great Britain set the trend for elaborate funeral etiquette and mourning customs, as well as for a cult of widowhood.[24] She wore a black mourning bonnet for the rest of her life and often communed with Prince Albert at his grave in the Royal Mausoleum, where she herself would be laid to rest after her death in 1901.

Through more than a thousand years in Western culture, attitudes toward death reflected a progression from an emphasis on collective destiny in which "we all shall die," to the personal awareness of "one's own death," and then to a preoccupation with the deaths of loved ones, "thy death." Despite these changes in emphasis, French historian Philippe Ariès characterizes virtually the whole of this period as one of "tamed death." Death was an ordinary human experience, not something to be hidden away from view or excluded from social life.

According to Ariès, the long era of "tamed death" came to an end in the twentieth century. World War I (1914–1918) was a major turning point in modern history. It marked the advent of "total war," which affected civilians as well as combatants. It also demonstrated the increasing importance of technology in virtually every aspect of life. In health care, technology brought about the "medicalization" of dying and death. Dying had been a public and communal event; now it became private.[25] Events that had been part of people's ordinary lives were placed under the control of professionals. The deathbed scene moved from home to hospital. Customary signs of mourning all but disappeared. In the twentieth century, the prevailing attitude toward death could be described by such terms as "forbidden death," "invisible death," and "death denied."

With this historical summary in mind, we are prepared to take a closer look at how changing attitudes toward death influenced specific customs and practices, such as the manner of dying and the deathbed scene, burial customs and memorialization of the deceased, and the cultural expression of the Dance of Death.

Dying and the Deathbed Scene

"I see and know that my death is near": Thus did the dying person during the Middle Ages acknowledge impending death. Anticipated by natural signs or by inner certainty, dying was understood as manageable. On pious deathbeds, the dying offered their suffering to God, with the expectation that all would take place in a customary manner. Sudden death was rare; even

This deathbed vigil in a Spanish village is characteristic of the way in which human beings have responded to death for thousands of years. Only recently have such scenes been superseded in modern societies by the specter of dying alone, perhaps unconscious, amid the impersonal technological gadgetry of an unfamiliar institutional environment.

wounds in battle seldom brought instantaneous death. (The possibility of unexpected death was fearful because it caught victims unaware and unable to properly close earthly accounts and turn toward the divine.) Those who kept vigil around the deathbed could confidently say that the dying person "feels her time has come" or "knows he will soon be dead."

Marked by simple and solemn ceremony, dying occurred within the context of familiar practices. Ariès describes a typical Christian death during the early Middle Ages: Lying down, with the head facing east toward Jerusalem and arms crossed over the chest, the dying person expressed sadness at his or her impending end and began "a discreet recollection of beloved beings and things." Family and friends gathered around the deathbed to receive the dying person's pardon for any wrongs they might have done, and all were commended to God. Next, the dying person turned his or her attention away from the earthly realm and toward the divine. Prayer requesting divine grace followed confession of sins to a priest, and then the priest granted absolution. With the customary rites completed, nothing more need be said: The dying person was prepared for death. If death came more slowly than expected, the dying person simply waited in silence. Elizabeth Hallam writes, "The deathbed was a space which developed a rich visual and aural texture where each word and gesture became meaningful in physical, social, and spiritual terms."[26]

Dying was more or less a public ceremony, with the dying person in charge. The recumbent figure in the deathbed, surrounded by parents, friends, family, children, and even mere passersby, remained the customary deathbed scene until the late nineteenth century, although subtle changes did occur over time. For example, as the destiny of the individual gained emphasis around the twelfth century, there were corresponding changes in the deathbed scene. Besides the entourage of public participants, there now hovered an invisible army of celestial figures, angels and demons, battling for possession of the dying person's soul. *How* a person died became profoundly important. Death became the *speculum mortis,* the mirror in which the dying person could discover his or her destiny by tallying the moral balance sheet of his or her life. The time of dying was a unique opportunity to review one's actions and make a final decision for good or ill. The moment of death became the supreme challenge and ultimate test of an entire lifetime. This emphasis on individual responsibility for the destiny of one's soul was communicated in the *memento mori* of the time, "Remember, you must die!"

In later centuries, scientific rationalism came to share the stage with religion. There was little change in the outward aspects of the deathbed scene; family and friends still gathered as participants in the public ritual of a person's dying. But religion was less prominent in the thoughts of the dying person or the grief of survivors. People now compared the act of dying to the emergence of a butterfly from its cocoon. A secular hope for immortality and eventual reunion with loved ones became more important than churchly images of heaven and hell. Gradually, the focus changed from the dying person to his or her survivors.

By the mid-twentieth century, the rituals of dying had been overtaken by a technological process in which death occurs by "a series of little steps." Ariès says, "All these little silent deaths have replaced and erased the great dramatic act of death." Writing in the 1970s, he added, "No one any longer has the strength or patience to wait over a period of weeks for a moment which has lost a part of its meaning." At the turn of a new millennium, this assessment is challenged by initiatives in end-of-life care, such as hospice and palliative care, which offer opportunities for dying persons and their families to find meaning in the last acts of a human life.

Burial Customs

As with the deathbed scene, changes in burial customs reveal transformations in attitudes toward death over time. In the Roman era, graveyards were situated on the outskirts of the settlements they served, and burial within the town's precincts was permitted only as a special honor.[27] With the rise of Christianity in the early Middle Ages, however, such burial customs began to change as believers adopted the idea that the saintliness of Christian martyrs was powerful, even in death, and that these saints of the Church could help others avoid the pitfalls of sin and the horrors of hell.[28] Thus, it became advantageous to be buried near the grave of a martyr to gain merit by proximity. (A modern analogy might be that of a movie fan being buried near a film star at Forest Lawn or a veteran requesting burial near a Medal of Honor winner, although medieval folk were generally more concerned with the welfare of their soul than with earthly prestige.)

As Christian pilgrims began journeying to venerate and honor the martyrs, altars, chapels, and eventually churches were built on or near the martyrs' graves. Initially, only notables and saints of the Church received such burial, but eventually ordinary folk came to be buried in common graves located in the churchyards and surrounds of churches and cathedrals. In later centuries, the great urban cathedrals allowed burials within their precincts. In this way, the state of the dead was intimately linked with the Church.

Charnel Houses

Burial within churchyards led to the development of *charnel houses,* arcades and galleries where the bones of the dead were entrusted to the Church. Limbs and skulls were arranged along various parts of the churchyard, as well as within and near the church. (In Paris, it is possible to visit catacombs where, as one visitor exclaimed, "piles of femurs and skulls" are "stacked eight feet high and ten yards deep, as neatly as lumber in an Oregon mill yard.")[29] The bones in these charnels came from common graves, which were periodically opened so that the bones could be safely kept by the Church until the Resurrection.

The public nature of these charnel houses reflects a familiarity with death and with the dead. As Romans had congregated in the Forum, their counterparts in the Middle Ages met in charnel houses, which functioned as public squares. There, they would find shops and merchants, conduct business, dance, gamble, or simply enjoy being together.

"As yet unborn," Ariès says, "was the modern idea that the dead person should be installed in a sort of house unto himself, a house of which he was the perpetual owner or at least the long-term tenant, a house in which he would be at home and from which he could not be evicted."

Memorializing the Dead

About the twelfth century, as part of an increasing emphasis on individualism, a desire arose to preserve the identity of the person buried in a particular place. Prior to this time, except for burials of members of the upper classes or notables of the Church, graves had no markers identifying who was buried there. Now, simple grave markers of the "Here lies John Doe" variety began to appear, as did elaborate effigies of the dead at the burials of notables. The thirteenth-century sepulchral effigy of Jean d'Alluye depicts a recumbent knight in chain mail, sword girded and shield at his side, feet resting on the image of a lion, a vivid expression of the intellectual and social milieu of the

Library of Congress

This ossuary located at a European monastery is a survival of the medieval charnel house, a gallery of skeletons and skulls and bones.

age of chivalry, with its tension between faith and heroism. Although effigies were created only for people at the highest social rank, they give us clues about how people of the time viewed death.

Effigies reflect the emerging belief that the bereaved could maintain bonds with the deceased by perpetuating their *memory*. Over time, such memorialization became increasingly important. By the time of the Renaissance, as secular ideas competed with religious beliefs, burials began to take place in cemeteries that were not associated with churches. The opening of the Cemetery of Père Lachaise outside Paris in 1804 signaled the culmination of a radical change in Western attitudes toward life and death.[30]

In the United States, the rural cemetery movement began in the 1830s with the aim of replacing the simple, untended graveyards of the Puritans with lush, well-kept cemeteries like Mount Auburn in Cambridge, Massachusetts, and Woodlawn in New York City. Places like Spring Grove in Cincinnati, Ohio, established in 1844 and occupying 733 acres, including a large undeveloped area of woodland at its center, promoted a new concept of cemetery design in which landscape took precedence over monuments.[31] In parklike settings, the bereaved visited private graves and communed in memory with the deceased.[32] Ornate monuments were erected to honor the dead, and elaborate funeral rituals included an extensive assortment of mourning paraphernalia. The deceased were imagined to be in a heaven where survivors hoped to be eventually reunited with their loved ones. An interest in occult practices, such as séances and communication with spirits, grew popular.[33] These mourning customs of the nineteenth century are marked by a sense of sentimentality that made death seem less final or severe. By the mid-twentieth century, such "excessive" mourning customs gave way to an apparent desire to mute the reality of death. Glennys Howarth says,

> The elaborate mourning rituals of the nineteenth century carried the expectation that people would adhere to the etiquette of mourning paraphernalia (such as the wearing of "widows weeds") and resulted in an outwardly public expression of grief. By contrast, the twentieth century has been marked by a reluctance to indulge public demonstrations of grief.[34]

In the modern era, except for occasional memorials to the war dead, most cemeteries do not encourage monuments interrupting the flat expanses of embedded "grave markers." Architectural historian James Curl says:

> The neglected cemeteries, poorly designed crematoria, and abysmal tombstone designs of the present insult life itself, for death is an inevitable consequence of birth. By treating the disposal of the dead as though the problem were one of refuse-collection, society devalues life.[35]

The Dance of Death

With origins in the ecstatic dances of pre-Christian times, artistic themes involving the *danse macabre*, or Dance of Death, came to fullest expression in the late thirteenth and early fourteenth centuries.[36] Partly a reaction to horrors of war, famine, and poverty, the Dance of Death was influenced primarily by the mass deaths caused by the plague, or Black Death, which came to Europe via a Black Sea port in 1347.[37] When the first wave of pestilence ended in 1351, a quarter of the European population had died. As a cultural and artistic phenomenon, the Dance of Death reflects ideas about the *inevitability* and *impartiality* of death.

The *danse macabre* was expressed through drama, poetry, music, and the visual arts. It was sometimes performed as a masque, a short entertainment in which actors costumed as skeletons danced gaily with figures representing people at all levels of society. Paintings of the Dance of Death depict individuals being escorted to graveyards by skeletons and corpses, a grim reminder of the universality of death. The Dance of Death conveys the notion that, regardless of rank or status, death comes to *all* people and to *each* person. In the oldest versions of the Dance of Death, the figure of death seems scarcely to touch the living as it singles them out. Death has a personal meaning but is part of the natural order. In later versions, people are depicted as being forcibly taken by death.

By about the fifteenth century, death is portrayed as causing a radical, violent, and complete break between the living and the dead. This is reflected in macabre themes that involve cadavers and the deterioration of the corpse. Along with the display of skeletons, naked corpses, and figures of the grim reaper, the Dance of Death eventually includes erotic connotations. The radical disruption of death is likened to the momentary break with ordinary consciousness that occurs during sexual intercourse.[38] It's as if the grim reaper has become a deadly lover.

Hans Holbein the Younger, authors' collection

MIGUEL Y LA CRIADA.

José Guadalupe Posada, Swann Collection, Library of Congress

The somber mood of Hans Holbein's depiction of Die Totentanz, *or Dance of Death, contrasts with the treatment of the same theme by Mexican artist José Guadalupe Posada. In Holbein's medieval woodblock print,* The Child, *we see the anxiety of family members as the skeletal figure of Death ominously takes a child; in Posada's print, there is a sense of gaiety and festivity. Although expressed differently, the two works convey a common message: Death comes to people in all walks of life; no one is exempt.*

This is also the era of public anatomy dissections, which were attended by ordinary townspeople as well as surgeons and medical students. At the University of Leiden, an "Anatomical Theater" was held in the apse of a church, where human remains were artistically displayed and posed in dramatic gestures. Frank Gonzalez-Crussi cites the example of a child's arm "clad in an infant's lace sleeve" and, held in the child's hand, "between thumb and index finger—as gracefully as an artist's model might hold a flower by the stem—a human eye by the optical nerve."[39]

By the eighteenth and nineteenth centuries, the blatant eroticism in the Dance of Death had been sublimated into an obsession with the "beautiful death." The relationship between love and death, which had been confined mostly to religious martyrdom, was extended to include romantic love. Antecedents of this notion are found in the code of chivalry and in the ideals of courtly love. Romances like those of Tristan and Isolde or Romeo and Juliet promoted the idea that, where there is love, death can be beautiful, even desirable.

Originally a reaction to fear of sudden death caused by an epidemic of plague, the *danse macabre* emphasizes the uncertainties of human existence, the knowledge that death can come when least expected and disrupt the most loving relationships. These themes of death's universality and inevitability are also portrayed in the Mexican celebration of *el Día de los Muertos,* the Day of the Dead, and modern artists draw upon these themes to convey the epidemic nature of AIDS as well as threatening aspects of other potential catastrophes. More subtly, images associated with the *danse macabre* persist in the form of skeletons and other scary regalia found on children's Halloween costumes.

Invisible Death?

In tracing the manner in which attitudes and behaviors change relative to dying and death, a common theme emerges: Human beings seek to manage death in ways appropriate for their cultural and historical circumstances. If we compare our present practices with those of earlier generations, dying and death are in many respects less visible, less part of our common experience. As mentioned in Chapter 1, care of the dying and the dead is now largely the domain of hired professionals. Deathbed scenes are often dominated by efforts to delay death. The role of family and friends as witnesses to a loved one's dying has diminished. Mourning customs that held sway in the past now seem excessive. Funerals and memorial services are shorter, more discreet, and private. Robert Fulton says, "From the end of the First World War until the late 1950s, death in America, it could be said, took a holiday."[40]

Death-related attitudes and practices continue to evolve, however. There are signs that people are becoming dissatisfied with the late twentieth century's tendencies to compartmentalize, professionalize, and medicalize dying and death. Present attitudes and practices relative to dying and death increasingly reflect a diversity of choices and options. Neil Small points out that "the modern exists as a layer on top of other ways of making sense of experience," many of which are pre-modern.[41] We are not satisfied with "one size fits all" answers and explore more meaningful ways of encountering death, both historically and cross-culturally.

Cultural Case Studies

Even when another culture initially appears exotic in comparison with what is most familiar to us, closer examination usually reveals significant correspondences between the "foreign" and the "familiar"—correspondences that evoke learnings about behaviors and attitudes that, because they are familiar, we have not really considered. Exploring other cultures provides perspectives that allow both appreciation and criticism of our own attitudes and customs.[42]

Native American Traditions

In discussing the indigenous peoples of North America, we first must recognize the fact that more than 500 tribal groups live in the United States, "each a separate people and each endowed with unique traditions."[43] In addition, historical practices were affected by social upheavals that accompanied the "westward expansionism" of white society.[44] Nevertheless, these tribal peoples share a "common body of thought," or "Indian worldview," that allows us to examine certain themes associated with Native American attitudes toward dying and death.

One of these themes is reverence toward the dead, who are often believed to serve as guardian spirits or special envoys to the spirit world. Chief Seattle, leader of the Suquamish people in the 1800s, said, "To us the ashes of our ancestors are sacred and their resting place is hallowed ground. . . . Be just and deal kindly with my people, for the dead are not powerless. Dead, did I say? There is no death, only a change of worlds."[45] Wandering far from the graves of one's ancestors, seemingly without regret, is not the Native American way. The land, the whole of the physical environment, is the basic source of American Indian identity and ultimate source of spiritual power.[46]

Within Native American societies, there is an emphasis on "living one day at a time, with purpose, grateful for life's blessings, in the knowledge that it could all end abruptly."[47] This relationship to death is typified in the Lakota battle cry: "It's a good day to die!" Stephen Levine says,

> This embodies the possibilities of a life reviewed and completed. A life in which even death is not excluded. I am speaking here of a whole death that succeeds a whole life. . . . When everything is brought up to date, and the heart is turned toward itself, it is a good day to die.[48]

Because death may come at any time, we are wise to be prepared, an outlook evident in the emphasis the Cree people place on being careful to say farewells before going away on a lengthy or difficult journey; unforeseen death may intervene.[49]

There are numerous stories of Native Americans whose preparation for death enabled them to face it stoically, even indifferently, sometimes composing "death songs" as they confronted their own death. In some cases, a death song was "composed spontaneously at the very moment of death" and "chanted with the last breath of the dying person."[50] These death songs express a resolve to meet death fully, to accept it with one's whole being, not in

Two Death Songs

In the great night my heart will go out
Toward me the darkness comes rattling
In the great night my heart will go out

        Papago song by Juana Manwell
        (Owl Woman)

The odor of death,
I smell the odor of death
In front of my body.

        A song of the Dakota tribe

defeat and desperation, but with equanimity and composure. Death songs summarize a person's life and acknowledge death as the completion of being, the final act in the drama of earthly existence.

Among most Native Americans, time is viewed not as linear and progress-oriented, but rather as cyclic. Åke Hultkrantz says that Native Americans are "mainly interested in how this cycle affects people in this life"; they have "only a vague notion of another existence after death."[51] Rigid beliefs about the state of the dead or the afterlife tend to be of little or no importance. Instead, Hultkrantz says, "One individual might hold several ideas about the dead at the same time [because] different situations call for different interpretations of the fate of humans after death." The Wind River Shoshoni, for example, have a variety of beliefs about death: The dead may travel to another world or may remain on earth as ghosts; they may be born again as people or may transmigrate into "insects, birds, or even inanimate objects like wood and rocks." Hultkrantz says that "most Shoshoni express only a slight interest in the next life and often declare that they know nothing about it."

Among some Native Americans, the soul or spirit of the deceased is thought to linger for several days near the site of death before passing on to the other world. Great care is required during this period, both to ensure the progress of the deceased toward the supernatural realm and to safeguard the living. The Ohlone of the California coast adorned the corpse with feathers, flowers, and beads, and then wrapped it in blankets and skins. Dance regalia, weapons, a medicine bundle, and other items owned by the deceased were gathered together and, with the corpse, placed on a funeral pyre. Destroying the deceased's possessions helped to facilitate the soul's journey to the "Island of the Dead." This action also removed reminders that might cause the ghost to remain near the living. This belief is echoed in a Yokut funeral chant

Warrior Song

I shall vanish and be no more
But the land over which I now roam
Shall remain
And change not.

        Hethushka Society, Omaha tribe

that says, "You are going where you are going; don't look back for your family." During the dangerous period, which lasted from six months to a year, the Ohlone considered it disrespectful to utter the deceased's name. In *The Ohlone Way,* Malcolm Margolin writes, "While the mere thought of a dead person brought sorrow, the mention of a dead person's name brought absolute dread."[52] Destroying the deceased's belongings and avoiding his or her name helped confirm the separation of the dead from the living.

Cherokee elders describe a multiple-soul concept that involves four souls and four stages of death.[53] The "soul of conscious life" leaves the body at death and stays nearby for a time as a harmless ghost before traveling the "trail of Kanati" to the land of the dead. When this soul departs the body at the moment of death, the other three souls begin to die. The second soul, located in the liver, takes about a week to die; the third soul, located in the heart and concerned with bodily circulation, takes about a month to die; the fourth soul, located in the bones, takes a year to die. In light of this understanding, Cherokee elders advise that graves should be tended for a year after death but can be neglected afterward "because there is nothing of any significance left in the grave." Formal mourning ends after a year because the process that separates the dead from the living is complete.

In the Great Plains, it was customary to expose the corpse on a platform aboveground or to place it in the limbs of a tree. This not only hastened decomposition of the body, but also aided the soul's journey to the spirit world. Later the sun-bleached skeleton would be retrieved for burial in sacred grounds. As Old Chief Joseph of the Nez Percé lay dying, he told his son, "Never forget my dying words. This country holds your father's body. Never sell the bones of your father and mother." These words were remembered by Younger Chief Joseph as he led warriors into battle to preserve the sanctity of the lands that held the bones of the ancestral dead. (Disputes about the disposition of artifacts and bones retrieved from sacred burial places by archaeologists and others led the U.S. Congress to enact the Native American Graves Protection and Repatriation Act in 1990 with the purpose of reuniting Native American skeletal remains, funerary items, and ceremonial objects with living members of the cultures that produced them.)[54]

Sedentary tribes, such as the Pueblo and Navajo, appear to express more fear of the dead than do tribes that are nomadic hunters and gatherers, such as the Sioux and Apache.[55] This contrast is found in a study conducted by David Mandelbaum among the Cocopa and Hopi.[56] When a Cocopa dies, surviving family members wail in an "ecstasy of violent grief behavior" that lasts twenty-four hours or more, continuing until the body is cremated. Clothes, food, and other items are burned with the body. Although the deceased needs these goods in the afterlife, the Cocopa also hope this will help persuade the spirit of the dead person to pass on from the earth. Later, a ceremony is held commemorating the deceased. The deceased's name cannot be spoken at other times, but, at this special mourning ceremony, those who have passed into the spirit world are publicly summoned, and their presence may be impersonated by living members of the tribe. A house constructed es-

L. A. Huffman, Coffrin's Old West Gallery, Bozeman, Montana

*In January 1879, frontier photographer L. A. Huffman recorded this scene
showing the burial platform of a Sioux warrior who had died and been
placed on the scaffold only a few days before. Surrounding the gravesite
is a vast plain, crisscrossed with the trails of wild herds of buffalo.*

pecially for the spirits may be burned as a gift. The ceremony is intended to
both honor the dead and persuade lurking spirits to come out into the open
and leave the earthly realm. Whereas the initial cremation ritual is focused
on the grief of the bereaved family, the subsequent mourning ceremony is focused on affirming the integrity of the family and the community.

Unlike the Cocopa, the Hopi keep death at a distance. Death threatens
the "middle way" of order, control, and measured deliberation. This attitude
is reflected in Hopi funeral rituals, which are attended by few people and

Burial Oration

You are dead.
You will go above there to the trail.
That is the spirit trail.
Go there to the beautiful trail.
May it please you not to walk about where I am.
You are dead.
Go there to the beautiful trail above.
That is your way.
Look at the place where you used to wander.
The north trail, the mountains where you used to wander, you
    are leaving.
Listen to me: go there!

Wintu tribe

held privately. Mourners are reticent about expressing grief. The Hopi want the whole matter to be "quickly over and best forgotten." They do not wish to invite dead ancestors to a communal gathering. Once a person's spirit leaves the body, it is a different class of being, no longer Hopi. Thus, it is important to make sure that the "dichotomy of quick and dead is sharp and clear."

As these descriptions of the Cocopa and the Hopi show, different social groups may create distinctive responses to death even when they occupy a similar cultural situation. Both Hopi and Cocopa fear the dead, but they cope with this fear differently: The Hopi want to completely avoid the dead, whereas the Cocopa invite the spirits of the dead to join them in ritual celebration, even if only temporarily and under controlled circumstances.

Although rites of passage surrounding death share common elements—themes of separation, transition, and reincorporation—the way in which these elements are actualized through ceremony and other mourning behaviors reflects a society's unique path toward resolution when death comes to a member of the community. Reflecting on the different emphases within Hopi and Cocopa societies can help us evaluate our own attitudes and values relative to death. What do you find valuable about each of these ways of coping with death?

Native Americans inhabit a world described by a sense of sacred time and sacred space, where experiences of place are infused with mythic themes and everything is related to every other being or thing. This worldview is expressed by the phrase "All my relations." As one native person remarked, "We do not believe our religion, we dance it!"[57]

African Traditions

The term *ancestor worship* is used to describe customs such as prayer, sacrifice, or libation, and other acts of respect or reverence shown to the deceased members of a community. "A starting point is the premise that death does not extinguish a person's participation in the life and activities of his family and community, but rather opens a way to a mode of participation that is different from the mundane mode of the living."[58] The dead are assumed to still have a stake in the society of the living, and it is crucial to give them ritual attention in prescribed ways.

It may be helpful to compare such communion with the "living dead" in African societies to our own relationships to deceased loved ones. When some event or stimulus evokes the memory of a person who was dear to us, we may pause a moment and think about the qualities that made that person beloved. Such momentary reverie often evokes a sense of communion with the deceased, and it may bring insights that are helpful in our lives.

Reverence for the dead in African culture involves the deceased members of a community who are still remembered by name. As generations come and go, and memory fades, the long-dead ancestral members of the community are replaced by the more recently deceased.[59] Thus, the ongoing community of the "living dead" consists of ancestors who are recalled in the minds of the living. This is illustrated by the system of age grouping: Among the Nandi in Kenya, for example, once past childhood, a male member of the tribe moves through the junior and senior warrior levels and eventually enters the age group of senior elders; he next becomes an old man and ultimately, at death, an ancestor, one of the living dead, whose personality is remembered by survivors. When he is no longer remembered, he merges with the anonymous dead. The Nandi believe that, by this time, the dead person's "soul stuff" may have reappeared in a newborn child of the tribe, thus continuing the recurrent pattern of a person's passage through the levels of the age-group system.[60]

Kofi Asare Opoku says that the traditional African attitude toward death is essentially positive because "it is comprehensively integrated into the totality of life."[61] In the African tradition, "the opposite of death is birth, and birth is the one event that links every human being, on the one hand, with all those who have gone before and, on the other, with all those who will come after." This basically optimistic attitude can be found in the festive sounds of trumpets and drums played at African funerals. "Music," says Francis Bebey, "is a challenge to human destiny; a refusal to accept the transience of this life; and an attempt to transform the finality of death into another kind of living."[62]

African funeral rituals prepare the dead to enter the abode of the ancestors. Mourners may give messages to the deceased to take to the other side, just as one might give a message to a person going on a trip to convey to those he meets at his destination. The traditional African concept of the afterlife reflects a "this-world orientation." Kwasi Wiredu says, "The land of the dead is geographically similar to our own [and] its population is rather like us."[63] It has been said that, for Africans, life is afterlife.[64]

In Africa today, reverence toward the dead retains its importance. When the body of a Nigerian villager of the Ibo people was shipped by air from the United States to her home village, the coffin arrived in a damaged condition. Somewhere in transit her body had been wrapped in burlap and turned upside down—violating strict tribal taboos concerning abuse of a corpse. Despite the family's offerings of yams, money, and wine to appease the insult,

*A woman and child in mourning are depicted in this Yombe
memorial figure from Zaire. Installed in a shed constructed on
the grave, such adornments are thought to provide the deceased
with companionship or protection in the afterlife.*

members of the tribe reported seeing the woman's spirit roaming about, and
relatives began to experience reversals of fortune, which they characterized
as a "curse" due to mistreatment of their dead relative. The woman's son said,
"My mother was treated as if she were nothing." Thus, her spirit was angry
and not at peace. In bringing suit against the airline to which the body had
been entrusted, the son said, "If this had been done to us by an individual,
my whole tribe would have gone to war. If I win the case, it would be like bringing back someone's head. It would prove I'm a warrior . . . it will show the
gods I have done something against someone who shamed my mother."[65]

The richness of traditional African funeral customs is illustrated by the practices carried out among the LoDagaa of northern Ghana.[66] Among the LoDagaa, funeral ceremonies span at least a six-month period and sometimes continue over several years. They occur in four distinct, successive phases, each focusing on specific aspects of death and bereavement.

The first stage begins at a person's death and lasts six or seven days. During the first several days, the body is prepared for burial, the deceased is mourned by the community, rites are performed to acknowledge the separation of the deceased from the living, kinship ties are affirmed, and some of the social and family roles occupied by the deceased are redistributed. The public ceremonies, which last about three days, conclude with the burial of the corpse. The remaining three or four days of this first stage are devoted to private ceremonies in which preparations are made for redistributing the dead person's property.

About three weeks later, in a second ceremony, the cause of death is established. Rather than considering a snakebite, for example, to be the cause of a person's death, the LoDagaa view the bite as an intermediate agent, but not the final cause of death. The real cause of death lies in a network of spiritual and human relationships. Inquiries are made to uncover any tension that may have existed between the deceased and others.

At the beginning of the rainy season, a third stage of the funeral is held. These rites mark a transitional period in the deceased's passing from the role of the living to that of an ancestor. At this stage, a provisional ancestral shrine is placed on the grave.

The fourth and final stage of LoDagaa ceremonies occurs after the harvest. A final ancestral shrine is constructed and placed on the grave, and close relatives of the deceased are formally released from mourning. The care of offspring is formally transferred to the deceased's tribal "brothers," and final rites conclude redistribution of the deceased's property.

These extended mourning ceremonies serve two purposes: First, they *separate* the dead person from the bereaved family and from the wider community of the living; social roles formerly held by the deceased are assigned to living persons. Second, they gather together, or *aggregate;* that is, the dead person joins with the ancestors and the bereaved are reincorporated into the community in a way that reflects their new status. This rhythm of separation and gathering together is common to funeral rites of all cultures. LoDagaa funeral practices are noteworthy because of the formality with which these functions are accomplished. They provide a model of explicitness in mourning that can be compared and contrasted with our own.

This explicitness is evident in the LoDagaa's use of "mourning restraints" made of leather, fabric, and string. These restraints, which are usually tied around a person's wrist, indicate the degree of relationship of the bereaved to the deceased. At a man's funeral, for example, his father, mother, and widow wear restraints made of hide; his brothers and sisters wear fiber restraints; and his children wear restraints made of string, tied around the ankle. Notice that the strongest restraints are worn by mourners who had the

> If we knew the home of Death, we would set it on fire.
>
> Acholi funeral song

closest relationship with the deceased, usually through kinship and marriage but sometimes through friendship bonds. Persons with less intimate relationships to the deceased wear weaker mourning restraints. In all cases, one end of the mourning restraint is attached to the bereaved while the other end is held by a "mourning companion," who assumes responsibility for the bereaved's behavior during the period of intense grief.

The LoDagaa mourning restraints serve two related purposes. First, as objects that can be seen and felt, they validate that the intensity of the bereaved person's grief is appropriate for his or her relationship with the deceased. Second, they discourage expressions of grief that exceed the norms of the community.

In Africa, as elsewhere, the social and economic forces of modern times threaten traditions. But customs are carried forward in innovative ways. Among the Yoruba of southwestern Nigeria, for example, obituary publication provides a modern forum for an ancient custom. In newspaper obituaries paid for by family and friends, the deceased's status and prestige are denoted by, among other things, the size of the obituary, which can occupy a full page. Olatunde Bayo Lawuyi says it is common to "mark the return of the dead [through obituary publications] every ten years," although this practice lessens over time.[67] The publication of obituaries, Lawuyi says, "demonstrates the possibility of continuity in ancestral beliefs" and "is a symbolic manifestation of a tradition that has taken a new cultural form."

Traditions such as those discussed here are part of the heritage of African Americans. In the black church, pastors, sermons, and songs frequently refer to themes related to death and "homegoing." The terminology of dying— that is, the use of the terms *passed* or *crossed over*—evokes, as Mary Abrums points out, "an image of passing across a fragile invisible line, almost a sleight of hand, where the loved one walked gently into an invisible space."[68] Members of the black church often express belief in the possibility of an ongoing relationship with someone who has passed and of one day being reunited with deceased loved ones.

In recent years, the black church—itself a hybrid of Protestantism and West African traditionalism—has been joined by newer religious communities with roots in African traditions. These include the Afro-Caribbean religions of *Santería, Espiritismo,* and *Orisha-Voodoo,* as well as traditional Yoruba religion (*Anago*). Ancestors typically hold an important place in such religions. Santería (from the Spanish word *santo*), for example, literally means "the way of saints." It recognizes that there can be no orishas (quasi-deities) without the dead, the *egun.* Thus, no ceremony in Santería can be conducted without first thanking the spirits of the ancestors or appeasing the egun.[69] As these traditions become part of the cultural mosaic of today's world, the Internet plays an important role in facilitating development of new African American religious communities.[70] This suggests the possibility of combining traditional worldviews and present circumstances to create a response to dying and death that is personally and culturally meaningful.

Mexican Traditions

From early times, Mexican culture has embodied themes of death, sacrifice, and destiny. For Aztecs, the creation of the world was made possible by sacrificial rites enacted by the gods, and human beings were obliged to return the favor. Sacrificial victims in Aztec rites were termed *teomicqueh,* the "divine dead." Within the divine-human covenant, they were participants in a destiny that had been determined at the origin of the world. Through sacrifice, human beings took part in sustaining life on earth as well as in the heavens and the underworld.[71] When the Spanish came, they may have brought elements from the medieval tradition of the Feast of Fools (associated with Carnaval, *carne vale,* "farewell to the flesh"), where everything is open to criticism, ridicule, and mockery. This humorous tradition became part of *el Día de los Muertos,* the Day of the Dead.[72]

In Mexican culture, people often confront death with humorous sarcasm. Death is cast as an equalizer that not even the wealthiest or most privileged can escape. The emotional response to death is characterized by impatience, disdain, or irony. The skeleton has been called "Mexico's national totem."[73] The popular engravings of Mexican artist José Guadalupe Posada resemble the medieval *danse macabre,* in which people from all walks of life dance with their own skeletons. Posada illustrated verses, like this, written by poet Constancio S. Suárez:

> It is a most sincere truth
> that this adage makes us see:
> only one who was never born
> can never a death's-head be.[74]

A striking awareness of death is displayed in graffiti and ornaments that decorate cars and buses. Newspapers revel in accounts of violent deaths, and obituaries are framed with conspicuous black borders. The suffering Savior is portrayed with bloody vividness. Mexican poetry is filled with similes comparing life's fragility to a dream, a flower, a river, or a passing breeze. Death is described as awakening from a dreamlike existence.[75]

Commenting on how these themes are displayed in modern-day Mexico, Octavio Paz says, "Death defines life. . . . Each of us dies the death he has made for himself. . . . Death, like life, is not transferable."[76] Folk sayings confirm this connection between death and identity: "Tell me how you die and I will tell you who you are." Surrounded by references to death, the Mexican, says Paz, "jokes about it, caresses it, sleeps with it, celebrates it [and makes it] one of his favorite toys and his steadfast love."

Every year, in November, Mexicans celebrate death in a national fiesta known as *el Día de los Muertos,* the Day of the Dead.[77] Blending indigenous ritual and Church dogma, the fiesta—which coincides with All Souls' Day, the

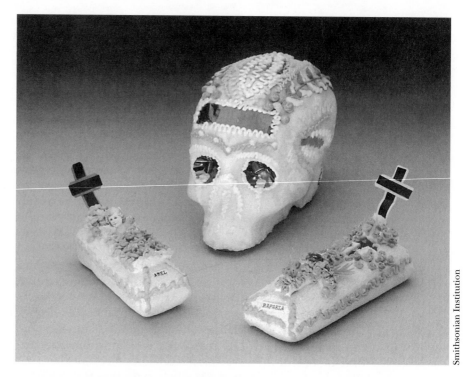

Smithsonian Institution

An ironic attitude toward death characterizes the Day of the Dead fiesta in Mexico. Death is satirized while memories of deceased loved ones are cherished by the living. Family members often place the names of deceased relatives on ornaments such as this candy skull and these candy coffins. This practice assures the spirits of the dead that they have not been forgotten by the living and provides solace to the living in the form of tangible symbols of the presence of deceased loved ones.

Christian feast of commemoration for the dead—is a special occasion for communion between the living and the dead. Bread in the shape of human bones is eaten; sugar-candy skulls and tissue-paper skeletons poke fun at death and flaunt it. Among the most traditional observances of the fiesta are those on the Island of Janitzio in Michoacán and in the Zapotec villages in the Valley of Oaxaca. The following account of *el Día de los Muertos* in the village of Mixquic is representative of observances throughout Mexico.[78]

The fiesta begins at midday on October 31, as bells toll to mark the return of dead children, *angelitos* ("little angels") "whose purity of heart makes them especially effective in mediating between the world of the living and the realm of the supernatural."[79] In each house, the family "sets a table adorned with white flowers, glasses of water, plates with salt (for good luck), and a candle for each dead child." The next day families gather at San Andres Church. Bells are rung at noon to signify the departure of the "small defunct ones" and the return of the "big defunct ones." Then, before nightfall, several thousand graves near the church are swept clean and decorated with ribbons, foil, and marigold-like cempaszuchitl flowers ("flower of the dead"). Maria Nuñez, a caretaker of the village, says:

> The celebration kicks into high gear on the evening of November 1 and into the next morning, when thousands file into the small candle-illuminated graveyard carrying tamales, pumpkin marmalade, chicken with "mole"—a spicy sauce of some 50 ingredients including chili peppers, peanuts, and chocolate—and "pan de muerto," or bread of the dead—sweet rolls decorated with "bones" made of sugar. People sit on the graves and eat the food along with the dead ones. They bring guitars and violins and sing songs. There are stands for selling food for the visitors. It goes on all night. It's a happy occasion—a fiesta, not a time of mourning.[80]

Octavio Paz observes that *el Día de los Muertos* is a time for revolting against ordinary modes of thought and action; the celebration reunites "contradictory elements and principles in order to bring about a renascence of life."[81] Jorge Valadez says,

> The rituals honoring and remembering the dead not only bring members of the community together; they also reinforce the belief that death is a transitional phase in which individuals continue to exist in a different plane while maintaining an important relationship with the living.[82]

Celebrants challenge the boundaries that ordinarily separate the dead from the living. Davíd Carrasco says, "The souls of the dead reassure the living of their continued protection, and the living reassure the dead that they will remember and nurture them in their daily lives."[83] It is important that families pay their respects to the dead, but mourners are cautioned against shedding too many tears; excessive grief may make the pathway traveled by the dead slippery, burdening them with a tortuous journey as they return to the world of the living at this special time of celebration. Although a heightened awareness of death is part of everyday life in Mexican culture, it is given special emphasis during *el Día de los Muertos* as people gather to commemorate enduring ties between the living and the dead.

Asian Traditions

A key concept in Asian philosophy is *harmony,* which is manifested in proper conduct, especially in interpersonal relationships. This emphasis on harmony stems from the fact that descendants of a common ancestor share a lineage that may go back centuries. Important in this regard is the Chinese ideal of *hsiao,* which translates as filiality or filial piety. In Asian societies, ancestors typically occupy a central place in the family as deceased members who continue to have reciprocal relationships with the living members of the household.[84] Life is a whole that embraces both the world of the dead and the world of the living; there is eternal reciprocity between dead ancestors and their heirs.[85] The living and the dead are dependent on each other; the living perform the necessary ancestral rites while the dead dispense blessings to their descendants. The Chinese philosopher Mencius said that the most unfilial act was to leave no heirs because there would be no one to perform the necessary ancestral rites.

Chuang Tzu's wife died. When Hui Tzu went to convey his condolences, he found Chuang Tzu sitting with his legs sprawled out, pounding on a tub and singing.

"You lived with her, she brought up your children, and grew old," said Hui Tzu. "It should be enough simply not to weep at her death. But pounding on a tub and singing—this is going too far, isn't it?"

Chuang Tzu said, "You're wrong. When she first died, do you think I didn't grieve like anyone else? But I looked back to her beginning and the time before she was born. Not only the time before she was born, but the time before she had a body. Not only the time before she had a body, but the time before she had a spirit. In the midst of the jumble of wonder and mystery, a change took place and she had a spirit. Another change and she had a body. Another change and she was born. Now there's been another change and she's dead. It's just like the progression of the four seasons, spring, summer, fall, winter.

"Now she's going to lie down peacefully in a vast room. If I were to follow after her bawling and sobbing, it would show that I don't understand anything about fate. So I stopped."

Chuang Tzu

In Chinese funerals, specific mourning garments show the degree of kinship between the bereaved and the deceased (similar to the LoDagaa use of mourning restraints). Following Taoist traditions, Chinese death rituals make use of ancient principles of *fĕng-shui* (literally, "wind-water"), an art of divination concerned with the proper positioning of elements in harmonious relation to one another. It is crucial to determine the most auspicious siting of human dwellings, for both the living and the dead; failure to do so can cause sorrow. Chinese cemeteries are usually situated on elevated, sloping ground— preferably with mountains behind and the sea in front—with a view of fertile fields the ancestors are leaving for their descendants. During funeral ceremonies, the foot of the casket is usually positioned facing the door so that the spirit or soul of the deceased will have an unobstructed pathway into the next world. Attention to such details assures the bereaved family that everything is done in the proper way to facilitate the ancestor's journey to the afterlife.

The Chinese celebrate the return of deceased ancestors in a spring festival known as *ch'ing ming*, which has been called a kind of Chinese Memorial Day. Families visit graves and burn paper replicas of money, clothes, jewelry, and even modern necessities like video cameras and cell phones as a way of showing regard and care for their ancestors.

The Japanese festival of *bon* or *o-bon* is similar in many respects to the Chinese *ch'ing ming*. Usually observed each year in August, *o-bon* marks the return of ancestral spirits to their families. Known in English as the Festival of the Dead, the Feast of Lanterns (because lamps are lit to guide the spirits on their journeys home), the Feast of All Souls, or simply as the midsummer festival, *o-bon* is a modern expression of ancient customs relating to the souls of the dead and the reverence due them by the living.

> Empty-handed I entered the world
> Barefoot I leave it.
> My coming, my going—
> Two simple happenings
> That got entangled
>
> Kozan Ichikyo

O-bon is a fusion of indigenous Japanese beliefs and Buddhist concepts. Based on a sutra, or discourse of the Buddha, known as the *urabon-kyo,* the festival weaves together traditions from Indian Buddhism, Chinese Taoism and Confucianism, and Shinto, Japan's indigenous religion. The strands of these traditions are woven almost seamlessly into "the Japanese way." In Japan, practicing one religious tradition does not require rejecting all others. A person might feel close to a number of different traditions insofar as they become an integral part of his or her way of life.

Japanese funeral and memorial practices, like those of other Asian cultures, are notable for both their duration and the strong association between the ancestor's spirit and the well-being of the family. Following a death, the family invites Buddhist priests to the home for prayers that help emancipate the deceased's spirit. After the body is cremated, the ashes and some pieces of bone are placed in an urn, which will be interred at the family's grave. Prior to interment, a funeral service is held, during which incense is offered and priests read Buddhist scriptures. At this time, the deceased is given a special posthumous or "Buddhist name," which indicates that the material aspect of the person is extinguished. This name (*kaimyo*) is eventually inscribed on an *ihai,* or memorial tablet, that is placed in the family's *butsudan,* or household altar.

The Funeral (1987), a Japanese film directed by Juzo Itami, offers a glimpse into Japanese death rites, along with elements of comic relief, through its portrayal of a modern family's experiences in rural Japan. American viewers have noted particularly how young children are incorporated into rituals and taught the proper way to behave. For example, after the coffin is closed but before it is taken from the family home, each member of the family uses a stone to strike a blow on the lid of the coffin, symbolically sealing it. A child of perhaps three or four, apparently fond of the sound the stone makes as it hits the wood, starts banging the stone on the coffin lid repeatedly, whereupon he is admonished kindly by an older relative, and the stone is passed along to the next family member.

In the traditional Japanese view, the spirit of the dead is thought to linger at the family home for the first forty-nine days after death. During this period, rites are held to remove the pollution of death and prepare the soul for enshrinement in the *butsudan,* where the family's ancestors are honored. Although these rites may be abbreviated today, they traditionally include seven

This butsudan, *prominently situated in the home of a Japanese American family in California, is representative of altars found in Japanese homes, where deceased relatives and ancestors are honored through prayers, gifts of food, and other ways of showing respect. As a focal point for ongoing relationships between the living and dead members of a household, the* butsudan *is a place where such relationships are demonstrated through concrete actions.*

weekly ceremonies, culminating, on the forty-ninth day after death, in the deceased person's transformation into a benevolent ancestor.

Memorial services continue to be held for the deceased at periodic intervals—typically, on the hundredth day after death, on the first anniversary, the

Death-Song

If they ask for me
  Say: He had some
  Business
In another world.
      Sokan

third anniversary, and at fixed intervals thereafter (the seventh, thirteenth, and twenty-third), until the thirty-third, or sometimes the fiftieth, anniversary. The memorial tablets (*ihai*) placed in the Buddhist altar in the home are regularly honored by the family with simple offerings and scripture readings. The priest of the family's temple may be requested to perform memorial masses in the home, especially on anniversaries of the person's death.

Besides the family *butsudan* in the home, the other main focus of Japanese ancestral rites is the *haka,* the family grave, where ashes of family members are interred. The grave must be maintained properly, which includes cleaning it and making offerings to the dead. As with the *butsudan,* the *haka* is a place of ritual. Incense and flowers are offered to the ancestors, and water is poured over the gravestone, a gesture of purification that dates back to antiquity and that some people now perform without fully recognizing its ancient meaning and symbolism. For the Japanese, it is quite ordinary to talk to their ancestors, either at the gravesite or at the family altar in the home, often in conversational ways, telling the deceased about things that are going on in life or asking for advice. Through such activities, the connection between the dead and the living is maintained.

The Chinese follow similar practices in honoring their ancestors. Traditionally, each ancestor's soul was embodied in a spirit tablet—a rectangular piece of wood, upon which was engraved the deceased's name, title, and birth and death dates—that was kept on the family's home altar. Many Chinese families maintain memorial walls in their homes, sometimes substituting photographs for spirit tablets, as a way to maintain the presence of the dead within the family.

Of particular importance in Chinese traditions is the ultimate destination of the deceased's bones. Many Chinese immigrants to America believed that their souls would not rest unless they had living descendants to care for their spirit tablets and graves. To allay such concerns, the passage contracts for Chinese workers often contained a clause specifying that, if they died while in the United States, their remains would be returned to ancestral plots in China.[86] Among overseas Chinese, it was customary to exhume the bones of the deceased after ten or twenty years and send them back to their ancestral villages in China. However, it sometimes happened that lack of funds or health department rules caused the bones to remain in America. For this reason, Chinese cemeteries in the United States often have a "Bone House," where the bones of deceased Chinese patiently await return to the homeland.

Celtic Traditions

It is commonly agreed that all European cultures can trace their roots to Celtic origins.[87] In ancient times, Celtic people occupied much of central and western Europe, ranging from the British Isles in the west to Turkey and the Black Sea coasts in the east, from Belgium in the north, south to Spain and Italy. The tribal societies of the Celts were led by warriors who justified their authority by skill, courage, and good fortune in battle. Fame after death was the hallmark of human achievement. As someone larger than life, but less than divine, the hero was viewed as being in contact with supernatural powers and the Otherworld.

With deep reverence for nature, the Celts relied on the powers ruling sky, earth, and sea to bring them strength and luck and to protect them from hostile forces. Sacred groves and sacred springs, lakes and bogs, figure prominently in Celtic religion and were among the earliest places of worship. The Celts believed everything was alive, inhabited by soul or spirit, which could be helpful or harmful.

The part played by battle-goddesses, battle-maids, or *valkyries* is important in both Nordic and Celtic traditions and can be traced back before the Viking Age. Valkyries were thought to haunt the battlefield, where they rejoiced in the bloodshed and deaths of warriors. Described as wearing swords, carrying spears, and riding over air and sea, they were viewed as apportioning victory or defeat in battle and welcoming fallen heroes into *Valhalla*, a place of heavenly honor and glory. The phrase "being a guest in Valhalla" was synonymous with death. Valhalla literally means "the hall of the slain." Of great height, it is roofed with golden shields and its rafters are spears. Valhalla was not viewed as the dwelling place of all the dead; it was intended for outstanding heroes. The Celtic attitude toward death in battle can be summarized as follows: "To be a warrior among warriors was the ideal life for the Celt, but to die in a fight surrounded by friends, poets and a hundred dead enemies was the supreme consummation."[88]

Both burial and cremation were practiced at various times in Celtic history. The Celts were often buried with personal effects, clothes, jewelry, and other items that apparently reflect belief in immortality. Articles held dear by the deceased were burned or buried so that they could continue to serve in another life. The status of the deceased and his or her place in the community were indicated by the extent and type of grave goods. Based on archaeological evidence, scholars believe that the Celts enacted elaborate funeral ceremonies involving clan gatherings and feasting at funeral banquets. In one especially lavish burial, probably of a chieftain, tomb furnishings include a large bronze couch on which the body was placed, as well as a four-wheeled vehicle that may have been a hearse or have represented a chariot for traveling to the Otherworld. The tomb contained bronze dishes and drinking horns, enough to accommodate nine people, the number considered ideal for a drinking party, suggesting a ritual feast.

The Celtic attitude toward the dead appears to have been somewhat ambivalent. Despite fearing the dangerous dead, the Celts also regarded the dead as guardian spirits who could help and support the living. Dead heroes and warriors were viewed as a source of power and inspiration. There was a strong sense of communication between the world of the living and the world of the dead. Memory toasts were drunk in honor of the dead. Generally, the dead were helpful to their descendants, especially when reverence was paid to them.

The realm of the dead was not seen as a static place; rather, the emphasis was on the journey to and from it. The life of the soul was not interrupted by the death of the individual, but could continue in a world apart from that in which mortals dwelled. Death was viewed as simply a changing of place. Life went on in all its forms in another world, a world of the dead, the Otherworld. When people died in that world, they could be reborn in this world. Thus, a constant exchange of souls took place between the two worlds: Death in the Otherworld brought a soul to this world, and death in this world took a soul to the Otherworld.

Contact between the living and the dead was especially possible during the breach in time known as *Samhain* (November 1), which marked the end of one year and the dawn of the next according to the Celtic calendar. As the most important festival of the year and a precursor to modern-day Halloween, the harvest feast of *Samhain* lasted several days, a time when supernatural communications with the gods as well as the dead could take place. At that time, the walls between this world and the "other" are most transparent, the souls of the dead driven toward the living "like swirling leaves."[89]

The Celtic priesthood, known as the *Druids,* presided over the sacrificial rites and interpreted omens.[90] They acted as intermediaries between the world of humankind and the domain of the supernatural. Their main teaching appears to have been immortality of the soul as a future bodily life, not merely as spirit or shadow of life after death. Indeed, the Celts seem to have been among the first peoples to develop a belief in personal immortality. Such beliefs helped the Celts face the fear of death and made them brave in battle.

The Celtic heritage continues to be evident in such observances as Halloween. In addition, the Celts, who valued skill in words nearly as much as skill in battle, delighting in word-games and intricate poetic language, also made notable contributions to world literature, perhaps most famously in the legend of King Arthur. Traces of Celtic myth are also found in Chaucer and in Shakespeare's *The Tempest* and *As You Like It,* as well as more recently in Tolkien's *Lord of the Rings,* which contains strong echoes of the Otherworld and includes Druid-like characters in the forms of magicians Gandalf and Saruman. In Tolkien's *The Hobbit,* the ring lord is called the *Necromancer,* a name from Nordic mythology meaning "enchanter" or "wizard" and which refers to the sorcerer's skill of speaking with the dead to gain knowledge. There is an elegiac note in Old English poetry, like *Beowulf,* in which there is a sense of grief at the awareness that all things are passing away and life is on loan.[91]

Today, interestingly, more people claim some sort of Celtic identity than at any other time in history. Celtic religious beliefs are being rediscovered as part of the modern resurgence of pagan, nature-venerating, polytheistic religions. (The literal meaning of the word *pagan* is "rural" or "country dweller.") The influence of Celtic culture is most clearly found in Wales, Scotland, and Ireland, where Celtic languages are still spoken by well over a million people.

Through emigration by the Irish and by Scottish Highlanders, Celtic traditions were carried to the United States, as well as to other parts of the world.

Celtic music is heard worldwide in pubs and taverns and at music festivals.[92] The keening sounds of dirges and laments played on bagpipes and *uilleann* pipes were part of many funeral processions held for firefighters killed as a result of the terrorist attacks in September 2001. The themes and techniques associated with Celtic music also survive as strong undercurrents in North American country and bluegrass music. The Celtic heritage is recognized as an important component of European and European-American culture.

Mixed Plate: Cultural Diversity in Hawaii

The population of Hawaii represents a rich ethnic and cultural blend. Eleanor Nordyke points out that Hawaii is "the only region where all racial groups are minorities and where the majority of the population has its roots in the Pacific Islands or Asia instead of Europe or Africa."[93] Hawaii was settled by Polynesians who sailed to the Hawaiian archipelago and whose first contact with Europeans came in 1778 with exploration of the Pacific by Captain James Cook.[94] Later, successive waves of immigrants came—including Chinese, Japanese, Portuguese, Okinawans, Koreans, and Filipinos—many arriving as temporary laborers in sugarcane fields and then remaining to make Hawaii their home. Today's residents include Caucasians from Europe and North America, Samoans, Vietnamese, Laotians, and Cambodians, as well as African Americans, Latin Americans, Pakistanis, Tongans, Fijians, Micronesians, immigrants from other parts of Oceania, and others. The pan-ethnic identity of being a "local" represents "the common identity of people of Hawaii and their shared appreciation of the land, peoples, and cultures of the islands."[95]

Each group has its own story, unique history, and corresponding traditions. Most also have their own cultural networks, with their own ways of keeping story, history, and tradition alive, as well as providing mutual support in times of need. With the Japanese, it's kin groups; the Portuguese have the church; the Chinese, clubs; and Filipinos have provincial clubs.[96] Hawaii illustrates the possibility of preserving the cultural richness of distinctive traditions by accommodating, and assimilating, their expression.

Characteristics of Hawaii's Peoples

Among native Hawaiians, the extended family group, or *'ohana,* is at the center of traditional values.[97] Children have an important place in family gatherings, including funerals. The intimate relationships of the *'ohana* involve close bonds between living family members and their ancestors.[98] Ancestral remains are sacred, especially those of the *ali'i,* members of the royal family. Indeed, as George Kanahele says, the Hawaiians' love of family is the basis of their love of the land:

> In a religious society in which ancestors were deified as *'aumakua* [gods] and genealogy elevated to prominent status, a place, a home, was much more valued because of its ties with the ancestors. A Hawaiian's birthplace was celebrated not

simply because he happened to be born there, but because it was also the place where so many generations of his ancestors were born before him. It was a constant reminder of the vitality of the bloodline and of the preciousness of life past, present, and future.[99]

In the spring of 1994, the Hawaiian community was shocked into mourning when two *ka'ai,* or woven caskets, containing bones believed to be those of deified Hawaiian chiefs were taken from the Bishop Museum in Honolulu.[100] A grief-filled ceremony was held at the Royal Mausoleum to inform the ancestors of the missing bones and express the desire for the bones' safe return. Chants and wailing laments asked the ancestors' forgiveness and formed part of a ceremony that reportedly was last held a hundred years ago.

Among the earliest immigrants to Hawaii were the Chinese.[101] Like those of native Hawaiians, Chinese cultural values emphasize the importance of family and relationships. They also retain elements of traditional funerals and mourning.[102] For example, in accordance with the belief that the needs of the dead resemble those of the living, Chinese funerals in Hawaii typically include offerings of food, money, and other items that will be needed by the deceased in the afterlife. Papier-mâché "servant dolls" are placed in front of the casket, and a Taoist priest chants instructions about how to take care of the deceased in Heaven. The boy servant might be told, "Take care of your master; fetch him water and firewood." To the girl servant, the priest might say, "Keep the house clean and, when you go shopping, don't waste your master's money." In the Taoist funeral, which lasts nearly all day, the priest chants and musicians play instruments while family members perform rituals at the priest's direction. Symbolic money (called "Hell Notes"), which the dead person will spend in the other world, is contributed by mourners and burned in a container during the service. The more money burned, the more the deceased has in the next life. Relatives and friends visit and express condolences. Following Taoist traditions, the ancient divinatory art of *fêng-shui* is called upon for auspicious placement of the casket during the service. Similarly, Chinese cemeteries in Hawaii are situated amid great natural beauty and on sloping ground, in accord with the principles of fêng-shui. A proper burial facilitates the journey of the deceased's spirit to the afterlife.

The Japanese also place high value on the family and its extended household.[103] Unlike the Chinese, who typically choose ground burial, the Japanese prefer cremation and then interment of the remains in a *haka,* or family memorial, which may have space for a dozen or more urns. At funerals, the primary mourner is often given *koden*—contributions of money to help defray expenses—with the donation increasing as kinship ties become closer. An elder son, for example, makes a larger contribution than, say, a cousin. Among the Japanese in Hawaii, most homes have a *butsudan,* or household altar, as a focal point for honoring the family's ancestors, and families participate in the midsummer *o-bon* festival honoring the dead. Celebrations like the Japanese *o-bon,* as well as the Chinese festival *ch'ing ming,* are community affairs in Hawaii, with people of diverse backgrounds and traditions joining together.

Most cultural groups living in Hawaii share a valuing of family ties and respect for ancestors. John F. McDermott says:

> In all groups, except perhaps the Caucasian, the extended family plays a central role. There is an emphasis on the family as a key social unit, and on family cohesion, family interdependence, and loyalty to the family as central guiding values. The individual is seen as part of a larger network, and duties and obligations, as well as much of the sense of personal security, derive from that context. . . . Caucasians, too, value the family, but they face the world as individuals.[104]

Although European American culture plays a major role in modern Hawaii, it is appropriate to think of Caucasians not as dominant, but as one of many groups that constitute the "ethnic mosaic" of the islands. Newcomers often find that this social reality requires some adjustment. Caucasians who move to Hawaii from mainland United States do not think of themselves as migrants; they view themselves as representing mainstream culture and usually expect others, not themselves, to adapt.[105] Those who remain in Hawaii, however, adapt to the unique culture of Hawaii and assume a "local" identity that reflects an appreciation of the land, peoples, and cultures of the islands.

Assimilation and Accommodation in Death Rites

The various ethnic groups in Hawaii tend to maintain a distinctive identity and culture while sharing elements of their identity and culture with the overall community. As different ethnic groups became part of the cultural mix in Hawaii, a common language, called "pidgin," developed and became a symbol of local identity. Borrowing words and grammar from the native tongues of its speakers, pidgin is not only an expressive means of communication among people of disparate backgrounds, but also a way for people to identify with their adopted homeland. Today, speaking pidgin allows people to transcend cultural boundaries and establish rapport with each other on the basis of "local" identity.

A Caucasian nurse describes how pidgin was useful in talking with a Filipino man who was dying. As the man's body wasted away, he was frightened. Offering comfort, the nurse told him, "Spirit good, body *pau* [finished]." In using a pidgin word, borrowed from the Hawaiian language, she was able to affirm, in a culturally appropriate and comforting way, the strength of his spirit while acknowledging that the life in his body was being consumed by disease.

Local identity is fostered by familiarity with customs practiced by the different ethnic groups and flexibility in adopting elements of those customs into one's own life. For instance, the native Hawaiian tradition of feasting at important ceremonial events is widespread among Hawaii's residents. At funerals, mourners often gather after the ritual to share food and conversation. Mortuaries in Hawaii accommodate this by having kitchen and dining facilities where food can be prepared, brought by mourners (potluck), or catered and served to gathered family and friends.

Similarly, funeral announcements in Hawaii usually include the notice "Aloha attire requested," to which mourners respond by wearing colorful shirts or *mu'u mu'u* (long "missionary" dresses), along with beautiful and fragrant flower leis. The lei is very special in Hawaiian culture, and different flowers and leis carry symbolic meanings. For example, a *hala* lei is associated

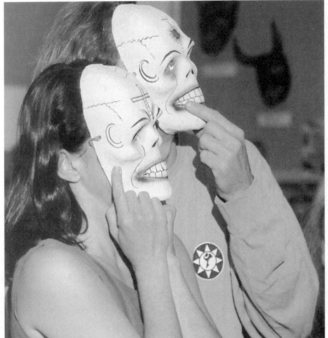

© Patrick Dean

In contemporary societies, where a variety of cultural traditions are practiced by different ethnic and subcultural groups, people may find themselves "trying on" customs and practices that differ from those of their own heritage group. The opportunity to participate in the rites and ceremonies of other cultures, to assume a "local identity," even if only temporarily, can broaden our understanding and expand our range of choices for revitalizing even those customs with which we are most familiar.

with the breath (*ha*) and connotes passing away or dying. The ginger, or *'awapuhi*, lei is a symbol of things that pass too soon, as indicated in the Hawaiian folk saying, "*'Awapuhi lau pala wale*," or "Ginger leaves yellow too quickly."[106] In the customs of "feasting" after a funeral and wearing flower leis, traditions associated with the indigenous Hawaiians have been adopted as expressions of local identity and community feeling.

Given the religions practiced in Hawaii—Christianity, Buddhism, and Taoism, among others—mortuaries are generally set up to offer appropriate accoutrements and symbols for all these traditions. The central portion of the altar at one mortuary is designed as a revolving display so that images and symbols of the appropriate religious tradition can be easily moved into view.

Hawaii's diverse inhabitants have not minimized differences between different ethnic groups so much as learned to appreciate and make room for their expression. The fastest-growing ethnic group in Hawaii is "mixed race," or *hapa*.[107] When people marry outside their heritage group, thereby joining in kinship with families from different cultural traditions, their customs,

beliefs, and practices blend together in a new family. As spouses from different traditions adopt elements of each other's culture, their children naturally
become acquainted with both cultures.

The boundaries between different groups are loosened through social interaction, becoming "soft instead of hard, often overlapping rather than
sharply defined," resulting in a situation wherein "no group has totally sur-
rendered the core of its traditional cultural identity."[108]

Death in Contemporary Multicultural Societies

Shared experiences and a sense of community shape the customs and beliefs
of a particular society. The ways we cope with death are not created out of
thin air. The root meaning of *tradition* is "to hand down." Each generation receives culture from the preceding generation, alters it, and passes it on.

Modern societies are composed of a number of social groups, each with
distinctive customs and lifestyles. The presence of a "cultural mosaic" created
by different ethnic and cultural groups can enrich a society.[109] People sometimes talk or write about "The American Way of Death," but this phrase conceals what, in fact, are many different "ways of death," reflecting attitudes,
beliefs, and customs of culturally diverse groups. David Olson and John De-
Frain remind us that "tremendous diversity exists among people who are commonly grouped together."[110]

In a cosmopolitan world, individuals may wrestle with the dilemma of
maintaining their cultural distinctiveness while also taking steps to broaden
the conventional terms of what it means to be a member of their culture. For
example, influenced by body disposition practices in the global context, an
individual might opt for cremation instead of burial, despite the latter being
the strongly held preference and traditional within her own group. Such
choices reflect the fact that today's societies are increasingly homogeneous
(similar) *across* cultures and heterogeneous (diverse) *within* them.[111]

Still, ethnicity and other cultural factors often have an impact on such
matters as coping with life-threatening illness, the perception of pain, social
support for the dying, manifestations of grief, mourning styles, and funeral
customs.[112] African American funerals and mourning practices illustrate how
customs can persist despite the passage of time and changed circumstance.
As Ronald Barrett points out, elements of traditional West African practices
retain their importance for many African Americans.[113] This is evident in
customs such as gathering at the gravesite to bid godspeed to the deceased
and referring to funerals as "home-going" ceremonies honoring the spirit of
the deceased. David Roediger says such customs "grew from deep African
roots, gained a paradoxical strength and resilience from the horrors of mid-
passage, and flowered in the slave funeral—a value laden and unifying social
event which the slave community in the United States was able to preserve
from both physical and ideological onslaughts of the master class."[114]

Similarly, Spanish-speaking people in northern New Mexico continue to
practice traditional forms of *recuerdo*, or remembrance, which memorialize

the dead and comfort the bereaved.[115] Presented as a written narrative or ballad, the *recuerdo* tells the story of a person's life in an epic, lyrical, and heroic manner. This is a kind of farewell, a leave-taking, or *la despedida*, on behalf of a deceased person. Such memorials frequently contain reminders of the transitory nature of life and express the notion that life is on loan from God for only a short time.

When everyone in a society shares the same beliefs and customs, there are known and socially accepted ways of dealing with death and grief. Cultural diversity may jeopardize this comforting situation because there is less agreement about which practices are socially sanctioned for managing death and minimizing "existential dread."[116] Uncertainty about the social norms for dealing with death is apparent when people at modern funerals are anxious about how they should act or what they should say to the bereaved.

In rediscovering the commemoration of death, we must beware the temptation to take "recipes" for coping with death or disposing of the dead from other cultures or a nostalgia-infused past. It can be worthwhile, however, to foster an appreciation of how other cultures relate to death and to adapt aspects of those "deathways" into one's own life and practice.[117] Ronald Grimes advises, "Our definition of death rites must be large enough to include not only ritualized preparation for death and rites performed near the time of a death, but also ritual activities that follow long after the occasion of a person's death."[118] Moreover, as Robert Harrison reminds us, mourning rituals are missing something important if they do not "provide the means, or language, to cope with one's own mortality even as they help one cope with the death of others."[119]

Further Readings

Lynne Ann DeSpelder. "Developing Cultural Competency." In *Living with Grief: Who We Are, How We Grieve*, eds. Kenneth J. Doka and Joyce D. Davidson, 97–106. Washington, D.C.: Hospice Foundation of America, 1998.

Anne Fadiman. *The Spirit Catches You and You Fall Down: A Hmong Child, Her American Doctors, and the Collision of Two Cultures.* New York: Farrar, Straus and Giroux, 1997.

Geri-Ann Galanti. *Caring for Patients from Different Cultures: Case Studies from American Hospitals,* 2nd ed. Philadelphia: University of Pennsylvania Press, 1997.

Ronald L. Grimes. *Deeply into the Bone: Re-Inventing Rites of Passage.* Berkeley: University of California Press, 2000.

Robert Pogue Harrison. *The Dominion of the Dead.* Chicago: University of Chicago Press, 2003.

Bert Hayslip, Jr., and Cynthia A. Peveto. *Cultural Changes in Attitudes Toward Death, Dying, and Bereavement.* New York: Springer, 2005.

Allan Kellehear. *A Social History of Dying.* New York: Cambridge University Press, 2007.

Claudio Lomnitz. *Death and the Idea of Mexico.* Cambridge, Mass.: MIT Press, 2005.

Colin Murray Parkes, Pittu Laungani, and Bill Young, eds. *Death and Bereavement Across Cultures.* New York: Routledge, 1997.

Mike Parker Pearson. *The Archaeology of Death and Burial.* College Station: Texas A&M University Press, 2000.

With federal support lacking, local and state death systems in Louisiana are overwhelmed. Bodies of the dead lay in the streets of New Orleans for days following Hurricane Katrina's devastation, a scene that most of the U.S. population thought could never occur in their country.

CHAPTER 4

Death Systems: Mortality and Society

*J*ust as society has a natural interest in the way its health care systems are organized to provide services to individuals, it also has an interest in such matters of public policy as procedures for legally defining and making a determination of death, rules governing organ donation and transplantation, ways of classifying different modes of death into useful categories, the manner in which investigative duties are carried out by coroners and medical examiners, and the criteria that apply to performing autopsies. These various aspects of public policy are sometimes interrelated, mutually affecting one another. For example, new legal and administrative procedures for defining death had to be created when medical technologies led to organ transplantation. These matters of public interest are all aspects of what Robert Kastenbaum calls the "death system"—that is, the elements of a society that have an impact on how people deal with dying and death. Kastenbaum says: "We may think of the death system as the interpersonal, sociophysical, and symbolic network through which an individual's relationship to mortality is mediated by his or her society."[1]

According to Kastenbaum, the components of a death system include *people* (for example, funeral directors, life insurance agents, weapons designers, people who care for the dying), *places* (for example, cemeteries, funeral homes, battlefields, war memorials, disaster sites), *times* (for example, memorial days and religious commemorations such as Good Friday, anniversaries of important battles, Halloween), *objects* (for example, obituaries, tombstones, hearses, the electric chair), and *symbols* (for example, black armbands, funeral music, skull and crossbones, language used to talk about death).

How the death system functions varies among different societies and at different times in the same society. The functions of a death system include

1. Warnings and predictions about potentially life-threatening events (for example, storms, tornadoes, and other disasters, as well as advice to specific individuals, such as doctors' reports of laboratory results or mechanics' warnings about faulty brakes)
2. Preventing death (for example, emergency and acute medical care, public health initiatives, antismoking campaigns)
3. Caring for the dying (for example, nurses, trauma workers, family caregivers, hospice staff)
4. Disposing of the dead (for example, mortuaries, cemetery plots, memorialization processes, identification of bodies in disasters)
5. Social consolidation after death (for example, coping with grief, maintaining community bonds, settling estates)
6. Making sense of death (for example, religious or scientific explanations, support groups, consolation literature, last words)
7. Killing (for example, capital punishment, war, hunting, raising and marketing of animals)

In practice, there are many interconnections and mutual influences among these functions. It should be clear from this brief listing, however, that the elements composing the death system touch on virtually every aspect of social and individual life.

Disasters

Although the term is sometimes applied loosely to any event with negative consequences, disasters are generally defined as life-threatening events that affect many people, usually within a relatively brief period of time, bringing sudden or great misfortune. Disasters result from natural phenomena—floods, earthquakes, and other "acts of God"—as well as from human activities. This latter category could include airplane crashes, chemical spills, terrorist acts, and nuclear contamination.

In the United States, the incidence of disaster has increased in recent decades. One reason is that more than half the U.S. population now lives within fifty miles of the coastline, an area that, in the West, is vulnerable to fires, floods, earthquakes, and landslides and, in the Southeast, is prey to storms, hurricanes, and tornadoes. Population growth and industrialization increase our exposure to disasters related to human activities—for example, fires, explosions, and chemical pollution. "This translates into virtually all of us having a direct stake in our national capacity to mitigate the risks associated with these perils.[2]

Risk theorists point out that modern technological systems are complex and fail in ways that cannot be anticipated, with minor events unexpectedly interacting to produce a major problem, a phenomenon that Charles Perrow calls a "normal accident."[3] As one writer concludes, "We have constructed a world in which the potential for high-tech catastrophe is embedded in the fabric of day-to-day life."[4] As the assumption of stable and predictable reality is undermined in disaster, collective behavior follows a characteristic "disaster cycle" from first warning, through impact and then rescue, to rebuilding and rehabilitation.

Reducing the Impact of Disasters

Communities can decrease the risk of injury and death by taking precautionary measures to lessen the impact of a potential disaster. In Japan, for example, where the Great Kanto earthquake of 1923 killed more than 100,000 people, some 8 million people nationwide have participated in emergency exercises to prepare for a major earthquake that officials say could occur at any time. Even when such precautions are taken, however, the effects of a potential disaster may be difficult to anticipate. For example, prior to a devastating earthquake that hit Mexico City in 1985, killing almost 10,000 people, city officials had enacted building codes based on the possibility of low-frequency earthquake waves, which are associated with the ancient lake beds on which Mexico City is built. Despite this effort to ward off disaster, however, the codes did not include specifications for the number of shaking cycles buildings should be constructed to withstand, a factor that experts determined contributed to the large number of fatalities.

Adequate warnings of an impending disaster can save lives. Yet such information may be withheld due to greed, political expediency, uncertainty about the nature and extent of the threat, or concerns about causing panic. The tragedy that followed the eruption in 1902 of the Mount Pelée volcano, on the island of Martinique in the West Indies, illustrates how information that could warn potential disaster victims is sometimes mismanaged, with disastrous consequences. The officials of the nearby community of Saint-Pierre were alerted to the likelihood that the volcano would erupt. But, concerned that the population would panic if notified and thus thwart their plans for an upcoming local election, officials withheld warning of the danger from the populace. As a result, almost the entire population of the small community was incinerated. The May 1980 eruption of Mount St. Helens provides an instructive comparison. Even though this eruption was larger, only 60 lives were lost compared with the 30,000 casualties resulting from the eruption of Mount Pelée. In part, this difference was due to adequate warnings of the hazard and timely establishment of a restricted zone of access.[5]

People do not always respond to threats in a prudent fashion. Just as the risks associated with smoking or drug abuse may be ignored, people may believe they are immune to disaster. Individuals living in areas where natural disasters are a common occurrence—earthquake or hurricane country, for example—may rationalize the danger as "playing the percentages." Similarly, predictions of potential disasters are often met with the response "I've never been affected before. Why should I worry now?" This is the apparent attitude

© Al Diaz

Shared support can help the bereaved cope with the traumatic impact of a disaster. Here, survivors embrace during the funeral services for passengers and crew of an airliner crash in the Florida Everglades.

of people who, when they learn of a chemical spill, travel to the disaster area for a closer look and of those who, hearing about an incoming tsunami, head for the ocean.[6] As Philip Sarre points out, "It seems that most people deliberately underestimate the risks to themselves."[7]

Warnings are not always timely or adequate, however, as with the 2004 tsunami triggered by an earthquake off the Indonesian island of Sumatra. Traveling at a speed of 500 miles an hour, the tsunami brought huge waves to coastal areas across the Indian Ocean, killing at least 225,000 people in a dozen countries. Relief workers had to get food, water, and medical supplies into remote areas where roads had been destroyed, as well as identify dead and missing, a job made difficult by the large number of non-Asian tourists vacationing in the region. As plans were put into practice for a more adequate warning system, experts concluded that equally needed were more-effective systems of evacuation and disaster relief.

Coping with the Aftermath of Disaster

What can be done when disaster strikes? What kind of help is needed in its aftermath? Imagine the situation: People are injured, some are missing, others are dead. In the wake of a disaster, the survivors may experience an "existential crisis" that is marked by a profound sense of emptiness and despair.[8] They are likely to be in a state of shock, uncertain about the whereabouts of loved ones and about the future.[9]

Meeting the immediate needs of survivors—providing food and shelter, caring for medical needs, and restoring vital community services—is essential. Even as attention is being focused on physical needs, however, the emotional needs of survivors must be addressed. Ministering to these needs might include forming a missing persons group to help alleviate the anxieties of survivors worried about the safety of relatives. Locating and caring for the dead is another important aspect of helping survivors cope with the trauma of disaster. The comment of one relief agency worker, "It doesn't really make too much sense to dig up the dead and then go and bury them again," reveals an unfortunate ignorance of the human emotions that surround disposition of the dead. As a former health director in New Orleans said, "You take care of the living by taking care of the dead."[10] Although most efforts directed toward coping with disaster are focused on the emergency or crisis period, regaining emotional stability may take years. Unfortunately, the disaster-response team that comes to assist survivors in recovering from disaster is usually present for only a brief time; it rapidly dissolves with the end of the emergency period.

Helping personnel who come to the aid of the survivors of a disaster may also become "survivors" because of their intense encounter with human suffering and tragedy. Consider the experience of a Kansas City doctor who arrived at the scene of a hotel disaster to find, among the debris left when a balcony collapsed onto the lobby below, bodies chopped in half, decapitated, and maimed. He watched as a critically injured man's leg, trapped under a fallen beam, was amputated with a chain saw. When things returned more or less to normal, he told officials that he felt the need to spend some time away from reminders of the disaster to cope with his own experience as a survivor. Often, those who provide care and support during disasters are themselves given little support for their own coping needs.[11]

When a storm dumped twenty inches of rain in one night on a coastal community in California, residents awoke the next morning to the news that twenty-two people had been killed, more than a hundred families had lost their homes, and another 3000 homes had been severely damaged. Within a few days, an impromptu organization was set up to help survivors deal with the psychological trauma of their losses. Known as Project COPE (Counseling Ordinary People in Emergencies), it provided counseling to disaster victims and coordinated the services of more than a hundred mental health professionals.[12] Counselors found that people who had lost loved ones or property were experiencing grief reactions heightened by the sudden, capricious nature of their losses. Some who had lost only material possessions felt guilty for mourning the loss of property when others had lost family members. Some felt guilty for surviving the disaster. Those made homeless by the storm felt isolated and alone. Bureaucratic delay and uncooperative insurance companies and government agencies caused people to feel angry and frustrated. Many victims felt anxious, vulnerable, and depressed. For some, old problems related to personal or relationship issues reemerged in the aftermath of the disaster.

COPE set up programs to respond to each of these problems. Survivors were reassured that their reactions were normal and their grief legitimate. Counselors helped them sort out their priorities so they could begin to solve problems created by the disaster. Emergency crews and relief workers were included in these efforts to provide critical incident stress debriefing. Although we cannot eliminate the encounter with death that accompanies disaster, steps can be taken to reduce its impact, preserve life, and demonstrate compassion for survivors.

Hurricane Katrina: A Case Example

On Monday, August 29, 2005, Hurricane Katrina came ashore in southern Louisiana. It killed more than 1500, left hundreds of thousands homeless, laid waste to 90,000 square miles of land, and ravaged one of America's most storied cities.[13] The storm surge obliterated coastal communities. The suffering of survivors continued for days and weeks after the storm passed. A Senate investigation reported a "failure of government at all levels to plan, prepare for, and respond aggressively to the storm."[14]

In New Orleans, levee failures, which caused flooding that left survivors homeless and destitute, had roots long predating Katrina. Taking responsibility, the Army Corps of Engineers said the levee system was "built disjointedly, using outdated data."[15] Nor was there adequate planning for the 100,000 people believed to lack the means to evacuate themselves. Despite strongly worded advisories from the National Hurricane Center and personal warnings from its director, top officials "did not appear to truly grasp the magnitude of the storm's potential for destruction before it made landfall."[16] One critic said, "As Katrina built, the local and state governments hesitated, and the federal government seemed to fiddle while Rome was burning."[17] Another commentator, noting that "for the whole week of the hurricane most people in the city had no access to official help," suggested that "society and nature were co-conspirators in the tragedy."[18]

The Coast Guard and certain private businesses had conducted planning and training for disasters, and this was put to good use when disaster struck.

> Both moved material assets and personnel out of harm's way as the storm approached, but kept them close enough to the front lines for quick response after it passed. Perhaps most important, both had empowered front-line leaders who were able to make decisions when they needed to be made.[19]

These strategies were the exception in the Hurricane Katrina disaster. Security expert Stephen Flynn summarizes the lessons of Katrina as they apply to being prepared for future disasters:[20]

1. The natural environment is undergoing changes that elevate the risk.
2. We have allowed protective measures that earlier generations constructed to deal with catastrophic events to erode.
3. We have embraced unfettered urban and coastal development, especially of housing, which exacerbates risk.
4. We have been unwilling to invest in mitigation measures or contingency planning to deal with a major disaster.

5. There are insufficient resources available to respond effectively when disaster strikes.
6. Last, when the dust clears (or the water recedes), we go right back to "business as usual."

Homicide and Capital Punishment

Some people believe that, unwittingly or not, Americans have fostered the notion that violence can be used to solve one's problems and, in support of this thesis, they cite the historical record of violence against Native Americans and African Americans. With few legal restraints during the great westward expansion across the continent, attitudes arose that promoted arbitrary justice and encouraged people to do whatever it took to ensure survival, whether inside or outside the law.

Assessing the Homicidal Act

Community standards of justice play a major role in determining how an act of killing is assessed by a society and its legal-political-judicial system. As Figure 4-1 illustrates, *homicide*—the killing of one human being by another—is separated into two main categories, criminal and noncriminal, and these categories encompass further distinctions. For example, an act of homicide is considered excusable or justifiable when a person who kills another is found to have acted within certain legal rights, such as that of self-defense, or when the killing is judged an accident involving no gross negligence.

Thus, although a murder is necessarily a homicide, a homicide is not always a murder. The law has traditionally recognized two main distinctions within the category of *criminal* homicide: murder and manslaughter. Murder is associated with acts carried out with deliberate intention ("malice aforethought"), and the category of first-degree murder is used to designate killings that are carefully planned or that take place in conjunction with other serious crimes, such as rape. Manslaughter, however, is defined as wrongful, unplanned killing, done without malice. An example of *voluntary* manslaughter is that of a person who, after being provoked, kills another person in a fight. Such a person is said to have acted in the heat of passion, without considering the consequences. When homicide results from criminal carelessness but is unintentional, it is termed an act of *involuntary* manslaughter, as in the case of a fatal automobile accident caused by reckless driving or a death caused by gross negligence.

The circumstances surrounding a killing, the relationship between the killer and the victim, and the killer's motivation and intention are all weighed to determine how an act of homicide is assessed within the judicial system. In a study by Henry Lundsgaarde of more than 300 killings that occurred in a major American city, it was found that more than half of the suspects were released before reaching trial.[21] To understand why some homicide cases are not brought to trial, it is necessary to look at how the circumstances of a homicidal act influence its investigation and how the judicial processes determine whether an accused killer is brought to trial.

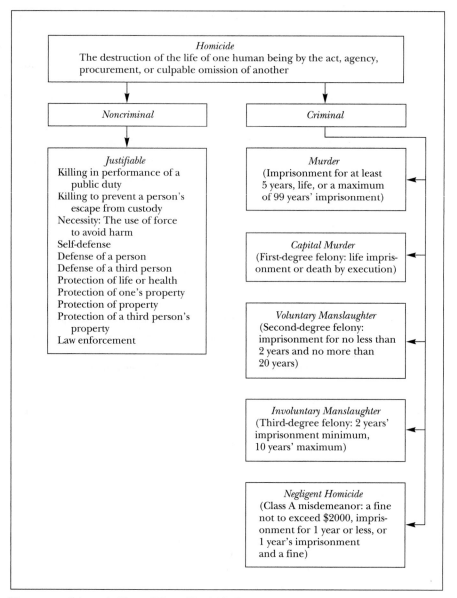

Figure *4-1 Schematic View of Texas Homicide Statutes*
Source: Vernon's Texas Codes Annotated: Penal Code, 1974. From Henry Lundsgaard, *Murder in Space
City: A Cultural Analysis of Houston Homicide Patterns* (New York: Oxford University Press, 1977), p. 213.

The medical-legal investigation of an act of homicide generally includes three components: (1) an autopsy to determine the official cause of death; (2) a police investigation to ascertain the facts and gather evidence pertinent to the killing; and (3) various judicial and quasi-judicial procedures, carried out by the district attorney's office and the court system, to determine whether there is sufficient cause to bring a case to trial.

Fundamental to this investigation is the acknowledgment that homicide is an interpersonal act. That is, it involves a relationship between the killer and the victim: They may have had close domestic ties, being members of the same family or otherwise related; they may have been friends or associates; or they may have been strangers. In the study conducted by Lundsgaarde, it was found that "the closer, or more intimate, the relationship is between a killer and his victim, the less likely it is that the killer will be severely punished for his act." In other words, killing a stranger was more likely to result in a stiff penalty than was killing a friend or family member.

The response of the criminal justice system to homicide reflects cultural attitudes about killing. Lundsgaarde says, "What appears so shocking, or understandable, as the case may be, about many killings depends upon our personal understandings of and assumptions about the rules that 'should' and 'ought' to govern a particular kind of relationship." Basing its standards on cultural attitudes, the criminal justice system in a community sets about its task of determining whether an act of homicide is lawful or unlawful. If it is lawful, the killer is released and the case is closed. If it is unlawful, a further determination is made as to whether the killing in question was an act of murder, manslaughter, or negligent homicide—and there are various degrees of criminal intent within each of these categories as well. In making these determinations, the criminal justice system, including the police investigation, takes into account the intention, motivation, and circumstances surrounding the homicide. The following set of figures is instructive:[22]

- 22,000—Number of *criminal homicides* reported (murder and non-negligent manslaughter)
- 15,000—Number of *arrests* reported of persons charged with criminal homicide
- 13,500—Number of homicide cases *prosecuted* (about 90 percent of persons arrested)
- 10,000—Estimated number of homicide *convictions* (about two-thirds of those arrested and nearly three-fourths of those prosecuted)
- 2000–4000—Estimated number of *death-eligible defendants* convicted of first-degree murder because of "aggravating circumstances" on which a jury can impose a death sentence
- 300—Average number of *death sentences* imposed annually (about one-tenth of death-eligible defendants)
- 55—Average number of *executions* per year

What are the cultural assumptions by which an act of homicide is judged? Lundsgaarde's research showed that the legal outcome for a person who kills his wife's lover is quite different from the outcome for a person who combines killing with theft, robbery, or similar criminal acts. An extensive investigation conducted by the *Los Angeles Times* found that people who killed strangers were more likely to get tough treatment from the criminal justice system than those who killed lovers, relatives, or other people they knew. One police investigator said, when "innocent victims, God-fearing people, end up murdered," other cases "take a back seat" because such killing causes

> When death is unreal, violence also becomes unreal, and human life has no value in and of itself.
>
> Vine Deloria, Jr.

neighborhood terror and therefore must be resolved quickly. However, he added, referring to gang shootings, "When 'Snoopy' kills 'Chilly Willie,' nobody cares."[23]

Society is usually reluctant to become involved in matters that fall within the domain of the family. This appears to be true even with family homicide involving a child victim. Situational elements within a family may result in penalties being imposed on the basis of statutes defining manslaughter or child abuse rather than murder.[24] A close relationship is believed to involve its own set of mutual responsibilities and obligations—its own "code of justice," if you will—that provides social sanctions for acts that occur within the relationship. In contrast, says Lundsgaarde, "The killer who chooses a stranger as his victim overtly threatens the preservation of the social order."

To put it another way, an individual who kills a stranger is not likely to be constrained by personal concern for the victim. Thus, society devotes its attention to acts of homicide that threaten the preservation of law and order within the larger society. Killings that occur within the family unit or between persons who know one another tend to be viewed as less of a threat to society at large.

Capital Punishment

Some people believe that violence is "contagious" in American society. This reasoning can be developed along several lines: First, it may be that a violent society creates an environment in which disturbed individuals are encouraged to act out their antisocial behaviors in more harmful ways than they might if other ways of releasing such violent tendencies were available. Second, each violent incident may spawn others, thus spreading the contagion of violence. Third, some believe that if an act of violence is not properly resolved, it will be repeated. Regarding this last point, a "proper resolution," according to Fredrick Wertham, is "for society to make clear what it wants: "Society must say, *No, this we will not tolerate,*" and this statement must be affirmed and upheld by a judicial process that emphasizes accountability for one's acts.[25]

Is capital punishment the strong statement that is needed? In theory, capital punishment serves a twofold purpose: (1) It punishes the offender and (2) deters other potential offenders. "The theory of deterrence is based on the idea that criminal behavior can be deterred if punishment is swift, certain, and severe enough to counter the benefits or pleasure gained from commiting crime."[26]

In 2005, sixty individuals were executed in the United States and, at year's end, about 3250 were under sentence of death.[27] Most murderers who receive the death penalty are involved in intraracial offenses—that is, cases of whites killing whites or blacks killing blacks.[28] Hanging, electrocution, the gas chamber, and lethal injection have all been used to carry out executions at various times in the United States.

Herb Haines observes that "executions have become highly ritualized affairs," as death-row prisoners are moved to special cells for their final visits and last meals, and then transferred from one prison staffer to another as they are taken to the place where the death sentence is carried out.[29] Haines says, "The modern orchestration of death lends assurance that everything is in order, everything is humane and civilized and that we aren't, after all, barbarians."

Although the death penalty has been applied to various offenses since ancient times, many people argue that it is needlessly cruel and overrated as a deterrent to murder. According to Glenn Vernon,

> Investigations into the ineffectiveness of the death penalty as a deterrent to murder revealed that some murderers were so busy with other things during the events preceding the murder that they simply did not think of the death penalty, and that others were interacting with their victims in such an extremely emotional manner that the consequences of their murderous acts were not even taken into account.[30]

In the United States, most statutes require that a sentence of death be imposed only after evidence is submitted to establish that "aggravating," as opposed to "mitigating," factors were present in the crime. If "aggravating" factors are found and the sentence is death, then the case is reviewed by an appellate court. Apart from certain crimes on which the Supreme Court has not ruled (the most notable being treason), the only capital crime in the United States is murder.[31]

Is it inconsistent for society to try to eradicate or prevent murder by itself engaging in killing? Does capital punishment reinforce the idea that violence solves problems? Citing evidence from psychology and behavioral therapy, which emphasizes the effects of positive reinforcement, Robert Kastenbaum and Ruth Aisenberg say "there is little evidence to suggest that imposing massive punishment on one individual will 'improve' the behavior of others"; on the contrary, it may reinforce hostile fantasies and murderous tendencies.[32] The greatest risk for a potential murderer, they contend, is not the risk of execution, "but the risk of being killed by the police, the intended victim, or some bystander."

Yet another argument against capital punishment is the concern for the number of death-row inmates who have been released after evidence of their innocence has been discovered, some of them just days before being executed. As of 2002, more than one hundred death-row inmates had been released due to evidence of their innocence since 1973.[33]

If capital punishment is not an effective deterrent to murder, are there other options? Comparing our present-day system with early Anglo-Saxon and English law and with many non-Western legal systems as well, Lundsgaarde says, "Modern criminal law has completely transformed the ancient view of homicide as a wrong against a victim and his family to its modern version that views homicide as an offense against the state."[34] In short, the modern tendency is to view crime as a social problem. The separation of civil and criminal law—or, more specifically, the separation of personal obligation and criminal liability—eliminates the killer's liability to the *victim as person.* Instead, the violent act is viewed as having been committed against the public at large.

Defining Death

At first, the definition of death might seem obvious: A person dies, is dead, and the corpse is disposed of. But as soon as someone asks, "What do you mean by 'a person dies'?" this simple definition begins to unravel. Finding a reliable way to define death and to determine when it has occurred can become quite complex. Think about how you would define death. When would you consider yourself to be dead? How would you know that death had occurred in someone else? The answers to these questions range from the definite ("when decay and putrefaction have set in") to the subtler ("when I can no longer take care of myself"). A person using the first method for making a determination of death would hardly be pleased to be judged dead by the standards of the second.

There are historical accounts of people being considered dead who, in fact, were in a condition that only mimicked biological death. As a safeguard against the threat of being buried alive, some people in earlier times arranged for their bodies to be placed in coffins with bells or some other attention-getting device that the "corpse" could activate after burial should consciousness return after a mistaken determination of death (see Figure 4-2).

The present concern with defining death is, of course, more sophisticated and draws upon scientific data. Yet, even though it is possible to determine when death has occurred by observing certain signs that life has ceased, these signs may be interpreted differently depending on how death is defined. In other words, the way we define death establishes the criteria that are used to determine that a person has died. Five steps can be distinguished in the process of making decisions about the death of a human being:[35]

1. Establish a conceptual understanding of what constitutes death—that is, a *definition of death.*
2. Decide upon the *criteria and procedures that will be used in making a determination* that death has occurred.
3. Apply these criteria and procedures *in a particular case* to determine if a person's condition meets the criteria.
4. If the criteria are met, the person is *pronounced dead.*
5. Attest the person's death on *a certificate of record.*

Conventional Signs of Death and New Technology

Historically, the death of the human organism has been determined by the absence of heartbeat and breathing. Most deaths are still determined by

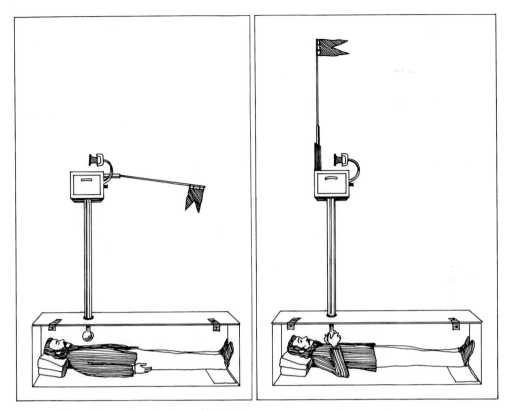

Figure 4-2 *Coffin Bell-Pull Device*
To prevent premature burial in cases of doubtful death, devices such as this French "life-preserving" coffin were invented and patented. If activated, the box above the ground opened to let in air and light, the flag raised, a bell rang, and a light came on to signal that the buried person was still alive. The person who had been mistaken for dead could also call out, and his or her voice would be amplified by the device. The fear of being buried alive stemmed from the period of great plagues and epidemics when, in the hasty disposition of the dead, a mistaken determination of death might result from a state of illness that only mimicked death.

the absence of these vital signs. However, when respirators, or ventilators, and other life-support systems are used to artificially sustain vital physiological processes, conventional means of determining death by absence of heartbeat and breathing are inadequate. By relying on the conventional vital signs, a patient with permanent loss of brain function, including loss of brain stem function, could be termed alive on the basis of *artificially* maintained cardiopulmonary functions.

Therefore, the concept of "brain death" was created as a means of determining whether a person is alive or dead when conventional vital signs are ambiguous because of supportive medical technology. (When brain death

When I was a junior physician in a hospital, we were once called urgently to the bedside of a lady of ninety. The nurse had used the term "cardiac arrest"—the old lady's heart had stopped (as hearts are apt to do, around ninety!). But because the cardiac arrest alarm was raised, I and the other houseman launched into a full-scale resuscitation. With violent drugs injected directly into the heart, blasts of electric current through her chest, noise and chaos, she had anything but a peaceful death. On reflection we realized that all this had been inappropriate, but nothing in our medical student training gave us any guide. Indeed once the emergency is in the air, there is not time to weigh up the pros and cons. The decision is rarely a doctor's anyway, because usually the only person on the scene when an emergency occurs is a nurse—probably a relatively junior one if it is night time—and she decides whether or not to resuscitate. Needless to say, it is a very courageous nurse who decides not to. Once things have started, it is very difficult for the doctor when he arrives to stop everything, particularly if the patient is showing signs of reviving.

Richard Lamerton, *Care of the Dying*

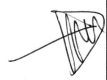

occurs, brain stem functions—including spontaneous breathing—are lost, but heartbeat and other vegetative functions related to internal homeostasis can continue because these functions are not completely dependent on the integrity of the brain stem.)[36] Rather than replacing the conventional clinical criteria for determining death—pulse, heartbeat, and respiration—the criteria for brain death supplement them.

In contrast to *clinical death*, which is determined by either the cessation of heartbeat and breathing or the criteria for establishing brain death, *cellular death* refers to a process that results when heartbeat, respiration, and brain activity cease. When a person's breathing and heartbeat are stopped temporarily, as occurs during certain surgical procedures, people sometimes say that the person was "clinically dead" for a period of time. However, such language is imprecise when the cessation of vital functions is reversible.

Cellular death encompasses the breakdown of metabolic processes and results in complete nonfunctionality. Thus, in this sense, the definition of death is "we die because our cells die."[37] Living cells require a continuous input of energy; without it, they degrade into a nonliving collection of molecules. Cellular death is an irreversible process of deterioration in the body's systems and organs. Without oxygen, cells vary in their survival potential. The cells of skin and connective tissues may survive for several hours; the neurons of the brain last only five to eight minutes. When there is a loss of neurons in the midbrain and medulla, the brain center that controls breathing is destroyed; the death of neurons in the cerebral cortex destroys intellectual capacity. The breakdown of metabolic processes, the sum of which is life, causes a loss of organic functions—that is, death. As the cells and tissues of the body die, advanced signs of death become evident: the lack of certain reflexes in the eyes, the fall of body temperature (algor mortis), the purple-red discoloration of parts of the body as blood settles (livor mortis), and the rigidity of

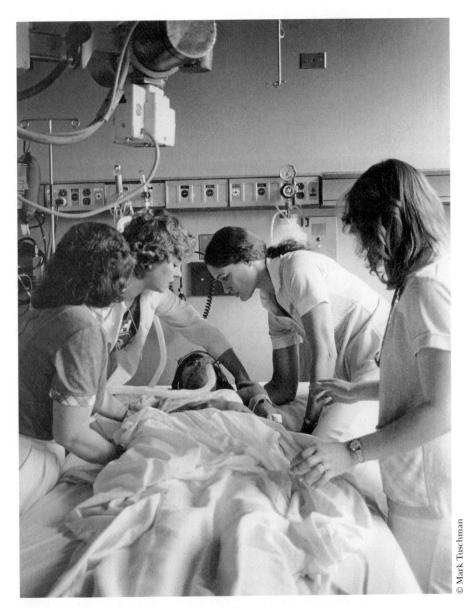

© Mark Tuschman

In the intensive care unit, both human and technical considerations combine to make necessary the evaluation of ethical questions regarding the meaning of life and death.

muscles (rigor mortis). In a biological sense, death can be defined as the cessation of life due to irreversible changes in cell metabolism.

Medical technologies make it possible to manipulate the dying process in such a way that some parts of the body stop functioning while other parts can be artificially maintained. Thus, cell death may affect some organs of the body, causing irreversible breakdown, while other organs of the body are still functioning. The capacity of modern medicine to alter the natural sequence and process of cellular death has created a need to rethink how death is defined and institute new procedures for determining when death has occurred.

Conceptual and Empirical Criteria

What is death? How can it be determined that a person has died? These questions, though closely related, involve separate issues that must be distinguished. Medical ethicist Robert Veatch outlines four levels that must be addressed in our inquiry concerning the definition and determination of death.[38] The first level involves formally defining *death*. Essentially, this is a conceptual or philosophical endeavor. According to Veatch, "Death means a complete change in the status of a living entity characterized by the irreversible loss of those characteristics that are essentially significant to it." Although this definition may sound rather abstract on first reading, it is really quite precise. It encompasses the deaths not only of human beings, but also of nonhuman animals, plants, cells, and indeed can even be understood metaphorically as applying to a social phenomenon such as the organization of a society or culture.

To flesh out this definition, we must turn to Veatch's second level of inquiry, again a conceptual or philosophical question: What is so essentially *significant* about life that its loss is termed death? Some possible answers include the flow of vital bodily fluids (breath and blood, for example), the soul, and, in more recent definitions, consciousness. Each of these possible answers will be examined more closely in a moment.

The third level that Veatch distinguishes has to do with the *locus* of death: Where in the organism should one look to determine whether death has occurred? This question moves us from the conceptual realm to an empirical inquiry—that is, one based on observation or experience. Notice, however, that the answer to this question depends on the conceptual understanding used to define death.

Veatch's fourth level deals with the following question: What technical tests must be applied at the locus of death to determine if an individual is living or dead?

So, to recap these levels of inquiry: Step one involves formally defining death. Step two adds further content to the definition by pinpointing the significant difference between life and death. Step three locates where one should look for signs of this significant change. And step four gives us some tests, or a set of criteria, that can be used to determine whether an organism is alive or dead. With this process in mind, we now have the tools to examine four different approaches to the definition and determination of death.

Four Approaches to the Definition and Determination of Death

All four of the following approaches to defining and determining death begin with the formal definition of death given by Veatch: "Death means a complete change in the status of a living entity characterized by the irreversible loss of those characteristics that are essentially significant to it." From that shared beginning, however, each approach finds its particular way through subsequent levels of inquiry. As you'll see, each of these approaches relates death to a loss: the first, of the flow of vital fluids; the second, of the soul by the body; the third, of the capacity for bodily integration; the fourth, of the capacity for social interaction. In considering the merits of the various approaches, notice how death is determined according to the way it is defined.

Irreversible Loss of Flow of Vital Fluids

The first approach focuses on the cessation of the flow of vital bodily fluids. With this conceptual understanding of death, one looks to the heart, blood vessels, lungs, and respiratory tract as the locus of death. To determine whether an individual is alive or dead, one would observe the breathing, feel the pulse, and listen to the heartbeat. In addition to these conventional tests, we can include the modern methods of electrocardiogram and direct measurement of oxygen and carbon dioxide levels in the blood because they focus on the same loci and criteria for determining death.

This approach to defining death is adequate for making a determination of death in most cases, even today. When vital functions are artificially sustained by machines, however, no clear determination of death can be made by this definition. Consider, for example, a patient connected to a heart-lung machine that keeps the vital fluids of blood and breath flowing through the body. According to this definition, the patient is alive. If the patient is disconnected from the machine, these vital functions cease and, by this definition, the patient is dead.

Thus, the ambiguity of this first approach results from defining death on the basis of physiological criteria that, although intimately related to life processes, do not appear to constitute the most significant criteria for identifying human life.

Irreversible Loss of the Soul from the Body

In the second approach to defining death—one used in many cultures worldwide and from time immemorial—the criterion is the presence or absence of the soul in the body. Within this framework, as long as the soul is present, the person is alive; when the soul leaves, the body dies. Some religious traditions define death in precisely this way.

The locus of the soul has not been scientifically established (nor has its existence), although some believe the soul is related to the breath or the heart or, perhaps, as seventeenth-century philosopher René Descartes believed, to the pineal body, a small protrusion from the center of the brain. For those who hold this concept, the criteria for determining death would presumably involve some means of ascertaining death at the particular locus where the soul is thought to reside. In a study done in 1907, dying people were placed on a sensitive scale to determine whether any weight loss occurs at the moment of death. Researchers noted a loss, averaging from one to two ounces, leading to speculations about whether the loss indicated the departure of the soul from the body at death.[39]

To people living in modern societies, in which secular beliefs are prominent, this approach to defining death seems irrelevant. Our first difficulty

[handwritten margin note: alternatives?, 1–2 oz of oxygen weight?]

Knowing What a Human Being Is

Rolling Thunder often repeated, "We do so many unnatural things, we don't know what's natural anymore." One day he and I were sitting on the ground out in the desert. He was describing a young Indian apprentice from another tribe and making designs in the sand with a stick. Suddenly he said, "You people don't even know what a human being is!" I did not see the connection between the subject at hand and that sudden exclamation, but I had learned to understand what he meant by "you people." It was not a judgmental finger-pointing to be taken personally, but a sort of generalized identification to be applied wherever it fit. "You can look right at someone's empty body and think that you're lookin' at the person when they're not even there. Time and time again, you people speed to the scene of an accident, pick up an empty body and take it down the highway at eighty miles an hour, leaving the person miles behind, not knowing what the heck is going on!"

As an example, he then described to me an episode in which he went into the hospital to assist a young lady—a friend of friends—who had been in a head-on collision and was a long time in a coma.

"But the moment I took a good look at the body, I could see she wasn't even there. I had to find her—go get her—and she was way out in the field where the car'd flipped over the cliff, and she was sittin' on a rock. Her friend who was driving was killed. And this one sittin' on the rock, she didn't even know where she was. But, boy, she was determined to stay there. She was totally disoriented. I had to pull her, nearly force her back. Only time we can do that is when we know their own will isn't working—otherwise we always leave it up to their own choice.

"Well, in the early days, most everyone could tell when a person wasn't in their body. That was just natural to see that. That's been lost now, mostly. Only thing I can say is, until you learn to understand these things, you should never, never move an unconscious body. Unconscious means the person is not in there. So treat the body on the scene and never, never move it. Not until you learn how. People can't find their own way back to the body—not when they've been pulled loose that way by some accident or something. Time and time again, traumatized people get abandoned that way. Time and time again, people die in a coma because of that."

Quoted in Doug Boyd, *Mystics, Magicians, and Medicine People: Tales of a Wanderer*

would be to adequately define the soul. And even if this difficulty could be overcome, we would need some way to ascertain whether the soul was present or absent at a given time. Moreover, this definition of death forces an examination of whether death occurs because the soul departs from the body or, conversely, whether the soul departs from the body because death has occurred. In other words, does the soul "animate" the body, giving it life, or do the physiological processes of vitality in the body provide a vessel wherein the soul resides? Such questions may lead to fascinating speculations, but they do little to solve the dilemmas posed by medical practice in a scientific age.

Irreversible Loss of the Capacity for Bodily Integration

In the third approach, death is defined as the irreversible loss of the capacity for bodily integration. That is, "an organism dies when it loses the

"You're confirmed for Sunday at 5:30 A.M. in your bed, sound asleep."

power to preserve and sustain its self-organizing organization permanently and irreversibly"; in other words, "death is the loss of syntropic capacity or ability."[40] This approach is more sophisticated than the first because it refers not just to the conventional physiological signs of vitality in the body (the flow of breath and blood), but also to the more generalized capability of the body to regulate its own functioning. The approach recognizes the fact that a human being is an integrated organism with capacities for internal regulation through complex homeostatic feedback mechanisms.

This definition at least partly resolves the ambiguity of the first definition because a determination of death would not be made merely because a person's physiological functioning was being maintained by a machine. Rather, a determination of death would be made when the organism no longer had the capacity for bodily integration. The locus for such a determination is currently considered to be the central nervous system—more specifically, the brain. The determination of death that results from this definition is often characterized as brain death (although this term is potentially misleading because it focuses attention on the death of part of the organism, not the whole organism).

According to standards published in 1968 by the Harvard Medical School Ad Hoc Committee to Examine the Definition of Brain Death, brain death involves four essential criteria:[41]

1. Lack of receptivity and response to external stimuli
2. Absence of spontaneous muscular movement and spontaneous breathing
3. Absence of observable reflexes, including brain and spinal reflexes
4. Absence of brain activity, as signified by a flat electroencephalogram (EEG)

The Harvard criteria require a second set of tests to be performed after twenty-four hours have elapsed, and they exclude cases of hypothermia (body temperature below 90 degrees Fahrenheit) as well as situations involving central nervous system depressants such as barbiturates. Procedures for applying these criteria, also known as the "whole-brain" definition of death, have been widely adopted when the conventional means of determining death are not conclusive.[42]

Some medical practitioners and ethicists believe that the clinical tests currently used to determine brain death do not actually satisfy all of the criteria; specifically, varying degrees and kinds of brain function have been found in some individuals pronounced brain dead according to the standard tests. This finding suggests that the tests may not always suffice to show "permanent cessation of functioning of the entire brain." As a result, some experts advocate returning to cardiorespiratory criteria as the definition of death. As debate over defining death goes on, simply abandoning current methods of determining brain death could create problems because, unless a more reliable and accurate method for determining death is substituted, the practice of organ donation and transplantation would involve a kind of legally sanctioned killing.

Irreversible Loss of the Capacity for Consciousness or Social Interaction

Although the Harvard criteria are widely accepted in clinical settings, some people believe that they fail to specify what is *significant* about human life. Veatch, for example, says that it is the higher functions of the brain—not merely reflex networks that regulate such physiological processes as blood pressure and respiration—that define the essential characteristics of a human being. Thus, the fourth approach to defining death emphasizes the capacity for consciousness and social interaction. The premise of this approach is that for a person to be truly human, not only must certain biological processes function, but the social dimension of life—consciousness or personhood—must also be present. Being alive implies a capacity for conscious interaction with one's environment and with other human beings. Therefore, according to this definition, death is determined by the irreversible loss of the capacity for social interaction. The death of a *person* is synonymous with the death of a human being.

Using this approach, where should we look to determine whether an individual is alive or dead? Current scientific evidence points to the neocortex, the outer surface of the brain, where processes essential to consciousness and social interaction are located. In this case, the EEG alone would provide an adequate measure for determining death.

In the debate about how death should be defined, this fourth approach is known as a "higher-brain" theory, which contrasts with the "whole-brain" theory. Karen Gervais represents the higher-brain approach when she writes, "It is loss of consciousness and not loss of biological functioning that should determine when human life is over."[43] Furthermore, "By emphasizing the brain's integrating role in the human organism, the whole-brain theory of

A number of years ago, before all the discussion about defining brain death and maintaining life on a respirator and so on, a patient of mine, a young pregnant woman at term, suddenly developed extremely high blood pressure. Then she had a stroke and the baby's heartbeat stopped, so we supported her by artificially maintaining blood pressure and other vital functions, including breathing. But she had had a complete brain death immediately. And she had lost the baby. We got an EEG [electroencephalogram], and it was completely flat. We repeated it twenty-four hours later, and again it was completely flat.

It was the worst tragedy I've ever seen, because in just a few minutes she was gone and the baby was gone—just within moments. I talked with her husband, her mother, and her father. (Now, this was long before the issues surrounding definition of death had become so contentious that the lawyers got involved.) I told them that the thing to do was turn off the machine. Just as I had not read about all this, they as a family had not read about it. It seemed quite logical to me.

So we picked a time when we were going to do it, and they all came and waited outside the door. I told them again what I was going to do, and they said to go ahead and do it. I went in and turned off the machine. The nurse and I watched her, and in five minutes her pulse rate had stopped. I think this is the proper way to handle this sort of situation when brain death is involved. I think it has a negative effect to continue life support systems for weeks and months. It was a tragedy, and given the tragedy, what options do you have? Continue the life support system or don't continue it. To me, there's no argument whatsoever to continue the life support system.

Quoted from *Death and Dying: The Physician's Perspective,* a videotape by Elizabeth Bradbury

death reduces to a lower-brain theory of death." In commenting on the search for a more precise definition of human death, Gervais concludes that we are confronted with a basic choice about the definition of human life—namely, whether we consider a human being as an *organism* or as a *person*.

The current whole-brain definition of death, says Robert Veatch, establishes a view of what is *essential* to being alive that is not shared by all ethnic or religious groups.[44] He argues that, rather than imposing one approach on everyone, the right to "opt out" could be made available to individuals whose beliefs about how to define the death of a human being are in conflict with the whole-brain approach of the Harvard criteria. Although these criteria have been part of medical practice for four decades, it is obvious that questions about defining death are not yet fully answered.

Legislation Defining Death

The definition of death touches upon many aspects of our lives. Criminal prosecution, inheritance, taxation, treatment of the corpse, and mourning are all affected by the way society "draws the dividing line between life and death."[45] After publication of the criteria for establishing brain death in 1968, public discussion began to take place about the need to revise the legal definition of death so as to reflect medical realities. In 1970, Kansas became the first state to adopt a statute that included brain-based criteria for determining death, and a number of other states subsequently adopted similar laws. These early statutes were potentially confusing, however, because they contained dual definitions for determining death: one based on cessation of vital signs and the other on brain functions.

In 1972, Alexander Capron and Leon Kass offered a proposal that related the two standards.[46] Capron and Kass said that the statute should

1. Concern the death of a human being, not the death of cells, tissues, or organs; and not the death or cessation of a person's role as a fully functioning member of his or her family or community
2. Move incrementally, supplementing rather than replacing older cardiopulmonary (heartbeat and breathing) standards
3. Avoid serving as a special definition for a special function such as organ transplantation
4. Apply uniformly to all persons
5. Be flexible, leaving specific criteria to the judgment of physicians

This proposal was adopted, with various modifications, by several states. But it was criticized for not addressing issues related to organ transplantation in that it did not require at least two physicians to participate jointly in determining death, nor did it require that the physician who pronounces death not be a member of the medical team seeking organs for transplantation. Capron and Kass replied that transplant considerations should be dealt with in separate legislation, such as the Uniform Anatomical Gift Act (discussed later in this chapter).

In 1975, the American Bar Association (ABA) proposed its own model statute, which offered a definition of death "for all legal purposes." This proposal virtually ignored conventional cardiopulmonary criteria and focused instead on "irreversible cessation of total brain function." Then, in 1978, yet another proposal was contained in a model statute that was part of the Uniform Brain Death Act. That model was followed the next year by a statute proposed by the American Medical Association (AMA). The fact that numerous proposals were put forward during the 1970s is evidence of the difficulty encountered at the time in trying to adjust to new medical technologies and their impact on determining when a person could (or should) be declared dead.

Finally, in the early 1980s, a presidential commission drafted a model statute that met with broad acceptance and eventually led to uniform laws throughout the United States: the Uniform Determination of Death Act (see Figure 4-3). In its report, the President's Commission for the Study of Ethical Problems in Medicine said that the Uniform Determination of Death Act "addresses the matter of 'defining' death at the level of general physiological standards rather than at the level of more abstract concepts or the level of more precise criteria and tests," because such standards and criteria change over time as knowledge and techniques are refined.[47] The Act acknowledges the fact that, in most cases, irreversible circulatory and respiratory cessation

❧ *Uniform Determination of Death Act*

1. [*Determination of Death.*] An individual who has sustained either (1) irreversible cessation of circulatory and respiratory functions, or (2) irreversible cessation of all functions of the entire brain, including the brain stem, is dead. A determination of death must be made in accordance with accepted medical standards.
2. [*Uniformity of Construction and Application.*] This act shall be applied and construed to effectuate its general purpose to make uniform the law with respect to the subject of this Act among states enacting it.

Figure *4-3* *Uniform Determination of Death Act*
Source: President's Commission for the Study of Ethical Problems in Medicine and Biomedical and Behavioral Research, *Defining Death: A Report on the Medical, Legal and Ethical Issues in the Determination of Death* (Washington, D.C.: Government Printing Office, 1981), p. 73.

provides an obvious and sufficient basis for making a determination of death. In other words, these cases permit death to be diagnosed on the basis that breathing and blood flow have ceased and cannot be restored. Thus, if a patient is not being supported on a respirator, there is no need to evaluate brain function before making a determination of death.

The Commission said that a statutory definition of death should be separate and distinct from any provisions concerning organ donation. In contrast to earlier proposals, which stated that a person would be "considered dead" when their stated criteria were met, the language of the Uniform Determination of Death Act is clearer and more direct. It states that a person who meets the standards set forth in the law "is dead."

Confusion about the definition of death had arisen, the Commission said, "because the same technology not only keeps heart and lungs functioning in some who have irretrievably lost all brain functions, but also sustains other, less severely injured patients." The result is a "blurring of the important distinction between patients who are *dead* and those who are or may be *dying.*" The Commission concluded that "proof of an irreversible absence of functions in the entire brain, including the brain stem, provides a highly reliable means of declaring death for respirator-maintained bodies." The Commission noted that the Harvard Committee's definition of brain death had been reliable and that "no case has yet been found that met these criteria and regained any brain functions despite continuation of respirator support."

Death is an absolute and single phenomenon, the Commission said, arguing that it would radically change the meaning of death to expand the definition of death to include persons who have lost all cognitive functions but are still able to breathe spontaneously. When brain stem functions remain—for example, when respiration occurs naturally but there is no cognitive awareness—the patient's condition is described as a "persistent vegetative state" (discussed in Chapter 6). Although one may observe involuntary movements and unassisted breathing in the person's body, the lack of higher-brain functions results in no awareness of self or the environment. Sustained by medical and nursing care, including artificial feeding and antibiotics to fight recurrent infections, such patients may survive for years without a respirator. (The longest such survival, according to the Commission's report, was over thirty-seven years.)

The Commission cited the nearly universal acceptance of the "whole-brain" concept by both the medical community and the general public. A higher-brain formulation, which would require agreement about the meaning of personhood, does not enjoy such consensus. At the present level of understanding and technique, the Commission said, "The 'higher brain' may well exist only as a metaphorical concept, not in reality." In summing up the work of the President's Commission for the Study of Ethical Problems in Medicine, Albert Jonsen says that it "brought conceptual clarity to a confused issue and helped to make good law."[48] However, because guidelines for brain death are implemented at the level of the hospital, a 2007 study found wide variability in practice, "differences that might have implications for determination of death and initiation of transplant procedures."[49]

Organ Transplantation and Organ Donation

Of all the innovative medical techniques for saving the lives of patients who were once considered hopelessly ill, perhaps the most dramatic is organ transplantation, which is defined as "the transfer of living tissues or cells from a donor to a recipient, with the intention of maintaining the functional integrity of the transplanted tissue in the recipient."[50] Since the day in 1954 when the first kidney transplant, from one identical twin to another, was performed at Peter Bent Brigham Hospital in Boston, organ transplantation has evolved to become part of standard medical practice. In 1967, public interest

© Albert Lee Strickland

Designed to increase public awareness of organ donation, this billboard on a Florida highway calls particular attention to donations that can save the lives of children.

was heightened as Christiaan Barnard accomplished the first successful adult heart transplant. Other noteworthy events in the history of transplantation include agreement on the definition of brain death in 1968 and discovery of the immunosuppressive drug cyclosporine in 1976.[51]

The subsequent success of organ transplantation is due largely to such factors as newer immunosuppressants, better patient selection, and earlier intervention, as well as better understanding of the issues related to histocompatibility, the ability of tissues to accept a transplant from a different individual without rejecting it. The growing number of patients on waiting lists for transplants involving the heart, kidney, liver, pancreas, and lung is indicative of the widespread acceptance of transplantation by the public today.

The ideal candidate for a transplant is a patient whose condition is deteriorating despite the best conventional medical treatment available and for whom a transplant offers a reasonable likelihood of recovery. For some transplants, most often a kidney, the donor is a living person; sometimes donor and recipient are members of the same family. When a living donor is unavailable, or when the needed organ (a heart, for example) cannot be taken from a living human being, the organ can be removed from the body of a person who has been declared dead (according to criteria for brain death) and whose organs are kept viable for transplantation by artificially sustaining physiological functions.

The Uniform Anatomical Gift Act, approved in 1968 by the National Conference of Commissions on Uniform State Laws and enacted in some form in all fifty states, provides for the donation of the body or specific body parts upon the death of the donor.[52] The main provisions of the Gift Act are presented in Table 4-1. Because of a chronic shortage of donated organs, the Gift Act was revised in 1987 to simplify organ donation by removing requirements that the next of kin give consent and that the document be witnessed. This revision also included a "required request" provision that requires hospitals to have procedures that encourage organ donations. Near the time of death, hospital personnel must ask if the patient agreed to be an organ donor; and, if not, the family must be informed about the option to donate organs and tissues.

T A B L E *4-1* *Major Provisions of the Uniform Anatomical Gift Act*

1. Any person over eighteen may donate all or part of his or her body for education, research, therapeutic, or transplantation purposes.
2. If the person has not made a donation before death, the next of kin can make it unless there was a known objection by the deceased.
3. If the person has made such a gift, it cannot be revoked by his or her relatives.
4. If there is more than one person of the same degree of kinship, the gift from relatives shall not be accepted if there is a known objection by one of them.
5. The gift can be authorized by a card carried by the individual or by written or recorded verbal communication from a relative.
6. The gift can be amended or revoked at any time before the death of the donor.
7. The time of death must be determined by a physician who is not involved in any transplantation.

DONOR   **STATE OF CALIFORNIA**
DMV
DEPARTMENT OF MOTOR VEHICLES

Pursuant to the Uniform Anatomical Gift Act.
I hereby give, effective upon my death:

A _____ Any needed organ or parts

B _____ Parts or organs listed _____

_____

Signature of Donor

DL-290 (REV 10/86)   D A T E

- -
DETACH HERE

To pledge a donation, fill out this card. Remove "DONOR" dot and affix it on the front of your license or I.D. card as shown in the diagram. Affix the card on the reverse of your license or I.D. card. If you change your mind, peel off the card and the dot. Whole Body donations require separate arrangements.
If you are unable to sign, instruct two witnesses to sign this card in your presence.

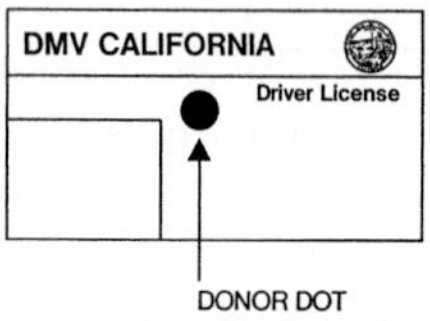

DMV CALIFORNIA
Driver License
DONOR DOT

NOTICE
If you are at least 18, you may designate on your driver license or I.D. card a donation of any needed organs or tissues for medical transplantation. Under the Uniform Anatomical Gift Act (Sec. 7150, Health & Safety Code) donation takes effect upon your death.
NEXT OF KIN (OPTIONAL)

NAME _____

ADDRESS _____

TELEPHONE NO. _____
—

DETACH HERE

Additional information regarding the Donor program may be obtained by writing or calling The Gift of Life:

National Kidney Foundation of Southern California
6820 La Tijera Blvd., Suite 111
Los Angeles, CA 90045
(213) 641-5245

3430 Fifth Ave., Suite C
San Diego, CA 92103
(619) 297-2470

National Kidney Foundation of Northern California
856 Stanton Road
Burlingame, CA 94010
(415) 697-0110

Figure *4-4 Donor Card*
Source: California Department of Motor Vehicles.

Organ donations can be made by completing a form such as the uniform donor card (see Figure 4-4). A donor may specify that *any* needed organs or body parts may be taken or that only certain body parts or organs are to be donated. Besides specifying how one's body may be used after death, the donor may also specify the final disposition of his or her remains once the donation has been effected. Although not legally required, most hospitals also obtain consent from the donor's next of kin. Nevertheless, twenty-seven states have passed laws barring family members from refusing to donate a registered donor's organs, although reports indicate that the rule is not always enforced.[53]

Every day, about sixty-eight people receive an organ transplant while another seventeen people on the waiting list die because not enough organs are available.[54] Because not enough organs are donated to meet the demand, physicians and organ transplant agencies must function as "gatekeepers" in choosing among prospective recipients. In 1984, the U.S. Congress enacted the National Organ Transplant Act, which instituted a central office to help match donated organs with potential recipients. The United Network for Organ Sharing (UNOS), under a contract with the federal government, maintains lists of people waiting for transplants and tracks the status of all donated organs with the goal of ensuring both the fairness of distribution and the competence of medical centers where organ transplants are performed.

Because many patients are on waiting lists for donated organs, and some die while waiting, questions have been raised about the effectiveness of the voluntary approach to organ donation of the Uniform Anatomical Gift Act. Some people suggest that donating one's organs after death is a moral duty and, therefore, the Gift Act should be changed to *require* organ donation except when a person intentionally "opts out" by signing an objection.

Questions about organ donation ultimately come down to personal values and particular views about the nature of the human body and the way it is perceived. Among the main views are[55]

1. *The body as machine.* A mechanistic view of the body in which organs are "extracted," "salvaged," and "replaced."
2. *The body as an ecological resource.* A form of recycling within the global biomass in which organs are "harvested" and "retrieved."
3. *The body as a potential gift.* A view that emphasizes ownership in which organs are "donated," "gifted," and "received."
4. *The body as a commodity.* The body is a profitable resource, and organs are "procured" and possibly bought and sold.

Because a human body is a valuable resource, one suggestion is to make commerce in human organs legal.[56] Under the provisions of the National Organ Transplant Act, it is currently illegal to buy or sell human organs and tissues (except blood). If this were changed, a person's heirs might earn money through selling the deceased's vital organs. Some people envision the possibility of a "futures market" in human organs, with prices fluctuating according to supply and demand. Those who favor making human organs a commodity argue that, as a result of market forces, shortages or surpluses of organs for transplantation would be eliminated. In some areas of the world, there already exists an active "black market" in transplantable organs (notably kidneys). In the United States, there appears to be growing support to indirectly compensate people who donate organs, possibly through tax credits or grants to help pay for funeral expenses. Generally, however, the consensus at present is that commercialization is not "ethically preferable to the gift model of organ donation."[57]

The scarcity of human organs for transplantation has also stimulated research into *xenotransplantation,* the use of animals—including baboons, chimpanzees, and pigs—as sources for needed organs.[58] The main technical difficulty in such cross-species transplants, as with transplantation generally, is rejection of donor tissue by the recipient's immune system. Currently, public policies reflect an era of transplantation in which organs are now from individuals who are legally pronounced dead while heartbeat and respiration are maintained artificially until organs can be removed. Artificially sustaining the body's functions necessarily raises complex medical, legal, and ethical questions about how life and death are defined. As we have seen, two issues become critical: (1) determining when death occurs and (2) deciding when it is permissible to remove the deceased's organs for transplantation. In reviewing how the advent of organ transplantation spurred a new definition of death, it is important to recognize that such a definition involves not only the presence or absence of a given set of physiological processes, but also social and cultural assumptions about life and death.[59]

Medical Ethics: A Cross-Cultural Example

In Japan, ethical, moral, and legal questions involving brain death and organ transplantation have been matters of public controversy for more than three decades.[60] Debate began in 1968, when Japanese surgeon Dr. Jurō Wada performed the world's second heart transplant using an organ from a brain-dead donor. Initially admired for his scientific achievement, Wada was soon subjected to intense questioning about alleged disregard for the rights of both donor and recipient. He was accused of illegal human experimentation and of poor judgment in the manner in which he made a determination of the donor's death. At the time, the criteria for establishing brain death were quite new, and no public consensus existed in Japan concerning this new definition of death. The Wada case left a legacy of mistrust about brain death and transplantation in Japan.

Among technologically advanced countries, Japan is unique in its reliance on living donors. Although most scientific and technological advances have been eagerly adopted in Japan, persistent questions about brain death have resulted in a reluctance to actively pursue organ transplantation. Only in 1997 did Japan pass an Organ Transplant Law that legalizes organ procurement from brain-dead donors. A condition of the legislation is that brain-dead patients are recognized as being dead only if they have given prior written permission for donation of their organs; otherwise, their heart must stop beating before they are considered to be dead. (Thus, in Japan, people effectively have an option about how to define their death.)[61] Family members also must approve the donation. Even with passage of this law, however, sixteen months elapsed before the first *legal* heart and liver transplantation was performed using organs from a brain-dead donor.

Japan's debate regarding brain death and organ transplantation illustrates how culture influences attitudes and practices related to dying and death. Although the circumstances surrounding the Wada case have had a lingering effect, a sense of mistrust between physicians and patients has long been prevalent in Japan. Until quite recently, most physicians practiced a kind of "closed door" medicine in which patients were neither given information about their health nor permitted to criticize their physicians. In the Japanese medical system, the consensus has been that patients should leave decision making to their physicians and family members. Many people feel this kind of paternalism is especially worrisome in the context of transplantation procedures. It is feared that, in determining brain death, doctors might give no information to family members and perhaps even lie to them. People also worry that the criteria for brain death may be applied too readily. There is widespread feeling that the definition of brain death is such a critical issue that it should not be decided solely by physicians. In addition, long-term

by who?

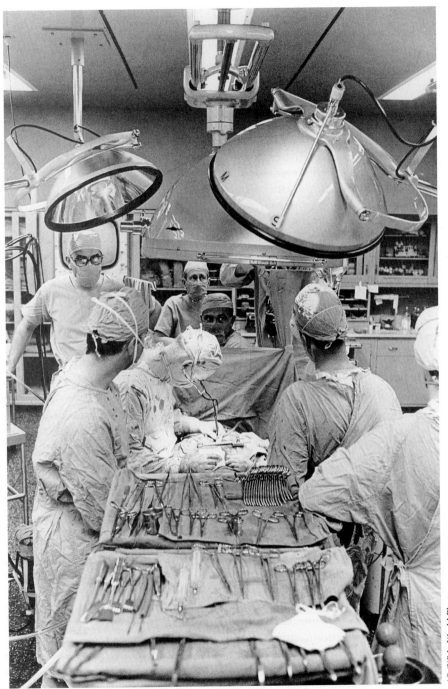

At the Stanford University Medical Center, Dr. Norman Shumway and his colleagues perform open-heart surgery. Advances in transplantation procedures and related medical therapies make such operations more feasible, yet they also raise questions that are difficult, at times quite painful, to resolve.

mistrust raises concerns that a market for organs could provoke abuses by physicians.

Traditional beliefs about death may have an even more important influence on attitudes. In Japan, death has been traditionally viewed as a social process, not a medically determined phenomenon. The respect shown to ancestors through various practices attests to an extended process of social death. Physicians may alter the conventional definition of death, but the persistence of traditional views reveals diverse opinions about the meaning of death.

Many Japanese are concerned about keeping the body intact, not only during life but also after death. The body is viewed as a gift from one's parents, one's ancestors. Removal of organs from brain-dead bodies violates the integrity of the body. An aversion to tampering with the corpse of a loved one is related to beliefs that body and soul must be intact as the person goes to the next world. The body must be perfect; if it is not, the soul may become unhappy. Organ transplantation is viewed as involving mutilation of the body. Whereas Americans tend to think of body organs as replaceable parts, the Japanese tend to find in every part of a deceased person's body a fragment of his or her mind and spirit. Related to this issue is Japan's historical concern about impurity. From this viewpoint, procedures involved in organ donation and transplantation defile the body. A person considering organ donation may be dissuaded by the notion that, if organs are taken, "My body is no longer mine."

Another important issue has to do with differing cultural ideas about the "seat of the soul" or "center of the self." In Western biomedicine, the brain—the locus of rational thought—tends to occupy the most important place among the various body parts. As the "seat of the mind," it represents the essence of humanness. In other traditions, the heart, not the brain, is considered the seat of life. Equating life with the functioning of the brain is alien to many Japanese, who place equal if not greater symbolic importance on the heart. A person's true center of spirit and consciousness, the "heart-mind," is traditionally located in the *hara,* or belly.

As this example illustrates, the notion of brain death is culturally constructed. The notion of death as absence of brain function, separate from other bodily functions, is inconsistent with the Japanese perspective on death of the whole person. Making a determination of brain death creates confusion because there remains a beating heart and a warm body. For many Japanese, the procedures involved in organ donation and transplantation result in a "death that cannot be seen," an invisible death. Furthermore, many people in Japan refuse to recognize brain death as biological death because they are skeptical about whether brain death can be determined with certainty and whether those who make such a determination can be fully trusted.

In addition to the cultural factors already mentioned, Japanese concerns about organ donation and transplantation relate to traditional practices involving the exchange of gifts. In Japan, there are fine-tuned rules governing the flow of gifts. Receiving a gift incurs an obligation to return the favor. With organ donation, giving is viewed as one-way. The recipient of an organ donation cannot offer a countergift. There is no way of repaying such a valuable gift. Moreover, the absence of a social relationship between donor and receiver clouds organ donation with a taint of commercialization.

The maintenance of cultural identity is important to most Japanese. Unquestioningly adopting Western practices of organ donation and transplantation would involve abandoning history and thereby diminishing cultural distinctiveness. A culturally appropriate bioethics would therefore incorporate the influences of Shinto, Buddhist, and Confucian thought, as well as modern Western traditions. In reflecting on the Japanese example presented here, we see that cultural differences need not be viewed as barriers that must be overcome, but as opportunities for learning about different ways that people deal with the complex issues surrounding dying and death.

Certification of Death

The official registration of death is considered the most important legal procedure following a death. A death certificate constitutes legal proof of death, and death certificates are required by all jurisdictions in the United States. Although death certificates vary somewhat from state to state, most follow the format outlined by the United States Standard Certificate of Death.

Death certificates reflect both a private and a public function. On the face of it, the document used to certify the facts of death is straightforward, a concise summary of the pertinent data regarding the deceased and the mode and place of death. However, this seemingly simple document has broader implications than one might imagine. Besides its value and purpose as a legal document that affects disposition of property rights, life insurance benefits, pension payments, and so on, the utility of the death certificate extends to such diverse matters as aiding in crime detection, tracing genealogy, and gaining knowledge about the incidence of disease and other aspects of physical and psychological health.

The typical death certificate (see Figure 4-5) provides for four different *modes* of death: accidental, suicidal, homicidal, and natural. However, as Edwin Shneidman points out, the *cause* of death isn't necessarily the same as the *mode* of death.[62] For example, if a death is caused by asphyxiation due to drowning, should it be classified as an accident, a suicide, or a homicide? Any of these modes might apply.

Underlying the distinction between mode and cause is the more complex issue of intentions and subconscious factors, the states of mind and actions, that may have contributed, directly or indirectly, to the death. For instance, if an intoxicated person jumps into a swimming pool with no one else present and drowns, is the death accidental or suicidal? Does it make a difference whether the alcohol abuse was related to emotional distress and despondency? Or what is the mode of death if the cocktails were served by a too-generous host? What if the person serving excessive alcohol were also an heir of the person who dies?

Obviously, intentions and subconscious factors can be more complex than allowed for by the relatively elementary distinctions concerning mode

CERTIFICATE OF DEATH
STATE OF CALIFORNIA
USE BLACK INK ONLY / NO ERASURES, WHITEOUTS OR ALTERATIONS
VS-11 (REV 1/03)

STATE FILE NUMBER   LOCAL REGISTRATION NUMBER

DECEDENT'S PERSONAL DATA

1. NAME OF DECEDENT --- FIRST (Given)   2. MIDDLE   3. LAST (Family)

AKA. ALSO KNOWN AS --- Include full AKA (FIRST, MIDDLE, LAST) | 4. DATE OF BIRTH mm/dd/ccyy | 5. AGE Yrs. | IF UNDER ONE YEAR Months / Days | IF UNDER 24 HOURS Hours / Minutes | 6. SEX

9. BIRTH STATE/FOREIGN COUNTRY | 10. SOCIAL SECURITY NUMBER | 11. EVER IN U.S. ARMED FORCES? YES NO UNK | 12. MARITAL STATUS (at Time of Death) | 7. DATE OF DEATH mm/dd/ccyy | 8. HOUR (24 Hours)

13. EDUCATION --- Highest Level/Degree (see worksheet on back) | 14/15. WAS DECEDENT SPANISH/HISPANIC/LATINO? (If yes, see worksheet on back.) YES NO | 16. DECEDENT'S RACE --- Up to 3 races may be listed (see worksheet on back)

17. USUAL OCCUPATION --- Type of work for most of life. DO NOT USE RETIRED | 18. KIND OF BUSINESS OR INDUSTRY (e.g., grocery store, road construction, employment agency, etc.) | 19. YEARS IN OCCUPATION

USUAL RESIDENCE

20. DECEDENT'S RESIDENCE (Street and number or location)

21. CITY | 22. COUNTY/PROVINCE | 23. ZIP CODE | 24. YEARS IN COUNTY | 25. STATE/FOREIGN COUNTRY

INFORMANT

26. INFORMANT'S NAME, RELATIONSHIP | 27. INFORMANT'S MAILING ADDRESS (Street and number or rural route number, city or town, state, ZIP)

SPOUSE AND PARENT INFORMATION

28. NAME OF SURVIVING SPOUSE --- FIRST | 29. MIDDLE | 30. LAST (Maiden Name)

31. NAME OF FATHER --- FIRST | 32. MIDDLE | 33. LAST | 34. BIRTH STATE

35. NAME OF MOTHER --- FIRST | 36. MIDDLE | 37. LAST (Maiden) | 38. BIRTH STATE

FUNERAL DIRECTOR/ LOCAL REGISTRAR

39. DISPOSITION DATE mm/dd/ccyy | 40. PLACE OF FINAL DISPOSITION

41. TYPE OF DISPOSITION(S) | 42. SIGNATURE OF EMBALMER | 43. LICENSE NUMBER

44. NAME OF FUNERAL ESTABLISHMENT | 45. LICENSE NUMBER | 46. SIGNATURE OF LOCAL REGISTRAR | 47. DATE mm/dd/ccyy

PLACE OF DEATH

101. PLACE OF DEATH | 102. IF HOSPITAL, SPECIFY ONE: IP ER/OP DOA | 103. IF OTHER THAN HOSPITAL, SPECIFY ONE: Hospice Nursing Home/LTC Decedent's Home Other

104. COUNTY | 105. FACILITY ADDRESS OR LOCATION WHERE FOUND (Street and number or location) | 106. CITY

CAUSE OF DEATH

107. CAUSE OF DEATH — Enter the chain of events --- diseases, injuries, or complications --- that directly caused death. DO NOT enter terminal events such as cardiac arrest, respiratory arrest, or ventricular fibrillation without showing the etiology. DO NOT ABBREVIATE. | Time Interval Between Onset and Death | 108. DEATH REPORTED TO CORONER? YES NO REFERRAL NUMBER

IMMEDIATE CAUSE (Final disease or condition resulting in death) (A) | (AT)

Sequentially, list conditions, if any, leading to cause on Line A. Enter UNDERLYING CAUSE (disease or injury that initiated the events resulting in death) LAST (B) (BT) | 109. BIOPSY PERFORMED? YES NO

(C) (CT) | 110. AUTOPSY PERFORMED? YES NO

(D) (DT) | 111. USED IN DETERMINING CAUSE? YES NO

112. OTHER SIGNIFICANT CONDITIONS CONTRIBUTING TO DEATH BUT NOT RESULTING IN THE UNDERLYING CAUSE GIVEN IN 107

113. WAS OPERATION PERFORMED FOR ANY CONDITION IN ITEM 107 OR 112? (If yes, list type of operation and date.) | 113A. IF FEMALE, PREGNANT IN LAST YEAR? YES NO UNK

PHYSICIAN'S CERTIFICATION

114. I CERTIFY THAT TO THE BEST OF MY KNOWLEDGE DEATH OCCURRED AT THE HOUR, DATE, AND PLACE STATED FROM THE CAUSES STATED. Decedent Attended Since / Decedent Last Seen Alive | 115. SIGNATURE AND TITLE OF CERTIFIER | 116. LICENSE NUMBER | 117. DATE mm/dd/ccyy

(A) mm/dd/ccyy (B) mm/dd/ccyy | 118. TYPE ATTENDING PHYSICIAN'S NAME, MAILING ADDRESS, ZIP CODE

CORONER'S USE ONLY

119. I CERTIFY THAT IN MY OPINION DEATH OCCURRED AT THE HOUR, DATE, AND PLACE STATED FROM THE CAUSES STATED. MANNER OF DEATH: Natural Accident Homicide Suicide Pending Investigation Could not be determined | 120. INJURED AT WORK? YES NO UNK | 121. INJURY DATE mm/dd/ccyy | 122. HOUR (24 Hours)

123. PLACE OF INJURY (e.g., home, construction site, wooded area, etc.)

124. DESCRIBE HOW INJURY OCCURRED (Events which resulted in injury)

125. LOCATION OF INJURY (Street and number, or location, and city, and ZIP)

126. SIGNATURE OF CORONER / DEPUTY CORONER | 127. DATE mm/dd/ccyy | 128. TYPE NAME, TITLE OF CORONER / DEPUTY CORONER

STATE REGISTRAR | A | B | C | D | E | FAX AUTH. # | CENSUS TRACT

Figure 4-5 *Certificate of Death in Use in California*

© Carol A. Foote

When death occurs under suspicious or uncertain circumstances, the coroner or medical examiner usually directs an investigation to determine the cause of death. If foul play is suspected, a police or sheriff's department investigation is undertaken.

and cause of death now listed on most death certificates. A study done in Marin County, California, to assess the conventional classifications of mode of death as well as the lethality of the deceased's intention revealed that some deaths classified as natural, accidental, and homicidal were also precipitated by the deceased's own actions; the deceased had lethal intentions against himself or herself. (The use of a *psychological autopsy* as an investigative tool for reconstructing the intentions and factors leading up to a death is discussed in Chapter 12.)

Death Notification

A notification of death "announces a void in the social fabric."[63] Medical personnel are not alone with the task of delivering "bad news" (the disclosure of a life-threatening diagnosis is covered in Chapter 5). Here, the emphasis is on sudden, unexpected, possibly traumatic death, such as from motor vehicle crashes and homicide. "Death notification is always traumatic. Difficult family dynamics and death scenarios can make it much more complex."[64] For military deaths, the governmental policy of sending a Western Union telegram has largely been replaced by a personal visit to the next of kin: "We are here to inform you that your son . . . ." Those devastating, dreaded words delivered by a stranger who seems to be the grim reaper launches survivors into the role of the bereaved, and grief is unpredictable. After being told that his son had been killed in Iraq, a Florida man used gasoline and a blowtorch to set fire to the Marines' van, severely burning himself.[65] One writer said, "Notifying officers must utter the first lines of a final chapter in a family's life."[66]

In a recent year in the United States, nearly 44,000 people were killed in motor vehicle crashes, many involving drunk driving, and more than 16,000 died by homicide.[67] Often, deaths occur away from the next of kin, who must be told the news. Selection of the notifier is important, although this task is frequently thrust expectedly on emergency or other first responders. More important than "who" is "how" and "when," and even "where."

In the hospital, the notifier is usually a physician who was involved in the life-saving efforts. If a physician is not available and family is already present, a nurse may give the notification. As the person ultimately responsible for treatment, however, the physician is thought to be able to best provide a detailed explanation, and families accept the reality more readily if a physician notifies. However, good arguments can be made for bringing in a social worker, chaplain, or counselor, perhaps even to deliver the initial news if the physician is unavailable or has just finished "running the code" and needs time to decompress.

When a death occurs "in the field," notification may be done by police officers, firefighters, EMTs, or coroners' staff. The primary notifier is preferably someone who has ample time to discuss the death and who was present with the victim or knows the details that led to the death because families often ask for more information. This may be someone who provided on-scene medical assistance if family members happen on the scene or survive the accident and ask about the condition of others.

Notification often does not occur at the scene of death, meaning that next of kin must be identified and contacted. This can present challenges when the deceased is, for example, an undocumented migrant, transient, or teenage runaway. It is crucial to be certain of the identity of the deceased to prevent an erroneous notification intended for someone else. Key elements in notification include timely announcement, control of the physical environment, details of the efforts to save the life, explanation of the cause(s) of death, appropriate emotional support, and other resources that could be helpful to the bereaved. Regarding timing, if it is necessary to make telephone contact, it is advisable to avoid making notification over the phone; the notifier should plan to direct the conversation and avoid telling more than is appropriate for the circumstance, especially if family dynamics and emotional stability are not known.[68] Plans can then be made to meet in person with the family.

R. Moroni Leash suggests a "sequential notification technique" that prepares the family for the ultimate statement of death. In meeting with the family (in this case at the hospital):

1. Ask the family members what they already know about the situation.
2. Bridging from what they know, give a brief description of events that led up to the patient's arrival at the hospital.

Death Notification Letter

Petersburg Va. Aug. 22, 1864

Mrs. E. H. Jones

Dear Madame

It becomes my painful duty to inform you of the death of your gallant husband E. H. Jones, who fell in the engagement near Deep Bottom on the 16th inst. In him we have lost a dear comrade, a true and noble soldier and one that did his whole duty cheerfully. He fell at his post endeavoring to repel a charge made by the enemy. He remained in the trenches after they had been abandoned by the greater part of his comrades and fell by a shot that caused instant death. He is buried near the spot he fell. I will take charge of his effects as soon as I can find someone to testify to them, and either send them to you, or make any disposition of them you may advise.

My personal and immediate attention will be given to any information or service you may desire. I feel a deep and earnest sympathy for you in your great affliction, and hope "God who doeth all things well" may comfort and console you.

Very respectfully,
T. M. Beasley Lieut. Comd. Co. F, 64th Ga. Rgt.

3. Give information regarding the resuscitative efforts made on behalf of the patient.
4. Conclude with the victim's response to treatment, the statement of death, and a brief explanation of the cause of death.

Leash advises, "Coordinate your statements with their emotional responses. By so doing, you allow them to control the flow of the conversation, preparing themselves as you proceed together."[69]

In thinking about the death system, as ennumerated at the beginning of this chapter, notification is important to the functions of disposing of the dead as well as social consolidation after death. Yet, police officers, emergency personnel, and even physicians often must seek appropriate resources on their own.[70]

The Coroner and the Medical Examiner

Most deaths in the United States result from disease. The physician attending the patient at the time of death completes and signs the death certificate. However, when death occurs in suspicious circumstances or is sudden and there is no physician to sign the death certificate, the cause of death must be determined by a coroner or medical examiner, also known as a *primary death investigator*.[71] Besides suspected homicides and suicides, circumstances of death that require investigation include accidents; deaths that occur on the job, in jails, and in other government institutions; deaths that occur in hospitals or other health care facilities when negligence is suspected or the death was un-expected; and deaths that occur at home when there is no attending physician who can sign a death certificate attesting to the cause of death.

Cause of death is determined by use of various scientific procedures, possibly including an autopsy (described later in this chapter), toxicology and bacteriology tests, chemical analyses, and other studies that are needed to arrive at adequate findings. Unlike autopsies performed as part of medical training or at a family's request, those done as part of an investigation conducted by a coroner or medical examiner are required by law. The results of such postmortem examination can play a crucial role in court cases and insurance settlements. The outcome of such proceedings may be important not only to law enforcement agencies, but also to the families involved: The mode of death—whether it is due to foul play, negligence, suicide, accident, or natural causes—can have a significant emotional effect on survivors. It may also have an economic effect; for example, some life insurance policies cover only accidental death, whereas others pay twice the face value of the contract in case of accidental death (double indemnity).

Coroners are usually elected officials; medical examiners are usually appointed. The main difference between the two positions, however, has to do with training. Whereas coroners may not possess any special background or training, medical examiners are qualified medical doctors, generally with advanced training and certification in *forensic pathology* (the application of medical knowledge to questions of law). Besides their responsibilities for investigating the cause of death in questionable circumstances, these officials often play a key role in community health programs such as suicide prevention and drug abuse education.

Autopsies

An autopsy (from the Greek *autopsia,* meaning "seeing with one's own eyes") is a detailed medical examination of a body after death to determine cause of death or to investigate the nature of changes caused by disease. Once the abdominal cavity is exposed, organs are removed for examination of their internal structure, and small samples may be taken for later analysis. After the autopsy is completed, organs not needed for further study are replaced in the body cavity and all incisions are closed.

An autopsy may be performed for legal or official reasons (as mentioned in connection with the role of the coroner or medical examiner) or as part of a hospital's teaching or research program. Sometimes, the deceased's family will request an autopsy to determine whether genetic or infectious conditions led to death or to help resolve questions about possible malpractice. Except when required by law, an autopsy can be performed only after the next of kin's consent is obtained or when the deceased has donated his or her body for autopsy under the provisions of the Uniform Anatomical Gift Act.[72]

Aided by the use of autopsies, forensic science has achieved noteworthy results in investigating human rights violations. In Argentina, for example, a team of forensic scientists helped to identify remains of the *desaparecidos,* the "disappeared," who had been buried in mass graves during a period of military rule and terrorism in that country. Many families were able to learn the fate of their missing loved ones. Furthermore, during the ensuing trials of several former military leaders, forensic scientists presented expert testimony that helped convict those responsible for the deaths.

Forensic techniques for identifying remains are also used by the Army Central Identification Laboratory at Hickam Air Force Base in Hawaii (CILHI), which is responsible for searching for, recovering, and identifying armed service members killed or listed as missing.[73] As part of a joint task force charged with resolving cases of Americans missing as a result of the Vietnam War, the unit investigated about 700 cases and inspected more than 360 crash sites or gravesites in Vietnam, Cambodia, and Laos.

Organized into three sections, CILHI includes teams devoted to search and recovery, casualty data analysis, and the lab itself. In the lab, recovered remains and other evidence are examined by physical anthropologists and other experts. Remains arrive at Hickam in flag-draped caskets with full military honors. Although CILHI does not expect to be able to recover or identify all of the roughly 2250 individuals unaccounted for from the Vietnam War, its perseverance in this task confirms the emotional importance that human beings attach to psychological closure when death occurs.

Techniques for identifying human remains have become increasingly sophisticated, allowing positive identification to be made not only from fragments of hair or bone, but also from DNA analysis based on relatively few cells. In 2003, when the space shuttle *Columbia* broke apart as it reentered the earth's atmosphere, search teams recovered remains from all seven astronauts and forwarded them to the Charles C. Carson Center for Mortuary Affairs at Dover Air Force Base in Delaware. Forensic analysis provided at the Carson Center also had been used to identify the remains of the *Challenger* astronauts in 1986 and the Pentagon victims of the September 2001 terrorist attack. Experts say that disasters such as the 2001 attack on the World Trade Center pushed the science of identification technologies to use new methods of chemical analysis and analytical software, enhancing their ability to identify burned or pulverized remains and to work with smaller biological samples of the genetic code that every human cell contains.[74]

As a method of conclusively establishing the cause of death, autopsies serve a number of important purposes in law and medicine. As a tool of medical investigation, autopsies are used to confirm diagnoses, train doctors, and conduct research. In this way, autopsies increase the understanding of disease, thereby leading to improved treatment and life-saving interventions. Because autopsies are required in just a few circumstances, however, many hospitals have discontinued the once-common procedure or no longer have full autopsy facilities. Valuable data regarding health and disease may go missing because autopsies are performed less frequently. Recent studies show that autopsy results contradict the presumed cause of death in about one-quarter to one-third of cases. John Lantos, a physician, says, "Postmortem examinations

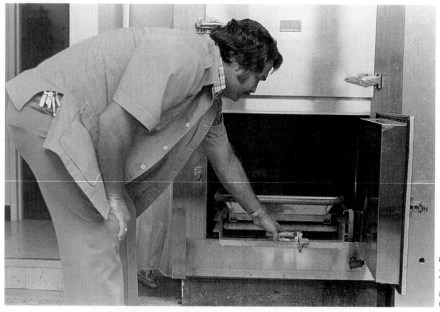

© Carol A. Foote

When a coroner's preliminary investigation reveals the need to scientifically determine the cause of death, the corpse is brought to the morgue, where it is held until an autopsy can be performed.

The autopsy, or medical examination to determine the cause of death, is conducted under the coroner's direction when the circumstances of a death are violent, suspicious, or unexplained, or when a death is medically unattended and a doctor is unable to certify the cause of death. All homicides, accidents, and suicides come under the coroner's or medical examiner's jurisdiction.

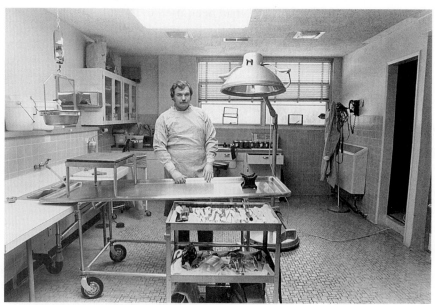

© Carol A. Foote

have long been recognized as one of the best teaching tools in medicine. They are the final check on whether what we did and what we thought we ought to be doing were correct or whether we missed something."[75]

Recently, private autopsy services have become available to conduct autopsies on behalf of hospitals and individual clients, many of whom are family members seeking information about hereditary diseases or who suspect malpractice and want evidence that may be obtained through an autopsy. With genetics being found to play a bigger role in a wider range of conditions, some experts believe that accurately knowing a family member's cause of death provides information that can potentially save lives.

The Impact of the Death System

Introduced by Robert Kastenbaum in 1977, the concept of the death system is a helpful model for contemplating how death shapes the social order and, in turn, our individual lives. As a network of people, places, and times, as well as objects and symbols, the death system affects our collective and personal relationships to mortality in many ways. All of the topics addressed in this text are aspects of the death system. In this chapter, we have seen how society develops public policies concerning the definition of death, organ donation and transplantation, certification of death, roles of coroners and medical examiners, and when and under what circumstances autopsies are performed. As you study topics related to dying and death, you may find it interesting to keep in mind how they fit into the death system. As Kastenbaum says, "Everything that makes a collection of individuals into a society and keeps that society going has implications for our relationship with death."[76]

Further Readings

Stuart Banner. *The Death Penalty: An American History*. Cambridge, Mass.: Harvard University Press, 2003.

Kai Erikson. *A New Species of Trouble: Explorations in Disaster, Trauma, and Community*. New York: W. W. Norton, 1994.

Renée C. Fox and Judith P. Swazey. *Spare Parts: Organ Replacement in American Society*. New York: Oxford University Press, 1992.

Sue Holtkamp. *Wrapped in Mourning: The Gift of Life and Organ Donor Family Trauma*. New York: Brunner-Routledge, 2002.

Howard M. Spiro, Mary G. McCrea Curnen, and Lee Palmer Wandel, eds. *Facing Death: Where Culture, Religion, and Medicine Meet*. New Haven, Conn.: Yale University Press, 1996.

Stuart J. Youngner, Robert M. Arnold, and Renie Schapiro, eds. *The Definition of Death: Contemporary Controversies*. Baltimore: Johns Hopkins University Press, 1999.

Stuart J. Youngner, Renée C. Fox, and Laurence J. O'Connell, eds. *Organ Transplantation: Meanings and Realities*. Madison: University of Wisconsin Press, 1996.

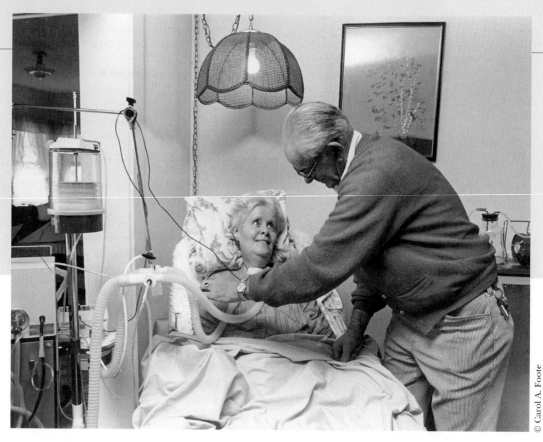

Home care may not come immediately to mind when one thinks of health care systems, yet this centuries-old tradition of care for the ill and the dying is once again emerging as an option for many. Innovations in sophisticated medical life-support equipment often make it possible for the seriously ill to be cared for using a high level of medical technology within the home.

CHAPTER 5

Health Care:
Patients, Staff, and Institutions

*I*n the past, most people died in their own beds, at home, surrounded by loved ones. In 1900, about 80 percent of deaths in the United States occurred in the home. Now, most deaths occur in institutional settings, mainly hospitals and nursing homes. (The percentage of deaths occurring at home has been growing as home hospice care becomes an option more widely available to dying persons and their families.)

Most people say they would want to live their last days amid the familiar surroundings of home. But the nature of an illness or lack of sufficient social support can oblige the dying person to be cared for in an institution. A long-distance phone call announcing the death of an aged relative may substitute for the more intimate experience of being present at a loved one's death.

Oriented toward the goal of sustaining life, the health care system sometimes falls short in meeting the needs of dying patients and their families. Think about the end of your own life. What are your fears about dying? Many people say they fear dying in pain, hooked up to machines in an impersonal institutional setting, as an "interventional cascade" surrounds the patient with technology. This is a chain of events, a series of tests and interventions, that results in unwanted aggressive care at the end of life. "The potential gain in survival even from perfect therapy may be small."[1] In the past, physicians did as much to console as to cure patients; indeed, consolation and comfort were often all that medicine could offer. Now, if treatment is not a cure, we may feel cheated. Physicians may become scapegoats if their therapies do not lead to the desired outcome.

Each of the three major categories of institutional medical care—hospitals, nursing homes, and hospices—is intended to optimally serve a specific purpose within the overall health care delivery system. Patients with life-threatening illness usually receive a combination of acute and supportive care. As conditions change, institutional care may alternate with home care.

Hospitals are devoted mainly to acute intensive care of a limited duration. Aggressive medical techniques are used to diagnose symptoms, provide treatment, and sustain life. The typical patient expects to regain well-being after a short period of treatment and then return to normal life. Patients with chronic or life-threatening illness may alternate between receiving acute care in hospitals and supportive care in nursing homes, hospices, or at home.

In recent decades, hospitals appear to be evolving toward an integrated approach in which outpatient and extended care, as well as home and hospice care, play important roles.[2] They are broadening their focus from acute care to a "portfolio" of health care services.[3]

Nursing homes (a category that includes convalescent and extended-care facilities) provide long-term residential care for people who are chronically ill and whose illness does not require acute, intensive care. Most patients will eventually return to the community. A smaller percentage of nursing home patients includes those who require ongoing supportive care, as well as those who die while being cared for in a nursing home. "Increasingly, the nursing home is the place of care and death for older Americans."[4]

Hospice care is distinguished by its orientation toward the needs of dying patients and their families. The mission of hospice care is to comfort the patient, rather than cure a disease. Hospice is not necessarily a place but, rather, a *program* of caring. Hospice care can be provided in various settings, including a palliative medicine department within a hospital, a nursing home or residential-care facility, a community hospice, or the home. These options for hospice care are examined in more detail later in this chapter.

Modern Health Care

A person admitted to a health care facility expects to receive medical and nursing care appropriate to his or her particular malady. The relationships among the patient, the staff, and the institution influence the quality of care provided. Each side of this health care triangle—patient, staff, and institution—contributes to the overall quality and nature of health care (see Figure 5-1). With the aim of efficient use of staff and facilities, procedures may become standardized and routine. As a result, the ability to meet the needs of a particular patient is inherently limited. When an elderly aunt was dying at home, she could be spoon-fed her favorite homemade soup by a family member. In a hospital or nursing home, she is likely to receive a standardized diet, perhaps served impersonally by a harried and overworked aide. One trade-off we make for sophisticated health care may be less personal attention. Charles

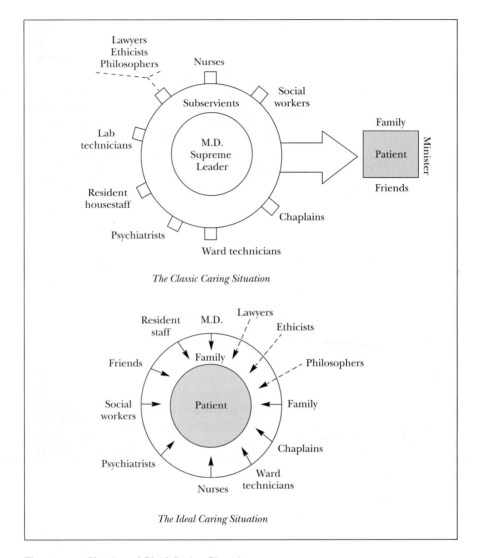

Figure 5-1 *Classic and Ideal Caring Situations*
Source: David Barton, ed., *Dying and Death: A Clinical Guide for Caregivers* (Baltimore: Williams & Wilkins, 1977), p. 181.

Rosenberg observes that "we expect a great deal of our hospitals: alleviation of pain, extension of life, [and] management of death and the awkward and painful circumstances surrounding its approach."[5]

A patient's experience is shaped by rules, regulations, and conventions—written and unwritten. Unwritten rules, no less faithfully executed than written ones, may contribute to a sense of alienation. The family of a dying patient may be relegated to maintaining a deathwatch in the corridor or the waiting room down the hall, with one person at a time squeezing into the patient's room to keep a bedside vigil. There may be no private space where relatives can meet to discuss their concerns with doctors or nurses. In public settings, grieving relatives may feel obliged to contain or repress their emotions. In the conventional medical model, patient and staff are central, while family members are less important. In the case of dying patients, however, "The goal must not be simply to provide expert medical care to an individual patient, but to help give voice and connection and meaning to a family."[6]

Abstraction, depersonalization, and standardization are aspects of the scientific method, which is the basis for many of the life-saving medical advances we applaud. Less welcome is the result when these mechanisms make medicine less humane. This occurs, for example, when an illness is not well understood and physicians show greater interest in the disease than in the patient. Depersonalization takes place when dying patients are given less attention because physicians and nurses believe "nothing more can be done" or avoid personal contact due to their own mortal fears. Some studies have found that nurses took longer to answer the bedside calls of dying patients than to answer the calls of patients less severely ill.[7] Although this finding may not be representative of the norm, such avoidance is lamentable whenever it occurs.

Health Care Financing

Our individual and social choices about financing health care influence the options available for care of the seriously ill and dying. In 1965, the Medicare and Medicaid programs were created to provide health care coverage to underserved populations, especially the elderly and poor. Despite persisting gaps in making adequate health care available to everyone, the United States spends more on health than any other industrialized country. In a recent year, national health expenditures totaled almost $1.3 trillion, more than 13 percent of the gross domestic product.[8] Health economists observe that spending for health care seems to be unlimited because "the richer a country becomes, the more it will tend to spend."[9]

As part of efforts to contain costs associated with health care, various policies have been instituted under the rubric of "managed care," including the use of diagnosis-related groups (DRGs) and prospective payment. The idea behind DRGs is that costs can be managed by a predetermined schedule of fees for reimbursing health care providers. The amount of reimbursement is based on the patient's disease, procedure, and medical history, as well as the complexity of services provided to the patient.

As a result, medical care tends to be viewed in terms of standardized "products." Managed care plans (by definition) involve efforts to control where, when, and from whom medical services can be obtained. Physicians are "providers" and patients are "consumers."[10] This is a dramatic change in the conventional understanding of the "medical encounter," which is inherently more complex than models of consumerism found in other commercial

Two great fears of the traditional Aboriginals are to be hospitalized away from their homelands and to die in the hospital and/or meet the "mamu" spirits of people who have died in the hospital. Aboriginals believe that good health results from harmonious relationships among physical, human, and supernatural environments; sickness results from disruption in these relationships and is directly attributable to the intervention of supernatural forces. These forces are known by various names, one of the most common is "mamu."

Generally, there are two types of forces, and both are potentially dangerous. The first is a kind of "devil," an indeterminate being capable of moving around the same space as ordinary people. . . . The second mamu is more fearful, from the adult Aboriginal's point of view. It is the spirit of the dead, particularly the recent dead. Although not hostile to people, these spirits are dangerous because they seek to rejoin the living. . . . This belief impels people to avoid using the dead person's name and to move camp as soon as a relative dies in camp, as the spirit will look for relatives in the last place they were seen in life.

Death at the time of hospitalization, in a hospital miles from home . . . means that the spirit of the Aboriginal child who dies cannot find its way to the tribal territory to await rebirth. It also means that the life force of adults who die, particularly those who have been repositories of tribal law and knowledge, are separated from their country; the strength of dreaming is weakened, to the eternal loss of all survivors. And a hospital in which many have died becomes a terrifying threat to Aboriginal patients because of the concentration of the mamu spirits of those who died and were unable to find their way back to their individual homelands.

Ruth Walker and Brenda Gameau, "Australia: Its Land, Its People, Its Health Care System, and Unique Health Issues"

transactions.[11] Some observers worry that patients may be neglected if "dollars saved" becomes the primary measure of outcome.

Medical technologies are expensive. The rising costs of health care are due partly to a "technological imperative" that promises an unprecedented range of tools for combating disease. Yet, medical innovations can be a mixed blessing. Earlier detection of disease, for example, may result in a cure that otherwise would not have been possible, or it may only result in the patient's being aware of his or her disease for a longer period of time.[12] The ability of medicine to predict death at an early stage in some diseases has led to the emergence of a category of experience called "terminal illness."[13] With earlier diagnosis and sophisticated medical techniques, the "terminal" stage of an illness may now last as long as 15 years.[14]

Do investments in medical technology result in a better quality of care? The answer seems to be yes. The impact of rising costs, however, is raising questions about whether society is obligated to provide every medical intervention that a patient believes might be beneficial. To alleviate pressures on the health care system, some experts suggest that resources must be rationed.

Rationing Scarce Resources

Rationing refers to the allocation of scarce resources among competing individuals. In health care, it is defined as any system that limits the amount of health care a person can receive. Rationing occurs when not all care expected to be beneficial is provided to all patients and, particularly, when a medical benefit valued by a patient must be withheld because of cost. Although physicians have always functioned as "gatekeepers" in decisions concerning access to therapies that are deemed best for a patient's welfare, the new era of managed care means that they now face the prospect of being forced to engage in "restrictive" gatekeeping and "bedside" rationing, roles that many people view as morally illegitimate in medicine.[15]

Daniel Callahan suggests that a "principle of symmetry" is useful in acknowledging the limits of medical care.[16] He says, "A technology should be judged by its likelihood of enhancing a good balance between the extension and saving of life and the quality of life." Conversely, "A health care system that develops and institutionalizes a life-saving technology which has the common result of leaving people chronically ill or with poor quality of life ignores the principle of symmetry."

Decisions about allocating scarce medical resources are not just the purview of experts and legislators. The choices each of us makes in pursuit of our well-being influence the health care system and contribute to shaping its character. Instead of facing costly and likely futile treatments at the end of life, for instance, we may choose to sign an advance directive that makes known our wishes about receiving life-sustaining medical therapies (advance directives are discussed in Chapter 6). "Medicine overreaches itself," Callahan says, "when it sets as its implicit goal that of curing all diseases and infinitely forestalling death."

Handwritten margin note: Italy = low birth + death rate also = ↓ cost of medical procedures, relationship?

"I think in the next 10–20 years we'll have 'warehouses' with patients on life support systems, if the American public and physicians don't come to grips with and resolve the inherent conflicts involved in the present 'common' method for handling the terminally ill patient." *General practitioner*

"I do not think anybody should have the right to be God and decide death. In view of age and circumstances life may be prolonged to the benefit of patient and family." *Orthopedic surgeon*

"I am a doctor and I feel I should do all in my power to diagnose disease and sustain life." *Internist*

"We should not prolong misery when it's not indicated for other reasons. Everyone has a time to die and should be allowed to die with some dignity." *Urologist*

"The Physician Speaks,"
The Newsletter of Physician Attitudes

The Caregiver-Patient Relationship

Aesculapius, the first physician according to Greek legend, was elevated to the pantheon of gods and, along with Hygeia and Panacea, ruled over health and illness. Given its association with the elemental experiences of birth, life, and death, medicine carries high symbolic importance. But the "Aesculapian authority" of physicians is diminishing. *Paternalism,* the assumption of parentlike authority by medical practitioners, is seen as infringing on a patient's autonomy or freedom to make medical decisions, and managed care is a reminder that the physician-patient relationship is influenced by its institutional and economic context.[17]

The social contract between physicians and patients includes qualities of a *covenantal* relationship, which implies a mutuality of interests between providers and patients and between medical professionals and society.[18] The physician-patient relationship can be viewed as an alliance wherein the physician is an educator, counselor, and expert, but not the sole decision maker.[19] Patients' experiences in coping with illness help shape the missions of health care.[20] Shared decision making is crucial in medicine generally and perhaps especially in end-of-life care. This kind of relationship is fostered when providers get to know the patient, empower him or her to share in decision making, and work within the constraints of the situation to respect and accommodate patient choices.[21] Arthur Frank says, "Medicine is a *play* of boundaries." It requires, on the one hand, the sensibility of the painter, who maintains distance and sees the whole, and the camera operator, who uses technology to penetrate realities and reassemble fragments. Frank explains, "Medicine requires both the aura of distance and the approachability that requires renouncing some measure of aura."[22]

Preferences or questions about end-of-life care should be part of the discussion when choosing a doctor. Does the doctor have experience caring for people at the end of life? Is he or she willing and able to provide care in a variety of settings—hospital, nursing home, hospice, or at home? Is the doctor familiar with community resources? Financial matters should be discussed, as should any preferences about limiting treatment at the end of life. The bottom line is, Will the system accommodate the patient's and his or her family's specific preferences and plans?

Disclosing a Life-Threatening Diagnosis

If you were diagnosed as having a life-threatening illness, would you want to know? Some people say, "Of course, I want to know about everything that's going on with me!" Others answer, "If I can be spared the truth, I'd rather not know that I could die; ignorance is bliss." Consider your own attitudes and preferences. The person who has spent a lifetime as a fighter against the odds is likely to have a different response from the person whose typical pattern of coping with difficulties involves efforts to shun stress.

"You will crawl out of here," he said.

My eyes widened, and so did my mother's. I was taken aback. He continued. "I'm going to kill you," he said. "Every day, I'm going to kill you, and then I'm going to bring you back to life. We're going to hit you with chemo, and then hit you again, and hit you again. You're not going to be able to walk." He said it point-blank. "We're practically going to have to teach you how to walk again, after we're done."

Because the treatment would leave me infertile, I would probably never have kids. Because the bleomycin would tear up my lungs, I would never be able to race a bike again. I would suffer immense pain. The more he talked, the more I recoiled at the vivid images of my enfeeblement. I asked him why the treatment had to be so harsh. "You're worse-case," he said. "But I feel this is your only shot, at this hospital."

Lance Armstrong, *It's Not About the Bike: My Journey Back to Life*

Surveys indicate that most people do want to be told if diagnosed with a life-threatening illness, but the questions of *when* and *how* such information should be communicated are more difficult to answer. Physicians need to present the news of a life-threatening diagnosis in a manner that will serve the best interests of the patient. In deciding how to do this, the doctor must consider the patient's personality, emotional constitution, and capacity for continued function under stress.

Doctors may worry that knowing all the details about a life-threatening illness could adversely affect a patient's ability to cope. Is minimizing the threat of an illness sometimes in a patient's best interest? Physicians generally subscribe to the belief that hope must be encouraged. Thus, although the general facts of a life-threatening illness are likely to be disclosed by physicians, details may be withheld until the patient takes the initiative by asking specific questions. Members of some cultural and ethnic groups prefer "concealment" rather than full disclosure.[23] Furthermore, a patient may not make all of the decisions about his or her medical care; family members may have the largest say.[24] In any case, patients (as well as medical and nursing staff) underscore the desirability of having a family member present during the disclosure.[25]

Communicating the diagnosis is a crucial event in patient care. How this is done can influence a patient's attitude toward the illness, response to treatment, and ability to cope. What is said depends on a number of factors, including the doctor's preferences for breaking bad news, the patient's receptivity to the facts, and the expected prognosis. In conversations that involve breaking the bad news of a terminal diagnosis, both physicians and patients tend to be cautious about mentioning dying and death.[26] Because uncertainty is inherent in medical practice, physicians who openly discuss the issues with patients may, in fact, promote trust and realistic expectations.[27] Rather than a single event, breaking bad news is better described as a process.[28]

Doctors generally should provide a truthful report of the diagnosis and offer advice about the proposed course of treatment and side effects,

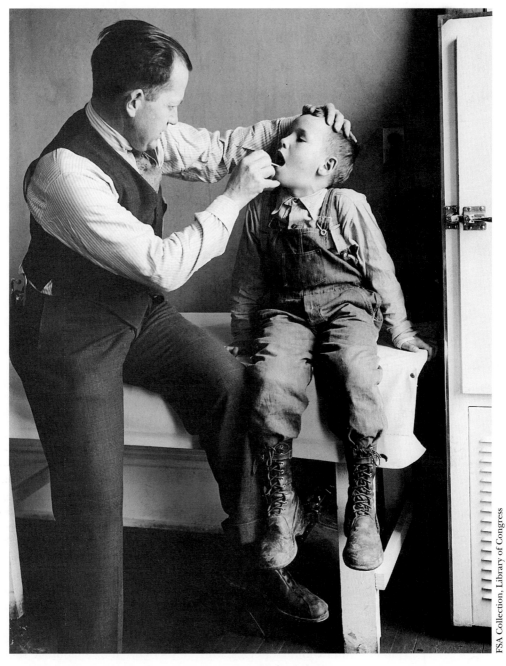

In 1935, medical care in Reedsville, West Virginia, seems less formal than that received in the urban clinics and hospitals of today. Although the practice of medicine has been enhanced by new methods of diagnosis and treatment, most people still believe that the relationship between physician and patient is central to the outcome of an illness.

providing as much detail as the patient desires. A good question to ask is "How much do you want to know about your illness?"[29] Ample time should be available to explore the patient's questions and concerns.[30] When first informed of a diagnosis of serious illness, patients may be too shocked to ask questions that will occur to them later; details can be given in segments.

Achieving Clear Communication

There is asymmetry in physician-patient communications, which challenges both parties to the dialogue.[31] Achieving clear communication in the physician-patient relationship does not happen automatically. Candace West, a sociologist who conducted a study of how doctors and patients relate to each other, found what she calls a "communications chasm" that hinders the healing process.[32] She observed a lack of "social cement"—the introductions, greetings, laughter, and use of patients' names—that is naturally part of ordinary social interactions. West also found that physicians tend to "advance questions which restrict patients' options for answers," and patients tend to be hesitant about questioning their doctors.

Physicians should "listen" with their eyes as well as their ears, paying attention to the nonverbal communication of gestures and body language that reveal a patient's unease or anxiety about what is being discussed. Highly technical diagnostic and therapeutic interventions can themselves be obstacles to effective communication.[33] Richard Sandor, a physician, says, "We detect subtle disturbances of heart rhythm, manipulate faltering blood pressure to within a few millimeters of mercury, and regulate minute changes in blood chemistry, but what about the *person who is dying*?"[34] In practicing the art of medicine, "Accurate communication is the single most valuable asset of the skilled doctor."[35]

Communication is an interactive and transactional process: One cannot *not* communicate. Think about the role that nonverbal communication plays. Nonverbal communication includes not only facial expressions, gestures, and body postures, but also *iconics*—objects that convey meaningful information (such as clothing and jewelry)—and *proxemics* (space and time). Consider, for example, the time it takes a caregiver to respond to a patient's request for help or the physical distance established when a physician stands behind a desk while talking to a seated patient. Labels such as M.D. and R.N., as well as titles such as doctor, nurse, and patient, are symbolic identifiers that can influence the process of communication.[36] For instance, in most medical communications, patients are addressed by their first names whereas doctors are addressed by their titles.[37]

When dying patients express a desire to talk about death, caregivers may respond with various strategies, which either curtail or encourage such conversations, including (1) reassurance ("You're doing so well"), (2) denial ("Oh, you'll live to be a hundred"), (3) changing the subject ("Let's talk about something more cheerful"), (4) fatalism ("Well, we all have to die sometime"), and (5) discussion ("What happened to make you feel that way?"). Trained to save lives, medical and nursing personnel may feel help-

I clearly made Dr. Mueh nervous. He was clearly up to his ears in patients and spread very thin.

He took 90 minutes to talk to me and my wife about my disease. He started out with terminal care and told me I'd get all the narcotics I would need to eliminate pain and that tubes could be used to provide nourishment.

I was amazed that he talked that way, as if I were dying.

Pierre Bowman, Honolulu *Star-Bulletin*

less when they are unable to offer a cure. Jeanne Quint Benoliel says caregivers need to be aware that "open communication does not necessarily mean open talk about death, but it does mean openness to the patient's verbalized concerns."[38]

Responding to the emotional and spiritual needs of patients and their families can be as important as caring for physical needs. A nurse who steps into the room, sits down by the patient's bed, and displays a willingness to listen is likely to be more effective in providing comfort than one who breezes in, remains standing, and quips, "How're we today? Did we sleep well?" Skillful communication helps in attaining the goals of health care for the whole person. One model suggested to caregivers for effective communication describes the "4Rs" of relate, review, revise, and reflect:[39]

1. *Relate* to patients. Sit next to them, make eye contact, respond to their feelings with empathetic statements, ask about their preferences for receiving information and making decisions.
2. *Review* treatment histories. Help patients recall the goals of treatment and understand the results, even when a treatment fails.
3. *Revise* the goals of care. Engage in an ongoing dialogue with the patients and plan treatment to achieve those goals.
4. *Reflect* on how roles and relationships change at the transition to hospice or palliative care.

Writing about his own experiences with serious illness, Norman Cousins points out that it is possible to communicate a life-threatening diagnosis as a "challenge rather than a verdict."[40] Communication can promote either a positive attitude, with faith in the ultimate outcome, or a negative attitude, with corresponding feelings of despondence and despair. Clear communication can play an important role in motivating the patient's own "healing system," creating the potential for a positive outcome regardless of the ultimate prognosis.

Providing Total Care

Caring for seriously ill and dying patients involves attending not just to a patient's physical needs, but also to his or her mental, emotional, and spiritual needs. This is referred to as "whole person" care.[41] The prerequisites include

The Patient's Story

In learning to think like a medical scientist, I was forgetting the whole patient. To help the patient in times of suffering, the physician must know the patient: not only as a case but as a person. Each patient has a history, a unique story to tell, which goes beyond the information in the medical history. Different patients have different senses of what makes life important to them, what they want out of life, and how far they are willing to go to preserve it. The patient's full story, like any person's story, includes his or her cultural background, childhood circumstances, career, family, religious life, and so on. It includes the patient's self-understanding, appearance, manner of expression, temperament, and character. In short, it includes those attributes that make the patient a person—and not only a person, but this particular person.

> Richard B. Gunderman,
> "Medicine and the Question of Suffering"

continuity of contact between at least one caregiver and the patient, opportunity for the patient to keep informed of his or her condition and prognosis, patient participation in decisions that affect him or her, and behavior by staff members that elicits the patient's trust and confidence.[42] When these guidelines are in place, there can be care that is both *personal* and *comprehensive*.

Accommodations sometimes must be made to help patients cope with inconvenient aspects of an illness. For example, it may be possible to adjust treatment schedules so that patients can continue to work, go to school, or care for their families. The entire family unit is affected when one of its members is seriously ill. As death approaches, the patient's family is likely to experience a transition that has been characterized as the patient's "fading away."[43] A period of chaos, confusion, fear, and uncertainty may ensue: "Nothing feels solid anymore." This transition involves a task of redefinition as family members cope with the burden of letting go of the old before picking up the new. Families often find themselves caring for a dying loved one while simultaneously trying to carry on with the normal business of life. Thus, total care also includes attending to the needs of the patient's family.

Care of the Dying

When Elisabeth Kübler-Ross set out to educate interns in an urban hospital about the dying, she wanted to let terminally ill patients make their own case. Informing staff members of her plan, she was told that no one was dying on their wards; there were only some patients who were "very critically ill."[44] Subsequently, Kübler-Ross's efforts to focus attention on the needs of terminally ill patients became an impetus toward compassionate care of the dying.

Dying, like birthing, is a natural event, sometimes better witnessed than managed. Caregivers are called upon to put aside their own beliefs to discover what's appropriate for a particular person in a particular situation. Care of the dying, as Balfour Mount observes, involves both heart and mind: "The dying need the friendship of the heart with its caring, acceptance, vulnerability and reciprocity. They also need the skills of the mind embodied in competent medical care. Neither alone is sufficient."[45]

Would you prefer to spend your last days or weeks at home, cared for by relatives and friends? Or would you rather have access to sophisticated medical technologies available in a hospital? The course of a disease may be unpredictable, preventing a person from choosing the place where he or she will die or the exact nature of medical care received. Even so, it is prudent to consider possible options. When death is expected, perhaps foreseen as the final chapter of a long illness, there is usually some choice about where death will occur. The end of life may involve a combination of home care, hospital stays, and hospice or palliative care. (Palliative care refers to treatment intended to relieve the symptoms or reduce the severity of a disease without curing the underlying disease.) Learning about the options for end-of-life care empowers us to make informed, meaningful choices.

Hospice and Palliative Care

According to the National Hospice and Palliative Care Organization (NHPCO), about 4100 hospice programs in the United States provided care to over a million patients in 2005 and about 800,000 Americans died while receiving hospice care, roughly one-third of all deaths in the United States that year.[46] In a recent survey, more than 98 percent of families indicated they would recommend hospice services to others.[47] Cancer diagnoses accounted for slightly less than half of hospice admissions, followed by heart disease, dementia, debility, and lung diseases. The growth of hospice reflects changing expectations about end-of-life care, "from cure to care, extension of life to quality of life."[48]

The Principles of Hospice and Palliative Care

For hospice and palliative care, the goal of medicine is *healing* rather than *curing* disease. This means restoring, or sustaining, a sense of equanimity and personal integrity despite the disturbances caused by illness.[49] The main aim of palliative care is to control pain and other physical distress.[50] It involves the active total care of patients whose disease is not responsive to curative treatment. As the phrase "total care" suggests, the mission of hospice and palliative care goes beyond the physical and seeks to relieve suffering by caring for all of a patient's needs: physical, psychological, spiritual, and existential.[51] At the end of life, a patient's personal story is not adequately told by what's written on the medical chart.

Often, the message heard by dying patients and their families is "nothing more can be done."[52] The response of hospice and palliative care is that, on the contrary, much can be done to help the dying person continue *living* until death, even though recovery or cure is not possible.

Palliative care involves a team approach that often includes physicians, nurses, social workers, pharmacists, physical and occupational therapists, chaplains, home health aides, and trained volunteers, as well as family members and friends. This team-oriented approach is intended to provide state-of-the-art care to treat pain and other distressing symptoms, as well as provide emotional and spiritual support tailored to the needs of the patient and his or her family. The goal is to help people live as fully as possible until the end of their lives.[53] As hospice and palliative care physician Ira Byock says, "Even when it is not possible to add many days to life, the opportunity exists to add life to one's days."[54]

The Origins of Hospice and Palliative Care

The roots of hospice and palliative care are found in age-old customs of hospitality and in "places of welcome" maintained by early Christians to care for pilgrims and travelers.[55] (The words *hotel, hospice,* and *hospital* derive from the Latin *hospitium,* meaning "a place that receives guests.") Whereas Roman hospitals were built on a "military model of efficiency" to provide quick repair of gladiators and slaves, Christian hospices aided injured travelers, the hopelessly ill, and victims of disasters. The dying received special honor, for they were seen as spiritual pilgrims close to God. Among the earliest hospices were those founded in the fourth century by a disciple of Saint Jerome named Fabiola, a wealthy Roman widow who became patron and nurse in caring for the sick and dying. Within the Judeo-Christian religious tradition, the basis for hospice care is found in the concepts of *diakonia* (serving and caring for others), *metanoia* (turning within to a deeper self or divine power), and *kairos* (a unique moment of fulfillment).[56]

The most influential model of modern hospice care is St. Christopher's Hospice in Sydenham, England, founded in 1967 by Dr. Cicely Saunders.[57] During the 1940s, while training as a medical social worker, Saunders met David Tasma, a Jewish refugee from Poland who was dying of inoperable cancer. They formulated the vision of a haven where people could find relief from pain and die with dignity. When Tasma died in 1948, he left a small bequest to Saunders, saying "I'll be a window in your home." Nineteen years later, with the opening of St. Christopher's Hospice, the vision became a reality as a window was dedicated to Tasma's memory.[58]

Named for the patron saint of travelers, St. Christopher's promotes acceptance of dying within an atmosphere of tranquility. St. Christopher's reflects what Dr. Saunders calls a "high person, low technology and hardware" system of health care.[59] The wards and rooms at St. Christopher's are filled with flowers, photographs, and personal items. Patients are encouraged to pursue their familiar interests and pleasures. Extensive visiting hours allow for interaction between patients and their families, including children and even family pets. When a patient is dying, family, friends, and staff members gather around the bed for farewells. After death, family and friends spend time with the body if they wish, and then it is bathed and taken to a small chapel.

Home care is an important adjunct to residential care at St. Christopher's; it allows the benefits of hospice care to be extended to nonresidential patients and families. The hospice staff plans medication schedules, and hospice nurses visit patients to monitor their conditions. A nurse is on call around the clock to answer questions from patients and family members. Over the years, St. Christopher's has exemplified many features associated with hospice care, such as providing adequate pain control, treating the patient and his or her family as the unit of care, and achieving the best possible quality of life for dying patients.

In 1963, a visit by Cicely Saunders to the school of nursing at Yale University stimulated interest in hospice care in the United States. When Saunders again visited Yale in 1966, Florence Wald, as dean of Yale's graduate school of nursing, organized a meeting attended by Saunders, Elisabeth Kübler-Ross, Colin Murray Parkes, and others interested in improving care of the dying. Wald, who had worked with terminally ill patients and their families for more than a decade, was instrumental in establishing the first American hospice, which opened in New Haven, Connecticut, in 1974. Its first medical director was Dr. Sylvia Lack, who had previously served at St. Christopher's.

Other key events in the modern history of hospice and palliative care include establishment of a hospital-based palliative care team at St. Luke's Hospital in New York City in 1974 and publication of assumptions and principles for terminal care by the International Work Group on Death, Dying, and Bereavement in 1979.[60] Also, in the early 1970s, at Hospice of Marin in California, Dr. William Lamers developed innovative approaches to home care for terminally ill patients. Hospice programs, Lamers says, were created out of a desire to improve the quality of life for patients with incurable illness, patients who were being "slighted" in "a health care system that stressed aggressive therapies aimed at cure or rehabilitation, but that seemed to offer disincentives for care aimed at relief of illness."[61]

Hospice Programs and Hospital-Based Palliative Care

Although the terms *hospice care* and *palliative care* are often used interchangeably, they can be differentiated by defining hospice care as a type of palliative care that focuses specifically on patients who are terminally ill.[62] Although the term *hospice* sometimes refers to a residential facility to which terminally ill patients are admitted, most of the time hospice care takes place in patients' homes with family members as primary caregivers. "Entering hospice care" usually means affiliating with a *hospice program*—that is, arranging to receive the services of a local hospice. Hospice care may be provided in nursing homes, residential-care facilities, senior housing, and hospitals, as well as in patients' homes.

Although it has sometimes been accused of promoting an idealized "happy death," hospice doesn't actually prescribe a particular "way of dying."[63] Rather, it seeks to create an environment in which the "seemingly disordered process of dying" can be lived out in a manner that fits the needs and beliefs of the person who is dying.[64]

Hospitals are increasingly incorporating principles of hospice and palliative care as part of their mission.[65] In some cases, palliative care is combined with cure-oriented treatments, allowing patients to continue to battle disease while benefiting from efforts to improve quality of life. When nurses are given

Dr. Elisabeth Kübler-Ross, seen here with a patient who has been diagnosed with a life-threatening illness, is widely recognized for her pioneering efforts toward increased awareness on the part of the patient, family, and medical staff relative to the issues that arise in caring for the dying.

time to get to know patients and their families, when caregivers are assigned responsibility for individual patients rather than tasks, when supportive relationships exist among staff members, and when there is a policy of open disclosure of diagnosis and prognosis, care of the dying in both hospitals and hospice programs embodies essentially similar ideals and philosophy regarding end-of-life care.[66] Richard Smith, editor of the *British Medical Journal,*

TABLE 5-1   *Questions for Contemporary Hospices*

1. *The question of access.* Is hospice care available to everyone who desires it? How can access to hospice care be improved for underserved populations such as minorities and people with AIDS?
2. *The question of spiritual care.* Is care related to the spiritual dimensions of life—that which "connects an individual to a sphere beyond himself or herself"—being adequately addressed by hospice?
3. *The question of finances.* What is the effect of the increasing imposition of bureaucratic regulation and budgetary controls on hospice care?
4. *The question of innovation.* How should present hospice services be expanded and new services created?
5. *The question of choice.* What is the role of hospice care in the growing debate about quality of life, euthanasia, and physican-assisted suicide?

Source: Adapted from Inge Baer Corless, "A New Decade for Hospice," in *A Challenge for Living: Dying, Death, and Bereavement,* ed. Inge B. Corless, Barbara B. Germino, and Mary A. Pittman (Boston: Jones & Bartlett, 1995), pp. 77–94.

points out that there is something paradoxical about creating a specialty for something that happens to us all, adding that "the trend now is for the lessons learnt by palliative care physicians to be reclaimed by everybody."[67]

Challenges to Hospice and Palliative Care

There are challenges in making hospice and palliative care more widely available at life's end (see Table 5-1).[68] First, because most care is provided in patients' homes, the presence of a primary caregiver available twenty-four hours a day is a near-requirement for receiving hospice services. A primary caregiver may be the patient's spouse, partner, or parent, although other relatives—as well as someone paid by the family or funded by public agencies—can fill this role. For men, this is usually a spouse or partner; for women, it is usually another relative, often a child or child-in-law. Home care is provided primarily by unpaid family members and friends and only secondarily by paid workers.[69] Caregivers must be able to accomplish a variety of health-related tasks, such as monitoring vital signs, assessing pain, and administering proper dosages of medications.

Another challenge for hospice and palliative care is funding. Hospice services are covered by Medicare/Medicaid programs as well as by most private health plans, but there are limits on who qualifies. Under the Medicare Hospice Benefit, enacted by the U.S. Congress in 1982, qualifying requires a doctor's certification that a patient's life expectancy is six months or less if the illness runs its normal course. Patients and their physicians must also agree to stop treatment aimed at prolonging life. A review of the accuracy of physicians' clinical predictions of survival in terminally ill patients found that they "consistently overestimate survival."[70] Because it is often difficult to state with certainty that a patient's expected prognosis is less than six months, the "six-month" rule tends to exclude patients who have conditions difficult to predict. This rule has the effect of causing patients to enter hospice care at a later stage of illness than would be preferable; in fact, a primary reason for nonadmission to a hospice program is death: The patient died before he or she could be certified as meeting the life-expectancy requirement.[71]

Hospice officials have been wary about the government questioning whether patients are sick enough to qualify for hospice care and penalizing hospice programs when patients don't die on schedule. In an attempt to offer clarification, the head of the Health Care Financing Administration, which administers the hospice benefit, said it is a misperception that patients who outlive the six-month rule automatically lose their coverage. The pertinent section of the law, she said, states "six months or less *if the illness runs its normal course.*"[72] Nevertheless, at times the government has reportedly emphasized the six-month part of the law.

Another challenge faced by hospice is broadening access for underserved patient populations. In a recent year, about 82 percent of patients were white and, of the remaining 18 percent, 7.5 percent were African American.[73] One explanation is that, for historical reasons, people of color tend not to trust social institutions.[74] Inequalities in health care are well documented.[75] For example, African American and Hispanic patients with severe pain are less likely than white patients to receive commonly prescribed pain medicines. Also, many ethnic groups have traditions of family and community support when coping with illness and death, whereas hospice programs have generally reflected white, middle-class values.[76]

Richard Payne, chief of the pain and palliative care service at New York's Memorial Sloan-Kettering Cancer Center, points out:

> African Americans are significantly less likely to prepare a living will, to talk to their doctors about end-of-life care, or to participate in a hospice program. When death is inevitable and imminent, blacks are twice as likely as whites to request life-sustaining treatments that can make dying a miserable experience for both patients and their families. . . . In my experience, many patients, especially African Americans and members of other medically underserved minority groups, tend to think of "palliative care" as "giving up hope." I suspect this is so because many African Americans fear their cultural and personal values will not be respected when they are dying.[77]

There is a need to recognize the potential conflict between European American values of individualism and self-determination and the Afrocentric emphasis on collectivity and family when end-of-life decisions are made. "Cookie-cutter services that fail to consider the contextual domain in which death and dying occur are likely to be rejected by those who most need assistance at the end of life."[78]

Hospice has also been challenged by an increasing bureaucracy. Might this lead to routinization of care? Experts note that "outcome measurement and evaluation is no longer just an option if a hospice or palliative care program is to succeed and establish credibility in the current environment."[79] In its early years, hospice was distinguished by the enthusiasm of pioneer-activists who sought to offer services not available from mainstream social service agencies or in conventional medical settings. With the growth of hospice or-

ganizations came increasing formalization and regulation. Inge Corless asks,
In our zeal to provide hospice care, are we becoming as paternalistic as the
medical practices we oft criticize? Do patients need to comply with hospice
ideology to receive services? Must all hospice clients engage in a dialogue
about death? What gives us the hubris to think we know best?[80]

Critics familiar with the evolution of hospice see a subtle shift from the
concept of striving for a "good" death to a more prescriptive "peaceful"
death.[81] In the beginning, hospices could experiment with various approaches
to the delivery of services. Now, says Corless, the "politicization of reimbursement for hospice care" brings regulations that require all programs which
want to obtain certification to comply with a set of standards based on one
model of care.[82]

A further challenge for hospice programs and palliative medicine is educating both the public and the professional about end-of-life care. Medical
and nursing schools and textbooks are deficient in topics involving end-of-
life care and death and dying.[83] If high-quality care is to be provided to dying
patients and their families, health care professionals not only must possess
necessary technical skills, but also must learn how to deal with their own anxieties about dying and death.[84]

In considering the future of hospice, William Lamers suggests that new
types of hospice care may be needed to meet some of the challenges.[85] He
outlines three "levels" of care that could be provided by hospice:

1. *Traditional* hospice care for persons with fairly definable short-term prognoses (for example, advanced, incurable cancers)
2. *Long-term* hospice care for persons with an indeterminate diagnosis who
   do not require expensive therapies to improve quality of life during a
   prolonged period of dying (for example, chronic, incurable neurologic
   disorders, such as Alzheimer's disease and amyotrophic lateral sclerosis,
   or ALS)
3. *High-tech* hospice care for persons who require expensive therapies to
   maintain reasonable relief of symptoms in the face of a limited, although
   uncertain, prognosis (for example, advanced AIDS)

Home Care

Simply defined, home care is medically supervised care that is provided
in a person's home. End-of-life care that is provided at home is often referred
to as "hospice home care." Such care is directed by physicians, coordinated
by nurses, and usually supported by an interdisciplinary team that may include volunteers, family members, and friends. In the United States, about
80 percent of the time, hospice care is provided by visiting nurses and other
staff in patients' own homes.[86]

Home care offers a number of potential advantages as a setting for terminal care, including the obvious fact that the patient is *at home,* which, for most
people, is a "center of meaningful activity and connectedness to family,
friends, and community."[87] It has been suggested that there is truly no place

like "home" because its image is constructed in memory and imagination. It is often defined in terms of relationships that people have (or would like to have) with others in the home. "Home is a representation of cultural identity" and provides a collective sense of security.[88]

At home, the dying person is in a familiar setting. Instead of having to comply with a schedule of visiting hours and other rules determined by institutional routine, the patient and his or her family enjoy greater flexibility. Home care lessens the need to "live to a timetable" and provides a sense of normalcy that enhances opportunities for the patient to maintain relationships and exercise self-determination. It also allows for reciprocity, a mutuality of care and concern, which families often find gratifying in caring for an ailing family member. It is not surprising, therefore, that most people express a preference to be cared for at home during the end-stage of an illness.

However, to realize these attractive features, home care requires adequate support. It depends on preparation and commitment. Home care can be a twenty-four-hour-a-day job. Whether family member, friend, paid home health aide, or outside volunteer, someone must be available to manage the various tasks that constitute appropriate care of the patient. These tasks are typically shouldered by women, who have traditionally filled the role of "family nurse" and continue to do so despite social progress in breaking down gender stereotypes in other areas.

Although the term *home care* sounds low key, it bears huge burdens in the health care system. Despite its domestic connotations, home care is often "high-tech," as central and peripheral intravenous lines are employed to administer fluids, drugs, and nutrition, and as side effects and complications are managed. Normal household routines may be disrupted as special equipment is set up and maintained, furniture moved or stored, and rooms rearranged to meet the needs of the patient.

The workload of patient care can be lightened by outside support services provided by visiting nurses and other caregivers. Home care may alternate with stays in the hospital or another health care facility. There may be times when it is appropriate to arrange *respite care*—temporary care that gives family members or other caregivers a welcome break—and it may be provided in a hospital, nursing home, hospice facility, or even in the home.

It isn't always possible to provide the necessary level of medical or nursing care at home. When a patient requires sophisticated medical procedures, does not have access to qualified caregivers, or intends to be an organ donor, other types of care may be more suitable. Although home care is not an option for everyone, people who have cared for a seriously ill or dying relative at home often say that the experience was positive and rewarding.

Social Support

Social support is a key component of care for patients with a life-threatening illness. Organizations dedicated to helping people with specific illnesses—for example, cancer or heart disease—can be found through hos-

Drawing by Jack Ziegler, © 2000 The New Yorker Collection

*"Sorry, Sylvia, but your mother's long-term care has been
going on just a little bit too long."*

pitals and other community agencies. Social support can decrease patients' feelings of helplessness while increasing their self-esteem and confidence. It can help them gain better understanding of their illness and provide a forum for sharing ways to cope with fears and enhance physical and emotional well-being. The Internet is another alternative that can be helpful. It offers health and medical information, and some sites provide social support. For example, online patient groups demonstrate a shared concern for a particular illness or malady and provide a forum for giving and receiving both information and support. Beyond these specific sources, Allan Kellehear proposes a "health-promoting palliative care" that enlists support "not merely in terms of support groups but also as a wider community issue."[89]

Social support services are often offered by hospices and other community groups. This is illustrated by the Zen Hospice Project, a program established in 1987 under the auspices of the San Francisco Zen Center.[90] Volunteers are trained in the fundamentals of hospice work, and care is provided at the Project's Guest House (a homelike residence providing twenty-four-hour care) as well as at Laguna Honda Hospital (a public facility with a twenty-eight-bed hospice unit). In addition, there is a regular schedule of community programs and services. In caring for individuals approaching death, caregivers cultivate the "listening mind" through regular meditation or spiritual practice. Frank Ostaseski, founding director of Zen Hospice Project, says, "As hospice workers, one of our central tasks is to be available when stories are ready to be told."[91]

Elder Care

Round-the-clock care is sometimes needed to manage illnesses and debilities that may accompany old age. Listen to conversations about care of a chronically ill older adult and you may notice language like this: "She couldn't live by herself so her son took her in," or "He was failing and had to be put in a nursing home." A question like "What will we do with Dad when he is too old and can't manage by himself?" reflects both loving concern and inadvertent disregard for the aged person. It is not surprising that old people report feelings of being put away, taken in, done to, and otherwise manipulated, their integrity ignored.

Institutional care is likely to be depersonalizing. Residents may feel deprived of self-esteem and integrity. Rules and regulations dictate a style of life that may be far from what the resident would choose for himself or herself. Even a cherished picture of a loved one may find no place in the resident's room: not the bedstand (that's for bedpans), not the wall (patients are frequently moved)—so where? The answer may be, "Nowhere." Of course, favoring institutional expediency over the needs of individuals cannot in the end be justified.

Gerontologists—persons who study the process and the problems of aging—describe how "psychological railroading" of routinized, bureaucratic environments can result in an *institutional neurosis,* the symptoms of which include "a gradual erosion of the uniqueness of one's personality traits so that residents become increasingly dependent on staff direction for even the most mundane needs."[92]

In the United States, social service programs for older people can be traced to the Depression of the 1930s and passage of the Social Security Act of 1935. The Old Age Assistance Act, enacted in 1950, became the first federal program to deal specifically with problems of the aged. Following adoption of the Medicare and Medicaid programs in the mid-1960s, federal assistance became a customary means of providing care for America's elderly. Nevertheless, questions about how to provide adequate, as well as cost-effective, care for the aged continue to be of public concern, and they become more important as life expectancy increases: Aged people are not only growing in numbers, but are also making up a larger proportion of the total population. (*Senescence,* the state or process of becoming old, is discussed in Chapter 11.)

Historically, the family has been a haven for ill and aged relatives, and families continue to provide the major portion of care for aged relatives. Indeed, most elders live in their own homes or with their families, who often highly value the care they provide to an older relative. But some aged people require more assistance than relatives or friends can realistically provide.

[handwritten marginal note:] Isn't this also when Americans began individualizing, breaking away from tradition and household?

I Know (I'm Losing You)

> *Have you ever touched your father's back?* No, my fingers tell me,
> as they try to pull up a similar memory.
>   There are none. This is a place we have never traveled to, as
> I try to lift his weary body onto the bedpan.
>   I recall a photo of him standing in front of our house. He is
> large, healthy, a stocky body in a dark blue suit.
>   And now his bowels panic, feed his mind phony information,
> and as I try to position him, my hands shift and the news
> shocks me more than the sight of his balls.
>   O, bag of bones, this is all I'll know of his body, the sharp ridge
> of spine, the bedsores, the ribs rising up in place like new islands.
>   I feel him strain as he pushes, for nothing, feel his fingers
> grip my shoulders. *He is slipping to dust,* my hands inform me,
> *you'd better remember this.*

Cornelius Eady

The decision for institutional care is usually made when a person is no longer able to live independently and his or her family is unable to provide the level of care needed. There may be several options to consider. *Personal care homes,* for example, provide care for residents who need minimal assistance and are otherwise able to care for themselves, whereas *skilled nursing facilities* provide more comprehensive care, furnishing medical and nursing services as well as dietary supervision. Other alternatives exist for older people who can continue living more or less independently in their own homes. *Home health care* may be available to assist the older person in a variety of ways, ranging from medical and nursing visits to helping with preparation of meals, exercise, and other maintenance needs, along with simple (but important) visitation.

Midway between institutionalization and independent living is a form of care known as *congregate housing.* This is usually a large facility with individual apartments or a group of small condominiums within a planned neighborhood. Congregate housing is distinguished by its organizational structure, which, like a series of concentric circles or graduated steps, provides the level of care needed by each resident. Within such a community, some individuals essentially live independently, preparing meals in their own apartments or eating in a common dining room when they wish. Others receive more help with the activities of daily living. This allows older people to enjoy a sense of security without losing their independence, knowing that help is available when needed.

Despite the image of old people being "dumped" in nursing homes by uncaring relatives, this is rarely the reality. On the contrary, families often delay obtaining care for elders because of reluctance to accept the fact that more help is needed. Entering into institutional care is usually viewed as a

T A B L E   *5-2*   *Steps in Choosing a Nursing Care Facility*

1. Make a list of local facilities offering the type of services needed.
2. Find out whether the facilities are licensed and certified.
3. Visit the facilities.
4. Prepare a checklist of desirable features and evaluate each facility in light of the needs of the person who would be moving in.
5. Determine the costs.
6. Make your decision.

Source: Adapted from Colette Browne and Roberta Onzuka-Anderson, eds., *Our Aging Parents: A Practical Guide to Eldercare* (Honolulu: University of Hawaii Press, 1985), pp. 204–209.

personal failure, for both the aged person and his or her family. It is pictured as the least desirable option, "a sort of confession to final surrender, a halfway stop on the route to death."[93] However, it may be the only reasonable course open to an aged person. The best outcome follows when adequate information is gathered before making a decision about a particular facility (see Table 5-2).[94] In coming decades, with the aging population on the rise, new types of elder care undoubtedly will be created to accommodate the "baby boomers."[95] Perhaps most important, for individuals and as a society, is the need to address the task of envisioning and creating a worthy "place" for the old who live among us.

Trauma and Emergency Care

In a recent year, nearly 109,000 Americans died from injuries sustained in accidents.[96] About 40 percent of these deaths involved motor vehicle accidents, with poisoning, fires, and drownings accounting for most of the rest. Experts in emergency care and *trauma* (defined as physical injury) refer to a "golden hour" following accidental injury, of which the first fifteen minutes are especially critical. Immediate surgery may be required, often to stop internal bleeding. When individuals receive appropriate care during the critical period, the survival rate is about 90 percent.[97]

The roots of modern emergency and trauma care can be traced back to the Civil War, when Army Major John Letterman developed a "triage" system for evacuating casualties. Aimed at reducing time between injury and care, triage involves assigning priorities to patients based on the seriousness of their injuries. Highest priority is given to patients whose injuries are serious but survivable. Lower priorities are assigned to patients with only a remote chance of survival and to those with comparatively minor injuries. Many of the procedures now commonplace in trauma care have been adapted from techniques used by the military in combat situations. These include the use of helicopter air ambulances, advances in team surgery and orthopedics, and treatment for burns and shock.

© Albert Lee Strickland

Emergency personnel, including search-and-rescue workers and police officers, engage in the grim task of recovering and identifying the bodies of two people who died in the crash of a helicopter about a thousand yards offshore. Such work is stressful and involves an extensive network of helping professionals who typically receive little or no formal training in methods of coping with the impact of multiple encounters with death, an inevitable consequence of the performance of their duties.

In the United States, modern hospital-based trauma care was initiated in 1966 by Robert Freeark at Cook County Hospital in Chicago and William Blaisdell at San Francisco General Hospital. Then, in 1969, R. Adams Cowley formed a comprehensive system of trauma and emergency care by bringing together the Maryland State Police and the Maryland Institute for Emergency Medical Services to create the first civilian helicopter medevac program. The first hospital-based helicopter program was established in 1972 at St. Anthony's Hospital in Denver. These innovations reflect the standard approach to emergency treatment in the United States, which is termed "scoop & run," meaning accident victims receive minimal on-site treatment from paramedics and are rushed to emergency rooms or trauma centers. "Stay & play" is used to describe an approach in which extensive on-site treatment and stabilization is performed by doctors who arrive at the scene of the accident in mobile hospital units. (This was the approach used to treat Diana, Princess of Wales, when her Mercedes crashed in the Alma tunnel in France.[98])

Generally, the doctor's announcement of the death was made within the first or first two sentences, usually in the course of one long sentence. An interesting feature of his presentation, more common in the DOA situation than in announcements of the deaths of hospital patients, was that in announcing the death he provided, in some way, that the death be presented as having followed a course of "dying." In nearly every scene I witnessed, the doctor's opening remarks contained an historical reference. . . . This was true in accident as well as "natural" deaths, and true whether or not the physician had any basis for assuming a likely cause of death. . . . Physicians seem to feel in such situations that historicizing their delivery of news, no matter how much their limited knowledge of the case may restrict the range of possibilities, helps not only reduce some of the shock values of "sudden deaths" but aids in the very grasp of the news. The correctness of the physician's supposed cause of death is of secondary significance relative to the sheer fact that he provides some sequential formulation of its generation, some means whereby the occurrence can be placed in a sequence of natural or accidental events. This is felt particularly to be necessary in the DOA circumstance, where many deaths occur with no apparent "reason," particularly the so-called "sudden unexpected death," not uncommon among young adults.

David Sudnow,
Passing On: The Social Organization of Dying

Think about the compelling images associated with the drama of life-or-death situations in the emergency room. As one ER staffer said, "You can be sitting there almost lulled to sleep during a quiet period, then suddenly everything is happening at once because there's just been a five-car crackup." Interventions must be rapidly and efficiently mobilized if life is to be sustained. For some caregivers, the pressure is overwhelming; the rhythm of patient care in other wards is less stressful. Others gain satisfaction from participating in situations in which their skills must be quickly brought to bear to save lives.

Trauma patients are frequently comatose or incoherent due to shock. The emergency room staff must take action that makes the difference between life and death while receiving little or no feedback from the patient. When a patient dies, members of the ER staff face the task of delivering bad news to relatives. A doctor usually provides news of a patient's death, perhaps with other staff members on hand. The manner in which such news is communicated often will remain with survivors. Ideally, information about a patient's death is presented both truthfully and compassionately (see "Death Notification" in Chapter 4).

The goal of saving every patient may be worthy, but it is not realistic or practical in the context of trauma care. When the circumstances of a death provoke the caregiver's own anxieties about death, or when a death is exceptionally tragic—the death of a child, for example, or the death of a family

Members of the Newburgh, New York, Volunteer Ambulance Corps are overcome with tears at the end of a memorial held for seven children killed at a local elementary school by a tornado. Emergency personnel who work in closely knit communities often have personal relationships with those they serve and thus may experience the tragedies that befall their neighbors with special intensity.

© Susan Ragan, AP / Wide World Photos

in an automobile accident on Christmas Eve—it is likely to profoundly affect caregivers.

Caregiver Stress

Medical, nursing, emergency, and other health care professionals work in environments where death occurs more often than in most other occupations.[99] This observation also applies to "first-responders" and search-and-rescue personnel, as well as firefighters and police officers who are at the scene of accidents or disasters.[100] The impact of working in a death-saturated environment is evident on the faces of rescue and recovery personnel in the aftermath of disasters, such as the terrorist attacks in 2001. Although it is sometimes suggested that individuals in jobs like these receive "critical incident stress debriefing" (CISD) following a traumatic event, the particulars of how best to provide support and psychosocial aid are not clear-cut.[101]

Even though professionals who care for seriously ill and dying people may be more exposed to death and thus more familiar with it than others, such intimacy with death is still stressful. Among the main sources of caregiver stress are feelings of inadequacy, nonreciprocal giving, and too many demands. The most stressful situations tend to occur when caregivers feel helpless, seemingly unable to improve the situation. The inability to produce a cure may be seen as an inability to provide adequate care. Providing care for patients with intractable pain or patients who are fearful about dying increases stress on caregivers. They may ask themselves, Was there something else that could have been done? Caregivers may experience a litany of "what ifs" when deaths occur.

In hospitals, nurses typically have more contact with patients than physicians do. Yet, as nurses are forced to take on administrative duties, they spend more time at desks and less time at patients' bedsides. As one physician comments, "We've devalued nurses by turning them into record keepers, and we've devalued patients, who need and deserve the attention of professional nurses."[102] How health care is managed thus becomes an additional stress for caregivers.

When caring is defined as curing, caregivers are vulnerable to feelings of failure when a patient dies.[103] The death of a patient whom caregivers have come to know well is likely to evoke grief. In working day in and day out with seriously ill and dying patients, caregivers may be fatigued by grief and be tempted to take refuge in hospital routine and standardized policies as a way of alleviating stress. This can lead to emotional exhaustion, "burnout," which is defined as a reaction to stress in which a caregiver goes beyond a state of exhaustion and depression to being "past caring." To maintain empathy for patients, caregivers need to have healthy ways to replenish themselves.

Perhaps most important is a supportive environment in which death or other stressors can be discussed by staff members. Social support is an antidote to harmful stress. Ways can be implemented that encourage caregivers to come together to discuss feelings and issues that come up in caregiving. The policy of one nursing home provides an example: After a death, everyone who cared for the patient—nurses, housekeepers, dietitians, recreational staff, special service personnel—gather to share their reactions to the patient's illness and death. When "care for the caregiver" is recognized as a crucial aspect of providing empathetic care to patients, positive ways of coping with stress can be created.

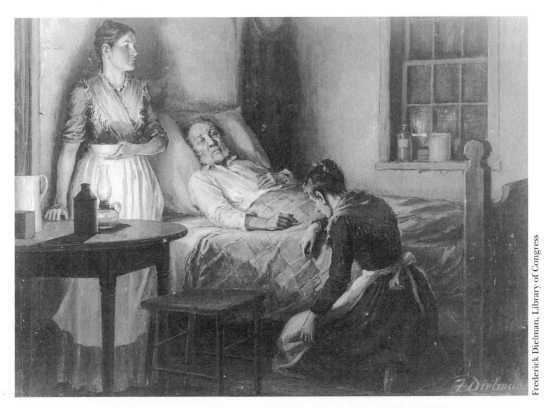

Frederick Dielman, Library of Congress

This 1895 illustration captures, in posture and expression, the weariness that accompanies round-the-clock care for the seriously ill and dying. Today's caregivers may feel this burden as much as ever while expecting themselves to put such feelings aside to conform to an image of professionalism.

Being with Someone Who Is Dying

We may feel uncomfortable in the presence of someone diagnosed with a life-threatening illness. What can we say? How ought we to act? Perhaps it seems that anything we might think of to express our thoughts or feelings would come out as nothing more than a stale platitude. Our discomfort may be exhibited through either excessive sympathy or obsessive avoidance while we shy away from real communication. As an antidote to such responses, it is helpful to keep in mind that the essence of caregiving is to leave your own agenda at the door and to be present to whatever the person needs. Charles Garfield says that one of the subtlest skills is knowing when to encourage someone to fight for life and when to accompany him or her to death's door.[104]

> A person's in the room with me and they're very close to dying and afraid. I can feel the fear of death in myself. I'm working through my fear. I give them an opportunity, silent though it may be, to work through theirs. If I come into a room saying, "Oh, there's nothing to be afraid of. We go through death and then into another rebirth," that's not very useful. That's a way of not dealing with the power of the moment—the suffering in that room in the fellow on the bed, and the suffering in the mind of the fellow next to the bed.
>
> Stephen Levine, *A Gradual Awakening*

Life review, a counseling tool used widely with older people, can open up possibilities for discussing issues of concern to someone facing death. Reviewing the course of a person's life can empower that person to make the choices he or she values in completing the last chapter of life.[105] Reviewing past relationships and events, the person gains an opportunity to complete unfinished business.

Often the only task that matters in being with someone who is dying is to sit still and listen to the stories. In a talk to volunteers at San Francisco's Zen Hospice Project, Tenshin Reb Anderson expressed it this way: "Stay close and do nothing."[106]

Being with someone who is seriously ill or dying, we confront our own mortality. We may come to appreciate how precious life is and how uncertain. Few occasions in life present us with the chance to be so vulnerable to aspects of ourselves that are usually kept hidden. Being with someone who is dying can surprise us with moments of grace and beauty. In describing the end of her mother's life and death, Janmarie Silvera describes how the blossoming of a "huge, luminous full moon" through a hospital window became an occasion of "wonderment," a moment of intimacy acknowledging both life and death.[107]

Further Readings

Joan Berzoff and Phyllis Silverman, eds. *Living with Dying: A Handbook for End-of-Life Healthcare*. New York: Columbia University Press, 2004.

Stephen R. Connor. *Hospice: Practice, Pitfalls, Promise*. Washington, D.C.: Taylor & Francis, 1998.

Marilyn J. Field and Christine K. Cassel, eds. *Approaching Death: Improving Care at the End of Life*. Washington, D.C.: National Academy Press, 1997.

Frank Huyler. *The Blood of Strangers: Stories from Emergency Medicine*. Berkeley: University of California Press, 1999.

Sharon R. Kaufman. *. . . And a Time to Die: How American Hospitals Shape the End of Life*. New York: Scribner, 2005.

Marcia Lattanzi-Licht, John J. Mahoney, and Galen W. Miller. *The Hospice Choice: In Pursuit of a Peaceful Death.* New York: Fireside, 1998.

Michael Rowe. *The Book of Jesse: A Story of Youth, Illness, and Medicine.* Washington, D.C.: Francis Press, 2002.

Carolyn L. Wiener and Anselm L. Strauss, eds. *Where Medicine Fails,* 5th ed. New Brunswick, N.J.: Transaction, 1997.

End-of-life decisions touch on many aspects of dying and death, ranging from legal matters relating to wills and the settling of estates to often emotionally charged issues such as advance directives, withholding or withdrawing treatment, physician-assisted suicide, and euthanasia. This young couple reviews the documents they have prepared with the help of their attorney.

CHAPTER 6

End-of-Life Issues and Decisions

Great-grandpa was born before Henry Ford put his first automobile on the road, and he died shortly after Neil Armstrong set foot on the moon. From Michigan to outer space, he experienced an unprecedented advance in the technological capacities of our society. At the time of his death, he was surrounded by technological innovations. The canvas-topped, hand-cranked, two-seater car he hand-built in 1922 had been replaced by a factory-built, vinyl-topped, four-door automatic, with power steering and power brakes. A retired autoworker, he had begun to question the consequences of the automobile on the quality of his life. If he had been conscious as he lay dying, he might have talked about the consequences the machines sustaining his life were having on the quality of his death.

In this chapter we examine issues and decisions that pertain to the end of life. Some of these involve matters that can be dealt with long before an individual is faced with the crisis of an illness or debility. These include activities like making a will, obtaining life insurance, and completing an advance directive to express wishes about medical treatment in the event one becomes incapacitated. Other issues and decisions are likely to come to the fore only after a patient is near death. These include such matters as choosing to withhold or withdraw treatments and considering physician-assisted suicide or aid-in-dying. Finally, some issues are initiated earlier in life by an individual but are not completed until after his or her death.

These include the settling of a person's estate through probate and the disbursement of proceeds from insurance and other death benefits to survivors.

All of the end-of-life issues and decisions discussed in this chapter ought to be considered at an early stage of life. By acknowledging the inevitability of death, we can begin to prepare for it. Adequate planning ensures that we do not add to the burdens carried by our survivors. Although some decisions cannot be made until one is in a particular situation, many issues can be anticipated, considered, and discussed with close relatives and trusted friends. Thus, it is prudent to begin considering end-of-life issues and decisions during the college years and to periodically review and revise one's choices throughout life.

Principles of Medical Ethics

To provide a framework for discussing informed consent, withdrawing or withholding medical treatment, euthanasia (defined as bringing about a gentle or peaceful death), physician-assisted suicide, and other issues that are relevant to end-of-life care, it is worthwhile to review some principles of medical ethics. To begin, *ethics* is concerned with the investigation of what is good and bad, especially as these concepts relate to moral duties and obligations. Such an investigation results in a set of moral principles or values that guide behavior. When we think of *morals,* or moral principles, we are dealing essentially with notions of right and wrong. Although the two terms—*morals* and *ethics*—are closely related, we can distinguish them, in one way, by noting that morals involve conforming to established codes or accepted notions of right and wrong, whereas ethics involve more subtle or challenging questions. The pursuit of ethics is characterized by efforts to answer the question "What is the good?" and its corollary, "What is to be done?"

In applying ethical principles to the realm of medicine, several concepts have importance. The first of these, *autonomy,* refers to an individual's right to be self-governing—that is, to exercise self-direction, freedom, and moral independence. Our personal autonomy is limited by the rights of others to exercise their autonomy, and it also may be limited by society, which exercises rights in the name of the community at large. A common example is the requirement that a traveler must obtain inoculations before being granted a visa to enter certain countries; the traveler's autonomy is restricted by concerns about public health imposed by the larger community.

A person may limit the extent to which his or her autonomy will be exercised. Cultural or religious beliefs can influence the degree to which individuals wish to exercise their autonomy.[1] For some ethnic and cultural groups, family members have a primary, or at least equal, voice in decisions about a patient's care. Individual autonomy is offset by respect for the values of others with whom one has a significant relationship. If decisions are made without adequately considering their effect on the "family commons," those choices

The doctor who fears being subjected to a malpractice suit if he doesn't tell the worst, and who tells the worst, may actually help to bring on the worst. . . . A serious diagnosis can be communicated as a challenge rather than as a verdict. The physician who volunteers a terminal date, for example, or allows himself to be pressured into offering a terminal date may actually be putting a hex on the patient.

Norman Cousins, "Tapping Human Potential"

may be overridden.[2] Thus, within certain limits, the principle of autonomy promotes "respect for persons" as people negotiate the medical system.

Another fundamental principle in medical care is *beneficence,* which involves doing good or conferring benefits that enhance personal or social well-being. This principle is sometimes expressed by its counterpart, *nonmaleficence,* or the injunction to "do no harm." In the context of caregiver-patient relationships, this principle requires that physicians not abandon a patient even when a patient makes decisions or takes actions that the physician believes are ill advised.[3]

Finally, medical ethics is concerned with the principle of *justice.* Like "the good," justice is not easy to define, although it includes qualities of impartiality and fairness, as well as right and proper action. Justice implies going beyond one's own feelings, prejudices, and desires to find an appropriate balance among conflicting interests. As you consider the issues discussed in this chapter, keep in mind the ethical principles of autonomy, beneficence, and justice.

Ideally, choices about end-of-life care and important medical matters are decided by individuals, families, and caregivers, who, acting together, form a community of interest, with firsthand knowledge about a particular case and the will to make moral decisions.[4] Physician John Lantos says, "The goal of medical ethics, it seems, should not be to develop rules that will minimize the need for individual virtues but to develop virtues that will minimize the need for rules."[5] However, traditional "virtue-centered" ethics may be challenged by the "businessification" of medicine.[6]

Informed Consent to Treatment

The relationship between patient and physician implies a contract whereby each party agrees to perform certain acts intended to achieve the desired results. Informed consent is generally considered essential to this contract. Patients have a right to be fully informed about a proposed plan of treatment so that they can decide whether to go forward with it. In practice, many people tend to rely on their physician's judgment, accepting the diagnosis and going along with the proposed course of treatment. We see our doctor to obtain medication to cure the flu or mend a broken arm, and we give little thought to other possible treatments. By following the doctor's advice, we expect to achieve a speedy recovery. The etiology, or cause, of the disease or injury generally concerns us less than obtaining relief from its symptoms. However, when an illness is serious or life-threatening, a patient's consent to treatment becomes more significant. Several treatment plans may be presented, each with its own set of potential risks and benefits, and it may be uncertain which treatment promises the best results or fewer potential side effects.

Principles of Informed Consent

Informed consent is based on three legal principles: First, the patient must be *competent* to give consent. Second, consent must be given *freely*. Third, consent must be based on an *adequate understanding* of the proposed treatment, including any potential risks. Although the phrase "informed consent" did not achieve legal definition until 1957, the antecedents of informed consent go back hundreds of years to English common law. The President's Commission for the Study of Ethical Problems in Medicine remarked that "the legal doctrine of informed consent imposes on physicians two general duties: to disclose information about treatment to patients and to obtain their consent before proceeding with treatment."[7]

Informed consent ideally occurs within a context of shared decision making based on mutual respect.[8] Because people differ in their attitudes toward autonomy in medical care, the process of obtaining informed consent must be flexible. Some studies indicate that patients are more interested in being *informed* than in being fully involved in *decision making;* this seems to occur most often when the decision involves a serious health risk.[9]

Most physicians believe they have a duty to truthfully inform patients about a life-threatening condition, but this has not always been the case. A study in 1961 found that most doctors had a strong and general tendency to *withhold* information.[10] None of the doctors surveyed at that time reported a policy of telling every patient about a life-threatening diagnosis. Only about 12 percent said they would usually inform patients about a diagnosis of incurable cancer. Even when patients were informed, the disease was often described euphemistically. Doctors might tell the patient that he or she had a "lesion" or a "mass." Some doctors were more precise, using a description such as "growth," "tumor," or "hyperplastic tissue." In many instances, the description was phrased to suggest that the cancer was benign, and adjectives were used to temper the impact of the diagnosis. Thus, a tumor was said to be "suspicious" or "degenerated." Such descriptions allowed physicians to give a general explanation about the medical situation while eliciting the patient's cooperation in the proposed course of treatment.

By the late 1970s, the climate of truth telling had changed significantly. A study done in 1977 found an almost complete reversal of attitudes, with about 97 percent of the doctors surveyed reporting that they would usually tell patients the truth about a diagnosis.[11] In a follow-up study, however, doctors reported that they were willing to engage in some deception when situations involved complicated or very sensitive ethical issues.[12] Researchers said that

[handwritten margin note: MDs withholding medical information was the norm in the 20th]

© Burton Steele, *Times-Picayune*

Informed consent is a fundamental ethical principle in medicine. Even fairly routine procedures, such as mending a small fracture, may become complicated when the patient is leukemic, as is this child: Alternatives must be weighed more carefully before a course of treatment is chosen.

physicians "appear to justify their decisions in terms of the consequences and to place a higher value on their patients' welfare and keeping patients' confidences than truth telling for its own sake." Offering information about *prognosis*—the expected course of the disease—can be especially problematic. It is often very difficult to predict life expectancy or how a disease will run its course in a particular patient. Statistics about the usual course of a disease can provide a rough idea of the odds of survival, and a doctor's clinical experience may be a guide. Still, because of uncertainty, "Some doctors prefer to offer hope by describing remarkable recoveries without also mentioning the high likelihood that most people who have such a condition will die."[13]

Informed consent can be especially important when medical care is provided by a team of specialists whose responsibilities are defined less by patients' needs than by particular diseases or organ systems. In some cases, it may seem as if no doctor has responsibility for the overall care of the patient. The patient may not be sure who to ask for information and advice. Situations like this can be a threat to the patient's well-being.

To the extent that a course of treatment is elective, the outcome uncertain, and the procedure experimental, informed consent becomes correspondingly more important. For example, drawing a blood sample is a common procedure that entails little risk to the patient. Consequently, we do not expect to receive a detailed explanation of risks when we roll up our sleeve for the insertion of the needle. However, a complicated surgical procedure, one that involves a nearly equal proportion of risks and benefits, makes a patient's informed consent crucial.

A gray area involving informed consent is the use of *placebos* in medical practice. A placebo is defined as "an inert substance given as a medicine for its suggestive effect."[14] Placebos are commonly used in testing new drugs to provide an evaluation by comparison, and such use is not normally questioned. In contrast, when doctors prescribe placebos in routine medical care, it raises questions about deceiving patients, even if the aim is worthy. Typically, placebos are prescribed when no organic cause for an ailment is found, and it is believed that the placebo will have a beneficial psychological effect. Some authorities estimate that perhaps one-third of all prescriptions are essentially placebos. "Those physicians who use placebos argue that the end, curing the patient, takes precedence over the means: in this case, the deception of the patient."[15]

Preferences Regarding Informed Consent

What constitutes sufficient information on which the patient can base a decision? Some patients take an active role in their treatment, even proposing methods of treatment to their physician. Others prefer to follow the treatment plan suggested by their doctor; they really don't want to know about potential risks or the percentage of failures. Full disclosure is a help to some patients, a hindrance to others. Such variation among patient attitudes presents a dilemma for the medical practitioner.

Additionally, members of a patient's family may have an agenda of their own that complicates issues of informed consent and medical decision making. Margot White and John Fletcher describe a case in which the spouse of a dying patient told doctors, "You can't tell my husband he's dying; it will kill him."[16] She insisted that the truth of her husband's illness be withheld from him, refusing the doctors' requests to speak with him about his condition and preferences for treatment. From the wife's point of view, she knew her husband better than anyone—certainly better than the doctors—and she knew what was best for him. For the staff, however, her "interference" created concerns about whether the patient's autonomy was being compromised. It is sometimes difficult to find solutions that satisfy all concerned parties.

Informed consent is closely tied to the quality of communication between physician and patient. A study to assess communication between physicians and seriously ill patients at the end of life found disturbing shortcomings.[17] (The study, known by its acronym, SUPPORT, was conducted as a multicenter "Study to Understand Prognoses and Preferences for Outcomes and Risks of Treatment.") Less than half of the physicians were aware of their patients' preferences for or against CPR (cardiopulmonary resuscitation). Researchers have found similar results in other studies.[18]

Patients at the end of life may not want disruptive medical interventions, preferring to be allowed to die as peacefully as possible. This preference can be recognized in the medical setting by designating the patient as "DNR" (Do Not Resuscitate), "No Code," or "CMO" (Comfort Measures Only)—all of which are intended to inform medical and nursing staff that the patient does not want attempts made to revive him or her in the event of cardiac or respiratory failure.[19] Unless a physician has written a DNR order, however, hospital policies generally require that CPR be initiated immediately if the patient experiences cardiac arrest or respiratory failure. "Hopitalized patients and their families generally do not realize that they must speak up if they do not want emergency resuscitation attempted."[20]

Even when a physician has entered a DNR order on the patient's chart, it may not contain specific guidance about which treatments should be initiated and which withheld. Does the order not to initiate CPR mean that *other* life-saving medical interventions should be done? Or should *all* such interventions be withheld? If medical heroics are to be avoided, who decides whether a particular intervention is "heroic" or "ordinary" in a given set of circumstances? When a patient's attending physician is not on the scene to determine the appropriate level of treatment, it can put other medical and nursing staff in a quandary about what to do.[21] It is not always straightforward to simply "follow doctor's orders."

The SUPPORT study shows that physicians tend to be unaware of their patients' preferences about resuscitation and that lack of communication may cause DNR orders to be ignored even when they exist. Many physicians have not been trained to move from aggressive to palliative care, nor are they familiar with the principles of care associated with palliative medicine.[22] The momentum in medicine naturally moves toward providing life-sustaining treatment. Thus, a patient's wish to refuse CPR or other life-sustaining interventions at the end of life may be an issue that is simply not on a doctor's "radar screen."

Although forced, coercive treatment is rare, caregivers can—unwittingly or not—exert undue influence on patients by means of subtle or overt manipulation. Once the patient is admitted to a health care institution, cooperation

Nurse: Did they mention anything about a tube through your nose?

Patient: Yes, I'm gonna have a tube in my nose.

Nurse: You're going to have the tube down for a couple of days or longer. It depends. So you're going to be NPO, nothing by mouth, and also you're going to have IV fluid.

Patient: I know. For three or four days, they told me that already. I don't like it, though.

Nurse: You don't have any choice.

Patient: Yes, I don't have any choice, I know.

Nurse: Like it or not, you don't have any choice. (laughter) After you come back, we'll ask you to do a lot of coughing and deep breathing to exercise your lungs.

Patient: Oh, we'll see how I feel.

Nurse: (emphasis) No matter how you feel, you have to do that!

President's Commission for the Study of Ethical Problems
in Medicine and Biomedical and Behavioral Research,
*Making Health Care Decisions: A Report on the Ethical and
Legal Implications of the Patient–Practitioner Relationship*

with caregivers is expected. The tacit communication may be that the patient has no choice. There is a tendency to assume that medical practices are to be faithfully followed as a matter of routine, without considering whether these conventions match the patient's preferences. In the SUPPORT study, for example, it seems that physicians tended to be oblivious to the fact that some patients, nearing the end of their lives, would not want CPR administered. Informed consent requires cooperation between patient and physician in seeking the common goal of optimal, and appropriate, health care.

Choosing Death

Medical advances take place because physicians take seriously the Hippocratic obligation to keep people alive. Named for the ancient Greek physician Hippocrates, the Hippocratic oath has been an enduring guide for the conduct of physicians since the fourth century B.C.E. But practicing this worthy maxim can lead to difficult choices. Advances in biomedical technology present us with new and sometimes confusing choices. Techniques for cardiopulmonary resuscitation (CPR) and artificial respiration allow physicians to intervene in the "normal" dying process. (It should be noted, however, that the portrayal of CPR on television medical shows generally presents a misleading picture of the frequency with which such resuscitation results in "miracles.")[23] Patients who are saved by such techniques may have their cardiac and respiratory functions restored but suffer irreversible damage to the brain. The human organism can be kept functioning despite the cessation of normal heart, brain, respiratory, or kidney function. Does the Hippocratic obligation apply when a person is saved only to be maintained in a hopeless condition? When medical technologies spare patients' lives and enable them to resume more or less normal functioning, the results are gratifying. But the same technologies that prolong life can also prolong dying.

The conventional understanding of the Hippocratic oath acknowledges that in some circumstances medical treatment is futile; that is, it has no reasonable possibility to "cure, ameliorate, improve, or restore a quality of life that would be satisfactory to the patient."[24] With the advent of modern medical technologies, however, the slogan often seems to be "Keep the patient alive at all costs." What is the proper balance between preserving life and preventing suffering when further treatment is likely to be futile? What is the effect of life-sustaining technologies on the *quality* of patients' lives? There is a growing recognition that, for some patients, "the available choices are between dying sooner but remaining comfortable and living slightly longer by receiving aggressive therapy, which may prolong the dying process, increase discomfort and dependence, and decrease the quality of life."[25]

If you were given a prognosis of a short time to live and told that any further treatment toward a cure was useless, would you want aggressive treatment to keep you alive, even if it meant that your vital bodily functions were maintained on life-support systems? The decision to limit treatment, to stop "doing everything that can be done," is often difficult for patients and their families. However, a stance that strives to keep people alive by all means and at any cost is increasingly questioned. Reviewing the range of modern medical technologies, the President's Commission for the Study of Ethical Problems in Medicine concluded, "For almost any life-threatening condition, some intervention is capable of delaying the moment of death. Matters that were once the province of fate have now become a matter of human choice."[26]

Some people argue that individuals have a "right to die" when suffering outweighs the benefits of continued existence. Surrounded by an array of machinery and tubes, the patient may seem less a human person than an objectified extension of medical technology. Patients themselves may "swallow Kleenex to suffocate themselves, or jerk tubes out of their noses or veins, in a cat-and-mouse game of life and death which is neither merciful nor meaningful."[27]

Should futile treatments be withheld or withdrawn, even when this is virtually certain to result in the patient's death? Alternatively, should treatment be continued even when a patient is in a persistent vegetative state (PVS) with no reasonable hope of any improvement? Are there circumstances in which a physician should actively hasten or assist in bringing about a patient's death?

Ethical questions about the "right to die" have become prominent since the landmark case of Karen Ann Quinlan in 1975. On April 15 of that year, at age twenty-one, after a party at a local bar, she was found not breathing in her bed. An ambulance was called, and Karen was admitted to the intensive care unit of a New Jersey hospital. She was in a coma. Soon her breathing was being sustained by a mechanical MA-1 respirator and she received artificial nutrition. When she remained unresponsive over the next several months, her parents asked that the respirator be disconnected so that nature could take its course. But hospital officials responsible for Karen's care denied their request. The request eventually reached the New Jersey Supreme Court, which ruled that artificial respiration could be discontinued.[28] Karen was taken off the respirator and, to the surprise of many, continued to breathe unaided. She was transferred to a nursing care facility, and lived in a persistent vegetative state until her death in June 1985 at age thirty-one, having become a focal point for issues pertaining to "death with dignity."[29]

(The terms "coma" and "persistent vegetative state" can be confusing. A *coma* is a state of profound unconsciousness usually lasting a few days or weeks, although there have been exceptions lasting years. Some patients eventually awaken, some progress to a vegetative state, and others die. "Brain death" is sometimes referred to as an irreversible coma. Of patients who enter a vegetative state [a sort of vegetative coma], some regain a degree of awareness while others remain in a vegetative state, which is described as "awake but unaware." *Persistent vegetative state,* a term coined in 1972, is defined as a wakeful unconscious state that lasts longer than a few weeks after acute brain injury.[30] Because the word "persistent" may suggest irreversibility, the phrase "post coma unresponsiveness" has been suggested as an alternative for PVS. The chance of recovery depends largely on the extent of injury to the brain. An important distinction between coma and PVS is that, in PVS, coma has progressed to a state of wakefulness; eyes may be open and the patient may respond reflexively to painful stimuli, but there is no detectable awareness.)

After Quinlan, both state and federal courts issued rulings concerned with removing life-sustaining treatment, including feeding tubes that supply nutrition and hydration to patients. Particularly noteworthy was the case of Nancy Beth Cruzan, heard before the United States Supreme Court in 1990.[31] As a result of injuries sustained in a car crash in January 1983, at age twenty-five, Nancy was left in a persistent vegetative state. Although she was resuscitated by paramedics, her brain had been deprived of oxygen for so long that she never regained consciousness. For nourishment, Nancy's physicians implanted a feeding tube in her stomach, the only form of life support she was receiving, a treatment that physicians said could prolong her life for as long as thirty years.

In 1987, after waiting for a recovery, Nancy's parents, who had been granted guardianship by the court, requested that the feeding tube be taken out, asserting her right to be free from "unwarranted bodily intrusions." The hospital refused, and the Missouri Supreme Court denied the Cruzans' petition, holding that, without "clear and convincing evidence" of Nancy's consent, her parents could not exercise her right to refuse treatment. Thus, the state's "unqualified" interest in preserving life should prevail.

The state court's decision was appealed to the United States Supreme Court, which ruled that the right to refuse treatment, even if life-sustaining, is constitutionally protected. However, the Court said that states are justified in requiring that only the patient herself or himself can make a decision to refuse treatment. Because Nancy apparently had not made a clear expression of her wishes prior to her injury and ensuing unconscious state, Missouri was not bound to honor her parents' request.

A few months later, however, in light of testimony from several of Nancy's friends that she had expressed her wish "not to live like a vegetable," a Missouri state court ruled that the standard of "clear and convincing" evidence of Nancy's wishes had been met, and permission was given for removing the feeding tube. Thirteen days later, in December of 1990, Nancy Cruzan died. In a statement to the press, her family said: "She showed no sign of discomfort or distress in any way. . . . There remains no question that we made the choice she would want."

The next case to capture public attention was that of Terri Schiavo, who collapsed in her home in February 1990, experiencing a cardiac arrest, which led to a diagnosis of PVS. In 1998, Michael Schiavo, her husband and guardian, petitioned a Florida court to remove her feeding tube, a move opposed by Terri's parents, who argued that she was conscious. From 1998 to 2003, there ensued a struggle in the courts to determine if life support should be withdrawn, a struggle compounded by the fact that Terri had not completed an advance directive, although the court found evidence that she would not want to be kept alive on a machine.

Terri's parents, however, argued that Terri was not in a PVS and, instead, was in a "minimally conscious state," saying that her actions showed response to external stimuli, not merely reflex behavior. This led to more court hearings to determine whether new therapies could help Terri restore cognitive function. By this time, the case was being played out in the media. Terri's feeding tube was removed and, within a week, the Florida legislature passed "Terri's Law," which gave Governor Jeb Bush authority to intervene on behalf of the parents and order reinsertion of the tube. A flurry of court hearings ensued and, in 2004, Terri's Law was overturned by the Florida Supreme Court.

A time and date for removal of the feeding tube was again set by the court, a ruling that sparked an upsurge of federal involvement in the case. Terri Schiavo was subpoenaed to testify at a congressional "field hearing" at Woodside Hospice, and President Bush signed a bill that transferred jurisdiction to the federal courts. (Critics pointed out that never before had Congress used its subpoena power to obtain testimony from someone in a persistent vegetative state.[32]) Within days, appeals were denied and the U.S. Supreme Court declined to grant judicial review, thus ending the legal options of Terri's parents.

The feeding tube was removed and, on March 31, 2005, Terri died. The subsequent autopsy revealed extensive brain damage, with Terri's brain only half the weight expected for a woman of her age, height, and weight. The report said the damage was "irreversible." However, because vegetative state is a clinical diagnosis made by observation at the bedside, an autopsy is not the tool to finally prove or disprove it, and so death was certified as

You know something? At this point, the opinions don't matter anymore. All that matters is whether people learned anything from *Schiavo*. Actually, let me set the bar a little higher. What matters is whether people learned anything that will make their life, or that of their loved ones, better. If the only legacy of *Schiavo* is bitterness that whichever side you're on didn't win, then Terri's loss is more tragic than I could have possibly imagined.

It's relatively easy to say that one lesson has to do with end-of-life directives, living wills, durable powers of attorney for health care—they go by many names, and each one means something a bit different. If you don't have one, and if everyone you know over the age of seventeen doesn't have one, you didn't learn much from *Schiavo*. Our ugliest battles were fought because Terri hadn't expressed her wishes in writing. Had she done so, odds are you wouldn't know her name.

Michael Schiavo, with Michael Hirsh, *Terri: The Truth*

"undetermined." William Colby, an attorney for the Cruzan family, said that "the hard questions raised by a case like Terri Schiavo's are blindingly new for humankind."[33]

As with Nancy Cruzan, Terri Schiavo brought attention to how important advance directives can be. The uniqueness of the case may lie, first of all, in the degree of public and political involvement it generated and, second, in bringing attention to the concept of a "minimally conscious state" (MCS), a condition considered distinct from either coma or vegetative state.[34] Although the evidence seems to show that Terri was in a persistent vegetative state, her parents argued that she was in a minimally conscious state. In this state, the patient shows deliberate behavior that clinicians determine goes beyond unconscious, reflexive responses, although it is inconsistent and erratic. It is common for family members to interpret small signs and movements as indicators of awareness or consciousness.

About the minimally conscious state, neurologist Ronald E. Cranford says, this may be "the era of patients who are substantially neurologically impaired but conscious to a variable degree."[35] For the present, it is perhaps not surprising that terms such as "permanent vegetative" and "minimally conscious" generate some degree of confusion among the public.

Withholding or Withdrawing Treatment

The right of a competent patient to refuse unwanted treatment is generally established in both law and medical practice. This can mean either withholding (not starting) a treatment or withdrawing (stopping) a treatment once it has been started. The consensus is that there is no medical or ethical distinction between withholding and withdrawing treatment. The choice to forgo life-sustaining treatment involves refusing treatments that would be expected to extend life. Such treatments include cardiopulmonary resuscitation (CPR), advanced cardiac life support, renal dialysis, nutritional support and

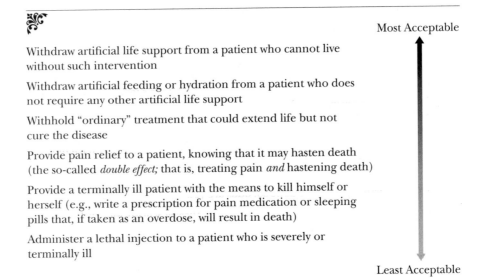

Figure *6-1* *Public Acceptance of Hastening Death*
Note: Involuntary euthanasia occurs when someone acts arbitrarily, without the patient's consent, to end the patient's life.

hydration, mechanical ventilation, organ transplantation and other surgery, pacemakers, chemotherapy, and antibiotics. Even when a patient decides not to receive life-sustaining treatments, ordinarily he or she continues to receive supportive medical care. The right to refuse treatment remains constitutionally protected even when a patient is unable to communicate. Although specific requirements vary, all of the states authorize some type of written advance directive to honor decisions of individuals unable to speak for themselves, but who have previously recorded their wishes in an appropriate legal document.

The distinction between "allowing to die" (withholding or withdrawing treatment) and "helping to die" (taking steps to cause a patient's death) is important in discussions about whether patients have a right to die, with many ethicists and physicians (as well as the general public) willing to permit the former but not the latter (see Figure 6-1). As you look at this figure, consider your own attitudes about the choices that hasten death.

Physician-Assisted Suicide

Assisted suicide refers to providing someone with the means to commit suicide, knowing that the recipient intends to use them to end his or her life. In *physician-assisted suicide (PAS)*, a physician intentionally helps a patient hasten his or her death by providing lethal drugs, offering advice on methods of suicide, or assisting with other interventions—at the patient's explicit request—with the understanding that the patient plans to use them to end his or her life.[36] The patient, not the doctor, administers the fatal dose or takes the action that causes his or her death.

Publicity surrounding the cases of physician-assisted suicide (PAS) conducted by Michigan pathologist Jack Kevorkian brought issues concerning intentionally hastened deaths of patients to widespread media and public attention. At the time of his sentencing in 1999 for the second-degree murder of Thomas Youk, Dr. Kevorkian had provided aid-in-dying to more than 100 individuals since he began his active crusade to legalize physician-assisted suicide in 1990.

In 1997, the U.S. Supreme Court reviewed two cases relating to physician-assisted suicide.[37] The decisions in these cases (*Washington v. Glucksberg* and *Vacco v. Quill*) are important for several reasons. First, the Court upheld the distinction between, on the one hand, withholding or withdrawing treatment and, on the other hand, physician-assisted suicide. In doing so, the Court clarified its ruling in the Cruzan case, noting that the right to *refuse treatment* is based on the right to maintain one's bodily integrity, not on a right to *hasten death*. When treatment is withheld or withdrawn, the Court said, the intent is to honor the patient's wishes, not cause death, unlike PAS, whereby the patient is "killed" by the lethal medication. Second, the Court affirmed the rights of states to craft policy concerning physician-assisted suicide, prohibiting it, as most states now do, or permitting it under some regulatory system, as is now happening in Oregon.

Oregon is currently the only state where PAS is permitted. The Death with Dignity Act (DWDA), a ballot initiative, was passed by Oregon voters in 1994 and, after surviving judicial challenges, was reaffirmed in 1997. The Oregon Death with Dignity Act allows physicians to prescribe lethal medication to terminally ill patients.[38] Doctors who are opposed to aid-in-dying can refuse to participate, and the provisions of the law are available only to individuals who are legal residents of Oregon. In March 1998, an elderly woman with breast cancer became the first known person to die under the law, taking a lethal dose of barbiturates prescribed by her doctor. During 2006, 65 prescriptions for lethal medications under the provisions of the DWDA were written; of these, 35 patients took the medications, 19 died of their underlying disease, and 11 were alive at the end of the year.[39] Since 1997, a total of 292 patients have died with the assistance of their physicians under the terms of the DWDA. The decision to request a prescription for lethal medication was associated mainly with patients' concerns about loss of autonomy and control. Specific concerns included their decreasing ability to participate in activities that make life enjoyable, losing control of bodily functions, and physical suffering.

A third finding of importance in the Supreme Court's 1997 rulings about physician-assisted suicide relates to the concept of *double effect* in the medical management of pain. The doctrine of double effect states that a harmful effect of treatment, even if it results in death, is permissible if the harm is not intended and occurs as a side effect of a beneficial action.[40] Sometimes the

Daymond J. Hartley, *Detroit Free Press*

Seen here testifying in a Michigan courtroom, Dr. Jack Kevorkian became a symbol of the public debate about ethical and legal issues surrounding physician-assisted suicide. After reportedly assisting in the deaths of at least 130 people over a period of nearly ten years, Kevorkian was found guilty of giving a man a lethal injection and sentenced to prison. The legal system touches on many aspects of dying and death, from advance directives and death certification to the making of wills and settling of estates.

dosages of medication needed to relieve a patient's pain (especially at the end-stage of some diseases) must be increased to levels that can cause respiratory depression, resulting in the patient's death, a practice sometimes termed "terminal sedation."[41] Thus, the relief of suffering (the intended good effect) may have a potential bad effect, which is foreseen but not the primary intention. The Court said that such medication for pain, even if it hastens death, is not physician-assisted suicide if the intent is to relieve pain.

In commenting on the 1997 U.S. Supreme Court decisions, Chief Justice William Rehnquist said, "Throughout the nation, Americans are engaged in an earnest and profound debate about the morality, legality, and practicality of physician-assisted suicide. Our [decision] permits this debate to continue, as it should in a democratic society."[42]

Ira Byock, a hospice and palliative care physician, welcomed the Supreme Court's decision but expressed concern that "the legalization of physician-assisted suicide is a particularly dangerous proposition unless fundamental changes are made in the care of the dying."[43] He emphasized the need for physicians and other caregivers to become more competent in pain management and other aspects of palliative medicine. Others—including John Pridonoff, former executive director of the Hemlock Society, which advocates assisted suicide and the "right to die"—believe that hospice care and aid-in-dying are not necessarily incompatible, that they can be complementary aspects of a comprehensive approach to end-of-life decisions.[44]

Although the trend has been toward greater freedom for individuals to choose when and how they will die, physician-assisted suicide continues to spark debate. In 2001, U.S. Attorney General John Ashcroft issued a directive stating that "prescribing, dispensing, or administering federally controlled substances to assist suicide violates the Controlled Substances Act." This interpretation authorized the Drug Enforcement Agency (DEA) to pursue criminal prosecution of Oregon physicians who write prescriptions under that state's Death with Dignity Act. Various court cases ensued and, in January 2006, the U.S. Supreme Court ruled in *Gonzales v. Oregon* that the attorney general (then Alberto Gonzales) was not empowered to prohibit doctors from prescribing drugs under Oregon's laws.

Euthanasia

In contrast to withdrawing or withholding treatment, assisted suicide and euthanasia refer to practices that intentionally hasten the death of a person. Although some ethicists argue that a right to euthanasia is found in the same constitutional basis as the right to refuse treatment, this argument has not been accepted by the U.S. Supreme Court nor by most health care practitioners.[45] Arthur Berger says, "Choosing to die naturally is one thing [but] asking the assistance of others to terminate a life is quite another."[46] Nevertheless, there seems to be increasing acceptance of the stance that it is ethically permissible for physicians to assist their patients in choosing death.[47]

When a treatment that could sustain life is withheld or withdrawn, some people have called this practice *passive euthanasia*, although this term is considered a misnomer because it tends to confuse the widely accepted practice of withholding or withdrawing treatment with the generally unacceptable and unlawful practice of taking active steps to cause death. It can be argued that "passive euthanasia" is not euthanasia at all but, rather, letting nature take its course.

Euthanasia involves a deliberate act to end another person's life. It is generally understood as the intentional act of killing someone who would otherwise suffer from an incurable and painful disease. An example is the case of "Debbie," a twenty-year-old woman with terminal ovarian cancer whose death

"Before we try assisted suicide, Mrs. Rose, let's give the aspirin a chance."

was hastened by a physician called to her bedside in the middle of the night, having previously not known the patient. Seeing her distressful condition and hearing her say, "Let's get this over with," he decided without further discussion to "give her rest" by preparing a fatal injection.[48] Were Debbie's words meant as a request for the physician's help in her dying? The circumstances in this case are ambiguous.

Euthanasia can be involuntary, nonvoluntary, or voluntary. *Involuntary* euthanasia refers to the death of a patient by a medical practitioner *without* the patient's consent. The most notorious example of this is the medicalized killing done by the Nazi regime. *Nonvoluntary* euthanasia occurs when a surrogate decision maker (not the patient himself or herself) asks a physician for assistance to end another person's life. This could occur, for instance, when a family member assumes life-or-death decisions for an ailing relative.

Voluntary euthanasia is the intentional termination of a patient's life at his or her request by someone other than the patient. In practice, this usually means that a competent patient requests direct assistance to die, and he or she receives assistance from a qualified medical practitioner.

At present, euthanasia has found greatest acceptance in the Netherlands, where physicians are legally permitted to give lethal injections to patients who request death.[49] The guidelines include the presence of a terminal diagnosis, the patient's unwavering desire to die, suffering that the patient finds unbearable, and a second medical opinion. Euthanasia is unlawful in the United States. Taking active steps to end someone's life is a crime—even if the motive for doing so results from good intentions as an act of mercy.

Palliative Care and the Right to Die

Decisions about hastening death are regularly arrived at on the basis of the pain and suffering experienced by the patient or perceived by caregivers and family members. In thinking about our options, we need to recognize that a "one size fits all" approach to medical treatment and decision making is likely to fit relatively few. Our preferences about these matters are influenced by both our individual beliefs and the cultural or ethnic traditions that help define who we are as human beings.

David Roy, director of the Center for Bioethics in Montreal and editor of the *Journal of Palliative Care,* argues that the distinction between allowing to die and active euthanasia should be maintained: "This distinction is a recognition of the limits of modern medicine's power, and of the limits of the medical profession's mandate; a recognition also that horrible and intolerable abuse is as much a possibility for us today as it has already proved to be a reality in the past."[50] The challenge, Roy says, is not to legalize euthanasia, but to transform care of the dying. Dame Cicely Saunders, founder of St. Christopher's Hospice (discussed in Chapter 5), says:

> We certainly cannot be complacent as we look at the pressures in hospital wards and nursing care facilities, the lack of community support for many in their own homes, and the frequently indifferent or negative attitudes toward the increasing number of elderly people. But surely this is the very climate in which euthanasia would not remain voluntary for long! Is there a society that will not exert pressure, however subtle, on the dependent to believe they are merely burdens with the responsibility to opt out or for exhausted care providers to beg or to act for their joint release?[51]

Proponents of euthanasia argue that it is morally permissible when it prevents an even greater cruelty— namely, preventing a person who is in unremitting pain or suffering from obtaining the release offered by death. Critics respond that, if euthanasia becomes a routine policy, it is likely to create significant ethical problems. How will physicians and others make sure that a patient has given his or her clear consent to a hastened death? What about the risk of an erroneous diagnosis? Objections to euthanasia also take the form of the "wedge" or "slippery slope" argument: One should not permit acts that, even if moral in themselves, would pave the way for subsequent acts that would be immoral. If euthanasia is permitted for people with incurable illness, it could be expanded to the aged, the mentally incompetent, the severely handicapped, or other "burdens on society," with the result that such acts become motivated by caprice or whim—or darker motives.

Charles Dougherty argues that questions about taking steps to intentionally hasten death should be placed within the context of society's "common good."[52] Excessive emphasis on individual choice can cause us to lose sight of the fact that no aspect of human experience is wholly personal and private. In fact, says Dougherty, "The way we die—when, under what circumstances, and from what cause or reason—is shaped in profound ways by relationships with others and by large social and institutional forces." If dying in the medical setting is accurately characterized as involving pain and suffering, and costs too much, the common good of society could be served best by taking measures that "add simplicity and dignity to the process of dying and contain unnecessary spending." Dougherty suggests that practical steps toward realizing this common good include

1. Increasing the use of home hospice care
2. Developing strategies for more aggressive pain management
3. Refining protocols for timely diagnosis of terminal illness
4. Making the right to refuse extraordinary care universally available to patients
5. Expanding the use of DNR orders to avoid prolonged, expensive, and unnecessary care at the end of life
6. Providing universal access to an appropriate combination of care options (home, hospice, and so on)
7. Instituting a health insurance system that ensures adequate and appropriate care for everyone

Nutrition and Hydration

The right of a competent patient to refuse unwanted treatment is generally established in both law and medicine. But should an exception be made for artificial nutrition and hydration? Answering this question requires examining the distinction between ordinary and extraordinary care. *Ordinary care* is generally defined as the use of conventional, proven therapies. In contrast, *extraordinary measures* usually involve some kind of life-sustaining intervention. Such measures are usually done as a temporary measure until the patient's own restorative powers allow the resumption of normal biological functioning.

Of course, therapies that are usually considered "ordinary" may be "extraordinary," or even intrusive, depending on the circumstances. Using antibiotics to treat pneumonia, a practice that generally fits into the category of ordinary care, may be viewed as extraordinary when such drugs are administered to a person who is actively dying. The distinction between ordinary and extraordinary therapies also becomes blurred in situations where a series of medical interventions, each one in itself "ordinary," combine in such a way

© Carol A. Foote

Assistance in providing nutrition to chronically ill and dying patients ranges from help with eating, as seen here in the case of these nursing home residents, to total reliance on artificial feeding. The issue of artificially providing nutrition to comatose, hopelessly ill patients is one of the newest ethical issues in medicine.

that the net result is an "extraordinary" effort to sustain life. Although some medical ethicists argue that a clear dividing line is needed between ordinary and extraordinary treatment, Thomas Attig makes the point that, in reality, it is likely that "a definitive rule dividing ordinary and extraordinary treatment will forever elude us."[53]

Removing artificial nutrition and hydration tends to evoke deep-rooted human feelings about the provision of food and drink, as well as the image of "starving" a person to death. This causes some people to believe that removal of artificial nutrition and hydration is really "intentional killing." The symbolic significance of nourishment seems to justify the continuation of artificial feeding even when all other medical treatments have been stopped.

Those who disagree with this view say that our normal, everyday sentiments about the symbolic meaning of food and water "cannot be transferred without distortion to the hospital world" and that, indeed, "authentic sentiment may demand discontinuance of artificial feeding."[54] Because we think of nourishment as ordinary care, withholding it brings up images of causing the patient's death by starvation. But these images may be inaccurate for several reasons. First, the invasive nature of delivering such nourishment, and the skills required to administer it, argue against the perception that artificial nourishment is merely providing simple care. Second, artificial nourishment causes discomfort to many patients, especially those who are close to dying. Feeding tubes and intravenous lines may actually add to a patient's suffering

[handwritten margin note: Symbolic meaning of food + water]

at the end of life. Acknowledging that issues around providing nourishment are highly charged emotionally, Dena Davis says, "We need to be very careful to sort out the physiological aspects of providing nutrition from the social phenomenon of 'feeding.'"[55] When a person is actively dying, the removal of artificial nutrition and hydration can be good palliative care.

Seriously Ill Newborns

In hospitals with specialized neonatal intensive care units (NICUs), newborns who are born prematurely or with serious medical problems are saved routinely. Unfortunately, some babies whose lives are saved will never be capable of living what most people consider a normal life. These infants suffer from cardiopulmonary ailments, brain damage, or other serious congenital defects or dysfunction. In the past, such conditions would have quickly resulted in death. Now, because of specialized neonatal care, babies born with life-threatening conditions often survive. Ethical issues that focus on the dilemma of whether to sustain life or to allow death are perhaps most sensitively realized in the case of seriously ill newborns.

These medical miracles raise questions. Should the infant's probable quality of life be considered? Is medical intervention the course of action to take in every case? For example, should a newborn with an intestinal blockage be spared by surgical intervention? Is the answer always "Yes, life should be saved," or does the answer change according to circumstances? Is the answer the same if the infant with intestinal blockage is also severely brain-damaged?

Consider the following case: An infant was born with his entire left side malformed, with no left eye and very little of a left ear; his left hand was deformed, and some of his vertebrae were not fused. Also afflicted with a tracheo-esophageal fistula (an abnormality of the windpipe and the canal that leads to the stomach), he could not be fed by mouth. Air leaked into his stomach instead of going to the lungs, and fluid from the stomach pushed up into the lungs. One doctor commented, "It takes little imagination to think there were further internal difficulties as well." In the ensuing days, the infant's condition steadily worsened. Pneumonia set in; his reflexes became impaired; and, because of poor circulation, severe brain damage was suspected. Despite the seriousness of all these factors, the immediate threat to his survival, the tracheo-esophageal fistula, could be corrected by a fairly easy surgical procedure. The debate began when the parents refused to give their consent to surgery. Some of the doctors treating the child believed that surgery was warranted and took the case to court. The judge ruled against the parents and ordered the surgery, declaring that "at the moment of live birth, there exists a human being entitled to the fullest protection of the law."[56]

In another case, which contrasts with the one just described, the mother of a premature baby overheard the doctor describing her infant as having Down's syndrome, with the added complication that the intestines were blocked. This kind of blockage can be corrected by ordinary surgery; without correction, the child could not be fed and would die. The mother felt that "it would be unfair" to her other children if a retarded child were brought into the home. Her husband supported this decision, and they refused their consent for surgery. One physician argued that the degree of mental retardation in children with Down's syndrome cannot be predicted; and, in the physician's words: "They're almost always trainable. They can hold simple jobs, and they're famous for being happy children. When further complications do not appear, a long life can be anticipated." In this case, however, the hospital staff did not seek a court order to override the parents' decision against surgical intervention. As a result, the child was placed in a side room and, over the following eleven days, starved to death.

Think about the differences between these two cases. In the first case, the severely malformed infant seemed to have less chance of survival or of living a normal life than the afflicted infant in the second example. Yet the hospital staff in the first case chose to seek a court order granting surgery, whereas the staff at the second hospital chose to abide by the parents' wishes, even though the child could probably have been saved. In the second case, did the physicians and the parents adequately explore the child's right to life? From the doctors' point of view, once the decision was made not to proceed with the operation, the child became terminal, and further means of sustaining life were therefore unwarranted. It could be argued, however, that the withholding of ordinary means of treatment (that is, surgery) was in fact an *extraordinary* nonintervention.

Whatever our feelings about the decisions described, a distinction between ethical issues involving infants and those involving adults should be noted. Generally, in the latter case, all procedures that might prolong life have been tried, or at least presented to the patient. In cases involving newborns, the question of whether to treat or withhold treatment cannot be discussed with the patient; thus, the decision is made by others, who will, it is hoped, act in the child's best interest. The tough part, of course, is defining "the child's best interest."[57]

The hard choices inherent in making decisions about the treatment of seriously ill newborns were highlighted in the study by the President's Commission for the Study of Ethical Problems in Medicine. While affirming that parents should have the power of decision making in most cases, the Commission also stated that medical institutions should pursue the best interests of an infant "when those interests are clear."[58] Using the example of an otherwise healthy Down's syndrome child whose life is threatened by a surgically correctable condition, the Commission said that such an infant should receive surgery. While stating that therapies expected to be futile need not be provided, the Commission added that, even in cases when no beneficial therapy is available, actions should be taken to ensure the infant's comfort.

Advance Directives

In a general sense, an *advance directive* is any statement made by a competent person about choices for medical treatment should he or she become unable to make such decisions or communicate them at some time in the future.[59]

Editor: If the governor signs the bill currently before him, this will become the first state to legalize suicide.

I believe this measure is immoral, bizarre, and tainted with Mephistophelian connotations.

Legislators, at all levels, should legislate laws pertaining only to life, as we know it. Death, in any manner, is nature's absolute domain, and no one should attempt to trespass on that domain.

I trust the governor is wise enough and sane enough to veto the bill presently lying heavily and cadaverously on his desk.

Editor: We have explored this bill and its implications in death and fully support the right of an individual, who wishes to do so, to be allowed to make a legally recognized written directive requesting withdrawal of life-support systems when these procedures would serve no purpose except to artificially delay the moment of death.

We reiterate our belief in the basic human right of an individual to control his destiny. We have communicated our support of this bill to the legislature and to the governor.

Editor: This bill, and all other natural-death or death-with-dignity bills, is based on a faulty premise. For when we react to tubes, oxygen and other paraphernalia, our concern is with daintiness, not dignity.

Dignity is the quality of mind having to do with worth, nobility, and forbearance. The dying, with the help of the living, can have dignity—no matter what functions of control are lost.

Instead of unplugging and abandoning our dying patients, we should work to achieve truly compassionate care for them in hospices like those in London, England, and New Haven, Connecticut.

Editor: No physician is required by law to use extraordinary means of preserving life, and none has ever been convicted for failing to do so.

So the real purpose of death-with-dignity or natural-death bills must be to set the stage for letting doctors take positive action: giving lethal injections or denying ordinary means of care to patients who may be handicapped or burdensome to society.

We must be suspicious of any trend which offers death as a solution to problems, no matter how heart-rending those problems may be.

Editor: The bill allowing an adult of sound mind to refuse extraordinary life-preservation measures reaffirms for me the value of life. Life is active choosing toward greater fulfillment and reduced suffering, not the beating of a heart in a pain-wracked and hopeless body. This bill is a public and legal recognition of that principle.

Figure *6-2* *Letters to the Editor*

Advance directives can be important in medical decision making, but they were quite controversial just a few years ago. Opponents argued that advance directives represented a step toward euthanasia, whereas proponents argued that advance directives could safeguard patients' rights to determine the manner of their care at the end of life (see the letters in Figure 6-2).

One type of advance directive is the *living will,* which enables individuals to provide instructions about the kind of medical care they want if they become incapacitated or otherwise unable to participate in treatment decisions. In 1967, Louis Kutner proposed the living will as a way for patients with terminal illness to document their wishes regarding medical care in the event of incapacitation.[60] Some people believe that living wills are appropriate only for stating a desire to forgo life-sustaining procedures or to avoid medical heroics when death is imminent. In fact, however, a living will can be drafted to express various wishes about treatment and to cover various contingencies.

Questions have been raised about whether living wills are the best choice to accomplish their stated goals. A presidential council on bioethics said, "Living wills make autonomy and self-determination the primary values at a time of life when one is no longer autonomous or self-determining, and when what one needs is loyal and loving care."[61] Another criticism is that, because living wills are not physician orders, they cannot be followed by emergency medical technicians (EMTs). An alternative to the living will, designed to counteract its potential deficiencies, is the Physicians Order for Life-Sustaining Treatments (POLST), which details a patient's wishes and is signed by his or her physician. Unlike the living will, the POLST governs medical issues considered likely to arise in the near term, usually within the year. Developed in Oregon and spreading into other states, the POLST is a two-sided pink form that "spells out directions for resuscitation, medical interventions, antibiotics, and artificial feeding" (current information can be found at POLST.org).

The second important type of advance directive is the *health care proxy* (also known as a durable power of attorney for health care). This document makes it possible to appoint another person, known as a proxy, to represent you in making decisions about medical treatment if you become unable to do so. (This decision maker is also known as a *surrogate.*) He or she may be a family member, close friend, or attorney with whom you have discussed your treatment preferences. As your representative, the proxy you appoint is expected to act in accordance with your wishes as stated in an advance directive or as otherwise made known. A court may take away the proxy's power to make decisions if he or she (1) authorizes any illegal act, (2) acts contrary to the patient's known desires, or (3) where those desires are not known, does anything clearly contrary to the patient's best interests. Completing a health care proxy can be an additional safeguard that preferences about life-sustaining treatment will be followed.

California was the first state to adopt a Natural Death Act, which permitted an individual to sign a declaration expressing his or her wishes for treatment and to appoint a health care proxy. The laws governing advance directives vary somewhat for different states, making it important to be sure you complete the proper forms that apply where you live (current forms for each state can be downloaded from Caring Connections at www.caringinfo.org).

Using Advance Directives

For advance directives to be of value, it is necessary to do more than merely complete the paperwork. Completing an advance directive is one step toward improving the chances that your treatment preferences will be honored if you become incapacitated. But physicians and other medical staff cannot follow advance directives if they don't know about them or if the instructions are too vague to give direction about what should be done. Also, because state laws may differ, if you completed an advance directive in one state and subsequently have moved to another state, you need to find out whether the requirements in your new residence require action on your part. After you have completed an advance directive, review it occasionally to be sure the preferences expressed in the directive continue to match your wishes.

Whether a patient's wishes, as expressed in an advance directive, are followed may depend on the policies of a given health care institution and the circumstances that bring the advance directive into play. Uncertainty about the course of a disease may cause doctors to be wary of deciding that a patient is in a terminal condition. In some cases, an advance directive may be less a directive than a request. Individuals should discuss issues of end-of-life care with their primary doctor and other physicians from whom they receive treatment, as well as with family members, *before* a situation occurs in which the advance directive becomes effective. Although advance directives are an important tool, there are other ways of expressing preferences for medical treatment, including communication between a patient and his or her physician, a letter written by the patient, or documentation of the patient's directives in his or her medical chart. All of these can be employed as methods for conveying advance directives to caregivers.[62]

Because advance directives are designed to become effective when a patient is unable to communicate his or her wishes, and when medical intervention is needed, there is a possibility that the directive might be implemented in a situation the patient had not foreseen.[63] Consider the case of a woman in her seventies who entered a hospital for hip replacement surgery and, along with other admission forms, was given an advance directive to sign. While recovering from surgery, she had an unexpected cardiac arrest. Rather than starting a resuscitation attempt, however, the medical staff assumed that—because she had signed a living will—she wanted no resuscitation and the woman died. Although this woman was not terminally ill, by signing a document providing evidence that she did not want to be kept alive if in a grave medical condition, the power to interpret her wishes was put into the hands of medical staff. Was the outcome what this woman intended?

In 1990, the United States Congress enacted the Patient Self-Determination Act (PSDA).[64] It requires providers of services under the Medicare and Medicaid programs to inform patients of their rights to appoint a health care proxy and draw up written instructions concerning limits to medical care to be activated if they become incapacitated. Health care providers are required to document in the patient's medical record whether the patient has executed an advance directive and ensure compliance with requirements of state law with respect to advance directives. The PSDA has been described as a "medical Miranda warning" (referring to the requirement that police officers advise arrested suspects of their legal rights) due to its requirement that patients be advised of their rights regarding advance directives and life-sustaining treatment.

Although the intent of the Patient Self-Determination Act is to help individuals determine their own medical care, some people are concerned that patients may become unduly alarmed about the state of their health when questioned about whether they have completed an advance directive. The elderly widow who enters a nursing home following the death of her husband may be frightened by what she perceives as a warning that she, too, is about to die, thus adding to the anxiety and depression caused by disruptions in her life. Thus, the PSDA—and matters pertaining to advance directives more generally—should be handled sensitively and with care for the particular patient's situation.

One should not be complacent in thinking that all will necessarily go smoothly so long as an advance directive has been completed and signed. Zelda Foster, a social worker and educator, describes the struggle to ensure that her ninety-three-year-old father's wishes were respected by medical personnel after he was brought to an emergency room and attached to life-support machines.[65] Despite having her father's health care proxy in hand, the staff seemed to be unfamiliar with its purpose and hospital administrators insisted that Foster's family obtain a court order to enforce the proxy's provisions. Ms. Foster noted that "the hospital has created one obstacle after another to challenge our rightful request that our father be allowed to die with dignity." As the Supreme Court made clear in the case of Nancy Beth Cruzan, advance directives offer a means for providing clear and convincing evidence of one's wishes for life-sustaining treatment in critical situations; however, they do not resolve all the difficulties that may accompany end-of-life care.

Advance Directives and Emergency Care

Do-not-resuscitate (DNR) orders are another type of advance directive. Unless given other instructions, hospital staff and emergency personnel will start cardiopulmonary resuscitation (CPR) to help patients whose heart has stopped or who have stopped breathing. As mentioned earlier in the chapter, a DNR is a directive that you don't want to be resuscitated. In the hospital, a DNR order is put in your medical chart by your doctor. But what about outside the hospital?

Emergency care provided by paramedics, EMTs, and other personnel is considered a boon when it helps save lives, but it may be less welcome when it results in interventions that save the lives of those who would rather die naturally. Once 911 is dialed, it sets in motion a response intended to save life. First-responders are generally not in a position to make decisions about who wants to be saved and who doesn't. In fact, they are legally *required* to initiate CPR unless there is clear evidence that the person has a valid DNR order provided by his or her physician.

Imagine a dying person, at home surrounded by family and close friends, prepared to let nature take its course. When the person begins to experience difficulty breathing, however, some of those watching this passage toward death may have an impulse to *do* something to relieve the apparent suffering. A spontaneous call to 911 can result in the dying person's being resuscitated and being placed on life-support equipment with the result that the last hours or days of life are played out as a crisis. Without preparation, unwanted treatment may be administered to a terminally ill patient.

To prevent this scenario, people who do not want CPR or other life-saving interventions must take steps to ensure that they have a valid DNR order and that it is readily available to emergency personnel who may be called to the scene. Medic-Alert bracelets or wallet cards may be helpful in signaling the fact that a person should not receive CPR. Because situations vary, patients who want to avoid such life-sustaining interventions should prepare and make sure that the necessary documents have been completed and are in place.

Wills and Inheritance

A *will* is a legal instrument expressing a person's intentions and wishes for the disposition of his or her property after death. It is a declaration of how a person's *estate*—that is, money, property, and other possessions—will be distributed to one's heirs and beneficiaries upon that person's death. Conferring a kind of immortality on the *testator* (the person making the will), a will can be thought of as the deceased's last words. During the life of the testator, a will can be changed, replaced, or revoked. Upon the testator's death, it becomes a legal instrument that governs the distribution of his or her estate. (A glossary of terms relating to wills and inheritance is provided in Table 6-1.)

A will can evoke powerful emotions, embodying as it does the testator's feelings and intentions toward his or her survivors, possibly affecting the intensity or course of grief.[66] People usually think of the will as simply a tool for estate planning, perhaps overlooking its comforting, and possibly therapeutic, effects for both the testator and his or her survivors.

Terminally ill patients and their families often turn to counselors and other mental health professionals to help explore their fears, uncertainties, and conflicts, as well as devise a plan to meet the prospects that lie ahead; an

And in a decade or two when death taps at the door, your estate may be far larger than you now envisage. It may be so already. One tends to think in terms of a few principal segments of one's estate. For purposes of planning, your "estate" includes everything of monetary value: your home and other real estate; all bank and savings accounts; usables including *objets d'art* and hobbies, such as a stamp collection; your carefully planned investment portfolio; life insurance; rights under a pension plan, if you enjoy that umbrella; as well as growing protection from social security. All must be arranged so as to afford maximum benefit to the beneficiaries.

Paul P. Ashley, *You and Your Will*

TABLE   *6-1*   *Terms Related to Wills and Inheritance*

Administrator: A person appointed by the court (in the absence of a will, or if no executor is named in one) to carry out the steps necessary to settling an estate. When an administrator is to be appointed, state law requires the drawing up of a preferential list of candidates. Assuming that the necessary qualifications are met, the order of preference typically begins with the spouse of the deceased and continues successively through the deceased's children, grandchildren, parents, siblings, more distant next of kin, and a public administrator.

Attestation clause: A statement signed by the persons who witness the testator's making of the will.

Codicil: An amendment to a will.

Conditional will: A type of formally executed will that states that certain actions will take place provided that a specified future event occurs. For example, suppose a testator wishes to bequeath money or property to a potential beneficiary who is incapable of self-care but who has a reasonable chance of recovery. With a conditional will, the money or property could be held in trust for that person until the conditions specified in the will (e.g., recovery) have been satisfied. A problem of conditional wills lies in the difficulty of stipulating with exactitude the nature of events and circumstances that might occur in the future.

Executor: A person named by the testator in his or her will to see that the provisions in the will are carried out properly.

Holographic will: A will written entirely by the hand of the person signing it. Some states do not recognize holographic wills as valid, and those that do generally have stringent conditions for such a document to be deemed valid. Not considered a substitute for a formally executed will.

Intestate: The condition of having made no valid will.

Mutual will: A type of formally executed will that contains reciprocal provisions. May be used by husbands and wives who wish to leave everything to the other spouse with no restrictions, although it limits the range of choices that are available when a will is executed individually.

Nuncupative will: A will made orally. Many states do not recognize a nuncupative will, or do so only under extremely limited circumstances. A few states admit an oral will if the person makes it in fear of imminent death or expectation of receiving mortal injuries, and the peril does result in death. A nuncupative will may also be valid when made by a soldier or sailor engaged in military service or by a mariner at sea; in these instances, the individual need not be in immediate peril. Generally, an oral will must be witnessed by at least two persons who attest that the will is indeed a statement of the testator's wishes.

Probate: The process by which an estate is settled and the property distributed. This process generally occupies an average of nine to twelve months, though it may be longer or shorter depending on circumstances and the complexity of the estate.

attorney can be an important part of that team. Estate planning not only optimizes survivors' financial security, but also helps ensure peace of mind, both for the bereaved and for the person who has taken steps to put his or her affairs in order. In addition, by preparing the legal documents, an attorney can help ensure that a person's wishes about organ donation or advance directives for medical care are carried out.

Barton Bernstein outlines three basic legal stages that apply in cases of terminal illness when death follows expected medical probabilities.[67] The *first* stage involves long-range planning, in which the terminally ill person arranges his or her legal and financial affairs for the eventuality of death. During the *second* stage, which occurs shortly before death, the survivors gather pertinent legal papers, obtain sufficient funds to cover immediate expenses, and notify the attorney and insurance representative so that they will be ready to make a smooth transition of the deceased's legal and financial affairs. Also at this time, if the dying person intends to make an organ donation or other anatomical gift (discussed in Chapter 4), the appropriate medical personnel are alerted.

In the *third* stage of legal activity, which follows the death, the will is delivered to an attorney for probate (the process of settling an estate). The effort that went into planning is now rewarded in the survivors' certainty that affairs have not been left to chance. The survivors can confront their loss without the distraction and worry of complex legal and financial entanglements.

Definitions and Elements of Wills

The privilege of determining how one's property will be distributed after death is not available in all societies, nor is it without limitations. In some countries, the government assumes control over the settlement of a person's affairs; in other countries, including the United States, a person has considerable liberty in determining how property will be distributed. Still, depending on the laws of a particular state, enforcing and carrying out the provisions of a will may be constrained by circumstances affecting one's heirs. For example, someone may try to avoid willing anything to his or her spouse, but, if the will is contested, a court may overturn it. State statutes usually stipulate that a surviving spouse cannot be disinherited. Some statutes require that dependent children be provided for in the will. As a rule of thumb, anything that conflicts with ordinary standards of social conduct may be abrogated or made invalid if the will is contested.

The person who makes a will must have the mental capacity to understand the nature of the document and the consequences of signing it. He or she must understand the nature and extent of the property being bequeathed by the will and be able to identify the persons who, by convention, ought to be considered when making a will, whether or not they actually become beneficiaries. Given these conditions, and in the absence of any significant delusions, the testator is said to be of sound mind, capable of executing a legal will. State laws generally specify a minimum age at which a person can make a legal will—usually eighteen, though in several states as young as fourteen—and various other requirements, such as the presence of witnesses and execution of the document in a proper form.

Besides standard clauses, such as a declaration that the document constitutes the person's last will and testament (along with a statement revoking previous wills, if applicable), a will may include information about the property to be distributed, the names of children and other heirs, specific bequests and allocations of property, as well as information concerning the establishment of trusts, the granting of powers to a trustee and/or guardian, other provisions for disposition of property, and payment of taxes, debts, and expenses of administration. Not all these items are necessarily part of every will, nor is a will limited to the items listed here.

In making a will, it is generally advisable to involve close family members, or at least one's spouse, to prevent problems that can arise when actions are taken without the knowledge of those who will be affected. When survivors discover that things are not as expected or customary, it may add to the burden of grief. In loving families, usually everyone has some idea of what is going to happen when the will becomes effective. There may be valid reasons for not disclosing the details of a will. But the *testator* can tell his or her survivors something like, "Call Rick, my attorney; he knows where my will is and can help you in handling my estate." Some experts suggest that there ought to be some kind of governmental or administrative program whereby wills, as well as other important documents such as advance directives, could be registered ahead of time and be readily available when they are needed.

The Formally Executed Will

The *formally executed will* is the conventional document used for specifying a person's wishes for the distribution of his or her estate after death (see Figure 6-3). If carefully prepared, it not only has sufficient clarity of purpose and expression to withstand a court's scrutiny, but also can help ease the burden and stress on survivors.

In making a formally executed will, most people find it beneficial to consult an attorney. A comprehensive review of an estate requires that legal records and other information be gathered. Several meetings may be required to carefully determine the nature of the property and the testator's wishes for its distribution. Once the will's content is determined and its provisions set, the attorney has it prepared and an appointment is made for its formal execution. On that occasion, the will is reviewed, two (or, in some states, three) disinterested persons are brought in to serve as witnesses, and the testator acknowledges that the document accurately reflects his or her wishes and signs it. Although preparation of the will may involve weeks or even months of thoughtful consideration and planning, the actual signing can take less than five minutes.

Amending or Revoking a Will

A will is not cast in stone; it can be changed as the testator's situation changes. A will can be revoked and replaced by an entirely new will, or only certain parts of it can be amended. Amending a will is a means of adding new provisions without having to rewrite it entirely. A testator who, after the will has been executed, acquires valuable property, such as an art collection, might want to make a specific provision for the new property without disturbing other parts of his or her estate plan. A *codicil*, which is executed in much the same manner as a will, accomplishes that objective. All wills should be reviewed periodically to determine if changed circumstances call for revision.

Will of Tomás Antonio Yorba

In the name of the Holy Trinity, Father, Son, and the Holy Ghost, three distinct persons and one true God, Amen.

1st Clause. Know all [men] who may read this my last will and testament: that I—Tomás Antonio Yorba, native born resident of this department of California, legitimate son of Antonio Yorba and Josefa Grijalva—being sick, but, by divine mercy, in the full enjoyment of my reason, memory and understanding, believing, as I firmly do, in all the mysteries of our holy Catholic faith, which faith is natural to me, since I have lived in it from my infancy and I declare that I want to live in it as a faithful Christian and true Catholic, trusting that, for this reason, his divine Majesty will have mercy on me and will pardon all my sins, through the mysteries of our Lord Jesus Christ and the intercession of his most holy mother, who is my protector and benefactress in these my last moments, so that together with my guardian angel, with St. Joseph, my own name's saint, and all the other saints of my devotion and all the other hosts of heaven, they will assist me before the grand tribunal of God, before which all mortals must render account of their actions—make and decree this my last will and testament as follows, in ordinary paper because of lack of stamped paper.

2nd Clause. Firstly, I commend my soul to God who created it, and my body to the earth, from whence it was fashioned, and it is my wish that I be buried in the church of the Mission of San Gabriel in the shroud of our father St. Francis, the funeral to be according to what my executors and heirs consider that I deserve and is befitting.

3rd Clause. Item: In regard to the expense of the funeral and masses, these should be drawn from the fifth of my estate, according to the disposition of my executors, and I leave the residue of this fifth to my son Juan.

4th Clause. I declare that with respect to my debts, my heirs and executors should collect and pay any legal claims that may turn up or be due according to law. Item: I declare to have been married to Doña Vicenta Sepúlveda, legitimate daughter of Don Francisco Sepúlveda and Doña Ramona Sepúlveda, of this neighborhood, by which marriage I had five children named: (1) Juan; (2) Guadalupe, deceased; (3) José Antonio; (4) Josefa; (5) Ramona. The first being 10 years old, the second died at the age of three, the third six years old, the fourth four years old, and the fifth two years old. Item: I declare to have given my wife jewels of some value as a wedding present, but I do not remember how many nor their value; but they must be in her possession, since I gave them to her. Item: According to my reckoning I have about 2,000 head of cattle, 900 ewes and their respective males, three herds of about 100 mares and their stallions, and three donkeys; about 21 tame horses, 7 tame and 12 unbroken mules; and lastly, whatever cattle, horses or mules may turn up with my brand which may not have been legally sold. Item: I declare to have the right—through inheritance from my father—to part of Middle Santa Ana and Lower Santana, known to be of the Yorbas. I have in Middle Santa Ana an adobe house, its roof being part timber and part thatched, consisting of 18 rooms, including the soaphouse. Item: I declare that I have two vineyards with wooden fences which are now planted with bearing vines and some fruit trees; also a section of enclosed land.

(continued)

Figure 6-3 *Historical Will*
Social custom plays a significant part in the making of a will. The will of Don Tomás Antonio Yorba, dating from the period of Mexican rule in California, presents an illuminating contrast to the modern will with its emphasis on the distribution of the testator's property. Although Yorba's estate was among the largest of the time—consisting of a Spanish land grant of 62,000 acres known as the Rancho Santiago de Santa Ana in Southern California—only a small fraction of his will relates to matters affecting the distribution of the estate to his heirs.

5th Clause. I declare that it is my wish to name as executors and guardians of my estate, first, my brother, Don Bernardo Yorba, and second, Don Raimundo Yorba, by joint approval, to whom I give all my vested power, as much as may be necessary, to go in and examine my property for the benefit of my heirs in carrying out this will, and I grant them the power to procure another associate [executor] to expedite its due execution, whom I consider appointed as a matter of course, granting him the same authority as those previously named.

6th Clause. I name as my heirs my children and my wife, in the form and manner indicated by the law, following the necessary inventory.

7th Clause. In this my last will, I annul and void whatever will or wills, codicil or codicils, I may have previously made, so that they may stand nullified with or without judicial process, now and forever, since I definitely desire that the present testamentary disposition be my last will, codicil, and final wish, in the manner and form most legally valid. To this effect I beg Don Vicente Sanchez, Judge of 1st *instancia,* to exercise his authority in probating this will.

To which I, the citizen Vicente Sanchez, 1st constitutional Alcalde and Judge of the 1st *instancia* of the city of Los Angeles, certify; and I affirm that the present testamentary disposition was made in my presence, and that the testator, Don Tomás Antonio Yorba, although ill, finds himself in the full command of his faculties and natural understanding, and, to attest it, I do this before the assistant witnesses—the citizens Ramon Aguilar and Ignacio Coronel—the other instrumental witnesses being the citizens Bautista Mutriel and Mariano Martinez; on the 28th day of the month of January, 1845. The testator did not sign because of physical inability, but Don Juan Bandini signed for him.

Figure 6-3 *(continued)*

When the addition of codicils makes a will unwieldy or potentially confusing, it is time to review the entire will and make a new one. States vary in their requirements for legally revoking a will. Generally, the testator's intent to revoke the will must be demonstrated; the accidental burning of a will, for instance, does not imply revocation. If someone turns up with an earlier will, it may be difficult to prove that it was revoked if a subsequent will does not explicitly say so. When in doubt, seek legal advice.

Probate

The period of *probate* allows time for the deceased's affairs to be resolved, debts and taxes paid, and arrangements made to receive funds that were owed to the deceased.[68] During the course of probate, the validity of the will is proved; an executor or administrator of the estate is appointed; the necessary matters for settling the estate are carried out; and, with the probate court's approval, the decedent's property is distributed to beneficiaries. If the deceased left a valid will, property is distributed in accordance with its terms.

**NOTICE OF DEATH OF
LEE D. WILLIAMS
AND OF PETITION TO
ADMINISTER ESTATE
Case Number: 11111**

To all heirs, beneficiaries, creditors, contingent creditors, and persons who may be otherwise interested in the will or estate of LEE D. WILLIAMS.

A petition has been filed by JANE DOE, in the Superior Court of Santa Cruz County requesting that JANE DOE be appointed as personal representative to administer the estate of the decedent.

A hearing on the petition will be held on March 22, 1982, at 8:30 a.m. in Dept III, located at 701 Ocean Street, Santa Cruz, California 95060.

IF YOU OBJECT to the granting of the petition, you should either appear at the hearing and state your objections or file written objections with the court before the hearing. Your appearance may be in person or by your attorney.

IF YOU ARE A CREDITOR or a contingent creditor of the deceased, you must file your claim with the court or present it to the personal representative appointed by the court within four months from the date of first issuance of letters as provided in section 700 of the California Probate Code. The time for filing claims will not expire prior to four months from the date of the hearing noticed above.

YOU MAY EXAMINE the file kept by the court. If you are a person interested in the estate, you may file a request with the court to receive special notice of the filing of the inventory of estate assets and of the petitions, accounts and reports described in section 1200 of the California Probate Code.

s/ JOHN P. SMITH
Attorney for the Petitioner

JOHN P. SMITH
9999 Pacific Avenue
Santa Cruz, CA 95060
March 7, 9, 14

Figure 6-4 *Newspaper Notice to Creditors*

When a person dies *intestate*—that is, without having left a valid will—property is distributed according to rules set up by the state.

The Duties of the Executor or Administrator

Someone has to be responsible for carrying out all the steps necessary to settling an estate through probate. As the decedent's personal representative, this person may be an *executor* named in the will or an *administrator* appointed by the court. Whereas an executor named by the testator is permitted to act more or less independently in the management of the estate provided that he or she acts prudently, a court-appointed administrator may be required to obtain the court's approval before proceeding with necessary decisions. In either case, executor or administrator, the personal representative generally must meet certain requirements stipulated by the law of the state in which probate occurs.

The personal representative's first duty is to notify interested parties of the death. This is generally accomplished in two ways. First, parties who are likely to be interested in the settlement of the estate are notified of the death by mail and, if they request it, are sent a copy of the will. Second, a legal notification of the death is published in appropriate newspapers (see Figure 6-4). This notice serves three purposes in the probate process: (1) It announces

The clock wound by Elizabeth still ticked, storing in its spring the pressure of her hand.

Life cannot be cut off quickly. One cannot be dead until the things he changed are dead. His effect is the only evidence of his life. While there remains even a plaintive memory a person cannot be cut off, dead. A man's life dies as a commotion in a still pool dies, in little waves, spreading and growing back towards stillness.

John Steinbeck, *To a God Unknown*

that someone is ready to prove the will of the decedent; (2) it acknowledges that someone is petitioning to be appointed by the court to begin probate; and (3) it gives notice of the death to creditors so that outstanding claims against the decedent can be submitted for settlement.

The estate is inventoried, including all personal and real property owned by the decedent. When a surviving spouse is the estate's primary or sole heir, the inventory of personal and household goods can be less meticulous, though items that have significant worth, such as paintings, jewelry, and antiques, are specified. Important papers are gathered, including insurance policies, Social Security and pension information, military service records, and other documents that require review and possibly action.

The executor or administrator is responsible for managing the estate pending its final disbursement to heirs. Tax returns may need to be filed on behalf of the decedent and the estate. An allowance may need to be paid to the deceased's spouse or to minor children for their support during probate. If the decedent was in business or was a stockholder in a corporation, the personal representative must manage a smooth transition that benefits the estate. When a personal representative is not knowledgeable about the law, he or she usually enlists the aid of an attorney to make certain that legal requirements are satisfied.

Finally, an accounting and schedule for distributing the estate's property to the beneficiaries is prepared and submitted for approval by the probate court. Once the court's approval is obtained, the property is distributed and receipts are obtained to certify that the distribution has been made correctly. Assuming that everything has been carried out properly, the court then discharges the personal representative. The estate is settled.

Avoiding Probate

Because probate involves delays and can sometimes be expensive, many people take legal steps to avoid or minimize it. For example, a husband and wife may own their house and other assets in joint tenancy, a form of property ownership that allows a spouse to take full legal possession of the property upon the other's death, without probate. Some approaches to avoiding probate, however, have serious pitfalls, particularly the do-it-yourself approach

> When it comes to divide an estate, the politest men quarrel.
>
> Ralph Waldo Emerson, *Journals* (1863)

taken without obtaining qualified legal counsel. For example, placing a minor's name on a deed may seem like a good way to avoid probate; but, if circumstances change, it can require going into court to request that a legal guardian be appointed to act on the minor's behalf, thus complicating, rather than simplifying, things.

Living trusts can minimize the costs of passing one's estate to heirs, and they can avoid the publicity about an estate that accompanies public proceedings. In fact, they can be a substitute for engaging in the complicated process of making a will and going through probate. In addition, living trusts may be used to avoid or minimize inheritance taxes that would otherwise have to be paid on the value of an estate. Of course, all decisions about wills and probate should be carefully considered and, in most cases, it is prudent to have the advice of an attorney who is well versed in such matters.

Laws of Intestate Succession

Statistics indicate that seven out of ten Americans die without leaving a will. Perhaps the failure to plan ahead by making a will is attributable to the discomfort many people feel about their own mortality. Or perhaps, overwhelmed by busyness, we neglect planning with the questionable excuse that we are not yet at an age when death is statistically probable. Whatever the reason, dying without having made a will can lead to unnecessary hardships for our survivors, even when an estate is modest in size.

Failure to prepare a will may result in a distribution of property that is not compatible with a person's wishes nor best suited to the interests and needs of heirs.

One of the chief reasons for making a will is to ensure that property will be disbursed according to one's wishes. In the absence of a will, property is distributed according to guidelines established in state law. The state generally tries to accomplish what it believes the deceased would have done had he or she actually made a will. Nevertheless, the laws that dictate the disbursement of property, the care of minor children, and all the matters that pertain to settling the estate reflect society's ideas of fair play and justice. Thus, the values of society, rather than the deceased's personal values, determine the outcome.

Although the laws of intestate succession differ among states, some general patterns prevail. In community-property states, for example, all community property goes to the surviving spouse. In separate property or non-community-property states, when there is only one child, an estate is generally divided equally between child and surviving spouse. If there is more than one child,

Burial in a national cemetery, such as the Black Hills National Cemetery in South Dakota, is a benefit made available to veterans who have served in American military forces during wartime. Such cemeteries have been established across the United States. Other death benefits for veterans include a lump-sum payment to help defray burial expenses and, under certain circumstances, direct payments to survivors.

© Albert Lee Strickland

usually one-third of the estate goes to the surviving spouse and the remaining two-thirds is divided equally among the children.

If there is no surviving spouse, property is divided among the lineal descendants (children and grandchildren who are in the decedent's "lineage"); if no lineal descendants, disbursement is made to the deceased's parents; if they are not living, property is likely to be divided among the deceased's surviving siblings; if there are none, the estate may be divided among the deceased's siblings' children. In attempting to settle an estate, the court will make a determined effort to locate surviving heirs. If none can be found, the proceeds from the estate go to the state.

Insurance and Death Benefits

In the United States, the first life insurance company was established in 1759 by the Presbyterian Synod of Philadelphia for its ministers. Although life insurance did not become common until the middle of the nineteenth century, it is now a huge industry. Most American households include at least one member who owns some form of life insurance.[69]

Depending on a person's age and health, life insurance can be a convenient way of leaving a basic estate for our beneficiaries after we die. It may represent a small portion of a large estate or the major portion of a smaller estate. Insurance plans can be designed in a number of ways and to suit many purposes. Some policies are part of a total investment portfolio that can be drawn upon during the insured's lifetime. Other policies provide benefit payments only after the death of the insured.

Life insurance offers some advantages not available with other investments. For example, life insurance benefits payable to a named beneficiary (not the decedent's estate) are not subject to attachment by creditors. Also, unlike assets that must be processed through probate, insurance benefits usually become available immediately following death. These benefits can have important psychological and emotional value, possibly providing relief and a sense of security to a surviving spouse or other dependents in the period soon after death. Knowing that money is available to cover anticipated expenses may help to reduce stress.

A recent development allows terminally ill patients to sell their life insurance policies to "viatical settlement companies" so that they can pay medical bills, travel, or purchase things they want to enjoy before dying. A *viatical settlement* allows a person with terminal illness to sell his or her life insurance policy before death and receive payment for a percentage of its face value. Viatical settlement companies typically pay about 70 percent of the face value of the policy, and the policy is cashed in for its full value after the policyholder's death. For example, on a policy with a face value of $100,000, the settlement company might pay $70,000 to the policyholder. Patients with less than a year to live usually receive a higher percentage of face value than those expected to live longer. When the patient dies and the policy is cashed in, the settlement company pockets the difference between what was paid to the policyholder and the face amount of the policy, less its operating expenses. Some mainstream insurers offer similar options. As with any area of financial planning, it is wise to compare choices.

Many survivors qualify for benefits from programs like Social Security and the Veterans Administration. To obtain current information about such death-benefit programs, call or write the appropriate government agency. A person entitled to benefits under one or more of these programs may not receive them unless a claim is filed. Moreover, delays in filing may result in a loss of benefits. A comprehensive estate plan includes consideration of benefits that accrue from government programs, as well as those related to employee or union pension programs.

When a death results from negligence, other death benefits may be payable to survivors. Such benefits sometimes result from court cases that attempt to place a value on the deceased's life and what the loss represents to his or her survivors. Although settlements of this kind may indeed be helpful to survivors, the monetary amount of a settlement, no matter how large, is poor compensation for the loss of a loved one (see Figure 6-5).

Dealing with the legal and financial issues surrounding dying and death can be a burden when a person is grieving the death of a loved one or coping with the impending death of a family member. Yet, crucial and even irrevocable decisions often must be made at times like these. Preparation can help ease the burden. Although one cannot plan for every contingency, it is possible to become aware of the range of legalities that may impinge on our experiences of death and dying and, acting out of that recognition, take appropriate steps to prepare ourselves for the inevitable eventualities.

Death of a Son

"I'm not happy because I no more my son already. . . . I miss him. Even if I get my money, I no more my loved one, my son. I'm not interested in money. Every day, after work, even if I feel tired, I no miss to go visit my boy. Sometimes I cry. Sometimes I give food [for his grave]. Soda. His favorite—Kentucky Fried Chicken. Sometimes fried saimin. Then I give an orange. Ice cream. . . . One day after the crash, my boy, he come my house in spirit. He tell me, 'Daddy, I miss you. I no more hands. I no more eyes.' Ho, I cry."

Figure 6-5 *Death of a Son*
Jovencio Ruiz of Molokai, responding to a question about a six-figure insurance settlement in the death of his 14-year-old son, Jovencio, Jr., in an air crash.

Inheritance

When I was ten years old, my father died. And at that time, of course, I thought my father was the best and finest man there ever was. And some years later when I was eighteen and I began to mingle in the adult community, I introduced myself to strangers and they would ask me if John Estrada was my father. When I said yes, they would say, "Well, let me shake your hand. He was a fine man and a good friend of mine." And then they would tell me wonderful stories about him. Since that time, I have hoped that when I am gone, some people might meet my children and say to them that I was a good man and a good friend. To me that is a finer inheritance than any material possession.

Fred Estrada

Considering End-of-Life Issues and Decisions

In reviewing the rapidity with which issues and decisions involving the end of life have come to public interest during the past few decades, bioethicist Leon Kass observes that "today the ethics business is booming," with medical schools offering courses in medical ethics, hospitals establishing ethics committees, courts adjudicating ethical conflicts, and blue-ribbon commissions analyzing and pronouncing on ethical issues.[70] Yet, Kass argues, much of this "action" is really just talk—philosophical theorizing and rational analysis—with comparatively little time devoted to "what genuinely moves people to act—their motives and passions." This is not to say that analysis and theorizing are irrelevant, but the "morality of ordinary practice" is where the rubber meets the road. Kass points out that every human encounter is an ethical encounter, an occasion for the practice and cultivation of virtue and respect.

Our choices about end-of-life issues result not only from our personal values, but also from values present within our particular ethnic or cultural group. Different value systems produce different attitudes about the end of life.[71] Concerns about issues pertaining to the end of life affect not just the realm of public policy, but also bear directly, often poignantly, on the lives of individuals and families.

Further Readings

Michael C. Brannigan and Judith A. Boss. *Healthcare Ethics in a Diverse Society.* Boston: McGraw-Hill, 2001.

Arthur L. Caplan, James J. McCartney, and Dominic A. Sisti, eds. *The Case of Terri Schiavo: Ethics at the End of Life.* Amherst, N.Y.: Prometheus , 2006.

Denis Clifford and Cora Jordan. *Plan Your Estate,* 6th ed. Berkeley, Calif.: Nolo Press, 2002.

William H. Colby. *Unplugged: Reclaiming Our Right to Die in America.* New York: Amacom, 2006.

Albert R. Jonsen. *The Birth of Bioethics.* New York: Oxford University Press, 1998.

Robert M. Veatch, ed. *Medical Ethics,* 2nd ed. Boston: Jones & Bartlett, 1997.

Matt Weinberg, ed. *Medical Ethics: Applying Theories and Principles to the Patient Encounter.* Buffalo, N.Y.: Prometheus, 2001.

Robert F. Weir, ed. *Physician-Assisted Suicide.* Bloomington: Indiana University Press, 1997.

Total care for the patient with a life-threatening illness includes warm, intimate contact with caring persons who are able to listen and share the patient's concerns.

CHAPTER 7

Facing Death: Living with Life-Threatening Illness

One day you wake up and notice symptoms in your body that you associate with a serious illness. What goes through your mind? Perhaps you just barely admit to yourself the possibility that you're "really sick," then quickly push away such thoughts and go on with your day's activities. "After all," you say, "there's no reason to suspect it's anything serious; it's probably just something minor." You don't want to tempt fate by looking too closely.

You forget about it for a while. But, more and more persistently, the symptoms demand your attention. "This better not be anything serious," you tell yourself, "I've got too much to do." Yet, in some part of your mind, you recognize that it could be serious. You begin to admit to your concern, feeling a bit anxious about what the symptoms might mean, how they might affect your life.

So you make an appointment with your doctor, describe your symptoms, submit to an examination, and wait for the results. Perhaps right away, or maybe only after additional tests are completed, you learn the diagnosis. Your doctor informs you that you have a tumor, a malignancy. Cancer.

Now your thoughts and emotions really become agitated. "What can be done? How are the doctors going to treat this illness? What kind of changes will I have to make in my life? Should I postpone the trip I've been planning? What course of treatment should be followed? Are there side effects? Can this kind of cancer be cured? What about the pain? Will

I die?" As the drama unfolds, you find ways to cope with the crisis. Earlier fears about symptoms are transformed into concerns about diagnosis, treatment, and outcome.

As time passes, you experience a remission: The tumor appears to have stopped growing. The doctors seem to be optimistic. Still, you wonder whether the cancer is really gone for good or just temporarily. You are in limbo. You're happy that things seem to be going well, but optimism is mixed with uncertainty and fear. Perhaps after a while you begin to relax and feel less anxious about the cancer returning. It seems "your" cancer was curable.

However, you may sooner or later again notice the onset of symptoms, signaling the cancer's return. You may fear metastasis, the spreading of the cancer to other areas of your body, as you wrestle with the questions "Is it going to be painful? What parts of my body will be affected? Am I going to die? How long do I have to live?" Cancer symbolizes the worst fears of our age: pain, wasting away, suffering, and death.

Some life-threatening illnesses are cured by relatively simple treatment. Others, with treatment, diminish or become stabilized. With yet others, there is little hope of survival. When life-threatening illness threatens one's well-being, the foregoing scenario resembles, by analogy, the experience of anyone diagnosed with life-threatening illness.

Once a disease is determined to be incurable, a person's fears may be focused on the uncertainty surrounding dying and death. These fears probably have been present from the beginning, underlying concerns about symptoms, diagnosis, and treatment. Yet, when life-threatening disease was just a possibility represented by a particular set of symptoms, attention was focused on what the symptoms might mean. After the disease has been diagnosed and as treatment proceeds, thoughts of death may become more predominant, although fear is balanced by hope. Attention is focused on carrying out all the various activities that accompany the role of being a patient with a life-threatening illness.

When nothing more can be done to stop the progression of the disease, the prospect of dying is difficult to avoid. Still, feelings of hopefulness may remain—the hope for a last-minute remission, some change for the better that the doctors haven't foreseen. We may fight to the end with the attitude "I've always outwitted the percentages. Why not now?" Or we may take a very different approach, coping with the end of life by making the most of the time we have left, being surrounded by those closest to us, and accepting our fate. The way we cope with dying will likely reflect the ways we've coped with living, the ways we've coped with other losses and changes in our lives.

Personal and Social Meanings of Life-Threatening Illness

A patient with acute leukemia compared her experience to that of someone facing the Black Death, which was caused by the plague during the fourteenth century in Europe. The origin of the disease is mysterious, the result of causes

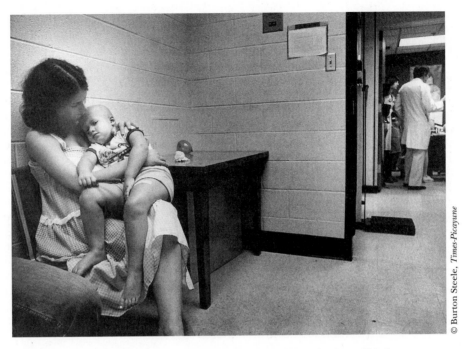

With her seriously ill daughter, this mother waits for the test results that will help determine the next step in care and treatment.

not easily discernible or completely understood. Nature seems somehow to have gotten out of control. Not fully comprehending the chain of events that has led to such a bleak fortune, the patient feels responsible for putting things right.

People coping with life-threatening illness may feel an added burden of social stigma. Such diseases are sometimes treated as taboo (from the Polynesian word *tapu,* meaning "marked off"), as if fraught with mystical danger.[1] This can lead to avoidance of people, places, and objects associated with the forbidden condition. Kay Toombs says:

> Diagnoses are permeated with personal and cultural meanings. The dread diseases—cancer, heart disease, AIDS—carry with them a particularly powerful symbolic significance. In living an illness, one is forced not only to deal with the physical symptoms of disease but also to confront the meanings associated with the diagnosis—particularly with respect to the response of others.[2]

Life-threatening diseases challenge our image of ourselves and threaten our plans for the future. They confront us with our mortality, exposing anxiety about being separated from all that we love, our fear of pain, and the imagined horror of dying. It takes courage to cope with such fears.

A pattern of taboo and avoidance can cause friends and relatives, as well as caregivers, to abandon the patient, creating a kind of "social death," with

When I first realized that I might have cancer, I felt immediately that I had entered a special place, a place I came to call "The Land of Sick People." The most disconcerting thing, however, was not that I found that place terrifying and unfamiliar, but that I found it so ordinary, so banal. I didn't feel different, didn't feel that my life had radically changed at the moment the word *cancer* became attached to it. The same rules still held. What had changed, however, was other people's perceptions of me. Unconsciously, even with a certain amount of kindness, everyone—with the single rather extraordinary exception of my husband—regarded me as someone who had been altered irrevocably. I don't want to exaggerate my feeling of alienation or to give the impression that it was in any way dramatic. I have no horror stories of the kind I read a few years ago in the *New York Times;* people didn't move their desks away from me at the office or refuse to let their children play with my children at school because they thought that cancer was catching. My friends are all too sophisticated and too sensitive for that kind of behavior. Their distance from me was marked most of all by their inability to understand the ordinariness, the banality of what was happening to me. They marveled at how well I was "coping with cancer." I had become special, no longer like them.

Alice Stewart Trillin,
"Of Dragons and Garden Peas:
A Cancer Patient Talks to Doctors"

the patient feeling "walled off" from the rest of society as somehow "in-valid." Negativity about the disease can lead to avoiding the person with the disease.

The "meaning" of a life-threatening illness is determined to a significant extent by the individual's social environment.[3] In societies that place high value on health, the pursuit of wellness becomes a kind of moral virtue, a way to set oneself among the "righteous."[4] A person who fails to achieve or retain good health may feel guilty: "Am I responsible for bringing this illness on myself?" In this regard, simplistic concepts about how the mind influences the body can be detrimental.

Magical thinking—assuming oneself responsible though it's unclear just how—can place an additional burden on a patient with life-threatening illness: "What did I do to bring this condition upon myself? If I had done this, or not done that, maybe I wouldn't be in this predicament." The person may feel helpless while trying to combat natural forces that have gone awry, forces that seem bent on destroying one's body.

Life-threatening diseases such as heart disease and cancer are expensive, with costs related to hospitalization, outpatient therapy, office visits, and medications. Besides medical care, there are incidental costs associated with transportation, support services, child care, and temporary housing for patients who must travel long distances to receive specialized care. Time lost from work may result in lost earnings. The patient's family shares these burdens. Looking at the family as a "system," as the illness affects family life, there is a reciprocal impact on the patient.[5]

I'm forty. So, obviously things happened to me before I came in here. . . . I was married—I had a wife, and I had a son. But my wife divorced me. I was served with the papers the day I went to the hospital for the operation. My son will be twelve this October, I guess. I've never seen him since.

In the beginning, I was bewildered-like. I didn't know what the hell was happening to me. I didn't know what was wrong. And I kept going from doctor to doctor—and getting worse all the time. Slipping and slipping. I was like up in a cloud—and I was cross then. And bitter. I couldn't see why God had made such a big decision on me. I saw my brothers and sisters walking around so healthy-like—and I couldn't understand why it had happened to me and not to them. Things like that. . . . But, after a while, I decided you've got to take what the Lord decides, and make the best of it. . . .

Quoted in Renée Fox, *Experiment Perilous*

Anxiety about treatment may compound fears about the disease itself. Education, counseling, support groups, and communication skills can help individuals cope with life-threatening illness. Acquiring information about the disease and its treatment, sharing experiences with others in an atmosphere of mutual support, using counseling services to clarify personal and emotional issues, and finding ways of communicating more effectively with caregivers as well as family members and friends—all of these are examples of positive approaches to dealing with life-threatening illness.[6] They can contribute to an understanding that places the crisis in a more affirmative context, making the experience less disturbing, perhaps less melodramatic, and restoring a sense of personal control over one's life.

Coping with Life-Threatening Illness

Every disease has its own set of problems and challenges, and each person copes in his or her own way.[7] How people respond to illness is shaped by personality, psychological makeup, family and social patterns, and environment. Much of the suffering experienced by people with life-threatening illness comes from overwhelming feelings of loss on all levels. "At the moment a diagnosis is confirmed and a lethal disorder identified, the patient becomes the focus of a potentially dramatic set of events."[8] Facing the prospect of dying and affirming this reality is not easy. Yet, as Arthur Frank points out, "Critical illness teaches us that to be alive is to be constantly at risk, but the risk greater than dying is living less than well."[9]

For many people, religious faith is an important ally in coping with life-threatening illness. Patients and their families may be comforted by a faith that helps them face the abyss of death and somehow make sense of existence.[10] Faith can promote a sense of self-confidence, peacefulness, and purpose. Many people with serious or life-threatening illness find constructive ways of adapting and, over time, come to see themselves as happier and better adjusted than they were before their illness.

Awareness of Dying

Observing family interactions in response to life-threatening illness, sociologists Barney Glaser and Anselm Strauss noted four distinctive ways in which a context of awareness about dying shapes communication styles.[11] In the *closed awareness* context, the dying person is not aware of his or her impending death, although others may know. This context is characterized by a lack of communication about the person's illness or the prospect of his or her death.

In the *suspected awareness* context, a person suspects his or her prognosis, but this suspicion is not verified by those who know. The dying person may try to confirm or deny his or her suspicions by testing family members, friends, and medical staff in an effort to elicit information known by others but not openly shared. Despite this secrecy, the patient observes the disruptions in family communication patterns caused by the illness and senses others' anxiety about the illness, thus tending to confirm suspicions.

The *mutual pretense* context is like a dance in which participants sidestep direct communication about the patient's condition. This can lead to complicated, though usually unspoken, rules of behavior intended to sustain the illusion that the patient is getting well. Everyone, the patient included, recognizes that death will be the outcome, but all act as if the patient will recover. Mutual pretense may be carried on right to the end, even when the unspoken rules are occasionally violated in ways that might have revealed the patient's condition.

Underlying mutual pretense is the notion that everyone should avoid "dangerous" or "threatening" topics, such as facts about the disease, its prognosis, medical procedures, the deaths of other patients with the same disease, and future plans and events that will likely occur after the patient dies. This eliminates from discussion a considerable portion of the patient's experience. Participants exchange subtle signals that the style of communication used to cope with the crisis is to pretend that things are normal.

"Bloom County," drawing by Berke Breathed, © 1985 by Washington Post Writers Group

When something happens that threatens to break the fiction and disclose the reality, the parties to mutual pretense act as if the threatening event did not occur. Distancing strategies preserve the illusion that the person is not seriously ill. People may respond to the risk of disclosure by becoming angry or withdrawn, or they may avoid further communication by saying they need to go out for a walk or make a phone call. In the short term, mutual pretense can be a useful strategy for coping with a difficult and painful situation.

Glaser and Strauss's fourth designation, the context of *open awareness*, is one in which death is acknowledged and discussed. Open awareness does not necessarily make death easier to accept, but it does allow for the possibility of sharing support in ways that are not readily available with the other awareness contexts. As new information about the course of the disease is presented to the patient or family members, the context of awareness may change. For example, mutual pretense may dominate through a succession of medical procedures; then, with receipt of new test results, the participants may begin to openly acknowledge the illness as life-threatening. As circumstances change, the awareness context may shift.

Agreement between beliefs and actions is an important determinant of how a crisis is experienced. If, in your belief system, mutual pretense is a useful way of coping with threatening or discomforting situations, and if this style of communication is customary in your family's interactions, then pretense may be an effective and helpful way to cope. Suppose, conversely, that you place a high value on openness and honesty, and your family has always been scrupulously honest with one another. If someone in your family is dying, yet everyone is pretending that this is really not happening—that the person is getting well—anxiety about the crisis will probably be made even more unbearable because of the conflict between beliefs and actions.

Adapting to "Living/Dying"

Living with an illness that is life-threatening and incurable can be described as a "living-dying" experience, during which patients and their families fluctuate between denial and acceptance as circumstances—and their responses to circumstances—change.[12] Psychiatrist Avery Weisman described this coping process as involving *middle knowledge,* with patients and their families seeking a balance between sustaining hope and acknowledging the reality.[13]

On the basis of her work with dying patients, Elisabeth Kübler-Ross developed the best-known description of the emotional and psychological responses to life-threatening illness.[14] Many people have some knowledge about the "five stages" associated with Kübler-Ross's model: denial, anger, bargaining, depression, and acceptance. This model has been portrayed in cartoons and on the television series *The Simpsons.* The acronym DABDA is even used by medical students while preparing for their examinations. The idea that these five stages occur in a linear progression—and that a person is supposed to move through them sequentially and eventually wind up at acceptance—is sometimes assumed to be a prescription for how people *ought* to cope with dying. On the contrary, Kübler-Ross pointed out that, during the course of an

I remember her as she lay in her hospital bed in July. Unable finally to deny the pain. And for the first time in our relationship of 21 years forced to allow someone else to take care of her. My father could not stand the sight and so he stayed outside, pacing up and down in the hallways. I could not help staring at her. Disbelief that this person with tubes running in and out like entrances and exits on a freeway was the same woman who just six months before had laughed gaily and danced at my wedding.

Ruth Kramer Ziony, "Scream of Consciousness"

illness, individuals tend to go back and forth among the various "stages" and may experience different stages at the same time.

Upon receiving the diagnosis of a life-threatening illness, a person may respond with avoidance or denial, suppressing the reality or trying to exclude it from consciousness. Even with acknowledgment, anger and feelings of vulnerability and dependency may be present. Sometimes anger is manifested as displaced hostility: "Maybe I could've done something to keep this from happening to me, but, damn it, if it isn't safe, why doesn't the government put a stop to it!" Often, the object of displaced hostility is the person's caregiver, as displayed in complaints about food or other aspects of care: "Why can't you fix me a good cup of tea? You know I can't do it for myself!" Expressions of anger can mask anxiety about the underlying problem: the encounter with serious illness and what it means for one's continued existence.

Bargaining, attempting to strike a deal with fate or with God, is another response that may occur as a patient tries to find some way to postpone or avoid the inevitable. Perhaps "good behavior" can be exchanged for an extension of life.

As the illness progresses, weakening the body, an individual's attempts to be stoic in the face of reality may be replaced by depression, a profound sense of loss. Kübler-Ross distinguished two kinds of depression: a *reactive* depression to disruptions caused by the disease and a *preparatory* depression related to the awareness that one must prepare for death.

As a person finds ways to cope with the realities of life-threatening illness and accompanying losses, he or she may find some sense of acceptance or resolution. This does not mean giving up or losing hope; rather, it implies facing one's mortality in a manner that is essentially positive. Consider the words of writer Harold Brodkey when he was confronted with the prospect of dying from AIDS:

I have liked my life. I like my life at present, being ill. I like the people I deal with. I don't feel I am being whisked off the stage or murdered and stuffed in a laundry hamper while my life is incomplete. It's my turn to die—I can see that that is interesting to some people but not that it is tragic. Yes, I was left out of some things and was cheated over a lifetime in a bad way but who isn't and so what? I had a lot of privileges as well. Sometimes I'm sad about its being over but I'm that way about books and sunsets and conversations.[15]

In coping with death, each person's pathway is determined by such factors as the specific nature of the illness, his or her personality, and the helping resources available in his or her environment.

The model of coping with life-threatening illness that Kübler-Ross devised four decades ago has been a stimulus toward a better understanding of how people experience the prospect of dying. But this, or any, model of how people cope with loss should not be applied indiscriminately. For example, people sometimes interpret denial as a "bad thing," something the dying person should move beyond. But this interpretation ignores the fact that denial can be a healthy and an effective way of coping. Whether denial is adaptive or maladaptive depends on the timing and duration of its use and on the nature of the perceived threat. Edwin Shneidman says, "Intermittent denial is the ubiquitous psychological feature of the dying process."[16] Facing reality about impending death is not always best; there are times when "game-playing," or acting "as if" circumstances were otherwise, is more appropriate.

Herman Feifel points out that "coping with a life-threatening illness or death threat varies in significant fashion not only among differing groups but among situations."[17] From the moment one notices unusual symptoms and questions what they mean, through the ups and downs of treatment, and on to the final moments of life, hope and honesty are often delicately balanced— honesty to face reality as it is, hope that the outcome is positive. The object of hope changes over time. Hope that the symptoms mean nothing gives way to hope that there will be a cure. When the illness is labeled incurable, one may hope for more time. When time runs out, one hopes for a pain-free and appropriate death. When hope no longer includes the expectation of a cure, it is crucial not to give up, but to retain other kinds of hope by focusing on meaningful aspects of life.[18]

Charles Corr identifies four primary dimensions in coping with dying: physical, psychological, social, and spiritual (see Table 7-1).[19] This approach highlights the fact that coping involves more than just body or mind. The spiritual dimension, it should be noted, is not exclusively religious; rather, it encompasses a person's basic values and sources of meaning about life and death. In presenting a broad view of coping, this model shifts our perspective from a linear or limited view of the dying process to one that is holistic.

T A B L E   7-1   *Four Primary Dimensions in Coping with Dying*

---

1. *Physical.* Involves satisfying bodily needs and minimizing physical distress in ways consistent with other values.
2. *Psychological.* Involves maximizing psychological security, autonomy, and richness in living.
3. *Social.* Involves sustaining and enhancing significant interpersonal relationships; and addressing the social implications of dying.
4. *Spiritual.* Involves identifying, developing, or reaffirming sources of spiritual energy or meaning and, in so doing, fostering hope.

Source: Adapted from Charles A. Corr, "A Task-Based Approach to Coping with Dying," *Omega: Journal of Death and Dying* 24, no. 2 (1991–1992): 81–94.

TABLE 7-2   *Tasks in Coping with Life-Threatening Illness*

Acute Phase	Chronic Phase	Terminal Phase
Understand the disease	Manage symptoms and side effects	Manage discomfort, pain, incapacitation, other symptoms
Maximize health and lifestyle	Carry out health regimens	Cope with health procedures and institutional stress
Optimize coping strengths	Manage stress and examine coping behaviors	Manage stress and examine coping behaviors
Develop strategies to deal with issues created by disease	Normalize life to extent possible in face of disease	Prepare for death and say goodbye
Explore effect of diagnosis on self and others	Maximize social support and preserve self-concept	Sustain self-concept and appropriate relationships with others
Express feelings and fears	Express feelings and fears	Express feelings and fears
Integrate present reality into sense of past and future	Find meaning in uncertainty and suffering	Find meaning in life and death

Adapted from Kenneth J. Doka, "Coping with Life-Threatening Illness: A Task Model," *Omega: Journal of Death and Dying* 32, no. 2 (1995–1996): 111–122.

Kenneth Doka provides another useful approach to understanding how people cope by focusing on the various tasks that individuals manage at different phases of a life-threatening illness (see Table 7-2).[20] This model describes an *acute* phase, initiated by the diagnosis; a *chronic* phase of living with the disease; and a *terminal* phase that involves coping with impending death. Doka points out that there are two additional phases that may occur in some cases: first, a *prediagnostic* phase, during which a person suspects the illness and may seek medical attention; and, second, a *recovery* phase following a cure or remission of a previously life-threatening disease. As you think about the tasks that pertain to each of these phases, it is important to keep in mind that serious illness doesn't automatically liberate a person from other, more ordinary problems and challenges of life. Doka says:

> Life-threatening illness is only part of life. Throughout the time of the illness, at whatever phase, individuals continue to meet many needs and to cope with all the issues and problems that they had prior to the diagnosis. . . . [Of course,] the experience of illness may affect the perception of these needs and issues. . . . All the previous challenges of life—dealing with family and friends, coping with

work and finances, even keeping up with the demands of a home or apartment—remain an ongoing part of the larger struggle of life and living.

After extensive studies of dying patients and the processes associated with "terminality," Avery Weisman observed that coping effectively with life-threatening illness involves three interrelated tasks: first, confronting the problem and revising one's plans as necessary; second, keeping communication open and wisely using the help offered by others; and, third, maintaining a sense of optimism and hope.[21] Based on his observations and analysis, Weisman also suggested that the process of coping with terminal illness consists of three phases: (1) from the time symptoms are noticed until the diagnosis is confirmed, (2) the time between diagnosis and the final decline, and (3) from decline to death.[22] Among the "landmarks" that characterize the journey through terminal illness are the following:

1. *Existential plight.* A crisis of self-identity begins with the initial shock of diagnosis as the person attempts to come to terms with the life-altering news.
2. *Mitigation and accommodation.* When treatment begins, the reality of the illness becomes part of the person's life as adjustments and accommodations are made.
3. *Preterminality and terminality.* When no cure or extension of life is in the offing, the individual confronts progressive decline and deterioration as the limits of life become increasingly clear. As the end draws near, palliative care replaces curative therapy as the dying person prepares for death.

We need to keep in mind the highly individual nature of coping styles, as well as the fact that any one person can have various ways of coping with life-threatening illness. Thus, it is not feasible to rely solely on some "standard" model of the dying process to tell us how a given individual is likely to behave or what she or he is likely to feel or think. We must pay attention to the dying person's own *life story* (see Figure 7-1). A person's death is as unique as his or her life.

Patterns of Coping

When confronted by a stressful situation, we evaluate the significance of the threatening situation and assess our resources for coping with it. Although we may not be fully aware of this process, this appraisal influences the way we subsequently cope.[23] Therese Rando identifies three major psychological and behavioral *patterns* that individuals use in coping with the threat of death: (1) retreat and conservation of energy, (2) exclusion from the threat of death, and (3) attempting to master or control the threat of death.[24] It is important to recognize that coping includes not only psychological (cognitive and emotional) processes, but also behavioral efforts.

The threat of a potentially fatal illness evokes a variety of responses to make the threat somehow manageable. These responses can be divided into two main categories: defense mechanisms and coping strategies.[25] *Defense*

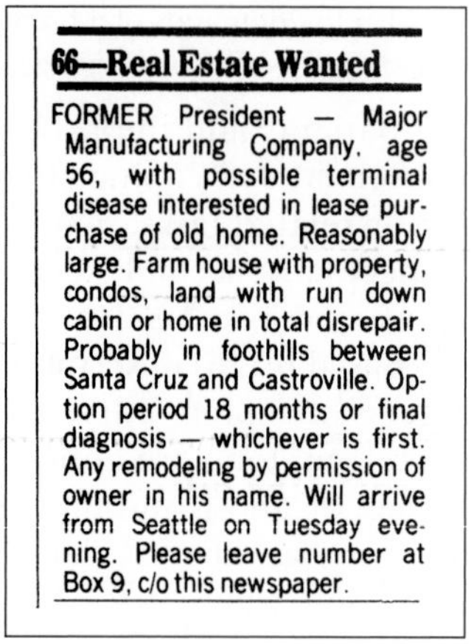

66—Real Estate Wanted

FORMER President — Major Manufacturing Company. age 56, with possible terminal disease interested in lease purchase of old home. Reasonably large. Farm house with property, condos, land with run down cabin or home in total disrepair. Probably in foothills between Santa Cruz and Castroville. Option period 18 months or final diagnosis — whichever is first. Any remodeling by permission of owner in his name. Will arrive from Seattle on Tuesday evening. Please leave number at Box 9, c/o this newspaper.

Figure 7-1 *Life Change with Life-Threatening Illness: Real Estate Want Ad*
The confrontation with a life-threatening illness may activate desires to accomplish in the present plans that previously had been visualized as occurring in the future.
Source: Register-Pajaronian (Watsonville, Calif.), March 11, 1981.

mechanisms occur unintentionally and without conscious effort or awareness; they function to change a person's internal psychological states, not the external reality. *Coping strategies* involve conscious, purposeful effort; they are employed with the intention of solving a problem situation. Although coping strategies are generally viewed more positively than defense mechanisms, both involve psychological processes that can help ease a distressful situation. Denial, for example, is a defense mechanism that is sometimes adaptive and sometimes not, depending on the person and the situation. In the short term, denial can give a person "breathing room" in living with a distressing situation; over the longer term, however, defenses may hinder a positive outcome if they prevent a person from mobilizing needed resources and taking appropriate action. Consider, for example, a person who uses denial to delay seeking medical attention because of his or her fear about illness.[26]

The main aim of the mental processes and behaviors involved in coping is to establish control over a stressful situation.[27] This generally requires different coping strategies working in concert. As with an orchestra, wherein particular instruments come to the fore at a given time while other instruments await their turn, the various coping strategies may be employed at different times to achieve different purposes. One way of distinguishing different strategies is to examine their purpose and focus. *Emotion-focused coping,* for example, helps regulate the level of distress. It allows a person to escape the impact of the stressful situation by reframing it or distancing oneself from it. Reframing a situation to put it in a positive light can reduce the sense of threat. Another strategy, *problem-focused coping,* deals with managing the problem that is causing distress. A cancer patient who seeks out information about her disease and takes an active role in determining her options is engaging in problem-focused coping. A hallmark of this style of coping is the person's pursuit of personally meaningful goals. Recalling that the main aim of coping is to establish a sense of control, it is noteworthy that a greater sense of control is associated with problem-focused coping. A third strategy, *meaning-based coping,* helps maintain a person's sense of positive well-being. Examples include giving up goals that are no longer achievable and formulating new ones, making some sense of what is happening, and, where possible, finding benefit in the distressing situation. In searching for meaning, people often turn to spiritual beliefs for insight in making the best of a bad situation. Finding some redeeming value in loss can make the burden easier to bear (see Figure 7-2).

How individuals respond to stressful circumstances is largely determined by who they are—by their enduring dispositions and personalities.[28] People vary their styles of coping depending on opportunities for problem solving, the intensity of their emotional responses and their ability to regulate them, and the changes in their environment as the distressing situation unfolds. Thus, the various coping strategies are dynamic rather than static, with the overall pattern of coping resembling a more or less continual flow or oscillation among the various styles. It is a mistake to pit one style against another because they are interdependent and work together, each supplementing the others.[29] Therefore, we should be careful about judging the coping process of another person as good or bad.

People who apparently cope best with life-threatening illness often exhibit a "fighting spirit" that views the illness not only as a threat, but also as a challenge.[30] Such people strive to inform themselves about their illness and take an active part in treatment decisions. They are optimistic and try to discover positive meaning in ordinary events. Holding to a positive outlook despite distressing circumstances involves creating a sense of meaning that is bigger than the threat. In the context of life-threatening illness, this encompasses a person's ability to comprehend the implications an illness has for the future, as well as for his or her ability to accomplish goals, maintain relationships, and sustain a sense of personal vitality, competence, and power. Although life-threatening illness disrupts virtually all aspects of a person's life, there is a vital link between finding meaning and achieving a sense of mastery.[31]

Maintaining Coping Potency

The capacity to maintain a sense of self-worth, to set goals and strive to meet them, to exercise choice out of an awareness of one's power to meet challenges, to engage in active interactions with one's environment—all of these reflect a "coping potency" that sustains the will to live in the face of death. Reportedly, both John Adams and Thomas Jefferson, although gravely ill, managed to live until July 4, 1826, the fiftieth anniversary of the signing of the Declaration of Independence. According to his physician, Jefferson's last words were "Is it the Fourth?" This story raises the question whether human beings have the capacity to delay death long enough to mark an anniversary or other important event.[32]

It has long been a truism in medicine that hope plays a key role in a patient's ability to live with illness. Doctors often attempt to instill hope in patients by the manner in which they discuss a disease and its treatment. In difficult cases, doctors may talk about taking things "one step at a time," first controlling the pain or other symptoms and then working on various

Dear Friends,

In company with our dear Mother Earth, I have arrived at the time of autumn in my worldly life, that time of transition between life and death. Before long, just as the leaves drop from the trees to continue Life's cycle of generation and regeneration, so will my body be shed and become part of the muttering earth. Like the tree gathering in energy to prepare itself for winter, I feel a need to gather energy for the process of dying. Also, I want to share a last celebration with you dear friends. To do this, I have planned a ritual of transition to take place on Sunday, November 3, at 2:30 p.m. here at my home.

I would love it if you can participate with your presence; and if you cannot, I would appreciate your joining us in spirit with loving energy via the ethers that afternoon.

If you can come, please bring a pillow to sit on and a symbolic gift of your energy and blessing for me in this process I am going through— something from nature (rock, shell, feather, etc.); a poem, picture or song; something written or drawn; or whatever you are inspired to bring. Please also bring a casserole, salad or dessert or beverage to contribute to our potluck supper following the ritual.

There is a new joy that is beginning to be realized in me as I acknowledge the prospect of having a spirit float free of my tired body. I look forward to sharing this with you too.

Love and blessings,

Joan Conn

Figure 7-2 *Invitation to a Going-Away Party*
Ritual and companionship can assist in dealing with impending death. This celebration was attended by close friends and family, who said the occasion was an extremely moving experience. Knowing that she would soon die from cancer, Joan created a ritual that involved drawing a line on the floor and, in her weakened condition, she was helped across it by her ex-husband and her children while members of the gathering played music and sang. Although such an event would not be appropriate for everyone, Joan's farewell party aptly reflected her lifestyle and values. She died seven months later.

treatment options. Or they may liken the process of coping with a serious illness to climbing a mountain, which can be arduous but potentially successful if one keeps advancing to the top. This metaphor suggests that the doctor can help "pull the patient to safer, higher ground." As one oncologist explains, "You have to give people something to wake up for in the morning, otherwise they might as well take some cyanide."[33] In putting the best face on bad news, doctors see themselves in the role of "the patient's cheerleader." Yet it is also the case that "sometimes the only real hope you can offer a dying person is that you will accompany them to their death and respect their wishes to the best of your ability."[34]

Essential to maintaining a positive attitude despite the stress of life-threatening illness is the patient's self-image. The late Orville Kelly, founder of Make Today Count, described his own response and the reactions of others after he was diagnosed with cancer.[35] After receiving a terminal prognosis, Kelly contemplated suicide, fearing that he might become a burden to his family. Relatives and friends were uncomfortable in his presence. One woman asked his wife, "How is he?"—although Kelly was just a few feet away. Though still alive, he was experiencing a kind of social death. Despite the frightening prognosis, Kelly soon realized that in fact he was still alive. He could still love and be loved. No matter how short a time he might have to live,

"You've got one foot in the grave. Further testing will determine if it's your left or your right."

he could make the most of each day. Recognizing that the mortality rate of every generation is 100 percent, Kelly began to talk about his feelings and express his concerns as a person with terminal illness. An article he wrote for his local newspaper elicited such a positive and sizable response that it led to Kelly's founding of Make Today Count, a nationwide support group for the terminally ill. Kelly's message is a crucial one: Everyone, whether diagnosed with terminal illness or not, is challenged to make each day count.

Treatment Options and Issues

The options for treating life-threatening illness vary with the nature of the disease and the patient's particular situation. As new medicines and medical technologies become available, treatment options change. Yet the range of life-saving choices for treating disease also depends in part on decisions made by society at large. Heart attack—which typically occurs when a blockage in a coronary artery cuts off the blood supply to a region of the heart—is a medical emergency. Half of the deaths from heart attack occur in the first three to four hours after the onset of symptoms. The sooner treatment begins, the better the chances of survival. Heart attack victims who reach a hospital and receive early treatment have a survival rate of about 90 percent. The key to life-saving help is a rapid emergency response. Some communities, recognizing that sudden cardiac death is a pressing public health problem, have funded sophisticated mobile cardiac care units; other communities consider these units too costly.

In discussing treatment options, we focus particularly on cancer for two reasons: First, it symbolizes for many people the nature of "life-threatening" or "terminal" illness; and, second, many of the medical and palliative care options now available to patients with life-threatening diseases were initially developed as a result of efforts to improve cancer care.

As a general term, *cancer* encompasses many types of malignant, or potentially lethal, growths that occur in the body. Among women, the most common malignancy is breast cancer; among men, it is prostate cancer. Briefly defined, a cancerous cell is one that has lost its normal control mechanisms and therefore reproduces in a manner unregulated by the body's normal controls on cell growth. Such cells can develop in any tissue within any organ. First affecting tissues in one part of the body, cancer may spread either by invading adjacent tissues or by *metastasis,* a process whereby diseased cells travel in the blood or lymph system or through body tracts, to more distant parts of the body.

Because there are many categories and types of cancer, some experts propose that cancer is best understood as a process, with *time* as a critical dimension.[36] Cancer growth may be fast or slow; it may take weeks or years. The speed at which cancer progresses affects how the patient and his or her family copes with the illness.[37] Successful treatment of cancer requires that all cancerous tissue be destroyed or removed; otherwise, the disease recurs.

   In treating cancer, attention is focused on the primary tumor and its metastases. No single therapy is effective for all types of cancer. A therapy that has a high success rate with one type of cancer may be ineffective with another. Some cancers require a combination of therapies. In some cases, there is also a need for *adjuvant therapy* (an auxiliary remedy that aids or assists another). (Key terms used in cancer care are defined in Table 7-3.) When a cure is not possible, palliation of symptoms using some or all of these therapies may improve the quality and duration of life.[38] Patients need to have enough information to clearly understand the risks and benefits of each therapy, as well as to assess the consequences of pursuing a different course of action.[39]

Surgery

   Surgery is the oldest and most common form of cancer therapy, and some cancers are curable in early stages with surgery alone.[40] The diagnosis of cancer is usually established by a biopsy, a tissue sample surgically removed and examined for the presence of cancerous cells. Although surgery is a routine medical practice, it can also be seen as a "violation of the body" whose

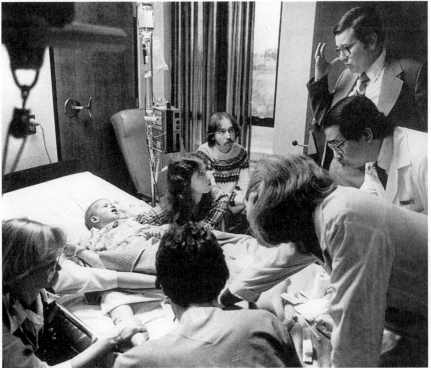

© Burton Steele, *Times-Picayune*

Family members and consulting physicians gathered around the bedside of a seriously ill child discuss the impending brain surgery that everyone hopes will bring a favorable prognosis.

TABLE 7-3   *Medical Treatment Word List*

Alkylating agents: A family of chemotherapeutic drugs that combine with DNA (genetic substance) to prevent normal cell division.

Analgesic: A drug used for reducing pain.

Antimetabolites: A family of chemotherapeutic drugs that interfere with the processes of DNA production and thus prevent normal cell division.

Benign: Not malignant.

Biopsy: The surgical removal of a small portion of tissue for diagnosis.

Blood count: A laboratory study to evaluate the number of white cells, red cells, and platelets.

Bone marrow: A soft substance found within bone cavities, ordinarily composed of fat and developing red cells, white cells, and platelets.

Cancer: A condition in which there is the proliferation of malignant cells that are capable of invading normal tissues.

Chemotherapy: The treatment of disease by chemicals (drugs) introduced into the bloodstream by injection or taken by mouth as tablets.

Cobalt treatment: Radiotherapy using gamma rays generated from the breakdown of radioactive cobalt-60.

Colostomy: Surgical formation of an artificial anus in the abdominal wall so the colon can drain feces into a bag.

Coma: A condition of decreased mental function in which the individual is incapable of responding to any stimulus, including painful stimuli.

Cyanotic: A blue appearance of the skin, lips, or fingernails as the result of low oxygen content of the circulating blood.

Diagnosis: The process by which a disease is identified.

DNA: Abbreviation for deoxyribonucleic acid, the building block of the genes, responsible for the passing of hereditary characteristics from cell to cell.

Hodgkin's disease: A form of tumor that arises in a single lymph node and may spread to local and then distant lymph nodes and finally to other tissues, commonly including the spleen, liver, and bone marrow.

Immunotherapy: A method of cancer therapy that stimulates the body defenses (the immune system) to attack cancer cells or modify a specific disease state.

Intravenous (IV): Describing the administration of a drug or of fluid directly into a vein.

Leukemia: A malignant proliferation of white blood cells in the bone marrow; cancer of the blood cells.

Lymph nodes: Organized clusters of lymphocytes through which the tissue fluids drain upon returning to the blood circulation; they act as the first line of defense, filtering out and destroying infective organisms or cancer cells and initiating the generalized immune response.

Malignant: Having the potentiality of being lethal if not successfully treated. All cancers are malignant by definition.

side effects may include disfigurement, disability, or loss of bodily function. To stop the growth of cancer and prevent it from spreading, surgery usually involves removing not only the malignant organ or tissue, but also adjacent healthy tissue. In addition to its role as a primary treatment for many types of cancer, surgery is used as a therapeutic option in treating pain in cancer patients.[41]

TABLE 7-3 *(continued)*

Melanoma: A cancer of the pigment cells of the skin, usually arising in a preexisting pigmented area (mole).

Metastasis: The establishment of a secondary site or multiple sites of cancer separate from the primary or original site.

Multimodality therapy: The use of more than one modality for cure or palliation (abatement) of cancer.

Myelogram: The introduction of radiopaque dye into the sac surrounding the spinal cord, a process that makes it possible to see tumor involvement of the spinal cord or nerve roots on X-ray.

Oncologist: An internist (specialist in internal medicine dealing with nonsurgical treatment of disease) who has subspecialized in cancer therapy and has expertise in both chemotherapy and the handling of problems arising during the course of the disease.

Parkinson's disease: Degenerative disease of the brain resulting in tremor and rigid muscles.

Prognosis: An estimate of the outcome of a disease based on the status of the patient and accumulated information about the disease and its treatment.

Prosthesis: An artificial structure designed to replace or approximate a normal one.

Regression: The diminution of cancerous involvement, usually as the result of therapy; it is manifested by decreased size of the tumor (or tumors) or its clinical evidence in fewer locations.

Relapse: The reappearance of cancer following a period of remission.

Remission: The temporary disappearance of evident active cancer, occurring either spontaneously or as the result of therapy.

Sarcoma: A cancer of connective tissue, bone, cartilage, fat, muscle, nerve sheath, blood vessels, or lymphoid system.

Subcutaneous cyst: A cyst located beneath the skin; usually benign.

Symptom: A manifestation or complaint of disease as described by the patient, as opposed to one found by the doctor's examination; the latter is referred to as a sign.

Terminal: Describing a condition of decline toward death, from which not even a brief reversal can be expected.

Therapeutic procedure: A procedure intended to offer palliation (abatement) or cure of a condition or disease.

Toxicity: The property of producing unpleasant or dangerous side effects.

Tumor: A mass or swelling. A tumor can be either benign or malignant.

Source: Excerpted and adapted from Ernest H. Rosenbaum, M.D., *Living with Cancer: A Guide for the Patient, the Family and Friends* (St. Louis: Mosby, 1982).

Radiation Therapy

Soon after the discovery of radium in 1898, it was recognized that radiation could be used to treat cancer. Radiation therapy uses ionizing radiation to preferentially destroy cells that divide rapidly.[42] Although radiation affects both normal and cancerous tissues, cancer cells are damaged more seriously because they usually grow more rapidly than normal cells. Radiation plays a key role in the treatment of some cancers, and it is used as an adjunct to chemotherapy in others. Even when radiation does not provide a cure, it may be used as a palliative therapy to relieve symptoms and improve quality of life.

Patients who receive radiation therapy are usually scheduled for frequent treatments over a period of several months. The radiation dose is prescribed on the basis of the stage of the disease and the patient's ability to withstand the side effects, which depend on the region being radiated and on how particular tissues tolerate the effects of radiation. Side effects can include nausea, vomiting, tiredness, and general weakness.

Chemotherapy

Chemotherapy has been called the leading weapon for increasing the number of patients who can be cured of cancer. *Chemotherapy* involves the use of toxic drugs to kill cancer cells.[43] It developed from the observation that toxic effects of mustard gases during World War I included damage to bone marrow. Clinical trials with chemotherapy began after World War II. Today, chemotherapeutic agents are employed in various combinations for treating cancer. The dose must be strong enough to kill the cancer or slow its growth, but not so potent that it seriously harms the patient. The ideal chemotherapeutic agent would attack cancerous cells in the body without affecting healthy tissue.

All chemotherapeutic agents basically work by blocking metabolic processes involved in cellular division. As a result, they damage healthy as well as diseased tissue. However, because cancer cells divide more rapidly than do most normal cells, chemotherapy preferentially affects cancerous cells. Whether a particular drug prevents cells from making genetic material (DNA), blocks nucleic acid synthesis, or stops cell division and induces other cellular changes, chemotherapeutic agents owe their effectiveness to the fact that they are poisonous.

Chemotherapy is an important treatment in many types of cancers, although it may cause discomforting side effects, including hair loss, nausea, sleeplessness, problems with eating and digestion, mouth sores, ulceration and bleeding in the gastrointestinal tract, and other toxic effects. To counteract side effects, other drugs may be prescribed. Some cancers are cured by chemotherapy; others respond but aren't cured; and yet others are resistant. The palliative effects of chemotherapy may help patients lead relatively normal, even prolonged, lives.

Alternative Therapies

Some people find mainstream medicine lacking in its ability to address the patient as a whole person, not just the recipient of a "doctor-centered" treatment regimen. As a result, there is growing interest in so-called *alternative therapies*.[44] Alternative health care encompasses a broad range of therapeutic approaches (see Table 7-4).

Cross-cultural issues are becoming more important in medicine.[45] Instead of viewing such beliefs as irrational or wrong, physicians are increas-

TABLE 7-4 *Alternative and Complementary Therapies*

Mind-Body Interventions	Systems-Oriented Approaches	Manual Healing Methods
Psychotherapy and support groups	Traditional Chinese medicine	Osteopathic medicine
Meditation	Acupuncture and acupressure	Chiropractic treatment
Imagery		Massage therapy
Hypnosis and biofeedback	Herbal medicine and diet/nutritional approaches	Biofield therapeutics (that is, laying on of hands)
Yoga, dance therapy, other movement therapies	Community-based practices (for example, Native American "sweat lodges" and Latin American *curanderismo*)	Reflexology
Music therapy and art therapy		"Body work" (for example, Rolfing, Trager, Feldenkrais method, Alexander technique, Shiatsu)
Prayer and mental healing	Ayurveda (India)	
	Homeopathic medicine	Bioenergetics
	Naturopathic medicine	

ingly recognizing that optimal care is often achieved by judiciously combining conventional biomedicine and folk beliefs, or *ethnomedicine*. This means physicians must entertain the possibility that practices other than the "culture of biomedicine" may be effective. Arthur Kleinman says, "If you can't see that your own culture has its own set of interests, emotions, and biases, how can you expect to deal successfully with someone else's culture?"[46]

Physician Lori Arviso Alvord, for example, integrates conventional medical training with traditional tribal beliefs to offer a holistic approach to her Navajo patients.[47] Similarly, among some Mexican immigrants and Mexican Americans, traditional practices of *curanderismo* (from the Spanish verb *curar*, "to heal") are an important part of total health care.[48] A study comparing folk healing and biomedicine in Mexico concluded, "In the search for the alleviation of pain, pragmatism prevails; people judge the treatments they are given by their effects."[49]

The establishment of the Office of Alternative Medicine within the National Institutes of Health is a sign of the acceptance of such issues in health care. A standard medical text says, "If the goal is the maintenance of or a return to health, all available mechanisms should be used."[50] However, despite more widespread acceptance of alternative approaches, their popularity causes some physicians to worry that people may be getting ripped off by quacks and charlatans. Quacks exploit people's misery while jeopardizing their health, and charlatans promise miracle cures for those with sufficient money.

Even in the best circumstances, alternative approaches typically make use of unproved therapies—that is, therapies that have not been subjected to rigorous scientific testing. Physicians warn that patients, "often grasping at straws, need to be informed and wary of those who falsely promise cure."[51] Conventional medical practice is based on randomized clinical trials and on "evidence-based medicine," whereby the scientific method establishes the efficacy, or value, of therapies. Physicians point out that "respect for multiculturalism should not be used as a sentimental excuse to abandon one's professional obligation to serve the patient's best interest."[52]

Complementary Therapies

Many of the therapies listed in Table 7-4 are used alongside conventional approaches to treating illness. In managing pain, adjuvant methods may include psychotherapy and other mind-body interventions (meditation, imagery, biofeedback, and so on), as well as physical therapy and other forms of manual healing. In conjunction with chemotherapy, patients may use *visualization* to imagine the therapeutic agent inside the body as it helps to restore well-being. Such techniques help patients mobilize their inner healing resources by imagining the diseased parts of the body becoming well again (see Figure 7-3).

At Shibata Hospital in Japan, conventional treatment is accompanied by a psychotherapeutic technique called *ikigai ryoho*, or meaningful-life therapy.[53] The idea behind meaningful-life therapy is that, despite fears or quirks of personality, even when we are terminally ill, we can "take responsibility for what to do in the time remaining to us." Thus, patients at Shibata Hospital begin by acknowledging their own suffering and gradually proceed, first, to the recognition that others also suffer, then to an acceptance of the reality of the illness and the fight that must be carried on, and, finally, to "an ability to live fully and deeply within the realistic limits posed by the illness."

Anson Shupe and Jeffrey Hadden use the term *symbolic healing* to identify the varied therapies known under such names as "faith healing," "supernatural healing," and "folk healing."[54] What we take to be meaningful—what we believe—potentially affects the functioning of our bodies. As human beings, we live within a series of overlapping environments: biological, social, and cultural. Cross-culturally, most healing systems describe illness as "an imbalance among different realms of a patient's life." When alternative therapies help restore this balance, they are an adjunct to conventional medical treatment. Adjunctive therapies of this kind are characterized as "complementary therapies." As one physician points out, complementary therapies only become "alternative," in a negative sense, when they are promoted as "cure-oriented alternatives to conventional treatment."[55]

Unorthodox Treatment

What comes to mind when you hear the word *unorthodox*? Outside the establishment? Ineffective? Unorthodox therapies are methods of treatment that the medical establishment considers unproved or potentially harmful.

Figure 7-3 *Good Cells and Bad Cells: A Child's Drawing*
In this drawing by a child with cancer, the health-giving good cells are
depicted as being victorious over the diseased bad cells. Such imaginative
techniques can be ways of enlisting the patient's internal resources as an
adjunct to conventional therapies.
Source: Center for Attitudinal Healing, *There Is a Rainbow Behind Every Dark Cloud*
(Millbrae, Calif.: Celestial Arts, 1978), p. 71.

The advocates of such remedies may be branded as quacks or charlatans, and
their methods characterized as updated editions of Dr. Feelgood's Medicine
Show, a form of snake oil medicine that, even if intrinsically harmless, diverts
individuals from conventional medicine, which could help them.

That a cure could be found in the pits of apricots or shark cartilage
stretches credibility; and, indeed, such "cures" may be not only controversial
but also dangerous. Yet many of our most common medications derive from
seemingly unlikely sources. Digitalis, in continuous use for more than two
hundred years and prescribed for heart ailments, derives from the plant fox-
glove. Penicillin is naturally produced from molds. The active ingredient of
common aspirin is close kin to a substance found in the bark and leaves
of the white willow. Perhaps the source of a proposed medicinal substance
ought to concern us less than the question "Does it work?" In China, about
1700 plants are commonly used as medicines, and in India that number is

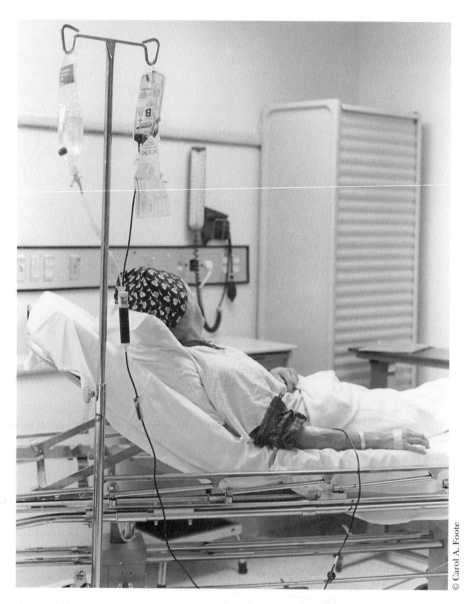

As part of her medical treatment, this chemotherapy patient is receiving a blood transfusion. Some treatments of life-threatening illness create the need for adjuvant therapies to counteract the side effects of the primary mode of treatment.

© Carol A. Foote

about 2500. The study of medicinal plants is increasingly important to pharmacology, as scientists investigate "undiscovered" drugs that are used by healers around the world.[56]

The debate over the medical use of marijuana has involved conflicts between law and medicine because the substance in question is not only an unproved therapy but also an illegal one.[57] However, this situation may be

changing in response to both public pressure to allow the
juana and ongoing scientific studies. A recent review by t
cine concluded that marijuana appears to have a natura
and easing pain as well as in treating wasting syndrome, r
and anxiety. It noted that marijuana and other cannab
useful adjuncts to existing medications."[58]

Shortly before his death, Norman Cousins said, "The
is not death but what dies inside us while we live."[59] The
serious or terminal illness can wreak damage on the human spirit, damage
that conventional medical therapies alone may not repair. It may be a mistake
to confront patients with an "either/or" situation, forcing them to choose between conventional and alternative treatments. There may be times when
rigidly defending standard practices can do more harm than good.

Pain Management

Pain is the most common symptom in terminally ill patients. Advocates of
hospice and palliative care point to the need for adequate pain management,
not only for patients with terminal illness, but for all patients with untreated
or undertreated pain. Increasingly, pain is viewed as a "fifth vital sign," one
that should be added to the four vital signs—temperature, pulse, respiration,
and blood pressure—now recorded and assessed as a standard part of patient
care.[60] Inadequate management of pain has been characterized as "the
shame of American medicine."[61]

Pain is a complex, multidimensional phenomenon; the type and severity
of pain can be an important diagnostic tool.[62] Two main types of pain can be
distinguished: *Acute pain* is "an essential biological signal of the potential for
or the extent of injury."[63] It is a protective mechanism that prompts the suf-
ferer to remove or withdraw from the source of the pain.[64] *Chronic pain*, the
second type, is usually defined as pain that persists longer than three to six
months. When pain lasts this long, it loses its adaptive role. Chronic pain may
be accompanied by sleep disturbances, loss of appetite, weight loss, diminished sexual interest, and depression. It may result from physical mechanisms
(somatogenic pain), psychological mechanisms (psychogenic pain), the acti-
vation of pain-sensitive nerve fibers (nociceptive pain), or nerve-tissue damage (neuropathic pain).

The Language of Pain

People often speak of pain as if it were a well-defined entity, but, in fact,
as Linda Garro points out, pain is "subjective in nature and ultimately un-
shareable."[65] Garro says, "Pain cannot be directly measured or observed; it is
a perceptual experience that can only be communicated through verbal
means and/or by behavior interpreted as indicating pain." Culturally related
belief systems have a dramatic impact on how patients "represent" their illness, as well as on their coping responses.

Languages differ in their "lexicon" for talking about pain. When describing pain, English speakers use such terms as *pain, hurt, sore,* and *ache.* Quali-
fiers are added to make the description match the actual experience. We talk

But You Look So Good

It's with me each day.
I wake, thinking
Today it will go away.
But the pain seems to stay . . .
Persistent, resistant, consistent.
People say,
But you look so good.
If only I could
Feel like I look.
Or, should
I look bad?
So they'll know
How I feel
is real.
Do they doubt?
I wish the pain
Was on the outside—
something you see.
Not only the pain
Do I need to survive,
But also my
Paranoid imaginings
Of others' disbelief.

Judy Ellsworth

about having a "burning" or "stabbing" pain or about "unbearable ache" or "soreness in the shoulder." Notice the tendency to treat pain as an object: "I have a pain." For Thai speakers, however, the basic terms for describing pain are verbs. They refer to the active perception of sensations and often convey the location of the pain as well; for example, "suffering focused abdominal pain" or "feeling irritated by an abrasion." Pain is described not as an object but as a perceptual process. Language reveals how our response to pain is, at least in part, culturally shaped.

Treating Pain

Effective treatment of pain requires attention to its severity, location, quality, duration, and course, among other factors, including the "meaning" of the pain to the patient. Furthermore, it is important to distinguish between pain and *suffering*, especially with cancer patients, "whose suffering may be due as much to loss of function and fear of impending death as to pain."[66]

Pain is generally managed in a stepwise approach, beginning with basic non-opioid pain medications and, if necessary, moving on to powerful opioids like codeine and morphine.[67] Morphine is the drug most commonly used to treat severe cancer pain. It affects both the perception of pain and the emotional response to it. The good news is that (1) it is not especially difficult to assess and treat cancer pain and that (2) physicians and other medical personnel are paying more attention to pain.[68] The not-so-good news is that there are doctors, nurses, and pharmacists whose misunderstandings about opioid analgesics, such as morphine, prevent patients from receiving adequate pain control. This is partly because many caregivers underestimate the pain experienced by patients and partly because of unfounded concerns about patients becoming addicted to such opioids. Strangely, there are even some hospice nurses who worry about the possibility of addiction in their dying patients.[69]

Pain experts point to a fundamental distinction between addiction (in which drug-seeking behavior occurs in an effort to reproduce the "high") and physical dependence (which simply results in an "abstinence syndrome" after the patient stops taking the drug). In fact, patients who experience severe pain rarely obtain pleasant, euphoric sensations from drugs. Morphine works effectively to manage pain because it taps into the body's own pain relief system, the neurotransmitters, one class of which is chemically similar to morphine. Heroin, which has an ill-deserved reputation as the "hardest drug" known to humankind, is a useful pain remedy. It is considered by many experts to be indispensable for managing pain, and many argue that it should be available to physicians in the United States, as it is in Great Britain.[70] Pain specialists say that medicine has the means to alleviate the pain and suffering of almost all dying patients, but the will to treat pain effectively is lacking (see Table 7-5). Thus, the "politics of pain management" may determine whether pain is treated adequately.

Advances in pain management are occurring as the pathways of pain and its mechanisms are understood more completely. Epidural and intraspinal drug delivery—placing a slow, steady stream of morphine directly into the

T A B L E 7-5 *Factors That Inhibit Adequate Pain Control*

- Medical personnel have concerns that patients may become addicted, so they either don't prescribe appropriate drugs or prescribe only low, insufficient doses of medications that would be helpful in adequate dosages.
- Physicians are afraid to prescribe powerful narcotics due to concern about prosecution by overzealous law enforcers.
- Patients feel they should silently live with pain as a sign of moral strength or stoicism.
- Patients worry that, if they use strong painkillers now, nothing will be available later when pain may become worse; in fact, however, for most people there is no upper limit to the ability of narcotics like morphine to control pain.
- Many doctors really don't know much about how to control pain. There is a severe lack of training and information about the principles of pain management and palliative medicine.

Adapted from Shannon Brownlee and Joannie M. Schrof, "The Quality of Mercy" (Special Feature), *U.S. News & World Report,* March 17, 1997, pp. 54–67.

The family of an elderly terminal cancer patient sued a nursing home that unilaterally reduced his pain medication without seeking approval from his doctor, a decision that caused the 75-year-old patient increased suffering. Deciding that the patient was "addicted to morphine," the nursing home staff substituted a "mild tranquilizer," which failed to control his pain. In response to the lawsuit, the nursing director at the facility said: "I have never heard of giving such high doses, at such frequent intervals. . . . The staff and I did not think he needed that much morphine."

Maureen Cushing, "Pain Management on Trial"

spinal column—is often used with late-stage cancer patients to provide effective pain control.[71] "Drug cocktails"—small amounts of several different drug compounds—are used to block different pain channels in the body. Patient-controlled analgesia, a mechanism that allows patients to determine for themselves the best timing of pain relief, is often more effective than relying on others for an injection or a tablet after pain has worsened. Pain is also treated with a variety of other medical techniques, including nerve blocks, electrical stimulation of nerves, acupuncture, and neurosurgery. In addition, antidepressants and other drugs are often prescribed to relieve anxiety, confusion, and depression that may be experienced by patients.[72] Finally, drugs can be given to minimize the discomforting effects of constipation, nausea, respiratory depression, and other physical symptoms commonly experienced by dying patients.

Hospice and palliative care practitioners have led the way in calling attention to the importance of adequate pain management, especially in terms of responding to a patient's "total pain," which includes physical, psychological, social, and spiritual components.[73] Controlling pain in patients who are nearing the end of life can present a formidable challenge, requiring specialized attention by skilled professionals. However, effective techniques for pain control are known and accessible. Failure to institute adequate delivery systems to make them widely available only perpetuates situations in which people die in needless pain.

The Dying Trajectory

Our expectations about dying may be quite different from what most people actually experience. Young adults tend to imagine themselves living into old age and then quickly dying at home, alert and lucid until the end.[74] Pain and discomforts of dying tend to be absent from these imagined deathbed scenes. Our pictures of dying may be influenced more by images from movies and other media than by what is likely to actually occur.

The concept of a *trajectory of dying* is useful for understanding patients' experiences as they near death. Although sudden death from an unexpected cause—a massive heart attack or an accident, for example—is one type of dying trajectory, our focus here is on deaths that occur when there is fore-

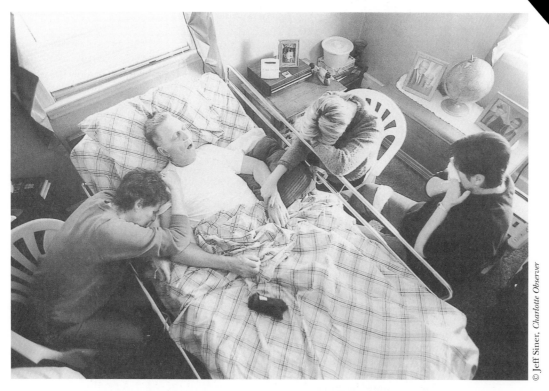

After being diagnosed with a recurrence of cancer, Vernon Nantz chose to be cared for at home by family and friends, with the support of hospice. In his last days, Vernon's family united in tears and prayers, sharing a vigil around his bedside, as he drifted away to the peaceful end he sought.

warning. Among these, some trajectories involve a steady and fairly predictable decline. This is the case with many cancers, which tend to follow the course of a progressive disease with a terminal phase. Other kinds of advanced, chronic illness involve a long period of slow decline marked by episodes of crisis, the last of which proves to be "suddenly" fatal.

We can also distinguish between different stages in a dying trajectory: namely, a period when a person is known to be terminally ill but is living with a life expectancy of perhaps weeks or months, possibly years; and a later period when dying is imminent and the person is described as "actively dying." The way in which such trajectories are estimated—their duration and expected course—can affect both patients and caregivers and influence their actions. Deaths that occur "out of time" (too quickly or too slowly) may pose special difficulties.

Two patterns of dying trajectories are particularly important: (1) the *lingering* trajectory, when a patient's life fades away slowly and inevitably, and (2) the *expected quick* trajectory, when an individual makes a sudden exit, as in emergency situations where life or death hangs in the balance.[75] The expectations

TABLE 7-6 *Signs of "Active Dying"*

Common Symptoms During Last Days or Hours . . .
- Body systems slow down.
- Breathing pattern changes and becomes irregular (for example, shallow breaths followed by deep breath; periods of panting).
- Difficulty breathing (dyspnea).
- Congestion (noisy and moist breathing; gurgling sounds).
- Decrease in appetite and thirst.
- Nausea and vomiting.
- Incontinence.
- Sweating.
- Restlessness and agitation (for example, jerking, twitching, pulling at bed linen or clothing).
- Disorientation and confusion (for example, about time, place, identity of people).
- Decreased socialization; progressive detachment.
- Changes in skin color as circulation decreases (limbs may become cool and perhaps bluish or mottled).
- Increasing sleeping.
- Decrease in consciousness.

At Time of Death . . .
- Relaxing of the throat muscles or secretions in the throat may cause noisy breathing ("the death rattle").
- Breathing ceases.
- Muscle contractions may occur and the chest may heave as if to breathe.
- Heart may beat a few minutes after breathing stops, and a brief seizure may occur.
- Heartbeat ceases.
- Person cannot be aroused.
- Eyelids may be partly open with the eyes in a fixed stare.
- Mouth may fall open as the jaw relaxes.
- Bowel and bladder contents may be released.

Adapted from "Preparing for the Death of a Loved One," *American Journal of Hospice and Palliative Care* 9, no. 4 (1992): 14–16; Robert Berkow, ed., *The Merck Manual of Medical Information: Home Edition* (Whitehouse Station, N.J.: Merck Research Laboratories, 1997), p. 21; and Robert E. Enck, "The Last Few Days," *American Journal of Hospice and Palliative Care* 9, no. 4 (1992): 11–13.

that medical professionals, family members, and others have about a patient's course toward death are likely to be important in determining the nature and kind of care received by the dying person. Although proposals appear from time to time concerning an *ars moriendi,* or art of dying, the notion that there is a "right way to die" that applies to everyone is unlikely to be valid within modern pluralistic societies that place a high value on individualism.

When a person is at the end-stage of a terminal illness, death is expected to occur within hours or, at most, a few days. The end of life is characterized by what is termed "active dying" (see Table 7-6). During the last phase of a fatal illness, a dying person may exhibit irregular breathing or shortness of breath, decreased appetite and thirst, nausea and vomiting, incontinence, restlessness and agitation, disorientation and confusion, and diminished consciousness. These symptoms usually can be managed by skilled palliative care.

Pain, if it is present, should be treated aggressively as part of a comprehensive approach to comfort care. Even when pain can be controlled by drugs and other therapies, some patients, even as they near death, still have concerns about addiction or want to delay pain medication "until it is really needed," or they want to maintain control by "using the pain as a reminder that they are still living."[76] Dying patients may also experience depression, anxiety, confusion, delirium, and unconsciousness.[77] Because people nearing the end of life are often more comfortable without eating or drinking, forcing food or liquids is usually not beneficial. As death becomes more imminent, relaxation of the throat muscles or secretions in the throat may cause the person's breathing to become noisy, resulting in a sound called the "death rattle." Dying patients usually are not aware of this noisy breathing. If it unnerves family or caregivers, medication or repositioning the person can help. Just before death, the person may take a breath and sigh or shudder. After death, unless the person had a rare infectious disease, family and friends may stay with the body for a time as they make their farewells.

The Social Role of the Dying Patient

When death is made to seem less a natural event than a medical failure, biological death, the cessation of physical functions, may be preceded by *social death*. Eric Cassell writes, "There are two distinct things happening to the terminally ill: the death of the body and the passing of the person."[78] The death of the body is a physical phenomenon, whereas the passing of the person is a nonphysical (social, emotional, psychological, spiritual) one.

As a person begins to recognize his or her impending death, this acknowledgment may stimulate a period of life review, an assessment of one's accomplishments in life: What have I achieved or failed to achieve? How have I contributed to others' well-being or to the betterment of humankind? Have I met my expectations for a life well lived? How will my reputation fare after I'm gone? Has life been "fair"? Has my "good luck" outweighed the bad? In short, what is the "balance sheet" of my life? As a person realizes that he or she is nearing the end of life, the most important thing may be "to believe that life has, if not a purpose, at least a singularity that makes it memorable."[79] The "narrative," or story, of a person's life is important.

In coping with life-threatening illness, individuals often find ways of redefining their situation so that they still feel "healthy." A woman with metastatic cancer said, "I am really very healthy. I just have this problem, but I am still me." Her statement shows a sense of self-integrity that demonstrates an ability to go on with life despite the disease.[80]

"Being healthy" is a vital characteristic of our social world. Illness, according to sociologist Talcott Parsons, is accompanied by a particular social role.[81] The obligation of the sick person is to engage in a supervised attempt to get well. Like all social roles—parent, child, student, employee, spouse—the role of the "person who is sick" includes rights and responsibilities. Illness tends

I have never understood the purpose of a newspaper obituary. As a published notice of death, it certainly works well enough. As a biography filled with concrete facts—achievements, mostly—it gives the life in question a one-sided loftiness devoid of the flaws and failures that make it whole. And where is the mention of an individual's spirit, his effectiveness as a human being, his courage in adversity? What about people who successfully battle illness for many years before they succumb? What are their achievements in this regard, or do they simply "die after a long illness"?

Spencer Nadler, *The Language of Cells: A Doctor and His Patients*

to excuse a person from his or her usual tasks. We may stay home from work, and someone else may take on our share of domestic or social commitments. We are granted the right to be sick. Other people make allowances for our behavior. Whereas taking off from work just to enjoy a day in the sun is frowned upon, absence due to illness elicits sympathy rather than reprimands. The sick person not only enjoys exemptions from usual social obligations, but also is given special consideration and care. Such care is part of the social role of being sick, of being a patient. But these "rights" are balanced by responsibilities. The sick person must cooperate with caregivers. You've got to take your medicine.

The terminally ill or dying person does not neatly fit the parameters of the "sick role" described by Parsons because terminal illness is not a temporary condition that is expected to be followed by a return to wellness. However, our society has not clearly defined a social role for the dying person. Even when circumstances are clearly contrary, the dying person may be urged to hope for recovery, to deny the reality of his or her experience. This sometimes results in actions that are incongruous. Consider, for example, the situation of an end-stage terminally ill person being rushed to the ICU (intensive care unit) and subjected to heroic medical attempts to sustain his or her life.

What would an appropriate social role for the dying look like? First, the dying person would not be expected to maintain an appearance of expecting to live forever, of getting well again, of sustaining false hope. He or she would be encouraged to mobilize the necessary resources for attending to the prospect of death. Relatives and friends, accepting this changed perspective as natural, would allow the patient to set his or her own agenda about activities and relationships as the end of life draws closer.[82] In a study of "farewells by the dying," most wanted to express their farewells through giving gifts, writing letters, and informal conversations with those closest to them.[83] Valued relationships are important for most people right to the end of life.

The social role of the dying encompasses spiritual as well as physical and emotional needs, including[84]

1. *The need for meaning and purpose.* This involves reviewing one's life (including relationships, work, other achievements, and religious concerns) and

[margin annotation: MODERN Society]

attempting to make sense of it, to place it with[...]
has meaning.

2. *The need for hope and creativity.* Whereas the fir[...]
looking back over one's life to discover meani[...]
oriented toward the future. It may involve th[...]
well-being, for being free of pain; the desire[...]
goal or to achieve reconciliation with others;[...]
This need may also center on the hope "that th[...]
ing and purpose to the individual may be aff[...]
portant to him or her."

3. *The need to give and receive love.* As Roderick Cosh says, "We all need to be reassured that we are loved and that others need our love."[85] Reconciliation is a key element in satisfying this human spiritual need.

In an essay, "The Eyes of a Dying Man," Japanese writer Yasunari Kawabata suggests that the human longing for beauty is realized in a special way by persons who are dying, and this theme is echoed in his stories: In "The Moon in the Water," a dying man finds an enhanced appreciation of the beauty of nature; in *The Sound of the Mountain,* an aged man, approaching death, enjoys an intensified awareness of the beauty of the heroine Kikuko; in *The House of the Sleeping Beauties,* the "beauties" are all the more beautiful because they are seen through the eyes of old Eguchi, who knows his days are numbered.[86]

Further Readings

Lance Armstrong. *It's Not About the Bike: My Journey Back to Life.* New York: Putnam, 2000.

Joan Berzoff and Phyllis R. Silverman. *Living with Dying: A Handbook for End-of-Life Healthcare Practitioners.* New York: Columbia University Press, 2004.

Ira Byock. *Dying Well: The Prospect for Growth at the End of Life.* New York: Riverhead, 1997.

Maggie Callanan and Patricia Kelley. *Final Gifts: Understanding the Special Awareness, Needs, and Communications of the Dying.* New York: Bantam, 1997.

Pauline W. Chen. *Final Exam: A Surgeon's Reflections on Mortality.* New York: Knopf, 2007.

Joanne Lynn and Joan Harrold, eds. *Handbook for Mortals: Guidance for People Facing Serious Illness.* New York: Oxford University Press, 1999.

Nancy Manahan and Becky Bohan. *Living Consciously, Dying Gracefully: A Journey with Cancer and Beyond.* Edina, Minn.: Beaver's Pond Press, 2007.

David B. Morris. *The Culture of Pain.* Berkeley: University of California Press, 1991.

Ernest H. Rosenbaum and Isadora Rosenbaum. *Supportive Cancer Care: The Complete Guide for Patients and Their Families.* Naperville, Ill.: Sourcebooks, 2001.

L. Eugene Thomas. "Personal Reflections on Terminal Illness After Twenty Years of Teaching a Death and Dying Course," *Omega: Journal of Death and Dying* 43, no. 2 (2001): 119–127.

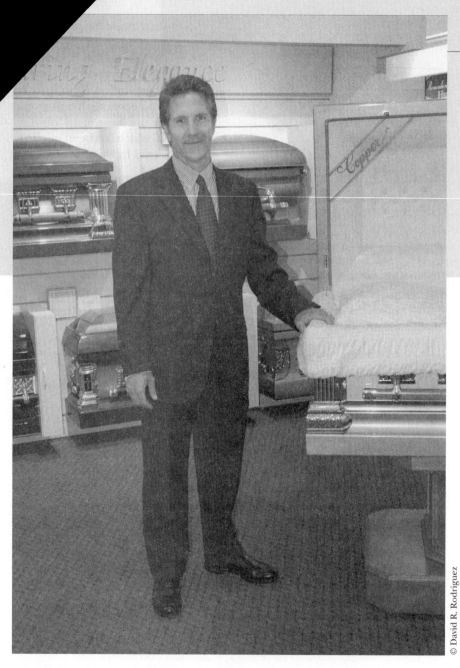

Familiarity with the choices available in funeral services can help us appreciate our many options, perhaps alleviating some of the stress of making such choices in the midst of crisis. The roles of the funeral director and others who can provide assistance in coping with the practical matters of death may also be better understood.

CHAPTER 8

Last Rites: Funerals and Body Disposition

The ceremonies that a community enacts to mark the passing of one of its members express, through symbol and metaphor, how death is perceived within a particular social group. A young musician describes the ceremony he would choose to mark his death: "My body would be cremated and the ashes put into an Egyptian urn. My friends would place the urn on stage at a concert and, as the band plays on, everyone will dance and celebrate the changes that we all must pass through eventually."

Some people find the musician's choice lacking in solemnity. "That's not a funeral," they say. "It's a party." The friends of the musician, however, might respond that his death style is consistent with his lifestyle. His funeral celebrates the joys of life. His preference for cremation may reflect a belief that existence is transitory. It's as if he were saying, "Life is a passing show. When the movie's over for me, why should my body be preserved?" The urn in which the ashes are placed symbolizes the view that he is part of a historical continuity that transcends death. Each part of the musician's death ceremony tells us something about his concept of death. Mike Parker Pearson says,

> It may be that the origins of ritual for the human species lie in disposing of the corpse, helping the bereaved, and adjusting to the community's loss. Death is the most significant of the rites of passage in our progress from womb to tomb.[2]

273

As you begin to think about the significance of funeral ceremonies, consider these questions: Who does the funeral serve—the living or the dead? What is the purpose—socially and psychologically—of last rites? What do funeral customs of other cultures tell us about their attitudes toward death?

Examining the death customs of the ancient Egyptians, we see a culture focused on acquiring mortuary goods and preparing for the afterlife.[3] A dominant theme in Egyptian religion was belief in life after death. The body was mortal. Yet, within it were immortal elements: the *Ba*, a soul or psychic force, and the *Ka*, a spiritual double representing the creative and sustaining power of life. At death, the *Ka* flew to the afterlife while the *Ba* lived on in the body.

As the permanent dwelling place of the *Ba*, the body was preserved by mummification and protected by wooden coffins, sometimes placed within a stone sarcophagus, or limestone coffin. The tomb was built to resemble an earthly home. Providing a home for the *Ba* (often depicted in the form of a bird hovering above the mummy of the deceased) ensured that the deceased would enjoy the afterlife. However, if the *Ba* were destroyed, the deceased would suffer "the second death, the death that really did come as the end." Thus, preserving the physical form, as mummy or statue, was necessary for survival.

In contrast to cultures in which the funeral is seen as a vehicle for preparing the dead to successfully migrate to the afterworld, funerals in the United States are mainly focused on the welfare of the survivors. Socially, funerals provide a setting wherein the bereaved family makes a public statement that one of its members has died. The wider community uses the occasion to respond with sympathy and support for the bereaved. According to Vanderlyn Pine, the funeral has historically addressed four major social functions:[4]

1. It serves to acknowledge and commemorate a person's death.
2. It provides a setting for the disposition of the dead body.
3. It assists in reorienting the bereaved to their lives, which have been ruptured by the death.
4. It demonstrates reciprocal economic and social obligations between the bereaved and their social world.

Traditionally, funeral rites begin with the gathering of family and friends for a "deathwatch" to say farewells and accompany the dying person in his or her last hours of life, and they formally end with the disposition of the corpse (see Table 8-1). Modern funerals do not always include all of the traditional elements, or some may be abbreviated, depending on individual and cultural preferences. The various elements of funeral ritual have both social and psychological significance in helping the bereaved deal with a loved one's death. Review the descriptions given in Table 8-1 and consider which of the elements you believe would have value in planning a funeral for a loved one or which you would want to have included as part of your own last rites.

TABLE 8-1 *Elements of Funeral Ritual*

1. *Deathwatch* (also known as the "death vigil" or "sitting up"). As death nears, tives and friends gather to say farewells and show respect for the dying person, as well as give support and care to his or her family. Historically, a deathwatch might continue for hours, days, or even weeks or months.

2. *Preparation of the deceased.* Involves various tasks associated with preparing the corpse for ultimate disposition, usually burial or cremation.

3. *Wake* (also known as "visitation" or "calling hours"). Traditionally held on the night after death occurs, this practice involves laying out the corpse and keeping a watch or "wake" over it. Historically, wakes were observed as a safeguard against premature burial, as an opportunity for paying respects to the deceased, and, in some cultures, as an occasion for lively festivities focused on allaying fears by "rousing the ghost."

    With changes in the social patterns of mourning, the traditional wake has been transformed into the practice of setting aside time for viewing of the body prior to the funeral service. As with traditional wakes, the modern "visitation" offers opportunities for social interactions that can be healing in the aftermath of loss.

4. *Funeral.* As the "centerpiece" of the ritual surrounding death, the funeral is a rite of passage for both the deceased and his or her survivors. Services are usually held in a mortuary chapel or church, although they may be held in the home or at the gravesite. The body may or may not be present; if it is present, the casket may be open or closed. Funeral services typically include music, prayers, readings from scripture or other poetry or prose, a eulogy honoring the life of the deceased, and, less frequently, a funeral sermon focusing on the role of death in human life generally. In modern times, funerals are usually held within a few days after death, and they are increasingly scheduled in the evening or on weekends so mourners who work during the week can attend the service.

5. *Procession.* Traditionally, funerals include a procession conveying the corpse from the site of the funeral to the place of burial. It is considered an honor to be among the friends and relatives chosen to carry the deceased's body to its final resting place. Funerals for national leaders and other notables may include a lengthy procession, or cortege, with the corpse attended by honorary pallbearers.

6. *Committal.* A ceremony held at the grave or crematorium, the committal service is held after, or sometimes in lieu of, the funeral service. When it follows a funeral service, it usually consists of a brief ceremony focusing on disposition of the deceased's remains.

7. *Disposal of the corpse.* In modern societies, disposition usually means burial or cremation.

Psychosocial Aspects of Last Rites

Just as people gather to commemorate other major transitions in a person's life, such as birth and marriage, funerals and memorial services are rites of passage that commemorate a person's life in a community and acknowledge his or her passing from that community. Funerals and memorial services provide a framework that allows survivors to support one another as they cope with the fact of their loss and express their grief. The presence of death rites in every human culture suggests that they serve innate human needs. Thomas

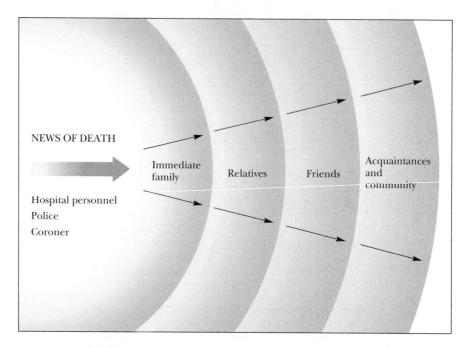

NEWS OF DEATH

Hospital personnel
Police
Coroner

Immediate family

Relatives

Friends

Acquaintances and community

Figure *8-1* *Widening Circles of Death Notification*

Lynch, author of *The Undertaking: Life Studies from the Dismal Trade,* makes the observation that "funerals are the way we close the gap between the death that happens and the death that matters."[5]

Death Notification

When a person dies, the first to learn about it, besides the attending medical team, are usually members of the person's immediate family. Then, in a widening circle of relatives, friends, and acquaintances, others affected by the death are notified. In his classic study, *Passing On: The Social Organization of Dying,* David Sudnow observed that death notification generally occurs in a consistent pattern from the immediate family to the wider community (see Figure 8-1).[6] Those with closest relationships to the deceased are notified first, followed by those with less intimate relationships. Sudnow also found that death notification generally takes place between people in a peer relationship. For example, a bereaved mother might first call the child who had been closest to the deceased, and that person then calls the other brothers and sisters. They, in turn, notify more distant kin. A similar pattern of notification occurs among people not directly related to the deceased. For instance, a coworker or neighbor informed about the death notifies others who had a similar relationship with the deceased. Ideally, this process of notification—taking in a gradually widening circle of relatives, friends, and acquaintances—continues until everyone affected by the death is notified.

Obituaries

Spirit Bird Benton

HAYWARD – Spirit Bird Benton, 17, Rt. 5, Hayward, died Friday, April 19, 1991, in Albuquerque, N.M. in an automobile accident.

Spirit Bird was born August 22, 1973 in St. Paul, Minn., the son of Edward J. and Delma (Arrow) Benton. He was a student at Lac Courte Oreilles High School.

He is survived by his father, Edward, Hayward; his mother, Delma, Tama, Iowa; three brothers, John Wedward and Ramon, both of Hayward and Eddie, Green Bay; four sisters, Marilyn, Nancy and Sherrole, all of Hayward and Natalie, Oneida; and a grandmother, Elizabeth Arrow, White River, S.D.

Tribal rites were held on Tuesday, April 23 at the Eagle Lodge, Hayward. Burial was in the Hayward Indian Cemetery in Historyland.

Anderson-Nathan Funeral Home of Hayward was in charge of arrangements.

Figure *8-2 Newspaper Obituary*
Source: The County Journal (Bayfield County, Cable, Wis.), April 25, 1991.

Notification also takes place by means of death notices and obituaries that appear in newspapers (see Figure 8-2). Human beings have an inherent need to respond to the death of someone significant to them. Thus, it is important for the notification process to occur in a timely fashion so that those affected by the death are able to come together in a spirit of mutual support to grieve their loss. When an announcement of death does not appear in a timely fashion, it can be upsetting. The following complaint is typical: "The obituary did not appear in the newspaper until the morning of the funeral. . . . We had a number of calls and letters from people who didn't know about the funeral until it was too late to attend."

Because the mutual support of the community of bereaved persons is not likely to be as available after the initial period of mourning has passed, the belatedly notified person may feel that he or she is alone in dealing with grief. The value placed on timely notification within the African American community is underscored by Ronald Barrett. He says, "The immediacy of notification is equated with importance and respect. To not be informed of the death in a timely manner is considered insensitive, lacking respect, and an insult."[7]

When the deceased is well known, news of the death is broadcast more widely because it affects more people. Thus, notification about the deaths of public figures is carried out on a grand scale. The death of President John F. Kennedy, for example, was known by about 90 percent of the American people within an hour of its official pronouncement at Parkland Hospital in Dallas.[8] A similar response occurred with the deaths of Diana, Princess of Wales, and John F. Kennedy, Jr.

The process of death notification also helps to set apart the bereaved during the period of mourning. In some societies, the black armband, mourning colors and garb, as well as various other signs and symbols, distinguish the bereaved person from those not in mourning. Such traditional signs of mourning have all but vanished in North America. Yet most people still feel that the bereaved deserve special consideration during their distress.

A woman who became involved in a minor automobile accident several days after the death of her child said later that she wished she could have had a banner proclaiming her status as a "mother whose child has just died." With no outward symbol of her bereavement, she was subjected, as any of us would be, to the strain of waiting around and filling in seemingly endless accident report forms. Had she lived in a small town, the process of notification itself might have set her apart in such a way that the task of completing the paperwork would have been made easier.

The process of death notification is important. It can elicit support that is helpful to survivors in dealing with their loss, and it provides an impetus for coming to terms with the fact that a significant loss has taken place.

Mutual Support

When people learn about the death of a person who is significant to them, they tend to gather together, closing ranks to provide support and comfort in their mutual bereavement. This emotional and social support is directed primarily toward the bereaved family. When a small child asked her mother why they were going to visit a bereaved family, the mother replied, "It's important for people to know that you care." What we think we can or cannot do for the bereaved family matters little; what counts is that we show our care and concern. J. Z. Young says, "Probably the very act of coming together symbolizes communication."[9] Assembling as a community reassures us that we are part of a larger whole, thereby strengthening our individual lives.

Funeral rituals embody the rhythms of separation and integration. Death is a change of status both for the person who dies and for his or her survivors. This change of status is reflected in language when we refer to someone as a "widow" or "widower." This special designation for a bereaved spouse affirms the social and psychological impact associated with the death of a mate. Based on a cross-cultural investigation of funeral rites, Vernon Reynolds and Ralph Tanner conclude:

> The importance of the rituals of death is that they are socioreligious requirements which have to be carried out by the bereaved within the social context of friends, relatives, and neighbors who are less bereaved. The bereaved are not left alone to generate and multiply the psychosomatic symptoms of their grief, but are required to be active, and in many cultures there is a special role for bereaved persons over quite a long period . . . at the end of which their recovery from bereavement is well advanced.[10]

Gathering at the home of the bereaved is a unique social occasion. Some people stay only a short time, express condolences, and leave. Others, usually relatives or close friends, stay for a longer time, perhaps assisting with the

Visiting with a family in a funeral home one night, we witnessed a woman enter the visiting room. She approached the casket and burst into convulsive tears. Two men stood up and supported her on either side as she sobbed loudly. The mother of the deceased man leaned over to me and said, "Brother Wayne, do you know that woman?" I had never seen her before. Everyone in the room was whispering and looking. "Who is that?" they were asking.

After this loud display, the men escorted the woman to a folding chair, where she gradually calmed herself. Finally, one of the men asked her how she was acquainted with his brother, Bill.

She raised her head and asked, "Bill?"

"Yes, that's my brother Bill."

The mystery lady stood, looked in the casket, and said, "Oh, I'm sorry . . . I'm in the wrong room," and quickly exited.

As we all doubled over with laughter, Bill's widow said, "I was fixin' to get up there and find out WHO she was and WHY she was so upset that Bill was dead!"

Wayne Delk, *U.S. Gospel News*

preparation of food, caring for children, helping with funeral arrangements, greeting visitors, and doing whatever else needs doing. This process of gathering together to support and comfort the bereaved continues throughout the events of the funeral. Such social interaction is psychologically important for the bereaved. The coming together of the friends and relatives to support one another confirms the significance of the loss.

Impetus for Coping with Loss

The death of a loved one is confronted not only within the social setting in which it occurs, but also within the psyche of the bereaved person. Death notification, visitation, and other after-death rituals are forms of social interaction that provide a potent psychological impetus for realizing a loss.

When death occurs, one of the immediate concerns of survivors is the disposition of the corpse. This involves both a mental process (deciding what is to be done) and a physical activity (carrying out the action decided upon). The final disposition of a dead body is surrounded by a web of social, cultural, religious, psychological, and personal considerations that determine how this task is accomplished. Making arrangements for the final disposition of the body engages survivors in a process that helps reinforce the recognition that the deceased person is really dead. This acknowledgment of the loss occurs whether the survivor simply talks with someone about funeral arrangements or actively constructs the coffin and digs the grave.

The funeral itself offers a range of opportunities for the bereaved to engage in activities that promote expression of grief. Survivors may place items that are significant to the deceased in the casket. The practice of burying "grave goods," or funerary artifacts, with the dead is found in many cultures.[11] Jewelry, photographs, rosaries, Bibles, favorite hats, military medals, stuffed

© Albert Lee Strickland

Located in a setting of great natural beauty on the Hawaiian island of Oahu, this Chinese cemetery is situated on a hillside that gently slopes down toward the city of Honolulu and the ocean beyond. Following Chinese custom, care is taken to ensure proper siting of the grave so that the deceased's spirit can easily depart this world. As in the case of this cemetery, located above a bustling, metropolitan city, certain aspects of traditional practices retain their importance even in modern social settings.

grave goods

animals, and organizational emblems are among the items commonly placed in the casket or buried with the deceased. Tobacco, alcohol, and articles related to a favorite activity such as golf or fishing are other examples of grave goods. The placing of such grave goods is a mourning practice that can be meaningful to survivors.

Funerals in the United States

Few people personally care for their own dead in modern societies. Most of us hire professionals, known as funeral directors or morticians, to provide services and merchandise for conducting a funeral service and handling various tasks involved in caring for the dead. As a result, the funeral business is generally viewed as a "mystery business," about which the average person knows little. Critics of the modern American funeral claim that, because of this widespread lack of familiarity, funeral directors are in a position to take advantage of their customers. This claim is made despite the fact that most people give funeral directors high marks for the services they provide at a distressing time.

Figure 8-3 *City Directory Listing for a Cabinet Maker and Supplier of Funeral Furnishings, circa 1850*

To counteract the possibility of abuses, the U.S. Federal Trade Commission (FTC) implemented the "Trade Regulation Rule on Funeral Industry Practices" in 1984.[12] The Funeral Rule, as it is called, stipulates that funeral service providers must give detailed information about prices and legal requirements to people who are arranging funerals. It requires the disclosure of itemized prices, both over the telephone and in writing. Misrepresentations about the disposition of human remains are prohibited, as are certain practices such as embalming for a fee without prior permission, requiring customers to purchase caskets for a direct cremation, or making the purchase of any funeral good or service conditional on the purchase of any other funeral good or service. The FTC Funeral Rule can be viewed as the natural outcome of a historical process that removed death from the purview of family and friends and placed it in the hands of professionals.

The Rise of Professional Funeral Services

When families themselves took care of the disposition of their dead, any criticism would have been irrelevant. And, of course, there was no profit motive. Disposition of the dead was simply a human task to be carried out by the family and community. At a time when the family's ceremonial occasions involving death were held within the home, the "undertaker" mainly functioned as a merchant who supplied materials and funeral paraphernalia—such items as the casket and carriage, door badges and scarves, special clothing, memorial cards and announcements, chairs, robes, pillows, gauze, candles, ornaments, and so on—that were used for mourning rituals (see Figure 8-3). From such humble beginnings, the funeral service "industry" became more commercialized.[13]

By the later decades of the nineteenth century, the undertaker was assuming a larger role in caring for the dead. No longer merely a tradesman who furnished goods to bereaved families, the undertaker became a provider of services. He began to actually take part in the disposition of the dead: laying out the body for the wake, transporting it to the church for the funeral, and, finally, taking it to the cemetery for burial. With the coming of smaller houses and increased urbanization, the viewing of the body moved from the parlor of the family home to a room reserved for such use by the tradesman-undertaker. The funeral "parlor" in town became a substitute for the ceremonial room that people no longer had in their own homes. This one-room funeral parlor was the forerunner of the present-day funeral home or mortuary.

Also around this time, undertakers were becoming "morticians" and were starting to view themselves as "funeral *directors*."[14] The Funeral Directors' National Association, established in the 1880s—now the National Funeral Directors Association (NFDA)—was among the first of the new trade organizations designed to promote funeral service businesses as well as establish standards. Early trade publications, such as *The Casket* and *Sunnyside*, helped to facilitate communication among funeral directors.

Professionalism in funeral service continued with the founding, in 1917, of the National Selected Morticians (now known as Selected Independent Funeral Homes), a limited-membership group dedicated to the ideal of excellent service. In 1945, the National Foundation of Funeral Service was formed to conduct research, establish a library of funeral service information, and sponsor an institute providing professional education for funeral directors.

More recently, many funeral directors have expanded their services to include "aftercare" programs, which can range from simply telephoning a bereaved spouse after the funeral to see how he or she is doing to offering counseling or support groups for bereaved individuals. Staff members may attend training programs to prepare themselves for offering aftercare; and, in some cases, the funeral establishment hires a certified psychologist or grief counselor to manage such services. In some communities, a local hospice and funeral home join forces in providing support groups. Many funeral directors view this offering of aftercare service—this extension of their professional services—as a contemporary expression of "old-fashioned neighborly concern."[15]

Traditionally, the clergy has played a large role in assisting bereaved families in making funeral arrangements. Whereas funerals were once commonly held in churches, they are now more likely to be held in funeral homes. The move from church to mortuary chapel (along with the more dominant role of mortuary personnel) has sometimes put a strain on relationships between clergy and funeral directors. Some members of the clergy are now bringing funeral services back into church and generally assuming a greater presence in funeral arrangements. In fact, some churches have started operating their own "funeral businesses" or have contracted with corporations that agree to provide funerals for parishioners at a discounted cost.

During the past couple of decades, conglomeration in the funeral industry has become a major trend and a much-debated topic. Large multinational corporations that own hundreds of funeral homes are purchasing neighborhood "mom-and-pop" funeral homes, many of which have been family owned and operated for generations. Many observers wonder whether the "personal touch" provided by locally owned funeral homes will be lost with corporate ownership. In some communities, long-time customers of funeral homes that were once family owned but are now owned by corporations are "voting with their feet" as they switch to mortuary establishments that remain devoted to local ownership and personal service.

Even though we are now accustomed to turning over care of our dead to professionals, the idea of profiting from such services may seem somehow macabre. When a corpse belongs to someone we loved, the common aversion to touching a dead body may be mixed with guilt. Unconscious resentment may be felt toward the funeral director or mortician who prepares the body of our loved one for final disposition. Pulled in opposing directions, we may experience a confusing range of emotions regarding our dead: aversion, guilt, resentment, anxiety, and affection. Lack of familiarity with the dead can result in funeral directors and funeral establishments becoming a lightning rod for criticisms.

Criticisms of Funeral Practices

Funerals have attracted criticism of various kinds since ancient times. The Greek philosopher Herodotus, in the fourth century B.C.E., spoke critically about what he called lavish displays for the dead. American funeral practices have received their share of criticism as well, as funeral ceremonies and care of the dead became professionalized, no longer a standard part of domestic life. One of the earliest criticisms was directed not just at funeral practices, but at the funeral itself. Published in 1926, Bertram Puckle's *Funeral Customs: Their Origin and Development* argued that the modern funeral was merely the vestige of a "pagan" superstitious fear of the dead. Like Herodotus, Puckle was especially critical of elaborate ceremonies for the dead.

In 1959, the commercialism and conspicuous display connected with funerals were documented by LeRoy Bowman in *The American Funeral: A Study in Guilt, Extravagance, and Sublimity.*[16] Bowman was especially interested in the social and psychological value of funerals, and he was concerned that modern funerals were overlaid with such ostentation that the essential meaning and dignity of funeral rites had all but disappeared. The American funeral, Bowman said, "appears to be an anachronism, an elaboration of early customs rather than the adaptation to modern needs that it should be." In Bowman's view, the funeral director was a tradesman, selling wares that were unnecessary and unwanted. Bowman believed that consumers could avoid the potential for exploitation associated with the materialistic features of contemporary practices by becoming aware of the essential social, psychological, and spiritual functions of funeral rituals. The function of the funeral director, said Bowman, should be to help the family fulfill its own wishes. He also argued for greater flexibility in funeral service: "The uniformity of present usage," he said, "should give way to individually adapted procedures, whatever they may be."

In 1963, two books appeared that brought widespread public attention to funeral practices in the United States: Jessica Mitford's *The American Way of Death* and Ruth M. Harmer's *The High Cost of Dying*. Both Mitford and Harmer were critical of what they viewed as excessive materialism in funeral practices. These publications, especially Mitford's *The American Way of Death*, stimulated

Drawing by P. C. Vey, © 2004 The New Yorker Collection

"That's the fourth husband she's put in the ground without any concern for what it's doing to the environment."

efforts by consumer advocates to lobby for greater governmental regulation of funeral businesses.

To Mitford, who employed a heavy dose of satire in making her case, conventional funeral practices were bizarre and morbid; efforts to disguise and prettify death made it more grotesque. The language used by funeral industry personnel became a special target of Mitford's wit. She took issue with the euphemisms employed to soften the reality of death: the metamorphosis of coffins into "caskets," hearses into "coaches," flowers into "floral tributes," and cremated ashes into "cremains." The corpse lies in state in the "slumber room." The undertaker, now a "funeral director," displays a solid-copper "Colonial Classic Beauty" casket, replete with "Perfect-Posture" adjustable mattress, in a choice of "60 color-matched shades." The deceased wears "handmade original fashions" from a "gravewear couturiere" and "Nature-Glo, the ultimate in cosmetic grooming."[17] Mitford's use of wry humor in her critical examination of funeral practices was reminiscent of Evelyn Waugh's earlier novel, *The Loved One* (1948), in which Waugh employed satire to poke fun at what he believed were hypocritical and death-avoiding attitudes relative to funerals.

Despite criticisms of American funeral practices by Mitford and others, most people appear to be satisfied with the quality of service provided by their local mortuaries. Funeral directors often receive expressions of gratitude from the people they serve for their help in sorting out the events that immediately follow the death of a loved one. The typical funeral director is committed to meeting the needs and wishes of bereaved families, even when they vary from "standard" practices, as the following story illustrates.

When a Dutch couple died unexpectedly while traveling in South America, their relatives felt that the couple's intimacy and sharing in life should be carried through to their death rites. They wanted the couple buried together in one coffin and in one grave. Although this request had never been made before, the funeral establishment checked applicable laws and found that they did not prohibit the family's wishes being carried out. There were practical problems, however. No company made a double casket. Acting quickly, the funeral home found a craftsman who was able to make a special casket by working overtime and, with a few adjustments, all went smoothly. The funeral director said, "We are proud that we have been able to arrange this committal for the couple in which, for the children, the love between their parents was confirmed."[18] A willingness to "go the extra mile" is typical of funeral directors.

Selecting Funeral Services

Symbolism in death rites

In commemorating a person's life and death, the choice of last rites may involve a traditional funeral ceremony or a simple memorial service. Whereas the casketed body is typically present at a funeral, it is not at a memorial service. In some cases, both a funeral and a memorial service are held, the former occurring within a few days after death and the latter being held sometime later (perhaps in a different town, where the deceased had a large social network). Although some individuals and families express a preference that no funeral services be held, bereaved relatives and friends usually benefit from having an opportunity to honor the deceased and express their grief through ceremony.

Decisions about one's own last rites are ideally made with a view to the needs and wishes of one's survivors. In making plans or arrangements, you may want to review the various elements that are traditionally part of after-death rituals (see Table 8-1, earlier in this chapter). Religious and cultural traditions play a major role in shaping the way people honor their dead. A meaningful funeral or memorial service can be designed in many different ways.

The purchase of funeral services is a transaction unique in commerce. Most people give it little or no thought until they find themselves in the midst of an emotional crisis. As with other purchases, however, the customer who winds up with the fewest regrets is likely to be the one who takes time beforehand to investigate his or her options. When arrangements for funeral services are made during a crisis, the customer must make an on-the-spot decision about a purchase that cannot be returned. Caskets do not bear a notice saying, "Return in thirty days if not completely satisfied." Once made, the decision is final.

Selecting funeral services differs from the way we make most other purchases. When purchasing a new car, for example, you can shop around and test-drive various makes and models. If you encounter a salesperson who uses high-pressure tactics, you can either submit or walk away: You have a clear choice. Yet the emotional circumstances surrounding the purchase of funeral services rarely allow for such objectivity or coolheadedness. The bereaved is usually not in a position to simply walk away and compare prices elsewhere. In some towns, there is just one funeral business to serve the entire community. Once a death has occurred, it may be too late to fully investigate the options. (However, there is no law that prohibits moving a body from one funeral home to another.)

It is unfortunate when an expensive casket or lavish display becomes the focal point of a funeral merely because survivors are attempting to assuage guilt or compensate for unresolved conflict with the deceased. Spending a huge sum of money on a funeral may, in some circumstances, thwart the real purpose of last rites—namely, to effect closure on the deceased's life and comfort the bereaved. As Thomas Lynch, a funeral director and poet-essayist, says, "In even the best of caskets, it never all fits—all that we'd like to bury in them: the hurt and forgiveness, the anger and pain, the praise and thanksgiving, the emptiness and exaltations, the untidy feelings when someone dies."[19]

The funeral is a setting for private sorrow and public loss in which the burden of grief is reduced by sharing with others. It effects the disposition of the corpse while acknowledging that indeed a life has been lived. The funeral is a statement from the family to the community: "We have lost someone, and we are grieving." It is a statement based on felt needs and values, and it is worth remembering that the purpose of the funeral can be realized whether it is garnished with diamonds and rubies or with poetry and a song.

Funeral Service Charges

The National Funeral Directors Association distinguishes four categories of costs related to the conventional American funeral. The first category includes services provided by the funeral director and mortuary staff, the use of mortuary facilities and equipment, and the casket and any other funeral merchandise selected by the customer.

The second category pertains to the disposition of the body. This can include the purchase of a gravesite and costs for opening and closing the grave; or, if aboveground entombment is chosen, the cost of a mausoleum crypt; or, if the body is cremated, the cost of cremation and subsequent interment, entombment, or scattering of the cremated remains, as well as the cost of an urn to hold the ashes, if desired.

The third category involves costs related to memorialization. For burials, this can include a monument or marker for the grave; for cremated remains, it can include an inscription or plaque for the niche (recessed compartment) in a *columbarium*, an aboveground structure with a series of niches for urns.

The fourth category involves miscellaneous expenses. These may include a clergy member's honorarium, the use of limousines and additional vehicles

William E. Rosemund, U.S. Army Photo

Thousands of American citizens joined in the funeral observance honoring the Unknown Serviceman of the Vietnam Era. Here the procession is crossing Memorial Bridge between a Marine honor cordon, on its way to Arlington National Cemetery. Replete with full military honors, the funeral was an occasion for expressing national gratitude and grief in response to the ultimate sacrifice of those who died in the wartime service of their country.

If you have an uncomfortable feeling about funerals, which are the accepted social pattern for confronting death in our culture, if you try to avoid or eliminate them, that might be a sign that you're dealing with major residual death anxiety. That's one of the things that shows up in our culture: the way people delude themselves and retreat from the major therapeutic resources that are provided culturally. There's a notion that if we have a mini-funeral, we'll have mini-grief. But we know that the exact opposite is true.

The more you reduce your emotional acting out at the time of the event, the more you prolong the pain of grief and postpone the therapeutic work of mourning.

That's why in a culture such as ours, where you have an unwise management of grief, you have a very large proportion of illness responses after the death experience. People act it out physically, rather than doing it psychologically or socially. That's a very heavy weight.

But in primitive cultures, such as the aboriginals in Australia, where you have almost a two-week funeral process, where there are all kinds of acting out of deep feelings, you come to the end of that two weeks and a major portion of the grief work has been done, and the survivor is ready to move into the period of resolution through the mourning process, which takes quite a bit longer usually.

Edgar N. Jackson, from an interview with the authors

(if not included in the funeral services category), flowers, death notices in newspapers, and transportation of the body outside the local area, if necessary.

With the advent of the Federal Trade Commission's Funeral Rule in 1984, it has become a requirement for all funeral businesses to provide itemized price information on a general price list so that customers can compare prices or choose only those elements of a funeral they want. It is important to note that FTC requirements do not prohibit funeral directors from also offering "package" funerals for a single price.

Funeral costs vary among regions of the country, as well as between rural and metropolitan areas. The average cost of an adult funeral, including casket but excluding cemetery costs, is about $6500.[20] With about 2.4 million Americans dying each year, expenditures for funeral, cemetery, and other such "death care" services total about $15 billion.[21] Although many funeral service firms are small businesses, considered in the aggregate, disposition of the dead is big business.

Comparing the Costs

Even when itemized, costs quoted by different funeral homes may be difficult to compare. Funeral providers do not always offer exactly the same goods and services, and they may have different ways of presenting prices. Nevertheless, it is useful to distinguish the usual charges. In reading the following discussion of funeral goods and services, notice that national price ranges for funeral services and merchandise are given. You will find it interesting to compare prices in your own area with these national ranges by obtaining information from local funeral homes.

Professional Services

Funeral costs include a basic charge for the services provided by mortuary staff, such as arranging the funeral, consulting with family members and clergy, directing the visitation and funeral ceremony, and preparing and filing necessary notices and authorizations related to body disposition. The latter may include filing the death certificate and certain claims for death benefits.

The fee for professional services ($400–$3000) also must cover a share of the overhead and business expenses required to maintain facilities and staff. Mortuary facilities usually require a large capital investment because of their specialized design. The typical funeral business is located in a large, possibly colonial style, building. The floor plan may be designed especially to function as a funeral home. Funerals have been compared to theatrical presentations, with certain activities taking place "off stage." The backstage area, hidden from the public's gaze, is where the body is prepared by embalming and application of cosmetics for its eventual role in the funeral drama. There is generally no hint of these backstage regions to those who enter by the front door. The funeral chapel itself has been described as "a model of theatrical perfection" that might well "make a Broadway star envious."[22] Usually arranged in such a way that there are several entrances and exits, it "may be served by back doors, halls, tunnels, and passageways that lead from the preparation room without ever trespassing frontstage areas."

Besides the fee for professional services, mortuaries usually charge an "intake fee" ($50–$1850) for transferring remains from the place of death to the mortuary, and there may be a surcharge for after-hours (night or weekend) pickup. Cemetery or crematory services, flowers, placement of newspaper notices, and other incidental costs are usually billed separately.

As an alternative pricing method, the FTC rule allows funeral providers to include the professional service fee as part of the cost of caskets. When this is done, however, a description of such services must appear on the casket price list.

The FTC Funeral Rule also specifies that, with direct cremation or immediate burial, the fee for professional services must be included in the price quoted for those methods of disposition. Similarly, the fee for professional services must be included in prices quoted for forwarding remains to another funeral home or receiving remains from another funeral home.

Embalming

A body destined for burial or cremation may or may not be embalmed ($185–$990). If the body will be viewed during a wake or will be present at the funeral, however, embalming is generally done (although facilities with "cold rooms" may substitute for embalming). Embalming methods have differed among cultures, and results have varied correspondingly with respect to

What sounds downright oxymoronic to most of the subspecies—a *good* funeral—is, among undertakers, a typical idiom. And though I'll grant some are pulled into the undertaking by big cars and black suits and rumors of riches, the attrition rate is high among those who do not like what they are doing. Unless the novice mortician finds satisfaction in helping others at a time of need, or "serving the living by caring for the dead" as one of our slogans goes, he or she will never stick it. Unless, of course, they make a pile of money early on. But most of us who can afford to send our kids to the orthodontist but not to boarding schools, who are tied to our brick and mortar and cash-flow worries, who live with the business phone next to our beds, whose dinners and intimacies are always being interrupted by the needs of others, would not do so unless there were satisfactions beyond the fee schedule. Most of the known world could not be paid enough to embalm a neighbor on Christmas or stand with an old widower at his wife's open casket or talk with a leukemic mother about her fears for her children to be motherless. The ones who last in this work are the ones who believe what they do is not only good for business and the bottom line, but good, after everything, for the species.

Thomas Lynch,
The Undertaking: Life Studies from the Dismal Trade

preservation of the corpse. In *Death to Dust,* Kenneth Iserson says, "Originally, embalming meant placing balm, essentially natural sap and aromatic substances, on a corpse."[23] In modern usage, embalming involves removing the blood and other fluids in the body and replacing them with chemicals to disinfect and temporarily retard deterioration of the corpse.

In the United States, embalming was adopted around the time of the Civil War, as funeral homes like Brown & Alexander in Washington, D.C., began to make embalming available to their clientele. Brown was a medical doctor whose interest in embalming grew out of his training in anatomy and his marriage to the daughter of the man who founded Kirk & Nice in Philadelphia, the oldest funeral home in the United States, which began operation in 1761. After witnessing embalming demonstrations by a French doctor in New York City, Brown decided to offer this service at no charge to "soldiers who may be so unfortunate as to die or be killed while at the seat of war and away from their families and friends."[24] The funeral procession for President Abraham Lincoln, which traveled by train from Washington, D.C., to Springfield, Illinois, was a public event that greatly increased awareness of the practice of embalming.[25] During this period, however, other means of temporarily retarding decomposition of the corpse remained in use (see Figure 8-4).

Embalming is such an accepted practice in America that few people question it, and it is usually considered a practical necessity by most mortuary establishments when a body will be viewed. With few exceptions, however, the FTC Funeral Rule requires that mortuaries obtain express permission to embalm from the family in order to charge a fee for the procedure.[26] Further-

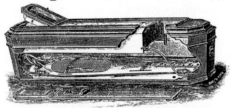
Figure 8-4 *Refrigerated Casket Advertisement, 1881*
Undertakers of the 1880s could keep a body for viewing over a longer
period of time by using an ice casket, such as the one shown in this
advertisement. When embalming became widespread, these cold-air
preservation devices became obsolete.

more, the mortuary's price list must include the following disclosure next to
the price for embalming:

> Except in certain special cases, embalming is not required by law. Embalming
> may be necessary, however, if you select certain funeral arrangements, such as a
> funeral with viewing. If you do not want embalming, you usually have the right to
> choose an arrangement which does not require you to pay for it, such as direct
> cremation or immediate burial.

Some mortuaries have a combined fee for both embalming and body preparation; others itemize the procedures separately. In addition to basic antisep-
tic hygiene procedures, body preparation services may include cosmetology,
hair styling, and manicuring, as well as dressing the body, placing it in the casket, and composing it for viewing.

If refrigeration or a "cold room" is available, a mortuary may offer the alternative of storing a body for a short time without embalming. A refrigerated, unembalmed body will remain relatively preserved for about three days,
although some mortuaries stipulate that they will not hold an unembalmed

body for longer than forty-eight hours. Refrigeration usually costs somewhat less than embalming.

Caskets

Most people feel that the casket is the centerpiece of a funeral because of its symbolic and emotional value in honoring the deceased. The average amount spent on a casket is about $2300. However, when it comes to buying a casket, customers have a wide range of choices, and prices are highly variable. Choices range from inexpensive cardboard containers all the way to solid mahogany, copper, or bronze caskets that cost thousands of dollars. Most funeral homes display caskets in a range of prices. Because funeral businesses determine their own methods of pricing caskets, customers may find that a casket selling for $1500 in one funeral home costs twice that amount in another. This price difference may be due to a higher markup by the second fu-

Library of Congress

The funeral has traditionally been a time when family and friends come together to pay respects and to say farewells. It is a time of mutual support for the bereaved and of tribute to the deceased. The display of flowers surrounding this coffin bespeaks the affection felt for the deceased while she was alive and the sense of loss at her absence from the community.

neral home; or, as mentioned earlier, the fee for professional services may be included in the casket price rather than charged separately.

Caskets at the lower end of the price range are typically made of cloth-covered plywood or pressboard and contain a mattress that is likely to be made of straw covered with an acetate sheet. At the next pricing level, refinements appear. The casket may be covered with copper or bronze sheathing, and the mattress constructed with springs and topped by a layer of foam rubber with a covering of acetate material. In this mid-range, gasketed steel caskets are available with devices intended to ensure an airtight environment within the casket. (Although this provides solace for some people, any added protection is debatable.) The gasketed steel casket is the most popular choice in the United States.

The price for a "top-of-the-line" casket ranges from about $5000 upward to $25,000 or more. For this sum, there are caskets constructed of mahogany, copper, or bronze and fitted out with all the embellishments of the casket manufacturer's art.

The FTC rule requires funeral providers to supply customers with a list of the prices and descriptions of available caskets. This may be done either on the general price list or on a separate casket price list. In addition, the FTC rule stipulates that customers have the right to buy a casket from a different supplier than the funeral home contracted to handle all the other aspects of the funeral service and burial. In addition, mortuaries may not charge handling fees on caskets purchased elsewhere.

The FTC rule has led to an increase in the number of casket discounters, some of which are operated as small chains. Although many discounters are storefront businesses or are even located in shopping malls, some are set up so that customers can order caskets via a toll-free number or on the Internet. Some mortuaries are joining this trend by opening their own "funeral shops," where caskets and funeral accessories are sold at discounted prices. Despite having the opportunity to avoid part of the markup on caskets, most people do not feel comfortable about buying funeral merchandise at discount. Not only do funeral homes provide "one-stop shopping" for merchandise and services, but the notion of "skimping" on a loved one's funeral also may be troubling. Nevertheless, for some people, casket retailers appear to be an idea whose time has come. The Regale Funeral Store in London, England, a "funeral supermarket," offers flowers, memorials, caskets, urns, and other funeral paraphernalia in a supermarket-style shopping hall, with the prices of all products and services clearly itemized and priced.[27]

People are usually surprised to learn that there is no law requiring that a body destined for cremation must be placed in a casket. Most crematoria require only that the body be delivered in a rigid container. Mortuaries can provide a body-sized cardboard box that suffices for this purpose. The FTC rule prohibits funeral providers from telling consumers that state or local law requires them to purchase a casket when they want to arrange a direct cremation (that is, a cremation that occurs without formal viewing of the remains or any visitation or ceremony with the body present). The FTC rule stipulates that firms offering direct cremation provide the following disclosure:

> If you want to arrange a direct cremation, you can use an unfinished wood box or an alternative container. Alternative containers can be made of materials like heavy cardboard or composition materials (with or without an outside covering), or pouches of canvas.

Outer Burial Containers

If outer burial containers (vaults or grave liners) are offered for sale by a funeral home, prices must be listed ($250–$17,800), either separately or on the general price list, and the following disclosure must be made:

> In most areas of the country, no state or local law makes you buy a container to surround the casket in the grave. However, many cemeteries require that you have such a container so that the grave will not sink in. Either a burial vault or a grave liner will satisfy these requirements.

Because many funeral businesses do not sell burial vaults or grave liners, this item may not appear on the price lists of mortuaries in your area.

Facilities and Vehicles

The use of a visitation or viewing room ($50–$1100) is a common component of most American funerals. In the itemized listing of prices, the funeral establishment may use whatever method of pricing it prefers or follow common practice in its area. For example, various settings in the funeral home might be listed, along with the charges for each by day, half day, or hour. Similarly, if funeral ceremonies can be held in a chapel at the funeral home, a charge for its use will be specified ($75–$3100). When other facilities are made available to customers (for example, tent and chairs for graveside services), the charges must be stated on the price list.

According to the FTC rule, charges for the use of a hearse, limousine, or other automotive equipment provided by the mortuary must be itemized separately on the general price list ($50–$600). Family members, pallbearers, or other participants such as clergy often use vehicles provided by a funeral home. A "flower car" (or van) may be engaged to transport floral arrangements from the place where the funeral is held to the cemetery or crematorium. A fee will also be assessed when a motorcycle escort is hired to be part of the procession.

Miscellaneous Charges

In the miscellaneous category are charges for goods or services provided directly by the funeral home, as well as charges incurred on behalf of the customer from outside sources. The latter include cash-advance items, such as floral arrangements and newspaper notices. The customer may be billed for the actual amounts of the items, or the funeral provider may add a surcharge for arranging these cash-advance items. If an additional charge is made, a notice to that effect must be shown on the general price list.

As a testament to changing times, funeral-cremation providers must be reminded that valuables on bodies might no longer only include ordinary items such as rings, watches, earrings, necklaces, bracelets, anklets, and toe rings nor be confined to ears, toes, fingers, necks or wrists. Body piercing is common. Diligence now requires thoroughly inspecting other parts of the body that may contain valuables. The tongue, chest, navel, pubic areas and nasal cavity must be inspected.

Michael Kubasak and William M. Lamers, Jr.,
Traversing the Minefield—Best Practice:
Reducing Risk in Funeral-Cremation Service

The FTC rule specifically mentions that acknowledgment cards ($10–$150) must be itemized if the funeral provider sells those items or performs the service of filling out and sending them for customers.

The "miscellaneous charges" category may also include the cost of burial garments purchased from the mortuary, any fees or honoraria for pallbearers, or an honorarium for the clergyperson who conducts the funeral service.

Direct Cremations and Immediate Burials

Not all funeral homes offer direct cremations and immediate burials to customers, but most do offer these options. These methods of body disposition generally do not involve any formal viewing of the remains or any visitation or ceremony with the body present. (Some mortuaries respond to requests for viewing or informal ceremonies by placing the body on a cloth-covered gurney.)

If direct cremation or immediate burial is offered by a funeral home, the cost—which includes the fee for professional services—is shown on the general price list ($300–$5000). When direct cremation is selected, the customer must be given the option of providing the container or of purchasing an unfinished pine box or alternative container (such as a box made of cardboard, plywood, or composition material). Similarly, for immediate burials, the customer can provide a container or purchase a simple casket, such as one made of wood and covered with cloth. (If a funeral home offers immediate burials but does not offer direct cremations, the FTC rule does not require the firm to make available an alternative container or unfinished wood box, although a funeral director might choose to do so.)

Funeral and Memorial Societies

Funeral and memorial societies are nonprofit, cooperative organizations that offer body disposition to members at a reduced cost by offering simplicity and economy in after-death arrangements. They are generally minimalist with respect to disposition of the corpse—either immediate cremation or immediate burial—although some offer other options at a higher cost. Funeral and memorial societies represent a response to consumers' wishes for low-cost and simple methods of body disposition.

Assume that we are confronted with the dead body of a man. What disposition shall we make of it? Shall we lay it in a boat that is set adrift? Shall we take the heart from it and bury it in one place and the rest of the body in another? Shall we expose it to wild animals? Burn it on a pyre? Push it into a pit to rot with other bodies? Boil it until the flesh falls off the bones, and throw the flesh away and treasure the bones? Such questions provoke others which may not be consciously articulated, such as: "What do men generally think this body is?" And, "What do they think is a proper way of dealing with it?"

Robert W. Habenstein and William M. Lamers,
The History of American Funeral Directing

Body Disposition

Think for a moment about the manner you would choose for the disposition of your body after you die. Corpses must be disposed of for sanitary reasons, though it is unlikely that a person's choice of *how* to accomplish disposition is influenced by that fact. The method chosen is more likely to involve social, cultural, religious, psychological, and personal considerations. Reynolds and Tanner point out that "dead bodies have to be disposed of and religions often provide the rules and personnel for this, even when the dead and their survivors are not specifically religious."[28] When Americans are asked their preferences, responses usually fall into one of the following categories: earth burial, entombment in a mausoleum crypt, cremation, or donation to science.

Religious beliefs often influence the method of body disposition. For example, Judaism, Christianity, and Islam typically practice ground burial, whereas Hindus and Buddhists prefer cremation. Each method of disposing of the corpse has symbolic meanings that are important to followers of the respective religions. For example, among Hindus, cremation is seen as a gesture of purification and symbol of the transitory nature of human life. Orthodox Judaism, in contrast, views cremation as a form of idolatry; burial returns the body to the "dust" from whence it was created by God. Other branches of Judaism have a less strict view of the ban on cremation. The Christian prohibition against cremation is no longer universal, having been replaced by a diversity of viewpoints; some churches support or at least tolerate cremation whereas others require, or strongly prefer, ground burial.

In *Death to Dust*, Kenneth Iserson reports that "an unembalmed adult body buried six-feet deep in ordinary soil without a coffin normally takes ten to twelve years to decompose down to the bony skeleton; a child's body takes about half that time."[29] Environmental conditions can delay or hasten decomposition; for example, corpses buried in coffins or caskets take longer to decompose than those buried without such containers, and bodies exposed to the environment will generally be reduced to skeletons rather quickly.

The decomposition of the body is hastened in some societies by washing the flesh from the bones when the corpse is partially decomposed; parts of

Burial at sea is a naval tradition the world over, particularly during times of war. Here the body of a seaman is committed to the deep during burial services aboard the USS Ranger *in 1963.*

India —
Tower of silence
dahkma
Zuroaster

the body are then retained as a memorial. In other societies, open-air disposal is practiced, with the body left to the elements, where it generally decomposes quite rapidly (except in very dry, desert climates, where heat removes the moisture from the body, acting thereby to preserve it). Some Indian tribes of the American plains constructed platforms on which the corpse was exposed to the effects of the sun, wind, and rain. In some societies, vultures or other animals consume the remains of the dead. In India, for example, one can see scaffolds known as high *dakhmas* (towers of silence) on Bombay's fashionable Marabar Hill, where the Parsi community disposes of its dead by leaving corpses to be devoured by birds of prey. As followers of Zoroaster, they regard earth, fire, and water as sacred and, therefore, not to be defiled by the dead.

A method of body disposal practiced by mariners since ancient times is water burial, or burial at sea. Depending on circumstances and cultural practices, this form of body disposition might involve either ceremonially sliding the corpse off the side of a ship or placing the corpse inside a boat that is set aflame and then set adrift. The Norwegian ship burials of the Viking Age present an interesting twist on this method of body disposal by combining the "burial at sea" theme with ground burial.[30] The dead were laid in a wooden

U.S. Navy Photo

Elmer Ruiz: Gravedigger

Not anybody can be a gravedigger. You can dig a hole any way they come. A grave-digger, you have to make a neat job. I had a fella once, he wanted to see a grave. He was a fella that digged sewers. He was impressed when he seen me diggin' this grave—how square and how perfect it was. A human body is goin' into this grave. That's why you need skill when you're gonna dig a grave.

The gravedigger today, they have to be somebody to operate a machine. You just use a shovel to push the dirt loose. Otherwise you don't use 'em. We're tryin' a new machine, a ground hog. This machine is supposed to go through heavy frost. It do very good job so far. When the weather is mild, like fifteen degrees above zero, you can do it very easy.

But when the weather is below zero, believe me, you just really workin' hard. I have to use a mask. Your skin hurts so much when it's cold—like you put a hot flame near your face. I'm talkin' about two, three hours standin' outside. You have to wear a mask, otherwise you can't stand it at all. . . .

The most graves I dig is about six, seven a day. This is in the summer. In the winter it's a little difficult. In the winter you have four funerals, that's a pretty busy day. . . .

The grave will be covered in less than two minutes, complete. We just open the hoppers with the right amount of earth. We just press it and then we lay out a layer of black earth. Then we put the sod that belongs there. After a couple of weeks you wouldn't know it's a grave there. It's complete flat. Very rarely you see a grave that is sunk. . . .

I usually tell 'em I'm a caretaker. I don't think the name sound as bad. I have to look at the park, so after the day's over that everything's closed, that nobody do damage to the park. Some occasions some people just come and steal and loot and do bad things in the park, destroy some things. I believe it would be some young fellas. A man with responsibility, he wouldn't do things like that. Finally we had to put up some gates and close 'em at sundown. Before, we didn't, no. We have a fence of roses. Always in cars you can come after sundown. . . .

A gravedigger is a very important person. You must have hear about the strike we had in New York about two years ago. There were twenty thousand bodies layin'

grave chamber and placed in a ship along with grave goods, and the whole was covered by an earthen mound.

Donation to medical science is another method of body disposition. The person who chooses this method may gain satisfaction from the notion that he or she is making a contribution to the advancement of knowledge: "My body will serve a useful function even after I'm gone." This is a somewhat limited option, however, because medical schools and other such institutions require few cadavers. When a body has been donated to science, the final disposition of the remains may be left to the discretion of the institution that received the donation. The next of kin is usually given a say in determining the final disposition once the medical or scientific purposes of the donation have been achieved. When the next of kin does not request return of the remains for private disposition, most medical schools and other such institutions have policies to ensure that cadavers are treated ethically and that human remains are and nobody could bury 'em. The cost of funerals they raised and they didn't want to raise the price of the workers. The way they're livin', everything wanna go up, and I don't know what's gonna happen.

Can you imagine if I wouldn't show up tomorrow morning and this other fella—he usually comes late—and sometimes he don't show. We have a funeral for eleven o'clock. Imagine what happens? The funeral arrive and where you gonna bury it? . . .

There are some funerals, they really affect you. Some young kid. We buried lots of young. You have emotions, you turn in, believe me, you turn. I had a burial about two years ago of teen-agers, a young boy and a young girl. This was a real sad funeral because there was nobody but young teen-agers. I'm so used to going to funerals every day—of course, it bothers me—but I don't feel as bad as when I bury a young child. You really turn. . . .

This grief that I see every day, I'm really used to somebody's crying every day. But there is some that are real bad, when you just have to take it. Some people just don't want to give up. You have to understand that when somebody pass away, there's nothing you can do and you have to take it. If you don't want to take it, you're just gonna make your life worse, become sick. People seems to take it more easier these days. They miss the person, but not as much.

There's some funerals that people, they show they're not sad. This is different kinds of people. I believe they are happy to see this person—not in a way of singing—because this person is out of his sufferin' in this world. This person is gone and at rest for the rest of his life. I have this question lots of times: "How can I take it?" They ask if I'm calm when I bury people. If you stop and think, a funeral is one of the natural things in the world. . . .

I believe I'm gonna have to stay here probably until I die. It's not gonna be too bad for me because I been livin' twelve years already in the cemetery. I'm still gonna be livin' in the cemetery. (Laughs.) So that's gonna be all right with me whenever I go. I think I may be buried here, it look like.

Quoted in Studs Terkel, *Working*

disposed of properly. In some cases, a memorial service is held to acknowledge the gift that is represented by the donation of the body to science.[31]

Cryogenic suspension is not a method of body disposal in the sense used so far, but it has nevertheless attracted attention as a unique way to deal with a body after death. Cryogenic suspension involves preserving a corpse by freezing it to the temperature of solid carbon dioxide and keeping the body frozen until some future time when medical science is sophisticated enough to allow for resuscitation of the body and continued life.

From the burials of prehistory to space-age cryonics, human beings have chosen from a variety of alternatives for disposing of the dead. Although few people give much thought to the subject of body disposition, it is nonetheless fraught with emotional and psychological importance, as the following story illustrates: When Major Edward Strombeck was killed in a plane crash while on duty in Vietnam, the military cremated his body and forwarded the ashes, by mail, to his home in Hawaii.[32] Shocked at the lack of proper ceremony, his mother and other family members expressed their dismay and gained the attention of U.S. Senator Daniel Inouye. The result was a change in policy, which ordered that the ashes of military personnel must be escorted home with dignity and honor. Proper disposition of human remains is a matter of considerable significance not only to the immediate survivors but also to the larger community. What do your own preferences regarding body disposition tell you about your attitudes and beliefs toward death?

Burial

In the Western European tradition, and in most societies associated with that tradition, including the United States, the preferred method for disposing of the corpse has been burial, at least until recently. Now, with a growing number of cremations, traditional cemetery burial is becoming more of a lifestyle choice.[33] The term *burial* encompasses a wide range of practices. It may involve digging a single grave in the soil, or it may refer to entombment in a mausoleum (of which the Taj Mahal and the pyramids are examples). The whole body can be buried, or just the bones or even cremated remains. In some parts of the world, cemetery plots are purchased outright; elsewhere, a burial plot is merely rented for a number of years.[34] In some cemeteries, we are all equal in death; in others, the social distinctions that held sway in life are perpetuated by dividing burial space into classes with better placement of graves for those who occupy the first-class ranks.[35]

In addition to the cost of a cemetery plot, which can range from less than $100 to more than $5000, cemeteries usually require a grave liner or vault to support the earth around and above the casket. On average, this adds about $950 to the cost of ground burial, although vaults that are designed (but not guaranteed) to seal out moisture can cost considerably more.

The cost of entombment in a mausoleum or outdoor crypt averages about $2000 although, again, prices vary. Historically, the term *crypt* denotes a subterranean burial vault or chamber, often situated beneath the floor of a church. In modern usage, the term also refers to space in a *mausoleum,* an aboveground structure of concrete, marble, or other stone in which one or more bodies are entombed. The most expensive crypt spaces are usually those at eye level, with less expensive spaces at the top and bottom. (The Queen of Heaven mausoleum complex in Chicago, the world's largest Catholic mausoleum, has space for 33,000 bodies.)[36] The opening and closing of a grave or crypt normally involves additional charges, which range from about $75 to $350, depending on the particular facility.

Simple bronze or stone grave markers generally cost about $300, with nameplates for mausoleum crypts costing a bit less. More elaborate memorials, if they are permitted by a cemetery (some permit only flat-on-the-ground markers), cost from several hundred to many thousands of dollars.

Finally, some cemeteries assess an endowment or "perpetual care cost" that subsidizes upkeep of the cemetery. These costs range upward of $100, although this fee is sometimes included in the basic cost for burial or entombment.

© Albert Lee Strickland

Burial vaults, such as those seen here in Oaxaca, Mexico, represent an alternative to underground burial that is found in many parts of the world. When space is at a premium, bodies may be removed from the vaults after a certain period of time and given underground burial.

Cremation

Cremation involves subjecting a body to intense heat, thereby reducing its organic components to a mineralized skeleton. In the United States, the practice of cremation as a method of body disposal dates from the nineteenth century (although it had been customary for some Native American cultural groups for centuries). In Europe, the practice is considerably older, going back at least to the Bronze Age. Cremation is the most common method of body disposal in many countries, including India and Japan, and it has found growing acceptance in the United States in recent decades.[37] Currently, cremation is the method of body disposition chosen in about 40 percent of final dispositions in the United States.[38]

Cremation involves a process of dehydration and oxidation of the organic components of the body by subjecting a corpse to extreme heat, approximately 2000 to 2500 degrees Fahrenheit. Cremation has been accomplished by means ranging from a simple wood fire to sophisticated electric or gas retorts. In the United States, natural gas is the most commonly used fuel. An average-size body takes about one and one-half hours to be reduced to a mineralized skeleton, which is put through a "cremulator" that reduces the bone fragments to a granular state, often referred to as "ashes." (The term *ashes* leads some people to believe that the cremated remains will look and feel like wood or paper ashes. Actually, they include pieces of bone, which look and feel like coarse coral sands whose shell-like components are worn by the wind and waves.)

Cremated remains can be buried, placed in a columbarium niche, put into an urn kept by the family or interred in an urn garden, or scattered at sea or on land. State and local laws may restrict how some of these options are carried out. Although scattering cremated remains is a popular method of final disposition, and usually the least costly, some people who have decided to scatter "ashes" later regret it because, as one woman said about her husband, "I have no place to take him a flower." When remains are scattered at sea, over a forest, or in some similar locale, people may find that they miss the emotional power of a *specific place* where one can visit the deceased loved one. In Japanese cemeteries, *haka*—small, private family mausolea that fit on a standard cemetery plot—hold a dozen crematory urns. This setting has been called "the Asian equivalent of a European family plot with a hedge growing around it."[39] As land for burials becomes more expensive, mainstream cemeteries may respond to the increasing popularity of cremation by offering landscaped "garden" plots that have space for several urns, thereby allowing several generations to be buried and memorialized in a family plot.

Survivors may choose to memorialize the deceased in conjunction with cremation, just as with traditional burials. Urns to hold cremated remains can be purchased at prices from about $50 to $400, though more expensive urns are available. If ashes are to be entombed, columbarium niches (a small vault in which the urn is placed) are available, with the cost depending on the size and location of the niche. Among some families and ethnic groups, a family tomb is the resting place for the ashes of several generations of the dead.

Memorialization

Grave markers and monuments are examples of ways in which people have traditionally chosen to honor and remember their dead. For cremated remains, such memorialization may include an inscription or plaque on a columbarium niche or a special urn to hold the ashes. With the growing popularity of cremation, entrepreneurs have developed, or rediscovered, innovative ways of memorializing a deceased loved one. For example, several firms offer "cremation jewelry," locket-style pendants that hold a small bit of cremated remains. These pendants can be worn around the neck or displayed in special holders.

In some inner-city areas, T-shirts are worn as a way of memorializing victims of violence, as well as persons who died in accidents or from illnesses. The custom apparently began in New Orleans and has since been adopted elsewhere. As "wearable tombstones," these shirts are characterized as "a uniquely modern twist on the ancient ritual of honoring the dead." One young woman in her early twenties has memorial T-shirts for eight family members and friends murdered in and around her neighborhood. A man in his early thirties says, "Now I got more T-shirts than friends." The shirts are worn to wakes and funerals, on the anniversaries of the deaths, the victim's birthday, when visiting the gravesite,

[handwritten margin note: Wearing of T-shirts began in NOLA / victims of violence, accident, illness]

A papier-mâché bull symbolizing the deceased's caste is a focal point of this cremation ceremony in a Balinese village. According to local custom, corpses are buried until families accumulate the necessary funds to pay for the cremation ritual; at that time, the body is disinterred, wrapped in cloth, and placed, along with various offerings, in ritual objects such as the bull shown here at the cremation site.

or just when someone is missed.[40] Memorials are also found in the form of "memorial wall art" that is painted on buildings.[41] Roadside accident crosses represent another adaptation of memorial culture.[42]

High-tech innovations are resulting in new styles of electronic gravesite memorials. One such offering allows survivors to compile a "visual eulogy"

Epitaph

The Body of
B. Franklin, Printer,
(Like the cover of an Old Book
Its contents torn out
And stript of its Lettering and Gilding)
Lies here, Food for Worms.
But the work shall not be lost;
For it will, (as he believ'd) appear
once more
In a new and more elegant Edition
Revised and Corrected
By the Author.

of the deceased loved one, whereby photographs, his or her life story and family history, and other such gleanings of a life well lived are electronically stored and can be displayed on a small video monitor that is installed into a traditional grave marker. Containing up to 250 pages of information, this personalized memorial "allows a person's life story to be remembered for generations to come."[43]

Laws Regulating Body Disposition

As a general rule, the deceased's next of kin is responsible for arranging for the final disposition of the body. State laws and local ordinances, however, may govern the manner in which disposition can be effected. For example, some communities have ordinances prohibiting burial within city limits.

When the deceased has left no money to cover the cost of body disposition, and his or her relatives are unwilling or unable to pay, the state may be forced to step in and handle the details. Counties generally have an "indigent burial fund" for such cases. Depending on the circumstances, the public administrator's office may make a determination that distinguishes between "inconvenient to pay" and "unable to pay." When funds are not available from private sources, the county picks up the cost. The county may have a contract with a local mortuary that provides direct cremation and burial of the cremated remains. If the next of kin opposes cremation, the corpse may be placed in a casket and buried in a plot donated by a cemetery for indigent burials (or, again, paid for out of community funds).

Making Meaningful Choices

The funeral has been defined as "an organized, purposeful, time-limited, flexible, group-centered response to death."[44] In light of the varied and diverse styles of funeral service now available, does this definition apply to our current approaches to caring for the dead? What values guide our actions in memorializing the dead and meeting the emotional needs of survivors? The choices we make concerning funerals and body disposition increasingly reflect personal rather than community judgments.

If the monolithic and perhaps stereotypical "American funeral" is disappearing, it is being replaced by a much broader range of options. Reflecting the cultural diversity in modern societies, most funeral directors have at least some familiarity not only with the rituals practiced in Judaism and Christianity, but also with Buddhist, Hindu, and Muslim services, as well as non-religious humanistic and fraternal rites.[45] Thus, rather than being locked into a "conventional funeral," people are now choosing from a wide range of resources that allow them to create or adapt funeral customs from both religious and secular traditions.

In pluralistic societies, there are many ways to deal meaningfully and appropriately with death. Among recent innovations in body disposition are making cremated remains part of a "memorial reef" and burying a body or ashes in a natural woodland or "green" cemetery.[46] Becoming aware of the alternatives enables us to make meaningful choices.

Some people prefer a minimal role in caring for their dead; others seek to participate actively. The experience of a family following the death of a young son is illustrative. There were no plans for a formal funeral ceremony. The body would be cremated and the ashes scattered. On the day before the body was to be cremated, the family found themselves experiencing the acute grief that comes with a sudden and intimate loss. As they tried to come to terms with their emotions and the loss of their son, someone in their circle of friends suggested that they put their energy into building a coffin. Soon, friends and members of the family, including the five-year-old brother of the child who was killed, were busily engaged in the task of constructing a coffin. Later they said they were relieved to have had the opportunity to "do something." Building the coffin became a meaningful way to honor the dead child as well as a means of working through their feelings (see Figure 8-5).

Traditional practices with respect to funerals and disposition of the body are being altered by the fast pace of modern life. Attendance at funerals is down; fewer people seem to "have the time" to take off from work or other pressing activities for a mourning ceremony that seems somehow optional. Yet the desire to participate in such ceremonies persists, as is evident in the advent of new technologies that allow distant mourners to feel they are included even when they can't be physically present at the funeral itself. Videotapes may be provided for friends and relatives who are unable to attend the funeral. Cameras in the funeral chapel can transmit live video of the funeral to "cybermourners" via the Internet.[47] Memorial pages on the Internet allow mourners to post their condolences and share their grief online. Web sites known as "virtual cemeteries" provide space for photographs and biographical information about the dead, and visitors have opportunities to sign the guest book and leave "digital flowers." One Web site offers a choice of virtual cemeteries to accommodate people from "all walks of life, including

Figure 8-5 *Three Views of a Child's Coffin*

Top View: When the wooden coffin constructed by the family and friends had been completed, the surviving child ran his hand over the surface and voiced his approval but said that it "needs something more." He gathered his marking pens and began to ornament the coffin with drawings. The inscriptions on the outer surface of the lid show the child's interest in identifying by name and by picture the fact that this coffin was built for his brother. His own participation in the making of the coffin is also connoted by the inclusion of his name and by the demonstration of his newly developed skills with the use of numerals and letters.

Detail of Lid Interior: In this close-up of a portion of the interior lid, viewed from left to right, one can see a chrysalis—indicating a transition from caterpillar to butterfly—along with some of the younger brother's favorite television characters: Big Bird, Oscar the Grouch, and the Cookie Monster.

Interior of Lid: In contrast to the matter-of-fact inscriptions placed on the outer surface, the inside of the coffin lid is filled with representations of experiences, events, and objects that brought joy into the life of the child's younger brother. Many of the dead child's favorite activities, such as listening to the stereo with headphones and sitting on a horse at grandma's house, are depicted. The surviving child depicts himself as sad because of his brother's death, yet also as happy because of the shared experiences he enjoyed with his brother. It is interesting to notice the degree of detail and the variety of images placed on the interior of the coffin lid.

those with religious, ethnic, military, national, and alternative lifestyle affiliations."[48] Thus, a person who was both Catholic and a Navy veteran might have a memorial placed on both the "Catholic" and "U.S. Navy Veterans" virtual cemeteries.

Internet memorial pages and other high-tech options appear to meet a basic human need for participation in rituals surrounding death. Whether these options are adequate substitutes for the intimate, face-to-face social support provided by conventional funeral services can be questioned. What does it say about how we manage our lives when we are too busy to join together with other mourners to acknowledge the passing of a person who was loved and respected as part of our community of friends and family? These new options attest to the strength of the bonds between the living and the dead and the human desire to make connections with others in our bereavement.

William Lamers points out that substituting a "memorial service" for a traditional funeral is lacking in several respects: First, it usually does not take place when feelings about a loss are most intense. Second, members of the family are not as exposed to the fact that death has occurred, nor do they participate as fully as they would in making funeral arrangements and going through the funeralization process. Third, the body is not present at a memorial service, thus removing the therapeutic benefit that comes with fixing the fact of death in the minds of mourners.[49] Alan Wolfelt, director of the Center

© Pütz-Roth

Figure *8-6* Mourners at Pütz-Roth in Bergisch Gladbach, Germany, are given opportunities to sit with their deceased loved ones in a serene, home-like environment that aids their coming to terms with the death. This innovative funeral establishment is a model for helping the bereaved find a place in the heart for grief.

for Loss and Life Transition, says, "Opponents of viewing [the body] often describe it as unseemly, expensive, undignified, and unnecessary. Yet, seeing and spending time with the body allows for last good-byes and visual confirmation that someone loved is indeed dead."[50]

At Pütz-Roth, an innovative funeral establishment in Bergisch Gladbach, Germany, mourners are encouraged to give themselves sufficient time to grieve after a loved one's death. In a homelike environment, the bereaved family and friends are offered the opportunity to spend time with the deceased's body over a period of several days prior to final disposition of the remains (see Figure 8-6). At Pütz-Roth, the bodies of the dead are not embalmed but are instead kept in a "cool room." When family and friends come, the body is moved to a sitting room, where the bereaved have access to a kitchen facility for keeping beverages or making snacks. In addition to comfortable seating and soothing artworks, each sitting room has windows that look out on natural surroundings and that also let in the sounds of running water and birdsong. Amid this natural setting, as the body begins to show signs of deterioration, the mourners are subtly encouraged to recognize that all things have a beginning and an ending and that grief involves letting go of the physical aspects of the deceased loved one while finding a "place in the heart for grief."[51]

The social support that accompanies meaningful ritual need not be limited to the period immediately following a death. In traditional Hawaiian culture, for example, the bereaved community holds a memorial feast on the first-year anniversary of the day of death for any person—man, woman, child, even a newborn baby.[52] For the extended family, this is considered "one of the three greatest occasions, the others being the feasts of rejoicing for the first-born and the marriage festival." Although this memorial occasion is called the *'aha'aina waimaka* or "feast of tears," because it embraces everyone who had shed tears out of respect and love for the deceased, it is in fact "a happy occasion, a joyful reunion of all who had previously shed tears together." In the words of one participant: "There was drinking, eating, singing and dancing. We had a *lu'au* when all the grief was done."

Further Readings

Katherine Ashenburg. *The Mourner's Dance: What We Do When People Die*. New York: North Point Press, 2002.

Xavier A. Cronin. *Grave Exodus: Tending to Our Dead in the 21st Century*. New York: Barricade, 1996.

Lisa Takeuchi Cullen. *Remember Me: A Lively Tour of the New American Way of Death*. New York: HarperCollins, 2006.

Douglas L. Davies. *Death, Ritual, and Belief: The Rhetoric of Funeral Rites*, 2nd ed. London: Continuum, 2002.

Robert W. Habenstein and William M. Lamers. *Funeral Customs the World Over*, rev. ed. Milwaukee: Bulfin Printers, 1974.

Mark Harris. *Grave Matters: A Journey Through the Modern Funeral Industry to a Natural Way of Burial*. New York: Scribner, 2007.

Kenneth V. Iserson. *Death to Dust: What Happens to Dead Bodies?* 2nd ed. Tucson: Galen Press, 2001.

Gary Laderman. *Rest in Peace: A Cultural History of Death and the Funeral Home in Twentieth-Century America*. New York: Oxford University Press, 2003.

Thomas Lynch. *The Undertaking: Life Studies from the Dismal Trade*. New York: Norton, 1997.

Family members leave the church after attending the funeral of a son and brother. Providing community support for the bereaved, such social rituals exhibit a blending of private grief and public mourning that offers solace during the early days of grief.

CHAPTER 9

Survivors: Understanding the Experience of Loss

Wᵉ are all survivors. Even if we have not experienced the death of someone close, we are survivors of losses that occur in our lives because of changes and endings. The loss of a job, the ending of a relationship, transitions from one school or neighborhood to another— such losses are sometimes called "little deaths," and, in varying degrees, all can involve grief. As you recall some of the "little deaths" in your own life, think about how you responded. Shock, disbelief, anger, sadness, and relief are all natural reactions.

A study of "sport career deaths" of college athletes found that grief was experienced by athletes who made an involuntary and unanticipated exit from sports because they were cut from the team or suffered a career-ending injury, or because their sport program or team was terminated. In transitioning to the status of a "normal student," these athletes mourned the loss of camaraderie with teammates, the loss of self-image and social reputation as athletes, and the loss of "what might have been."[1]

Similarly, when the Chicago White Sox played their last game at Old Comiskey Park, many fans were acutely aware that their grief was a response to losses associated with their memories of attending games at "the world's greatest baseball palace."[2] One fan recalled attending a game at the Park with six of his friends before leaving for Vietnam. He said, "Three of those guys eventually were killed over there and I guess I'm sayin' goodbye to them. This Park was my bond with them and now I'm gonna lose that tie." Another fan said that his fondest memories of his father were associated with the ball games they attended together at the stadium. He said, "As a son, I went back to recapture the warmth and contentment I always had felt sitting in those 'special' seats—I went back to visit my father. . . . When Old Comiskey closed that autumn day . . . I lost something. I lost a very real connection to the feelings a six-year-old boy has for his father."

Bereavement, Grief, and Mourning

Knowing the definitions of bereavement, grief, and mourning broadens our understanding of what it means to be a survivor. Although these terms are often used interchangeably, each refers to a distinct aspect of the encounter with loss.[3]

Bereavement is defined simply as the objective event of loss. It comes from a root word meaning "shorn off or torn up"—as if something precious had been suddenly yanked away by a disruptive force. Thus, at root, bereavement conveys a sense of being deprived, of having some part of ourselves stripped away against our will, of being robbed. Although bereavement can be defined as an event that disrupts our lives, it is also appropriate to define it as an event that is normal in human experience. For us to understand bereavement, these two definitions need to be kept in balance. As Dennis Klass observes, "Bereavement is complex, for it reaches to the heart of what it means to be human and what it means to have a relationship."[4]

Grief is the reaction to loss. It encompasses thoughts and feelings, as well as physical, behavioral, and spiritual responses. These reactions may appear immediately after the bereaved learns of the death, or they may be delayed; they may even be absent. No particular survivor will necessarily experience all of them, nor must all be present. Grief is highly variable. It is an evolving process with multiple dimensions.

Mental or cognitive distress in grief may manifest as disbelief, confusion, anxiety, tension or pain, a pervasive sense of disorganization, and depression. Things and events may seem unreal, sensory responses undependable and erratic. Especially in the early period after a loss, survivors may seem depressed, although this reaction is distinguished from clinically defined depression.[5] They may experience periods of euphoria, with heightened perceptual and emotional sensitivity to people and events. The bereaved person may be preoccupied with images of the deceased, experienced in dreams or hallucinations, or may feel a vague sense of the deceased's presence. Paranormal or psychic experiences in which the dead appear to the living or seem to communicate with the living are not unusual in grief.[6]

Emotions in grief may include sadness, longing, loneliness, sorrow, self-pity, anguish, guilt and anger, as well as relief. The bereaved may express outrage at the apparent injustice of the loss. Inability to control events may leave the bereaved person feeling frustrated and impotent. If the world could be arranged more to his or her liking, it would not have included this loss. By recognizing that grief can involve a very wide range of feelings, even conflicting ones, we become better able to cope with it.

Comparing the extent and form of emotional responses to announcements of death in various circumstances, I found a considerable amount of variability. On some occasions there was no crying whatever; the doctor's mention of the death was responded to with downward looking silence. On other occasions, his utterance "passed away" or "died" spontaneously produced hysterical crying, screaming, moaning, trembling, etc. . . . In numerous instances I have seen men and women tear at themselves, pulling their hair, tugging at their garments, biting their lips.

David Sudnow,
Passing On: The Social Organization of Dying

physical symptoms of grief

Physically, grief may be exhibited in frequent sighing, shortness of breath, tightness of the throat, a feeling of emptiness in the abdomen, muscle weakness, chills, tremors, nervous system hyperactivity, insomnia or other sleep disruptions, and changes in appetite.

Behaviors associated with grief include crying and "searching" for the deceased. Bereaved people may talk incessantly about the deceased and the circumstances of the death. Or they may talk about everything but the loss. At times, survivors may be highly irritable or even hostile. They may exhibit a kind of frenetic overactivity and general restlessness, as if not knowing what to do with themselves.

Religious or spiritual beliefs may be reexamined as a person tries to find meaning in a loss. Bereaved people may also turn to such beliefs as a source of consolation and comfort in coping with loss. A significant loss can cause us to question our fundamental assumptions about the world and our place in it, undermining beliefs that we had taken for granted. When loss shatters our "assumptive world," healing the rifts may require us to *relearn* how to live in all the dimensions affected by the loss.[7]

Thus, grief involves the whole person and is manifest in a variety of ways: mentally, emotionally, physically, behaviorally, and spiritually. Limiting the definition of grief reduces our chances of accepting all of the reactions to loss that we may experience. Many kinds of thoughts, feelings, behaviors, and so on are a normal part of grief.

Mourning is closely related to grief and is often used as a synonym for it. However, mourning refers not so much to the *reaction* to loss but, rather, to the *process* by which a bereaved person integrates the loss into his or her ongoing life. How this process is managed is determined, at least partly, by social and cultural norms for expressing grief.[8] Considered together, grief and mourning are the natural pathways toward coping with the experience of bereavement.

Typical mourning behaviors include wearing black armbands or clothes of subdued colors and, if the deceased was a public figure, flying the national flag at half-mast. Following the death of George Washington, Congress led the nation in a thirty-day period of mourning, during which citizens wore black bands on which were stamped in white letters the inscription that appeared on the president's coffin plate: "General George Washington—Departed this life on the 14th of December, 1799."[9] In some cultures, widows wear black for years following the death of a spouse as a public way of acknowledging their loss, their changed status, and their grief. The *mater dolorosa*, a veiled woman dressed in black clothing, represented the socially prescribed way of mourning in earlier centuries. Altering one's appearance as a sign of mourning occurs in many societies. Among some Native Americans, a person's hair is shorn as a way of signifying that he or she is mourning. Long hair is a sign of status and wealth. Thus, as Terry Tafoya says, "To cut the hair short is a symbolic and actual sacrifice in memory and respect of the one lost. It is also an immediate sign to visitors that such a loss has taken place. It is a strong visual symbol of grief."[10]

There is a common theme to mourning behaviors cross-culturally—namely, that the bereaved are "different" and that this difference usually diminishes with time.[11] This is seen in customs that involve seclusion of the bereaved for a period of time. Seclusion enforces on survivors abstinence from social relationships. You may have heard someone say, "That family experienced a death in the family and is in mourning; they aren't going out socially." Seclusion serves two purposes during the period of mourning: First, it allows survivors to shelter their grief from the world, and, second, it prevents survivors from forgetting the deceased too quickly.[12]

Mourning customs are no longer as formal or as socially regulated as they were in the past. Lacking well-defined social rules, people who are recently bereaved sometimes experience conflict about what constitutes appropriate mourning behavior, as illustrated by the following anecdote: A young girl wrote to an advice columnist about a "sweet sixteen" party that her dying father asked the family to celebrate for her, even if the party should occur on the day of his funeral. The girl said that, although she had not felt like having a party, family members decided to honor the promise to her father. So the party was held two days after her father's death, and it turned out to be a good experience for all who attended. The problem, she said, arose when several relatives became horrified because, in their view, enjoying a party was not appropriate during a time of mourning. What advice would you have given to this girl?

"Appropriate" mourning behavior is difficult to define in modern societies, especially those that include diverse cultural groups and social influences. It is perhaps best to suspend judgments or preconceptions about what is "correct," recognizing that many different kinds of mourning behaviors can be appropriate for different people and circumstances.

Models of Grief

The belief that there is a consistent pattern to grief and mourning may bring solace to bereaved people.[13] Human beings appear to have an affinity for patterns and models that help them make sense of complex phenomena. However, although models provide a "snapshot" of a dynamic process, they tend to oversimplify and distort reality. This is surely the case with a complex phe-

> Working through our endings allows us to redefine
> our relationships, to surrender what is dead
> and to accept what is alive,
> and to be in the world more fully to face the
> new situation.
>
> Stanley Keleman,
> *Living Your Dying*

nomenon like grief. Various models have been proposed and refined, as theorists attempt to describe more accurately how people grieve. It is exciting to see these pictures develop, even as we recognize that they are not complete.

Working Through Grief

The concept of "working through grief" has been an important theoretical perspective at least since Sigmund Freud's 1917 paper, "Mourning and Melancholia."[14] The central message of the *grief work* perspective, as it is usually understood, is that the bereaved must "let go" of his or her bonds of attachment to the deceased by gradually "working through" these attachments and relinquishing them. Therese Rando points out that, according to this model,

> Mourning is initiated by the need to detach from the lost object, and the reason mourning is such a struggle is that the human being never willingly abandons an emotional attachment, and only does so when he or she learns that it is better to relinquish the object than to try to hold on to it now that it is lost.[15]

The nature of our attachments and the process by which those attachments are relinquished were central concerns in the work of John Bowlby.[16] According to *attachment theory*, when a person recognizes that an object (someone loved) to which he or she is attached no longer exists, grief arises, along with a defensive psychological demand to withdraw libido (energy) from the object. This demand to withdraw energy is likely to meet with resistance, causing the survivor to temporarily turn away from reality in an attempt to cling to the lost object. As the survivor continues to do grief work, the energy previously invested eventually becomes detached from the love object, and the ego (personality) is freed of its attachment so that new relationships can be formed.

In "The Symptomatology and Management of Acute Grief," a landmark article published in 1944 and based on the author's involvement as a psychiatrist in treating the survivors of a nightclub fire in which 492 people died, Erich Lindemann observed:

> The duration of a grief reaction seems to depend upon the success with which a person does the *grief work,* namely, emancipation from the bondage to the deceased, readjustment to the environment in which the deceased is missing, and the formation of new relationships.[17]

Lindemann added that the main obstacle to successful grief work was the fact that many people "try to avoid the intense distress connected with the grief experience and to avoid the expression of emotion necessary for it."

The grief-work model incorporates several important points about mourning a loss: First, it describes grief as an *adaptive response* to loss. Second, it states that the reality of the loss must be *confronted and accepted*. Third, it acknowledges that grieving is an *active process that occurs over time*.

The grief-work model has been widely accepted as the standard formulation for understanding and helping people accommodate to loss. However, its apparent emphasis on the need for bereaved individuals to break their relational bonds with the deceased has been questioned. Colin Murray Parkes points out: "Each love relationship is unique, and theoretical models which assume that libido can be withdrawn from one object in order to become invested in another similar object, fail to recognize this uniqueness."[18] It is perhaps more useful to think of bereavement, as Parkes suggests, as one category of "psychosocial transition."

With recent studies offering evidence that coping with loss is more complex than simply severing affectional bonds with the deceased and getting on with one's life, a review of the literature finds similar ideas, albeit expressed less prominently, in the writings of many early theorists.

The conventional formulation of the grief-work model seems to imply that "one size fits all," that everyone needs to work through grief in a similar fashion to recover from a loss. Cross-cultural studies, however, attest to diversity in grief and mourning.[19] Although certain patterns of grief are commonly found within a particular social or cultural group, there may be no universal or standard process of coping with grief. The idea that there is some standard method of grieving is being replaced by the recognition that grief is both highly individualistic and influenced by a variety of situational factors, such as the type of death, circumstances of the loss, and so on.

In a comprehensive review of the literature on grief, Margaret Stroebe points to a number of significant questions about the grief-work model: Is it really necessary to work through grief in order to adapt to a loss? Could suppression not lead to recovery? Are there occasions when, or persons for whom, grief work is not adaptive? And where does one draw the line between healthy grief work and unhealthy rumination? Stroebe says, "Within the range of normal grief reactions, it is possible that suppression or avoidance of confrontation with memories related to the deceased can be as effective a strategy as 'working through' grief. For some people, and in some circumstances, it may even be more effective."[20] In short, there is more than one way to cope effectively with loss.[21] One bereaved father said, "Living without my son has meant adding another room onto the house in my mind; not so I can shut the door on his death, but so I can move in and out of the experience of my loss."[22]

Tasks of Mourning

In William Worden's description of the "tasks of mourning," the first task involves *accepting the reality* of the loss.[23] "Denying the facts of the loss," says

Worden, "can vary in degree from a slight distortion to a full-blown delusion." One signpost at this point in the journey is the survivor's choice of words when talking about the deceased person. Most significant is the transition from present to past tense, from *is* to *was*, as, for example, from "Randy is a wonderful carpenter" to "Randy was a wonderful carpenter."

The second task involves *working through the pain* of grief. This includes physical as well as emotional and behavioral pain. As Worden says, "Not everyone experiences the same intensity of pain or feels it in the same way, but it is impossible to lose someone you have been deeply attached to without experiencing some level of pain." In accomplishing this task, humor can lighten the weight of grief, providing respite as survivors cope with loss.

The third task involves *adjusting to a changed environment* in which the deceased is missing. It takes time to make this adjustment, especially when a relationship was of long duration and exceptional closeness. The many roles fulfilled by the deceased in the bereaved's life may not be fully recognized until after the loss. The "changed environment" encompasses physical, emotional, mental, behavioral, and spiritual dimensions of life. Changes in one's environment are symbolized by actions such as rearranging the furniture or changing the place settings at the dining table.

The fourth task has to do with *emotionally relocating the deceased and moving on with life.* Accomplishing this task involves the recognition that, although one does not forget or necessarily stop loving the deceased person, there are other people one can love.

Therese Rando offers another perspective on the tasks of mourning.[24] She calls these tasks the "Six R's":

1. Recognize the loss (acknowledge and understand the death).
2. React to the separation (experience the pain; feel, identify, accept, and express the reaction to loss; and identify and mourn secondary losses).
3. Recollect and reexperience the deceased and the relationship (review and remember realistically; revive and reexperience the feelings).
4. Relinquish the old attachments to the deceased and the old assumptive world.
5. Readjust to move adaptively into the new world without forgetting the old (develop a new relationship with the deceased, adopt new ways of being in the world, form a new identity).
6. Reinvest (the emotional energy that was invested in the relationship with the deceased needs to be reinvested where it can return some of the emotional gratification that was lost with the death).

In the tasks of mourning outlined by both Worden and Rando, notice that accomplishing these tasks involves "relocating" the deceased in one's ongoing life and "developing a new relationship" with the deceased.

Maintaining Bonds with the Deceased

The view that coping with grief means relinquishing affectional ties with the deceased is giving way to a paradigm that is both more encompassing and

Edward V. Gillon, Jr.

© Albert Lee Strickland

The nineteenth-century Romantic view of death is reflected in the Lawson memorial, which characterizes both the devotion of the bereaved to the deceased and the belief that loving relationships continue beyond the mortal framework of the human lifespan.

Contemporary memorial stones often reflect a similar emphasis on the unending love felt by survivors for the deceased and on the faith that bonds forged during a person's lifetime can remain strong despite death.

deception of the bereaved "get over it"

more accurate in describing the range of behaviors and emotions elicited by loss. Recognizing the variability in grief, we need to be careful about generalizing. What expectations do we communicate to the bereaved when we speak about grief as a "time of healing" and talk about "getting over it"? By focusing on "resolving" grief, we may unwittingly perpetrate what Phyllis Silverman calls "a major deception of the bereaved as they try to conform to the expectations of their social network." When it turns out that grief is not so readily "resolved," the bereaved may feel somehow deficient, as if "something must be wrong with them." Silverman observes that our way of talking about grief influences both how we understand it and how we cope with it.[25]

Margaret Stroebe and her colleagues suggest that we "search for an appreciative understanding of grief in all its varieties."[26] Rather than severing ties, grief usually involves a process whereby the bereaved person incorporates the deceased into his or her ongoing life. In some cultures, this occurs in the context of rituals that locate the deceased in the realm of beloved ancestors. In others, it means keeping a special place for the deceased in one's heart and mind.[27]

Based on an extensive survey of "communications" between the living and the dead as expressed in art, literature, and song, Sandra Bertman observes that "the dead do not disappear from the lives of the living. They stay connected; and lively communications continue between the two worlds."[28] Whether maintaining continuing bonds with the deceased reflects a "healthy" adjustment to loss may depend on two criteria: First, does the mourner truly recognize that the person is dead and understand the implications of the death? Second, is the mourner moving forward adaptively into his or her new life?[29]

Dennis Klass says that bereaved parents often find solace by maintaining bonds with their children who died untimely deaths.[30] "Memory," Klass says, "binds family and communities together." Through religious beliefs and objects that link the parents with memories of the child, a kind of immortality is granted to the child in the lives of surviving family members. Klass points out that the death of a child challenges parents' worldviews—that is, their basic assumptions about how the universe functions and their place in the world. Making sense of such a loss is facilitated by maintaining an "inner representation" of the dead child that allows for continuing interactions so that the significance of the child's life is not forgotten or diminished.[31] Work done by Phyllis Silverman, Steven Nickman, and William Worden supports the notion that children likewise maintain connections with deceased parents through memories and linking objects.[32]

David Balk and Nancy Hogan point out that "a remarkable bit of evidence for ongoing attachment is the millions and millions who visit the Vietnam War Memorial each year to remember and leave literally tons of connections for their deceased loved ones."[33] Therese Rando says, "The development of a healthy new relationship with the deceased is a crucial part of the mourning process when the person lost has been integral to the mourner's life."[34]

Maintaining bonds with the deceased would not be surprising to people living in cultures where ties between the living and the dead are sustained as a matter of tradition. Recall, for example, the Japanese custom of maintaining a household shrine to the ancestors or African traditions that celebrate relationships with the "living-dead." In commenting on the social bond between human beings, Lyn Lofland suggests that the following are just some of the "threads of connectedness" or "ties that bind" us to one another:

> We are linked to others by the *roles* we play, by the *help* we receive, by the wider *network* of others made available to us, by the *selves* others create and sustain, by the comforting *myths* they allow us, by the *reality* they validate for us, and by the *futures* they make possible.[35]

Telling the "Story": Narrative Approaches

When someone we love dies, we face the prospect of revising and re-forming our life story. John Kelly suggests that, by contemplating mourning in terms of a narrative, or story, we find a way to cope with loss by re-forming our story so that we integrate the deceased into our lives in a new way and adjust our relationships in ways that restore wholeness.[36] Narratives, says Jerome Bruner, are "a version of reality" that reflects how we organize our experience and our memory of human happenings.[37] Carolyn Ellis describes how telling the story of her brother's death from an Air Florida crash into the Potomac

shrines = "living dead"

All that day I walked alone. In the afternoon I looked for a church, went into a cafe, and finally left on the bus, carrying with me more grief and sorrow than I had ever borne before, my body in tatters and my whole life a moan.

Oscar Lewis, *A Death in the Sanchez Family*

River after takeoff from Washington National Airport not only gives meaning to the loss, but also helps in "reconstructing" her life.

> Each writing and reading of my text has permitted me to relive my brother's death from an aesthetic distance, a place that allows me to experience the experience but with an awareness that I am not actually again *in* this situation, and thus I muster the courage to continue grieving.[38]

In telling the story of loss, Ellis says, "We can make true a plot in which we play the part of, and become in the playing, actual 'survivors.'"

The story of grief can be told without the constraint of having to conform to a particular model of how it should be or what it should feel like or what should be thought. In a sense, it is the "real" story. In telling and retelling it, the story gradually reveals the varied dimensions of grief in a way that allows survivors to carry on despite loss. Mary Anne Sedney and her colleagues note that "every death creates a story, or a set of stories, to tell."[39] Sharing the story of a loss provides emotional relief, promotes the search for meaning, and brings people together in support of one another.

Part of coping with grief is talking about the dead. "Through storytelling, the diverse meanings of life experience and existence are woven into a whole."[40] In conversation with others, we not only gain a fuller appreciation of the deceased's life, but also come to a revised assessment of our own life. Describing how this process occurred with the death of a former girlfriend, Tony Walter says, "This was not social support for an intrinsically personal grief process, but an intrinsically social process in which we negotiated and re-negotiated who Corina was, how she had died, and what she had meant to us."[41] One way we "keep" those we have lost to death is to talk honestly about them with family, friends, and neighbors who knew them.

In emphasizing the *personal meaning* of a loss, Stephen Fleming and Paul Robinson observe:

> It is our opinion that survivors seldom, if ever, are able to make sense of a loss or find meaning in a death. . . . You do not find meaning in *death,* you find meaning in the *life* that was lived. Central to the struggle to find meaning in the life that was lived is the notion of the deceased's legacy. The legacy is the appreciation of how knowing and loving the deceased has irrevocably changed the survivor, thus realizing the transition from losing what one has to having what one has lost.[42]

"Giving grief voice" by telling our stories about the dead and listening to the stories that others tell helps us move on with our lives without leaving our loved ones behind.[43]

Toward an Integrated Model of Grief

As Paul Rosenblatt notes, "Defining grief is in some ways self-defeating, because there are many different kinds, forms, and expressions of what might be called grief."[44] In reformulating our understanding of grief, attention is being given to the role of the family system in coping with loss. Nancy Moos says, "Families and family grief processes are inextricably linked to individual grief and recovery."[45] The family and its patterns of interaction are often crucial determinants of whether grief is dealt with in a healthy or a dysfunctional manner.[46]

In this connection, it is important to understand that, although gender influences patterns of grief and mourning, it does not determine them. People sometimes believe that "men don't cry, women do," thus associating a behavior that applies to human beings generally with only one gender. Gender stereotypes portray women as more emotional than men, a notion that is sometimes interpreted as a sign that women are better able to cope with grief. Terry Martin and Kenneth Doka point out, however, that there are many effective ways of expressing and adapting to loss, and that women as well as men make use of various coping strategies.[47] They identify two patterns of grieving: *intuitive* and *instrumental*. In the first, individuals experience and express grief in an affective way (feelings or emotions as distinguished from thought or action); in the second, grief is experienced physically, such as in restlessness or mental activity. Although the first pattern tends to be associated with women and the second with men, Martin and Doka reject the notion that one pattern is inherently better than the other, along with the bias that correlates these patterns with gender. In fact, both patterns can be effective ways of coping, and both men and women make use of them.

In developing a comprehensive understanding of how people cope with loss, one of the most interesting contributions is the dual process model proposed by Margaret Stroebe and Henk Schut.[48] According to this model, the bereaved person expresses, in varying proportions (depending on individual as well as cultural variations) both *loss-oriented* and *restoration-oriented* coping behaviors. This model avoids getting stuck in an "either/or" framework whereby the bereaved must either "let go" of the deceased or "hold on" to memories. Instead, there is "oscillation," or movement back and forth, between the two aspects of coping.

Examples of loss-oriented coping include the grief work of conventional theories: yearning for the deceased, looking at old photographs, crying about the death, and so on. Restoration-oriented coping includes mastering tasks that had been taken care of by the deceased (such as cooking or handling the finances), dealing with arrangements for reorganizing one's life (such as selling the house or moving to another area), developing a new identity (such as changing status from spouse to widower or from parent to parent of deceased child), and so on.

Thus, on the one hand, loss-oriented coping involves "concentrating on, dealing with, [or] processing some aspect of the loss experience." Restoration-oriented coping, on the other hand, involves making the changes that are required to cope with the "secondary consequences" of loss—all those aspects of the bereaved's life that require rearrangement in the wake of the loss.

Central to this model is the understanding that grief is a dynamic process. It involves movement—oscillation or alternation—between loss-oriented and restoration-oriented coping. In coping with loss, the bereaved at times will be actively confronting the loss; at other times, he or she will avoid troubling memories, be distracted, or seek relief by turning attention to other things. Over time, movement between these ways of coping leads to adjustment. As a theoretical construct, the dual process model has a broad range of applications, including its ability to help explain patterns of grief in diverse cultural settings as well as at different times within the same person.

Grief occurs within a social context, and individual grievers differ in their styles of grieving. This leads to the recognition that there is no standard way of coping with loss. Colin Murray Parkes points to three main influences on a person's course of grieving:[49]

1. The urge to look back, cry, and search for what is lost
2. The urge to look forward, explore the world that emerges out of the loss, and discover what can be carried forward from the past into the future
3. The social and cultural pressures that influence how the first two urges are inhibited or expressed

As these influences interact in various ways, at times the bereaved tries to avoid the pain of grief and at other times confronts it.

The Experience of Grief

Newly bereaved individuals may be alarmed by the flood of grief reactions they experience. As Stephen Fleming and Paul Robinson point out, "Grief, at times, may be experienced as frightening, overwhelming, even 'crazy-making.'"[50] People often ask, What is normal grief? How long should a person mourn? If the bereaved is not "over" the loss by a certain time, does it mean he or she is grieving or mourning inappropriately? Such questions require us to consider the circumstances of a death as well as other factors that influence a person's experience. It is also helpful to have a basic understanding of the dynamics of grief and how it is likely to be expressed over time.

Mental Versus Emotional Responses

When there is a substantial difference between a survivor's emotional and mental responses to death, and the survivor believes that only one response can be right, the result is conflict. To expect the head and the heart to react exactly the same to loss is unrealistic; disparity between thoughts and feelings is likely. When a person is grieving a loss, many different emotions will be felt, and many different thoughts will arise. By allowing them all and withholding judgment as to the rightness and wrongness of particular emotions or thoughts, a bereaved person is more likely to experience grief as healing.

Survivors often have rigid rules about what kind of emotions can be expressed in grief, and when—such as where and when it is acceptable to be angry or to open to the pain and release an intense outburst of sadness. Permission to have and express feelings is important in coping with loss. Intellectually, we may think, "How can I be mad at someone for dying?" Yet anger may indeed be a component of grief. Consider the example of someone who died as a result of driving while intoxicated or suicide. Of course, the survivor may be angry even if death was seemingly unavoidable and beyond the victim's control. One young mother told of walking past a photograph of her recently deceased child and noticing, amid the grief and pain, a small voice within her blurting out, "Brat! How could you die and leave me as you did!" We might be tempted to think this mother's behavior out of place. How could she be angry at her child for dying? Yet survivors need to give themselves permission to experience their feelings, to feel anger at the person for having died and anger at themselves for not having been able to prevent the death.

The Course of Grief

To describe the course of grief as a set of stages or phases seems to suggest a linear progression from the first stage, through the second, and so on, until the process has been completed. This notion might be comforting to those who would like to have a ready-made schema for evaluating a survivor's journey after loss, but we need to be cautious about applying any such schema to the experience of a particular survivor. The different phases of grief "may overlap, may be of varying and unpredictable duration, occur in any order, may be present simultaneously, and may disappear or reappear at random."[51]

In the first hours or days following a death, grief usually manifests in shock and numbness, feelings of being stunned, as well as of disbelief. There may be an expression of denial—"No! This can't be true!"—especially if the death was sudden and unexpected. Even when a death is anticipated, however, grief is not necessarily diminished when the loss becomes real. During the initial period of grief, the sense of confusion and disorganization can be overwhelming, as if the bereaved person, motionless and helpless, is stranded in the middle of a fast-flowing stream while water and debris rush about him or her. Bewildered by the shock of the loss, the bereaved may feel vulnerable and seek protection by withdrawing. The confusion of this early phase of grief is set against the need for survivors to attend to decisions and activities directed toward the disposition of the deceased's body. This is normally a time when the bereaved are occupied with arranging for funeral services, as well as starting to sort out the deceased's personal and family affairs. As relatives and friends gather to offer mutual support, the funeral can be a focal point that helps reintegrate distraught and disoriented grievers after the disruption caused by death.[52] Engaging in such ceremonies within the context of community can help promote acceptance of the reality of the death and allow survivors to begin moving beyond the acute period of grief.

In its middle phase, grief is characterized by anxiety, apathy, and pining for the deceased. Despair is likely to be felt, as "feelings of disbelief give way to the realization that there will be no reprieve and that the reality is neither a horrible hoax nor a bad dream."[53] Pangs of grief are felt as the bereaved deeply experiences the pain of separation and yearns intensely for the person who died. Bereaved individuals may repeatedly go over the events surrounding the loss, wishing to undo the calamity and make everything as it was before.

During this phase, which can last some time, survivors often experience volatile emotions, which suggests the image of a volcano, at times giving off steam, at other times appearing relatively dormant. Rage and resentment may

be felt and expressed toward persons or institutions that might have somehow prevented the death, "if only things had been different." Anger may be
directed toward the deceased whose "abandonment" causes such pain, as well
as toward God ("How could you let this happen?") or the situation itself
("How could this happen to me?"). Family members or friends may become
the targets of displaced anger. Hostile or negative feelings may, in turn, give
rise to guilt.

The predominant emotion during this middle phase of grief is likely to
be sadness, accompanied by longing and loneliness, as various needs and de-
pendencies that had been satisfied by the deceased become painfully apparent. Much of this time is filled with "if-onlys" and "what-ifs," as the bereaved
comes to terms with the reality: The loved one is dead. In beginning to accept the unwelcome fact that the loss is real and cannot be changed, the bereaved person is likely to review and sort through all the "bits" of interaction
that created his or her relationship with the deceased. This can involve an intense reexperiencing of the history of the relationship. Over a period of weeks
or months, the process goes on, as the bonds of the relationship that *was* are
gradually undone and a new form of relationship with the deceased is created as part of the survivor's ongoing life.

This is usually a painful time in grieving. Yet it is a time when the bereaved
may not have much social support from relatives and friends, who were more
present during the earlier period. After the funeral is over, the bereaved may
be left alone with his or her grief. In providing support to a grieving person,
it's helpful to remember that an absence of social support limits the bereaved's opportunities for talking about the loss and expressing grief.

There is no predetermined timetable for completing the grieving process.
In moving toward the restoration of one's well-being, however, the last phase
of "active" grief is marked by a sense of resolution, recovery, reintegration,
and transformation as the bereaved person moves forward with a life that is
irrevocably changed but worth living. The earlier turmoil of grief subsides;
it no longer dominates every waking hour. Physical and mental balance is
reestablished. This is not to say that sadness goes away completely; rather, it
gradually recedes into the background. Grief is no longer so "heavy"; a weight
has been lifted. Adapting to loss may at times feel like a betrayal of the deceased loved one, but it is healthy to once again engage life and become oriented toward the future.

Even though the focus is now mainly on the present, not the past, anniversaries and other reminders of the loss are likely to stimulate active grieving
from time to time. New losses also may reactivate grief for an earlier loss. Coming to terms with loss doesn't mean forgetting or minimizing the significance
of the lost relationship. It is not a matter of "getting over the grief" in some
absolute or final sense but, rather, a process of "living with the grief." The journey of grief allows us to incorporate the loss into our ongoing lives. There is
no absolute end point so long as the deceased is kept alive in memory.

When you recall a loss in your life, you may remember the emotions,
thoughts, physical reactions, and behaviors associated with grief. Perhaps it

Tears stream down the face of accordion player Graham Jackson as the body of President Franklin Delano Roosevelt is carried to the train at Warm Springs, Georgia, the day after his death—a poignant example of how bereaved persons express their loss in public as well as private.

felt as if all these reactions were happening at once. Part of you may have been in shock while another part was calm. Distinguishing certain aspects or waypoints of grief can help us better comprehend "how grief works," but the experience itself resembles a series of dance steps more than it does a cross-country walk.

The Duration of Grief

People sometimes assume that normal grief lasts only a short time, perhaps six months to a year. This assumption can lead to placing unrealistic expectations on a bereaved person when his or her grief appears to continue beyond some arbitrarily defined limit. Professionals who work with grieving people generally subscribe to the axiom that grief has no absolute end point or timetable. On the contrary, its duration varies among individuals and depends significantly on the circumstances surrounding a loss. Therefore, the notion that a particular individual is experiencing "prolonged grief" tends to be problematic.

It is preferable to take a cautious approach about labeling certain manifestations of grief as "prolonged" or "abnormal."[54] When signs of *acute* grief persist over a long period of time, however, they may be indicators of unhealthy grief. This may be the case, for example, when a bereaved individual exhibits symptoms of depression, especially if accompanied by emotional problems, substance abuse, or suicidal thoughts. Help is warranted when unhealthy grieving puts bereaved individuals at risk.

The onset of intense grief years after a loss may be mistaken as abnormal when it is actually a normal response to a new loss and, therefore, a time-appropriate, rather than delayed, response.[55] This is illustrated in the experience of a young woman who reported intense grief over the death of her husband, despite the fact that he had died nearly four years earlier. Bewildered, she said, "I don't understand myself; it feels almost like the day he died." In conversation with a counselor, she discovered the event that triggered her pain: Within a few days, the couple's seven-year-old daughter would be celebrating her first communion. Although happily remarried, successfully back to work, and obviously healing from her loss, this devoutly religious woman grieved the absence of her child's father from a celebration that had been discussed and anticipated since the child's birth.

Individuals may also experience a resurfacing of grief stimulated by a public death. Researchers call this a "ripple effect." For example, in the week following the sudden and highly publicized death of Diana, Princess of Wales, South Australia's largest cemetery reported having more visitors than on Mother's Day, which is traditionally the busiest visitation day of the year.[56]

Perhaps in your own life you recognize a recurrence of grief for earlier losses. For example, individuals sometimes grieve the loss of childhood and its special experiences. A woman mentioned visiting her parents after some years of living on her own; one day, while poking around in the attic, her mother opened a trunk and pulled out a collection of dolls that had belonged to the daughter when she was a child. Seeing the dolls evoked grief for the childhood that had ended years earlier. She said, "I looked at those dolls and their tiny clothes, and I got in touch with the loss of that time in my life when my mother had taken care of me and had made clothes for my dolls. There I was, sitting in the attic, just bawling." Most of us have experienced similar situations in our own lives. Some event, picture, place, song, or other stimulus provokes grief related to something or someone no longer present.

Survivors may experience a recurrence of grief for a significant loss at various times throughout their lives when something brings freshly to mind the recognition that what once was is no more. For example, a person who was bereaved as a child by a parent's death may grieve that death anew many years later when his or her own child is born. A study of bereaved spouses found that the effects of loss can be sustained over an extended period of time that is more appropriately termed a "life transition" than a "life crisis," with survivors grieving in some fashion for the rest of their lives.[57]

An Elegy on the Death of John Keats

Ah, woe is me! Winter is come and gone,
But grief returns with the revolving year;
The airs and streams renew their joyous tone:
The ants, the bees, the swallows reappear;
Fresh leaves and flowers deck the dead Seasons' bier;
The amorous birds now pair in every brake,
And build their mossy homes in field and brere;
And the green lizard, and the golden snake,
Like unimprisoned flames, out of their trance awake.

Alas! that all we loved of him should be
But for our grief, as if it had not been,
And grief itself be mortal! Woe is me!
Whence are we, and why are we? of what scene
The actors or spectators? Great and mean
Meet massed in death, who lends what life must borrow.
As long as skies are blue, and fields are green,
Evening must usher night, night urge the morrow,
Month follow month with woe, and year wake year to sorrow.

Percy Bysshe Shelley, "Adonais"
(excerpt)

Complications of Grief

The journey through grief may be affected by various influences that hamper its satisfactory resolution and the bereaved's ability to adapt to life without the deceased. Therese Rando lists the following as examples of situations that heighten the risk of *complicated mourning*:[58]

1. Sudden and unanticipated death, especially when it is traumatic, violent, mutilating, or random
2. Death from an overly lengthy illness
3. Death of a child
4. The bereaved's perception that the death was somehow preventable
5. A relationship between the bereaved and the deceased that was markedly angry or ambivalent, or markedly dependent
6. The bereaved's prior or concurrent mental health problems or unaccommodated losses and stresses
7. The bereaved's perceived lack of social support

Determining whether grief is complicated is not as simple as taking a checklist and marking off the appropriate items. Rando says, "What may be an appropriate response in one circumstance for an individual mourner may be a highly pathological response for a different mourner in other circumstances." In reviewing the circumstances that may complicate grief, notice that complicating circumstances alone do not justify labeling a person's grief as "abnormal" or "pathological." For example, a parent who experiences the death of his or her child due to random violence may be confronted by a mode of bereavement that is inherently complicated, but this fact alone should not lead us to conclude that the parent's grief will be dysfunctional.

When grief is suppressed and emotional engagement with the loss is absent or diminished, or when grief is so boundless that it becomes totally overwhelming, it sets the stage for a poor adjustment to the loved one's death.[59] Rando says, "In all forms of complicated mourning, there are attempts to do two things: (1) to deny, repress, or avoid aspects of the loss, its pain, and the full realization of its implications for the mourner; and (2) to hold onto, and avoid relinquishing, the lost loved one." Rando believes the prevalence of complicated mourning is increasing due to a variety of social processes, including urbanization, secularization, and deritualization, as well as violence, availability of guns, social alienation, substance abuse, and a sense of hopelessness.[60]

Holly Prigerson and her colleagues have been developing criteria for distinguishing between normal and pathological grief, which they call *traumatic grief*.[61] At the core of traumatic grief is *separation distress,* a cluster of symptoms such as yearning, longing, or searching, which the researchers believe indicates an intrusive, distressing preoccupation with the deceased. A second cluster of symptoms, known as *traumatic distress,* includes "efforts to avoid reminders of the deceased; feelings of purposelessness and futility about the future; a sense of numbness and detachment resulting from the loss; feeling shocked, stunned, or dazed by the loss; having difficulty acknowledging the death; feeling that life is empty and unfulfilling without the deceased; having a fragmented sense of trust, security, and control; and experiencing anger over the death."[62]

Although the proposed criteria for diagnosing traumatic grief have not been finalized, many of the *symptoms* being associated with traumatic grief are similar to the *signs* of normal grief.[63] What differentiates traumatic from normal grief, say Prigerson and her colleagues, is the severity of the reactions and their duration: Individuals who are adapting to life without the deceased are considered to be grieving normally, whereas individuals who have persistent impairments in their social, occupational, and other areas of functioning for longer than two months (the duration currently stated in the criteria) are considered to be grieving abnormally.

Phyllis Silverman points to a tension "between those who focus on grieving behavior as symptoms of psychiatric problems and those who see mourning as an expected life-cycle transition, the pain that is to be expected under the circumstances."[64] Futhermore,

> The view of grief as an illness permeates many layers of society as a continuation of the invisible death [Philippe] Ariès describes. Grief is taken to the "doctor's office," where it can be contained and controlled and will not intrude on the life of the community.[65]

On the one hand, the effort to define criteria for diagnosing traumatic grief is commendable insofar as it seeks a reliable means of identifying individuals who are experiencing abnormal grief so that they can receive appropriate treatment. On the other hand, it risks "medicalizing" grief by blurring the line between dysfunction and normality. The criteria for making such a distinction must be unambiguous to avoid creating an environment in which people make hasty and ill-informed judgments about their own, or someone else's, grief.

The Mortality of Bereavement

Can a grieving person die of a "broken heart"?[66] The death of a loved one involves many concurrent changes, or secondary losses, that add to a survivor's vulnerability. What determines the outcome is not so much stress itself as the person's ability to cope with it. During the fifteenth century, grief was a legal cause of death that could be listed on death certificates. Stephen Oppenheimer, a neurologist, says, "It's an old wives' tale that a person can die of a broken heart. . . . But, many old wives' tales are true."[67] Oppenheimer believes that unresolved mental stress can throw the heart into an irregular and fatal heartbeat. He is studying the brain's insular cortex, an area of the nervous system that controls breathing and heartbeat and that links up with the limbic system, which deals with anger, fear, sadness, and other emotions. Damage to the insular cortex may render a person susceptible to a chaotic heartbeat called ventricular fibrillation, leading to cardiac arrest and, thus, a "broken heart."

In reviewing the "broken heart" phenomenon, Margaret Stroebe concludes that "both the direct consequences of loss of a loved one, or a broken heart, and secondary effects, or the stress of bereavement, are responsible for the bereavement-mortality relationship."[68] She adds, "When extreme grief coincides with severe life stresses during bereavement, the risk to life is likely to be greatest of all."

In some cases, the stress of bereavement appears to aggravate a physical condition that may have been latent, causing symptoms to manifest or develop more rapidly. Hans Selye's studies point to the existence of an acute alarm reaction, or mobilization of the body's resources, in situations of high emotional stress.[69] According to Selye, the alarm reaction is a "generalized call to arms" of the body's defenses, and it manifests in physiological changes that prepare the organism to cope with the agent or situation eliciting the reaction. If this reaction is not followed by either adaptation or resistance to the agent eliciting it, dysfunction or death may ensue.

A study of a small community in Wales found that the death rate among bereaved individuals during the first year of bereavement was nearly seven times that of the general population.[70] Other research has shown a higher incidence of chronic diseases in the recently bereaved.[71] A study at Mount Sinai School of Medicine found that there was a diminished immune response among widowers during the first few months following bereavement.[72] Other studies have shown significant depression of lymphocyte (T-cell) function following bereavement.[73]

The upper <u>middles</u> would probably drink themselves silly at the funeral. Although a few years ago this would have been frowned on. When my husband in the sixties announced that he intended to leave £200 in his will for a booze-up for his friends, his lawyer talked him out of it, saying it was in bad taste and would upset people. The same year his grandmother died, and after the funeral, recovering from the innate vulgarity of the cremation service when the gramophone record stuck on 'Abi-abi-abi-abi-de with me', the whole family trooped home and discovered some crates of Australian burgundy under the stairs. A rip-roaring party ensued and soon a <u>lower middle</u> busybody who lived next door came bustling over to see if anything was wrong. Whereupon my father-in-law, holding a glass and seeing her coming up the path, uttered the immortal line: 'Who is this intruding on our grief?'

WTF

Jilly Cooper, *Class*

George Engel investigated the possible relationship between stress and sudden death.[74] After compiling a number of case reports, Engel classified stressful situations into eight categories, four of which can be considered as either a direct or an indirect component of grief and mourning: (1) the impact of the death of a close person, (2) the stress of acute grief, (3) the stress that occurs with mourning, and (4) the loss of status or self-esteem following bereavement.

At first glance, loss of self-esteem may not seem especially relevant. Guilt, however, tends to lower self-esteem, and guilt is a common component of grief. Consider the bereaved person who says, "If only I had tried harder or done something differently, my loved one might not have died." The changed circumstances of daily life may also tend to diminish a survivor's self-esteem. A widower who used to attend social functions with his spouse may now be left off the guest list; a widow may decline social events that she believes are for "couples only." Tighter finances may lower self-esteem. Loss of status that had been enjoyed due to a deceased mate's professional or community standing may have a similar effect.

Although no direct cause-and-effect link has been established between bereavement and the onset of disease, there is intriguing evidence which hints of the possibility that the reaction to loss can contribute to illness and even death. So, can a grieving person die of a broken heart? For now, the answer seems to be "the fact that bereavement may be followed by death from heart disease does not prove that grief itself is a cause of death."[75]

Variables Influencing Grief

Just as no two persons are alike, no two experiences of grief are alike. The circumstances of death, the personality and social roles of the bereaved, the relationship with the deceased—these are among the factors that influence grief and mourning. These factors offer clues about why some deaths are especially devastating to survivors. In thinking about some of the variables that can influence a survivor's grief, the following are some basic questions: Who died? How did the death occur? What was the quality of the survivor's relationship to the deceased? Is there still "unfinished business" from the relationship? What prior losses has the survivor experienced? Were there any complicating factors about the death? Was this loss socially sanctioned? (See "Social Support and Disenfranchised Grief" later in this chapter.) What financial and legal matters remain to be dealt with in the wake of the death? Each of these questions opens up an area for further consideration.

Survivor's Model of the World

A survivor's response to loss is conditioned by his or her model of the world—that is, by his or her perception of reality and judgment about how the world works. How a person copes with loss—the death of a mate, other family member, or close friend—tends to be consistent with how that person copes with the everyday stresses and small losses of daily living. In considering how a person's model of the world applies to bereavement, four factors identified by Edgar Jackson are especially important: personality, social roles, perception of the deceased's importance, and values.[76]

Personality

The person with an immature or dependent personality is especially vulnerable to the loss of someone in whom much emotional capital has been invested, perhaps in an attempt to compensate for feelings of inadequacy by projecting part of his or her identity onto the other person. With the death of that person, more of the survivor's projected self is involved in the loss. In contrast, the person with greater self-esteem and stronger self-concept is not as prone to such overcompensation; thus, grief is likely to be less devastating. People who report a high degree of purpose in life tend to cope more effectively with bereavement than do people who report a low purpose in life.[77] Self-concept is an important determinant of how a person responds to death.

Cultural Context and Social Roles

Grief is shaped by the social context in which it occurs.[78] In examining bereavement and loss in two Muslim communities—one in Egypt, the other in Bali—Unni Wikan concludes that culture is a potent shaper and organizer of how people respond to loss.[79] Although both societies share a common religious heritage, one encourages mourners to express their sorrow in wails and lamentations, whereas the other encourages mourners to contain their sorrow and maintain a quiet and essentially cheerful countenance.

In combat, a soldier is expected to perform assigned duties despite personally grieving when comrades die. In some societies, a widow knows well in advance what kind of behavior is expected when her husband dies, and the members of her society gather to ensure that her grief is expressed in specific and appropriate ways. People who live in modern societies generally have

Bereaved persons in most cultures may dream that a beloved person has come back. In the early stages of bereavement, this, as well as hallucinating the dead, is a normal manifestation of grieving. However, Hawaiians usually see the dead in dreams more often, for more reasons, and for longer periods after a death than do, for example, Western Caucasians. In modern Western culture, when dreams (or hallucinations) of the dead continue too long, they are usually symptoms of pathological grief: the process or "work" of grieving has not progressed through the normal stages.

For the Hawaiian who is emotionally close to his ethnic roots, such prolonged dreaming or envisioning of the dead may or may not be a sign of blocked grief work. In the Hawaiian tradition, the dead do return: in dreams and visions, in sensations of skin, in hearing the voice or smelling the perfume or body odor of the one who has died.

The difference between what is culturally normal and what may be pathological is only partly spelled out by the dream content. We must also know what is going on in the life and family life of the dreamer; we must know how much and what kind of emotion the dream aroused. Especially, we must know what were the relationships in life between the one who died and the survivor who dreams.

Mary Kawena Pukui, E. W. Haertig, and
Catherine A. Lee, *Nana I Ke Kumu (Look to the Source)*

greater flexibility in determining for themselves what behavior is appropriate in different social contexts. Even so, the cultural environment is an important factor in shaping a person's grief and mourning.

Perceived Relationship with the Deceased

The survivor's perception of the relative importance of the deceased also shapes the experience of grief. Was the deceased an important person in the bereaved's life? Is the bereaved's life likely to be significantly changed by the death? Think for a moment about the various relationships in your life—parents, children, neighbors, coworkers, teachers, friends, lovers, and so on. Generally speaking, the death of a family member or other close relative is perceived as more important than the death of a coworker or neighbor. But the outward form of the relationship is not the only determinant of the deceased's importance to a survivor. The death of a close friend may parallel the mourning patterns associated with surviving a death within the family.[80] Reports of death in the media may even prompt "vicarious grief" experiences, especially if they involve events or circumstances that have special poignancy to the griever.[81]

Whatever the outward form—kin, friend, neighbor, or mate—relationships vary according to degree of intimacy, perception of each other's roles, expectations of the other person, and the quality of the relationship itself. In some instances, a person's relationship with his or her parents may reflect socially defined roles of "parent" and "child" more than feelings of friendship or personal intimacy. For others, a parent may occupy additional roles of business

David Des Granges, Tate Gallery, London

This portrait of the Saltonstall family, painted in 1611 by David Des Granges, pro-vides a record of living family members and their relational links with the deceased, whose influence is still felt. The husband and father, Sir Richard, is portrayed as if standing at the bedside of his dead wife, whose arm reaches toward their two children. Seated in the chair and holding her baby, the newest member of the family, is Sir Richard's second wife, whom he married three years after the death of his first wife.

associate, neighbor, and friend. These differing roles and expectations result in different perceptions that are likely to shape the experience of grief when a parent dies.

A number of factors determine whether a relationship is central or peripheral to a person's life. In his influential 1977 paper, "Human Grief: A Model for Prediction and Intervention," Larry Bugen observed that a death involving someone central to the survivor's life generally will be more affecting than the death of someone who is perceived to be on the periphery.[82] Bugen added that grief can also be predicted to some extent by a survivor's belief about the circumstances of the death—that is, whether the death was preventable or unpreventable. For instance, given a *central* relationship between the survivor and the deceased and the belief that the death was *preventable*, mourning would be expected to be both intense and prolonged. However, if a survivor had a *peripheral* relationship with the deceased and also believed that the death was *not preventable*, mourning would be expected to be less intense as well as of shorter duration.

© James Van Der Zee

Many people believe the death of a young child to be the most heartrending of all bereavement experiences—what researchers term a high-grief death because it tends to elicit a tremendous sense of loss.

The deceased's importance may also be considered in terms of a survivor's *perceived similarity* to the deceased. This hypothesis suggests that the more similar to the deceased a survivor believes he or she is, the greater the grief reaction is likely to be.[83] (Perceived similarity is also a factor in the formation of support groups that are composed of people who have experienced similar losses.)

It is also important to mention the role of *ambivalence* on the course of grief. Ambivalence about a relationship reflects a push-pull struggle between love and hate, and it may be subtle or dramatic. Perhaps no relationship is entirely free of ambivalence, but when it is intense and ongoing, confusing emotions can complicate grieving.

Relationship issues and the circumstances of a death appear to influence whether a particular death is likely to involve *high grief* or *low grief*.[84] A high-grief death is characterized by intense reactions; a low-grief death is perceived as less devastating, and thus grief is likely to be less intense. The death of a child is often cited as the classic example of a high-grief death.

Values and Beliefs

A person's value structure—that is, the relative worth he or she assigns to different experiences and outcomes—is another influence on the course of grief. We sometimes hear people say things like, "Of course, his wife misses him terribly, but she is also relieved that he is no longer enduring such pain and suffering." In other words, knowing the husband's suffering is over mitigates the wife's grief at his death. Edgar Jackson cites the example of a husband who, knowing that he will soon die from a terminal illness, prepares his wife for the time when he will not be present to manage their financial affairs. The value this couple placed on being prepared was a factor in their grief as they faced the husband's dying and, subsequently, in the wife's grief after his death.

More generally, value structures that include a place for death in a person's philosophy of life can be a factor in how that person experiences loss and grief. Religious and spiritual beliefs, for example, influence how individuals relate to the meaning of death and, thus, play a role in shaping the experience of loss and grief. Even when there is hope of an eventual reunion with the deceased loved one, however, the immediate reality must be recognized. Richard Leliaert says, "To suggest that faith itself can drive out the pain of bereavement is to counsel badly."[85] Although religious faith may be consoling and comforting, the path of grief still must be trod. Leliaert says, "Good spiritual caregiving for bereaved persons needs a fine balance between the human need to grieve adequately and the spiritual grounds for hope provided by formal religions or spiritual belief systems."

Mode of Death

How a person dies affects a survivor's grief. Consider the ways in which people die: the grandmother, dying quietly in her sleep; the child pronounced DOA after a bicycle crash; the bystander caught in the crossfire of violence or terrorism; the despondent person who dies by suicide; the chronically ill patient who dies a lingering death. The mode of death—natural, accidental, homicide, or suicide—has an impact on the nature of grief, as does the survivor's previous experience with that type of death.[86]

Anticipated Death

The phenomenon of *anticipatory grief,* or anticipatory mourning, can be understood as a reaction to the awareness of an impending loss. Therese Rando points out that this awareness may also be accompanied by a recognition of associated losses.[87] Some people believe that an expected or anticipated death, as is often true with chronic or long-term illnesses, is easier to cope with than a death that occurs suddenly, without warning.[88] Others believe that grief experienced before a death occurs does not diminish the grief experienced when the anticipated loss becomes an objective fact. Nevertheless, disbelief and shock tend to be more intense when a death is unexpected.

A Letter from the Canadian Prairie

Heather Brae, Alberta
January 12, 1906

Miss Jennie Magee
Dear Sister:

You will be surprised to hear from me after so many years. Well I have bad news for you. My Dear little wife is Dead and I am the lonelyist Man in all the world. She gave Birth to little Daughter on the 27th of December three Days after she went out of her mind and on the 7th of January she took Pnumonia and Died about half past three in the afternoon. We buried her tuesday afternoon in a little cemetary on the Prarry about 15 miles from here. I am writing to you to see if you will come and keep house for me and raise my little Baby. I would not like to influence you in any way as I am afraid you would be lonely when I have to go from home as I will now and again. You are used to so much stir in the city. I have 400 acres of Land and I have 9 or ten cows and some hens. If you come you can make all you can out of the Butter and eggs and I might be able to Pay you a small wage . . . Write and let me know as soon as Possible what you think about the Proposition. I am writing to the rest tonight to let them know the bad news. I think this is all at Present from your affectionate Brother.

William Magee

Linda Rasmussen, Lorna Rasmussen,
Candace Savage, and Anne Wheeler,
A Harvest Yet to Reap: A History of Prairie Women

A phenomenon associated with anticipatory mourning is *secondary morbidity,* which refers to "difficulties in the physical, cognitive, emotional, or social spheres of functioning that may be experienced by those closely involved with the terminally ill person."[89] The strain of caring for a dying relative may cause the caregiver to be inattentive to his or her own health care needs, with the result that the caregiver becomes sick or run-down. Secondary morbidity can affect professional or volunteer caregivers as well as family members and friends of the dying person.

Sudden Death

In an address before a group of death educators and counselors, Yvonne Ameche described her experience on the night two policemen came to her door with news of her son's unexpected death. Despite having experienced the deaths of her grandparents during her childhood and, later, the deaths of both her parents, Ameche said, "I don't know if anything prepared me for the knock on the door the night Paul died. . . . I remember reeling back [and feeling] like I had been physically assaulted."[90] The sense of overwhelming shock caused by the unexpected nature of her son's death was accompanied by feelings that her own familiar sense of self had been "lost" as well. The journey of survivorship from head to heart, as Ameche describes it, "where I started to internalize what I had so carefully intellectualized," took a long time and, she adds, "it was a long time before I felt like myself."

Survivors who are bereft because of a sudden death usually want information quickly, often in considerable detail, to help them begin to make sense of the loss. Hospital staff, emergency personnel, and others who deal with traumatic deaths need to offer this information in a sensitive, compassionate manner and provide a supportive environment for the grief that ensues following a notification of sudden death. (See "Death Notification" in Chapter 4.) The abrupt breaking of ties between the deceased and his or her survivors makes sudden deaths a category of bereavement that many people consider especially difficult.

Suicide

People who survive a loved one's death by suicide are often left feeling bewildered, "Oh, my God, he did it to himself!" The impact of suicide can intensify survivors' feelings of blame and guilt.[91] If someone close to us was in such pain that he or she died by suicide, we may be burdened by guilty questions: "Why didn't I see the predicament and do more to help? What could have been done to respond to the cry for help?" In a series of interviews with individuals bereaved as a result of suicide, Carol Van Dongen concluded:

> A consistent theme throughout survivors' experiences was an intense need to understand why the suicide had occurred and what were the implications of the death for themselves and their family. Survivors agonized over possible reasons for the suicide, as well as how the death was affecting them now and what it might mean in the future.[92]

Besides guilt and self-questioning, survivors may direct feelings of anger and blame toward the person who died by suicide. Suicide is seen as the ultimate affront, the final insult—one that, because it cannot be answered, compounds survivors' frustration and anger. When a suicide is actually witnessed by family or friends, it is likely to add to the trauma of the loss.[93]

Feelings of guilt and blame may be made more difficult to cope with because of societal attitudes. Survivors are more likely to be "held responsible" for a death by suicide than for a death by illness. This kind of negativity may be even directed toward the parents of a child who died by suicide.[94] Gordon

 The other day I heard the father of a boy who had committed suicide say, "Everyone has a skeleton in their closet. But the person who kills themselves leaves their skeleton in another's closet." The grief and guilt that arise in the wake of suicide often leave a legacy of guilt and confusion. Each loved one wracks the mind and tears the heart questioning, "What could I have done to prevent this?"

Stephen Levine, *Who Dies? An Investigation of Conscious Living and Conscious Dying*

Thornton and his colleagues point out that such attitudes can result in a comparative lack of social support for individuals who are bereaved by suicide.[95] As with other categories of sudden death, because suicide is usually unexpected, the shock magnifies the bereaved's sense that the death occurred "out of time" or was inappropriate.

Homicide

When a loved one dies as a victim of homicide, the survivor may experience the world as dangerous and cruel, unsafe and unfair. The suddenness and apparent injustice of a violent death have an impact on the experience of grief. Furthermore, as Lula Redmond points out, "The raw wound of the grieving homicide survivor is overtly and covertly affected by the performance of law enforcement officials, criminal justice practitioners, media personnel, and others after a murder."[96] Dealing with the criminal justice system extends the normal mourning period as the case drags on, with no assurance that the result will give the survivor a sense of justice being done. Among the "trigger events" that Redmond cites as restimulating grief are

1. Identification of the assailant
2. Sensing (hearing, smelling, and so on) something that elicits recollection of an experience acutely associated with the traumatic event
3. Anniversaries of the event
4. Holidays and other significant events in the life of the family (such as birthdays)
5. Hearings, trials, appeals, and other criminal justice proceedings
6. Media reports about the event or about similar events

Survivors of someone who was murdered face a number of obstacles in adjusting to the loss. The survivor may have to give depositions to attorneys and possibly testify in court. He or she may be surprised to learn that the charge of murder is a crime against the *state,* not against the *loved one* for whom the survivor grieves. Prosecutors may decide to plea bargain or reduce the charge to a lesser offense, and they may do so without consulting the bereaved family. As the case proceeds through the judicial system, survivors can find themselves facing the defendant in the courtroom or in the corridor or waiting room. Character witnesses may describe the defendant as a good and honorable person. Survivors may have to contend with the defendant's receiving a light sentence or even being released. In other instances, the crime may never be solved, or it may not be prosecuted because of insufficient evidence to bring the case to trial.

In considering the effects of homicide on survivors, we should also think about those who deal with such deaths in an official capacity. Although dealing with violent death becomes a way of life for those who investigate homicides, the constant exposure to death not only is stressful but also can evoke intense feelings of grief. One homicide detective says, "Every cop maintains that detachment is the key, but the truth is that he gives up a section of his soul to every corpse and he dies a little death at the beginning of every case."[97]

Disaster

People who survive a disaster in which others died become survivors twice over—survivors of a catastrophic event that could have ended their own lives and survivors of the deaths of others, often friends or relatives.[98] Because such survivors may feel that they did not deserve to live when others did not survive, a sense of profound guilt can accompany the anguish and sorrow of grief. Relief at having survived catastrophic and threatening circumstances— a natural human response—may be accompanied by intense questioning: Why did I survive while others very much like me perished? Survivors of the Nazi Holocaust, for example, often express a deep sense of guilt about having survived the camps and torture while others did not survive.[99] Combat veterans whose comrades were killed in war often feel much the same way. Similar responses are common among those who survive disasters, and they were reported among individuals who managed to survive the September 11, 2001, terrorist attack while others did not. Although such feelings are intensified by catastrophic events that involve the untimely or unwarranted deaths of others, *survivor guilt* at being alive while others died can be felt, in varying degrees, in other situations.[100] (Other aspects of coping with the aftermath of disaster are discussed in Chapter 4.)

Multiple Losses and Bereavement Burnout

The experience of multiple losses can intensify grief and mourning. Catastrophe, whether natural or human-caused, can result in multiple losses that complicate mourning. Overwhelmed by loss, survivors can be so devastated that they become emotionally numb and disoriented, preventing the expression of normal grief.

Genocide, the deliberate and systematic destruction of a racial, religious, political, cultural, or ethnic group, is often an accompaniment to war, as in the Nazi Holocaust and, more recently, in the mass killings in Rwanda and the Balkans. Terry Tafoya points out that Native Americans "hold in common a heritage of death following initial contact with Europeans."[101] Within two generations of white contact, it is estimated that 80 percent of the Native people of the Pacific Northwest had died from newly introduced diseases to which they had no immunity. Natives throughout the Americas experienced a similar pattern.

In the wake of multiple losses, such as many people experienced as a result of September 11, 2001, or because of AIDS, survivors may feel that they have "run out of tears," that they are bereft of emotional resources to express further feelings of grief.[102] The experience of multiple losses can result in what has been termed *bereavement burnout*. It's as if the normal expression of grief is short-circuited by an ongoing experience of loss.

Social Support and Disenfranchised Grief

The experience of grief and mourning also varies according to the kind of social support available to the bereaved. In some communities and religious traditions, such social support is provided within an organized framework that ensures caring concern for the bereaved. Among Jewish religious families, for example, there are specific customs associated with *aninut,* the period between death and interment; *keriah,* the rending of the garment by the bereaved, which allows expression of deep anger in response to grief in a controlled, religiously sanctioned manner; the *hesped,* or eulogy, in which the virtues of the deceased are recounted in a way that elicits the natural expression of grief; *seudat havraah,* the meal of condolence, which recognizes that the first meal after the interment should be provided by the mourner's friends or neighbors as a way of offering consolation; the *kaddish* prayer, which subliminally transfers the focus from the deceased to the living; and *shiva,* the seven days of mourning that give structure to the early period of grief.[103] Social support of this kind can be immensely helpful to mourners.

Conversely, when social support is lacking, mourners may experience an added burden in dealing with a loss. For example, after the death of an unborn child, whether through miscarriage or induced abortion, bereaved persons may receive little or no social support of the kind that comforts survivors of other types of bereavement. In most cases, there is no funeral or other formal observance of the death; the loss may not be acknowledged at all by the larger community. Occurrences of this kind can involve what has been termed *disenfranchised grief*—that is, grief experienced in connection with a loss that is not socially supported or acknowledged through the usual rituals.[104]

When grief is disenfranchised, either because the significance of the loss is not recognized or because the relationship between the deceased and the bereaved is not socially sanctioned, the bereaved person has little or no opportunity to mourn publicly. Bereaved same-sex mates of persons who die may face this situation. Survivors may receive comparatively little support from the broader community as they cope with their loss. How many community resources, such as spousal support groups, are welcoming of persons with a different sexual orientation? Obviously, the answer to this question varies depending on the community and the mind-set of a particular support group. For example, in one community, a support group for parents who experienced neonatal loss integrated a lesbian couple whose baby had died, thus providing a measure of community support. When a death is treated by society as if it were not a significant loss, the process of adjustment is unnecessarily made difficult for survivors.

Grief may also be disenfranchised not because of the circumstances of the loss, but because of certain qualities that others may wittingly or unwittingly associate with the bereaved himself or herself. Darlene Kloeppel and Sheila Hollins point out that complications may occur when a death in the family is combined with a family member's having a mental handicap.[105] These complications may affect both the family's functioning and the handicapped person's mourning. Kloeppel and Hollins add that "death and mental retardation are both taboo subjects in our society" and that "taboos elicit fear and avoidance."

Family support can be central to determining whether the bereaved feels encouraged to cope not only with grief, but also with the many practical issues that accompany bereavement. An illustration of this is the situation faced by widows in western Nigeria, where the custom is that a widow has no rights of inheritance to her deceased husband's estate; all of their joint possessions revert to the husband's family. Kemi Adamolekun points out that the social support provided by in-laws, or the lack of it, is an important factor in how these widows mourn their loss.[106] Complicated grieving was especially noted when in-laws held the widow somehow responsible for her husband's death and when in-laws took steps to dispossess the widow and her children of property. One observer at an African funeral said, "When a widow cries uncontrollably at her husband's burial, she is not crying only for the loss, but for herself, because of the ordeal ahead of her." Indeed, a common saying is that widowhood should not be wished even for an enemy.

Unfinished Business

Unfinished business can be aptly termed "business that goes on after death." Something is incomplete. The content of unfinished business, how it is handled, and how the survivor is affected by it all have an impact on mourning. Unfinished business can be thought of in one or both of two ways relative to its effect on survivors: first is the fact of death itself; second is the relationship between deceased and survivor. As to the first, perhaps an earlier death of a parent, child, sibling, or someone else close continues to be a vivid reminder of the survivor's uncertainty and fears about death. Regardless of an individual's particular beliefs or values, the more "finished" the business of death is—that is, the more a survivor feels resolved within himself or herself toward it—the easier it will be to accept death and to cope with it. If a person rails against death, refusing to make a place for it, grief is likely to be more difficult to accept. Accepting death, giving it a place in our lives, allows us to be finished with otherwise unresolved issues about death itself.

Second, and perhaps more crucial, is the unfinished business between the deceased and the survivor. Something in the relationship was left incomplete—perhaps some long-standing conflict was never resolved while the deceased was alive, and now it's too late. Unfinished business can include things that were and were not said, things done or not done. Bereaved people often say that the things left unsaid or undone seem to come back to haunt them and make mourning more painful. The sense of never being able to resolve conflicts left by unfinished business amplifies the suffering. Consider the image of a son standing over his father's grave saying, "If only we had been closer, Dad. We ought to have taken more time to visit each other." It may be possible to resolve unfinished business by dealing with unresolved issues through the help of creative or therapeutic interventions, but it is generally better to resolve unfinished business daily, in all our relationships and especially our intimate ones.

Another category of unfinished business relates to the plans and dreams that the bereaved person had shared with the deceased. Perhaps there were places they had talked about going together at some time in the future; now, these travel plans will never be fulfilled. Perhaps the survivor and the deceased shared dreams related to family matters—plans about their children or retirement years, for example. Such plans and dreams can touch on a number of areas in a survivor's life. Death brings an end to all the plans and dreams that had involved the presence of the deceased.

Deathbed promises constitute a particular kind of unfinished business. Picture the classic scene in which the person who is dying elicits some promise from the survivor to perform a particular action after the person dies. Most survivors agree to enact the promise, whether or not they really want to comply with the deathbed request. Thus, a deathbed promise can later create conflict for the survivor, who may be torn between fulfilling the promise and taking another course of action. Whereas some people carry through a deathbed promise and find it to be a gratifying choice, others find that deathbed promises need to be reevaluated in the light of their own wishes and circumstances.

Support for the Bereaved

When a person experiences a significant loss, he or she may initially feel and behave much like a frightened child. A hug may be more comforting than words. Having someone who can "simply listen" can be helpful. The key to being a good listener is to refrain from making judgments about whether the feelings expressed by a bereaved person are "right" or "wrong," "good" or "bad." The emotions and thoughts evoked by loss may not be expected, but they can be appropriate and valid within a survivor's experience.

In some circumstances, survivors may seek professional help in understanding and coping with their grief. William Worden differentiates grief *counseling*, supportive help that people may need as they deal with their grief, from *grief therapy*, which might be required by a minority of people with extreme emotional problems.[107]

In recent years, several articles have been published in both scholarly journals and the popular press suggesting that grief counseling may be more harmful than helpful. One article states, "Grief counseling does not appear to be very effective, most probably because many of the people who receive it would do just as well (and perhaps in some cases better) without it."[108] In a recent study, Dale Larson and William Hoyt conclude that this pessimistic view of grief counseling originated in an unpublished dissertation and did not enjoy the benefits of peer review. They say, "There is no empirical or statistical foundation for these claims."[109] According to Larson and Hoyt, there is no reason to believe that grief counseling is less effective than other forms of counseling or psychotherapy, which have positive outcomes for various forms of psychological distress. With limited data available at present, additional research is needed to clarify whether or not grief counseling is an effective treatment for normally bereaved people. In the meantime, Phyllis Silverman reminds us that the bereaved "need comfort, support, and help as they deal with their grief and find a new direction for their lives. . . . Who should that helping person be in our postmodern society—grief counselor, family, and/or friend?"[110]

In offering support to the bereaved, a basic guideline is do not urge them to hold back their feelings or try to be "strong" and "brave." Talking and crying, even yelling in rage, are ways of coping with intense emotions.[111] Expressing grief is healing. The role of the wake in Hawaiian culture illustrates how support from others provides an opportunity for the bereaved to engage in a "controlled expression of anger and hostility and also for a lessening of guilt and anxiety."[112] Everyone in the *'ohana*, or extended family, attends the wake, including children. With each new arrival, a relative might say—as if telling the dead person—"Here comes Keone, your old fishing companion," or "Tutu is coming in now; remember how she used to massage you when you were sick." The assembled mourners address the dead, recalling their memories and sometimes describing their feelings of abandonment or even scolding the deceased. A fishing companion might exclaim, "Why you mean, go off when we gon' go fishing! Now who I go fish with?" Or a wife might say, "You had no business to go. You should be ashamed. We need you."[113] Scolding the corpse gives survivors an opportunity to vent hostility toward the dead who abandoned them. What a contrast to the idea that one should "not speak ill of the dead," which encourages suppressing feelings of anger at the deceased.

As a culturally condoned vehicle for expressing grief, funerals and other death-related community gatherings facilitate mourning by providing a social framework for coping with the fact of death. Funerals and other rituals can help survivors gain a sense of closure and begin to integrate a loss into their lives. For some, funerals are occasions of weeping and wailing; for others, stoic and subdued emotions are the rule. Different styles of mourning behavior can be equally valid and appropriate. Whereas dense social networks—small or medium-sized Israeli kibbutzim, for example—have social structures that allow mourning to take place within an intimate circle of family, friends, neighbors, and coworkers, looser social networks may need funerals and other rituals to provide a structure wherein support can be offered to the bereaved.[114]

Social support is critical during the later course of grief, just as it is during the first days and weeks after a loss. Bereaved people should be able to rely on receiving support from those they trust. They may need to be reassured that their grief is normal and that it is appropriate to express grief. They may also need permission to occasionally give themselves a break from grieving. As they move forward with life, bereaved individuals may be helped by encouragement from others to face the world confidently. The need for this kind of support can extend beyond the initial period of grief. The first anniversary following a significant loss is usually a time of renewed grieving, when the support of others is important and appreciated. Knowing that others remember and acknowledge the loss, and that they take time to "touch base," is usually perceived as very supportive.

Advice for the Bereaved

Realize and recognize the loss.

Take time for nature's slow, sure, stuttering process of healing.

Give yourself massive doses of restful relaxation and routine busy-ness.

Know that powerful, overwhelming feelings will lessen with time.

Be vulnerable, share your pain, and be humble enough to accept support.

Surround yourself with life: plants, animals, and friends.

Use mementos to help your mourning, not to live in the dead past.

Avoid rebound relationships, big decisions, and anything addictive.

Keep a diary and record successes, memories, and struggles.

Prepare for change, new interests, new friends, solitude, creativity, growth.

Recognize that forgiveness (of ourselves and others) is a vital part of the healing process.

Know that holidays and anniversaries can bring up the painful feelings you thought you had successfully worked through.

Realize that any new death-related crisis will bring up feelings about past losses.

The Centre for Living with Dying

Besides receiving social support from individuals who form their network of friends and relations, bereaved people may want to share their stories and concerns through organized support groups. Most such groups are based on perceived similarity. Having experienced similar losses, members of support groups come together to talk with each other as they integrate those losses into their lives. Widow-to-widow groups, for example, provide opportunities for women to share experiences of being a woman alone and encourage one another in the task of coping with the death of a spouse. Military families receive bereavement support through the Tragedy Assistance Program for Survivors (T.A.P.S.), which offers peer-to-peer support, counseling referrals, survivor seminars, and other types of help.[115] Other organizations, such as The Compassionate Friends (TCF) and Bereaved Families of Ontario (BFO), assist families who are coping with the death of a child. BFO also provides assistance to children, adolescents, and young adults who lose a parent or sibling. In describing the aims of BFO, Stephen Fleming and Leslie Balmer note that it is "designed to facilitate the grieving process, emancipate the bereaved from crippling attachments to the deceased, assuage fears that one is 'going crazy,' educate the survivors about the nature and dynamics of grief to normalize their experience, and promote the usual curative qualities found in groups (the installation of hope, altruism, group cohesiveness, catharsis, and insight)."[116] Some support groups are composed entirely of peers; others are led by a trained professional or lay counselor. Many hospice and palliative care programs have trained volunteers to help families cope with grief.[117]

Bereaved people may also find solace through leave-taking rituals that differ from, or become an adjunct to, conventional funerals and memorial services. These forms of "directive mourning therapy" allow the grieving survivor to take symbolic leave of the deceased.[118] Ritual can also help individuals move from a maladaptive to an adaptive style of grieving.[119] These rituals typically use *linking objects* that symbolize in some way the relationship between the bereaved and the deceased.[120] An example is writing a farewell letter to the deceased and subsequently burying or burning it. An activity like this can be followed by a "reunion" ritual, perhaps in the form of a ceremonial dinner with family and friends. In this way, the rhythms of separation and joining found in traditional rituals can be adapted to the circumstances of a particular survivor.

The impact of change on recently bereaved people may affect virtually every detail of life: The family unit is different; social realities are no longer the same; legal and financial matters require attention. Newly bereaved people face the question "How can I make the necessary adjustment in each of these areas?" Survivors are sometimes urged to take a hand in the practical management of their everyday affairs soon after bereavement, but it can be useful to limit, insofar as possible, the number of changes made, especially in the first few months after loss. It is usually appropriate to strike a balance between the *linking* activities that maintain the survivor's familiar ties to the past and the *bridging* activities that lead the survivor to a future without the deceased.

Bereavement as an Opportunity for Growth

Viewing bereavement as an opportunity for growth can be difficult at first, but this perspective can promote gradual movement toward accommodating the loss. As the bereaved person begins to reformulate the loss, it frees up energy that had been bound to the past. As John Schneider says, "There is a change in perceptual set from focusing on limits to focusing on potential; from coping to growth; and from problems to challenges."[121] The tragic event of a loved one's death is reformulated in a way that doesn't shut out new possibilities. This reframing can carry over into other areas of the person's life so that beliefs and assumptions that were once limiting are reassessed with greater self-confidence and self-awareness, making possible significant and rewarding life changes.

The loss is transformed in a way that places it within a context of growth. Grief becomes a unifying rather than alienating human experience. The lost relationship is changed but not ended. Becoming a survivor can allow for changes in beliefs and values—understanding about death and about life— that might not have been possible otherwise. Recalling their grief and mourning, bereaved individuals often describe themselves as stronger, more competent, more mature, more independent, better able to face other crises; and, for many, bereavement leads to more positive experiences in the context of family and friends.[122] Georges Bataille writes:

> It is a naive opinion that links death closely to sorrow. The tears of the living, which respond to its coming, are themselves far from having a meaning opposite

to joy. Far from being sorrowful, the tears are the expression of a keen awareness of shared life grasped in its intimacy.[123]

Turning to inner sources of creativity gives form to the experience of grief. Creatively responding to loss can bring forth remarkable results. Those who work with the bereaved can spark a grieving person's creative response, as in the case of a young woman who had experienced the sudden, unexpected death of her son at birth. Overwhelmed by feelings of sadness, depression, and an inability to do anything other than grieve, she was despairing of words to communicate her feelings. In a counseling session six months after her son's death, she remarked, "I haven't touched a lump of clay since Justin died." The obvious question was, What had she done with clay before his death? She said that her sculptures of whales and seals had sold at a local seaside crafts shop. The counselor pointed out that the reason for her inability to return to her art might lie in the products of her creative energies. Although whales and seals might one day reemerge from the lumps of clay, her creativity at present might take a different form. The client agreed to find a quiet moment when she would put her hands to the lump of clay as an experiment to see what might emerge.

Both the bereaved mother and the counselor were amazed at the results (see Figures 9-1 a,b,c). Over the course of twelve months, a series of some twenty-two figures emerged. The earliest were naked; later works were draped with a blanket; and, with the final pieces, the fabric of the blanket had been turned into clothing. The mother's creativity not only gave form to her loss, but also manifested an unconscious understanding of the process of recovery and the integration of her loss. Subsequently, the sculptures were photographed and published, along with her prose, giving comfort to other survivors.[124]

People maintain connections with deceased loved ones through memories, as well as through personal and social rituals that provide a "space" in their ongoing lives for acknowledging affection and love for the deceased. Because society is increasingly diverse, Glennys Howarth observes that we cannot simply construct a "new model" of grief or easily determine what may, or may not, be "healthy grieving." Rather, the task is to recognize difference and develop new, complex concepts and approaches that can aid in understanding the *differentiated* experiences of bereaved people.[125] Bereavement, grief, and mourning are complementary threads in the fabric of life, part of the warp and weft of human experience.

Further Readings

Thomas Attig. *The Heart of Grief: Death and the Search for Lasting Love.* New York: Oxford University Press, 2000.

Joan Didion. *The Year of Magical Thinking.* New York: Knopf, 2005.

Sandra M. Gilbert. *Death's Door: Modern Dying and the Ways We Grieve.* New York: Norton, 2006.

Figure *9-1*(a)   *Anguish of Loss*

Figure *9-1*(b)   *Sharing the Grief*

Figure *9-1*(c)   *Collapsing*

"The anguish of loss is overpowering and vast," begins the prose accompanying the sculpture by Julie Fritsch pictured here, part of the series created following the death of her son. "Sharing the grief" states the theme of the second sculpture, acknowledging that "together we must comfort and be comforted." The third sculpture portrays the bereaved artist "collapsing from the weight of emotions I cannot control." The prose accompanying this sculpture continues: "Drained of any ability to cope or carry on, I must collapse now. And feel myself overcome by absolute grief."

Robert E. Goss and Dennis Klass. *Dead but Not Lost: Grief Narratives in Religious Traditions.* Walnut Creek, Calif.: AltaMira Press, 2005.

Nancy R. Hooyman and Betty J. Kramer. *Living Through Loss: Interventions Across the Life Span.* New York: Columbia University Press, 2006.

Janice Winchester Nadeau. *Families Making Sense of Death.* Thousand Oaks, Calif.: Sage, 1997.

Robert A. Neimeyer, ed. *Meaning Reconstruction and the Experience of Loss.* Washington, D.C.: American Psychological Association, 2001.

Colin Murray Parkes. *Bereavement: Studies of Grief in Adult Life,* 3rd ed. New York: Rout-
    ledge, 2001.
Margaret S. Stroebe, Robert O. Hansson, Wolfgang Stroebe, and Henk Schut, eds.
    Handbook of Bereavement Research: Consequences, Coping, and Care. Washington, D.C.:
    American Psychological Association, 2001.
Froma Walsh and Monica McGoldrick. *Living Beyond Loss: Death in the Family,* 2nd ed.
    New York: Norton, 2004.

A child feels the death of a parent or other close family member or friend as deeply as do adult survivors of a close death. This young girl finds solace and a means of coming to terms with the death of her father by bringing a favorite drawing to the gravesite and spending some time alone with her thoughts and memories of her father and what his loss represents in her life.

Death in the Lives of Children and Adolescents

*C*hange is pervasive in the lives of children and adolescents. Families move. Children leave familiar playmates and friends, their neighborhood, school, and the people and places they have come to know and to which they feel attached. A parent may say, "But, dear, it's only for a year," or, "We'll come back to visit next summer." To a child, however, a year or next summer can seem a very long time indeed. Change can bring a very real loss.

Changes in family relationships—divorce or separation, for instance—may be experienced as a kind of death. The child senses that the known relationship has changed, but exactly what the future holds is uncertain and possibly bewildering. Even though such changes do not have the finality that adults reserve for death, children can experience a lingering uncertainty, a kind of "little death."

Change is experienced as older brothers and sisters grow up and move away from home. As the composition of the family shifts, a child is faced with the need to adjust to new and unfamiliar situations. Perhaps the child delights in the change because it means having one's own room. However, with the departure of an older sibling, a child may lose an advocate or a confidant who provided support and understanding. Change can bring both gains and losses.

An addition to the family, a new baby brother or sister, can give rise to both excitement and anxiety. The new family member can represent an intrusion upon the child's place in the family, a loss of attention from parents and other family members. Yet the child may also enjoy the adventure and the more mature responsibilities that accompany change. Change requires readjustments.

In addition, children and adolescents may experience significant losses: the death of a brother or sister, a parent, or a friend; or confrontation with an illness that threatens his or her own life. As much as we may wish it were otherwise, children are exposed to events of change and loss, experiences of bereavement and grief.

Early Childhood Encounters with Death

When does a child first become aware of death? By the time children are four or five, death-related thoughts and experiences are usually evident in their songs, their play, and their questions. The infant's experience of the difference between sleep and wakefulness may involve a perception of the distinction between being and nonbeing.[1] Children begin to experiment with this difference at a very early age, as in the "peekaboo" game, for instance. The infant's experience of having a cloth thrown over her face, shutting out sensory awareness of the environment, is analogous to death. The "boo," when the cloth is removed, is like being alive again. Thus, death may be experienced in games of this kind as separation, disappearance, and return.

The ability to distinguish between the animate and the inanimate is among a child's earliest encounters with death. The child perceives whether or not something has life. The following story illustrates how this may occur in quite ordinary circumstances. An eighteen-month-old boy was out walking with his father when the father inadvertently stepped on a caterpillar. The child kneeled down, looked at the dead caterpillar lying on the sidewalk, and said, "No more!" That is the typical genesis of a child's awareness of death: *No more*.

Similar experiences may produce quite different responses in different children. Encountering a dead caterpillar or dead bird may set off a reaction in one child that lasts for several days, during which time the child is eager to find answers. Another child may pay such an encounter little heed, apparently without a moment's reflection about an event that the first child found provocative and mysterious. Some theorists believe that much of the behavior shown by infants and very young children is *protothanatic*—that is, preparation for concepts about life and death that will eventually emerge in the child's later interactions with the environment.

For older children, play activities can help them deal with evolving concerns about death. Games like cowboys and Indians and cops and robbers reflect, in part, a child's efforts to reach some understanding about the place of death in his or her world. Play can be a means of exorcising fears, trying out roles, making decisions, investigating consequences of actions, experimenting with value judgments, and finding a comfortable self-image.

Death-Experienced Children, Ages One to Three

A study conducted by Mark Speece to investigate the impact of death experiences on children ages one to three suggests that very young children

Death has a different emotional meaning to young children. In the game of Cowboys and Indians death is not final; the game must continue. The common threat when angered may be, "I'll kill you." One can readily see that the concept of killing is not viewed as final and that there is no association of pain with killing. Perhaps the following example will best prove the point. Upon arriving home from a business trip, a young child's father brought her a gun and holster set. After buckling on her new present she took out the gun, pointed it at her father and said, "Bang, bang, you're dead! I killed you." Her father replied, "Don't hurt me." His daughter's innocent answer was, "Oh, Daddy, I won't hurt you, I just killed you." To many children death is seen only as something in the distant future; "only old people die."

Dan Leviton and Eileen C. Forman,
"Death Education for Children and Youth"

make efforts to come to terms with death-related experiences.[2] Speece says, "It seems safe to conclude that death experiences occur in the lives of a sizable proportion of children of this age and that those children who do have such experiences attempt to deal with and integrate their specific death experiences into their understanding of the world in general."

Speece found that slightly over half of the children he studied had some experience with death: in some cases, a human death (for example, a grandmother, a cousin, a neighbor); in others, a nonhuman death, such as that of a pet (most often birds, dogs, and fish). Speece found that these young children responded to death in observable ways. One child became angry when a pet bird that had died would not come back to life. Some children actively looked for the deceased pet or person. They questioned the immobility of the deceased and what happens after death, and expressed concern about the welfare of the living.

The Very Young Child and Death: An Example

So, how does one answer the question "When does the understanding of death begin, and what influences its development?" The dialogue between a twenty-seven-month-old child and his psychologist father provides an illuminating case study.[3] (Notice how the father's professional skills in listening and his sensitivity to his child's behavior helped him engage in this kind of conversation.)

For two months the child had been waking several times each night and screaming hysterically for a bottle of sugar water. The father describes getting up one night, for the second or third time, and deciding with his wife to use firmness in refusing to meet the child's demand. He went into his son's room and told him that he was too old to have a bottle and would have to go back to sleep without it. The father, his mind made up that enough was enough, started to leave the room.

But then he heard a frightened cry, one of desperation that sounded like the fear of death. Wondering what could be causing the child such alarm, the father turned back into the room, took his son out of the crib, and asked, "What will happen if you don't get your bottle?" The child, no longer hysterical, but very tearful and sniffling, said, "I can't make contact!" The father asked, "What does that mean, 'you can't make contact'?" His son replied, "If I run out of gas, I can't make contact—my engine won't go. You know!"

The father then remembered several family excursions during the previous summer, when vehicles had run out of gas. "What are you afraid will happen if you run out of gas?" Still crying, the child replied, "My motor won't run and then I'll die." At that point, the father recalled another incident his son had witnessed. Some time earlier, when they were selling an old car, the prospective buyer had tried to start the engine, but the battery was dead and the engine wouldn't turn over. The child had heard remarks like "It's probably *not making contact*," "the *motor died*," and "I guess *the battery's dead*."

With this incident in mind, the father asked, "Are you afraid that your bottle is like gasoline and, just like when the car runs out of gas, the car dies; so, if you run out of food, you'll die?" The child nodded his head, "Yes." The father explained, "Well, that's not the same thing at all. You see, when you eat food, your body stores up energy so that you have enough to last you all night. You eat three times a day; we only fill up the car with gas once a week. When the car runs out of gas, it doesn't have any saved up for an emergency. But with people it isn't anything like that at all. You can go maybe two or three days without eating. And, even if you got hungry, you still wouldn't die. People aren't anything like cars."

This explanation seemed to do little toward alleviating the child's anxiety, so the father tried a different tack. "You're worried that you have a motor, just like a car, right?" The child nodded, "Yes." "So," continued the father, "you're worried that if you run out of gas or run out of food you'll die, just like the motor of a car, right?" Again, the child nodded yes. "Ah, but the car has a key, right? We can turn it on and off anytime we want, right?"

Now the child's body began to relax. "But where is your key?" The father poked around the boy's belly button: "Is this your key?" The child laughed. "Can I turn your motor off and on? See, you're really nothing like a car at all. Nobody can turn you on and off. Once your motor is on, you don't have to worry about it dying. You can sleep through the whole night and your motor will keep running without you ever having to fill it up with gas. Do you know what I mean?" The child said, "Yes."

"Okay. Now you can sleep without worrying. When you wake in the morning, your motor will still be running. Okay?" Never again did the child wake up in the middle of the night asking for a bottle of warm sugar water.

Think of the impressive reasoning that goes on in a child's mind—the way of stringing together concepts. In this case, the father speculates that two experiences contributed to his child's understanding: First, the child had decided that sugar water would give him gas because he had overheard his parents saying that a younger sibling had "gas" from drinking sugar water; second, when the child's parakeet died, his question "What happened to it?" was answered by his father: "Every animal has a motor inside that keeps it going. When a thing dies, it is like when a motor stops running. Its motor just won't run anymore."

A child's understanding of death is composed of a series of concepts, strung together like beads in a strand that is worked with until it eventually becomes a necklace, a coherent understanding of death. The description of this twenty-seven-month-old's complex associations of language and death demonstrates that children are capable of formulating an elementary understanding of death very early in life.

Children with Life-Threatening Illnesses

Seriously ill children need "mental first aid" to help them cope with their thoughts and feelings. This may mean simply comforting the child and being supportive through a difficult or painful procedure, or it may require more substantive intervention to deal with anxiety, guilt, anger, or other conflicting or unresolved emotions. Caring for children requires a flexible approach. A child who feels unsupported or unsure about what is happening may have fantasies that are more frightening than the truth. A supportive atmosphere in which the child feels free to express his or her fears diminishes feelings of separation and loneliness.

Parents and other adults may find it painful to respond to a child's questions about a serious disease and its prognosis. Such questions can evoke uncertainty and may be met with silence or other forms of avoidance. Is it ethical, or even possible, to withhold information about a serious or life-threatening illness from a child? This question poses a dilemma for those who might wish to keep troubling news from a child. William Bartholome observes that "the most daunting problem facing parents and caregivers who are caring for a terminally ill child is that the person they are caring for lives in a different reality."[4]

The Child's Perception of Serious Illness

Based on a study of children in a leukemia ward, Myra Bluebond-Langner observed that seriously ill children are usually able to guess their condition by interpreting how people behave toward them.[5] Crying or avoidance behaviors are interpreted as indicating the serious nature of the disease and the likelihood of dying. The children in the leukemia ward, most of whom were between the ages of three and nine, were able to accurately assess the seriousness of their illness even though the adults in their lives had not shared this information with them. Although they sometimes discussed their illnesses with their peers, these children refrained from doing so with adults. Recognizing that such conversations made adults uncomfortable, the children talked about the taboo topics among themselves, much as children discuss other forbidden topics, out of range of an adult's hearing.

Over time, the children's interpretations of their conditions changed. At first, the illness was seen as acute, then chronic, and finally fatal. Similarly, medications were first "healing agents," then "something that prolongs life."

As their perception of the drugs changed from being "always effective" to "effective sometimes" to "not really effective at all," their behaviors toward taking medication likewise changed. Generally, the children on this leukemia ward knew a great deal about the world of the hospital, its staff and procedures, and the experiences of other leukemic children, making comments like "Jeffrey's in his first relapse" and noticing when other children died. Although the children did not always know the exact name of the disease afflicting them, they typically displayed considerable knowledge about its treatment and prognosis.

The main concerns experienced by seriously ill children generally match their understanding of death (see Chapter 2). For example, children under five years old tend to be most distressed by separation from the mother. Children from roughly ages five to nine tend to be most concerned about the discomforting and possibly disfiguring effects of the disease and related medical procedures. Older children tend to be anxious in response to other children's deaths. The way a child copes with such concerns is influenced by his or her perception of the meaning and likely consequences of an illness.

The Child's Coping Mechanisms

Seriously ill children are not passive participants in the medical and social events that occur because of their illness. How a child perceives the illness and the manner in which he or she responds to it depend on age, the nature of the illness and its treatment, family relationships, and the child's own personal history. A child's illness can result in absences from school, changes in family patterns, increased dependency on others, and financial or emotional strain on the child's family. Other sources of stress and grief include medical concerns, such as the presence of pain and, possibly, the visible effects of the disease or treatment, which may have symbolic significance depending on the child's age and the part of the body affected.

To cope with the anxiety and confusion that accompany serious or life-threatening illness, children use various coping mechanisms. Even very young children exhibit a wide range of coping mechanisms, although the child's stage of development influences his or her capacity for drawing on both internal and external resources. Some children use distancing strategies to limit the number of people with whom they have close relationships, thus reducing the number of opportunities for a distressing interaction. In this way, a child selects from the whole situation just those aspects or those people that seem least threatening. This coping mechanism allows the child to construct as safe and secure an environment as possible given the circumstances.

Children may cope with a painful medical procedure by making a deal that allows some desire to be fulfilled once the pain is endured: "After I get my shot, can I play with my toys?" In dealing with an overwhelming situation, sick children may regress to behavior patterns that recall a less demanding, more comfortable time in their lives. Children may revert to baby talk or "forget" their toilet training during stressful times. A child whose illness prevents him or her from engaging in a competitive sport may cope by using sublimation,

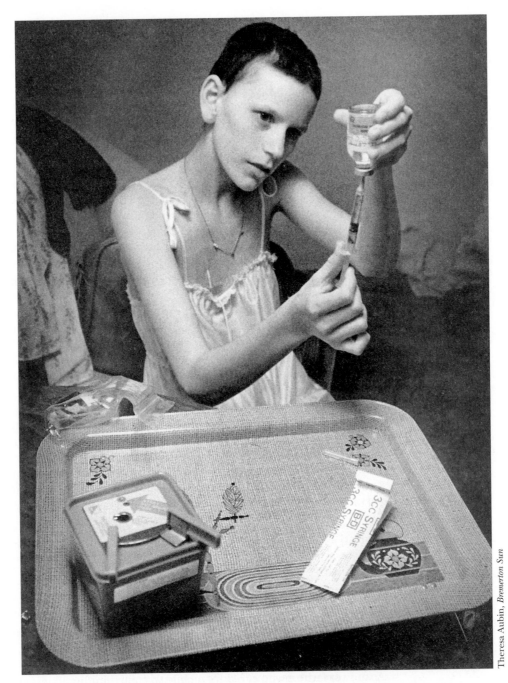

Theresa Aubin, *Bremerton Sun*

Adolescents and older children with life-threatening illnesses may take on increasing responsibilities for their daily treatment regimes. Here, a young cancer patient flushes her venous access catheter, the route used to administer chemotherapy, which must be cleaned nightly.

perhaps finding a substitute for the desired activity by playing board games in a highly competitive way. One might envision scenes of sick children racing through the hospital corridors, IV bottles swinging from their wheelchairs, in a spontaneous competition. As with adults, children use varied coping mechanisms as they confront uncomfortable and frightening aspects of a potentially life-limiting illness. Even very small children know when they are very sick, and they are often far more aware of death than adults realize.[6]

Pediatric Hospice and Palliative Care

Caring for a child who is dying involves more than just medical treatment. The child and his or her whole family should receive appropriate social, psychologicial, and spiritual care. Researchers note that "children's spiritual growth appears to parallel physical and psychosocial growth."[7] Providing optimal care involves implementing the principle of whole-person care, for children as well as adults. An Institute of Medicine report found that "too often, children with fatal or potentially fatal conditions and their families fail to receive competent, compassionate, and consistent care that meets their physical, emotional, and spiritual needs."[8]

Dying children receive care in children's hospitals, hospices with established pediatric programs, and other institutions that care for children with life-limiting conditions, as well as at home. There are few residential hospice care programs intended to specifically serve dying children and their families. The world's first was Helen House, which was founded in England in 1982; George Mark Children's House, in the San Francisco Bay area, was the first freestanding children's respite and end-of-life facility in the United States. One goal of residential hospice care is to offer an alternative to hospitalization when a child requires more intensive assessment, symptom management, and care planning than can be successfully provided at home.

Home-based palliative care programs are indeed an important option in the care of terminally ill children.[9] Ida Martinson, a nurse-educator who helped pioneer such care, observes:

> The greatest barrier [to providing effective care to dying children and their families] is the difficulty in accepting the reality of the dying child by the parents and physicians as well as the nurses. No one wants a child to die, so continued treatment goes beyond what is desirable and useful for the child.[10]

Martinson says, "Parents may have difficulty in realizing that the care they are providing their child in the home is as good—and most likely better than—what we health care professionals could provide in the hospital."

Caring for a Seriously Ill Child

A study of fathers who cared for a child with life-limiting illness characterized their experience as "living in the dragon's shadow" and "battling the dragon."[11] It was a continuous process that required strength, willpower, and work. In the fathers' perceptions, they (and their ill child) "struggled valiantly to overcome the dragon's power."

The ill child is thrust into a more or less alien world of hospitals and medical paraphernalia. Illness separates children from their familiar surroundings and the people they love. Even as a child becomes accustomed to the rhythms of life in and out of hospital, new therapies or unfamiliar medical settings or personnel can make everything again seem out of whack. Changes in expected routine can be upsetting, adding to the child's anxieties and fears.[12] "Each time a child returns to the hospital he is literally a different person. He is at a wholly new stage of development with correspondingly different fears and expectations."[13] Some children are resilient in response to the stressors of treatment, debilitating side effects, and the day-to-day experience of living with serious illness; others have difficulty coping with all the varied acute and chronic stressors that accompany a life-threatening illness.[14]

The participation of family members in some aspects of care can be comforting to a child. Although professionals are usually better equipped to care for a child's medical needs, parents have special expertise in the nontechnical aspects of care. Parents can be involved in activities like bathing the child, assisting at mealtimes, tucking the child in at night, and emotionally supporting the child. Parents should carefully consider whether it is in the child's best interest for them to be involved in performing medical procedures that might cause the child pain. Generally speaking, parents should focus on their parenting role, rather than trying to perform the role of a nurse.

Children as Survivors of a Close Death

Nearly all parents would wish to spare their children the pain of bereavement. When a loss occurs in a child's life, attempts are often made to minimize its effects. The death of a pet, for example, may be swiftly followed by its replacement with another animal. Such an action may have limited usefulness, however. A more constructive approach is to help children explore their feelings about death and develop an appropriate understanding of it. Death is a fact of life that eventually cannot be ignored.

The Bereaved Child's Experience of Grief

Bereaved children experience grief reactions similar to those experienced by adults. However, children differ from adults in cognitive abilities, need for identification figures, and dependence on adults for support.[15] A particular child's response to loss reflects the influence of such factors as age, stage of mental and emotional development, patterns of interaction and communication within his or her family, relationship with the person who has died, and previous experiences with death. Although children tend to be resilient in coping with tragedies in their lives, adults can play a crucial role in guiding a child through grief by listening to the child's concerns and communicating support for the child's well-being. Deaths that are sudden and unexpected or that result from suicide or homicide complicate the issues the child faces in coping with loss.[16]

Hasse Persson, UPI/Corbis-Bettmann Newsphotos

The classmates of a murdered child carry his coffin to the grave. The rituals and ceremonies surrounding death can provide an avenue for children and adolescents to express their grief and to begin the process of coming to terms with loss.

If a child believes he or she may have played a role in the events that led to the death, guilt might predominate among emotions experienced after the loss. In such cases, it is important to openly discuss the circumstances surrounding the death and give the child opportunities to explore the troubling aspects of his or her grief. When children are left on their own to figure out how to cope with confused feelings of guilt and blame, the loss may have traumatic effects that persist into adulthood. To illustrate, in one situation, which involved three brothers playing with a loaded gun, the youngest pushed the oldest, who held the gun, as a bullet was discharged, killing the third sibling. "I have always struggled with myself about whether my brother would have died if I hadn't tried to push my other brother away," said a thirty-year-old man, recalling events that had taken place more than a quarter of a century earlier. "I always thought I did the right thing in trying to prevent the accident, but no one ever talked with me about my feelings of confusion and doubt. For years, I cried myself to sleep alone in my bed at night." Even when it is obvious to others that a child bears no responsibility for a death, he or she should be encouraged to share his or her perceptions and beliefs about how the death occurred. The child's experience may be different from that of the adults in his or her environment.

In coping with loss, children sometimes selectively forget or try to reconstruct reality in a more desirable and comfortable way. A child may not recall how frightened she was by the sight of a sibling lying ill in a hospital bed surrounded by awesome medical paraphernalia; or the child may remember a protracted illness with long stays in the hospital as if the sibling were away from home only briefly for a few tests. The forgotten details or reconstructed images provide a way to cope with the experience without being overwhelmed by painful memories. Although age and cognitive development affect a child's response to loss, many other variables are at work, not least of which are the attitudes exhibited by the significant adults in the child's life.

The Death of a Pet

When a pet dies, adults may wonder how best to help a child cope with the loss. Should one minimize the loss? Or should the death be seen as a natural opportunity to help the child consider what death means and explore his or her feelings about the loss? Research has shown that the death of a pet has a strong impact on the lives of children, and even more so on adolescents.[17]

One mother described the responses of her daughters to the deaths of a new litter of baby rabbits.[18] Upon learning the news, the seven-year-old burst into tears and howled, "I don't want them dead." The five-year-old at first stood silently and then asked to call her father at work. She told him, "If you had been here, Daddy, you could have been the rabbits' doctor," reflecting a belief, appropriate for her age, that it should have been possible somehow to save the baby rabbits or restore them to life. Later, when the children began to dig a grave to bury the dead rabbits, the seven-year-old stopped crying for the first time since learning the news, while the five-year-old kept repeating, "The baby rabbits are dead, the baby rabbits are dead," in a monotone.

Suddenly the feeling that this was all just a dream ended. Christopher was angry. It wasn't fair. Why did that dumb man have to hit Bodger?

"I ought to run *him* over with a truck."

"Oh, honey, Bodger ran right in front of him. The man didn't have time to stop."

They took Christopher home to bed where he relived the accident over and over in his mind. He tried to pretend that the truck had missed the dog, or that he hadn't called and Bodger had stayed on the other side. Or he pretended that they hadn't left the dirt road where there were hardly ever any cars. Or that they had stayed home and waited.

But the bad dream always rolled on out of his control until the moment when Bodger was lying in the road.

Carol and Donald Carrick, *The Accident*

In the days following the rabbits' deaths, the girls asked many questions. The seven-year-old was particularly interested in questioning a family friend who was a widow about her dead husband. How often did she think about him and why did people have to be taken away from those who loved them, she wanted to know. The five-year-old, meanwhile, continued to mourn silently until her mother encouraged her to express her feelings. Then she began to sob. Finally, she said, "I'm glad I'm only five; you only die when you're old."

The younger child's first concern was for herself, the fear that she herself could die. The older child worried about the durability of relationships. Although each child had a distinctive response to the loss, both children showed a need to be close to their parents during the days following the deaths of the rabbits, and they told the story of the rabbits' deaths again and again as they dealt with their experience.

Of course, it is not just children who are affected by the death of a pet. Kelly McCutcheon and Stephen Fleming note that "the loss of a pet often involves responsibility for life and death which can make grieving especially difficult. When a pet is seriously ill, the owner is faced with the major decision of whether the pet's life is worth continuing or if the pet should be euthanized."[19] A woman described the reaction of her husband to the death of Iggy, a desert iguana.[20] When the iguana died, her husband "cried throughout the shoebox burial in the backyard." He later said that he was crying "for every pet he had ever loved and lost." The death of a pet can evoke numbness and disbelief, preoccupation with the loss, being drawn toward reminders of the pet, anger, depression, and the whole range of mental and emotional qualities associated with grief following a significant loss. Rather than viewing a pet as a possession, many people feel that a pet is not only a companion, but "part of the family."[21]

Attachments between humans and pets can be very strong. Yet mourning the loss of a pet sometimes elicits ridicule. Some people may say that the bereaved pet owner is overreacting. After all, "It was only an animal, a mere pet."

Jack Delano, FSA Collection, Library of Congress

Children can feel strong attachment to their pets. Involving a child in the experience of a pet's death through ritual or discussion provides a means of coping with the loss.

However, as Allan Kellehear and Jan Fook point out, "Despite the popular tendency in some quarters to trivialize such loss, the general literature on pet-human relations portrays bereaved owners as every bit as beset with the same power and range of emotions as for other kinds of human loss."[22]

Those who counsel individuals who are grieving over the loss of a pet emphasize that feelings should be expressed by adults as well as children. Sufficient time for mourning the loss should be allowed before a new animal is acquired. "For some owners, grieving may be facilitated by the presence of another pet, but for others, replacement may never be appropriate."[23] The right time is likely to be when grief has been integrated enough to be able to reinvest emotionally in a new pet.

When the bond between a pet and its owner is broken by death, the significance of that loss is increasingly recognized as a natural occasion for mourning.[24] Indeed, as Avery Weisman observes, "The depth of a human-animal bond often exceeds that between a person and close kith and kin."[25]

The Death of a Parent

Of all the deaths that may be experienced in childhood, the most affecting is likely to be the death of a parent.[26] A parent's death is perceived as a loss of security, nurture, and affection—a loss of the emotional and psychological support upon which the child could formerly rely. Based on data obtained from the Child Bereavement Study, Phyllis Silverman and her colleagues conclude that children who have lost a parent typically establish a set of memories, feelings, and actions that the child draws on in "reconstructing" an image of the dead parent.[27] This involves building an "inner representation" that allows the child to sustain his or her relationship with the deceased parent, and "this relationship changes as the child matures and as the intensity of grief lessens." The child negotiates and renegotiates the meaning of the loss over time. The loss is permanent; the process of coping with it changes.

When the death of a parent occurs when a child is very young, an important component of grief may involve mourning the years of relationship that were lost due to the parent's premature death. There can be a lingering sense of "never having known" the deceased parent. Consider, for example, the situation of a parent who dies as a result of war. Powerful emotions may lie buried for years until some stimulus—perhaps the discovery of the parent's military papers or a visit to a war memorial—brings the loss to the surface. Sharing the loss with others can aid healing. Ways of understanding the loss may include talking to other veterans, allowing the child to fill in the picture of a deceased parent whom he or she had not been able to fully know.

Children sometimes take responsibility as they struggle to understand a close death. For example, a child whose parent died of cancer might remember times when she was noisy and her parent needed to rest. "Maybe if I had been less noisy," the child thinks, "Mom would have gotten well." The very fact that the parent is dead while the child is alive may cause children to experience "survivor's guilt." A drawing made by a four-year-old whose father had died of leukemia illustrates this (see Figure 10-1, page 366). Some time after his father's death, as the child was playing with pencils and drawing paper, he asked his mother how to spell various words. Attracted by the child's activity, his mother noticed that he had drawn a picture of his father. In the

The Lesson

'Your father's gone,' my bald headmaster said.
His shiny dome and brown tobacco jar
Splintered at once in tears. It wasn't grief.
I cried for knowledge which was bitterer
Than any grief. For there and then I knew
That grief has uses—that a father dead
Could bind the bully's fist a week or two;
And then I cried for shame, then for relief.

I was a month past ten when I learnt this:
I still remember how the noise was stilled
In school-assembly when my grief came in.
Some goldfish in a bowl quietly sculled
Around their shining prison on its shelf.
They were indifferent. All the other eyes
Were turned towards me. Somewhere in myself
Pride, like a goldfish, flashed a sudden fin.

Edward Lucie-Smith

drawing the father was saying to the child, "I am mad at you!" Surprised at this depiction of her husband's anger toward her son, the mother asked, "Why should your father have been mad at you?" The child explained, "Because you and I can still play together and Dad isn't with us anymore." Amid the confusing feelings resulting from his father's death, the child was attempting to come to terms with the fact of his survivorship.

Now, in working with this child as a survivor, his mother did a very wise thing. She said, "Tell me about this picture." She asked open-ended questions, which allowed her to elicit information about the child's feelings and respond directly to the child's concerns. Spontaneous drawings and other forms of art therapy are excellent methods for working with young children; they help them explore and express feelings that otherwise might remain hidden, yet be disturbing to them.[28] Using art with bereaved children helps them to work through grief by providing a safe, focused environment for expressing their concerns and feelings.[29]

The Death of a Sibling

Unlike a parent's death, a sibling's death rarely represents a loss of security for the surviving child. Yet the effect of such a close death may increase the surviving child's sense of vulnerability to death, especially when siblings are close in age. Betty Davies points out that relatively little attention has been devoted to sibling bereavement.[30] When a child dies, most of the attention is focused on the parents, rather than on the dead child's surviving siblings. Yet,

Figure *10-1* *A Four-Year-Old's "I Am Mad at You"*
Drawing
Following the death of his father, a four-year-old has
depicted his father saying, "Donovan, I am mad at
you." Notice that the father is portrayed as being
bald due to chemotherapy treatments. Whereas baldness is an accurate representation of the father's
appearance, the absence of arms reflects the child's
emotional perception of the situation. Arms reach out;
they hug and enfold; they are a common means by
which human beings express affection for one another.
In the later stages of the father's illness, the pain was
so great that he was unable to gather the child into his
arms. The child's experience of this has been depicted
in his drawing. Also notice that the drawing shows
the father's body facing the viewer, yet his feet are
drawn at an angle as if they are walking off the page.
Again, the drawing reflects the child's experience,
this time showing the father's movement out of his
life. Importantly, the child's mother used the occasion
of this drawing as an opportunity to talk with the child
about his present feelings regarding his father's death.

in countries like the United States, where families tend to be small in size, the
death of a sibling can make the surviving child an *only* child. Losing a brother
or sister can be a lonely experience. As one child said, "It was like my mom
and dad had each other, and I had no one." The brother or sister may have
been a protector or caregiver, as well as a playmate. The surviving child may
be grieving the loss of this unique relationship, worried that the protection
and care given by the sibling is no longer available, and yet relieved or even
pleased that, with the sibling's absence, he or she is now more the center of
attention in the family. This mixture of emotions can produce guilt and confusion as a child comes to terms with the sibling's death.

For adolescents bereaved by a sibling's death, their efforts to cope with the loss may be intertwined with the developmental task of formulating a personal sense of the meaning of life, a task that usually includes intense questioning about the value of religious beliefs and the existence of God. David Balk points out that the death of a sibling shatters "trust in a benign, innocent universe" and "questions about the nature of life and death, about good and evil, and about the meaning of life become personal."[31] Coping with a sibling's death can bring about a greater maturity in cognitive development, social reasoning, moral judgment, identity formation, and religious understanding. Indeed, bereaved young people often cite religion as an important resource for coping with loss, a source of meaning that provides solace as they search for significance in the aftermath of tragedy. A sense of the "ongoing presence" of the sibling bond is also reported by bereaved adolescents, as they continue the "conversation" with a deceased brother or sister and take time to "catch up" on things that have been going on in their lives.[32]

Children typically look to their parents for help in understanding and coping with a sibling's death and its effects on the family. Sometimes the parents' response to a sibling's death sets into motion dysfunctional family patterns that impair the surviving child's ability to cope. Such dysfunctional responses range from overt resentment of the surviving child to attempts to re-create in that child the qualities of the deceased child. Parental responses like these may be present to a lesser extent even in families that appear to be coping successfully. As parents try to come to terms with a child's death, they may unintentionally minimize contact with the surviving child. The living child can be a painful reminder of the child now lost. Conversely, parents may become overprotective of the surviving child.

The bereaved child must be given opportunities to acknowledge and express his or her grief. If a child talks about feeling guilty, one can ask, "What would it take to forgive yourself?" Feelings of guilt are often related to normal sibling rivalry. The sister at whom one angrily yells, "I hate you!" in the morning may be lying dead at the morgue in the afternoon, the victim of a bicycle accident. To a young child, anger directed toward a person and that person's subsequent death might be viewed as a cause-and-effect relationship.

This assumption of responsibility is sometimes displayed as a preoccupation with the "should haves." One five-year-old whose younger brother was run over by a truck while they were outside playing told his mother later, "I should have . . . I should have." He saw himself as his younger brother's protector, responsible for his safety. His mother asked him, "You should have what?" He replied, "I just should have!" His mother then asked, "What do you mean, you 'should have'?" The boy answered, "I should have looked, I should have known, I should have . . .": a flood of "should haves" about being his brother's guardian and protector. Taking the child into her arms, his mother said, "I understand, honey. Daddy's got the 'should haves.' Mommy's got the 'should haves.' We all have them. It's okay to have them. And it's okay to know that everybody could have done something differently, and that they *would* have if they'd had a choice."

© Karen Saltzman

Siblings enjoy a special relationship, one conjoining both rivalries and mutual affection and love. The death of a brother or sister thus severs a unique human relationship. The surviving child may feel the loss more intensely because of an identification with the deceased brother or sister. The surviving child recognizes that he or she is also not immune to dying at an early age.

Figure *10-2* *A Five-Year-Old's "Crooked Day" Drawing*
In this drawing of "The Crooked Day," a five-year-old boy depicts his experience of the events that transpired on the day his brother received fatal injuries in an accident. Contrary to what might be assumed about this drawing, the places on the line where the greatest stress is indicated occurred after the accident itself. The sharp dip in the line at the left-hand side of the drawing represents the accident; the point at which the line crosses back on itself denotes the time when the surviving child was left with a neighbor while his parents were at the hospital with his brother. This was a period of uncertainty and confusion, and the child was angry about not being with the other members of his family. The point at which his parents returned and informed him of his brother's death is indicated by the vertical slash marks, which were literally stabbed onto the paper. The jagged line connoting the remainder of the day represents the emotional upheaval that occurred as the child and his parents together focused their attention on coping with the initial shock of their loss. Importantly, the drawing ends with an upward slanting line that is indicative of an essentially positive attitude—the child's ability to deal constructively with his experience of loss. This drawing demonstrates that even a simple artistic expression, such as a line depicting the chronology of events, can reveal a wealth of detail about a child's experience of a traumatic event such as death.

Allowing a child to be a participant in the family's experience helps the child cope with crisis, as we see exemplified in a drawing by the five-year-old who saw his younger brother killed (see Figure 10-2). The drawing represents "the day my brother was killed"; the point of greatest stress is shown to be the period of time when he was left at a neighbor's house while his parents were at the hospital. Even more frightening than seeing the wheel of the truck roll over his brother's head was the feeling of being left alone, separated from the rest of his family, not knowing what was happening with his parents and his younger brother.

This child's parents not only encouraged the child to express his feelings, but also sought out resources as additional support for coping with the tragedy. Just as the child's work with spontaneous drawings helped bring to light his anger at being left out, the parents received support by sharing their experience with others who had survived similar experiences and by calling on therapeutic resources in their community. In studies of adolescent sibling bereavement, the support considered most helpful by the bereaved teenagers was perceived as "people being there for me."[33]

Support Groups for Children

Community support can be an important supplement to a family's own internal support system. Many organizations that offer support during the crises of life-threatening illness and bereavement have programs for all members of a family, including children. For example, The Compassionate Friends and the Bereaved Families of Ontario not only serve bereaved parents, but also help children and adolescents cope with loss. The Dougy Center for Grieving Children has been so successful in providing bereavement support programs to its community in Portland, Oregon, that it conducts facilitator trainings and distributes its publications worldwide.[34] In Maryland, the Hospice of Frederick County has an innovative outreach program, "Camp Jamie," in which bereaved children are paired with a group of caring adults, many of whom are recovering from losses.[35] Named after a hospice patient who died before his third birthday, Camp Jamie provides children with "a haven to learn about coping with grief." In an idyllic mountain setting, participants enjoy recreational activities and have opportunities to explore their losses in a safe environment among peers and "big buddies."

An organization called HUGS: Help, Understanding, and Group Support for Hawaii's Seriously Ill Children and Their Families offers a wide range of services, provided free of charge, including twenty-four-hour crisis support, hospital and home visits, transportation to medical appointments, recreational activities, and respite care. Children and families can avail themselves of counseling, and bereavement support is provided when a child dies. With a professional staff and a network of trained volunteers, the mission of HUGS is "to help families stay together in the face of overwhelming adversity."[36]

Telephone support groups are another type of organized social support that has been effectively used with varied populations, including children. The telephone was first used as a method of outreach for suicide prevention by the Samaritans in London in 1953.[37] The Pediatric Branch of the National Cancer Institute created a telephone network to offer social support to HIV-infected children. Organizers said the telephone offered "a sense of confidentiality not afforded in face-to-face groups," thus providing "a creative and therapeutic way to help HIV-infected children and their family members cope with the impact this disease had on their lives."

Another type of psychosocial support is offered through computer networks that function as virtual environments where children can share their concerns in an interactive online community.[38] Yet another support for seriously ill children is organizations that exist to grant the wishes of children who have been given a limited or uncertain prognosis. The Sunshine Foundation, founded in 1976, and the Starlight Foundation, founded in 1983, are two examples.[39] Through the efforts of such groups, seriously ill children

Even young children sense that they are different from other kids after a parent dies. During one of The Dougy Center's "Littles" groups for three to five year olds, Luke got a splinter in his finger while climbing on the playhouse outside. He went inside with an adult facilitator for a Band-Aid, trailed by his buddy, Mario. Both of these preschoolers' fathers had died in car accidents. As Luke's finger was washed and the Band-Aid applied, Mario said that he too had a "boo-boo" and needed a Band-Aid. When the facilitator asked him where his boo-boo was, he replied, "It's invis'ble. All of us kids at The Dougy Center have invis'ble boo-boos, 'cause we all had someone die." He knew, even at four, that he was different from other kids.

Donna Schuurman, *Never the Same: Coming to Terms with the Death of a Parent*

and their families are able to take a vacation together or fulfill some other wish that seems impossible without outside help.

Helping Children Cope with Change and Loss

How can we help a child cope with the experience of loss? How do family patterns and styles of communication influence a child's ability to cope with death? Children usually cope more easily with their feelings in a crisis when they feel included as participants in the unfolding experience. If they are excluded, or their questions go unanswered, uncertainty creates more anxiety and confusion. When an adult is also struggling to cope with a traumatic experience, it may be difficult to provide an explanation of the painful circumstances to a child. The child's feelings and concerns may be dismissed or ignored. Even when adults agree with the notion that children have a right to know the truth, they may feel uncomfortable about giving them painful and disturbing news. They may ask themselves: Would knowing the truth cause the child more harm than good? In most instances, the child's natural curiosity effectively eliminates the option of withholding such information.

Guidelines for Sharing Information

Responding to a child's natural inquisitiveness and concern does not mean that one needs to overwhelm the child with excessive detail, nor does it mean "talking down" to the child, as if he or she were incapable of comprehension. Nevertheless, a child's manner of perceiving, experiencing, and coping with change needs to be considered by parents and others who wish to be helpful to children in crisis. This implies responding to the child's questions and concerns on the basis of his or her ability to understand. As a general guideline for discussing death with a child, it is important to keep the explanation simple, stick to basic facts, and verify what the child has understood.

Discussing Death Before a Crisis Occurs

Parents have natural concerns about what to tell their children about death. What can the child understand? How should I start the discussion? We

"Peanuts," drawing by Charles Schulz, © 1995 United Features Syndicate, Inc.

have seen that children develop their own concepts about death, whether or not they receive parental instruction, even when the topic is considered taboo. Children want to know about death, just as they want to learn about all the things they encounter in their lives. One child wrote, "Dear God, what's it like when you die? Nobody will tell me. I just want to know. I don't want to do it."

In explaining death to children, honesty is foremost. Be aware, however, that a parent who sets a ground rule that it's okay to be open and honest in talking about death may find that there are times when the child wants to initiate a discussion and the parent is tired or would rather avoid the subject. If talking about death is part of normal life and not a reaction to crisis, choosing a good time is more of a possibility.

Second, don't put off introducing the topic of death. When a close death precedes the discussion, the parent is faced with the need to provide an explanation in the midst of crisis. This unfortunate situation arises when a parent puts off discussing death "because it's not really going to happen," only to find that "it's happening right now and my child has to be told something." In these circumstances, the explanation to the child is likely to be charged with all the emotions the parent is dealing with, making the aim of clear communication more difficult to attain. Thus, it is a good idea to make use of "teachable moments," occasions that come up in everyday activities, for talking with children about death (see discussion of teachable moments in Chapter 2).

Third, set the explanation to the child's level of understanding. By using as a guide the child's interest and ability to understand, the parent can provide an explanation that is appropriate to the child's particular circumstances.

When talking with children about death, it is important to verify what it is they think you've told them. Have them tell you what they learned or heard you saying about death. Children generalize from known concepts to make new experiences fit. This may lead to a very literal-minded interpretation of new information, especially among young children, who tend to emphasize the concreteness of things. Recognizing this, strive to keep your communication free of associations that could be confusing. Metaphorical explanations about death may help you draw a child-sized picture as an aid to understanding, but unless fact and fancy are clearly distinguished, the child may grasp the

He lived a long way from here
Lew's mother explained.
You never asked
so I never told you
Grandpa died.

I want him to come back.
I miss him, Lewis said.
I have been waiting for him
and I miss him especially tonight.

I do too
said Lew's mother.
But you made him come back
for me tonight
by telling me what you remember.

Charlotte Zolotow, *My Grandson Lew*

fanciful details instead of the underlying facts the analogy was meant to convey. This is illustrated in the following story: A five-year-old girl was told that her grandfather's cancer was like a seed that grew in his body; it grew and grew until he couldn't live in his body anymore and he died. Her parents didn't notice that ever afterward, all through childhood, she never ate another seed. Not one. Not a cucumber seed, watermelon seed, no seeds. Finally, at age twenty-one, she was asked, "Why are you avoiding the seeds? Isn't that a little bizarre? What's wrong with the seeds?" Her automatic response was, "You swallow them and you die." After all those years, she saw the fallacy of her compulsion to avoid eating seeds. It would have been useful if someone had asked her when she was five, "What will happen if you swallow that seed?"

When a Family Member Is Seriously Ill

When a member of a child's family is seriously ill, family routine is disrupted. If the truth about the illness is kept from the child, he or she may become confused about the reasons for changes in the family's usual pattern of interactions. The child may feel rejected, left out of family activities, or ignored for no apparent reason: "Why are my parents so nice to my sister, but they ignore me all the time?" or "Geez, I get into trouble about every little thing while my brother gets off scot-free no matter what he does!" Siblings of a seriously ill child may be alarmed by changes in the sick child's appearance due to disease or side effects of treatment.[40] When a sibling is afflicted with human immunodeficiency virus (HIV), there may be multiple losses to endure and mourn, possibly including the deaths of family members, unpredictable living arrangements, and changes of school, as well as issues involving stigma, secrecy, and shame.[41]

Although open communication is important in helping a child cope with the crisis, explanations must be suited to the child's cognitive capacity. A very young child whose parent is seriously ill might be told simply that "Mommy has an ouch in her tummy which the doctors are trying to fix." A school-age child could be given a more complex explanation, such as the parent needs medical treatment because something is growing in her stomach that doesn't belong there.

Anxiety about a parent's or sibling's illness may be displayed in varied ways. Children may feel neglected and resent adjustments they must make in their own lives. A child may be angry because "Mommy isn't here," yet feel guilty because he or she imagines somehow "causing Mommy's illness." To counteract these feelings, help the child feel that he or she is a fully participating member of the family. Encourage the child to be part of the process of dealing with the illness.

The child can participate in caring for the sick family member in appropriate ways. For example, a child might pick a bouquet or make a drawing as a gift. Such activities allow the child to express his or her feelings in a creative way. Although children cannot be protected from the reality of death, their experiences of it can be made less difficult if they have sensitive, caring support from those closest to them.

In the Aftermath of Loss

We tend to assume that others share our experience of the world. In fact, each of us perceives the world uniquely. Understanding another person's experience requires the art of listening. The aim is to discover what the other person thinks, feels, and believes: What does he or she find important? What are his or her concerns, fears, hopes? If a need for support or assistance is being expressed, what kind of help is he or she asking for? Questions of this kind are important in helping children cope with loss. We need to be willing *to listen and to accept the reality of the child's experience.*

When death disrupts familiar patterns of living, the result can be confusion and conflict, creating a tangle of emotions and thoughts that are hard to sort out. In the midst of this, children may be asked to remain "unseen and unheard," thus thwarting their natural tendencies to explore and grapple with the emotions and thoughts generated by change. Paying attention to a child's behavior is useful for gathering information about his or her experience of crisis. Crying, for instance, is a natural response to the loss of someone significant. Admonishing a child to "Be brave!" or "Be a little man and buck up!" denies the validity of the child's spontaneous human emotion.

In helping children cope with loss, adults must strive to *answer the child's questions honestly and directly.* Explanations should be truthful to the facts and should be as concrete as possible. Telling a child that her goldfish "went to heaven" may cause her to make an elaborate picture of the pearly gates and different sections of heaven: Here is goldfish heaven, cat heaven, and over here is people heaven—a very logical concept that makes sense to a child. We need to be careful that the concepts we convey to a child don't turn out to be dysfunctional.

One woman recalled that when she was three or four a favorite old black dog had to "go away for a long sleep." Not until she was about seven years old did she realize that the dog wasn't just away napping someplace, at the puppy farm having a nice long sleep. If Rover was just "off somewhere to sleep," then a casual goodbye was fine. But, when she realized that in fact her beloved dog was dead, she felt angry and upset that she hadn't had the opportunity to give it a proper farewell.

Exemplifying the age-old oral tradition of elders transmitting culture to the young, this Native American grandmother shares memories and stories as her grandson learns about his deceased grandfather and his place in the family's heritage. Occasions for discussing death with children arise naturally out of our interactions; the most important contribution an adult can make in talking with a child about death is often simply to be a good listener.

Similarly, religious beliefs are an important part of how death is understood in many families. Parents want to share these beliefs with their children when coping with the death of a family member or friend. Children may indeed be comforted by such beliefs, but they deserve to be told that these are *beliefs.* Talk about them in a way that avoids confusing the child. For example, a parent's concept of an afterlife may be different from what a child is able to understand. A child who is told that "God took Daddy to be with him in heaven" may not feel very kindly toward a being who could be so capricious and inconsiderate of the child's feelings.

For the same reason, fairy tales, metaphors, and the like should be avoided or used with care because children may take such explanations of death literally. Consider the case of a four-year-old whose brother (nine) told him that daddy had gone to heaven. The four-year-old promptly went and told his mother, "My daddy's on the roof!" She said, "What? Who told you that?" He said, "Andrew did." The older brother then explained, "We were looking out the window and I told him that daddy was in heaven up there." To the four-year-old, the highest "up there" was up on the roof. If you tell a four-year-old that someone who has died is "up there" and you also say that Santa Claus lands on the roof on Christmas Eve, he may decide that Santa Claus and the person who has died are great buddies. He might make up stories about how they work together, making toys, feeding the reindeer, and so on.

The concreteness of a young child's concepts about death is also illustrated in the experience of a woman whose first experience with death occurred when she was three and a half years old and her mother died. It seemed that her mother had just disappeared; she didn't know what had happened to her. Some time later, she began to realize that her mother had died and she started asking questions. Some people told her that her mother had been buried, and her thought was, "Why don't they dig her up?" Others said that her mother had gone to heaven, so she kept looking at the sky, watching for her. With both of these concepts running through her young mind, she did her best to figure out, "How can my mother be buried in heaven?"

When asked about their experiences involving a close death, children often say that the most difficult times were when they did not know what was happening. A child whose diagnosis of serious illness was withheld from her by her family said later, "We'd always done everything with each other knowing what was going on. Suddenly, it was different. That scared me more than what was happening to my body. It felt like my family was becoming strangers."[42] Sudden change in family communication patterns can be alarming to a child, heightening anxiety about the crisis. A child who is kept from the funeral of a close friend or relative may feel anxious about not being included in an activity that had obvious importance to the significant adults in his or her life. Some children may not want to attend a funeral. Those who do, however, tend to report that it helped them acknowledge the death, provided an occasion for honoring the deceased person, and made it possible for them to receive social support and comfort.[43]

The crisis of a child's illness can lead to a serious breakdown in communication. A young girl told a hospital staffer, "I know I'm going to die. I want to talk to Mother, but she won't let me. I know she's hurting, but I'm the one who's dying." When told of this conversation by the staff member, the girl's mother replied angrily, "She wouldn't be thinking of dying if you hadn't made her talk about it." The communication between mother and daughter went from bad to worse. Still refusing to discuss her daughter's feelings, the mother's style of communication degenerated into baby talk: "Her doesn't feel goody today . . . her doesn't want to talk." A lack of openness was hampering satisfaction of normal human needs for affection and reassurance.

The best gauge of a child's readiness to be informed about a potentially painful situation is the child's own interest, usually expressed through questions. Using these questions as a guide, caregivers can give straightforward answers without burdening the child with facts irrelevant to his or her understanding of the situation. Most important, children in crisis situations need to be reassured that they are loved.

Children are apt to point out any inconsistencies in what we tell them about death. When one three-year-old's playmate was killed, his mother explained to him that Jesus had come and taken his friend to heaven. His re-

Small boy. "Where do animals go when they die?"
Small girl. "All good animals go to heaven, but the bad ones
    go to the Natural History Museum."

Caption to drawing by E. H. Shepard, *Punch,* 1929

sponse was, "Well, that's an awful thing to do; I want to play with him. Jesus isn't very nice if he comes down here and takes my friend from me." In discussing death with a child, it is crucial to consider the child's belief system, the kind of thought processes he or she uses to understand the world. Then, from your very first statement, ask yourself, "If I explain death in this way, how will it be understood by the child?"

Using Books as Tools for Coping

Bibliotherapy—that is, using books as an aid to coping—facilitates discussion between adults and children and creates opportunities for sharing feelings. Libraries and bookshops are stocked with a variety of children's books about dying, death, and bereavement. In choosing a book to read with a younger child or suggest to an older child or teen, it is important to first read or review the book yourself to evaluate its literary merit and how it presents information about death. Books for children and teens should be appropriate for a particular situation. For example, *When Dinosaurs Die: A Guide to Understanding Death,* a picture book for young children, can be used to facilitate a child's understanding of death in the context of the feelings people experience when someone they love dies. When one young boy's kindergarten teacher died unexpectedly, each time he read and reread this book with his parents, he raised different questions about his teacher's death.

It is also important to pay attention to the language the author uses to describe dying, death, and bereavement. Euphemisms such as "closure," "moving on," or "getting over the loss" may signal that an author is not familiar with the theories and insights that apply to understanding grief. A story that refers to death as sleep should probably raise a "red flag" about the ideas it is communicating to children. Straightforward words such as died, dead, sorrow, and funeral suggest the use of honest and accurate terminology. Both fiction and nonfiction books are published on such topics as the death of a parent, grandparent, sibling, and other relatives and friends, as well as pets (see Figure 10-3). A book can give adults and children an opportunity to begin talking about each other's experiences.[44]

Adults tend to worry about children's encounters with death. Are they doing all right? Will they be okay? Is death going to be too hard for them to handle? Can they survive this particular loss? In general, children do remarkably well. As Erik Erikson said, "Healthy children will not fear life if their parents have the integrity not to fear death."[45]

Books for Younger Children

Nicholas Allan. *Heaven*. New York: HarperFestival, 1997. When Dill the dog dies, he shares a whimsical view of heaven with his owner, Lily. Ages 4–up.

Mary Bahr. *If Nathan Were Here*. Illustrated by Karen A. Jerome. Grand Rapids, Mich.: Eerdmans, 2000. After his best friend dies, a boy is comforted by the memories he retrieves and stores in a memory box containing "all the best things we remember about Nathan." Ages 4–8.

Mary Bahr. *The Memory Box*. Illustrated by David Cunningham. Morton Grove, Ill.: Albert Whitman, 1995. A young boy and his grandfather, who has Alzheimer's, create a box to store family tales and traditions. Ages 4–8.

T. A. Barron. *Where Is Grandpa?* Illustrated by Chris K. Soentpiet. New York: Philomel Books, 2000. As his family reminisces about his grandfather's death, a young boy copes with his feelings and thoughts by recognizing that his grandfather is still with him in a special way in all the places they shared. Ages 4–7.

Marc Brown. *When Dinosaurs Die: A Guide to Understanding Death*. Illustrated by Laurie Krasny Brown. Boston: Little, Brown, 1996. This cartoon-like book offers comfort and reassurance to children by addressing their fears about death and explaining in simple language the feelings people may have when a loved one dies and ways of remembering someone who has died. Ages 3–8.

Margaret Wise Brown. *The Dead Bird*. New York: Morrow, 2004. A simple story in which children find a dead bird and conduct a funeral and burial. Ages 4–8.

Eve Bunting. *The Happy Funeral*. Illustrated by Dinh Mai Vo. New York: Harper and Row, 1982. The funeral of a Chinese American child's grandfather. Ages 3–6.

Eve Bunting. *The Summer of Riley*. New York: HarperTrophy-Cotler, 2002. A boy adjusts to his parents' divorce and his grandfather's death by establishing a relationship with a dog. Ages 9–12.

Carol Carrick. *The Accident*. Illustrated by Donald Carrick. New York: Seabury/Clarion, 1976. A young child copes with the death of a pet. Ages 3–8.

Jo Carson. *You Hold Me and I'll Hold You*. Illustrated by Annie Cannon. New York: Orchard Books, 1992. A young girl and her father comfort each other at the funeral of her great-aunt. Ages 4–8.

Seymour Chwast. *Ode to Humpty Dumpty*. Illustrated by Harriet Ziefert. Boston: Houghton Mifflin, 2001. The ultimate book for understanding rituals. A town comes together to memorialize Humpty's death. Ages 4–13.

Andrea Fleck Claudy. *Dusty Was My Friend: Coming to Terms with Loss*. Illustrated by Eleanor Alexander. New York: Human Sciences Press, 1985. An eight-year-old boy grieves the loss of his ten-year-old friend who died in a car accident. Ages 6–9.

Eleanor Coerr. *Sadako and the Thousand Paper Cranes*. Illustrated by Ronald Himler. New York: Putnam, 1977. The story of a Japanese girl's illness and death from leukemia resulting from the Hiroshima bomb, her courage, and the memorial to her by her classmates and community. Ages 7–10.

Miriam Cohen. *Jim's Dog Muffins*. Illustrated by Lillian Hoban. New York: Greenwillow, 1984. A friend and a teacher help a boy cope with the loss of his dog. Ages 3–8.

Janice Cohn. *I Had a Friend Named Peter: Talking to Children About the Death of a Friend*. Illustrated by Gail Owen. New York: Morrow, 1987. When Betsy's playmate dies from an accident while chasing a ball into the street, her parents, teacher, and classmates help her cope with the loss and describe the coming funeral and burial, inviting her to attend if she wants to; includes two sections, one for parents and one for children. Ages 4–7.

Figure *10-3 Books for Helping Children Cope with Loss*
Prepared with the assistance of Carol F. Berns, Co-Founder and Director of the Children's Bereavement Center, Miami, Florida.

Janice Cohn. *Molly's Rosebush: A Concept Book.* Illustrated by Gail Owen. Morton Grove, Ill.: Albert Whitman, 1994. Through the story of Molly, whose mother suffers a miscarriage, this book offers guidance to parents about how children are affected by such a loss and provides a way of explaining the loss to young children. Ages 3–6.

Bill Cosby. *The Day I Saw My Father Cry.* Illustrated by Varnette P. Honeywood. New York: Scholastic, 2000. The sudden death of a family friend brings lessons in experiencing and expressing grief. Ages 4–10.

Tomie DePaola. *Nana Upstairs & Nana Downstairs.* New York: Penguin, 1978. A boy learns to face the eventual deaths of his grandmother and great-grandmother. Ages 3–8.

Dyanne DiSalvo-Ryan. *A Dog Like Jack.* New York: Holiday House, 2001. Story of loving and losing an aged pet. An epilogue contains suggestions for parents about pet loss. Ages 4–8.

Mem Fox. *Tough Boris.* Illustrated by Kathryn Brown. New York: Harcourt and Brace, 1994. When Boris's parrot dies, he shows that even he, a scary pirate, can express his sadness and grief. Ages 4–8.

Jason Gaes. *My Book for Kids with Cansur: A Child's Autobiography of Hope.* Aberdeen, S.D.: Melius & Peterson, 1987. A boy's gift to other children with cancer. Ages 6–up.

Mordicai Gerstein. *The Mountains of Tibet.* New York: Harper & Row, 1987. Inspired by the Tibetan Book of the Dead, this illustrated tale uses the theme of reincarnation to tell the story of a Tibetan woodcutter who, after dying, is given the choice of going to paradise or living another life anywhere in the universe. Ages 7–up.

Charlotte Graeber. *Mustard.* Illustrated by Donna Diamond. New York: Macmillan, 1982. A young boy deals with the increasing infirmity and eventual death of a cat that had been part of the family since before he was born. Ages 3–6.

Kathleen Hemery. *The Brightest Star.* Illustrated by Ron Bolt. Omaha, Neb.: Centering Corporation, 1998. A girl grieving the death of her mother shares memories with her father. Ages 6–14.

Anna Grossnickle Hines. *Remember the Butterflies.* New York: Dutton, 1991. Children recall the special times they had with their deceased grandfather, including what he taught them about butterflies. Ages 3–7.

Margaret Holmes. *A Terrible Thing Happened.* Washington, D.C.: Magination Press, 2000. Helps children express their feelings after witnessing a trauma. Includes a caregiver's resource section. Ages 4–11.

Deborah Hopkinson. *Bluebird Summer.* Illustrated by Bethanne Anderson. New York: Greenwillow Books, 2001. Two children work on grandpa's farm after grandma's death, nurturing and maintaining her garden. Ages 4–8.

Eiko Kadono. *Grandpa's Soup.* Illustrated by Satomi Ichikawa. Grand Rapids, Mich.: Eerdmans, 1999. After Grandma's death, Grandpa fixes her soup recipe for his friends, including his mice friends. Ages 4–8.

Lee Klein. *The Best Gift for Mom.* Illustrated by Pamela T. Keeting. New York: Paulist Press, 1995. Jonathan doesn't remember his father, who died when he was a baby. After hearing lots of "dad stories" from his mom, he gives her a surprise gift, including a message and a memory. Ages 4–8.

Sandy Lanton. *Daddy's Chair.* Illustrated by Shelly O. Haas. Rockville, Md.: Kar-Ben Publishing, 1991. A young boy's lessons in coping with the death of his father. Ages 4–8.

(continued)

Books for Younger Children (continued)

Gloria H. McLendon. *My Brother Joey Died.* Photographs by Harvey Kelman. New York: Simon & Schuster, 1982. The issues surrounding a sibling's death as told from the perspective of a nine-year-old. Ages 8–up.

Miska Miles. *Annie and the Old One.* Illustrated by Peter Parnall. Boston: Little, Brown, 1971. The story of a Navajo girl's efforts to prevent the inevitable by unraveling each day's weaving on a rug whose completion she fears will bring her grandmother's death. Ages 6–10.

Jane Mobley. *The Star Husband.* Illustrated by Anna Vojtech. New York: Doubleday, 1979. This adaptation of a Native American myth affirms the natural cycle of life, death, and rebirth. Ages 3–8.

Marjorie Blain Parker. *Jasper's Day.* Illustrated by Janet Wilson. Tonawanda, N.Y.: Kids Can Press, 2002. Knowing that their beloved dog, Jasper, is dying and in pain, the family plans a day to celebrate before bringing him to the vet to be euthanized. Ages 4–8.

Barbra Ann Porte. *Harry's Mom.* Illustrated by Yossi Abolafia. New York: Greenwillow, 1985. A story for young children about a mother's death. Ages 3–8.

E. Sandy Powell. *Geranium Morning.* Illustrated by Renee Graef. Minneapolis: Carol Rhoda Books, 1990. Two friends who experience the death of a parent, one suddenly and one from a life-threatening illness, help each other with loss and regrets. Ages 5–12.

Fred Rogers. *When a Pet Dies.* Photographs by Jim Jukis. New York: Putnam, 1988. Portrays a family whose dog dies and another family whose cat dies; the grieving children ask questions of their parents and adjust to their losses. Ages 3–8.

Jane Resh Thomas. *Saying Goodbye to Grandma.* Illustrated by Marcia Sewell. New York: Clarion, 1988. A seven-year-old girl attends her grandmother's funeral and examines the rituals with her cousins and other children. Ages 6–9.

Benette W. Tiffault. *A Quilt for Elizabeth.* Illustrated by Mary McConnell. Omaha, Neb.: Centering Corporation, 1992. When her father gets sick and dies, a little girl and her grandmother decide to make a quilt from his clothes. Ages 4–8.

Susan Varley. *Badger's Parting Gifts.* New York: Lothrop, Lee & Shepard, 1984. The story of an old animal's dying and the grieving of those who loved him. Ages 5–9.

Judith Vigna. *Saying Goodbye to Daddy.* Morton Grove, Ill.: Albert Whitman, 1991. A kindergarten girl whose father dies in a car accident has a difficult time living with the loss. With the help of her mother and grandmother, she comes to understand his absence. Ages 4–8.

Judith Viorst. *The Tenth Good Thing About Barney.* Illustrated by Erik Blegvad. New York: Atheneum, 1971. A boy thinks of the ten best things about his pet cat, who has died. Ages 3–9.

E. B. White. *Charlotte's Web.* Illustrated by Garth Williams. New York: Harper & Row, 1952. This classic story describes the grief experienced at the death of a close friend—Charlotte, a spider—and the continuing of life through her offspring. Ages 3–up.

Judy Williams. *Mrs. Magruder and the Purple Hat.* Illustrated by Jack Williams. Warmister, Penn.: MarCo Products, 1993. A story of a special relationship between a young girl and an aging neighbor who dies suddenly. Through the legacy and with her mother's help, Chelsea copes with her grief. Includes a four-session program to use with children to help them understand grief.

Charlotte Zolotow. *My Grandson Lew.* New York: Harper & Row, 1974. Lew learns the value of memories of his deceased grandfather. Ages 3–7.

Books for Older Children and Teens

Arno Bohlmeijer. *Something Very Sorry.* New York: Putnam, 1997. Based on a true story about a girl whose whole family is in a serious car crash, this novel describes with loving sensitivity how Rosemyn and her family cope with the accident's aftermath, including the mother's death after being removed from life support. Ages 9–12.

Penny Colman. *Corpses, Coffins, and Crypts: A History of Burial.* New York: Henry Holt, 1997. Ranging from ancient Chinese history and the embalming of soldiers during the Civil War to today's Internet memorial parks and e-mail tributes, this book describes how diverse cultures and religions honor their dead, allowing readers to view death as a universal experience that connects them to others. Ages 9–up.

The Dougy Center. *After a Murder: A Workbook for Grieving Kids.* Portland, Ore.: The Dougy Center, 2002. An interactive workbook in which children learn from other children who have experienced a death by murder. Encourages children to express their thoughts and feelings through a variety of activities, including drawings, puzzles, word games, and helpful stories and advice from other kids and adults. Ages 9–up.

The Dougy Center. *After a Suicide: A Workbook for Grieving Kids.* Portland, Ore.: The Dougy Center, 2001. An interactive workbook in which children learn from other children who have experienced a death by suicide. Encourages children to express their thoughts and feelings through a variety of activities, including drawings, puzzles, word games, and helpful stories and advice from other kids and adults. Ages 9–up.

Paula Fox. *The Eagle Kite.* New York: Dell/Laurel-Leaf, 1996. When Liam, a high school freshman, learns that his father is dying of AIDS, he experiences feelings of shame and betrayal heightened by family secrets as he reckons with the truth and ultimately finds a healing in his relationship with his father. Ages 11–14.

Barbara Snow Gilbert. *Stone Water.* Arden, N.C.: Front Street, 1996. After Grandpa Hughes suffers a massive stroke and lies unconscious in a nursing home bed, 14-year-old Grant is sure that his grandfather is ready to die and struggles with his decision to take matters into his own hands in this story of assisted suicide. Ages 10–up.

Kevin Henkes. *Sun & Spoon.* New York: Greenwillow, 1997. A ten-year-old boy wrestles with grief during the first summer after his beloved grandmother's death and finds the healing power of remembering a deceased loved one. Ages 9–12.

Davida Wills Hurwin. *A Time for Dancing.* New York: Puffin, 1997. In this novel about how terminal illness affects the lives of friends and those around them, two teenage girls who have been best friends since childhood face mortality when one of them is diagnosed with histiocytic lymphoma, a deadly form of cancer. Ages 12–up.

Hadley Irwin. *So Long at the Fair.* New York: McElderry-Macmillan, 1988. Joel Logan, a high school senior, finds that he must remember and work through the past to come to terms with the suicidal death of his girlfriend. Ages 12–up.

Jill Krementz. *How It Feels When a Parent Dies.* New York: Knopf, 1981. A photographic essay with children's descriptions of their experiences. Ages 10–up.

Madeleine L'Engle. *A Ring of Endless Light.* New York: Farrar, Straus & Giroux, 1980. A teenage girl copes with the experience of loss, grief, and terminal illness by discovering underlying spiritual and moral dimensions. Ages 10–up.

(continued)

Books for Older Children and Teens *(continued)*

John Mayled. *Death Customs.* New Jersey: Silver Burdett, 1987. Overview of religious and cultural death customs worldwide. Ages 10–up.

Joyce McDonald. *Swallowing Stones.* New York: Delacorte, 1997. A bizarre Fourth of July accident, which leaves an innocent man dead, draws together four teens, whose lives are drastically changed as they deal with guilt, anxiety, and grief. Ages 12–up.

Donna Jo Napoli. *Stones in Water.* New York: Dutton, 1997. Based on the life of a survivor and told from the point of view of a young Venetian boy forced into the war by the Nazis, this story leads readers through a gradual unfolding of events until they come face to face with the scope of the atrocities that occurred in Europe during World War II. Ages 10–up.

Ann Novac. *The Beautiful Days of My Youth: My Six Months in Auschwitz and Plaszow.* New York: Henry Holt, 1997. A memoir of the Holocaust that poignantly describes life, death, and survival in Hitler's camps. Ages 12–up.

Katherine Paterson. *Bridge to Terabithia.* Illustrations by Dona Diamond. New York: HarperTrophy, 1987 (reissue). In this Newberry award-winner, fifth-grader Jess's rural world expands when he meets his new neighbor, a tomboy named Leslie. After a rocky start, they become best friends and create a secret kingdom in the woods named Terabithia, which can be reached only by swinging on a rope across a creek. When Leslie drowns trying to reach their special hideaway while alone, Jess's life is changed forever as he struggles with anger and grief in coping with the loss. (A guidebook for using this story in the classroom is available from Teacher Created Materials.) Ages 9–12.

Elizabeth Richter. *Losing Someone You Love: When a Brother or Sister Dies.* New York: Putnam, 1986. The experience of sibling loss as related in interviews with young people. Ages 10–up.

Gary D. Schmidt. *The Sin Eater.* New York: Dutton, 1996. After Cole's mother's death from cancer and the subsequent suicide of his father, Cole's grandfather guides him in exploring the immediate and enduring benefits of preserving family history and helps him recognize how the past holds keys to the present and how stories can keep loved ones alive. Ages 10–14.

Staff of the New York Times. *A Nation Challenged: A Visual History of 9/11 and Its Aftermath (Young Reader's Edition).* Combines stories published in the newspaper and Pulitzer Prize–winning photographs to present an intimate account of terrifying events in an age-appropriate fashion. Ages 9–14.

Yukio Tsuchiya. *Faithful Elephants: A True Story of Animals, People, and War.* Illustrated by Ted Lewis. Boston: Houghton Mifflin, 1988. A poignant story of the horror of war and its effect on animals and people. Ages 9–12.

Alan Wolfelt. *Healing Your Grieving Heart for Teens.* Boulder, Colo.: Companion Press, 2001. Offers tips and ideas for expression of grief. Activity oriented. Ages 12–up.

Kazumi Yumoto. *The Friends.* Translated by Cathy Hirano. New York: Farrar, Straus & Giroux, 1996. In this story that is both universal and rooted in the country and culture from which it comes, three young boys' fascination with death leads them to form an unexpected friendship with an old man through which they confront their fears and learn to accept the inevitable with a sense of joy in life. Ages 9–up.

Further Readings

David W. Adams and Eleanor J. Deveau. *Beyond the Innocence of Childhood.* 3 vols. Amityville, N.Y.: Baywood, 1995.

Myra Bluebond-Langner. *The Private Worlds of Dying Children.* Princeton, N.J.: Princeton University Press, 1978.

Betty Davies. *Shadows in the Sun: The Experience of Sibling Bereavement in Childhood.* Washington, D.C.: Taylor & Francis, 1998.

Kenneth J. Doka, ed. *Children Mourning, Mourning Children.* Washington, D.C.: Hospice Foundation of America, 1995.

Marilyn J. Field and Richard E. Behrman, eds. *When Children Die: Improving Palliative and End-of-Life Care for Children and Their Families.* Washington, D.C.: National Academies Press, 2003.

Donna Schuurman. *Never the Same: Coming to Terms with the Death of a Parent.* New York: St. Martin's, 2003.

Phyllis Rolfe Silverman. *Never Too Young to Know: Death in Children's Lives.* New York: Oxford University Press, 2000.

J. William Worden. *Children and Grief: When a Parent Dies.* New York: Guilford Press, 1996.

Leigh A. Woznick and Carol D. Goodheart. *Living with Childhood Cancer: A Practical Guide to Help Families Cope.* Washington, D.C.: American Psychological Association, 2002.

Holding their dead baby, this Harlem couple finds comfort in the sharing of their memories and their grief as they acknowledge the death of their firstborn child. Of all the losses that can be experienced during adult life, most people feel that the death of a child is the most painful.

Death in the Lives of Adults

*H*uman development does not stop with childhood's end. The patterns of coping with loss continue to evolve throughout a person's life span. Just as we associate certain developmental tasks and abilities with children of different ages, so too we can distinguish distinctive phases and transitions during adult life. In Chapter 2, we discussed the first five stages of psychosocial development proposed by Erik Erikson—namely, those pertaining to the years of childhood and adolescence. The last three stages of psychosocial development, according to Erikson's model, occur during adulthood. As in childhood, each stage of adult life requires a particular developmental response, and each stage builds on previous ones.

Young adulthood (20 to 40 years) is represented by tension between intimacy and isolation. This stage involves various forms of commitment and interaction, including sex, friendship, cooperation, partnership, and affiliation. Because mature love takes the risk of commitment, the death of a loved one may be most devastating during this stage and the next.[1]

The next psychosocial stage is *middle adulthood* (40 to 60 or 65 years), which, according to Erikson, involves the crisis of generativity versus stagnation. This stage is characterized by a widening commitment to take care of the people, things, and ideas one has learned to care for. Michele Paludi says, "Middle adulthood appears to be a prime period for experiencing fear of death since it is during this stage of the life cycle that the death of one's parents typically occurs."[2]

BLOOM COUNTY **by Berke Breathed**

"Bloom County," drawing by Berke Breathed, © 1984 by Washington Post Writers Group

When we reach the stage of *maturity,* the eighth and final stage of the life cycle, the turning point or crisis to be resolved is that of integrity versus despair. Some developmentalists divide this stage into several periods, *young old* (60 to 75 years), *middle old* (75 to 85 years), and *old old* (85 years and older). Viewing all the developmental phases as connected, each building on the ones before, the crisis of this stage is especially powerful, as it includes physical decline, outward signs of aging, and vulnerability to chronic diseases. It is marked by the end of our "one given course of life." Successfully negotiating this developmental task gives us the strength of wisdom, which Erikson describes as "informed and detached concern with life itself in the face of death itself."[3]

You may find it useful to consider the losses that have occurred in your own life, both as a child and as an adult. How have they differed, and in what ways are they similar? Notice how your orientation to loss changed as you got older. What coping mechanisms were you able to bring into play to move through the experience of loss successfully? Questions of this kind can form a framework for examining typical losses in adult life.

Parental Bereavement

What makes the loss of a child a high-grief death? To most people, the death of a child represents the unfinished, the untimely loss of a potential future. We expect that a child will outlive his or her parents. Death may be viewed as appropriate in old age, but a child's death underscores the truth that no one is immune to death. These attitudes about the death of a child are related to advances in health care that have greatly reduced infant and child mortality during the past century. In earlier times, and in parts of the world today, a newborn or infant child is not really viewed as a "person" until he or she has lived long enough to exhibit a strong likelihood of ongoing viability. In the context of modern societies, however, the death of a child is generally considered the least natural of deaths.[4] A child's death upsets the expectation that the old die first and are replaced by the young. With the death of a child, parents become survivors of what seems an untimely and unwarranted death. When the basic function of parenting is understood as protecting one's child and nurturing his or her well-being, this responsibility is thwarted by a child's death.

Parents envision their children playing on the local youth soccer team, graduating from school, getting married, raising their own children—all the various milestones and occasions that comprise a sense of continuity into the future. Death brings an end to the plans and hopes for a child's life. Moreover, a child's very existence grants a kind of immortality to the parent; this is taken away when the child dies.

The interdependency between parent and child makes the death of a child a deep experience of loss.[5] Grief may focus on issues of parental responsibility. Symbolically and actually, a child's death is opposed to the nurturant psychosocial task of adulthood. Parenting is generally defined as protecting and nurturing a child until he or she can act independently in the world. Thus, the death of a child may be experienced as the ultimate lack of protection and nurture, the ultimate breakdown and failure in being a "good parent." Among the Cree of North America, infants were given "ghost-protective" moccasins to wear. Holes were cut in the bottom of the moccasins to safeguard the baby from death. If the spirit of an ancestor appeared and beckoned, the infant could refuse to go, pointing out that his or her moccasins "needed mending."[6]

Many issues of parental bereavement span the adult life cycle. They are present for thirty-year-old parents and eighty-year-old parents. They are experienced by parents of grown children as well as by parents of infants. A parent's fantasies and plans can be as strong for an unborn infant as for an older child. A sixty-five-year-old divorced or widowed mother may feel considerable loss of security when her thirty-five-year-old child dies suddenly. One such woman said, "He was going to take care of me when I got old; now I have no one." Whether or not her son would have indeed taken on the responsibility she envisioned, his death represented the loss of *her* imagined future.

Parental bereavement is a powerful experience that relates to both sociobiological and psychological explanations of grief. Studies of human bonding and the psychodynamics of family systems contribute to a comprehensive model of parental grief. Bereaved parents often maintain an inner representation of the dead child sustained through memories and spiritual beliefs.[7]

Coping with Parental Bereavement as a Couple

In counseling bereaved parents, clinicians sometimes note the presence of a kind of "general chaos," a pervasive sense that the parents have been robbed of a past and a future. With such a traumatic event, parents expect, and are expected, to support each other. But the energy expended by each partner in coping with his or her own grief can deplete the emotional resources needed for mutual support. Some bereaved parents report that, in addition to losing a child, they felt they had lost their spouse for a time. Studies indicate that the death of a child has the potential to either improve or worsen a marital relationship.[8] A child's death may have the paradoxical effect of creating a feeling of estrangement and a strong bond between parents at the same time.[9]

Käthe Kollwitz, Library of Congress

The overwhelming grief of parental bereavement is expressed in the soft-ground etching Überfahren (Passing Over), *by Käthe Kollwitz, whose art became a means of working through her own sorrow following the death of a child. The dead child is carried by adults bent with the burden of grief; other children look on.*

Even though they share the same loss, parents typically have different grieving styles, which can leave each of them feeling isolated and unsupported by the only person who shares the magnitude of the loss. Individual differences in values, beliefs, and expectations may cause conflicts in coping styles, thereby reducing the sense of "commonality" in a couple's grief experience.[10] Although husbands and wives do not always or necessarily grieve in an asynchronous or "roller coaster" pattern, it is not uncommon for bereaved parents to find themselves grieving "out of synch" with one another at times.[11]

The sense of commonality in a couple's grief is also affected by their view of themselves as a *couple*. They may have difficulty reaching agreement about the best way to regain a sense of stability and meaning in life after their child's death. Despite each partner's desire and expectation to "go through grief" together, differences in grieving styles may create conflict about whether one's partner is behaving appropriately.

Conflict can arise out of each partner's *interpretation* of the other's behavior. A husband who contains his grief so that he can "be there" for his wife may be perceived by the spouse as cold and unfeeling. His desire to be caring and protective may be misinterpreted, resulting in conflict rather than comfort. Disagreement or misunderstanding can also relate to issues about what constitutes "proper" mourning behavior, the couple's "public face" of grief.

Reducing conflict and promoting positive interactions between grieving partners requires the willingness of each to engage in open and honest communication. In this way, each partner's emotional expression of loss helps validate the reality of the other's perceptions. Simply crying together can be helpful in resolving conflict and working through the loss. A characteristic of couples who report little conflict is their positive view of each other and their relationship. Accepting differences and being flexible about roles also contribute to sharing grief.

Coming to terms with a grieving spouse's behavior is enhanced by the ability of partners to *reframe* each other's behavior in a positive way. For example, a husband who views his wife's sobbing as "breaking down" can alter his perception so that crying is seen as emotionally cleansing and therefore valuable. Reframing a spouse's behavior makes it possible to explain the behavior in positive terms, rather than judging it as inappropriate or dysfunctional. When previously unsettling behavior is seen as providing emotional release, it allows a mate to support the expression instead of trying to curtail it by urging the spouse to "get it together." As always, it is often the little things spouses do that cause their partners to feel supported and loved.

Childbearing Losses

Pregnancy represents a major life transition for adults. The expected result is the birth of a viable, healthy baby. Miscarriage, stillbirth, or neonatal death is not the anticipated outcome. Yet, in a recent year, 63,153 fetal and infant deaths were recorded in the United States, with about 45 percent of these deaths having been stillbirths, another 34 percent neonatal deaths, and the remaining 21 percent postneonatal deaths.[12]

According to medical definition, *stillbirth* refers to fetal death occurring between the twentieth week of gestation (pregnancy) and the time of birth, resulting in the delivery of a dead child. *Neonatal* deaths are those occurring during the first four weeks following birth. According to this definition, *postneonatal* deaths occur after the first four weeks and up to eleven months following birth.

The statistics given do not include deaths from *miscarriage,* which occurs prior to the twentieth week of pregnancy. Miscarriage, also termed *spontaneous abortion,* is defined as "loss of the products of conception before the fetus is viable."[13] The distinction between miscarriage and stillbirth is based on the logic that most fetuses are viable—that is, able to survive outside the mother's body—after the twentieth week of pregnancy. In contrast to miscarriage, or spontaneous abortion, which occurs naturally, *induced abortion* (sometimes called artificial or therapeutic abortion) is brought about intentionally with the aim of ending a pregnancy by mechanical means or drugs.

Pregnancy, induced and spontaneous abortion (miscarriage), stillbirth, and infant death all take their meanings from the lives of those who experience them and the social worlds in which they occur. The distinction between a miscarriage and a late period, like that between a miscarriage and a stillbirth, can be seen as socially negotiated. . . . The physical reality (at what point a death occurs), the social reality (the definition *as* death as well as the significance of that death), and the psychological reality (the grief associated with that death) are all constructed within particular, and various, social contexts.[14]

Broadly considered, reproductive loss also includes losses resulting from infertility and sterility. Whereas *infertility* refers to "diminished or absent capacity to produce offspring," *sterility* denotes "complete inability to produce offspring," due to inability either to conceive (female) or to induce conception (male).[15] Despite advances in medical treatment for infertility, many couples remain childless, their biological and social urges to reproduce thwarted by forces beyond their control.

Another example of reproductive loss involves giving up a child for *adoption.* Although this might not initially be thought of as a childbearing loss because it usually results from choice, grief may nonetheless accompany such decisions. Psychologists point out,

> In a society that defines women as mothers, mothers-to-be, or childless, the woman who has given birth and then relinquished her child for adoption is an enigma. Having signed away her legal claim to the child, she is often perceived as the most unnatural of women, a rejecting mother. [But] the maternal experience does not end with the signing of surrender papers.[16]

Although the grief following adoption is often unrecognized, unsupported, and unresolved, it can nonetheless have deep emotional effects on birth parents.[17] Seeing a child at play or walking down the street can spur the reaction of wondering what the relinquished child might be like at that age.

A comprehensive view of childbearing losses also includes losses that ensue when a child is born with severe disabilities, such as congenital deformities or mental retardation. Parents may have difficulty accepting the reality that their child is not as they had dreamed; they may grieve the loss of the "perfect" or "wished-for" child.[18] These lost expectations need to be acknowledged and mourned.

Childbearing loss involves grief for "unlived" lives. Judith Savage says, "Childbearing losses are mourned not only for what was, but also for what might have been."[19] Grief is felt not only for the physical loss, but also for symbolic losses. Parents mourn "the child of the imagination, that part of themselves which seems now to have no possibility of embodiment in the world." Writing from the perspective of a Jungian psychologist who by age thirty-three had experienced multiple losses (her adoptive and biological parents, her two brothers, and her infant son), Savage says:

> By unraveling the mystery of the imaginative relationship, that is, the projections of the self onto the unborn child, it becomes clear that primary relationships are not composed merely of interchangeable functional attributes and roles but are uniquely personal bonds that are generated from deep within and are as much a reflection of the individual soul as they are an accurate reflection of the other.[20]

When we bury the old, we bury the known past, the past we imagine sometimes better than it was, but the past all the same, a portion of which we inhabited. Memory is the overwhelming theme, the eventual comfort.

But burying infants, we bury the future, unwieldy and unknown, full of promise and possibilities, outcomes punctuated by our rosy hopes. The grief has no borders, no limits, no known ends, and the little infant graves that edge the corners and fencerows of every cemetery are never quite big enough to contain that grief. Some sadnesses are permanent. Dead babies do not give us memories. They give us dreams.

Thomas Lynch,
The Undertaking: Life Studies from the Dismal Trade

It is important to be aware of two distinct yet related realities: the *actual* relationship and the *symbolic* nature of the parent-child bond. Grieving parents often talk about lost companionship, lost dreams—all the ways in which the child would have enriched their lives. Such discussion is concerned with the actual loss. The symbolic loss relates to the meaning attached to the relationship, as when an individual, by parenting a child, becomes a nurturing, supportive guide. A bereaved father said, "Not only have I lost a son who might follow in my footsteps, but, without him, I have no feet." It was important for this father to acknowledge and mourn both the loss of his son and the loss of meaning and purpose in his own life. The image of the lost child activates powerful associations, which become part of a natural process guiding the bereaved parent's journey toward wholeness.

With a childbearing loss, blame can be turned inward as well as directed outward. A parent may ask, "Didn't I want this baby enough?" Questions about the cause of the tragic outcome abound: Was it that glass of wine, the aspirin, or, as one mother asked in desperation, "Was it the nutmeg I put on my oatmeal?" Even inconsequential actions may be scrutinized.

Anger may be focused on the dead child, resulting in confusing and tangled emotions. After all, what kind of person could be angry at an innocent infant? Yet anger is a natural response to loss. As one woman said of her stillborn daughter, "Why did she just drop in and out of my life? Why did she bother coming at all?" Emotional responses may be accompanied by auditory or kinesthetic hallucinations: A baby cries in the night, waking parents from sleep; the baby kicks inside the womb, yet there is no pregnancy, no live child.

Absent a baby, the mother may be confronted by physical reminders of the loss, such as the onset of lactation. One bereaved mother said, "I wanted to go to the cemetery and let my milk flow onto my daughter's grave." Meanwhile, the father may feel culturally constrained to "be brave" so that he can support the mother, who is recuperating physically as well as emotionally. As a result, the father's need to grieve may go unmet, his emotions pushed below the surface.

Small Son

They have gone.
The last mourner,
the last comfort,
last cliche.

I wrap a pillow
in your blanket.
Lie burying my face
to hold your fading
milk sweet smell.

The silence swells.

    I run

to where the stand
of saplings wait
for clearing.

Chopping, slashing,
small limbs
dragged and pulled
and piled for burning.

I turn away
consumed,
the taste of ashes
in my mouth.

                Maude Meehan

Grief following a childbearing loss is also potentially influenced by the parents' perceptions that the loss is neither understood nor acknowledged by others. Bereaved parents report hearing insensitive comments, such as "It must be easier since you didn't get too attached." Well-intentioned family members and friends may attempt to minimize the death in an effort to console the bereaved parent. They may say, "You're young; you can have another baby," unaware that such a comment, though possibly true, is inappropriate: No other baby will replace the one who died. Advice such as this is especially difficult for couples who postponed having children—they may feel an added constraint of time that compounds the experience of loss.

Parents who have suffered a childbearing loss benefit from programs like the one sponsored by the Reuben Center for Women and Children at Toledo Hospital in Ohio.[21] The program has a variety of bereavement protocols, including guidelines for bereavement support, photographic techniques (photos are taken of all deceased infants and are given to parents either at the time of the death or at whatever time they want them), use of hospital chaplains and trained support group volunteers, distribution of printed materials on bereavement and grief (including a brochure written expressly to educate relatives and friends of the bereaved about what they can do), various funeral and memorialization options, and the availability of support groups for families who do not live near the hospital. Educational programs and mutual support are also provided for staff members who care for newly bereaved families. In this way, comprehensive support is provided to families, staff, and the community.

As always, it is important to keep in mind that there is considerable individual variation in the expression and, indeed, experience of grief. This may be especially true of childbearing losses. Irving Leon points out:

> Not long ago the death of a baby was an unspeakable event in a hospital. Hushed silence greeted the delivery of a stillborn. The baby was whisked away before parents could see and hold their child. They were told to forget what happened and have another baby as soon as possible. The mother was given tranquilizers

if she became too upset, if she "lost it" (meaning that she was grieving over what she *had* lost).[22]

Today, in most hospitals, the situation is different and grief for childbearing loss is respected. We must remember, however, that people are different, as are their attachments to their newborn and unborn children. Bereaved parents should not be expected to "follow a script" or enact some "right way" to grieve. Social support should be offered in ways that recognize individual differences and that promote genuine empathy.

Miscarriage

People may assume that the loss of a baby during the early stages of pregnancy evokes feelings of disappointment, but not grief. To parents who have dreamed about the baby even before its conception, however, miscarriage evokes pain and confusion. Parents may be told that the loss is simply "Nature's way" of weeding out genetic anomalies. Such a remark offers little or no consolation to grieving parents; it was *their* baby that Nature decided to sort. Platitudes that minimize or deny the loss are unhelpful. When parents experience a series of miscarriages, loss is compounded upon loss.

Parents may have difficulty identifying their loss precisely or making sense of what has happened. After a miscarriage, one young mother's grief was complicated because she had no remains to be buried. "I didn't know where my baby was," she said. Even though a miscarriage may have occurred many years ago, grief for an unborn baby can recur with other significant life events—for example, at the birth of a subsequent child or the onset of menopause. A particular marker, such as reaching age forty or age sixty-five, can reawaken feelings of grief.

Induced Abortion

Although induced abortion is also termed "elective" abortion, in many cases it is less a choice than a medical necessity. Some people assume that women who *elect* to terminate a pregnancy do not experience a grief reaction, but this is not always true. Grief after elective abortion can be just as real as grief after involuntary fetal or infant loss.[23] It may depend on a person's perception of the pregnancy: Does she perceive herself as simply pregnant or as a potential mother? Similar questions apply to men who participate in decisions about elective abortion.

The emotional reaction to induced abortion varies. "For a woman who experiences a pregnancy loss as a tragedy, it is a tragedy; and for a woman who experiences a loss as relief, it is a relief."[24] In some cases, the repercussions are not felt until much later. One woman, who had chosen to abort a pregnancy as a young adult because she and her husband felt their relationship couldn't withstand the pressures of raising a child at that time, experienced great remorse when she and her husband later found themselves unable to have other children. "That may have been our only chance," she lamented. Subsequent pregnancy loss may be experienced as "retribution" for an earlier abortion. In addition, personal and social attitudes toward abortion can affect the resolution of grief. When social support is lacking, people have fewer opportunities to express their feelings about a loss.

When the decision for an abortion is made because of adverse information about the baby's health, the inherent conflict about the choice may add to parents' grief. Many genetic diseases are identified by tests during the early stages of pregnancy; and, when the results are unfavorable, terminating the pregnancy may seem the best or only choice. Some tests can be done only well into the pregnancy, after the mother has already felt the baby moving. Parents who decide in favor of a therapeutic abortion may worry that no one will understand their "choice" and that they will be judged harshly. Furthermore, in this situation, couples may face not only the loss of a particular baby, but also the possibility of a childless future; biological considerations or genetic risk may preclude the choice to conceive again.

In Japan, at places like Hase Temple near Kamakura and Shiun Jizo Temple north of Tokyo, thousands of tiny stone statues called *mizuko* represent children conceived but never born.[25] Some of these "water children" wear bibs and stocking caps. Placed alongside them are toy milk bottles, dolls, and twirling pinwheels, along with memorials written by their sponsors—women who chose to have an abortion rather than give birth. The statues, each one costing several hundred dollars, are erected as repositories for the souls of unborn babies. At Hase Temple, more than 50,000 *mizuko* are watched over by a thirty-foot-tall wooden statue of the "Goddess of Mercy," who is also the patroness of safe birth. Even though abortion is common in Japan, "*mizuko* worship" bears witness to an intense desire to acknowledge the unborn fetus.

Conflicting views about abortion may place the bereaved in a dilemma: Those who believe a loss occurred may not sanction the act, whereas those who sanction the act may not recognize that grief in response to a perceived loss needs to be expressed and legitimized. Complications in grieving may be exacerbated when customary sources of solace and social support are not readily available.[26]

Stillbirth

"Instead of giving birth, I gave death," said a mother whose daughter died in childbirth. Instead of a cradle, there is a grave; instead of a receiving blanket, there are burial clothes; instead of a birth certificate, there is a death certificate. After a stillbirth, "A family's wishes and hopes and dreams—the individuals' illusions about what life *ought* to be—are quickly shattered by the reality of what life really *is*."[27] Those who counsel newly bereaved parents of a stillborn baby emphasize the importance of acknowledging the child's birth. Rather than whisking away the stillborn infant as quickly as possible, hospital staff can encourage parents to see and hold their baby. Acknowledging the reality of the baby's life and death facilitates healthy grief. A postmortem photograph of the child may assist in the process of grieving.[28] Parents may hold a memorial service for the stillborn baby, a choice that not only acknowledges the reality of what has happened, but also provides an opportunity to find meaning and solace by sharing grief with others.

Some hospitals give bereaved parents an information packet that includes a "Certificate of Stillbirth," which acknowledges the birth as well as the death of the child. Linking objects, such as a lock of hair, a photograph, and the receiving blanket, can be comforting to parents. Nearly 90 percent of the parents included in a study by John De Frain named their stillborn baby, thereby recognizing that it was indeed part of the family, no matter how briefly: "Naming seemed to help show others that the baby really existed and was important, not just something to be thrown away and forgotten."[29] The hurt may fade as time passes, the memories do not.

Neonatal Death

When a baby is born alive but with life-threatening disabilities due to prematurity or congenital defects, the ensuing period of uncertainty about the baby's survival can be a nightmare for parents. Parents may experience an overwhelming sense of frustration and futility as medical interventions are discussed, attempted, and perhaps fail. Sometimes a baby born with one or more life-threatening conditions embarks on a life-or-death struggle that lasts

© Albert Lee Strickland

The items placed around the grave of this infant in Hawaii—balloons, flowers, and jars of baby food—bespeak the parents' loss and acknowledge the enduring bonds of even a short-lived relationship.

weeks. During this time, parents may have to make difficult ethical choices that determine whether the baby lives or dies. Meanwhile, the costs incurred in keeping the baby alive continue to mount. If the baby does die, parents may resent the medical institution and its personnel, feeling as if they survived a painful and futile ordeal only to be billed later for the experience.

In circumstances involving a critically ill newborn, *any* decision may haunt parents as they repeatedly ask themselves if they made the right choice. Caregivers who appreciate the heart-wrenching ethical dilemmas that occur in the context of neonatal intensive care are in a position to provide sensitive care and support to parents facing the prospect of making and living with these difficult decisions. When the life of a critically ill infant is being sustained by extraordinary medical means, the decision to terminate artificial support ought to be handled with as much grace as circumstances allow. One young neonatologist remarked, "One of the most difficult and important things for me to learn was to hand over the baby to the parents so it could die in their arms."

Sudden Infant Death Syndrome

Sudden infant death syndrome (SIDS) is defined as "the sudden and unexpected death of any infant or young child between 2 weeks and 1 year of age in which a thorough postmortem examination fails to show cause."[30] The unexpected nature of the death, age of the child and of the parents (who are generally young and may be experiencing an intimate death for the first time), and uncertainty about the cause of death combine to make SIDS deaths a difficult loss for the whole family.

Because the cause of death is not certain, and because of generalized concerns about the possibility of child abuse, law enforcement personnel may question whether the parents are responsible. Tragically, parents do sometimes murder their own infants and try to pass the deaths off as natural or accidental. The search for a cause of death in SIDS cases is often characterized by ambiguity. Because of this, and because SIDS support groups have circulated information about the adverse effects of misdirected accusations on grieving parents, police and other investigators are usually sensitive in handling cases that may involve SIDS. Even so, parents may question themselves just as sternly: Was the death in any way due to something they did or left undone? Could it have been prevented? The unexplained nature of SIDS deaths can lead survivors to embark on a quest for answers that may not be available.

The Death of an Older Child

Many of the issues discussed in the preceding section pertain as well to parents' grief following the death of an older child or adolescent. The meaning of such a death is usually more complex, however, because the relationship between parent and child has been of longer duration, with a correspondingly larger store of memories. A child represents many things to a parent. As Beverly Raphael reminds us, a child is "a part of the self, and of the loved partner; a representation of generations past; the genes of the forebears; the hope of the future; a source of love, pleasure, even narcissistic delight; a tie or a burden; and sometimes a symbol of the worst parts of the self

Last year, a fourteen-year-old boy who suddenly collapsed on the street was rushed to our hospital emergency room. Even though there were no clinical signs of life, at least six physicians frantically attempted resuscitative measures. In the hallway outside the emergency room, I came upon two stunned parents who were standing absolutely alone. None of the physicians wanted to leave the dramatic scene to obtain a history, let alone provide any solace. I did not want to either, the boy was dead (possibly from a cardiac conduction defect—even the autopsy later was unrevealing); but I forced myself to sit down in an adjoining room and listen while they talked of their hopes and their son's aspirations. I am used to talking with parents whose children die of sudden infant death syndrome; this was different and I was overwhelmed. Afterward, I went to my office and cried. I later thought that I should have let my interns and residents witness me cry to learn that professionalism does not preclude expression of human feeling.

Abraham B. Bergman, "Psychological Aspects of Sudden
Unexpected Death in Infants and Children"

and others."[31] Over time, the bond between parent and child takes on increasing complexity.

Among the major causes of death among children between the ages of five and fourteen, accidents top the list.[32] As the most prominent cause of death during the first half of the human life span, injury is characterized as "the last major plague of the young."[33] Although more children and adolescents die from injuries received in accidents than from the effects of disease, the situation of a child with life-threatening illness is usually viewed as especially poignant. Perhaps we feel, justifiably or not, that an accident is something that just "happens" and is, therefore, not preventable, whereas we expect medicine to provide a cure for disease.

As mentioned in Chapter 10, when a child's life is threatened by serious illness, it affects the whole fabric of family life. Parents and siblings, along with other relatives, are all involved in coping with the illness. Few families are able to sustain total openness to the reality of a child's terminal illness throughout what may be a long process from diagnosis of the disease to the child's death. At times, a seriously ill child may function quite normally, and the routine of medical care becomes just another aspect of family life. At other times, the illness requires parents and other family members to deal intensely and decisively with changes in the child's condition. Those around the child may feel challenged as they try to adjust to fluctuations between hope for recovery and acceptance of terminality, all while trying to support the child in the best way possible.

Parents seem to have a somewhat easier time coping when they do not derive their personal identities solely from their role as parents. In other words, although parenting is an important part of their lives, it is not the totality of their self-image, which encompasses other accomplishments and values as well. Some parents not only manage to cope and survive the devastating loss of a child; they also grow from the experience. Such parents are able to "respond to a [child's] severe illness by making a more mature reevaluation of their lives and achieving a truer vision of what counts," says Jerome Schulman. "They learn to make each new day more enriching."[34]

The Death of an Adult Child

For a young or middle-aged adult to die while his or her parents live on seems unnatural. It is a death "out of sequence." With the death of an only child, the consequent loss of parenthood may become a kind of "perpetual bereavement," in which the struggle to understand the meaning of the child's death continues all through life.[35]

The older parent who survives the death of an adult child may also have lost a caregiver. The child may have been a source of comfort and security that is now gone. This may make coping with the bereavement more complicated, as may the sense of "competing" with the dead child's spouse or children for the role of "most bereaved." Who has priority in receiving care and comfort? The death of an adult child sometimes involves circumstances that require parents to assume care of grandchildren, a result of the loss that may be emotionally as well as economically disruptive.

Parents who suffer the death of a child already grown to adulthood may find themselves alone in coping with their grief. In contrast to the situation of parents who lose younger children or individuals who survive the death of a spouse, few social support resources are available to help parents cope with the death of an adult child. Yet the death of a child—at whatever age—is always a significant loss.

Social Support in Parental Bereavement

A variety of support groups exist to offer information and help to parents who are coping with the serious illness or death of a child. Some groups support all categories of parental bereavement; others focus on particular losses or specific purposes. The Compassionate Friends, which has chapters across the nation, offers support to bereaved parents across a broad spectrum of losses. Another group, the Candlelighters Childhood Cancer Foundation, focuses more specifically on providing support for children with cancer, their parents, and other family members. Two groups, Mothers Against Drunk Driving and Parents of Murdered Children, combine social support with political

---

 We had waited, agonizing through the nights and days without sleep, startled by nearly any sound, unable to eat, simply staring at our meals. Suddenly in a few seconds of radio time it was over. My first son, whose birth had brought me so much joy that I jumped up in a hall outside the room where he was born and touched the ceiling—the child, the scholar, the preacher, the boy singing and smiling, the son—all of it was gone. And Ebenezer was so quiet. All through the church as the staff learned what had happened, the tears flowed, but almost completely in silence.

Martin Luther King, Sr.

advocacy. Organized groups of bereaved parents who have experienced similar losses constitute what some people have called "communities of feeling" within which grief is shared.[36]

In addition to such organizations, the relatives and friends of bereaved parents have many ways to offer support, including simply listening, sending cards or letters of condolence, bringing food, doing housework or other chores, caring for other children in the family, sharing their own grief over the loss, giving the parents time to be alone, and so on. Individuals who are willing to talk openly with a parent about his or her grief in the wake of a child's death are important sources of support in parental bereavement.

Death of a Parent

Many people say that a parent's death is one of the hardest things they have ever dealt with in their lives. Even when the parent had been ill beforehand, the ensuing grief may include a variety of emotions: sadness over the loss; relief at the ending of the parent's suffering; anxiety because a kind of "protection against death" symbolized by a parent is gone; and memories, painful as well as comforting, of the deceased parent. The death of a parent typically represents the loss of a long-term relationship characterized by nurture and unconditional support. Parents are often described as "always there when the chips are really down, no matter what."

For midlife adults, a parent's death is an important symbolic event.[37] It may initiate a period of upheaval and transition. Most people report that the death of a parent changes their outlook on life, often spurring them on to examine their lives more closely, to begin changing what they don't like, and to appreciate more fully their ongoing relationships.[38] Any death reminds us of our own mortality, but a parent's death may cause a person to realize, perhaps for the first time, that he or she has become an adult. Thus, the death of a parent can result in a "developmental push," which may lead to a "more mature stance in parentally bereaved adults who no longer think of themselves as children."[39]

When both parents have died, there may be a consequent role change for the adult child, who no longer has his or her parents to "fall back on," even if only in imagination. When parents are alive, they may represent a source of moral support. There is often a sense that, if real trouble comes, a child can call on his or her parents. With the deaths of one's parents, that sense of security is gone. The bereaved child may feel that there is no longer anyone who would be willing to answer his or her call for help unconditionally. After the deaths of both her parents, one woman said that, although she knew friends and other relatives loved and cared about her, she felt that the love from her parents had been unique and irreplaceable. Adjusting to the death of one's parents can involve both "holding on" and "letting go," as the bereaved child simultaneously recognizes the reality of death and treasures comforting memories of the deceased.[40]

Perhaps because of a mother's traditional status as primary nurturing caregiver, many people believe that the death of a mother is harder to cope with

You Don't Miss Your Water

At home, my mother wakes up and spends some of her day talking back to my father's empty chair.

In Florida, my sister experiences the occasional dream in which my father returns; they chat.

He's been dead and gone for a little over a year. How it would please me to hear his unrecorded voice again, now alive only in the minds of those who remember him.

If I could, if as in the old spiritual, I could actually get a direct phone link to the other side, I could call him up, tell him about this small prize of a week I've had teaching poetry at a ski resort a few miles from Lake Tahoe, imagination jackpot, brief paradise of letters.

How could I make him believe that I have gotten all of this, this modern apartment, this pond in front of my window, all from the writing of a few good lines of verse, my father, who distrusted anything he couldn't get his hands on?

Most likely, he would listen, then ask me, as he always did, just for safety's sake, if my wife still had her good paying job.

And I can't tell you why, but this afternoon, I wouldn't become hot and stuffy from his concern, think "old fool" and gripe back *Of course I'm still teaching college. It's summer, you know?*

This afternoon, I miss his difficult waters, and when he'd ask, as he always would, *how're they treating you?* I'd love to answer back, *fine, daddy. They're paying me to write about your life.*

Cornelius Eady

than the death of a father.[41] Another factor may be the fact that, statistically, due to shorter life expectancy, fathers tend to die before mothers. Thus, a mother's death often represents the loss of having "parents," as the bereaved adult child experiences reactive grief over the death of the other parent as well.

When a relationship has been dysfunctional, a parent's death ends the hope of creating a better, more functional parent-child bond. Upon the death of her alcoholic mother, one middle-aged woman lamented, "With her death, dead also is the dream that she would eventually go into treatment and that we would finally heal the wounds our family suffered. I'm relieved that I can no longer be hurt by her drinking, but I wish it could have turned out differently."

Generally, for adult children, a parent's death is less likely to evoke intense grief than, for instance, the death of a child. The reason for this is probably related to the fact that an adult child is involved in his or her own life; feelings of attachment to parents have been redirected to some extent toward others, such as spouse and children. Nevertheless, it can put a strain on a marriage when the person whose parent has died feels that his or her partner is not offering as much emotional support as needed or expected or does not understand the impact of the loss.[42] The parent-child bond has unique symbolic importance and, with the death of a parent, the bereaved child mourns the loss of the special relationship that existed with the deceased parent.

Spousal Bereavement

The ties between two persons in a paired relationship are usually so closely interwoven that, as Beverly Raphael says, the death of one partner may "cut across the very meaning of the other's existence."[43] Even though we may recognize the likelihood that one spouse will die before the other, leaving the survivor to carry on alone, such thoughts are usually kept safely in the background. The pressing activities of daily life occupy our attention until one day the possibility becomes a reality that can't be ignored.

The aftermath of spousal bereavement has been described as follows: "Everyday occurrences underscore the absence of your mate. Sitting down to breakfast, or dinner, opening mail, hearing a special song, going to bed, all become sources of pain when they were formerly sources of pleasure. Each day is full of challenges and heartbreaks."[44]

A spouse's death requires an adjustment from being a couple to being single, a transition that is likely to be especially hard for the survivor who is also a parent. With children to care for and nurture, there is the added burden of single parenthood. The way a particular person adjusts to the role of a newly widowed person depends on a host of sociocultural, personal, and circumstantial factors.

Factors Influencing Spousal Bereavement

Although the death of a mate is the most intensively studied of all loss experiences during adulthood, research has generally focused on a brief time span immediately after bereavement; there are few studies of the enduring effects of spousal death.[45] It is also noteworthy that studies of spousal, or conjugal, bereavement have generally focused on heterosexually paired relationships while mostly ignoring homosexual couples who make lifelong commitments to each other. In same-sex relationships, grief following the death of a partner may be exacerbated by conflict with a mate's parents who never made peace with their son's or daughter's sexual orientation or lifestyle. "If I was effectively nonexistent to them before," one surviving mate said, "I really vanished after my partner died. For years, they denied our commitment to each other; now they acted as if they could completely erase me! They claimed everything: the body, our home, and, seemingly, my right to grieve." It is important to recognize that grief over the loss of a mate is independent of legal or social sanctions about the nature of relationships.

The patterns of intimacy and interaction between spouses are an important determinant of how the loss of a partner will be experienced by a survivor. Whereas one couple may derive their primary satisfaction from shared activities, another couple enjoys greater independence. In some relationships, the focus is on children; in others, the adult partners take precedence.

Mr. and Mrs. Andrew Lyman, Polish tobacco farmers living near Windsor Locks, Connecticut, exemplify some of the qualities that contribute to a close relationship. When such a bond is severed by death, the effect is felt in every area of the survivor's life.

Jack Delano, FSA Collection, Library of Congress

Furthermore, the patterns of a given relationship tend to be in flux as circumstances change over time.

Consider the differences in outlook between an older couple, who have shared their lives over many years, and a young couple, who have been together only a short time. The death of a mate in old age typically follows a lifetime of mutual commitment and shared experiences. In contrast, a young couple is just setting out to build a world together and, when a partner dies, the survivor must reconstitute previously shared aims. During the years from youth to old age, a person's standard of living and overall quality of life are also likely to change, thus affecting the meaning and reality of loss.

Spousal bereavement also elicits distinct behaviors related to culturally sanctioned gender roles. In one culture, a widower might avoid crying publicly because doing so would be viewed as weak and shameful. A widower in another culture, conversely, might express his grief through many tears and loud crying because not doing so would suggest a weakness in ability to love.

Individuals who have lived out traditional sex roles may find the transition to widowhood especially hard. Learning to manage unfamiliar role responsibilities in the midst of grief can be a formidable task, intensifying feelings of helplessness. The widow who has never written a check or the widower who has never prepared dinner is confronted not only with grief at losing a loved one, but also with major role readjustments. New skills must be learned to manage the needs of daily life. Widowed persons whose lifestyles include multiple roles—such as parent; employee; friend; student; hobbyist; or participant in community, political, and religious organizations—appear to make an easier adjustment than do those with fewer role involvements.

In the first year after the death of a mate, there are higher rates of illness and death among widows and widowers, with aged people particularly at risk. This is partly explained by the observation that individuals tend to neglect health problems while caring for an ailing spouse, thereby making surviving spouses more prone to disease and death. In addition, a survivor's ties to the outside world may have diminished while caring for his or her spouse, thus increasing feelings of loneliness following bereavement. A recent study of over 55,000 widows found that women widowed less than a year reported "substantially higher rates of depression and poorer social functioning, overall mental health, and general health than longer term widows."[46] After a three-year period of time, however, these widows showed marked improvements in their functioning, which researchers attributed to the "resilience of older women" and their capacity for reestablishing social connections.

Adverse effects of spousal death appear to be more common among widowers, perhaps because men with conventional gender roles find it difficult to manage domestic matters that were once left to the now-deceased spouse. Widowers also may be less likely than widows to seek help from others, a trait of "self-reliance" that may be associated with gender roles. As Judith Stillion points out, men who care for an ailing partner over an extended period of time may be at a disadvantage in coping with the onset of normal physical and psychological problems of bereavement if "their socialization prohibits

your hair is falling out,   and
you are not so beautiful:
your eyes have dark shadows
your body is bloated;   arms covered with
      bruises and needlemarks;
legs swollen and useless . . .
                  your body and spirit
are weakened with toxic chemicals
urine smells like antibiotics,
                  even the sweat
that bathes your whole body
      in the early hours of morning
reeks of dicloxacillin   and methotrexate.

            you are nauseous all the time
i am afraid to move on the bed
for fear of waking you   to moan
and lean over the edge
                  vomiting into the bag

      i curl up fetally
                  withdraw into my dreams
with a frightened back to you . . .
                  and i'm scared
                  and i'm hiding
but i love you so much;

them from asking for help, showing strain, or even, in some instances, recognizing and discussing their feelings with helping professionals."[47]

Relief following the death of a spouse, although little discussed, is an emotion that may be experienced by people who have cared for an ailing spouse over a long period of time. In such cases, death may be viewed as ending an ailing loved one's suffering. Less socially accepted, or acknowledged, is relief experienced when a mate's death is the welcome end to an unsatisfactory relationship.

Because women statistically live longer than men, it is estimated that three out of every four married women will be widowed at one time or another. Widows who want to remarry face not only social pressures, but also a situation wherein there are few eligible men. However, it has been suggested that widowhood is less difficult for women than retirement is for men. This is because there are many other widows with whom to share leisure time and activities; thus, a woman's status may increase with widowhood, whereas a man's status usually decreases at retirement.

Social Support for Bereaved Spouses

The death of a mate results in the loss of a primary source of social interactions and alters a person's social role in the community. The availability of

this truth does not change . . .
                        years ago,
when i met you, as we were falling in love,
your beauty attracted me:
        long, golden-brown hair
clear and peaceful green eyes
high cheekbones   and long smooth muscles
        but you know—and this is true—
i fell in love with your soul
        the real essence of you
and this cannot grow less beautiful . . .

        sometimes   these days
even your soul is cloudy
        i still recognize you

we may be frightened
        be hiding our sorrow
it may take a little longer
to acknowledge the truth,
but i would not want to be   anywhere else
        i am here   with you
you can grow less beautiful to the world
    you are safe
        i will always love you.

Christine Longaker

a stable social support network can be crucial in determining how bereaved spouses adjust to their changed status. Because friendships are based on common interests and lifestyles, maintaining relationships with nonrelatives appears to be especially important. Participation in leisure activities with friends may help widowed people cope with role transitions and maintain a sense of resiliency and positive morale despite difficult life changes.[48]

Family relationships, in contrast, may pose a potential psychological threat to the widowed elderly because they contain elements of role reversal between the adult child and the aging parent that suggest or demand dependency from the aged widow or widower. Furthermore, an adult child's experience of the loss differs from that of the bereaved spouse, who is likely to value the loss as more significant than does the child and to feel the effects of the loss more intensely with respect to physical and emotional health.[49]

One of the most valuable resources for the recently widowed is contact with peers—that is, other bereaved people who have lost a mate and who can serve as role models during the subsequent period of adjustment. Exposed to the role model's accepting attitude, the newly widowed person learns to live with the painful or difficult feelings of grief and gain perspective on them.

In 1973, following the pioneering work of Phyllis Silverman at Harvard University Medical School, the Widowed Persons Service (WPS) began

"What would you like for breakfast, Jack?" I asked my son-in-law on Sunday, the day after the funeral.

"A fried egg, over," he replied.

Such a simple thing. Yet, I'd never fried an egg.

Oh, we often had them on weekends; but my husband was the breakfast cook, while I dashed up and down the steps putting clothes in the washer, running the vacuum, and all the other tasks always awaiting a working wife.

I stood there, the frying pan in one hand, the egg in the other.

How many times in the future would I find myself standing the same way? How many things had I never done? How many things had I taken for granted?

Maxine Dowd Jensen, *The Warming of Winter*

to implement a concept of mutual help to widowed individuals.[50] The Widowed Persons Service, whose parent organization is the American Association of Retired Persons (AARP), offers newly widowed people help provided by trained volunteers who themselves have been widowed, the key to the effectiveness of such programs.

Death of a Friend

The death of a close friend is a loss that evokes grief similar to the reaction following the death of a relative.[51] Yet there are few opportunities to openly mourn the death of a friend. Whereas most employers provide at least some type of bereavement leave when death occurs in an employee's family, such leave is unlikely to be provided when a close friend dies, even when the mourner and the deceased have been best friends for years. We tend to believe that the most important human relationships are found within families. But friendship involves similar bonds. Because of changes in family structure, social and geographical mobility, and other psychological or cultural factors, friendship ties are increasingly important for many people.

The term "friend" encompasses many different kinds of relationships. Most people have casual friends, close friends, and best friends, as well as "special-purpose" friends such as colleagues, associates, and acquaintances. Many people identify a spouse as their best friend; when death ends the marital relationship, it packs a double whammy because it also means the loss of the surviving partner's best friend. Some friends do not see each other often but, when they get together, their friendship "picks up where we left off."

For older adults, friendships are sometimes more important than family relationships. For example, despite the fact that many older women live alone, they often say that they are not lonely because of the mutually supportive relationships they have developed and maintained with a circle of friends.[52]

At any age, however, friendships are important to people. When a friend dies, grief should be acknowledged. Even when society tends to disenfran-

What Personnel Handbooks Never Tell You

They leave a lot out of the personnel handbooks.
Dying, for instance.
You can find funeral leave
but you can't find dying.
You can't find what to do
when a guy you've worked with since you both
     were pups
looks you in the eye
and says something about hope and chemotherapy.
No phrases,
no triplicate forms,
no rating systems.
Seminars won't do it
and it's too late for a new policy on sabbaticals.

They don't tell you about eye contact
and how easily it slips away
when a woman who lost a breast
says, "They didn't get it all."
You can find essays on motivation
but the business schools
don't teach what the good manager says
to keep people taking up the slack
while someone steals a little more time
at the hospital.
There's no help from those tapes
you pop into the player
while you drive or jog.
They'd never get the voice right.

And this poem won't help either.
You just have to figure it out for yourself,
and don't ever expect to do it well.

         James A. Autry

chise such grief, it is nonetheless important to make time to mourn the death of a friend.

Aging and the Aged

Aging doesn't begin at fifty, or sixty-five, or eighty-five. At this moment, we are all aging. A person festively celebrating his or her thirtieth or fortieth birthday may find that these milestones of life also bring sobering reflections about the meaning of growing older and the lost opportunities that occur in taking one particular path in life rather than another.[53] Interestingly, the expectations most people have about aging or being old differ from the actual experience. Young adults typically expect problems among older people to be more serious than they actually are for those who experience them. Bernice Neugarten reports that when she first developed a course on Adult Development and Aging, "It was generally assumed that you reached a plateau simply called adulthood and you lived on that plateau until you went over the cliff at age sixty-five."[54]

The stereotyped image of an aged person is marked by such outward signs as dry and wrinkled skin, graying hair, baldness, failing eyesight, hearing loss, stiff joints, and general physical debility. Indeed, the physical signs of *senescence*, or the process of becoming old, are rightly associated with the aging of the human organism. (Senescence can be thought of in terms of vulnerability; the risk that an illness or an injury will prove fatal increases with age.)[55] Many illnesses and disabilities—with accompanying losses in many areas of life—occur most commonly among people in the seventh or eighth decade of life or older. (However, age alone is a poor predictor of outcome for a particular individual.)[56] As we age, we not only experience with increasing frequency the deaths of others, we also come closer to our own death. Some of the reasons given by aged people for preferring death to continued existence are found in Table 11-1.

There is a push toward improving the quality of life while "compressing" morbidity, or illness, and extending "active" life expectancy.[57] Making the period of debilitating illness briefer enables people to enjoy good health and stay active until quite near the end of their lives. The changing health status of older adults is acknowledged in the National Council on Aging's use of the terms *young old* for people ages 60 to 75, *middle old* for those 75 to 85, and *old old* for those over the age of 85. This last group is the fastest-growing segment of the aged population. As a "highly selected" group of survivors, they tend not to match stereotypes of advanced age as a time of fragility and dependency.[58]

In contrast to their stereotypical image, old people tend to be more individually distinct than any other segment of the population: They have had more years to create unique life histories. Neugarten says, "People are 'open systems,' interacting with the people around them. All their experiences leave traces."[59] Mutual respect, faith, communion with others, and concern with existential issues of life are essential to the well-being of the aged.[60]

TABLE 11-1   *Some Reasons Given by Aged People for Accepting Death*

Death is preferable to inactivity.
Death is preferable to the loss of the ability to be useful.
Death is preferable to becoming a burden.
Death is preferable to loss of mental faculties.
Death is preferable to living with progressively deteriorating physical health and concomitant physical discomfort.

Source: Adapted from Victor W. Marshall, *Last Chapters: A Sociology of Aging and Dying* (Monterey, Calif.: Brooks/Cole, 1980), pp. 169–177.

After a lifetime together, spouses engage in the activities of daily living out of a history of habit and familiarity. Preserving independence becomes a crucial goal of people in the years of maturity.

As a society, we provide for the physical care of older people through programs like Social Security and Medicare. We appear to be less interested, however, in providing a place for the aged in society. The societal wish seems to be only that the old "age gracefully." As Daniel Callahan observes, the impulse to rid ourselves of stereotypes about old age may have the ironic effect of leading us "away from fruitful and valid generalizations about the elderly and fresh efforts to understand the place of old age in the life cycle."[61] While acknowledging individual *differences* among the aged, says Callahan, we should also appreciate the "*shared* features of old age, the features that make it meaningful to talk about the aged as a group and about old age as an inherent part of individual life." In seeking what Callahan terms a "public meaning" of aging, important questions need to be discussed:

1. Aging is often accompanied by "private suffering" caused by physical and psychological losses—how can such suffering become a meaningful and significant part of life?
2. What moral virtues (for example, patience, cultivation of wisdom, courage in the face of change) should properly be associated with preparing for and living old age?

While There Is Time

I carry the folding chair
for my mother
I carry the shawl
the large straw hat
to shield her from the glare
She leans her small weight
on my arm   Frail legs unsteady
feet now cramped with pain

Each day we sit for hours
at the ocean   The sun is hot
but she is wrapped and swathed
her hands are icy cold
they hide their ache
beneath the blanket

Her eyes follow the
movement that surrounds us
the romp of children
flight of gulls
the strong young surfers
challenging the sea

When the visit is ended
when my mother leaves
I will burst from the house
run empty-handed to the beach
hold out my arms
and swoop like a bird
my hands will tag children
as I pass

I will run and run
until I fall
and weep
for the crushed feet
the gnarled fingers
for her longing
I will run for both of us

Maude Meehan

3. What are the characteristic moral and social obligations of the elderly? Is old age a time for devoting one's life to pleasure and well-being, or is it a time for active involvement in the civic life of society?

4. What medical and social entitlements are due to the elderly? If we cannot meet every medical need or pursue every possible line of medical research, how can we arrive at an equitable level of support?

As Callahan suggests, our answers to such questions need to reflect both "what kind of elderly person we want ourselves to be and what ideal character traits we would like to promote and support." In considering one's own future status as an elder, it is worth noting that attempts to meet *all* the needs of the elderly must inevitably fail, especially if those needs are defined as the avoidance of disease and frailty. The obvious truth, says Callahan, is that "it will *always* be impossible to meet such needs" despite an implicit social ideology that apparently "seeks to neutralize any inevitability about the process of aging and decline."

The positive images and meanings of growing old are eroded when we regard old age as a pathological state or as an avoidable affliction. In some societies, the aged hold special status as the "elders" of a community. Elderly women in the African American community, for example, occupy a special place as they continue the oral traditions of passing on cultural meanings to succeeding generations.[62] Respect for elders is similarly found among Native American peoples.[63]

Old age is a time for bringing plans to completion or relinquishing the responsibility for uncompleted projects to others younger than oneself, for reflection and summing up, and for preparing for one's own death. Jay Rosenberg says, "The fact that each of us will someday die shapes and colors our consciousness."[64] Rosenberg adds that one sign of a rational person

> is that he lives a life appropriate to a dying being—that he acknowledges without denial and without complaint the unavoidable transitoriness of his own existence, accepts with dignity and with grace the inevitable passage from youth to old age, which is the outward sign of that transitoriness, and prudently plans and provides for his own death and, to the extent that he can, for the well-being and betterment of those whose lives will continue after his life, and thus his very being, has come to an end.[65]

Growing old is not essentially a "medical problem." Robert Butler says, "None of us knows whether we have already had the best years of our lives or whether the best are yet to come. But the greatest of human possibilities remain to the very end of life—the possibilities for love and feeling, reconciliation and resolution."[66] As the culminating phase of human life, the period of old age or maturity is an appropriate time to focus on the tasks specific to that part of the human journey. Butler says:

> After one has lived a life of meaning, death may lose much of its terror. For what we fear most is not really death but a meaningless and absurd life. I believe most human beings can accept the basic fairness of each generation's taking its turn on the face of the planet if they are not cheated out of the full measure of their turn.[67]

Further Readings

Donna S. Davenport. *Singing Mother Home: A Psychologist's Journey Through Anticipatory Grief.* Denton: University of North Texas Press, 2002.

Sharon R. Kaufman. *The Ageless Self: Sources of Meaning in Later Life.* Madison: University of Wisconsin Press, 1995.

Donald M. Murray. *The Lively Shadow: Living with the Death of a Child.* New York: Ballantine, 2003.

Therese A. Rando, ed. *Parental Loss of a Child.* Champaign, Ill.: Research Press, 1986.

Paul C. Rosenblatt. *Parent Grief: Narratives of Loss and Relationship.* Philadelphia: Brunner/Mazel, 2000.

Catherine M. Sanders. *Grief, The Mourning After: Dealing with Adult Bereavement.* New York: Wiley, 1989.

Phyllis R. Silverman. *Widow to Widow: How the Bereaved Help One Another,* 2nd ed. New York: Brunner-Routledge, 2004.

Debra Umberson. *Death of a Parent: Transition to a New Adult Identity.* New York: Cambridge University Press, 2003.

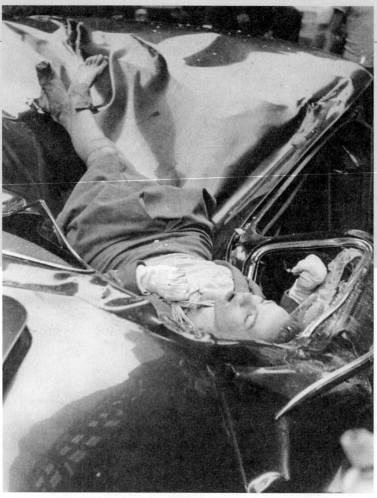

After plummeting eighty-six floors from the observation deck of the Empire State Building—visible in the metallic reflection at lower left—this young woman lies dead, the victim of suicide.

CHAPTER 12

Suicide

A person giving up his or her life for others or for a greater good—altruistic suicide—probably has occurred since human beings first banded together in clans. We can imagine situations in which one individual volunteered to draw the attention of a herd of animals to himself, thereby allowing other members of a hunting party to more easily trap the animals. Although the likelihood of surviving the onrushing herd was low, the reward for the clan was survival. Among nomadic peoples, suicide among the elderly or infirm was accepted as a way to maintain the mobility needed for the survival of the group. Honor was given to the person who, recognizing that the end of life was near, willingly left the community for certain death. Historically and across cultures, suicide also has been recognized as a way for a person to express his or her ultimate commitment to a moral or philosophical principle. Judith Stillion observes that "suicide is arguably the most complex and the least understood of all human behaviors, although it has been documented throughout recorded history."[1]

Suicide can be studied in relation to its cause or purpose, the individual and cultural meanings attached to suicidal behaviors, and the specific populations affected by suicide. "Why," it is asked, "would someone end his or her own life?" People are uncomfortable with the awesome fact that each of us has the power to decide whether or not we live. Questions about *intention* and *choice* are central in understanding suicide and other self-destructive behaviors. Suicide is influenced by a person's culture as well as by the unique qualities of his or her personality and life situation. It involves such factors as depression, negative life experiences, low self-esteem, and chronic physical pain. There is usually not one single answer that explains *why* a person dies by suicide. Kay Redfield Jamison says:

> Suicide is a death like no other, and those who are left behind to struggle with it must confront a pain like no other. They are left with the shock and the unending "what if's." They are left with anger and guilt and, now and again, a terrible sense of relief. They are left to a bank of questions from others, both asked and unasked, about Why; they are left to the silence of others, who are horrified, embarrassed, or unable to cobble together a note of condolence, an embrace, or a comment; and they are left with the assumption by others—and themselves—that more could have been done.[2]

Comprehending Suicide

At some time in their lives, most people have briefly entertained fantasies about the possibility of suicide. Such thoughts are not uncommon during childhood and adolescence, and they may crop up from time to time in later life as well. They may occur as a kind of "trying out" or "testing" of the notion of deliberately ending one's life rather than as serious plans for suicidal behavior. As you consider what might influence a person to die by suicide, you may think, "There's nothing that could cause me to think seriously about ending my own life." For individuals who are confident about their resources to deal effectively with the demands of life, suicide seems a radical solution indeed. Yet, as a complex human behavior, suicide involves diverse motives and intentions. In the search for answers about suicide, our first step must be to find a framework for organizing this complexity into manageable form. The four definitions of suicide given in Table 12-1 help establish a framework that is useful for all of these approaches.

TABLE *12-1*   *Four Definitions of Suicide*

Suicide is . . .

The act or an instance of taking one's own life voluntarily and intentionally, especially by a person of years of discretion and of sound mind. (*Webster's New Collegiate Dictionary*)[a]

Self-killing deriving from one's inability or refusal to accept the terms of the human condition. (Ronald W. Maris)[b]

All behavior that seeks and finds the solution to an existential problem by making an attempt on the life of the subject. (Jean Baechler)[c]

The human act of self-inflicted, self-intentioned cessation. (Edwin Shneidman)[d]

[a]Used by permission. From *Merriam-Webster's Collegiate Dictionary, Eleventh Edition*, © 2003 by Merriam-Webster, Inc., publisher of the Merriam-Webster® Dictionaries.
[b]Ronald W. Maris, *Pathways to Suicide: A Survey of Self-Destructive Behaviors* (Baltimore: Johns Hopkins University Press, 1981), p. 290.
[c]Jean Baechler, *Suicides* (New York: Basic Books, 1979), p. 11.
[d]Edwin S. Shneidman, ed., *Death: Current Perspectives*, 2nd ed. (Mountain View, Calif.: Mayfield, 1980), p. 416.

Notice that each definition emphasizes certain aspects of suicidal intention and behavior. The standard dictionary definition is a good starting point for understanding suicide, but it is vague. As you carefully review the different definitions, pay particular attention to how each explains the dynamics of suicide. Ask yourself, What kinds of human behavior does the definition include? Is suicide a specific act, or is it a behavioral process? What is the context of suicide? What are the circumstances in which it occurs?

For example, Ronald Maris's definition focuses on the cause or rationale for suicide. French social scientist Jean Baechler's definition emphasizes suicide as a means of resolving problems. Notice that suicide is defined as a behavior rather than as a specific act. Notice also that suicidal behavior may be immediate or long term. Thus, alcohol abuse can be a suicidal behavior because, in attempting to solve existential problems, it makes use of something that, over time, can have fatal consequences. Finally, Edwin Shneidman's definition emphasizes intention and action, along with the concept of ending one's conscious existence.

Statistical Issues

Nearly 32,000 people die by suicide every year in the United States.[3] For the nation as a whole, suicide ranks eleventh among all causes of death, and it ranks third among persons fifteen to twenty-four years old. Among those who die by suicide, males outnumber females by about four to one. It is estimated that more than 700,000 people attempt suicide each year, with about twenty-five attempts being made for every death that occurs by suicide. In contrast to the male-female ratio for *deaths* by suicide, about three females attempt suicide for every male who makes an attempt.[4]

 You may notice that I have not used the common terminology "committed suicide." It's because I believe this phrase incorrectly and unfairly accuses the suicide victim of an act over which they had no control. (If they had control, they would not have suicided. If they had, in other words, been in their right mind, they would not have taken their life.) The topic of "rational suicide" or physician-assisted suicide/death with dignity, as in the case of debilitating terminal illness, is a whole other topic of its own and outside the scope of these comments. The word "commit" is frequently paired with negatively judged acts: commit adultery, commit murder, commit a crime, commit a felony. I strongly believe that, because the suicidal person's mind is not working properly, there is a moment where suicide is no longer a choice. . . . If at that moment the person has access to the means to die, the suicide will happen. If at that moment the person is prevented from suiciding because he or she does not have the means, the suicide can be prevented. People refer to suicide as an "easy way out," but if you think about it, would it be easy for someone who is thinking clearly to slit their wrist, jump off a bridge, or pull the trigger of a gun?

Donna Schuurman, *Never the Same: Coming to Terms with the Death of a Parent*

Besides the cost in terms of lives lost, suicide has a powerful impact on those who are left to grieve a death by suicide. Edwin Shneidman says the person who dies by suicide "puts his psychological skeleton in the survivor's emotional closet."[5] It is estimated that each suicide affects at least six other people. These survivors of suicide include family members, friends, significant others, and loved ones. Based on an average of one suicide every eighteen minutes in the United States, this means that there are at least six new survivors every eighteen minutes as well. "Those who are left behind in the wake of suicide are left to deal with the guilt and the anger, to sift the good memories from the bad, and to try to understand an inexplicable act."[6]

Because talking openly and honestly about suicide is difficult or even taboo for many people, the actual number of suicide deaths that occur each year is likely to be much higher than statistics indicate. There is general agreement that official counts understate the number of suicides, perhaps by as much as half. A death is unlikely to be classified as a suicide unless the coroner or medical examiner suspects it because of the deceased's history of suicidal tendencies or acts of self-injury, or because the deceased left a suicide note, or because the circumstances of death so clearly point to suicide.

When the circumstances of a death are equivocal (meaning that the causes are uncertain or unclear) and there are questions about whether the cause was suicide or accident, it is likely to be classified as accidental unless a careful investigation proves otherwise. In some cases, for example, a detailed examination of circumstances surrounding an automobile accident leads to the conclusion that what seemed an "accident" is really a "suicide in disguise." In fact, some authorities believe that if such "autocides" were added to known statistics, suicide would be ranked as the number-one killer of young people.

Similarly, victim-precipitated homicide may mask a person's suicidal intent. Someone who deliberately provokes others by flashing a knife or wielding a gun, or by goading others with threats of violence, may be attempting to enlist the unwitting help of others in causing his or her own death. Individuals sometimes create violent situations in which they are likely to be killed, thereby possibly "dying as heroes."[7] A subcategory of victim-precipitated homicide, known as "suicide by cop," occurs when individuals engage in life-threatening and criminal actions that force police to shoot and kill them.[8] Similarly, research indicates that some individuals murder others and then seek the death penalty as a form of suicide, a situation that has been termed the "murder-suicide syndrome."[9] These kinds of victim-precipitated deaths usually are not included in suicide statistics.

In summarizing the difficulties in compiling accurate suicide statistics, Edwin Shneidman says,

> Because of religious and bureaucratic prejudices, family sensitivity, differences in the proceedings of coroner's hearings and postmortem examinations, and the shadowy distinctions between suicides and accidents—in short, the unwillingness to recognize the act for what it is—knowledge of the extent to which suicide pervades modern society is diminished and distorted.[10]

The Psychological Autopsy

Developed in 1961—primarily by Norman Farberow, Edwin Shneidman, and Robert Litman—the psychological autopsy is an impartial investigation by behavioral scientists to look for the motivational or intentional aspects of cases of equivocal death.[11] The findings of a psychological autopsy improve the accuracy of death classification. It attempts to re-create the personality and lifestyle of the deceased and the known circumstances of his or her death. Information gathered from interviews, documents, and other materials is used to determine the mode of death: natural, accident, suicide, or homicide.[12] With this information in hand, "The historical gestalt that emerges from the data can clarify the most probable mode of death."[13]

Of particular importance is the information pieced together from interviews with the deceased's friends and relatives, as well as other members of the community. This involves learning about current and previous stresses, psychiatric and medical histories, and the general lifestyle of the deceased, as well as any communication about suicidal intent. The person's routine in the days and hours before death is considered carefully as investigators try to create a picture of the person's character, personality, and state of mind. Based on an assessment of all the data gathered, a judgment is made about the mode of death (see Table 12-2).

In 1989, an explosion aboard the USS *Iowa*, which killed forty-seven sailors, brought increased public attention to the use of psychological autopsies.[14] Based on an "equivocal death analysis" conducted by the FBI, the U.S. Navy attributed the tragedy to alleged suicidal acts by Gunner's Mate Clayton Hartwig. Because of questions about the investigation, the House Armed Services Committee convened a panel of distinguished psychologists to conduct a peer review of the FBI's report and the Navy's subsequent conclusion. After weighing the evidence, the Committee rejected the Navy's allegation that Hartwig intentionally caused the explosion and characterized the inquiry as

TABLE *12-2* *Four Purposes of the Psychological Autopsy*

1. To help clarify the mode of death: natural, accident, suicide, or homicide (a classification system known by the acronym NASH). Note that *mode* of death differs from *cause* of death. The mode of death may be uncertain while the cause is clear.
2. To determine why a death occurred at a particular time; in other words, to examine the possible connection between the individual's psychology or state of mind and the timing of his or her death.
3. To gain data that may prove useful in predicting suicide and assessing the lethality of the suicidal person, thus helping clinicians and others identify trends in suicidal behavior and high-risk groups.
4. To obtain information that can be of therapeutic value to survivors in resolving emotional turmoil and questions that follow upon a loved one's death by suicide.

Source: Adapted from Thomas J. Young, "Procedures and Problems in Conducting a Psychological Autopsy," *International Journal of Offender Therapy and Comparative Criminology* 36, no. 1 (Spring 1992): 43–52.

TABLE *12-3*   *Limitations of the Psychological Autopsy*

1. *Lack of standardized procedures.* Several guidelines for conducting a psychological autopsy have been proposed, but a set of standardized procedures does not exist. Thus, critics question the reliability and validity of psychological autopsies. Proponents, on the other hand, argue that wide latitude is needed to accommodate unique situations.
2. *Retrospective nature.* Examiners are required to offer observations or opinions about a person's past mental state.
3. *Third-party informants may distort representations of the decedent for a variety of reasons.* Everyone who participates in a psychological autopsy has some stake in its outcome. Information from friends or relatives may be biased; public agencies may shape the story to fit certain preconceived parameters.
4. *The individual of interest is not available for examination,* a fact that makes this the greatest limitation of the psychological autopsy.
5. *There are few studies examining the reliability and validity of data obtained by psychological autopsies.*

Source: Adapted from James R. P. Ogloff and Randy K. Otto, "Psychological Autopsy: Clinical and Legal Perspectives," *Saint Louis University Law Journal* 37, no. 3 (Spring 1993): 610–614; and Thomas J. Young, "Procedures and Problems in Conducting a Psychological Autopsy," *International Journal of Offender Therapy and Comparative Criminology* 36, no. 1 (Spring 1992): 47–48.

an "investigative failure," particularly with respect to the FBI's analysis. Later tests indicated that the blast may have been due to mechanical error. The Navy ultimately recanted its allegations of Hartwig's responsibility, and the Chief of Naval Operations issued a formal apology to Hartwig's family.

In commenting about the case, the Committee's psychologists cited several limitations of reconstructive psychological procedures, such as the FBI's equivocal death analysis and psychological autopsies (see Table 12-3). They concluded that such psychological reconstruction should not result in an assertion of "categorical conclusions about the precise mental state or actions suspected of the actor at the time of his or her demise."[15] At present, the judiciary appears undecided about the admissibility of psychological autopsies as evidence: Some courts admit them into evidence whereas others exclude them.

The Hartwig case demonstrates that a lack of scientific precision may result in erroneous conclusions about the data collected through the use of psychological autopsies. However, as proponents of such investigative techniques point out, even *medical* autopsies are not perfect—yet they are viewed as having the potential to clarify circumstances surrounding death.

Despite its limitations, the psychological autopsy has proved to be a useful tool in assessing risk factors for suicide, especially factors that place young people at risk.[16] As both an investigative approach and a research tool, the psychological autopsy deepens our understanding of suicide and suicidal behavior.

Explanatory Theories of Suicide

The study of suicide has mainly followed two lines of theoretical investigation: (1) the sociological model, which has its foundation in the work of nineteenth-century French sociologist Emile Durkheim, and (2) the psychological model, based on the work of Viennese psychoanalyst Sigmund Freud. Most scholars pursue an integrated approach to understanding suicide, one that combines sociological and psychological insights (see Figure 12-1).

The Social Context of Suicide

The sociological model, as its name implies, focuses on the relationship between the individual and society. People live within networks of social relationships, ranging from the family to society as a whole, and social forces influence the circumstances surrounding suicide. Durkheim theorized that these social forces are manifested in the degree of integration and regulation present in a given society.[17]

Degree of Social Integration

The degree to which a person is part of (integrated into) his or her society is important. At one extreme we find situations in which the individual feels alienated from the institutions and traditions of his or her society. This is known as low integration or low belongingness.[18] The person has too few ties with his or her community. Without an adequate sense of social connectedness, a person becomes overly dependent upon his or her own resources. In this type of social environment, the suicides that occur are termed *egoistic*. An individual's mental energies are concentrated on the self to such an extent that social sanctions against suicide are ineffective. People who are disenfranchised or who live at the fringes of society may have no reason to hold to life-affirming values because they do not experience themselves as meaningfully related to the community. In Durkheim's view, when a person is detached from society, individual personality takes precedence over collective personality. Egoistic suicide is a type of suicide that springs from excessive individualism.

Conversely, when a person has a strong degree of social connectedness and integration, he or she may identify with its values or causes to such an extent that the sense of his or her own personal identity is diminished. Under certain circumstances, the values or customs of the group may demand suicide. This is the case in what Durkheim called *altruistic* or institutional suicide, which has been defined as "the self-destruction demanded by a society . . . as a price for being a member of that society."[19]

In feudal Japan, for example, when samurai warriors sacrificed their lives to maintain the honor or reputation of their lords, their society viewed such suicide as heroic. In certain circumstances, ritual disembowelment, called *seppuku* or *hara-kiri*, was culturally accepted, and expected, and it was accomplished by a prescribed etiquette.[20] When a warrior experienced disgrace in battle, *seppuku* was a way to regain honor. It demonstrated devotion to a superior, and the samurai might be expected to exhibit his devotion in this manner upon the death of his lord. At other times, *seppuku* could be an honorable way for a samurai to make a public statement of disagreement with a superior. The custom of suicide as protest also occurred during the Vietnam War, when

Thurs July 10
1:35 PM

My Darling Wife,

This afternoon I am going to make a 3rd attempt at bringing my turbulent life to an end. I hope that it is successful.

I dont know what I want from this world of ours, but you see I am due to go soon anyway. My Mother died at 60 ish as did her brothers and father. Also Alf has gone now.

Please dont get Margaret to come over here. — but you go as planned It will do you good. Put the Bungalow on the market and have a sale of the chattels. Then buy a smaller one.

The field will have vacant pos in nov if you want to sell that.

The wills are in the safe.

My love to you, Margaret, Michael and Janice.

I love you all & you have been so good to me

Tommy

X . X . X . X . X .
X X . X . X . X . X .

Dial Police 999
Also Bill   891459.

IT IS NOW 2.00 PM
Tommy xx.

Figure 12-1 *Suicide Note and Report of Death*
Even when a newspaper account is as detailed as this British report (*facing page*), the facts of suicide as described in the newspaper may reveal very little of the intense human factors—the personal and social dynamics—that precipitated the suicidal act.

Retired man's suicide

A HYTHE man aged 64 killed himself because he could not stand old age, an inquest heard yesterday.

Retired maintenance engineer Aubrey Heathfield Aylmore, who lived at Forest Front, Hythe, was found dead in his car by his wife.

The inquest heard that Mrs. Heathfield Aylmore had been to a WI meeting and returned home an hour later than planned.

She found her husband's body in the garage with a length of hose pipe running from the exhaust into the car.

A note was found in which Mr. Heathfield Aylmore said that this was his third suicide attempt and that he wanted to "put an end to my turbulent life."

Dr. Richard Goodbody, consultant pathologist, said cause of death was asphyxia due to carbon monoxide poisoning.

Coroner Mr. Harry Roe said that Mr. Heathfield Aylmore had been depressed at the thought of growing old.

Buddhist monks died by self-immolation to protest their country's governmental policies. According to Durkheim, highly integrated societies naturally encourage altruistic and fatalistic suicide.[21]

Similarly, in the past, certain castes in India were expected to practice *suttee,* which called for the wife to throw herself upon her husband's cremation pyre. Such self-immolation, or "following into death," was condoned by religious and cultural beliefs.[22] Reluctance to enact such ritual suicide could meet with social disapproval. Indeed, a reluctant widow might be "helped" onto the burning pyre. To these examples of *seppuku* and *suttee* could be added the deaths of kamikaze pilots in Japan's air attack corps during World War II and the example of the dedicated captain who goes down with the ship. In discussing altruistic suicide, Durkheim introduced the concept of "heroic suicide" in referring to deaths in combat, such as that exhibited by Medal of Honor recipients who voluntarily sacrificed their own lives to save the lives of others.[23]

Mass suicides also occur within a highly integrated social context. For example, on November 20, 1978, at a previously little-noticed jungle clearing in Jonestown, Guyana, more than 900 persons died in what is considered the largest mass suicide in history.[24] Family members died in one another's arms as, in hypnotic tones from his throne above the crowd, the Reverend Jim Jones instructed the followers of his Peoples Temple community to drink cyanide-laced fruit punch.

Malcolm Brown, AP / Wide World Photos

Flames engulf the body of a Buddhist monk, Quang Duc, whose self-immolation before thousands of onlookers in downtown Saigon was a protest against alleged persecution of Buddhists by the government of South Vietnam.

Degree of Social Regulation

In Durkheim's model, insufficient social regulation creates the conditions for *anomic* suicides. In the typical example, the relationship between an individual and society is suddenly shattered or disrupted. Such social estrangement is characterized by the term *anomie* (meaning "lawlessness"). The classic example of this situation occurs when societies undergo rapid social change and people lose their moorings to traditional values and ways of life. Suicide among youth worldwide is partly attributed to cultural changes whereby individualism and autonomy tend to loosen bonds between individuals and society. Anomie (lack of regulation) and egoism (lack of integration) reinforce each other.

Sudden trauma or catastrophe can also weaken the ties between an individual and society. The loss of a job, the amputation of a limb, the death of a close friend or family member—any of these losses can be an anomic event. Indeed, any disruptive change—whether positive or negative—can precipitate a state of anomie. Sudden wealth may contribute to suicidal behavior if the newly rich person is unable to cope with his or her changed status.

For more than 900 Americans who left their home to join a religious fanatic called the Reverend Jim Jones, death came in the jungles of Guyana with these comforting words from the man who engineered the largest mass suicide the world has witnessed:

> What's going to happen here in a matter of a few minutes is that one of those people in the plane is going to shoot the pilot. . . . So you be kind to the children and be kind to seniors, and take the potion like they used to in Ancient Greece, and step over quietly, because we are not committing suicide—it's a revolutionary act.
>   Everybody dies. I haven't seen anybody yet didn't die. And I like to choose my own kind of death for a change. I'm tired of being tormented to hell. Tired of it. (Applause)

A few cultists protested. Some women screamed. Children cried. Armed guards took up positions around the camp to keep anyone from escaping:

> Let the little children in and reassure them. . . . They're not crying from pain, it's just a little bitter-tasting. . . . Death is a million times more preferable to spend more days in this life. If you knew what was ahead of you, you'd be glad to be stepping over tonight . . . quickly, quickly, no more pain. . . . This world was not your home. . . .

Here the tape runs out. The sound stops before the report of the pistol that killed Jim Jones, presumably fired by his own hand.

Robert Ramsey and Randall Toye, *The Goodbye Book*

At the other extreme of regulation we find a society characterized by excessive social constraints. Lack of freedom and absence of choice can generate a sense of fatalism, a feeling that there is nowhere to turn and that nothing good can be achieved. This produces what Durkheim termed *fatalistic* suicide. Suicide in jail is due partly to the rigid regulation found in such environments. (When three Guantanamo Bay detainees died by hanging themselves with fabricated nooses made from clothes and bed sheets, another detainee explained what led to their deaths by saying, "I would rather die than live here forever without rights.")[25]

Viewed from a social perspective, suicide is caused by a disturbance in the ties between an individual and society. An imbalance in the degree of social regulation or social integration, or both, heightens the potential for suicide. Thus, according to the sociological explanation, each form of suicide—egoistic, altruistic, anomic, fatalistic—is related to a particular kind of interplay between society and the individual.

Psychological Insights About Suicide

Drawing on theories proposed by Sigmund Freud, the psychodynamic model of suicide focuses attention on the mental and emotional processes, both conscious and unconscious, occurring within the mind of an individual.[26] It assumes that a person's behavior is determined by both past experience

Suicide Note Written by a Married Man, Age 45

My darling,

May her guts rot in hell—I loved her so much.

Henry

and current reality. Among the key insights from psychological studies of suicide are the following:

1. The *acute* suicidal crisis is of relatively brief duration; that is, it lasts hours or days rather than weeks or months—though it may recur. A person is at the peak of self-destructiveness for a short time and gets help, cools off, or dies.
2. The suicidal person is likely to be *ambivalent* about ending his or her life. A person on the brink of suicide both wants to die and doesn't want to die. While plans for self-destruction are being made, the person also entertains fantasies of rescue or intervention.
3. Most suicidal events are *dyadic* events—that is, two-person events. In some way, they involve both a suicidal person and a significant other.

In the psychodynamic view, suicide involves strong, unconscious hostility. Under conditions of enormous stress, the intrapsychic pressures impelling a person toward self-destruction increase to the point that they overwhelm the defense mechanisms of the ego, or self. This, in turn, causes a regression to primitive ego states, which involve powerful forces of *aggression*. Whereas murder is aggression turned upon another, suicide is aggression turned upon oneself. In this sense, suicide may be viewed as murder in the 180th degree. In the German language, suicide is a murder of the self, *Selbstmord*.

Even with aggressive forces mobilized, however, the urge toward self-preservation works against the self's acquiescence in its own death. Thus, another psychodynamic process comes into play: *ambivalence*. Analysis of suicidal behavior usually reveals the presence of conflicting forces that compete for the greater share of the person's mental energies. Suicidal persons tend to be indecisive. They may even count on being rescued. Shneidman says the prototypical suicidal person wants "to cut his throat and to cry for help at the same time."[27]

Even when a person appears to be intent on suicide, the natural urge toward self-preservation works against the self accepting its own death. At issue is the will to live versus the will to die. "Most people who commit acts of self-damage with more or less conscious self-destructive intent do not want either to live or to die, but to do both at the same time."[28]

The balance between these opposing polarities may be delicate, with an otherwise minor incident tipping the scales one way or the other. Although one of these forces is eventually stronger than the other, the weaker one

Richard Cory

Whenever Richard Cory went down town,
    We people on the pavement looked at him:
He was a gentleman from sole to crown,
    Clean favored, and imperially slim.

And he was always quietly arrayed,
    And he was always human when he talked;
But still he fluttered pulses when he said,
    "Good-morning," and he glittered when he walked.

And he was rich—yes, richer than a king—
    And admirably schooled in every grace:
In fine, we thought that he was everything
    To make us wish that we were in his place.

So on we worked, and waited for the light,
    And went without the meat, and cursed the bread;
And Richard Cory, one calm summer night,
    Went home and put a bullet through his head.

Edwin Arlington Robinson

nevertheless affects the person's behavior. Most suicidal acts are examples of risk-taking behavior or gambles. The outcome of the conflict between the self-destructive and life-preserving impulses depends on a variety of factors, some of which are outside the individual's control.

Toward an Integrated Understanding of Suicide

Because suicidal behavior is multidimensional and multifaceted, the social and psychodynamic explanations of suicide interact in an integrated fashion. After devoting a lifetime to studying suicide, pioneering suicidologist Edwin Shneidman distilled his learning into five words: *Suicide is caused by psychache*.[29] Shneidman says: "Psychache is at the dark heart of suicide; no psychache, no suicide."[30] The term "psychache" refers to unbearable mental pain that is caused by the frustration of a person's most important needs, which are unique to each individual. Shneidman believes that most suicide cases tend to exhibit themselves in one of four clusters of frustrated psychological needs:[31]

1. Thwarted love, acceptance, or belonging
2. Fractured control, helplessness, and frustration
3. Assaulted self-image and avoidance of shame, defeat, humiliation, and disgrace
4. Ruptured key relationships and attendant grief and bereftness

Suicide has been called "a very bad decision on a very bad day." It is the outcome of a person's desire to reduce intolerable mental pain. An individual who is suicidal is likely to be in a state of isolated desperation, a dark corner where it seems there is no hope of relief. A common theme among the various paths to suicide is that it is seen as an ultimate form of gaining control over insurmountable difficulties in life.

The sequence leading to suicide often begins with interactions between biochemical imbalances in the brain, personality factors, and life stress. Most suicides are the outcome of a disease in the brain, an illness such as depression, anxiety, schizophrenia, bipolar (manic-depressive) disorder, or some other mood disorder. Clinical depression, a state of intense sadness and self-reproach, is a major risk factor. A key aspect of depression is the person's sense of *hopelessness.* Suicide risk is also higher with some personality disorders, such as borderline and antisocial personality, especially when combined with substance abuse. (Alcohol or substance abuse is a contributing cause in many suicides.) Whereas mental illness is an *ongoing* risk factor for suicide, the specific *timing* of suicidal acts tends to be related to stressful life events.

In studies of attempted and completed suicides, there appears to be a neurobiological determinant related to the brain's reduced ability to make and use serotonin, a key neurotransmitter. Serotonin is lower in suicide attempters, and postmortem studies of suicide victims reveal decreased serotonin activity in the prefrontal cortex.[32] Low levels of serotonin (5-HT) or its neurotransmitter metabolite (5-HIAA) may be correlated with suicidal behavior. Serotonin levels appear to be related to a calming influence on the mind and, when levels are low, an increased risk of suicide. As scientists learn more about the role of biological markers like serotonin, it may be possible to reduce vulnerability to suicide by identifying individuals at risk and offering appropriate therapy.

Many people are not aware of the role of brain disease in suicide. As a result, they tend to treat suicide as a failure of personal responsibility and as a matter of shame. This mistaken attitude can severely limit an understanding of suicide. In fact, once we recognize the strong connection between diseases of the brain and suicide, it challenges the conventional notion that suicide is chosen by a person out of his or her free and rational choice.

Some Types of Suicide

Various classification schemes have been applied to suicide to comprehend its personal and social meanings (see Table 12-4). To provide a more complete picture of suicide and other self-destructive behaviors, it is worthwhile to look more closely at some "types" or categories of suicide. Notice that an instance of suicide may include elements from more than one category.

Suicide as Escape

Suicide may be a means of escape from some intense physical pain or mental anguish. A person with a severely debilitating or terminal illness may view suicide as a way to gain release from burdensome suffering. Ending one's life in such a situation is sometimes termed "rational suicide" because the reasoning used—death will bring release from pain—conforms to normal logic.

T A B L E *12-4* *Meanings of Suicide*

Some Cultural Meanings of Suicide

Suicide is sinful: A crime against nature, a revolt against the preordained order of the universe.

Suicide is criminal: It violates the ties that exist, the social contract between persons in a society.

Suicide is weakness or madness: It reflects limitations or deviancy ("He must have been crazy" or "He couldn't take it").

Suicide is the Great Death, as in *seppuku, suttee,* and other culturally approved forms of ritual suicide.

Suicide is the rational alternative: The outcome of a "balance-sheet" approach that sizes up the situation and determines the best option.

Some Individual Meanings of Suicide

Suicide is reunion with a lost loved one: A way to "join the deceased."

Suicide is rest and refuge: A way out of a burdensome and depressing situation.

Suicide is getting back: A way of expressing resentment and revenge at being rejected or hurt.

Suicide is the penalty for failure: A response to disappointment and frustration at not meeting self-expectations or the expectations of others.

Suicide is a mistake: The attempt was made as a cry for help and was not intended to be fatal, but there was no rescue or intervention and the outcome was death.

Source: Adapted from Robert Kastenbaum, *Death, Society, and Human Experience,* 2nd ed. (St. Louis: Mosby, 1981), pp. 239–255.

Physician-assisted suicide (discussed in Chapter 6) can be considered an example of this type of suicide.

In other instances, a desire to escape through suicide results from destructive logic. When an individual's self-concept or sense of identity is confused, and when this confusion is coupled with problems in relating to others, it can result in the person's self-perception as a failure. In this case, suicide may be termed "referred," bringing to mind the analogy of a physical pain that is experienced at some distance from its source. An inflammation of the liver may be experienced as pain in the shoulder. Just as this physical phenomenon is characterized as referred pain, so the root causes of referred suicide are likewise only indirectly related to the end result—namely, suicide. The intention to end one's life is not based on a dispassionate or rational assessment of the situation but, instead, results from an overwhelming sense of anguish and confusion about one's options.

Not performing up to expectations or role definitions may provoke a crisis of self-concept that ultimately leads to a desire to escape the unsatisfactory situation. These expectations may be related to something outside the person ("If I can't be a good enough daughter to please my parents, I give up!") or to inward feelings of frustration ("Everybody thinks I'm doing okay, but I feel rotten").

Desire to escape may arise from loss of meaning in one's life. Despite significant accomplishments, a person may feel, "Okay, now what?" Accumulating successes one after another may seem a Sisyphean effort, a continual struggle for achievement without a corresponding sense of accomplishment. Conversely, success may be accompanied by feelings of ennui—"If this is success, it's not worth the effort." The causal chain begins with events that fall short of standards and expectations.[33] The individual seeks to escape from a negative sense of self. Drastic measures seem acceptable, with suicide becoming the ultimate step in the effort to find release.

Cry for Help

Considered as a *cry for help*, suicide aims to force a change. The person no longer wishes to continue living life as it is. The goal is not to die, but to solve some problem. Suicide is perceived, at least temporarily, as a means of eliminating the problem. Suicidal behavior is, in effect, a message that "something has to change in my life; I can't go on living this way."

Youthful suicide often reveals this pattern in such actions as cutting one's wrist or taking a drug overdose. The intent may be to express frustration or gain attention, but the potential danger of a fatal outcome is not really acknowledged. Many suicide attempts represent a kind of communication that says, in effect, "I am deadly serious; you'd better pay attention!" This message may be directed inwardly to oneself or meant for others.

In this regard, it is useful to make a distinction between *attempted* suicide and the *fait accompli*. According to Glen Evans and Norman Farberow, attempted suicide "refers to behavior directed against the self which results in injury or self-harm, or has strong potential for injury." Indeed, "Intention in the behavior may or may not be to die, or may or may not be to inflict injury or pain on oneself."[34]

There may be two distinct populations of individuals who engage in suicidal behavior: (1) *attempters* (who tend toward repeated, but not lethal, attempts) and (2) *completers* (whose first attempt typically results in death). Attempters and completers may have quite different aims with regard to their suicidal acts.[35] Some suicidologists believe that attempted suicide should be viewed as the norm, whereas completed suicide should be seen as a failed behavior in which a person inappropriately died.

A "cry for help" is associated with individuals who threaten or attempt suicide as distinct from those who actually kill themselves. Often, in the first

---

 Suicide Note Written by a Divorced Woman, Age 61

You cops will want to know why I did it, well just let us say that I lived 61 years too many.

People have always put obstacles in my way. One of the great ones is leaving this world when you want to and have nothing to live for.

I am not insane. My mind was never more clear. It has been a long day. The motor got so hot it would not run so I just had to sit here and wait. The breaks were against me to the very last.

The sun is leaving the hill now so hope nothing else happens.

group, the lethality of the attempt is low. It appears the aim of the behavior is to communicate to others how desperate or unhappy the person feels. When low-lethality suicidal behavior is met with defensive hostility or attempts to minimize its seriousness, however, the risk of suicide may increase, along with the possibility that a future attempt will be lethal. In responding to the cry for help, it is crucial to recognize that a problem exists and take steps toward expanding communication and proposing remedies. Whatever the intention, suicidal behavior can be deadly. Psychological autopsies indicate that some people who have died by suicide didn't intend for their actions to result in death, but help didn't arrive in time.

Attempted suicides outnumber completed suicides by a significant margin. As mentioned earlier, one estimate is that there are twenty-five attempts for every death by suicide. There are more suicide attempts among females than among males, while males die by suicide more often than do females.[36] These gender differences may be explained partly by the methods chosen, with males tending to use more lethal methods, such as a gun, whereas females tend to take pills or slash wrists. (Unfortunately, this gap may be narrowing as females appear to be adopting more-lethal methods, such as firearms.) Alcohol abuse, a risk factor for suicide, is also more common among males. Furthermore, it may be that males consider a "failed" suicide attempt to be cowardly or unmasculine and therefore make a special effort to be "successful." In addition to this "suicidal success syndrome," males are less likely than females to report suicidal thoughts or seek help. By trying to hide their feelings of depression or hopelessness, males are less likely to seek out suicide prevention or crisis intervention programs.

People who survive a suicide attempt may view their continued existence as a second chance or "bonus life." If this opportunity is used well, the person may arrive at a more positive self-identity and find ways to get beyond the pain that led to the attempted suicide. By altering the distressing situation or one's attitude toward it, a "cry for help" may lead to constructive change and healing.

Subintentioned and Chronic Suicide

As defined by Edwin Shneidman, a *subintentioned* death is "one in which the person plays some partial, covert, subliminal, or unconscious role in hastening his own demise."[37] Some fatalities reported as accidents result from the victim's taking unnecessary and unwise risks. Such behavior might be called careless or imprudent. Probing deeper into causes, however, reveals that accidents are sometimes the end result of a self-destructive pattern of behavior. Similarly, homicide investigations sometimes turn up evidence of subintentional factors that lead a victim to behave in ways that provoke his or her death at another's hands.

Besides subintentioned death, Shneidman delineates two other patterns of death-related behaviors: *intentioned* and *unintentioned*. Table 12-5 presents an outline of these three patterns. Notice that within each of these categories a person might exhibit a variety of attitudes and behaviors regarding death.

TABLE 12-5 *Patterns of Death-Related Behavior and Attitudes*

Intentioned Death: Death resulting from the suicide's direct, conscious behavior to bring it about. A variety of attitudes or motives may be operative:

The *death seeker* wishes to end consciousness and commits the suicidal act in such a way that rescue is unlikely.

The *death initiator* expects to die in the near future and wants to choose the time and circumstances of death.

The *death ignorer* believes that death ends only physical existence and that the person continues to exist in another manner.

The *death darer* gambles with death, or, as Shneidman says, "bets his life on a relatively low objective probability that he will survive" (such as by playing Russian roulette).

Subintentioned Death: Death resulting from a person's patterns of management or style of living, although death was not the conscious, direct aim of the person's actions:

The *death chancer*, although in many ways like the death darer, may want higher odds of survival.

The *death hastener* may expedite his or her death by substance abuse (drugs, alcohol, and the like) or by failing to safeguard well-being (for example, by inadequate nutrition or precautions against disease or disregard of available treatments).

The *death facilitator* gives little resistance to death, making it easy for death to occur, as in the deaths of patients whose energies, or "will to live," are low because of their illness.

The *death capitulator* is one who, usually out of a great fear of death, plays a subintentional role in his or her own death, as may a person upon whom a so-called voodoo death has been put, or as may a person who believes that someone admitted to a hospital is bound to die.

The *death experimenter* does not consciously wish to die, but lives on the brink, usually in a "befogged state of consciousness" that may be related to taking drugs in such ways that the person may become comatose or even die with little concern.

Unintentioned Death: Death in which the decedent plays no significant causative role. However, various attitudes toward death may shape the experience of dying:

The *death welcomer*, though not hastening death, looks forward to it (as might an aged person who feels unable to manage adequately or satisfactorily).

The *death accepter* is resigned to his or her fate; the style of acceptance may be passive, philosophical, resigned, heroic, realistic, or mature.

The *death postponer* hopes to put death off for as long as possible.

The *death disdainer* feels, in Shneidman's words, "above any involvement in the stopping of the vital processes."

The *death fearer* is fearful, and possibly phobic, about anything related to death; death is something to be fought and hated.

The *death feigner* pretends to be in mortal danger or pretends to perform a suicidal act without being in actual danger, possibly in an attempt to gain attention or to manipulate others.

Source: Adapted from Edwin S. Shneidman, *Deaths of Man* (New York: Quadrangle Books, 1973), pp. 82–90.

As you review this table, ask yourself: Where do I stand on this list? What does that tell me about my own regard for life and death?

Chronic suicide, a term coined by Karl Menninger, refers to individuals who destroy themselves by means of drugs, alcohol, smoking, reckless living, and the like. Although individuals who shorten their lives by chronic suicide may consciously find the idea of suicide repugnant or unacceptable, an analysis of their lifestyles typically reveals the presence of a "death wish."

Risk Factors Influencing Suicide

Another way to increase our understanding of suicide is to examine risk factors that influence suicide and suicidal behaviors. Besides the neurobiological and genetic factors discussed earlier in this chapter, here we focus on risk factors related to culture, personality, and the individual situation. Typically, various risk factors overlap and are mutually influential in a particular instance of suicidal behavior.

Culture

Cultural messages about suicide acceptability can influence the kinds of behavior engaged in by members of a social group. For example, a society or group may believe that suicide to end physical suffering from terminal disease is more acceptable than suicide to escape mental pain of other life problems.

Cultural disruption and stress appear to play a part in suicide among Native Americans.[38] Forced onto reservations, their cultures undermined, native peoples of North America have undergone severe dislocations. Conflicts

---

 Suicide Note Written by a Married Man, Age 74

What is a few short years to live in hell. That is all I get around here.

No more I will pay the bills.

No more I will drive the car.

No more I will wash, iron, & mend any clothes.

No more I will have to eat the leftover articles that was cooked the day before.

This is no way to live.

Either is it any way to die.

Her grub I can not eat.

At night I can not sleep.

I married the wrong nag-nag-nag and I lost my life.

W.S.

To the undertaker

We have got plenty money to give me a decent burial. Don't let my wife kid you by saying she has not got any money.

Give this note to the cops.

Give me liberty or give me death.

W.S.

between their traditional ways and the ways of contemporary white society can lead to feelings of powerlessness and anxiety. An added burden is experienced by Native Americans who live in large cities, where support systems, family ties, and traditional customs are lacking. These stresses, sometimes combined with dysfunctional behaviors such as alcohol and drug abuse, can heighten suicide risk.

Kathleen Erwin has examined how social factors may influence gay and lesbian suicide.[39] Explanations for the elevated rate of suicide among homosexual populations have been sought mostly in theories centering on individual psychology. More recently, however, the antecedents of gay and lesbian suicide have been located in a sociocultural model that highlights the role of social forces that have been intolerant and oppressive toward homosexuals. The earlier focus on individual psychology is being balanced by a recognition that social factors are important, perhaps decisive, in suicide among homosexuals.

Within African American communities, many young people consider suicide a weak, cowardly way out of their problems, a view that is also held by many of their elders. The rate of suicide among African Americans is lower than among white Americans, a phenomenon due at least partly to a common perception among African Americans that suicide is a "white thing." Kevin Early and Ronald Akers report that religion and family play important roles in "buffering" social forces that might otherwise promote suicide among African Americans. Early and Akers found that suicide is typically viewed as "inherently contradictory to the black experience and a complete denial of black identity and culture."[40]

The acceptability of violence as a solution to problems is another cultural factor that affects suicide risk. The availability of lethal weapons as well as the prevalence of violence in the media contribute to a sense that violence is an acceptable alternative when the going gets rough. Easy access to guns is an important factor in suicide among children and young adults, who are increasingly using guns to end their lives instead of methods that are more likely to fail. The apparent acceptance of violence in our lives can change posturing into deadly deeds.[41]

In considering cultural messages, the idea that suicide is contagious has a long history. Following publication of Johann Wolfgang von Goethe's *The Sorrows of Young Werther* in 1774, an epidemic of suicide among young people was thought to be stimulated by the book. The influence of suggestion on suicidal behavior has been termed the "Werther effect." The question of whether such a "contagious" or imitative effect actually exists remains controversial. (Suicide "clusters" are discussed later in this chapter.) What is clear is the fact that the social environment is a significant influence on suicide and suicidal behaviors.

Cultural factors in suicide are highlighted in what Brian Barry calls "the balance between pro-life and pro-death forces operating at any given time."[42] Pro-life forces include (1) the belief that problems can promote growth, (2) a perceived ability to solve life problems, (3) a willingness to struggle and suffer if necessary, and (4) a healthy fear of death and its aftermath. In contrast, pro-death forces include (1) the belief that problems are intolerable, (2) a perception that life problems are intractable or unyielding, (3) a sense of entitlement to a rewarding life, and (4) a philosophical stance that sees suicide as a means of obtaining relief. In Barry's view, people in modern societies have accepted two fundamental assumptions about life that no previous generation has embraced so thoroughly: first, the belief that we deserve significant fulfillment in our jobs, marriages, and overall lives; and second, the belief that, rather than accepting unalterable circumstances, we must live and die on our own terms. In other words, we not only aspire to a good life, but we have convinced ourselves that we are entitled to it. If this sense of entitlement is not realized, we may feel it's appropriate to protest by removing ourselves from an intolerable situation, even when the outcome is death.

Suicide bombings, too, reflect an understanding that the cultural collective—religion, sect, nation—is more important than the individual, leading to the terrorist's belief that he or she is engaged in a worthy struggle that makes suicidal sacrifice not only desirable but imperative (this topic is discused in Chapter 13).

Personality

Some people seem to have a "basic optimism," whereas others have a "basic pessimism." This personality difference can have an impact on the onset of suicidal thoughts. Fear or anxiety about death may also influence suicidal behavior. A higher degree of anxiety may inhibit suicidal behavior, whereas perceiving death as an attractive prospect may encourage it. Thus, the meanings attributed to death may influence the way individuals evaluate the possibility of suicide. Personality factors that contribute to suicidal thoughts and behaviors include low self-esteem, difficulties with intimate relationships, hopelessness, lack of coping skills, and feelings of stagnation, loneliness, and despair.

An individual's fascination with the "mystique" of death, especially self-willed death, can increase suicide risk. Some suicides appear to be related to a "poetic" or "romantic" attraction to death. Following the example of Thomas Chatterton, who killed himself in 1770 at the age of seventeen, the Romantics thought of death as "the great inspirer" and "great consoler." In other words, death is a lover to be courted. The poet Sylvia Plath wrote, "I will marry dark death, the thief of the daytime."[43] Do the suicides of such writers as Ernest Hemingway, Anne Sexton, Plath herself, and, more recently, musician Kurt Cobain, reflect a desire to embrace the mystery of death? Or do they result from commonplace human experiences? Investigated deeply, failure to find meaning in life and relationship problems are common threads.[44] As someone said, "The death of love evokes the love of death."

The Individual Situation

The intersection of culture and personality creates the unique life situation experienced by a particular person. Every person is subject to a constellation of environmental factors that involve varying degrees of suicide risk.

These include the social forces existing within society as a whole, as well as the particular characteristics associated with an individual's family, economic situation, and so on.

Stressful life events are associated with suicidal behaviors. For example, individuals who have been bereaved as a result of suicide may be vulnerable to an increased risk of suicide themselves.[45] Academic stress, when not adequately managed, is associated with suicidal behaviors. In *crisis suicide,* the typical pattern is that of an adolescent who experiences traumatic change in his or her life, such as the loss of a loved one or the threatened loss of status in school.

The influence of peers can also affect an individual's suicide risk, especially among adolescents and young adults. A study of suicide among young Micronesian males found an "epidemic-like" increase during a twenty-year period.[46] This period was marked by rapid sociocultural transformation, as traditional styles of living gave way to a capitalist economy and modern forms of education, employment, health services, and technology. Investigators found links among the suicides, with several occurring among a small circle of friends over several months. There were also cases of self-destructive behavior in reaction to the suicide of a friend or relative, as well as "suicide pacts" between two or more people. Taken together, these phenomena pointed to the existence of a "suicide subculture" wherein suicide begat suicide. In an environment characterized by a general familiarity with and acceptance of the *idea* of suicide, suicide had become a culturally patterned and partly collective response to personal dilemmas and problems.

Life Span Perspectives on Suicide

The risks and motives for suicide change through life as human beings encounter changing circumstances related to different periods of human development. The causes of suicide among adolescents, for example, tend to be distinct from those of people in old age. In studying various risks that pertain to different segments of the life span, notice which factors affect people of all ages and which factors tend to exert a particular influence on people in specific age groups.

Childhood

Suicide is rarely reported in young children, but many researchers and clinicians believe that suicidal behavior is found among even very young children. Because suicide risk is higher among those who have made an earlier attempt, children with a history of suicide ideation or attempt are at risk for multiple recurrence of suicidal ideas or acts.[47]

Researchers believe that the rate of suicide among children would be higher if childhood accidents were examined more carefully for intent. Some of the childhood deaths resulting from running in front of cars or plastic bag suffocation are probably intentional rather than accidental. Although young children usually do not have access to sophisticated means of self-destruction, as do people at older ages, they nevertheless engage in acts of self-harm, and

Henry Wallis, Tate Gallery, London

Unable to earn a living by writing and too proud to accept food offered to him by his landlady, this seventeen-year-old killed himself by taking poison. Painted in 1856 by Henry Wallis, The Death of Chatterton *depicts an adolescent suicide that was precipitated by crisis arising out of the developmental transition from child to adult.*

some kill themselves. In the case of young children, however, labeling a death as suicide may be problematic because of questions about whether a child possesses a mature concept of death and, thus, is fully aware of the consequences of his or her actions.[48] (Recall the discussion of childhood development in Chapter 2.) There is evidence that children who attempt suicide, especially those on the cusp between childhood and adolescence, tend to be in a transitional stage between concrete operational and formal operational thought, a period that may involve heightened vulnerability to suicidal ideation and behaviors.[49]

Adolescence and Young Adulthood

Suicide is the third leading cause of death for people ages fifteen to twenty-four in the United States.[50] Adolescent suicide begins to appear in the age group of ten- to fourteen-year-olds and increases significantly among older adolescents and young adults, which suggests that developmental changes play a role, possibly related to cognitive development and the conceptualization of death.

Suicide Note Written by a Single Woman, Age 21

My dearest Andrew,

It seems as if I have been spending all my life apologizing to you for things that happened whether they were my fault or not.

I am enclosing your pin because I want you to think of what you took from me every time you see it.

I don't want you to think I would kill myself over you because you're not worth any emotion at all. It is what you cost me that hurts and nothing can replace it.

Social disruption is an important factor in self-destructive behaviors among the young (see Table 12-6). Psychiatric diagnosis, dysfunctional personality traits, and psychosocial problems also increase the risk of suicide. Suicidal adolescents are linked with interpersonal conflict (with parents as well as boy- or girlfriends), interpersonal losses (including disruption of a romantic attachment, as well as other separations), and external stressors (most notably, legal or disciplinary problems, which are often related to tendencies to engage in impulsive violence).[51]

Family problems are significant. Suicidal young people tend to be exposed to family violence, disengaged families and deficient family support, physical abuse, parental suicidal behavior, instability in their living situation, and other acute and chronic stressors related to family life. The young person's response to such turmoil may give rise to a variety of affective and cognitive states, such as rage, hopelessness, despair, guilt, revenge, self-punishment, and retaliatory abandonment.[52] Substance abuse is a common theme, both in families and among young suicide-prone individuals. Active substance abuse, combined with depression and the availability of a handgun, is potentially lethal.

Upheavals in family life, and in lifestyles generally, add to the pressures experienced by young people. Suicide may be seen as a way to impose some control over confusing and upsetting events or to escape them. As Paulina Kernberg points out,

> An important meaning of suicide is that it can serve as an act of mastery, of ultimate control, of competency in individuals who are suffering loss of a sense of control over themselves and their lives. It is, as it were, the ultimate "locus of control."[53]

Substance abuse, delinquency, and suicide are linked on a continuum of "escape behaviors" that young people engage in to avoid feelings of depression and hopelessness. Risk-taking behavior may represent a "way out" for the individual who no longer cares whether he or she lives or dies. Flirting with death, as in "playing chicken," may be engaged in lackadaisically, with little concern for the outcome. When substance abuse and risky behaviors no longer provide sufficient distraction from painful lives, young people may opt for suicide to provide the ultimate numbness.[54]

T A B L E   *12-6*   *Risk Factors in Youthful Suicide*

1. Early separation from one's parents
2. Family dissolution, economic hardship, and increased mobility
3. Effect of highly conflicted families or families who are unresponsive to the young person's needs, or who are anomic (not accepting of the usual standards of social conduct) or depressed, alcoholic, and so on
4. Increased social isolation as compared to the support previously provided by the extended family, church, and community
5. Rapidly changing sex roles
6. Increase in relative proportion of young people in the total population, and corresponding increase in competition because of the large youthful cohort population
7. Pressure for achievement and success, perhaps resulting from parental expectations
8. Impact of peer suicides and role models of popular entertainers in terms of "copy cat" suicide
9. Media attention given to suicide, and the influence of self-destructive themes in popular culture, especially in popular song lyrics
10. Sense of lack of control over one's life
11. Low self-esteem and poor self-image
12. Devaluing of emotional expression
13. Lack of effective relationships with peers
14. Easy access to drugs and alcohol

Source: Adapted from William C. Fish and Edith Waldhart-Letzel, "Suicide and Children," *Death Education* 5 (1981): 217–220; Michael Peck, "Youth Suicide," *Death Education* 6 (1982): 29–47; and Judith M. Stillion, Eugene E. McDowell, and Jacque H. May, *Suicide Across the Life Span: Premature Exits* (New York: Hemisphere, 1989), pp. 95–100.

Adolescents and young adults may be susceptible to a kind of "contagion," whereby one person's suicide triggers another. So-called *cluster suicides* typically take place within the same locale, are closely related in time, and involve the same method.[55] (Mass suicide can be considered as a special form of clustering.) The term "copycat suicide" is also used to describe cluster suicides, especially when such imitation occurs in connection with the depiction of a suicide in the media. In a study of two Texas clusters, researchers concluded that exposure to reports of suicides may affect individuals who are already at risk. Sensational or romanticized media coverage may foster an affinity with those who die by suicide and confer an aura of celebrity on them. In suicide-susceptible individuals, this could evoke the impression that suicide will claim special—albeit posthumous—attention from their family and peers.

Suicide pacts are a similar phenomenon in that they relate to an arrangement between two or more people who determine to kill themselves at the same time and usually in the same place.[56] Four teenagers in New Jersey, two boys and two girls, decided to die together by sitting in a car with the motor running inside a locked garage. Reportedly, they were distraught over the death of a friend. They were discovered dead the next morning. Two days later, another suicide pact took the lives of two teenage girls in Illinois, who killed themselves in similar fashion.

Another instance of adolescents entering into a suicide pact involved a boy and girl who reportedly became obsessed with the possibility of reincarnation. They crashed their car into their old junior high school building, causing the boy to be killed instantly. The girl, who apparently had last-second doubts about reincarnation, barely survived by diving under the car's dashboard.

An unusual, and "one-sided," version of a suicide pact occurs in the phenomenon of graveside suicides, in which a pathological grief reaction leads a bereaved person to kill himself or herself at the grave of a deceased loved one. Cemeteries are symbolic of the reunion of the living and the dead, and graveside suicides are analogous to a death pact between two persons in which the second death occurs as a reaction to the first, without the knowledge of the first.[57]

Whereas the motives for suicide among adolescents often involve issues relating to family and peer relationships, for young adults the major issues tend to involve academic achievement, courtship, family formation, and career. A desire for perfection, whether socially or self-imposed, can lead to suicide ideation when accomplishments fall short of ideals. One study found an exceptionally high rate of suicide among men ages twenty to thirty-four years who had been recently widowed.[58]

At present, the most promising approaches for reducing suicide among young people appear to be in two major areas: first, providing treatment for disorders that increase the risk of suicide, such as depression, substance abuse, and family conflict; and, second, targeting prevention efforts at high-risk groups, such as affectively disordered young men who exhibit substance abuse and other antisocial behavior. The treatment options include hospitalization for psychologic evaluation, subsequent close outpatient follow-up, removal of firearms and securing of lethal medications from the home, and therapy for any associated psychiatric disorder.[59]

 Romeo and Juliet also embody another popular misconception: that of the great suicidal passion. It seems that those who die for love usually do so by mistake and ill-luck. It is said that the London police can always distinguish, among the corpses fished out of the Thames, between those who have drowned themselves because of unhappy love affairs and those drowned for debt. The fingers of the lovers are almost invariably lacerated by their attempts to save themselves by clinging to the piers of the bridges. In contrast, the debtors apparently go down like slabs of concrete, apparently without struggle and without afterthought.

A. Alvarez, *The Savage God*

Middle Adulthood

Middle age, roughly between ages thirty-five or forty and sixty-five, has been called the "terra incognita" of the human life span. This is a period of "generativity," of giving back to society some of the gifts of nurture and sustenance received during earlier periods of life. It is a time of shifting from valuing physical capabilities to valuing wisdom, of building new relationships as old ones are lost or altered, and of gaining greater flexibility in life. This part of the life span has also been characterized as "middlescence," suggesting that middle age may be as turbulent for many adults as the period of adolescence.

This is also a time of coping with the loss of dreams and ambitions, coming to terms with the realization that one may not reach the goal of being a great artist or writer, a company president, or whatever visionary goal one had for oneself earlier in life. It may not be possible to achieve the aim of attaining a perfect marriage or raising perfect children.

The motive for suicidal behavior may be related to difficulties in an individual's career or marriage. In some cases, the nature of the career itself has a particular impact on suicidal behavior, as may be the case with the relatively high rate of suicide among police officers.[60] The major factors influencing suicide among the middle-aged often include an accumulation of negative life events; affective disorders, especially major depression; and alcoholism.

Late Adulthood

Although teenage suicide attracts more media attention, elderly people are at higher risk for suicide than any other age group. This is especially true of elderly white males, particularly widowers. Some of the reasons given for suicide among those in later adulthood (generally defined as people over age sixty-five) are given in Table 12-7. Major risk factors include being divorced or widowed, living alone, and psychiatric or physical illness.[61] Older people are not as likely to have expressed suicidal ideation or to have made a previous suicide attempt as people in younger age groups.[62] Researchers seem to agree that elderly people who attempt suicide genuinely want to die, unlike younger people, whose attempts are often a cry for help.[63] Suicide may be

T A B L E *12-7* *Risk Factors for Suicide in Late Adulthood*

1. Social isolation and loneliness
2. Boredom, depression, sense of uselessness
3. Loss of purpose and meaning in life after retirement and separation from family and friends
4. Financial hardship
5. Multiple losses of loved ones
6. Chronic illness, pain, incapacitation
7. Alcohol abuse and drug dependence
8. Desire to avoid being a "burden" to others or to end one's life with "dignity"

seen as a rational choice that offers release from severe illness or other hardships of old age. Old age can be a period of increased life satisfaction and ego integrity, or one of dissatisfaction, despair, and disgust.

Double suicides (a type of suicide pact) occur with greatest frequency among the elderly. The typical double suicide involves an older couple with one or both partners physically ill. Heavy alcohol use by one or both partners is also common. Such couples tend to be dependent on each other and isolated from external sources of support. There seems to be a "special chemistry" between couples who die by suicide together, with the more suicidal partner dominant and the more ambivalent partner passive in the relationship.[64]

Contemplating Suicide

Imagine for a moment the progression of thoughts of someone considering suicide. Assume that in an untenable situation suicide seems the only recourse or at least an option to be considered further. The next step might involve formulating some means of killing oneself. At this point the means have not actually been acquired, but possibilities are considered.

Many people have reached this stage—perhaps through mere fantasizing or perhaps with serious intentions. For some, the shock of recognizing that one is harboring such thoughts is enough to force a more life-affirming decision. For others, the next step toward suicide is taken, a step that greatly increases the level of lethality with regard to suicidal intention.

This stage involves acquiring the means to kill oneself, thereby setting into motion the logistics that make suicide a real possibility. A change of mind away from suicide is still possible. Otherwise, the final step in the suicidal progression comes into play: actually using the means that have been acquired to proceed with the suicidal act.

These steps toward lethality have been described as occurring in a definite sequence, but they are likely to be experienced as anything but logical and orderly. Suicide typically involves a complex array of conflicting thoughts and emotions. Nevertheless, recognizing the steps that must be taken to carry out the suicidal act is helpful for understanding both the amount of sustained effort involved and the many decision points at which a change of mind or outside intervention is possible.

Once a suicidal decision is made, a choice must be made concerning the means to be used. Sometimes a particular method is chosen because of the image it represents to the suicidal individual. One might imagine drowning as a dreamy kind of death, a merging back into the universe. Or one might associate an overdose of sleeping pills with the death of a movie star. Whatever one's image of a particular method, the reality is likely to be different. Some people who overdose on drugs do so expecting a quiet or peaceful death. The actual effects of a suicidal drug overdose are usually far from peaceful or serene.

Sometimes a particular method of suicide is chosen for its anticipated impact on survivors. A study of suicide notes found that people using "active"

Resume

Razors pain you;
Rivers are damp;
Acids stain you;
And drugs cause cramp.
Guns aren't lawful;
Nooses give;
Gas smells awful;
You might as well live.

Dorothy Parker

methods of suicide often communicated that rejection was a critical factor in the decision for self-injury.[65] An individual who wants survivors to "really pay for all the grief they caused me" might select a method of suicide that graphically communicates this rage. Someone who did not want to "make a scene" might select a method imagined as being less shocking or disturbing to one's survivors.

Experience and familiarity also influence the choice of suicidal method. An experienced hunter, knowledgeable about rifles, might be inclined to turn to a firearm for suicide because of its accessibility and familiarity. Someone who understands the effects of various drugs might use them to concoct a fatal overdose. In short, the method of suicide tends to reflect a person's experience and state of mind. It may be a spontaneous choice, with the person using whatever lethal devices are readily at hand, or it may be the outcome of deliberate thought and even research.

Choosing a method of killing oneself can be likened to making travel arrangements for a cross-country trip. A person wanting to travel from the West Coast to the East Coast must consider the kinds of transportation available—automobile, train, airplane, and so on. Some of these are quite rapid; others are relatively slow and deliberate. For example, once you board an airplane and it lifts off the runway, there is no opportunity to change your mind and disembark before reaching the destination. However, someone bicycling from coast to coast has innumerable opportunities to decide on a different destination.

Similarly, some methods of suicide offer little hope of changing one's mind after the lethal act is initiated. Once the trigger is pulled on a revolver placed next to one's skull, there's virtually no possibility of altering the likelihood of a fatal outcome. However, the would-be suicide who cuts his or her wrists or takes an overdose of drugs *might* have time to alter an otherwise fatal outcome by seeking medical help. If help is not forthcoming, the likelihood of dying may be as great as with a gunshot wound to the head—but there is a chance of intervention. Among methods used for the suicidal act, then, there is an order of lethality.

Suicide Notes

Suicide notes have been called "cryptic maps of ill-advised journeys."[66] Such notes are usually written in the minutes or hours preceding suicide. Although it is often assumed that nearly all suicides leave notes behind for their survivors, in fact only about one-fourth of suicides write a final message. As a partial record of the mental state of suicides, such notes are of immense interest to scholars and helping professionals, not to mention bereaved families. Imagine yourself in circumstances that would lead to writing a suicide note. What kinds of things would you want to say in your last words to your survivors?

Actual suicide notes display a variety of messages and intentions. Some notes explain to survivors the decision to die by suicide. Others express anger or blame. Conversely, some notes emphasize that the writer's suicide is "no one's fault." The messages in suicide notes range from sweeping statements of the writer's philosophy or credo regarding suicide to detailed listings of practical chores that will require attention after the writer's death. For example, one note instructs survivors, "The cat needs to go to the vet next Tuesday; don't miss the appointment or you'll be charged for it. The car is due for servicing a week from Friday." Suicide notes represent the writer's "last chance to take care of business, decide who gets what, or to make funeral wishes known."[67]

Suicide notes may include expressions of love, hate, shame, disgrace, fear of insanity, self-abnegation; feelings of rejection; explanations for the suicidal act or defense of the right to take one's life; disavowal of a survivor's responsibility for the suicide; instructions for distributing property and possessions. They typically display dichotomies of logic, hostility toward others mixed with self-blame, the use of particular names and specific instructions to survivors, and a sense of decisiveness about suicide. Suicide notes often convey an intense love-hate ambivalence toward survivors, as expressed succinctly in the following note:

> Dear Betty:
>> I hate you.
>>> Love,
>>>> George

This example of ambivalence also points up the dyadic nature of suicide—here involving husband and wife. Suicide notes provide clues about the intentions and emotions that lead a person to suicide, but they rarely tell the whole story—and they often raise more questions than they answer. The message in a suicide note may come as a surprise to survivors who had no hint of the feelings described by the writer. Suicide notes can have a significant effect on survivors. Whether the final message is one of affection or blame, survivors have no opportunity to respond. Suicide represents the ultimate last word.

Suicide Prevention, Intervention, and Postvention

Starting in 1953, Chad Varah, an Anglican clergyman, developed a telephone service in London staffed mainly with volunteers whose goal is to "be-

Suicide Note Written by a Married Man, Age 45

Dear Claudia,

You win, I can't take it any longer. I know you have been waiting for this to happen. I hope it makes you very happy, this is not an easy thing to do, but I've got to the point where there is nothing to live for, a little bit of kindness from you would of made everything so different, but all that ever interested you was the *dollar.*

It is pretty hard for me to do anything when you are so greedy even with this house you couldn't even be fair with that, well it's all yours now and you won't have to see the Lawyer anymore.

I wish you would give my personal things to Danny, you couldn't get much from selling them anyway, you still have my insurance, it isn't much but it will be enough to take care of my debts and still have a few bucks left.

You always told me that I was the one that made Sharon take her life, in fact you said I killed her, but you know down deep in your heart it was you that made her do what she did, and now you have two deaths to your credit, it should make you feel very proud.

Good By Kid

P.S. Disregard all the mean things I've said in this letter, I have said a lot of things to you I didn't really mean and I hope you get well and wish you the best of everything.

Cathy—don't come in.

Call your mother, she will know what to do.

Love,
Daddy

Cathy don't go in the bedroom.

---

friend the suicidal and despairing." This service, called The Samaritans, has become an international movement, and Varah has been hailed as "suicidology's most powerful practitioner" and "the patron saint of the suicide prevention volunteer."[68]

In the United States, a comparable milestone was the founding in 1958 by Norman L. Farberow and Edwin S. Shneidman of the Los Angeles Suicide Prevention Center.[69]

> The importance of the Los Angeles Suicide Prevention Center cannot be overstated in any history of suicide. The work begun in that center by Shneidman and his associates, and expanded upon later when Shneidman became director of the Suicide Center in the National Institute of Mental Health, changed the nation's view of suicide and suicidal behavior. The most important change was a shift away from seeing suicide as an act committed by an insane person to seeing it as an act committed by a person who felt overwhelming ambivalence toward life.[70]

The typical suicide prevention center operates as a telephone-answering center with round-the-clock availability to people in crisis. Hotline services

Graffiti

I find a snapshot
buried in my father's drawer.
A picture of the grandfather I never knew.
Small, stooped yet dignified he stands
beside my brother's wicker pram
surrounded by his family.
My mother tells the story, hidden in the past
of the last time she saw him.
She was big with child, and so allowed to sit
while his two daughters served the sons
who gathered at the table.
Grandma who reigned as always at the head
arranged the seating of those sons
not in the order of their age
but of the weekly wage they earned
and without question brought to her.

I learn that you, mild gentle man
never at home in the new language, the new land,
subdued by failure, each passing year withdrew
further into old world memories, and silence.
Rising that evening from the table, as usual
scarcely noticed as you went to lie down
on your narrow bed, there was no sign, no signal.
Only that as you passed, you bent
with a shy unaccustomed show of tenderness
to murmur "*Liebchen*" and to kiss my mother's head.
She tells me that I leaped and struggled in her womb
when from your room you shattered silence
with a shot. Your life exploding
sudden messages across blank walls in bursts of red.

Maude Meehan

are mainly intended to serve as a short-term resource for people contemplating suicide. The caller's anonymity is respected, and his or her expressed need for help is accepted unquestioningly. Staff members—some of them professionals, many of them volunteers who receive training—use crisis intervention strategies to reduce the caller's stress. Like other public health services, suicide crisis centers vary in their standards of professionalism; overall, however, they have a positive impact on countless people.[71]

Some suicide intervention centers have expanded their services to encompass treatment for a broad range of self-destructive behaviors. For example, the Los Angeles Suicide Prevention Center offers counseling and community services. Low-cost counseling is available for potential suicide victims, as well as for survivors of a friend's or relative's suicide. Clinics provide treatment for depression and drug abuse. Community-based programs for troubled youths have been implemented to help individuals overcome destructive behaviors. The activities of the Los Angeles Suicide Prevention Center exemplify the understanding of suicide as a subset of a larger class of self-destructive behaviors, all of which require attention.

Prevention

There is little reason to be optimistic about the prospect of preventing suicide, at least in the sense of eliminating it from the repertoire of human behaviors. To do so, the causes of human unhappiness and dissatisfaction would have to be eliminated. Efforts to create a social utopia inevitably fall short of perfection. This is not to say that efforts to relieve human suffering are not worth pursuing, only that they are inherently limited.[72]

Education is an essential element in any program of suicide prevention. The lessons to be learned can be applied across the life span and include the following key points: First, it is crucial to acknowledge the reality that life is complex and that all of us will inevitably have experiences of disappointment, failure, and loss in our lives. Second, we can learn to deal with such experiences by developing appropriate coping techniques, including the skills of critical thinking. Individuals "who form a habit early of analyzing situations from a variety of perspectives, of asking appropriate questions, and of testing the reality of their own thinking are far less likely to settle easily into the cognitive inflexibility that focuses on suicide as *the* solution."[73] A corollary of such coping skills involves the cultivation of a sense of humor, especially the ability to laugh at oneself and at life's problems, to see the humor in situations. Finally, it is important to learn how to set appropriate and attainable goals. Positive self-esteem is a preventative against suicide.

Suicide prevention programs are sometimes aimed at particular populations. One native Ojibway/Cree community in Ontario, Canada, for example, the Muskrat Dam community, has organized a group known as Helping Hands to confront suicide.[74] Patterning its program on traditional Native American spiritual values, the Helping Hands project has several primary objectives: (1) instilling a sense of value within the general community population; (2) rebuilding the lives of disturbed youth, thereby enabling them to proceed with direction and purpose; (3) restoring pride and a sense of well-being to members of the community; (4) motivating young people to lead constructive and productive lives; (5) providing life-skills training that can be applied within the family and community; and (6) helping individuals develop good mechanisms for coping with mental health problems. Programs like this, which are sensitive to the needs of a particular community or risk-prone segment of the population, are an important part of suicide prevention.

Another strategy for preventing suicides involves setting up physical barriers in places where suicides are likely to occur. In Washington, D.C., the number-one jump site historically has been the Duke Ellington Bridge, a three-arch concrete structure with pedestrian lookouts. After three suicides from the bridge within a ten-day period, authorities ordered the construction

Käthe Kollwitz, Library of Congress

Despair, a common component of many suicides, is starkly depicted in this lithograph, Nachdenkende Frau, *by Käthe Kollwitz. If the potential victim's warning signals are observed by persons who take steps to provide crisis intervention, the suicidal impulse may be thwarted.*

of an eight-foot-high fence. However, the construction was opposed by neighborhood groups and by the National Trust for Historic Preservation because the fence would block scenic views and diminish the architectural aesthetics of the structure. Further, it was argued, such protective fences do not prevent suicides. The barrier was installed, however, and only one suicide occurred from the Ellington Bridge during the next four years. This is in comparison with ten suicides from the nearby Taft Bridge, which had no fence.[75] Although it appears the fence did prevent some suicides, there are too many variables and unknowns to reach a confident conclusion. It is possible that individuals who would have jumped from the Ellington Bridge simply found other ways to kill themselves. To a suicide-prone person, what is the meaning of a bridge barrier? Could it at least alleviate the sense of crisis that drove an individual to consider suicide? These questions are difficult to answer with certainty, but intervention during a suicidal crisis can reduce its lethality and give the would-be suicide an opportunity to reassess a painful situation and perhaps find a constructive and healthy solution.

Intervention

Suicide intervention emphasizes short-term care and treatment of persons who are actively experiencing a suicidal crisis. The aim is to reduce the lethality of the crisis. Although many suicide intervention programs are called "suicide prevention centers," such programs generally use theories and techniques common to crisis intervention. Antoon Leenaars notes:

> Suicide intervention is optimally practiced in cooperation with a number of colleagues, representing various disciplines, and even individuals outside the helping professions. . . . The treatment of a suicidal person should reflect the learning and response of individuals with different points of view.[76]

The cardinal rule in suicide intervention is to *do something*. The basic questions are "Where do you hurt?" and "How may I help you?"[77] Thus, suicide intervention involves (1) taking threats seriously; (2) watching for clues to suicidal intentions and behaviors; (3) answering cries for help by offering support, understanding, and compassion; (4) confronting the problem by asking questions and being unafraid to discuss suicide with the person in crisis; (5) obtaining professional help to manage the crisis; and (6) offering constructive alternatives to suicide. A key theme of suicide intervention is that talking is a positive step toward resolving the crisis.

Postvention

Suicide *postvention,* a term coined by Edwin Shneidman, refers to the assistance given to *all* survivors of suicide: those who attempt suicide as well as the families, friends, and associates of those who die by suicide. The bereaved survivors of suicide often experience feelings of guilt and self-blame.[78] When

Suicide Note Written by a Single Man, Age 51

Sunday 4:45 PM   Here goes

To who it may concern

Though I am about to kick the bucket I am as happy as ever. I am tired of this life so am going over to see the other side.

Good luck to all.

Benjamin P.

these feelings are not dealt with or are mismanaged, they may lead to dysfunctional relationships and emotional problems. Survivors who actually witnessed someone die by suicide may face special challenges.[79] (Grief issues for people bereaved by suicide are discussed in Chapter 9.)

Cases of "railway suicide" present an important example of postvention for unwitting survivor-victims of someone's suicide. In some cities, there are dozens of cases each year where people jump in front of trains in apparent attempts to kill themselves.[80] For drivers of these trains, such violent and unexpected events can result in a severe posttraumatic stress reaction.[81] Postvention can include not only debriefing and counseling sessions for the affected train drivers, but also preventive efforts designed to reduce the incidence of such suicides. Thus, postvention efforts often play an important role in suicide prevention.

Helping a Person Who Is in Suicidal Crisis

Warnings that an individual is considering suicide may be communicated in a variety of ways. Evans and Farberow point out that suicidal intent may be expressed in four main ways: (1) *verbal direct* ("I will shoot myself if you leave me"), (2) *verbal indirect* ("A life without love is a life without meaning"), (3) *behavioral direct* (for example, a chronically ill person hoarding pills), and (4) *behavioral indirect*.[82] Among the warning signs that fall under this last category, Evans and Farberow mention

1. Giving away prized possessions, making a will, or attending to other "final" arrangements
2. Sudden and extreme changes in eating habits or sleep patterns
3. Withdrawal from friends or family, or other major behavioral changes accompanied by depression
4. Changes in school or job performance
5. Personality changes, such as nervousness, outbursts of anger, or apathy about health or appearance
6. Use of drugs or alcohol

 When I was thirteen months old, my mother killed herself. So I eventually learned, as I learned her maiden name, Georgia Saphronia Collier, and where she was born, Sulphur Springs, Arkansas, and how old she was when she ended her life, twenty-nine. (And good lord, writing these words now, all these years afterward, for the first time in memory my eyes have filled with tears of mourning for her. What impenetrable vessel preserved them?) I didn't know my mother, except as infants know. At the beginning of my life the world acquired a hole. That's what I knew, that there was a hole in the world. For me there still is. It's a singularity. In and out of a hole like that, anything goes.

Richard Rhodes, *A Hole in the World: An American Boyhood*

The recent suicide of a friend or relative, or a history of previous suicide attempts, should also be taken as a warning sign of suicide risk.

A number of commonly held beliefs, or myths, have grown up about suicide and about the kind of person who is likely to die by suicide. Unfortunately, many of these beliefs—being false—are harmful, for they have the effect of depriving the suicidal person of needed help. For example, the notion that people who talk about suicide don't kill themselves has been called the "grand old myth of suicide," one that may be used to excuse the failure to respond to another person's cry for help. In fact, most people who engage in suicidal acts do communicate their intentions to others as hints, direct threats, preparations for suicide, or other self-destructive behaviors. When such cries for help go unheeded by friends, family members, coworkers, or health care personnel, the end result can be tragic.

If a person says, "I feel like killing myself," that statement should not be taken lightly or brushed aside with the quick response, "Oh, well, you'll probably feel better tomorrow." To the person in crisis, there may seem little hope of a "tomorrow" at all. Pay attention to the message being communicated.

Similarly, responding to a suicidal statement with a provocation—"You wouldn't be capable of suicide!"—or with a tone of moral superiority—

Stanley Forman, Boston Herald American

Once a person is this close to the suicidal act, the chance of a successful intervention is usually slight. Fortunately, in this dramatic instance intervention was successful.

"I don't want to hear such unhealthy talk!"—can worsen rather than ease the crisis. A litany of the "good reasons" why the person should not die by suicide may also offer little practical assistance to a person in crisis.

More helpful is listening carefully to exactly what the person is communicating; the tone and context of statements should reveal to the sensitive listener something about the communicator's intent. Often, remarks about suicide are made in an offhand manner: "If I don't get that job, I'll kill myself!" Perhaps the remark is intended as a figure of speech, much as in the joking threat, "I'll kill you for that!" There is a tendency to discount such statements in a culture where "talk is cheap" and "actions speak louder than words."[83] Suicidal threats need to be taken seriously. To do otherwise is to fall prey to the myth that "talking about suicide means the person will not really go through with it." Knowing the patterns of suicidal behavior can help distinguish facts from fallacies. It is also helpful to become acquainted with the crisis intervention resources available in your community.

Lastly, it is important to recognize that no one can take *ultimate* responsibility for another human being's decision to end his or her life. This recognition may go against one's inclination to preserve life, yet there are limits to what can be done to assist another person in crisis. In the short term, it may be feasible to keep someone from taking his or her life. Constant vigilance or custodial care can prevent suicide during an acute suicidal crisis. Over the longer term, however, taking responsibility for preventing someone else's suicide is likely to be unsuccessful. A terminally ill man dying in great pain said to his wife, "You'd better keep my medication out of reach, because I don't want to keep up this struggle any longer." The wife had to decide whether she could take responsibility for whether he would continue to live with pain or end his life by an overdose. After much soul searching, she concluded that, although she had compassion for his predicament, she could not take responsibility for safeguarding his medication, doling out one pill at a time, constantly fearful that he might locate the drugs and attempt suicide anyway.

Not taking responsibility does not mean that one must go to the opposite extreme: "Well, if you're going to kill yourself, then get it over with!" Although there are limits to how much one person can *protect* another, it is always possible to offer life-affirming support and compassion. A person who seems intent on suicide may be hoping for some intervention. The person who is cast in the role of helper in such a drama can affirm the fact that there are choices other than suicide. It is important to sustain or stimulate that person's desire to live. "The desperation of the suicidal moment has to be immense for anyone to carry it through. In the fact of that degree of agony, the only appropriate sentiment is sorrow that life reaches such passes for so many."[84]

One way to help people in crisis is to help them discover what about themselves *can* matter, however small or insignificant it may seem. It is important to find something that matters *to the person*. What are the possibilities of sustaining that value into the present? Asking the person what he or she needs in order to feel worthwhile may be a matter of survival. In the short term, external support can help to ensure survival during the height of crisis.

Suicidal thoughts and behaviors indicate a critical loss of a person's belief that he or she is someone who matters. The feeling that nothing matters, in the sense that one's life is in complete disarray, is not by itself the stimulus for suicide. More important is the person's belief that "*I* don't matter." Those two streams of thought in combination—the sense that the external situation is unsatisfactory and that one does not matter enough to improve it—can be lethal. As has been well stated, "Suicide is a permanent solution to what is most likely a temporary problem."[85]

Further Readings

Fred Cutter. *Art and the Wish to Die.* Chicago: Nelson-Hall, 1983.

Norman L. Farberow, ed. *Suicide in Different Cultures.* Baltimore: University Park Press, 1975.

Keith Hawton and Kees van Heeringen, eds. *The International Handbook of Suicide and Attempted Suicide.* New York: Wiley, 2000.

Kay Redfield Jamison. *Night Falls Fast: Understanding Suicide.* New York: Knopf, 1999.

Thomas Joiner. *Why People Die By Suicide.* Cambridge, Mass.: Harvard University Press, 2005.

Antoon A. Leenaars, ed. *Lives and Deaths: Selections from the Works of Edwin S. Shneidman.* Philadelphia: Brunner-Mazel, 1999.

Edwin S. Shneidman. *Autopsy of a Suicidal Mind.* New York: Oxford University Press, 2004.

Judith Stillion, Eugene McDowell, and Jacque May. *Suicide Across the Life Span: Premature Exits,* 2nd ed. Washington, D.C.: Taylor & Francis, 1996.

Calling attention to the threats posed by threatening encounters with death—accidents, violence, war, terrorism, and emerging epidemic diseases—this drawing depicts victims embraced by Azrael, the angel of death.

CHAPTER 13

Threats of Horrendous Death

The essayist E. B. White said, "To confront death, in any guise, is to identify with the victim and face what is unsettling and sobering."[1] Though we in modern societies tend to be insulated from firsthand experiences of death, we nevertheless encounter it in many guises. We are confronted by subtle, and sometimes dramatic, encounters with death as we engage in our life's pursuits—on our jobs and in our recreational activities, as well as more distantly in the media. The risk of death becomes evident in the form of our encounters with accidents, violence, war, terrorism, and emerging epidemic diseases. Anthony Giddens says, "We live in a world where hazards created by ourselves are as, or more, threatening than those that come from outside."[2]

In 1721, the novelist Daniel Defoe wrote *A Journal of the Plague Year*, a fictional account of the Great Plague that had devastated London in 1665. Drawing on published accounts and his recollection of tales heard during childhood, he vividly depicted a plague-stricken city and the terror of its helpless citizens, confronted by a horror they could not comprehend. What prompted Defoe to write about a plague that had taken place two generations earlier? He knew that a plague again threatened to sweep across Europe, a plague that could potentially cause death and destruction on the scale of the Great Plague of 1665. He wrote to alert a largely indifferent populace to the threat so that precautions could be taken to avert catastrophe.

Today we no longer fear the Black Death. Yet we seem to be confronted by a multidimensioned "plague" that is no less threatening than the more easily distinguishable plague of Defoe's time. Indifference to the threats of death that now plague us only increases the possibility of a disastrous encounter with death.[3]

No one is immune to risks. At home, on the job, or at play, threats confront us in varied ways. After a classroom discussion about various activities, one student said, "It seems we're coming around to the point that everything we do involves risks. You could even stab yourself with your knitting needle!" Perhaps, but usually when we consider activities involving risk, we think of pursuits whose risks we have acknowledged. The possibility of falling backward from a rocking chair while knitting strikes most people as less risky than, say, driving a formula race car or heading out on an expedition to the Himalayas.

Risk Taking

All life involves risks. However, the degree of risk we assume is often subject to our own choices about how we live our lives. In this sense, "Risk refers to hazards that are actively assessed in relation to future possibilities."[4] Our willingness to take risks is influenced by the images communicated in the media and popular culture. Risks frequently accompany our activities in pursuit of the "good life." In some cases, we can exercise considerable choice about the nature and degree of risk to which we are exposed. For example, smoking, drinking, taking drugs, and driving habits involve risks that can be controlled. Think about your own life. What risks do you face in connection with your job, leisure activities, and overall lifestyle? Are any of these risks potentially life-threatening? Do you take "calculated" risks? Are some risks avoidable?

Some occupations involve dangers that most people, if given a choice, would avoid. Examples of such jobs include high-rise window washer, movie stuntperson, explosives expert, test pilot, as well as police officer and firefighter, to name a few examples. Such a list could be continued almost indefinitely. We could add scientists who handle hazardous materials, mine workers, electricians, heavy-equipment operators, and farm workers using toxic pesticides. As you add your own examples to this list, notice whether they involve the risk of sudden death (as from an explosion or a fall from a high-rise building) or long-term exposure to hazardous materials or conditions. Sometimes risks are identified only after years of exposure to a hazardous condition. At other times, people accept risks as something that "comes with the territory," as in the case of the hazards encountered in professional sports like football.[5]

In Japan, job-related stress is legally recognized as a cause of death, affecting possibly thousands of victims a year. Mostly men in their prime working years, these victims of *karoshi*, or sudden death from overwork, are found in virtually every occupational category. *Karoshi* is characterized as a buildup of fatigue caused by "long hours of work that clearly exceed all normal physiological limitations," disruptions in an individual's normal daily rhythms

UPI/Corbis-Bettmann Newsphotos

To keep from tumbling through space at 125 miles per hour, this mile-high skydiver spreads his arms and legs to control his freefall before opening his parachute. Although risks are ever present in our lives, we expose ourselves to many of them by personal choice.

(often related to travel or lengthy commutes to and from the job), and other job-related strains placed on workers.[6] In some occupations, the rise of global markets (with their corresponding time differences) has forced workers to conduct business far into the night after the normal day's work has been completed. The incidence of *karoshi* is accompanied by a growing recognition that exhaustion induced by chronic overwork can aggravate preexisting health problems and harm even the healthiest person—sometimes causing a life-threatening crisis that ends in death.

The possibility of death may also be found in our recreational activities: mountain climbing, parachuting, scuba diving, motorcycle racing, and the like. Activities like these are sometimes characterized as thrill seeking, although this term suggests motives that some participants in these activities would not necessarily ascribe to themselves. Such activities present opportunities to test our limits and develop confidence. Risks can help us learn to deal positively with fear. One mountain climber said, "Without the possibility of death, adventure is not possible."[7]

Although mountain climbing involves obvious risks, two different climbers can relate to these risks in different ways. One climber displays an attitude of abandon that could only be called foolhardy or death defying. The other devotes many hours to obtaining instruction, preparing equipment, conditioning for the climb, and asking advice from more experienced climbers before deciding to set foot on a mountain. In short, risk can be minimized. An activity may be attractive to some individuals *because* of its inherent risk; other people accept the risk as inseparable from other attractive features of the activity. When behavior involves doing dangerous things just for the thrill of it, or as a way to "laugh in the face of death," it may represent an attempt to deny fear or anxiety about death.[8]

Often, we have choices that allow us to control or manage the element of risk. What automobile driver has not chosen at some time to drive just a bit faster in order to arrive at the destination sooner? Accident statistics, as well as common sense, tell us that speeding is risky. Yet we make a trade-off; the added risk is exchanged for the expected benefit of arriving at the destination sooner.

When death results from a high-risk sport or similar activity, it can have a strong impact on others who engage in the same activity. In addition to its effect on those who are most immediately involved (for example, people who had rented equipment or given instruction to the deceased), the death may affect the larger community of people who also participate in the sport. Such a death challenges the assumption that careful, cautious practice of the sport ensures safety.[9] Rumors may circulate that the deceased failed to take necessary precautions or followed an unwise or ill-considered course of action. These rumors attempt to fit what has happened into a manageable scheme

---

 I stared in a horrified trance as a figure appeared, frozen in the air for the briefest moment, its arms outstretched above its head as if in utterly hopeless supplication. Then it continued its relaxed, cart-wheeling descent, with only the thundering crashes attesting to its frightening impacts on the rock. It disappeared into a gully.

"Don't look!" I screamed to my wife, who was, of course, as helplessly transfixed as I was. And the sounds continued. After a time, the figure came into view at the base of the gully and continued down the pile of rubble below. My last view of it is frozen in time. The figure's arm was curled easily over its head, and its posture was one of relaxation, of napping. It drifted down that last boulder field like an autumn leaf down a rippling brook. Then it disappeared under the trees, and only the pebbles continued to clatter down the rock. Suddenly it was very, very still.

I looked down to Debby and had to articulate the obvious: "That was a man," I said quietly, numbly.

William G. Higgins, "Groundfall"

and may serve to mitigate feelings of guilt about having been unable to prevent the death. As a means of coping with such a death, "blaming the victim" may allow others to feel comfortable continuing the activity despite the risks.

Accidents

Do accidents happen because of "fate" or "bad luck"? Are they just the result of chance? If so, it follows that little if anything can be done to prevent them. However, the definition of an accident as an event that occurs "by chance or from unknown causes" can be broadened to include the recognition that an accident may be due to "carelessness, unawareness, or ignorance." Most accidents are events over which individuals do have varying degrees of control. Suppose a gun is brought into a person's household. The presence of the gun increases from zero the chance that there may be an accidental firing of the weapon. Of course, such an accident may never happen. But if a gun were *not* in the home, there would be *no* chance of an accidental firing.

The choices we make affect the probabilities of various kinds of accidents. Sometimes, perhaps jokingly, we call a person *accident-prone* because he or she seems to be involved in accidents more often than others. Although there may be no scientific way to describe a particular personality type as accident-prone, certain factors do affect the probability that an individual will be involved in an accident. It is an established fact that drivers who have been drinking tend to take greater risks than do sober drivers. It is also a fact that a driver's judgment and performance are inversely related to the amount of alcohol consumed, whereas a driver's tendency to overrate his or her driving abilities is directly related to the amount imbibed. About half of the drivers involved in accidents are under the influence of alcohol. Are such accidents the result of mere "chance" or "fate"? When we view accidents as simply random events, it lessens the probability that steps will be taken to prevent their occurrence.

Unsafe conditions that are present in the environment are sometimes called "accidents waiting to happen." Such conditions may be due to negligence or ignorance about the threat they pose to safety. Consider the situation of a swimming pool left unattended and easily accessible to young children; if a toddler happens by, falls into the pool, and is drowned, the owner of the pool and the child's guardians may be judged negligent.

Unsafe environmental conditions are frequently related to the attitudes and value systems of the person or group responsible, or of society as a whole. Accidents caused by drunk driving occur, for example, because of choices made by both the drinking driver and society. Despite the presence of threats to life and health, individuals and society as a whole often fail to take adequate steps to alleviate these problems. While it is naive to believe that the risks we encounter in our lives can be totally eliminated, risks can nonetheless usually be minimized. Lack of attention—or lack of resolve—about taking necessary actions to correct unsafe conditions prompts the question "How negligent must a society be before 'accidental' deaths are tantamount to homicide?"[10]

Violence

Violence is one of the most potent of our encounters with death. It can affect our thoughts and actions even when we have not been victimized ourselves. Potentially, anyone may become its unsuspecting victim. In the most recent year for which statistics are available, over 14,000 murders occurred in the United States; roughly half of the victims were under thirty years old.[11] Almost 30 percent of these murders were related to arguments—over money, property, "romantic" situations, or other issues—whereas slightly less than 15 percent were related to the commission of a felony. Other or "unknown" motives accounted for the remainder. In two-thirds of all murders, guns were used as the murder weapon.[12] In some urban areas, emergency room physicians have reported being besieged with patients whose injuries are identical to wounds incurred by soldiers in combat. These wounds result from semi-automatic assault weapons that fire dozens of bullets per minute at several times the velocity of an ordinary pistol: "Organs that would have been merely grazed or even cleanly pierced by a handgun bullet are exploded by assault weapon fire, requiring massive transfusions of blood."[13]

Young people are disproportionately represented among victims of violence.[14] Among the most troubling aspects of handgun violence, says a report by the American Medical Association, "is the fact that children very often are the victims of fatal gunshot wounds, self-inflicted either intentionally or accidentally, or received as innocent bystanders in scenes of domestic or street violence."[15] Rap musician Ice-T has drawn attention to the troubled condition of his hometown, South Central Los Angeles. Gang warfare, he says, is comparable to other wars: Members of gangs are like "veterans from war," and "thousands of people have died on each side of this bloody battlefield."[16]

Violence resulting from gang warfare has even intruded upon the serene setting of the cemetery. In Anaheim, California, two men died of multiple gunshot wounds they received while visiting the graves of two fellow gang members who had been murdered the previous year.[17] In Detroit, a mother whose sixteen-year-old son had been shot while walking to a neighborhood store with friends told a reporter that similar shootings occurred in her neighborhood every night. "They shoot like it's their job or something," she said. "All I want to do is move to someplace safe," she added. "Someplace where there's no shooting on your block or the next block over. That's all. That's good enough. Just two safe blocks."[18]

For some, guns are more than just weapons; they are potent symbols of power and energy. One young man said:

> When you are carrying a gun, I think other people can tell. Some kind of way a gun makes you light up. If you don't have a gun on you, a dude might mug you down. People don't mug you if you've got your gun on. They can detect something about you that wasn't there before.[19]

Children who witness violence have been called "silent victims"; they appear physically unharmed, but are nevertheless emotionally affected as they

At Columbine High School in Littleton, Colorado, distraught students grieve the violent deaths of friends in the aftermath of a shooting rampage carried out by two schoolmates who murdered 13 and wounded 23 before killing themselves.

The deepest grave on earth can never contain the violent death of a single decent soul.

John Nichols, *American Blood*

hear gunshots outside their homes, witness shootings on the playground, or have a family member (often an older sibling) involved with violence.[20] In describing a community-based approach to violence prevention in Richmond, California, Larry Cohen and Susan Swift remark:

> Interpersonal violence, although most concentrated among youth in densely populated, low-income communities, affects everyone in the United States. An awareness of violence permeates the environment, determining where people prefer to live, where they shop, how they respond to strangers on the streets, where they walk and drive, and how late at night they stay outside of their homes. Unlike any other environmental threat, violence has turned into a public health epidemic.[21]

Random Violence

The most threatening of violent acts are those that occur without apparent cause, when the victim is selected seemingly at random, thus heightening anxiety at the possibility that violence could unexpectedly confront anyone. A few years ago, in California, a number of murders were committed by someone whom the police dubbed the Trailside Killer because the killings occurred along several popular woodland trails. A woman who usually jogged every morning along one of these trails expressed feelings of being personally threatened because these violent acts had taken place "so close to home." In an area where she had previously felt safe and secure, she now felt fearful. Although she had no direct experience of the killings, she was nevertheless victimized by the violence because it occurred in her own familiar environment.

One woman described a potential encounter with death that began innocently enough when she answered a knock on her door. Recognizing a former schoolmate whom she hadn't seen in a long time, she invited him in and they began to chat. She began to feel uneasy, although she couldn't say why. About two months later, she heard on the news that her visitor had been arrested (and was subsequently convicted) for the brutal murders of several young women. The murders had been committed around the time of his unexpected visit. Recalling the experience, this woman commented, "I sometimes wonder how close we may be to death at times and just not realize it. It seems we really never know." In reviewing the motivations of serial killers, Dana DeHart and John Mahoney conclude that "one of the more disturbing aspects of serial murder is that virtually everyone is at some risk. Even cautious and circumspect persons are not safe from a serial killer; the victims need not provoke or even be acquainted with the killer."[22]

TABLE *13-1*   *Factors Favoring Violence*

Anything that physically or psychologically separates the potential killer from the victim. For example, the use of a gun leads to a concentration on the means (pulling the trigger) rather than the end result (the death of a person). Psychological separation occurs when the victim is perceived as fundamentally different from oneself.

Anything that permits the killer to define murder as something else, such as "making an example of the victim," "making the world safe for democracy," "implementing the final solution," or "exterminating the terrorists."

Anything that fosters perceiving people as objects or as less than human. This happens when victims become "cases," "subjects," or "numbers," as well as when the killing occurs from a distance as with high-altitude bombing or submarine warfare.

Anything that permits one to escape responsibility by blaming someone else: "I was just carrying out orders."

Anything that encourages seeing oneself as debased or worthless: "If I'm treated like a rat, I might as well act like one. What have I got to lose?"

Anything that reduces self-control or that is believed to have this effect: alcohol, mind-altering drugs, hypnotism, mass frenzy, and the like.

Anything that forces a hasty decision or that does not permit time for "cooling off." That is, a situation may force one to decide to shoot or not to shoot with no opportunity for deliberation.

Anything that encourages a person to feel above or outside the law: The notion that rank, prestige, wealth, or the like makes it possible for one to "get away with murder."

Source: Adapted from Robert Kastenbaum and Ruth Aisenberg, *The Psychology of Death: Concise Edition* (New York: Springer, 1976), pp. 291–294.

Steps Toward Reducing Violence

The term *psychic maneuvers* has been used to describe the factors that facilitate murder and other homicidal acts (see Table 13-1). You may find it interesting to review this list three times. First, consider how each of these psychic maneuvers might function in your own life. Notice that they do violence to ourselves and others even when they function far more subtly than the overt act of homicide. Second, note how these psychic maneuvers function within society, how they contribute to violence between individuals and between groups. The third time, consider how each of these psychic maneuvers may be a dysfunctional strategy found in conflicts between nations.

Victims sometimes play a role in encouraging violent acts against themselves. Homicide investigators have found that victims are not always as innocent as might initially be assumed. Consider the example of a husband who has been repeatedly threatened by his angry wife wielding a loaded revolver. His response to this threat is, "Go ahead, you might just as well kill me." What can be said about his role as a victim in such circumstances? Or consider another such incident: A daughter, overhearing her parents arguing, tries to intercede but is told by her mother, "Never mind, honey, let him kill me." After the daughter leaves the house to seek assistance, her father obtains a revolver from another room and shoots and kills the girl's mother.

Investigators note that, during domestic strife, wives have made statements like "What are you going to do, big man, kill me?" coupled with dares like "You haven't got the guts." Such statements combine "elements of seduction and lethality."[23] In some instances, there are indications that the victim not only seemed to be "asking for it," but also was the one responsible for escalating the conflict to the level of physical violence.

While recognizing that victims sometimes do contribute to bringing violence on themselves, we should be cautious about placing blame on victims. Lula Redmond underscores the fact that labeling victims as bad, careless, seductive, "with the wrong crowd," or as somehow "asking for it" denies the reality that everyone is vulnerable to victimization.[24] Blaming the victim is a convenient, albeit erroneous, way to overcome one's own sense of vulnerability and thereby regain a sense of personal security. If suitable "explanations" can be found to account for a victim's demise, they offer convincing evidence that a similar encounter *could never* happen in one's own life.

Far more effective than blaming the victim is to understand the factors that favor violence and take action to reduce their presence in our own lives and in society as a whole. Violence is reduced when residents of a community work together to create a safe and orderly environment and when neighbors themselves take a measure of responsibility for maintaining social order.[25] In addition, the sense of social isolation that helps breed violence is counteracted when families take care to communicate positive community values.[26] Cohen and Swift argue that "stopping the momentum of violence requires a 'critical mass' of people who are willing to speak out and to work together to change the structures and policies that frame the way we live."[27] In seeking ways to reduce the level of violence, it is useful to consider the factors that tend to *prevent* violent behaviors (see Table 13-2).

T A B L E 13-2   *Guidelines for Lessening the Potential for Violence*

1. Avoid the use of prejudicial, dehumanizing, or derogatory labels, whether applied to oneself or to others.
2. Avoid or eliminate conditions that underlie dehumanizing perceptions of oneself or others.
3. Promote communication and contact between potential adversaries, emphasizing similarities and common goals rather than differences.
4. Refrain from using physical punishment as the primary means of discipline.
5. Champion the good guys.
6. Teach children that violence is not fun, cute, or smart. Emphasize that they are responsible for their behavior.
7. Identify and foster the human resources that can provide alternatives to violence. For example, promote sharing among children, and encourage them to think before engaging in impulsive and possibly hostile actions against others.
8. Reduce the attractiveness of violence in the mass media.

Source: Adapted from Robert Kastenbaum and Ruth Aisenberg, *The Psychology of Death: Concise Edition* (New York: Springer, 1976), pp. 296–297.

War

Within the context of ordinary human interaction, our moral and legal codes stand in strict opposition to killing. In war, however, killing is not only accepted, but may be heroic. War abrogates conventional sanctions against killing by substituting a different set of conventions and rules about moral conduct. The expectation that one will kill and, if necessary, die for one's country is a concomitant of war. As Arnold Toynbee says, "The fundamental postulate of war is that, in war, killing is not murder."[28]

In Dalton Trumbo's classic antiwar novel, *Johnny Got His Gun*, we find a veteran "without arms legs ears eyes nose mouth" who devises a means of communicating with the outside world by "tapping out" messages on his pillow with his head.[29] He asks to be taken outside, where he can become an "educational exhibit" to teach people "all there was to know about war." He thinks

At Buchenwald, near Weimar, Germany, a few of the dead are piled in a yard awaiting burial following the invasion by the Allies. Starvation and disease due to unsanitary living conditions, as well as the incessant torture of prisoners, caused an average of two hundred deaths each day at this infamous Nazi concentration camp.

Col. Rex L. Dively, Signal Corps Photo

to himself, "That would be a great thing to concentrate war in one stump of a body and to show it to people so they could see the difference between a war that's in newspaper headlines and liberty loan drives and a war that is fought out lonesomely in the mud somewhere, a war between a man and a high explosive shell."

Chivalrous notions of combat, with mounted men-at-arms meeting gallantly to do battle on an uninhabited hill or plain, have been replaced in modern times by the reality of mass technological warfare. According to the International Red Cross, nine out of ten casualties in modern warfare are civilians—men, women, and children who simply "got in the way of somebody's war."[30] According to a United Nations report, during the 1990s, nearly 2 million children were killed and another 6 million were seriously injured or permanently disabled because of military conflicts.[31] The report goes on to say that, in the year 2000, an estimated 300,000 child soldiers, girls as well as boys, were forcibly recruited as combatants in 30 conflicts around the world. In the so-called postwar period since 1945, more than 20 million people have died in more than 100 conflicts, and another 60 million or more have been wounded, imprisoned, separated from their families, and forced to flee their homes or their countries.

In addition to the death and injury directly related to war, a worldwide "militarism" is singled out as having a variety of deleterious health effects, including poverty, environmental damage, social unrest, political instability, national debt, and military oppression.[32]

Technological Alienation

When we recall the epic battles of Achilles and Agamemnon, or of the legendary King Arthur and the Knights of the Round Table, or of the samurai in medieval Japan, we encounter a view of warfare as heroic. The enemy is seen as a worthy opponent with whom one is engaged in a "metaphysic of struggle."[33] This sense of chivalry is now largely absent from warfare, due in significant measure to technological advances in weaponry, leaving "only the abstract virtue of obedience to duty." Instead of individual initiative and courage, modern warfare emphasizes bureaucratic cooperation and calculation.

"Technological alienation" has been termed the "most characteristic feature of the modern war machine."[34] During the Spanish Civil War, the world was horrified by the aerial bombing of the Basque town of Guernica, causing the indiscriminate slaughter of civilians of both sexes and of all ages. Although it was not until World War I that warfare involved civilians on a large scale, by the end of World War II, civilian victims outnumbered military casualties. "The no-holds-barred incendiary and atomic bomb attacks on Japan marked the removal of all moral restraints. Total war had come at last, with no mercy, no quarter, and no limit to the capacity for destruction."[35] Distinctions between combatants and noncombatants had been blurred, if not erased.

Early warfare had limits: the bow and arrow, the bullet from a gun, the artillery shell. These conventional limits of warfare were radically altered with the advent of the atomic bomb, unleashed on Hiroshima in August 1945.

"Disarmament Talks," © 1987 Ralph Steadman, Swann Collection, Library of Congress

> By the time we reach the atom bomb, the ease of access to target and the instant nature of macro-impact [large-scale destruction] mean that both the choice of city and the identity of the victim have become completely randomized, and human technology has reached a final platform of self-destructiveness. . . . At Hiroshima and Nagasaki, the "city of the dead" is finally transformed from a metaphor into a literal reality.[36]

The bomb fell near the center of the city, and its explosive force, heat, and radiation engulfed all of Hiroshima. A soldier who saw the city the next day left this description:

> I could find nothing but a wide stretch of burned ruins with a lot of debris. Where had the former city of Hiroshima gone? . . . The seven rivers that ran through the city were full of corpses, soot, smoke, and charred driftwood, stretching like black lines through Hiroshima, which was reduced to ashes.[37]

The characteristic human response to such carnage is one of *psychic numbing*. Exposed to mass death, the self-protective psychological response is to become insensitive and unfeeling. Robert Lifton and Eric Olson observe that "jet pilots who coolly drop bombs on people they never see tend not to feel what goes on at the receiving end."[38] They add that "those of us who watch such bombing on TV undergo a different though not unrelated desensitization." Confronted by the death-dealing potential of modern weaponry, it is worth remembering the story of Dalton Trumbo's veteran, who wanted to be a living exhibit of the ravaging, destructive effects of war. His request was denied, the story explains, because "he was a perfect picture of the future and they were afraid to let anyone see what the future was like."

What kinds of images are evoked when you hear or read about combat and warfare? What makes the encounter with death in war different from other encounters with death? Images of the dead and dying, the emaciated, of terrified children, and ravaged cities seem not to fit the codes of noble sacrifice.[39] Glenn Vernon observes that "confrontation with wartime killing may be one of the most difficult experiences of those who have been taught to avoid killing."[40]

The Conversion of the Warrior

War activates a special set of conventions that make it psychologically possible for individuals to go against the grain of what they have learned about right and wrong—to put aside ordinary rules of moral conduct. As long as the combatant "keeps more or less faithfully to the recognized rules," Toynbee says, "most of humankind have been willing to alter their moral sense in such a way as to regard the killer in war as 'being righteous.'"[41] One convention of warfare, Toynbee points out, is to dress the part. The psychological effect of the uniform is that it "symbolizes the abrogation of the normal taboo on killing fellow human beings: it replaces this taboo by a duty to kill them."

A Marine who fought in the Gulf War describes the moments before combat:

> We are all afraid, but show this in various ways—violent indifference, fake ease, standard-issue bravura. We are afraid, but that doesn't mean we don't want to fight. It occurs to me that we will never be young again. . . . The supposedly anti-war films have failed. Now is my time to step into the newest combat zone.[42]

Joel Baruch, a combat veteran, says, "Changes in personality and mood are rooted in the special climate of the combat zone. These mutations evolve in such a wily fashion that the person who undergoes them is not aware of the alterations himself."[43] The conventions of war are mind- and personality-altering. Here is Baruch's account of his first encounter with death on the battlefield:

> Stone dead, he was. Eyes wide open, staring at nothing. A thin veneer of blood curling at the corner of his lips. Two gaping holes in his chest. Right leg half gone. My first combat fatality. A lifeless body where only moments before a heart beat its customary seventy pumps in one orbit of the minute hand. It is one thing to hear about death; to watch it happen is quite another. I went over to the nearest tree and vomited my guts out.

By his next experience of combat death, however, Baruch began to question whether he was becoming callous and unfeeling: "I was becoming impervious to the death of my fellow soldiers, and, in addition, I was negating the possibility of my own . . . demise." Another veteran explains:

> Social context is much more important than most people realize. We pretty much live within the boundaries of one social context. If you lived in a different society, you would consider a different set of behaviors as normal. What's bewildering and frightening in the combat situation is how quickly "normal" can change.[44]

Each of us experiences differences in our behavior according to the social context. How we behave among our relatives is likely to be different from how we behave among strangers or business associates. Usually, such differences are subtle and rarely meet head on. The contradictory values that exist for the soldier in combat, however, require what the veteran just quoted calls "a much more total 'schizophrenia'":

> When you're there you don't really remember what it's like to come back into the social context of a society where killing is abhorrent. And, when you come back home, you don't really remember the context of the combat situation, except perhaps in your nightmares.

When societies reflect on their participation in war, they often speak in terms of patriotism, the heroism of fighting for one's country, the need to defend the things that are held dear. When we listen to the words of those who have experienced combat, however, we hear a different value system at work. We hear about individuals fighting for their lives.

 The third plane came in, skimming the treetops, engine screeching. Two napalm canisters spun down from the Skyhawk's bomb rack into the tree line, and the plane pulled into a barrel-rolling climb as the red-orange napalm bloomed like an enormous poppy.

"Beautiful! Beautiful!" I said excitedly. "They were right on 'em."

The napalm rolled and boiled up out of the trees, dirty smoke cresting the ball of flame. The enemy mortar fire stopped. Just then, three Viet Cong broke out of the tree line. They ran one behind another down a dike, making for the cover of another tree line nearby. "Get 'em! Get those people. Kill 'em!" I yelled at my machine-gunners, firing my carbine at the running, dark-uniformed figures two hundred yards away. The gunners opened up, walking their fire toward the VC. The bullets made a line of spurts in the rice paddy, then were splattering all around the first enemy soldier, who fell to his knees. Letting out a war whoop, I swung my carbine toward the second man just as a stream of machine-gun tracers slammed into him. I saw him crumple as the first Viet Cong, still on his knees, toppled stiffly over the dike, behind which the third man had taken cover. We could see only the top of his back as he crawled behind the dike. What happened next happened very quickly, but in memory I see it happening with an agonizing slowness. It is a ballet of death between a lone, naked man and a remorseless machine. We are ranging in on the enemy soldier, but cease firing when one of the Skyhawks comes in to strafe the tree line. The nose of the plane is pointing down at a slight angle and there is an orange twinkling as it fires its mini-gun, an aerial cannon that fires explosive 20-mm bullets so rapidly that it sounds like a buzz saw. The rounds, smashing into the tree line and the rice paddy at the incredible rate of one hundred per second, raise a translucent curtain of smoke and spraying water. Through this curtain, we see the Viet Cong behind the dike sitting up with his arms outstretched, in the pose of a man beseeching God. He seems to be pleading for mercy from the screaming mass of technology that is flying no more than one hundred feet above him. But the plane swoops down on him, fires its cannon once more, and blasts him to shreds. As the plane climbs away, I look at the dead men through my binoculars. All that remains of the third Viet Cong are a few scattered piles of bloody rags.

Philip Caputo, *A Rumor of War*

A soldier who fought in the Iraq War with the 1st Infantry Division said, "I don't think we should be fighting a war there for any reason whatsoever, but . . . there's no politics involved when it actually happens, when it comes down to you having to exchange rounds with someone."[45] Heroic intentions and patriotic feelings may be reasons for donning the uniform, but in combat the emphasis is likely to be on survival.[46]

Genocide

Genocide, defined as the effort to destroy an entire nation or human group, occurred with horrendous results during the twentieth century.[47] Between 1941 and 1945, Nazi Germany exterminated 6 million Jews in the Holocaust and killed another 5 million people deemed to be political opponents, mentally ill, retarded, or somehow "genetically inferior." When the Khmer Rouge came to power in Cambodia, 2 million Cambodians died from execution and starvation, an example of "autogenicide," a group killing its own people. After the assassination of the president of Rwanda in 1994, up to a million people, mainly members of the Tutsi tribe, were massacred in an attempt to exterminate them.

In the wake of traumatic bereavement from such losses, the repression of grief may contribute to further genocide by perpetuating a cycle of violence focused on revenge. Colin Murray Parkes says, "It is not unreasonable to hope that any action to encourage people to grieve and express their discontent in controlled and safe ways might reduce the risk of uncontrolled violence."[48]

Coping with the Aftermath of War

Combatants do not necessarily resolve their losses merely by leaving the war zone or being discharged from military service. In the aftermath of war, many experience symptoms such as numbness, irritability, depression, relationship problems, and guilt at having survived when others did not. They may experience nightmares and flashbacks to traumatic scenes. Some "experience positive excitement when reviving memories of mortal risk and killing."[49] The tension and hyper-alertness of being in combat can produce an addictive "high."

The term *posttraumatic stress disorder* (PTSD) has been used to describe such symptoms, although such reactions have also been termed "delayed grief syndrome" or "posttraumatic grief disorder."[50] Known as "shell shock" during World War I and "battle fatigue" during World War II, PTSD first became prominent in the 1970s in the aftermath of the Vietnam War.

Psychiatrist Jonathan Shay finds parallels between the grief and rage experienced by modern combat veterans and the description in Homer's *Iliad* of similar symptoms experienced by warriors who fought in the Trojan Wars 3000 years ago.[51] Shay says, "There have been technological changes, but there have been no changes to the human mind and heart and soul." The chilling atrocities committed by Achilles in a berserk rage following the battlefield death of his friend Patroclus are echoed in episodes of grief-driven combat violence such as the My Lai massacre during the Vietnam War. One of the lessons to be learned from Homer's *Iliad,* says Shay, is that soldiers should be

Rites of Passage

. . . As a psychiatrist who has worked with Vietnam veterans, I know all too well the long-term effects of wartime traumas. Ten and fifteen years after the events, there remain nightmares, fears, depression and, most fundamentally, failures of loving in veterans of combat. The timelessness of the unconscious does not bend to political realities. National treaties mark the beginning, not the end, of the psychic work of mastery.

Primitive societies intuitively knew the value of cultural ceremonies that marked the end of hostilities. Rites of passage were provided for the soldiers and the society to make the transition from the regression of combat to the structure of integrated living. These rituals acknowledged and sanctioned the otherwise forbidden acts of war. They thanked the soldier for his protection, forgave him his crimes and welcomed him back to life.

Our failure to provide such a cleansing for our warriors and ourselves has left our culture struggling for closure. It has as well made the task of intrapsychic mastery so much more difficult for the individual soldier.

Harvey J. Schwartz, M.D.

allowed to grieve: "Snatching bodies off the battlefield in black bags and spiriting them back to stateside mortuaries without permitting comrades to mourn the fallen is profoundly damaging to survivors."

Combat leaves haunting memories. After the shooting stops, the mind must sort out the almost incomprehensible facts of war. One helicopter door gunner told his friends to stop boasting about achieving high casualties after he saw dead enemy troops for the first time. "It's different when you see their faces, with blood coming out of their wounds," he said.[52]

Some combat veterans find solace and renewed self-respect through innovative means of coming to terms with their experiences.[53] On Memorial Day, 1990, a group of Vietnam veterans began a 700-mile walk from Angel Fire, New Mexico, to the Pine Ridge Indian Reservation in South Dakota. At the end of their journey, the veterans (who called themselves "The Last Patrol") were welcomed by several hundred Oglala Sioux and invited to participate in traditional ceremonies for returning warriors. After participating in honoring dances, sweat-lodge rituals, and smoking the sacred pipe of the Oglala Sioux, one veteran had one of his few nights of restful sleep after years of nightmares and said, "This is a new life for many of us. . . . [This] was an opportunity to eliminate the things that have tortured us." Other veterans who participated in retreats led by the Vietnamese Buddhist monk Thich Nhat Hanh later reported that the Buddhist walking meditation reminded them of "walking point." Traumatic memories surfaced and were discussed during group sessions. One veteran said that the hours of silent meditation with the Vietnamese Buddhists "dissolved his mistrust of the 'enemy.'"

Since its dedication in 1982, the Vietnam Veterans Memorial in Washington, D.C., has become a "wailing wall" for the families and friends of the more than 58,000 whose names are engraved there, as well as for those who served and survived. Many visitors have left mementos, ranging from a pair of old cowboy boots found at the base of the Memorial shortly after its dedication, to teddy bears, baseball caps, newspaper clippings, diaries, and tear-stained letters. One of the first letters was left at the Memorial by the mother of an Army sergeant whose death had occurred nearly fifteen years before her visit. In the letter, she described finding her son's name for the first time:

> We had been looking for about a half-hour when your father quietly said, "Honey, here it is." As I looked to where his hand was touching the black wall, I saw your name, William R. Stock.
>
> My heart seemed to stop. I felt as though I couldn't breathe. It was like a bad dream. I felt as though I was freezing. My teeth chattered. God, how it hurt.[54]

The families of men and women in the military make sacrifices that may go unnoticed. In recalling her odyssey as the wife of a Marine Corps officer, Marian Novak says, "I watched my husband train for war; I waited thirteen months for him to return from it; and then I waited another fifteen years for him to truly come home."[55] War creates a "phantom army" that is composed of the spouses, children, parents, and friends who serve invisibly at home. Lee Woodruff, whose husband was seriously injured during the Iraq War, said,

> I bristled when, in an effort to make me feel better, people would say to me, "Things happen for a reason" or "God doesn't give you more than you can handle." It felt like greeting-card philosophy to try to package something so complex into bite-sized chunks.[56]

The euphemistic term "collateral damage" encompasses not only the civilian deaths that occur in a war zone, but also the grief experienced by families whose lives are disrupted by the loss or injury of loved ones serving in the war zone.

Making War, Making Peace

According to Karl von Clausewitz, a nineteenth-century military writer whose *On War* is considered a classic study, war is the continuation of political policy by other means. Generally speaking, war is defined as a condition of hostile conflict between opposing forces, each of which believes its vital interests are at stake and seeks to impose control on the opposing side through the use of force. Joining with others against a common enemy creates a sense of community and connectedness. Human beings may have an innate tendency to divide the world into "us" and "them." Sam Keen says:

> In the beginning we create the enemy. Before the weapon comes the image. We *think* others to death and then invent the battle-axe or the ballistic missiles with which to actually kill them. Propaganda precedes technology. . . . It seems unlikely that we will have any considerable success in controlling warfare unless we come to understand the logic of political paranoia, and the process of creating propaganda that justifies our hostility.[57]

Through their analysis of news stories, Debra Umberson and Kristin Henderson distinguished four major themes in how media reports generate public

Mickey Sanborn, U.S. Air Force Photo

Among the most poignant losses that can be experienced in adult life are those related to war. The Vietnam Veterans Memorial in Washington, D.C., is a focal point for coping with the grief of individual as well as national losses. For many who fought the war, as well as for other survivors, the effects are pervasive and felt daily. Here, visitors reflect on the names of the individuals engraved on the face of the black wall of the Memorial, following its official dedication in November 1982.

TABLE *13-3*   *Faces of the Enemy*

- The enemy as stranger. "Us" versus "Them."
- The enemy as aggressor. "Good" versus "Evil."
- The faceless enemy. "Human beings" versus "Dehumanized barbarians."
- The enemy as enemy of God; war as applied theology. "Holy" versus "Unholy."
- The enemy as barbarian (threat to culture, heathen, pagan).
- The greedy enemy (appetite for empire).
- The enemy as criminal, as committer of atrocities, as torturer (anarchists, terrorists, outlaws).
- The enemy as torturer or sadist.
- The enemy as rapist, desecrator of women and children. ("Woman as bait and trophy.")
- The enemy as beast, reptile, insect, germ. (Gives sanctions for extermination.)
- The enemy as death. ("The ultimate threat.")
- The enemy as worthy opponent. ("Heroic warfare or chivalry.") Examples: The epic battles of Achilles and Agamemnon, King Arthur and the Knights of the Round Table, the samurai in medieval Japan.

Source: Adapted from Sam Keen, *Faces of the Enemy: Reflections of the Hostile Imagination* (San Francisco: Harper and Row, 1986).

support for war while facilitating denial of death: (1) rhetorical devices that distance the reader from death and encourage denial of death in the war, (2) official denial of responsibility for war-related deaths and reassurance to the public that death would be "minimal," (3) rhetoric that prepares the public for death in war and to view the deaths as just, and (4) ambiguity and uncertainty about the actual death toll from the war.[58]

If we come to view other human beings as hostile, even their ambiguous actions may be perceived as threatening. When we act to defend ourselves against this perceived threat, their reaction confirms our initial assumption (see Table 13-3). It is important to recognize, however, that sometimes our images of the enemy are accurate. Keen says, "Short of utopia there are real enemies. It is a luxury of the naive and sheltered to think that right thinking, good intentions, and better communication techniques will turn all enemies into friends."[59]

Viewed symbolically, war allows us to ritually affirm our own deathlessness by killing the enemy who *is* Death. This idea is reflected in the promise made by some religions that warriors who fall in battle go directly to Valhalla or Paradise. "War as the bringer of death," says Keen, "wears the face of horror, but also of ecstasy."[60]

Terrorism

Speaking to the often random nature of terrorist acts, someone said, "It is not the bullet with my name on it that worries me; it is the one that says, To whom it may concern."[61] In this sense, terrorism is like other homicidal acts that occur between strangers. Yet many terrorist acts have more in common with warfare, which aims toward specific targets and goals. The complex nature of terrorism is apparent in the fact that, although there are more than one hundred definitions of terrorism, no single definition is universally accepted.

Among the common elements of terrorism is the use or threat of violence to create fear among both its direct victims and a wider audience. Even when apparently random, the victims and locations of terrorist attacks are often chosen for their shock value. The aim is to destroy the sense of security people normally feel in familiar places. Thus, terrorists frequently target schools, shopping centers, bus stops, restaurants, night clubs, and other locations where people gather. The definition developed by the U.S. State Department emphasizes the indiscriminate nature of terrorism, describing it as "premeditated, politically motivated violence perpetrated against noncombatant targets by sub-national groups or clandestine agents, usually intended to influence an audience."[62]

Although this definition captures key points, it is incomplete for several reasons. First, many terrorist acts do not target "noncombatants," or civilians, but rather are aimed against military or police forces. Second, terrorist acts may be perpetrated by states as well as "sub-national groups." Third, the phrase "politically motivated" is insufficient, because much of the worst terrorism has religious or quasi-religious sources. Another criticism is that such definitions tend to treat terrorism as a type of *crime* rather than defining it as *war*.[63] The proposal to treat terrorism as war is not universally accepted, however, because war generally has been defined as "a state of usually open and declared armed hostile conflict between states or nations."[64] Terrorist acts do not fit this definition. Furthermore, war is generally viewed as an activity conducted according to socially recognized rules. In other words, war is a social construct that is recognized in custom and law. The rules of war are spelled out in international agreements like the Geneva Convention, which describes such matters as the treatment of prisoners of war and of the sick, wounded, and dead in battle. In contrast, terrorism occurs outside the boundaries of social sanctions that regulate conduct between individuals and between groups.[65]

The debate about how to define terrorism, and whether it should be classified and prosecuted as a criminal act or an act of war, is being shaped by changes in the methods and manner of terrorist activities in the recent past. Terrorism has been called the "weapon of the weakest," but, increasingly, terrorists make use of sophisticated weapons and strategies. To attract publicity designed to generate widespread fear, they engage in dramatic and high-profile attacks, including hijackings, hostage takings, kidnappings, car bombings, and, frequently, suicide bombings. Although terrorism is not a new phenomenon in human affairs, having been carried out to achieve psychological and strategic goals at least since the Roman Empire, there is an element of the "new" with respect to both weaponry and how it is being used. The release of nerve gas into a Tokyo subway in 1995 by the doomsday cult *Aum Shinrikyo* is an example of the escalation of destructive power brought about through terrorists' use of weapons of mass destruction.

In the *Encyclopedia of Terrorism,* Cindy Combs and Martin Slann highlight some of the key features of present-day terrorism by observing that it is "a synthesis of war and theater, a dramatization of the most proscribed kinds of violence—that which is perpetrated on innocent victims—played before an audience in the hope of creating a mood of fear."[66] In achieving their goals, terrorists often rely on *amplification effect,* whereby their actions are broadcast through the media to a much larger audience than they would have in just the location where the action is occurring, thus giving their acts greater significance. From this standpoint, the media's interest in sensational news and the terrorists' desire for publicity are linked.

Terrorist attacks may seem to be directed at random targets, but they are also directed at politically or culturally important targets. The goals of terrorism are aided by the element of surprise and the pervasive sense of fear felt by the threatened population. According to terror management theory, human beings are confronted by the challenge to live with awareness of the inevitability of death while managing its potential (and ultimate) threat in such a way that life is nonetheless embraced as meaningful and significant.[67] Individuals manage the threat of death by adopting cultural worldviews, whether religious or secular, that lend a sense of continuity, permanence, and significance to life. This works quite nicely until some dramatic and unexpected threat to our well-being intrudes, shattering our assumptions about safety and security. In this sense, acts of terrorism threaten our assumptive world, heightening our awareness of mortality and increasing our feelings of vulnerability.

September 11, 2001

The events that culminated in the bloodiest day on U.S. soil since the Civil War began shortly before 9:00 A.M. on Tuesday, September 11, 2001, when terrorists piloted a hijacked jetliner into the North Tower of the World Trade Center (WTC) in New York City.[68] Roughly fifteen minutes later, a second airplane crashed into the South Tower of the WTC, erasing any doubt about whether the first crash was a horrible accident or an intentional act. As the nation went on alert and emergency personnel responded to the disaster in New York, a third jet was flown into the Pentagon, a symbol of U.S. military power, just outside Washington, D.C., and a fourth jet crashed into a field near Shanksville, Pennsylvania, a result of passengers on the flight thwarting the terrorists' apparent intentions to strike the U.S. Capitol or White House. It was determined that the hijackings and suicide attacks were perpetrated by nineteen militants associated with an Islamic extremist group known as al-Qaeda.

The most dramatic and devastating result of the attacks was the collapse of the 110-story Twin Towers of the WTC, killing more than 2400 workers and hundreds of firefighters. For thirty years the Twin Towers had stood above the streets of New York City. Now, in just one morning, they had been reduced to a few skeletal fragments because of a horrific attack by men wielding box cutters. In bringing down the Twin Towers and severely damaging the Pentagon, the terrorists had struck at the symbolic heart of the nation's economic

This photograph, taken by a tourist from Arkansas, shows United Flight 175 seconds before it crashed into the South Tower of the World Trade Center. In the background, smoke rises from fires caused by the earlier crash of American Flight 11 into the North Tower. Less than two hours later, both of the 110-story Twin Towers suffered catastrophic collapse.

wealth and military might. The attacks revealed the vulnerability of the United States and brought home the fact that terrorism was a very real threat not only to citizens living in distant places, but also to people on American soil.

Thousands of people witnessed the attacks firsthand, and millions more watched the tragedy unfold on television. The events were witnessed live, in real time, as the "terrorist moment" took place in a "global public space" created by extensive media coverage.[69] The most disturbing images were those of people falling or jumping to their deaths, most from the North Tower, the first tower to be hit. Later analysis of videotapes showed that at least sixty people died this way.[70] Having no way to escape, people trapped in the Twin Towers or on hijacked airplanes made telephone calls to loved ones or left poignant messages on answering machines in their last moments.

The Associated Press uses four levels of notification to signal a story's importance: The highest level is Flash, followed by a NewsAlert, a Bulletin, and an Urgent. On September 11, it sent two Flashes (reporting the collapses of the Twin Towers), twenty-five NewsAlerts, and eighteen Bulletins.[71] Harold Dow, a correspondent for CBS News, said, "The media were very much a part of the terrorists' plan. From the time the first plane went in, they gave the media time to get down there to record the second plane. These pictures were shown all over the world; that's their trophy."[72]

Besides conventional news media, the Internet was a major medium for disseminating news of the attacks. People used the Internet to seek information about what happened, who died, who survived, and the extent of the damage. Despite the massive death toll caused by the attack on the Twin Towers, more than 15,000 people managed to escape.[73] An online "survivor registry," where people could post their names to let friends and loved ones know they had survived, received more than one million "hits" on September 11 and the next day, as people turned to the Internet to exchange information.[74] The Internet also functioned as a virtual space where individuals who died were identified and commemorated. People from eighty countries around the world, engaged in ordinary life activities, became victims of someone's desire to make a point, weaken a government, express a grievance.[75]

Rescue, Recovery, and Mourning

Rescue and recovery operations began immediately, but the initial hope of finding a large number of survivors in the rubble was soon replaced by the grim realization that efforts would mainly involve retrieving and identifying the dead. Hundreds of photographs of the missing posted by friends and family members throughout New York City in the days after the attack became memorials to loved ones.[76] In the end, only eighteen people were recovered alive from the collapsed Twin Towers.[77] When the "unbuilding" of the World Trade Center officially ended in the summer of 2002, 1.5 million tons of ruins had been taken from the seventeen acres of the site, which became known as "Ground Zero." Only about half of the people who were missing and presumed killed had been identified, many of those due to an exceptionally ambitious program of DNA matching.

William Langewiesche, who was at the WTC site during its demolition, observed that "one of the unacknowledged aspects of the tragedy was the jealous sense of ownership that it brought about—an unexpected but widespread feeling of something like pride, that 'this is our disaster more than yours.'"[78] This bias resulted in differing treatment of the recovered human remains, with some granted elaborate ceremonies while work on the site was stopped as the remains were reverently carried away, and others subjected to a routine "bag 'em and tag 'em" approach. Elaborate rituals were associated with the remains of 343 firefighters, who were viewed as having died while performing acts of heroism. Acknowledging their sacrifice with appropriate ceremony was not only in keeping with firefighter tradition, but also a matter of paying due respects. Yet the greatest loss of life for a single organization took place at the financial firm Cantor Fitzgerald, where 658 people were killed, some of them undoubtedly dying as heroes as well. A growing "us versus them" mentality at the site, evident in dissimilar treatment of remains, led to what some called a "Battle of the Badges."

Even though the principle that human remains ought to be treated with dignity is almost universally accepted, the application of this rule in extraordinary situations can generate volatile emotions. In Israel, where the commandment to bury the dead is a basic rule in Jewish law, a volunteer organization known as Zaka (an acronym for *Zihui Korbanot Ason,* Hebrew for Identification of Disaster Victims) responds to terrorist incidents to collect remains and identify as many parts as they can, including blood, so that as much of a victim's body as possible can be buried. Doing this kind of rescue and "cleanup" work, seeing firsthand the gruesome violence done to human beings, is stressful and can trigger intense grief. To help volunteers cope with such traumatic experiences, Zaka regularly schedules counseling workshops, family days, and other programs where members can discuss their feelings in an atmosphere of mutual support.[79]

Whereas Israelis may be familiar with the stresses of life under terrorism, many of the people engaged in recovery at the WTC were much less accustomed to its grisly effects. Frustrated because of the awesome death toll and grieving the deaths of so many individuals both known and unknown, those who toiled at Ground Zero shared with the wider community a sense of uncertainty and confusion about how to cope. Problems in recovering and identifying victims' remains, as well as the scope and extent of devastation, were among factors that added to the impact of the terrorism of 9/11 (see Table 13-4).

Numerous charitable campaigns raised money to help families of those who died. Such fund-raising efforts were immensely successful and generated widespread response from the public, whose contributions allowed them to participate in the process of recovery and express gratitude for the sacrifice of lives lost. But these well-meant campaigns were also plagued by issues involving the allocation of funds and questions about which group was most deserving of help. Much as disputes over "ownership" of the loss surfaced among recovery workers, grieving families began to be identified as members of particular groups, each of which seemed to be vying for the distinction of who

TABLE *13-4*   *Factors Increasing Impact of Terrorism*

1. Scope and extent of physical and emotional devastation
2. Realization that destruction and horror was intentional and directed not just at individuals but also at the government and culture they represent
3. Age of victims, especially when many are young adults or children
4. Defenselessness of the victims and suddenness of the attack
5. Duration of the event, including the length of time it takes to rescue the injured and recover remains of the dead
6. Difficulties and delays in identifying and returning remains of victims, inability to recover identifiable remains of some victims, severe body fragmentation, and issues related to disposition of "common" or unassociated human tissue
7. Issues related to remains of terrorists mixing with remains of victims
8. Intrusiveness of media coverage, especially repetitive broadcast or publication of disturbing visual images
9. Speculation about the perpetrators and their motivations, who was really behind the attack, and whether the true architects of the terrorism can be apprehended and brought to justice
10. Speculation about the ability of official agencies to have prevented the attack and resulting loss of faith in government to protect its citizens
11. Difficulty in finding human service providers and mental health professionals who have knowledge and experience in working with violent injury and death, as well as the ability to handle the disturbing and gruesome content of victims' experiences
12. Large-scale memorials and anniversary commemorations

Source: Kathryn M. Turman, Program Director, Office for Victim Assistance, FBI Headquarters, Washington, D.C.

had suffered most from the terrorist attacks. Meanwhile, some individuals bereaved as a result of other terrorist acts, such as the bombing of a federal office building in Oklahoma City in 1995, or whose loved ones died in circumstances that received less public notice, wondered why their losses were not recognized as equivalent and granted similar levels of social support.

Just days after the attacks, the *New York Times* began publishing a special feature, "Portraits of Grief," which evolved into a kind of shrine that offered vignettes about people who had died. Unlike formal obituaries, these were quick sketches that suggested some spark of life that made each person special. They served to highlight a person's unique humanity and interests, not his or her status or achievements. This new form of reportage represented what one writer called a "kind of haiku obit"—journalism as tribute, as homage, as witness, and as solace.[80]

At homes and in schools around the world, children wrote letters, made drawings, and collected stuffed animals and other items that they mailed to the firefighters, police officers, rescue workers, Red Cross volunteers, and others who had suffered in the attacks or who rushed in to help in its aftermath. In their drawings, children often depicted rainbows, flowers, people holding hands, and other hopeful images. Some drawings depicting the attacks on the Twin Towers included positive messages directed to the victims or to rescue personnel (see Figure 13-1). In their cards and letters to families

Figure *13-1 Child's 9/11 Drawing*
A young child's portrayal of the terrorist attack on the Twin Towers in New
York City shows the towers in flames as individuals who were trapped in the
devastation on the upper floors jump to their deaths. At the far left, an airplane is depicted at what appears to be the moment of impact, while a fire
truck and rescue personnel approach the site from the opposite side. At
the top of the drawing, the child includes a written affirmation, "You are
the best," and she signs the drawing with an affectionate "Love, Briana."

whose loved ones had died, children sent messages of condolence and reassurance, and some shared loss experiences of their own. In creating their artworks and writing their messages, children expressed their anxieties and
feelings about the events of September 11 while also reaching out to others
in gestures of support.[81]

The Mind of the Terrorist

From the moment the second airplane hit the South Tower of the WTC,
confirming the fact that the events taking place were intentional, people
asked what could motivate human beings to perpetrate such acts of violence
against innocent citizens. Is it even possible to understand the mind of a terrorist? Despite the unparalleled military arsenal of the United States, a successful attack on the symbols of power and wealth in the Western world was
carried out by men wielding box cutters, creating the most spectacular terrorist event in history.[82] Yet such violence was not unprecedented, nor was it

merely a chance occurrence devised by nineteen amateurs acting on their own. On the contrary, the attacks were the deliberate result of careful planning by al-Qaeda, an organization with operations in as many as sixty countries worldwide.[83] In its use of sophisticated information technology and small cells of terrorists who operate for long periods independently, al-Qaeda is representative of a new kind of combat organization, one that operates on a global scale as a "fighting network."[84]

Why do organizations like al-Qaeda exist, and why do individuals become allied with them to the extent that they are willing to sacrifice their lives in suicide attacks? Much of the terrorism in recent decades has a religious or quasi-religious component whereby terrorists combine fanatical hatred of the secular state with a vision of themselves as defenders of an ancient faith. The secular world, having betrayed the true faith, is seen as "evil"; therefore, it is the duty of the "righteous" to engage in a moral and spiritual struggle between good and evil. Mark Juergensmeyer says, "Concepts of cosmic war are accompanied by strong claims of moral justification and an enduring absolutism that transforms worldly struggles into sacred battles."[85] Such views have developed as part of revivalist movements that promote a return to fundamentalism in religious matters. They are adopted by individuals who seek to impose their own concepts of right and wrong on those who fail to share their views. In the mind of the terrorist, it is permissible, even necessary, to kill because he or she is doing it for a higher purpose.

Suicide bombings exemplify the terrorist's belief that he or she is engaged in a worthy and just struggle, one that makes sacrifice not only desirable but also imperative. The collective—religion, sect, nation—is more important than the individual. Suicide missions are usually easy to plan because no escape route is needed and, once a suicide terrorist heads for the target, even if he or she does not succeed in reaching it, some damage likely can be inflicted on the enemy while being apprehended.[86]

Psychologist Aaron Beck describes terrorists as "prisoners of hate."[87] Harboring a profound sense of being wronged, they call for revenge against those whom they view as their oppressors. Beck says, "Terrorists who execute well-planned acts of destruction are not deranged"; rather, they are "possessed by a cool hatred toward the designated enemy," which allows them to be "cold and calculating in carrying out their grand design."

Throughout history, there have been struggles between competing religious and secular ideologies that, on one hand, provide security for those who accept them but, on the other, inspire violence against those who do not. From the perspective of terror management theory, conflict between individuals and groups occurs because those who hold beliefs about reality that differ from our own challenge our faith, threatening to undermine the promise of literal or symbolic immortality afforded by those beliefs.[88] Anxiety released by this threat drives the hostility and hatred felt toward those who view the world differently than we do. Aaron Beck argues that the antidote to this cycle of violence is to establish a "humanistic code" whereby the universality of humankind is emphasized as an alternative to the rigid perspectives of tribalism, nationalism, and militant religiosity.[89]

To despise another human being, to wound another human being, to open another human being's body in the name of proving a belief, requires denying those other human beings' essential humanity. Otherwise the wellsprings of compassion, of our profound and bodily identification with one another—all mothers, all fathers, all brothers and sisters and daughters and sons, all lovers and neighbors and friends—would flood the mechanism of alienation that cleaves us apart.

We distance those whom we fear, and we fear them more for their distance. We distance them psychologically by reducing them to epithets: Hun, kike, Jap, kulak, gook, nigger, fascist, liberal, communist, Sandinista, enemy of the people, queer. We distance them physically by refusing to acknowledge their common humanity or to attend their suffering. Only then can we bear to injure or destroy them.

Technology amplifies this effect. Destruction at a distance with projectiles and bombs short-circuits the identification with similarly embodied beings . . . that might otherwise stay our hand.

Richard Rhodes

Viewed from this perspective, the mission to combat terrorism—to make the world less threatening, to provide a safer environment for ourselves and our loved ones—is seen as a challenge calling for adaptive behavior. The goal is to replace destructive conflict with sensitivity to others' needs, responsibility for their welfare, and altruistic actions on their behalf. In describing the twenty-first century as "the global century," Shashi Tharoor argues that, as never before, "the tragedies of our time are global in origin and reach," and "tackling them is a global responsibility that must be assumed by us all." Tharoor says:

> Terrorism emerges from blind hatred of an Other, and that in turn is the product of three factors: fear, rage, and incomprehension. Fear of what the Other might do to you, rage at what you believe the Other has done to you, and incomprehension about who or what the Other really is. . . . If terrorism is to be tackled and ended, we will have to deal with each of these three factors by attacking the ignorance that sustains them. We will have to learn to see ourselves as others see us, learn to recognize hatred and deal with its causes, learn to dispel fear, and, above all, simply learn about each other.[90]

AIDS and Other Emerging Diseases

Another kind of threat is represented by emerging infectious diseases like AIDS (acquired immune deficiency syndrome). In the early twentieth century, infectious diseases predominated among the principal causes of death, and epidemic infections caused global havoc. The influenza epidemic of 1918–1919, for example, reportedly caused the deaths of 20 million to 40 million people worldwide.[91] Subsequent advances in public health and medicine so dramatically altered patterns of morbidity and mortality that people have become complacent about the threat of infectious diseases. Yet virologists fear that some of the currently emerging viruses are a bigger threat than the 1918 virus.[92] AIDS may be a harbinger of other emerging diseases that threaten the health of human beings worldwide in coming decades.

The Response to AIDS

For many people, AIDS is synonymous with death: a dread disease, contagious and epidemic, a modern plague. Robert Kastenbaum says that the symbolism of AIDS embodies the stigma of earlier forms of catastrophic dying: disfiguration, dementia, and skeletonization. It conveys multiple meanings about human vanity and pride, divine punishment, attack by an enemy from within, the terror of life in death and the despair of death in life, and the romantic exit of brilliant and beautiful doomed youth.[93] Many survivors—the friends, neighbors, business associates, and relatives of people who died from AIDS—have experienced multiple losses.

The first cases of AIDS, a disease that destroys the body's natural defenses against infection, were reported in 1981; by early 1982, researchers believed that AIDS was caused by an infectious agent. Discovery of HIV (human immunodeficiency virus) as the likely cause of AIDS was confirmed in January 1984 by Luc Montagnier at the Pasteur Institute in Paris and by Robert Gallo at the U.S. National Institutes of Health. Late in 1985, the genetic sequence of the virus was determined and a blood test devised to detect antibodies to HIV. In 2006, twenty-five years after the first AIDS cases emerged in the public arena, scientists traced the virus's origin to a community of wild chimpanzees living near Cameroon's Sanaga River.[94]

According to a United Nations report, HIV/AIDS has killed more than 25 million people since it was first recognized in 1981, making it one of the most destructive epidemics in recorded history, and nearly 40 million people worldwide are currently living with the AIDS virus.[95] Sub-Saharan Africa remains the most affected region. More than 2 million children under the age of fifteen, mainly in sub-Saharan Africa, are living with HIV.[96] Eleven million children have been orphaned by AIDS in sub-Saharan Africa, with the number threatening to reach 25 million by the year 2010.[97]

Peter Piot, director general of UNAIDS, says, "The main message of our report is that the AIDS epidemic is far from over. In fact, it's far worse."[98] Scientists say the next twenty-five years of AIDS threatens to be deadlier than the first. AIDS is concentrated in the developing world, where it is wiping out gains in life expectancy that had been made in recent decades. In the United States, AIDS mainly affects intravenous (IV) drug users, hemophiliacs, and recipients of blood transfusions, as well as the sexual partners of individuals infected with the virus. In other parts of the world, it is transmitted mainly through heterosexual contact.

The social and political response to AIDS has been mixed.[99] From the first inklings that AIDS was a new and challenging disease, debate began about how to mobilize and allocate economic, medical, and social resources. Some communities responded with a variety of health and public service programs. Others reacted by hampering efforts to help individuals affected by AIDS. When Elisabeth Kübler-Ross proposed a hospice for infants with AIDS in rural Virginia, the local community denied the necessary permits. Fear of contagion overruled the wish to help sick and dying infants. In Africa, years into the pandemic, governments and media tended to ignore the crisis, attributing victims' deaths to anything but AIDS.[100]

At a cultural level, AIDS has challenged our notions of how family is defined and who constitutes a family, with persons other than kin often playing important roles.[101] A hospice model of caregiving—usually with home care as a major component—has been widely adopted in caring for AIDS patients. Nevertheless, as Ronald Barrett points out, people with AIDS have sometimes exhibited social withdrawal and self-initiated isolation.[102] People who display this behavior have been termed "elephant people," a reference to the belief that dying elephants remove themselves from their herd and go away to a remote elephant burial ground to die.

Society has been unsure how to respond to AIDS. In California, the Department of Motor Vehicles (DMV) refused to provide a customized license plate, reading "AIDS RN."[103] The license plate was requested by a nurse who specializes in AIDS care. He wanted the new plate on his Thunderbird to show pride in his work and AIDS awareness. After the DMV deemed the plate offensive and turned down the request, he said, "What [the DMV] is kind of saying is the way the general society wants to deal with AIDS—they don't want to deal with it." Eventually, the DMV reversed itself, but it said some AIDS groups had told the DMV they didn't want plates issued bearing the words "AIDS" or "HIV" because they would be reminders for people with the virus. Meanwhile, the clinical supervisor of an AIDS project said the DMV's rejection of the plate was the "ultimate in political incorrectness." As a commentary on attitudes toward AIDS, this saga of a license plate exemplifies the conflicting and confusing responses elicited by the disease.

Viewing AIDS in historical perspective, Charles Rosenberg says:

> Mortality is built into our bodies, into our modes of behavior, and into our place in the planet's ecology. Like other epidemics, AIDS has served well to remind us, finally, of these ultimate realities.[104]

AIDS is a reminder that infectious diseases remain a threat and that human beings remain uncertain about how to respond to epidemic disease. When confronted by a new disease with an unknown mode of transmission, people become anxious and fearful. In this regard, the response to the outbreak of AIDS resembled historical patterns of social responses to epidemics. As the initial panic recedes, more thoughtful and helpful measures are implemented.

Living with AIDS

Acquired immune deficiency syndrome (AIDS) impairs the body's immune system.[105] It affects the body's ability to fight disease, making it more vulnerable to opportunistic infection, which is the usual cause of death in AIDS patients.

It is important to distinguish between AIDS and human immunodeficiency virus (HIV), which causes AIDS. Medically defined, HIV infection is

© Carolyn Jones, from *Living Proof, Courage in the Face of AIDS*

Zoë Lorenz and her daughter Candice are among the many people affected by AIDS. Zoë saw her father die from AIDS, plagued not only by the disease but by the humiliation and shame so often associated with it. Now afflicted with the virus herself, Zoë says, "I have a beautiful four-year-old daughter who has beat the odds and remains HIV negative. So many people have the attitude that I should go off and die somewhere alone. They don't see the tragedy of this child losing her mommy. I don't need to be proud that I have AIDS, but I won't be ashamed that I do. I don't want to feel that I have to tell people I've got cancer or some other acceptable disease."

caused by one of two related retroviruses that become incorporated into host cell DNA, progressively destroying white blood cells called lymphocytes and causing AIDS and other diseases that result from impaired immunity.

People infected with the virus are usually not aware of it until symptoms become evident years later. A blood test can be used to screen people for HIV infection. Although the pattern of progression from HIV infection to AIDS is not entirely clear, the consensus has been that almost all HIV-infected persons eventually develop AIDS.

One year ago today, I told my colleagues that I was dying of AIDS. I had been fighting it for years—the illness and the telling. . . . But now I was gaunt, tired, and rather sure I was losing the battle.

I was happily dying—and about to go on a Mexican vacation. I felt I had made my peace with death and, in a way, was looking forward to it. I had blown my mother's estate, about $180,000, on living for the moment, eating in the best restaurants and taking three or four foreign vacations a year. There was no time to lose, and I was determined to go out in style.

What has happened in the past year, at least for me, is a miracle that couldn't have taken place at any other moment. Thanks to the arrival of the new drugs called protease inhibitors, I am probably more likely to be hit by a truck than to die of AIDS.

I stopped the presses on my obituary. Oddly enough, the return from my near-death experience was at first very annoying. I had a few adjustments to make. I had to start thinking again about my bills. . . . We had to start living within our means. . . . I have had to re-energize myself for the daily grind. I'm even thinking about cleaning the basement.

But I'm not out of the woods.

Some HIV-negative men are guilt-ridden when they see so many of their friends dying. I feel guilty that I am getting the best possible medical care, because it is unavailable to most of the world's AIDS sufferers, and to the poor and uninsured in this country.

Figure *13-2 Back to a Future*

The prognosis for AIDS patients has much improved, as newer drugs have become available. Besides new drugs, there are advances in understanding the biology of HIV infectivity and the role of natural chemicals called chemokines in suppressing HIV's ability to infect cells.

With new treatment options, the focus is changing from "dying with AIDS" to "living with HIV and AIDS." Patients who have depleted their financial resources for care or other expenses at what had seemed the end of their lives are now confronted by the need to reappraise their planning for "last days" and reconstruct their lives so as to include a future that didn't seem likely until quite recently (see Figure 13-2). To make this future a reality, however, they must also cope with the fact that the new therapies are expensive, often limited in availability, involve various side effects, and may need to be taken over a long period of time to promote continuing improvement.

For AIDS patients who lack financial resources or access to sophisticated health care—a group that includes not only a significant portion of patients in the United States, but the majority of patients in many other countries as well—the future is bleaker. In recent years, the greatest impact of AIDS in the United States has been among African Americans and Hispanics.

Although AIDS is increasingly viewed as a treatable disease, if replication of the virus is not completely suppressed, drug-resistant mutants are given a chance to appear. As yet, there is no cure or preventive vaccine for AIDS.

Furthermore, newer drugs are not effective with all patients, and some have trouble complying with a regimen that requires daily doses of dozens of pills, many with serious side effects. AIDS researcher David Ho says, "We must dutifully avoid unwarranted triumphalism [as well as] the undue pessimism that prevails in some circles. The state of HIV treatment is neither black nor white. We must paint the situation in the proper shade of gray."[106]

The Threat of Emerging Diseases

If AIDS is a harbinger of things to come, what are the lessons that we need to learn? Three of the most important involve (1) early identification of people who are at risk for disease, (2) a shift to community and public health perspectives, and (3) the need to address health problems on a global scale.[107] Confronted by AIDS, North American and Western European countries tended to value individual citizens' privacy more highly than society's stake in controlling the disease. Thus, rather than forgoing patient confidentiality in order to promote public health efforts to prevent the spread of the virus, the decision was made to guard the privacy of HIV-infected individuals. In the case of AIDS, this approach was deemed appropriate because the virus is not transmitted by ordinary contact with infected individuals, and the carrier of HIV represents no risk to others in normal social and commercial life. This is not true of all viruses, however. The epidemiology and mode of infection of a disease are crucial in determining the ways in which societies cope with it.

In recent years, there have been localized epidemics of a number of emerging diseases, many of them related to hemorrhagic fever viruses such as the Marburg, Ebola, Lassa, and hantaviruses, as well as yellow fever, swine flu, Legionnaires' disease (*Legionella*), and cholera.[108] Bernard Le Guenno of the Pasteur Institute in Paris says:

> Hemorrhagic fever viruses are among the most threatening examples of what are commonly termed emerging pathogens. They are not really new. Mutations or genetic recombinations between existing viruses can increase virulence, but what appears to be novel viruses are generally viruses that have existed for millions of years and merely come to light when environmental conditions change. The changes allow the virus to multiply and spread in host organisms. New illnesses may then sometimes become apparent.[109]

Most outbreaks of hemorrhagic fevers result from disruption of the environment due to human activities. With expansion of the human population, forest clearing and other agricultural activities disturb previously stable ecosystems, thereby facilitating contact with pathogenic viruses that threaten life and health.

Patrick Olson, an epidemiologist at the Naval Medical Center in San Diego, theorizes that the plague that struck the Greek city of Athens in 430 B.C.E., which was reported by the Athenian general and historian Thucydides, was caused by the deadly Ebola virus (which is named after a river in the Congo, where it was first detected in 1976).[110] Olson finds parallels between the ancient and modern accounts. Fever, diarrhea, and severe weakness are prominent symptoms. As with the Athenian plague, Ebola claims almost all of its victims, and quickly, with most infected people dying within two weeks. Ebola outbreaks usually last only a few weeks because its victims die faster than they are able to spread the virus, which disappears for a time, only to reemerge later.

The worst infectious disease episode in modern times was the 1918 pandemic caused by an influenza virus that killed as many as 40 million people worldwide. In the United States, a quarter of the population had the flu and more than half a million people died. Many of the thousands of young men crammed onto World War I troop ships were just developing the flu as they left the United States. After a week's crossing of the Atlantic, the ships arrived in France with hundreds of sick servicemen, many of whom died.

Experts believe that many flu viruses reside harmlessly in birds and occasionally infect pigs, where they are changed into a new form of the virus that can affect humans.[111] Similar mechanisms involving "species jumping" have been suggested for AIDS and other viruses. William Clark points out that this phenomenon may be due to depletion of natural resources and extinction of species that have been the natural habitat of microbial organisms with whom they have previously lived in equilibrium. "Deprived of their natural hosts, some of these microorganisms . . . have begun to jump to humans where there is no such equilibrium. . . . The results, as we have seen with the Ebola and AIDS viruses, can be disastrous."[112]

In studying how newly emerging diseases like AIDS are disseminated in urban societies, Rodrick and Deborah Wallace conclude that physical and social disruption intensifies the pathological behaviors and conditions that promote the rapid spread of infectious diseases.[113] Political abandonment of inner-city areas results in what the Wallaces term "urban desertification" or "social thanatology."[114] The devastation and disintegration in some urban areas is characterized as "unprecedented in a modern industrialized state short of the aftermath of total war."[115] Among disadvantaged populations, a lack of crucial municipal services leads to what Richard Rothenberg of the U.S. Centers for Disease Control and Prevention calls "the metastasis of dangerous behavior."[116] For some marginalized people, the view of AIDS is quite different from the view held in society's mainstream: AIDS appears to be a form of race or class warfare, "a virus created in a government or CIA laboratory in an attempt to 'clean up' a seemingly dirty population."[117] The fact that such a view exists is itself evidence of the gap between the haves and have-nots of society.

Since the advent of penicillin, people have become complacent about infectious diseases, believing that epidemics are no longer a threat. But the pandemic of AIDS shows that complacency is ill advised. In addition to newly emerging diseases, some diseases that had seemed conquered are reemerging as a threat. For example, drug-resistant strains of tuberculosis are spreading, even in wealthy countries, due to migration as well as international business and tourist travel.[118] This upswing in a disease believed to be under

I grew up during the Depression; everything in the country had stopped; there was no work, the factories were cold and empty. People daydreamed about what this country was going to be like when it got going again—the kind of houses people would live in, the kind of cars they would drive, the kind of vacations they'd take, the kind of clothes they'd wear, and all that—and it was a dream for their descendants. I don't find anybody now who gives a damn about what kind of world their grand-children are going to inherit. . . .

All the ads tell you that your own life is short, enjoy it while you can: buy this right now, start drinking really good wines, just take a really swell vacation, drive a really fast car, do it right now. I think it's much more absorbing to plan a world for our grandchildren, but there are no ads that invite you to do that. In a way, the threat of the Bomb may be a boon to wine merchants, restaurateurs, manufacturers of fancy automobiles, salesmen of condos in Aspen. It's all going to blow up—that's part of the sales message.

Kurt Vonnegut, quoted in *Publishers Weekly*

control since the 1940s, when effective drugs were introduced, has been blamed on "worldwide medical chaos," which results in TB being pushed into the poorer sections of society, particularly among inner-city dwellers and the homeless. Malaria, which was subjected to a global eradication effort during the 1970s, has also staged a comeback, with as many as 500 million people in 90 countries affected each year.[119] The most ominous reason for this comeback, researchers say, is the ability of the mosquito-borne parasite, the *Plasmodium* protozoan, to develop resistance to antimalaria drugs. More money and other resources need to be invested in surveillance efforts to combat the threat of emerging and reemerging infectious diseases like malaria, tuberculosis, dengue fever, Ebola, and other plagues.

Coping with Threats

Daniel Leviton uses the term *horrendous death* to describe categories of death that affect large numbers of people.[120] He says, "The horrendous death concept is about preventable death and the process of prevention. It is about addressing causes as well as symptoms."[121] Horrendous death typically involves the motivation to kill, maim, injure, torture, or otherwise destroy another human being. Homicide, nuclear and conventional war, terrorism, assassination, genocide, and death resulting from racism and ethnic hatred are examples of horrendous-type deaths. The first step in eliminating, or at least reducing, such deaths involves confronting the wish to deny the reality of such deaths. Sometimes horrendous-type deaths are treated as an aberration, an anomaly. Yet they involve enormous costs for present as well as future generations.

It is hypothesized that the more horrible the type or style of dying and/or death is perceived, the greater the fear; the greater the fear, the greater the denial; and the greater the denial, the less change of action to eliminate the very causes of such torturous deaths.[122]

Threats of death—accidents, violence, homicide, war, epidemic diseases—affect us as we go about our daily lives. Sometimes the encounter is subtle; at other times it is overt, calling into action our ability to cope with threat. The failure to find adequate means of coping with these encounters with death represents a threat to the survival of society as well as the individual.

Further Readings

Roy F. Baumeister. *Evil: Inside Human Violence and Cruelty*. New York: W. H. Freeman, 1997.

Mia Bloom. *Dying to Kill: The Allure of Suicide Terror*. New York: Columbia University Press, 2005.

Craig Calhoun, Paul Price, and Ashley Timmer, eds. *Understanding September 11*. New York: New Press, 2002.

Jim Dwyer and Kevin Flynn. *102 Minutes: The Untold Story of the Fight to Survive Inside the Twin Towers*. New York: Times Books, 2005.

Albert R. Jonsen and Jeff Stryker, eds. *The Social Impact of AIDS*. Washington, D.C.: National Academy Press, 1993.

Walter Laqueur. *No End to War: Terrorism in the Twenty-First Century*. New York: Continuum, 2003.

Marcia Lattanzi-Licht and Kenneth J. Doka, eds. *Living with Grief: Coping with Public Tragedy*. Washington, D.C.: Hospice Foundation of America, 2003.

Daniel Leviton, ed. *Horrendous Death and Health: Toward Action*. New York: Taylor and Francis, 1991.

Albert J. Reiss, Jr., and Jeffrey A. Roth, eds. *Understanding and Preventing Violence*. Washington, D.C.: National Academy Press, 1993.

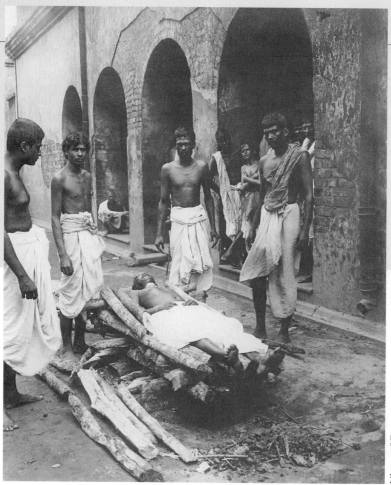

The corpse placed on the funeral pyre, these men prepare to light the crema-
tion fire. Cremation has been a traditional practice in India, where Hindus
believe that "even as the person casts off worn-out clothes and puts on others
that are new, so the embodied Self casts off worn-out bodies and enters into
others that are new."

CHAPTER 14

Beyond Death/After Life

*D*eath—and then what?

Some people have a ready answer to this question: "When you're dead, you're dead—that's it!" or "You go through a transition and take birth in another body," or "After you die you go to heaven." Each of these responses reflects a particular understanding of the meaning of human existence. Beliefs about life after death occupy a broad spectrum, from the notion that death spells the end to the notion that the "soul" or "self" lives on after death in some fashion. Answering the question "What happens after I die?" has occupied the attention of human beings since the dawn of consciousness. Concern with immortality—that is, survival after physical death—is cut from the same cloth as questions about the meaning of life and the corollary "How, then, should one live?" Responses to these questions reflect a person's values and beliefs about human experience and the nature of reality. Andrew Greeley says, "We are born with two incurable diseases: *life,* from which we die, and *hope,* which says maybe death isn't the end."[1]

Death can be a tricky question for people. Bob Dylan describes how reviewers of his album *Time Out of Mind* understood that it dealt with "mortality," but not a single critic applied this recognition to himself; it was, Dylan said, as if "whoever's writing about the record has got eternal life and the singer doesn't."[2] Our philosophy of life influences our philosophy of death. Conversely, our understanding of death and its meaning affects the way we live.

> Every time an earth mother smiles over the birth of a child, a spirit mother weeps over the loss of a child.
>
> Ashanti saying

According to Socrates, "The unexamined life is not worth living." Such self-investigation includes discovery of what one believes about the consequences of death. Ambivalence about belief in survival after death is aptly described in an anecdote related by Bertrand Russell: A woman whose daughter had recently died was asked what she thought had become of her daughter's soul. She replied, "Oh, well, I suppose she is enjoying eternal bliss, but I wish you wouldn't talk about such unpleasant subjects."[3]

Exploring your beliefs about immortality may not result in an easier acceptance of death—nor should it necessarily. After all, the prospect of immortality is not always looked upon favorably.[4] Nevertheless, such an exploration can lead to a more coherent philosophy of life and death, making possible a congruence between hopes and perceptions. Even when we are settled upon a belief system, exposure to other views can both broaden our understanding of different responses to death and enhance appreciation of our own beliefs. In this chapter we explore the meaning of mortality by investigating some of the ways that cultures, Eastern and Western, answer the question "What happens after death?" These answers provide grist for the mill of our own contemplation about this ultimate human concern.

Traditional Concepts About Life After Death

The notion that life continues in some form after death is one of the oldest concepts held by human beings. In some of the earliest graves, archaeologists have uncovered skeletons that were bound by hands and feet into a fetal position, perhaps indicating beliefs about "rebirth" into other forms of existence following death. (Rebirth, in one form or another, has been characterized as the "most persistent image of afterlife in the history of religion.")[5] In traditional societies death represents a change of status, a transition from the land of the living to the land of the dead.

Judgment is a key feature of many beliefs about what follows death. Among the various concepts of afterlife among traditional Hawaiians, for example, was the belief that a person who had offended a god or who had harmed others would suffer eternal punishment.[6] Such an unworthy soul became a wandering spirit, "forever homeless, forever hungry." The ancestor-gods had the power to punish or reward the released spirit, or even send it back to the body. Misfortune could result when a person had neither loving relatives to care for the corpse nor the guardianship of family ancestor-gods, who help souls find their way to the world of spirits. Those who had lived worthily were welcomed into eternity, whereas those who had done misdeeds, without repenting for or correcting them, were punished. The reward for a

William Hodges, Bishop Museum

The platform burial of a Tahitian chief is depicted in this drawing by William Hodges, made during Captain Cook's second voyage to the South Pacific in the 1770s.

In a world populated by unseen spirits who could exert their influence for good or evil upon the living, the death of a chief or other important person occasioned a spectacular display of grief, which was presided over by a chief mourner (right). Usually a priest or close relative of the deceased, the chief mourner wore an elaborate costume of pearl shells and the feathers of tropic birds. Rattling a pearl shell clapper and brandishing a long wooden weapon inset with sharks' teeth, the chief mourner was accompanied by other weapon-carrying men who could strike anyone in their way, thus helping ensure that funeral rites were carried out in a manner that would offend neither the living nor the dead.

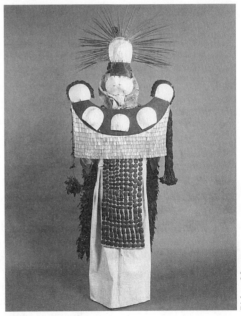

Bishop Museum

good life was reunion with those closest to the family-loving Hawaiians: one's own ancestors.

To understand the consciousness from which such a view of immortality arises, the notions of selfhood in Western cultures must be put aside momentarily. Against an emphasis on individual identity and the self, imagine a mentality in which group identity is all-encompassing. The family, the clan, the people—these social groups represent the loci of communal consciousness within which the thoughts and actions of the individual are subsumed. Thus, traditional beliefs are less concerned with individual survival than with continuation of the community and its common heritage. Having shared in the life of the group, the individual is part of its ultimate destiny, a destiny that transcends death.

Jewish Beliefs About Death and Resurrection

Although the Bible takes death seriously, it does not present a systematic "theology of death" or the afterlife.[7] The biblical story describes a people focused on their communal destiny. Individuals are actors in an unfolding drama, its final outcome foretold in the promises made by Yahweh (the biblical proper name for God). The emphasis is on faith—faith in the people of Israel as a community with a common destiny and faith in Yahweh, whose promises will be realized in the unfolding of the divine plan. For example, as the patriarch Abraham lay dying, his last thoughts were hope for the survival of his progeny so that these promises could be realized. Abraham's vision is reenacted by biblical heroes in one circumstance after another, as they affirm Israel's communal destiny. By contributing to this destiny, the righteous person is part of the continuing story of the people as a whole. "According to Jewish tradition, our lives are measured by our deeds and by whether we have lived up to our full potential."[8]

In the story of Job's encounter with adversity, the possibility of life beyond death appears bleak: "As a cloud fades away and disappears, so a person who goes down to the grave will not come up from it."[9] Resignation toward death is echoed in the other Wisdom books—including Proverbs, Ecclesiastes, and some of the Psalms—which present the thought of the ancient He-

"There is always hope for a tree:
    when felled, it can start its life again;
    its shoots continue to sprout.
Its roots may be decayed in the earth,
    its stump withering in the soil,
but let it scent the water, and it buds,
    and puts out branches like a plant new set.
But man? He dies, and lifeless he remains;
    man breathes his last, and then where is he?
The waters of the sea may disappear,
    all the rivers may run dry or drain away;
but man, once in his resting place, will never rise again.
    The heavens will wear away before he wakes,
    before he rises from his sleep."

Job 14:7–12, *The Jerusalem Bible*

brew sages on the question of human destiny. Righteous conduct is advised because it leads to harmony in the present life, not because it guarantees future rewards for the individual.

Between the time of Job and the later prophets, however, there was a gradual change from resignation to hopefulness in the face of death. In the apocalyptic, or visionary, writings of prophets such as Daniel and Ezekiel, we find the strands of thought that are eventually woven together in ideas about the resurrection of the body. Daniel envisions a future in which the "sleeping" dead will awaken, "some to everlasting life, some to everlasting disgrace."[10] This development in Hebrew thought would greatly influence Christian theology. Stated succinctly, it "consists in the belief that, at the end of time, the bodies of the dead will be resurrected from the grave and reconstituted."[11]

Hints of this change are also evident in the meanings ascribed over time to the Hebrew word *She'ol,* which in early usage is generally defined as the underworld of all the dead, a shadowy realm of ghostly, disembodied souls (much like the *Hades* of Greek mythology). A story gives an account of necromancy in which King Saul requests the witch of Endor to summon the spirit of the dead prophet Samuel. Asked by Saul to describe what she sees, the witch replies, "I see a ghost [*elohim* = superhuman being] rising up from the earth [*She'ol*]." With further refinement of these concepts, the shadowy underworld of *She'ol* is divided into two distinct realms: *Gehinom* (hell) and *Pardes* (heaven or paradise).[12]

In the main, ideas about resurrection of the body found in the prophets did not alter the essential understanding of the human person as an undivided

I knew my former father-in-law from the time I was thirteen. Although I had divorced many years ago, he remained a second father to me. Kurt was born in Germany. He left for Holland on the day of Kristallnacht. He arrived here penniless and went on to become an extremely successful business man. In coming to this country, he left his entire family. With the exception of an uncle, they all died in the Holocaust. He remained an observant Jew and did not talk much about the Holocaust until the last two years of his life. Since he never knew when his parents, sisters, and other loved ones died, he observed the *yahrzeit* (anniversary of their deaths) on Yom Kippur (the day of atonement).

Just before Rosh Hashanah two years ago, he became very ill and was hospitalized. Following an old European tradition, in the synagogue on Rosh Hashanah he was given a new Hebrew name (so that when the angel of death came looking for him, he wouldn't find him). I went to visit him in the hospital that day. He was in and out of consciousness. I doubt that he consciously knew who I was, and I'm sure was not aware of the day. When he did speak, he was speaking only in German. I said my good-bye to him and left. He remained alive for the entire ten-day period (often referred to as the Days of Awe) and (I believe) went to be with his loved ones on Yom Kippur.

Barbara J. Paul

psychophysical entity. Wheeler Robinson says, "The Hebrew idea of personality is an animated body, and not an incarnated soul."[13] In other words, it is not as if the soul *takes* a body; rather, the body *has* life. Concepts like body or soul cannot be abstracted from the integrity of the human person.

The consensus expressed by the biblical writers seems to be, "Our present existence is of God; if there is life hereafter, it will also be God's gift. Why be anxious about death? What matters is to live righteously." The faith of Israel is sustained through customs like the *minyan* (a quorum or minimum number of individuals required for communal worship) and the reciting of *kaddish* (a liturgical expression of praise to God, which functions as a kind of "memorial prayer"), as well as in the practice of *shivah* (period of formal mourning, traditionally seven days). An Aramaic doxology, *kaddish* is essentially a pledge from the living to dedicate one's life to the God of Life.[14] It is recited by mourners during the first eleven months after death of a loved one and then on the anniversary, or *yahrzeit,* of the death. In Judaism, the customary mourning rituals help the bereaved face the reality of death, give honor to the deceased, and engage in a reaffirmation of *life.*[15]

Classical Greek Concepts of Immortality

The ancient Greeks held a variety of views about what might follow the death of the body. Generally, however, the afterworld was not an attractive prospect. *Hades,* the realm of the dead, was typically pictured as a shadowy place inhabited by bloodless phantoms, an image that evoked despair. The heroes in Greek drama are often portrayed as raging against death.[16]

In the Athenian democracy, what mattered was the survival of the *polis,* the corporate existence of the city-state. Personal immortality was important only to the extent that it affected the survival of the community. A person could achieve social immortality by being a good citizen—that is, by performing actions directed toward the common good. Because the community remembers heroic acts, the hero achieves a renown that extends beyond his or her lifetime.

For those who sought more than symbolic immortality, assurances of happiness beyond death could be obtained by participating in one of the mystery religions (any of various secret cults that offered religious experiences not provided by the official public religions). By dedicating themselves to rites prescribed by the priests of the mystery cult, initiates exchanged the grim picture of bloodless phantoms in the afterworld for the more promising one of an idyllic future in paradise.

 For the whole world is the sepulchre of famous men, and it is not the epitaph upon monuments set up in their own land that alone commemorates them, but also in lands not their own there abides in each breast an unwritten memorial of them, planted in the heart rather than graven on stone.

Thucydides, *The Peloponnesian War*

Speak not smoothly of death, I beseech you, O **famous Odysseus**. Better by far to remain on earth the thrall of another . . . rather than **reign sole** king in the realm of bodyless phantoms.

Homer, *The Odyssey*

Among the early Greek philosophers, most thought of life and death as aspects of an ever-changing, eternal flux. They typically believed that the soul was a vital principle that continued in some fashion after death, but did not imagine it surviving as a distinct entity. If something of the "soul" continued beyond death, it merged with the stuff of the universe.

Later, Pythagoras taught that conduct during life determined the destiny of the soul after death. Through practicing discipline and purification, one could influence *transmigration*—that is, migration of the soul from one body or state to another in successive rounds of births and deaths—resulting in eventual union with the Divine or Universal Absolute. These beliefs drew upon the Orphic mystery religions of ancient Greece (dedicated to the hero Orpheus and emphasizing ideas about purification and the afterlife), which went back to the cult of Dionysus.

The idea that a person's conduct in this life somehow could influence existence in the afterlife contrasted with the predominant view of an indistinct immortality in which all human beings participated regardless of their actions. Eventually, the beliefs of Pythagoras and his followers would be adopted in somewhat altered form during the pre-Christian era, and the relationship between righteous conduct and immortality would be further refined during the early centuries of Christianity.

With Socrates, there are further signs of the shift from a social immortality predicated on the life of the community to the possibility of personal survival after death. Precisely what Socrates believed is unclear, although he apparently favored the notion that the soul survives the death of the body. On his deathbed, he describes a sense of anticipation at the prospect of communion with the spirits of the great in the afterworld. In the *Apology*, however, he describes death as *either* eternal bliss *or* dreamless sleep. In the *Phaedo*, Plato advanced a number of "proofs" that the soul is eternal and is released

. . . he who has lived as a true philosopher has reason to be of good cheer when he is about to die, and that after death he may hope to receive the greatest good in the other world. . . . For I deem that the true disciple of philosophy . . . is ever pursuing death and dying; and if this is true, why, having had the desire of death all his life long, should he repine at the arrival of that which he has been always pursuing and desiring?

Plato, *Phaedo*

> Become accustomed to the belief that death is nothing to us. For all good and evil consists in sensation, but death is deprivation of sensation. And therefore a right understanding that death is nothing to us makes the mortality of life enjoyable, not because it adds to an infinite span of time, but because it takes away the craving for immortality. For there is nothing terrible in life for the man who has truly comprehended that there is nothing terrible in not living.
>
> Epicurus, *Letter to Menoeceus*

from the body at death. The dualism of body and soul is emphasized, and their respective fates are distinguished: Because it is mortal, the body is subject to corruption; the soul is immortal and therefore not subject to death.

Christian Beliefs About the Afterlife

The principal insight of both Jewish and Christian thought has two main premises: first, "that human beings are creatures, composites of dust and God's animating breath," and second, "that they are created in the image and likeness of God, with a destiny—a royal dignity—that overtakes their finite status."[17] In the New Testament, writings about dying and death derive from Jewish traditions as interpreted in the light of Jesus' death and resurrection.

The life, death, and resurrection of Jesus is the model of ultimate reality for Christians, a model realized through faith. For early Christians like the Apostle Paul, death was vanquished by Christ's resurrection. "As Paul sees it, the Christian certainty of the life to come comes from the fact that the Christian's Saviour is one who was dead and is alive again."[18] Resurrection is presented in Paul's writings as a special kind of bodily existence, but it also has a symbolic or spiritual meaning. The promise of immortality, which was implicit in the Hebrew scriptures, is defined in the Christian view as personal and bodily resurrection from the dead."[19]

At the same time, a Greek understanding of body and soul was a persistent influence on early Christian thought. In this view, the soul is immortal; it is part of the human person that exists in a disembodied state after death.

> Behold, I show you a mystery; We shall not all sleep, but we shall all be changed. In a moment, in the twinkling of an eye, at the last trump: for the trumpet shall sound, and the dead shall be raised incorruptible, and we shall be changed. For this corruptible must put on incorruption, and this mortal must put on immortality. So when this corruptible shall have put on incorruption, and this mortal shall have put on immortality, then shall be brought to pass the saying that is written, Death is swallowed up in victory. O death, where is thy sting? O grave, where is thy victory?
>
> I Corinthians, 15

This understanding interacted richly with Hebrew thought during the formative years of Christianity. Milton Gatch says about this period:

> The notion of resurrection and of the restoration of an elect people continued to be prominent. But the idea of a disembodied afterlife for the soul was also current and led to the conception of some sort of afterlife between the separation and the reunion of soul and body. From a picture of death as the inauguration of a sleep which would last until the divinely instituted resurrection, there emerged a picture of death as the beginning of quiescence for the body and of a continued life for the soul, the nature of which remained more or less undefined.[20]

Gradually, Church doctrine began to accommodate the idea that an intermediate period of purification between death and resurrection provided for the removal of obstacles to "the full enjoyment of eternal union with God."[21] This intermediate state came to be known as *purgatory*.[22] In the writings of Dante and Thomas Aquinas, earlier concepts of death, which focused on eventual resurrection of the body, are subordinated to a more pronounced emphasis on the soul's immortality after death. Carol Zaleski says,

> The classical Christian view, expressed in countless catechisms and confessions, is that upon death the souls of the blessed enter immediately into the divine presence, where they enjoy the unmediated vision of God, join in the angelic liturgy, and attend to the needs of the living who turn to them for intercession. . . . They await the return of Christ, the resurrection of the dead, and the renewal of all creation. Their bliss is perfect after its kind; but until the soul regains its body, and the whole body of Christ is complete in all its members, this perfection is, paradoxically, an unfinished work.[23]

The interplay between the concepts of resurrection and immortality is illustrated by two tombstone inscriptions from the colonial period found in a cemetery in New Haven, Connecticut.[24] On the first tombstone, the inscription reads, "Sleeping, but will someday meet her maker." The second is inscribed, "Gone to his eternal reward." Whereas the first inscription suggests an intermediate state of "soul-sleep" followed by resurrection of the body at some time in the future, the second inscription proposes the immortality of the soul, which continues to exist even though the body dies. The apparent contrast between these inscriptions is incongruous when you consider that these two individuals were married to each other and are buried side by side. Yet, one is "sleeping," while the other is "gone." In these tombstone inscriptions we see a curious example of how contrasting ideas about the afterlife can coexist in time.

Indeed, both of these ideas about the afterlife can be found today, although comparatively few Christians believe in the literal "soul-sleep" of the dead, or waiting until the end of the world before experiencing their heavenly reward. The predominant view is

> After death and the separation of the soul from the body through death, the bodiless and intermediate state of the soul follows; after the intermediate state of the soul, the resurrection and judgment; after the resurrection and judgment, two-fold eternity: *Paradise* or *Hell*.[25]

Foto Biblioteca Apostolica Vaticana

This scene from Dante's Divine Comedy *shows the guide Charon ferrying worthy souls up the River Styx toward Paradise. Unable to reach the heavenly kingdom, the unworthy, immersed in the river, struggle in despair.*

As the nature of Paradise or Hell, figurative phraseology like "the heavenly Jerusalem" or "the great tribulation" is used to convey ideas about the *conditions* of souls after death, rather than exact descriptions. As a "pilgrim people," poised between the ascension of Christ and the realization of the

Go Down, Death—A Funeral Sermon

Weep not, weep not,
She is not dead;
She's resting in the bosom of Jesus.
Heart-broken husband—weep no more;
Grief-stricken son—weep no more;
Left-lonesome daughter—weep no more;
She's only just gone home.

James Weldon Johnson

kingdom of God, Christians see themselves as part of a "narrative of hope" that dawned at the beginning of human history, a journey of faith in which death can be understood as "coming home."[26]

The Afterlife in Islamic Tradition

The third of the great religious traditions stemming from the patriarch Abraham is Islam. Like Judaism and Christianity, Islam shares the Semitic religious heritage of monotheism, God's revelation through the prophets, and accountability for one's actions at the Day of Judgment. *Islam* means "peace" or "submission" (peace comes from submission to transcendent reality, the Divine). A *Muslim* is an adherent of Islam—that is, a person who has submitted to and is at peace with God.

The Islamic message came through Muhammad, who received his call to be a prophet in 610 when he was about forty. It is recorded in the Qur'an (meaning "readings," and more familiarly spelled phonetically as "Koran" in the West). According to Muslims, the Qur'an "does not abrogate or nullify, but rather corrects the scriptures preserved by the Jewish and Christian communities."[27] Frithjof Schuon notes that the doctrine of Islam hangs on two statements: First, "There is no divinity (or reality) outside the only Divinity (or Absolute)" and, second, "Muhammad is the Envoy (the mouthpiece, intermediary, or manifestation)."[28]

A basic premise of Qur'anic teaching about death is that God determines the span of a person's life: "He creates man and also causes him to die."[29] After death, Allah (God) judges a person's conduct. The Book of Deeds, wherein are recorded good and bad actions, will be opened and each person will be consigned to either everlasting bliss or everlasting torment. "For the Muslim, life on earth is the seedbed of an eternal future."[30]

The Islamic vision of the afterlife is both spiritual and physical. "Since the Last Day will be accompanied by bodily resurrection," says John Esposito, "the pleasures of heaven and the pain of hell will be fully experienced."[31] Heaven is a paradise of "perpetual peace and bliss with flowing rivers, beautiful gardens, and the enjoyment of one's spouses (multiple marriage partners are

> The happiness of the drop is to
> die in the river.
>
> Ghazal of Ghalib

permitted in Islam) and beautiful, dark-eyed female companions (*houris*)."
The terrors of hell are described in equally physical terms.

Some Muslims believe that, after a person dies, "two black-faced, blue-eyed angels named Munkar and Nakir visit the grave and interrogate the deceased about his beliefs and deeds in life." Depending on the answers, the deceased is comforted or punished. Thus, "At a Muslim funeral a mourner may approach a corpse as it is about to be laid in the tomb and whisper instructions for answering these questions."[32] It is also believed by some Muslims that "no one should precede the corpse in the funeral procession because the angels of death go before it."[33]

When death nears, the dying person may be read passages from the Qur'an to help ensure a righteous state of mind and facilitate an easy release. After death, a ritual washing, or ablution, is done—except in the case of a martyr, in which case washing is not done "in order not to remove traces of blood which are the hallmark of his martyrdom."[34] The funeral should be conducted without elaborate ceremony with the body wrapped in white cloth and laid in a simple, unmarked grave. No coffin comes between the body and the earth to which it returns. Some Muslims believe the grave should be deep enough for the dead person to sit up without his or her head appearing above ground when the time comes to answer questions at the Last Judgment. The grave is laid out in a north-south axis, with the deceased's face turned toward the East—that is, toward Mecca—so that it is symbolically in a state of prayer. Burial follows as soon as possible after death. On hearing of someone's death, it is customary to say, "Allah Karim": From God we came and to him we shall return.[35]

The goal of Muslims is to die in the knowledge that one has submitted to the transcendent reality and has passed the test of this life. The moment of death is considered a call to prayer. "The underlying belief is that one should and can take comfort knowing that life and death are in accord with God's will, that the soul returns to God, and that the community is supportive of the bereaved."[36]

Death and Immortality in Asian Religions

Western thought typically makes distinctions, points up contrasts, establishes differences. Experiences are analyzed as being *either* this *or* that. Life is the opposite of death, death is the enemy of life; life is "good"; death "evil." In Asian cultures, by comparision, the characteristic mode of thought emphasizes the integrity of the whole rather than distinctions between constituent parts. Whereas Western thought distinguishes between "either/or," Eastern thought subsumes such distinctions within a holistic "both/and" approach.

Before we were born we had no feeling; we were one with the universe. This is called "mind-only," or "essence of mind," or "big mind." After we are separated by birth from this oneness, as the water falling from the waterfall is separated by the wind and rocks, then we have feeling. You have difficulty because you have feeling. You attach to the feeling you have without knowing just how this kind of feeling is created. When you do not realize that you are one with the river, or one with the universe, you have fear. Whether it is separated into drops or not, water is water. Our life and death are the same thing. When we realize this fact we have no fear of death anymore, and we have no actual difficulty in our life.

Shunryu Suzuki, *Zen Mind, Beginner's Mind*

This view of reality is reflected in sacred texts of the East. In Chinese tradition, for example, the *Book of Changes,* or *I Ching* (Yijing), one of the greatest literary works of Asia, postulates the basic circumstance of change in the universe; life and death are different manifestations of a constantly changing reality. As depicted in the symbol of the *Tao* (literally, "the way"; the process of nature by which all things change), the contrasting aspects of reality interpenetrate one another. Thus, death and life are not mutually exclusive opposites but, rather, complementary facets of an underlying process revealed in cycles of birth, decay, and death. Like a pendulum swinging through its arc, the completion of one cycle heralds the beginning of another. Chuang Tzu expressed the traditional Chinese attitude toward death as follows:

> Life and death are fated—constant as the succession of dark and dawn, a matter of Heaven. I received life because the time had come; I will lose it because the order of things passes on.[37]

Observing this process, the sages of the East developed the concept of reincarnation, or transmigration (passing at death from one state of existence to another, or of the soul from one body to another). Some people understand this process in a physical way: "I will take birth in another body following the death of my present body." In other words, reincarnation implies a continuity of personal identity from incarnation to incarnation. Other people shun a materialistic understanding, adopting the view that there is, in fact, no "I" to be reborn. Something may indeed be carried over from one state to the next, but this "something" is impersonal, formless, and ineffable.

Hindu Teachings About Death and Rebirth

The terms "Hindu" and "Hinduism" refer to the beliefs, practices, and socioreligious institutions that developed from the civilization of the Indo-European-speaking peoples who settled in India in the last centuries of the second millennium B.C.E. In Hinduism, death has been called "the personification of time (*mahakala*) and the foundation of the cosmo-moral order (*dharma*)."[38] Among the distinguishing features of Hinduism is belief in transmigration of the soul. This is termed *samsara*, which refers to "wandering," "journeying" or "passing through" a series of incarnational experiences. What

The cosmic dance of the Hindu deity Shiva, an ever-changing flow of creation and dissolution, embodies the fundamental equilibrium between life and death, the under-lying reality behind appearances. As the Lord of the Dance, Shiva is portrayed with one foot on the demon of ignorance and poised for the next step.

links these experiences is *karma,* which can be roughly defined as the moral law of cause and effect. The thoughts and actions of the past determine the present state of being; and, in turn, present choices influence future states. This karmic process pertains to the ever-changing flow of moment-to-moment experience, as well as to successive rounds of deaths and rebirths. As each moment conditions the next, karma governs the reincarnational flow of being. In the *Bhagavad-Gita,* Krishna tells Arjuna:

> For death is a certainty for him who has been born,
> and birth is a certainty for him who has died.
> Therefore, for what is unavoidable thou shouldst not grieve.

In a commentary on this passage, Nikhilananda adds, "It is not proper to grieve for beings which are mere combinations of cause and effect."[39]

Behind the apparent separateness of individual beings is a unitary reality. Just as the ocean is composed of innumerable drops of water, undifferentiated being manifests itself in human experience as apparently separate selves. "Underlying man's personality and animating it is a reservoir of being that never dies, is never exhausted, and is without limit in awareness and bliss. This infinite center of life, this hidden self or *Atman,* is no less than *Brahman,* the Godhead."[40]

Hinduism teaches that it is possible to free ourselves from the illusion of separate selfhood, with its attendant pain. Attachment to, or identification with, the concept of "self" as separate and distinct causes suffering in the present life and perpetuates the endless wheel of births and deaths, the wheel of *karma.* Liberation (*moksha*) from fate and the cycles of history involves the recognition that life and death are beyond such mistaken notions of self-identity. "The one who has attained *moksha* can see the eternal in the temporal and the temporal in the eternal."[41] The *Bhagavad-Gita* says:

> Worn-out garments are shed by the body:
> Worn-out bodies are shed by the dweller.

Nikhilananda says, "In the act of giving up the old body or entering into the new body, the real Self does not undergo any change whatsoever. . . . Brahman, through Its inscrutable *maya* (illusion), creates a body, identifies Itself with it, and regards Itself as an individual, or embodied, soul."[42]

Death is inescapable. It is a natural corollary of conditioned existence. What is born passes away. Yet, for the person "whose consciousness has become stabilized by the insight that it is the very nature of things to come-to-be and pass-away," there is no "occasion either for rejoicing over birth or grieving over death."[43]

Hinduism offers various rites and practices that help in awakening to truth. For example, one practice involves imagining one's own death and the fate of the body, its return to elemental matter in the grave or on the funeral pyre. Another practice involves paying close attention to the transitory and ever-changing nature of one's own being, moment to moment. Other practices involve meditation in the presence of a dead body or at burial or cremation grounds. By consciously confronting mortality, one becomes reoriented toward the transcendent dimensions of reality. The aim is to let go of conditioned existence. This is "the death that conquers death."[44]

The Buddhist Understanding of Death

Buddhism is named after the historical Buddha ("the awakened one"), Siddhartha Gautama, who taught in India around the sixth to fourth centuries B.C.E. Like Hinduism, Buddhist doctrine explains that the universe is the product of *karma,* and the goal is escape from the suffering of *samsara,* the cycle of births and deaths. The aim is *nirvana,* which means "extinction," as when a flame goes out when deprived of fuel. *Nirvana* is described as an "unconditioned state beyond birth and death that is reached after all ignorance and craving have been extinguished and all karma, which is the cause of rebirth, has been dissolved."[45]

In this view, there is no "self" to survive after death or be reborn. Everything is transitory and impermanent (*anicca*), in continual unease and unrest (*dukkha*), and substanceless (*anatta*). In the Buddhist view, *karma* is seen as the universal principle of causality that underlies the stream of "psychophysical" events. Dōgen, founder of the Soto Zen sect of Buddhism, says, "Life constantly changes, moment by moment, in each of its stages, whether we want it to or not. Without even a moment's pause our karma causes us to transmigrate continuously."[46]

This transmigration can be likened to impressing a seal onto wax, or to transferring energy in a game of billiards when the cue ball strikes the cluster of balls, creating new energy events. "Rebirth does not involve the transfer of a substance, but the continuation of a process."[47] From the Buddhist perspective, it could be said that there are two kinds of death: continuous and regular. Continuous death is the "passing show" of phenomenal experience, constantly arising and passing away, moment by moment. Regular, or corporeal, death is the physical cessation of vital body functions at the end of a lifetime. "For the enlightened person, death happens; that is all. And one is in perfect accord with the event."[48]

Buddhist meditation is described as "in one sense a death rite, although it is seldom called that. Meditation practice is about sitting attentively on the abyss between life and death without clinging to life as if it were good or fleeing death as if it were bad."[49] Dōgen said, "The thorough clarification of the meaning of birth and death—this is the most important problem of all for Buddhists."[50]

Thus shall you think of all this fleeting world:
A star at dawn, a bubble in a stream;
A flash of lightning in a summer cloud.
A phantom, an illusion, a dream.

Buddha,
The Diamond Sutra

Like Hinduism, Buddhism teaches that it is necessary to renounce the desires and cravings that maintain the delusion of a separate self. When all attachments are dropped, the wheel of *karma,* the incessant round of birth-decay-death, is given no further fuel. How does one awaken to this reality, to *nirvana*? Dōgen says, "Simply understand that birth and death are in themselves *nirvana,* there being no birth-death to be hated or *nirvana* to be desired. Then, for the first time you will be freed from birth and death."[51]

The paradox of Dōgen's statement about birth-death and the importance of using death as a means of awakening to truth is echoed in the words of Hakuin, who is known as the reviver of the Rinzai sect, the other great Zen Buddhist lineage in Japan.[52] For those who wish to investigate their true nature, Hakuin advised meditation on the word *shi,* the character for death. To do this, he suggested a *koan* (a teaching question): "After you are dead and cremated, where has the main character [the chief actor or one's "original face"] gone?" Hakuin wrote:

> Among all the teaching and instructions, the word *death* has the most unpleasant and disgusting connotations. Yet if you once suddenly penetrate this "death" koan, you will find that there is no more felicitous teaching than this instruction that serves as the key to the realm in which birth and death are transcended, where the place in which you stand is the Diamond indestructible, and where you have become a divine immortal, unaging and undying. The word *death* is the vital essential that the warrior must first determine for himself.

The period immediately after death is considered to be an especially opportune time for gaining insight. The priest at a Buddhist funeral, for example, speaks directly to the deceased, expounding on the teachings that can awaken the intermediate being to the true nature of existence. Philip Kapleau says, "The funeral and subsequent services thus represent literally a 'once in a lifetime' opportunity to awaken the deceased and thereby liberate him from the binding chain of birth-and-death."[53]

After-Death States in Tibetan Buddhism

According to W. Y. Evans-Wentz, "Buddhists and Hindus alike believe that the last thought at the moment of death determines the character of the next incarnation."[54] On this point, the Buddha said, "Rebirth arises from two causes: the last thought of the previous life as its governing principle and the actions of the previous life as its basis. The stopping of the last thought is known as decease; the appearance of the first thought as rebirth."[55] Scriptures like the *Bardo Thödol,* or *The Tibetan Book of the Dead,* as it is better known in the West, are meant to influence the thoughts of the dying person during the transitional period of life-death-rebirth. Indeed, the *Bardo Thödol* is also known as "The Book of Natural Liberation." Here is an excerpt:

> Listen carefully; be attentive and alert. Death has come to you. It is time for you to depart this world. While you must face this reality alone, know that you are not the only one, for death comes to all. Do not cling to life because of sentiment, and do not fear to go on. You do not have the power to stay.[56]

© Albert Lee Strickland

In the Japanese section of this cemetery on the island of Oahu, graves holding the ashes of deceased members of the community are ornamented with Buddhist symbols of the Wheel of Dharma and the Lotus.

Although *bardo* is often interpreted as an intermediate or transitional state between death and rebirth, it can be translated as "gap" or "interval of suspension." In this sense, it refers to a number of "in between" or transitional conditions.[57] Chögyam Trungpa suggests that the term refers not only to the interval between death and rebirth, but also to "suspension within the living situation."[58] The *Bardo Thödol* and similar texts are commonly read as a person is dying. (A similar practice occurs in the Hindu tradition, with the *Bhagavad-Gita* being read.) Such texts can serve as a guide for the living as well as the dying. Chögyam Trungpa says that the *Bardo Thödol* deals with "the principle of birth and death recurring constantly in this life." Indeed, in this view, "The bardo experience is part of our basic psychological make-up."

The *Bardo Thödol* offers counsel about how to use these experiences—some terrifying, some benign—to awaken to a more enlightened incarnation. Although acknowledging that these experiences likely appear quite real to the *bardo* traveler, the text emphasizes that the deities or demons encountered are simply apparitions, the experiencer's own projections. They do not represent ultimate or transcendent perfection but, rather, steps on the way. (Some scholars believe, as Christopher Carr argues, that modern near-death experiences, or NDEs, "describe, at most, the beginning of death processes, whereas the Tibetan books of the dead describe entire death processes.")[59]

> Though it will die soon
> The voice of the cicada
> Shows no sign of this.
> Bashō

Secular Concepts of Immortality

In technology-oriented and economics-driven societies—both East and West—traditional religious and philosophical beliefs about the purpose of life or the nature of death no longer enjoy universal acceptance as they did when societies and communities were more cohesive. For many people, death has been divorced from religious and mythic connotations. *Secularization* is "the process in modern societies whereby religious ideas, practice, and organizations lose their influence in the face of scientific and other knowledge."[60] Traditional beliefs no longer carry the same weight in a social milieu that emphasizes rationalism and scientific method. Colin Murray Parkes says, "Secularism is essentially rational; it is the faith that we must rely on our reason in all matters, and that reason must take precedence over other ways of perceiving reality."[61] Theological or philosophical discussions about the afterlife may seem to resemble the famous debate about the number of dancing angels that will fit on the head of a pin. Yet vestiges of traditional concepts about death and the afterlife remain part of our modern consciousness.

The Abrahamic religious traditions—Judaism, Christianity, and Islam—present a linear picture of human history, describing a progression of events that begins with creation and eventuates in the resolution of the cosmic story at the end of time. Such an orientation leads to an interest in *eschatologies*—that is, pictures of the ultimate state, doctrines of last things. From the wellsprings of the Judeo-Christian tradition and Greek thought, people in Western culture have predominantly framed their beliefs about the afterlife in a historical context oriented toward the future. The predominant viewpoint in Western culture is that human beings live a single life; that the soul survives death, perhaps in a disembodied state; that at some future time each soul will be judged; and that, depending on one's conduct during earthly existence, the aftermath will be either hellish torment or heavenly bliss. This view is challenged by modern ways of thinking about human existence and death.

Among the most influential secular alternatives to religious orientations are humanism, positivism, and existentialism. *Humanism* (meaning a doctrine, attitude, or way of life centered on human interests or values) emphasizes human intellectual and cultural achievements rather than divine intervention and the supernaturalism of religion.[62] It tends to reflect an antireligious, even atheistic, stance in which human beings are the measure of all things. *Positivism,* a school of thought associated with science, reflects the belief that religious or metaphysical modes of knowing are imperfect and that "positive knowledge" is based on what can be directly observed in nature and in human activities. *Existentialism* is an intellectual and artistic movement that also influences secular attitudes about life and death. In its inquiry into the meaning of human experience, existentialism disavows the comforting answers offered by religion or social convention. Instead, it focuses squarely on our individual responsibility for making choices that define who we are and what we will become. The "human predicament" is such that we cannot shirk our responsibility for making difficult, but crucial, choices that shape our existence.

> We are self-creating creatures: we can choose what we want to be, and choose to be it. The moment of choice, the leap into existence, comes between two fixed points: the nothingness from which we come and the nothingness to which we return after we die. Our glory is the self-defining choice; our agony is that we need to make it.[63]

It is not unusual for a person to hold several competing worldviews at the same time, perhaps combining elements of religious faith carried over from childhood with elements of the viewpoints and attitudes represented by one or more of the secular alternatives just discussed.

Secular, or nonreligious, responses to questions about survival after death often reflect ideas about some kind of *symbolic immortality*.[64] These ideas include the biological continuity that results from having children who sustain a person's genetic legacy through succeeding generations, thus conferring a kind of personal immortality. Other "children" that symbolically convey personal immortality include those produced through creative works of art, contributions to a field of knowledge, and even heroic or helpful deeds. A person who has arranged for his or her body to be donated after death for the purpose of medical research gains a kind of "medical immortality" through training new physicians or advancing medical science. The fact that we are all members of one human race means that the good things we do and our contributions to the welfare of others extend beyond our deaths, thereby conferring a kind of "communal immortality" as our good deeds continue to resonate with a positive influence on humankind.

Today, despite the option of unbelief, most Americans affirm belief in God. Nearly 80 percent say they believe in life after death.[65] Researchers note that images of what the afterlife might be like generally involve union with God, peace and tranquility, and reunion with relatives.[66] One study of college undergraduates found that more than 90 percent believe that "one is reunited with family and friends, that the afterlife is comforting, that there is Heaven, and that the transition is peaceful."[67] It is apparent that religious ideas continue to play a role in both personal and social thought.

Although the assurances of religion can be comforting, Simone Weil presents a complementary approach:

> Not to believe in the immortality of the soul, but to look upon the whole of life as destined to prepare for the moment of death; not to believe in God, but to love the universe, always, even in the throes of anguish, as a home—there lies the road toward faith by way of atheism. This is the same faith as that which shines resplendent in religious symbols.[68]

The absolute certainty that death is a complete and definitive and irrevocable annihilation of personal consciousness, a certainty of the same order as our certainty that the three angles of a triangle are equal to two right angles, or contrariwise, the absolute certainty that our personal consciousness continues beyond death in whatever condition (including in such a concept the strange and adventitious additional notion of eternal reward or punishment)—either of these certainties would make our life equally impossible. In the most secret recess of the spirit of the man who believes that death will put an end to his personal consciousness and even to his memory forever, in that inner recess, even without his knowing it perhaps, a shadow hovers, a vague shadow lurks, a shadow of the shadow of uncertainty, and, while he tells himself: "There's nothing for it but to live this passing life, for there is no other!" at the same time he hears, in this most secret recess, his own doubt murmur: "Who knows? . . ." He is not sure he hears aright, but he hears. Likewise, in some recess of the soul of the true believer who has faith in a future life, a muffled voice, the voice of uncertainty, murmurs in his spirit's ear: "Who knows? . . ." Perhaps these voices are no louder than the buzzing of mosquitoes when the wind roars through the trees in the woods; we scarcely make out the humming, and yet, mingled in the uproar of the storm, it can be heard. How, without this uncertainty, could we ever live?

Miguel de Unamuno, *The Tragic Sense of Life*

Questions about immortality and "life after death" engage our thoughts. When religious answers do not suffice, a search for scientific proof of "something beyond" ensues. The search for satisfying answers about what lies beyond death is illustrated by widespread interest in near-death experiences.

Near-Death Experiences: At the Threshold of Death

Stories of travel to other worlds can be found in virtually all cultures. The traveler may be a hero, shaman, prophet, king, or even an ordinary mortal who passes through the gates of death and returns with a message for the living. Examples of such journeys include the heavenly ascent of the prophet Muhammad and the heavenly visions of Enoch and the Apostle Paul, as well as Odysseus's and Gilgamesh's epic adventures to the underworld, and the descent of the goddess Inanna.

Carol Zaleski identifies three forms of the *otherworld* journey: (1) the journey to the underworld, (2) the ascent to higher worlds, and (3) the fantastic voyage.[69] The common thread of all such journeys, says Zaleski, is the "story," which is shaped not only by what appear to be universal laws of symbolic experience, but also by the experiences of a given culture. Belief in a future life was historically based on religious experience; today, near-death experiences are often cited by people as a reason for such belief.[70] *Near-death experiences (NDEs)* are "profound psychological events with transcendental and mystical elements, typically occurring to individuals close to death or in situations of intense physical or emotional danger."[71]

"Calvin and Hobbes," drawing by Bill Watterson, © 1990 Universal Press Syndicate

The publication in 1975 of Raymond Moody's *Life After Life* sparked the current interest in otherworld journeys and, more specifically, in near-death experiences. These accounts by individuals who have come back from the edge of death provide fascinating glimpses into a paranormal, or scientifically unexplainable, order of existence that seemingly transcends the limits of biological life. Some people view near-death experiences as proof that the human personality survives death. Others assign psychological or neurophysiological causes to NDEs, describing them as naturalistic responses to the stress of facing a life-threatening danger. What are the components of a typical near-death experience?

NDEs: A Composite Picture

Suppose, in a horrific accident or acute medical crisis, you find yourself suddenly faced by an overwhelming encounter with death. Perhaps, almost beyond awareness, you begin to realize you're not going to make it, you're going to die.

It's like a dream, yet the experience seems more real than ordinary waking consciousness. Your vision and hearing are extremely acute. Sensory perceptions are heightened, and your thought processes are vividly clear, rational. Somehow, you are no longer bound to your body. Becoming aware of this feeling of disconnectedness, you realize that you are, in fact, separate from the body, floating free, as you look down at the mangled or suffering body and recognize it as your own.

You may feel a bit lonely, drifting in space, although there is a pervasive sense of calm, a serenity that was rarely if ever experienced in the body. The constraints of time and space seem irrelevant, unreal. As you move away from the once-familiar world of the now-dead body, you enter a darkness, a tunnel, a transitional stage in your journey.

Now you notice a light, more brilliant than could have been imagined during your earthly existence. It beckons, drawing you onward, its golden hues heralding your approach to the other side. The whole of your life is experienced in a nearly instantaneous matrix of flashbacks, impressions of your prior life, events, places, people: your life reviewed and projected on the transparent screen of consciousness.

As you begin to enter the light, you glimpse a world of unimaginable and unspeakable brilliance and beauty. Someone is greeting you, perhaps a loved one, or perhaps you become aware of Jesus or Moses or Muhammad or another being of ineffable grace. But now you realize that you cannot enter fully into the light, not yet, not this time.

Dimensions of Near-Death Experiences

Many people emerge from a near-death experience with a greater appreciation of life, a determination to make better use of the opportunities presented to them. Often, they are more self-confident, more able to cope with the difficulties of life. Relationships become more important and material comforts less important. NDE researcher Kenneth Ring says the typical near-death experiencer "has achieved a sense of what is important in life and strives to live in accordance with his understanding of what matters."[72] Near-death experiencers report dramatic reductions in death anxiety and fear of death, which leads to altered life goals and values and to enhanced health, well-being, tranquility, and zest for life.[73] People who experience NDEs exhibit many features associated with the "conversion" stories of life-changing religious experiences.

In outline, our imaginary near-death experience is typical of reports by those who have actually had such experiences. Four core elements have been identified as characteristic of NDEs—namely, the person (1) hears the news of his or her death, (2) departs from the body, (3) encounters significant others, and (4) returns to the body. However, this "typical" NDE is experienced variously by different individuals. In one sample, only about 33 percent of respondents experienced themselves as separate from their bodies, 23 percent experienced the entry into a dark tunnel or transitional stage, 16 percent experienced seeing a bright light, and 10 percent experienced themselves as actually entering the light (though only for a "peek" into the unearthly surroundings). Ring found that NDEs resulting from illness were more likely to be complete—to have all of these characteristic core elements—than were NDEs resulting from accidents. Over half of the NDEs related to accidents, however, included an experience of *panoramic memory*, or life review, compared to only 16 percent of those whose NDE was related to illness or attempted suicide.

Life review, in itself a fascinating feature of NDEs, usually consists of vivid and almost instantaneous visions of the person's whole life or "selected highlights" of it.[74] The life review may appear in an orderly sequence, or it may happen "all at once." Either way, it apparently occurs without any conscious control or effort on the part of the experiencer. Life "review" may include visions of the future, with experiencers visualizing their death, the reactions of friends and relatives, and events at the funeral.

The encounter with a presence—a feature of NDEs typically related to the "tunnel" experience—usually involves the experiencer seeing deceased

In Hieronymus Bosch's portrayal of the Ascent into the Empyrean—the highest heaven in medieval cosmology—the soul, purged of its impurities, approaches the end of its long journey and union with the Divine.

relatives or friends, or sensing a religious figure. This presence has often been understood as a representation of the "higher self," but this is not always the case.[75] William Serdahely describes an eight-year-old boy who was "comforted by two of his family's pets who had died prior to the incident."[76] These encounters with a presence are sometimes linked to the decision to return, to terminate the NDE. Some experiencers believe that the decision to return to earthly life is made for them; others report that they arrived at this decision themselves. Usually, the decision to return relates in some way to unfinished business or to responsibilities that the person must attend to before his or her death.

The majority of NDEs are characterized by feelings of joy, peace, and cosmic unity, but some are distressing and frightening.[77] These "hellish" NDEs may include imagery and sounds of torment, as well as demonic beings. An initial period of terror is, in some instances, followed by peaceful resolution. In other cases, the aftermath of the NDE brings a sense of emptiness and despair. In yet other instances, a benevolent guide accompanies the experiencer through the disconcerting experience. Some scholars think that hellish NDEs may be a truncated version of the typically radiant NDE; that is, hellish NDEs are *incomplete* NDEs. Another explanation highlights the fact that many saintly persons and mystics—St. Teresa of Avila and St. John of the Cross, to name two examples—reported frightening visions while engaged in deep prayer or meditation. A hellish NDE could therefore be a "purification experience," a kind of "dark night of the soul," as St. John of the Cross described his distressing religious experiences. What are we to make of near-death experiences? How should they be interpreted?

Interpreting Near-Death Experiences

Near-death experiences are fascinating. To some they suggest (or confirm) hoped-for possibilities of an afterlife or immortality. Others view near-death experiences as some sort of psychological phenomenon that may tell us something about the nature of human consciousness. To those who hold this view, NDEs are not "glimpses into a world beyond, but insights into the world within the human mind."[78] To yet others, NDEs are related to psychodynamic processes that occur when the self is threatened by annihilation. NDEs are initiated in the presence of a belief that one is dying—whether or not one is in fact close to death.[79] Some of the theories devised to explain near-death experiences are listed in Table 14-1.[80]

For early Hawaiians, observations of *apparent* death, or persons who had "left the body prematurely," were interpreted in accordance with their beliefs about the ancestor-gods.[81] On each island, there was a special promontory overlooking the sea; this was the *leina*, or leaping place, of the soul or spirit on its journey to the realm of the ancestors. If, on its way to the *leina*, a soul was met by an ancestor-god and sent back, the body would revive. Otherwise, the ancestor-god would lead it safely to and over the *leina*; once beyond that hurdle, the soul was safe with the ancestors.

TABLE 14-1   *Theories of the Near-Death Experience*

1. Neuropsychological theories:
   A. *Temporal lobe paroxysm,* or limbic lobe syndrome: Seizurelike neural discharges in the temporal lobe or, more generally, in the limbic system.
   B. *Cerebral anoxia,* or oxygen deprivation: Shortage of oxygen in the brain.
   C. *Endorphin release:* Release of certain neurotransmitters associated with analgesic (pain-killing) effects and a sense of psychological well-being.
   D. *Massive cortical disinhibition:* Loss of control over the random activity of the central nervous system.
   E. *False sight:* Hallucinatory imagery arising from structures in the brain and nervous system.
   F. *Drugs:* Side effects.
   G. *Sensory deprivation.*
2. Psychological theories:
   A. *Depersonalization:* Psychological detachment from one's body; in this case, a defensive reaction to the perceived threat of death. May be accompanied by hyperalertness.
   B. *Motivated fantasy:* A type of "defensive" fantasy that basically proposes that experiencers have an impression of surviving death because they desire to survive death.
   C. *Archetypes:* Images associated with various elements of the near-death experience are "wired" into the brain as mythological archetypes of our common humanity.
3. Metaphysical theories:
   A. *Soul travel:* Transitional journey of the soul or spirit to another mode of existence or realm of reality (e.g., "heaven"); proof of life after death.
   B. *Psychic vision:* Glimpses into another mode of reality, though not necessarily providing proof of soul-survival after death.

For various reasons (often, though not always, having to do with a person's behavior), an ancestor-god might delay a soul's acceptance into eternity. For instance, if a person died before his or her earthly work was done, the ancestor-god conducted the soul back to the body. "Sometimes when it is not yet time to die," reports Mary Pukui, "the relatives [ancestors] stand in the road and make you go back. Then the breath returns to the body with a crowing sound, *o'o-a-moa.*"[82]

Albert Heim, a Swiss geologist and mountain climber, is thought to have been the first to systematically gather data on near-death experiences.[83] During the early part of the twentieth century, Heim interviewed some thirty skiers and climbers who had been involved in accidents resulting in paranormal experiences. Heim's subjects experienced such phenomena as detachment from their bodies and panoramic memory, or life review.

The data compiled by Heim were subsequently reviewed by psychoanalytic pioneer Oskar Pfister, who explained NDEs as being caused by shock and depersonalization in the face of impending death. In other words, when a person's life is threatened, psychological defense mechanisms may come into play, giving rise to the phenomena associated with NDEs. Pfister's interpretation continues to be elaborated by present-day researchers who believe NDEs can be explained without resorting to the hypothesis that they prove life after death.

According to Russell Noyes and Roy Kletti, when the self is confronted by mortal danger, defensive reactions may result in a sense of depersonalization.[84] Their model, which may be the most comprehensive psychological explanation of NDEs offered thus far, distinguishes three stages in the typical near-death experience: (1) resistance, (2) life review, and (3) transcendence. The first stage, *resistance,* includes the processes of recognizing the danger, struggling against it, and finally accepting death as imminent. Such acceptance, or surrender, marks the beginning of the second stage, which is characterized by *life review.* As the self detaches from its bodily representation, panoramic memories occur and appear to encompass a person's whole life. Life review is often accompanied by affirmation of the meaning of one's existence and its integration into the universal order of things. The third stage, *transcendence,* occurs as there is further detachment from one's individual existence. It is characterized by an increasingly transcendental, or cosmic, consciousness that replaces limited ego- or self-identity.

Calm detachment, heightened sensory awareness, life review or panoramic memory, and mystical consciousness are all phenomena associated with the ego's protective response to the possibility of its own demise. In other words, the threat of death stimulates various psychological processes that allow the ego, or experiencing self, to "escape" the threat. Because these processes dissociate the experiencing self from the body, death is perceived as a threat only to the *body,* not to the perceiving "self." It is important to point out that a psychological interpretation of NDEs does not necessarily invalidate any possible spiritual meaning that may be associated with NDEs.

In seeking the meaning of NDEs, some researchers follow the lines of inquiry founded in the late nineteenth century by parapsychologists. To adequately understand NDEs, these researchers say, one must go beyond the usual boundaries of scientific inquiry. In short, we must be prepared to accept the possibility, which is not scientifically verifiable, that NDEs are in fact what they seem to be—that is, valid experiences of states of consciousness that transcend the death of the body. In this view, NDEs teach us that the *appearance* of death is not the same as the *experience* of death. In conducting cross-cultural studies of near-death experiences, Karlis Osis and Erlendur Haraldsson concluded that the evidence strongly suggests life after death.[85] They reported that "neither medical, nor psychological, nor cultural conditioning can explain away deathbed visions." Supporting this conclusion is the observation that some deathbed visions include apparitions contrary to the experiencer's expectations, such as "apparitions of persons the person thought were still living, but who in fact were dead," as well as apparitions that do not conform to cultural stereotypes, as with dying children who are "surprised to see 'angels' without wings." The idea that NDEs strongly suggest, or even prove, that there is life after death seems to resonate with many people. In national surveys, most adult Americans answer yes to the question "Do you believe in life after death?"[86]

It is wonderful that five thousand years have now elapsed since the creation of the world, and still it is undecided whether or not there has ever been an instance of the spirit of any person appearing after death. All argument is against it; but all belief is for it.

James Boswell, *Life of Johnson*

In summary, then, two distinct explanations have been offered to explain near-death experiences. In the first, NDEs offer proof of survival after death. NDEs are what they appear to be: experiences of life after death. In the second explanation, NDEs are a response to the threat of death and destruction of the self. This response focuses on the brain or nervous system and results from a ego-defensive reaction to a life-threatening situation.

Each explanation offers a model, or representation, of "how the world works." Louis Appleby, writing in the *British Medical Journal,* says that the explanations put forward to explain NDEs share one attribute: Each requires a form of faith.[87] The explanation that best suits your own perception of how things work is likely to be accepted most readily. There remains, however, another approach to interpreting the significance of near-death experiences. Perhaps both of the explanations are valid: There is life after death and there is also a psychological phenomenon involving various defense mechanisms whereby the personality is radically altered as the transition from one state to the next is negotiated. In Carol Zaleski's view, "We need to find a middle path between the extremes of dismissing near-death experience as 'nothing but' and embracing it as 'proof.'"[88]

Raymond Moody, who coined the term *near-death experiences,* now prefers to characterize NDEs as part of a "paranormal death syndrome," which includes apparitions of "death-bed escorts" frequently reported by individuals who are near death.[89] Concerning the way his findings about NDEs have been interpreted over the years, Moody is disturbed when people discuss NDEs as if they provide scientific evidence or proof of life after death. The prospect of finding scientific proof of life after death is, he says, "unthinkable." To Moody, NDEs represent a "wading out collectively into a domain of experience that has been closed for the most part to us until the past few decades and which is now opening up due to the developments and techniques of cardiopulmonary resuscitation." People who have experienced NDEs and shared their stories are enabling us all "to move across a frontier of consciousness."

On the subject of how best to interpret NDEs, Herman Feifel's remarks are pertinent:

> What is somewhat disquieting is the claim by some that near-death experiences are evidence for and proof of the existence of an after-life. There may well be life after death, but jumping to that conclusion from reported near-death experiences reflects more a leap of faith than judicious scientific assessment. This in no way minimizes the reality of these occurrences for the people who

declare them. I just think that in weighing the evidence in this area we have less far-fetched and more parsimonious interpretations within the canons of science that can explain these phenomena. What strikes me about many of these out-of-body reports is the hunger for meaning and purpose they suggest in this age of faltering faith.[90]

Robert Kastenbaum cautions us to be careful about readily accepting the "fantastic voyage" implied by most life-after-death accounts.[91] He says:

> The happily-ever-after theme threatens to draw attention away from the actual situations of the dying persons, their loved ones, and their care givers over the days, weeks, and months preceding death. What happens up to the point of the fabulous transition from life to death recedes into the background. This could not be more unfortunate. The background, after all, is where these people are actually living until death comes.

Finally, we should consider three points expressed by Charles Garfield, who has worked extensively with dying patients:[92]

1. Not everyone dies a blissful, accepting death.
2. Context is a powerful variable in altered-state experiences. A supportive environment for the dying person may be an important factor in determining whether the outcome is a positive altered-state experience for the dying.
3. The "happily ever after" stance toward death may represent a form of denial when what is really needed by the dying person is a demonstration of real concern and real caring in his or her present experience.

Whatever the beliefs that one may hold about life after death, Garfield says, "Let us have the courage to realize that death often will be a bitter pill to swallow."

Death Themes in Dreams and Psychedelic Experiences

Fascinating "hints" about afterlife possibilities have also been conveyed through "death dreams" and experiences with psychedelic or mind-altering drugs. "Dreams offer a vivid illustration of our lifelong awareness of death, giving voice to the unconscious fears, wishes, and desires that surround the brute fact of human finitude."[93]

Marie-Louise von Franz says that, compared to near-death experiences, which tend to be schematic and more culture-bound, the death imagery in dreams is richer in graphic detail and more subtle.[94] Among older people, dreams often appear to be psychically preparing them for impending death by symbolically indicating "the end of bodily life and the explicit continuation of psychic life after death." Using the medium of dreams, the unconscious communicates a comforting message—namely, that there *is* an afterlife.

> All of the dreams of people who are facing death indicate that the unconscious . . . prepares consciousness not for a definite end but for a profound transformation and for a kind of continuation of the life process which, however, is unimaginable to everyday consciousness.[95]

British Museum

The Egyptian papyrus of Hunefer depicts the Hall of Judgment and the Great Balance, where the deceased's soul is weighed against the feather of truth. Beneath the scales, the Devourer of Souls awaits the unjust while Horus is ready to lead the just to Osiris, the lord of the underworld, and to a pleasurable afterlife.

Death dreams incorporate a great variety of alchemical and mythological motifs, including themes associated with the growth of vegetation or flowering plants; the divine marriage of the soul with the cosmos; travel through a dark, narrow passageway, or through fire or water, to new birth; sacrifice or transformation of the old body; shifting ego- or soul-identity; and resurrection.

The journey through a dark passageway toward "a light at the end of the tunnel" is a common motif not only in dreams and NDEs, but in numerous mythological traditions. Indeed, many mythologies embody a comparison of the sun's path with the mystery of life and death. Among Egyptians, for example, the sun was viewed as the goal of the soul's journey along the pathway of the dead. The sun symbolizes the source of *awareness,* of becoming conscious. Franz says, "This also lies behind the widespread custom of lighting candles and letting them burn in mortuary rooms and on tombs and graves," which is a form of "analogy magic through which new life and an awakening to new consciousness is granted to the deceased."[96]

Turning to death imagery in connection with the use of psychedelic drugs, it is interesting to note that, although LSD (lysergic acid diethylamide) was first synthesized in 1938 by the Swiss chemist Albert Hoffman, its biochemical action on the brain is still not completely understood.[97] Nevertheless, its amplifying and catalyzing effects on the mind are well documented. From the earliest studies of LSD, researchers noticed that it activates "unconscious material from deep levels of the personality."[98] It apparently opens up areas of religious and spiritual experience that are intrinsic to the human personality but independent of a person's cultural or religious background. Most notably, it often leads to a "shattering encounter" with critical aspects of human existence: birth, decay, and death.

In the early 1960s, Eric Kast of the Chicago Medical School began studies of the pain-relieving effects of LSD and other psychedelic substances on patients who were suffering intense pain from a life-threatening illness.[99] Besides relieving the symptoms of physical pain and discomfort, LSD therapy diminished emotional symptoms, such as depression, anxiety, tension, insomnia, and psychological withdrawal. LSD seemed to accomplish these results by altering the patient's learned response to pain—that is, the patient's anticipation of pain based on past experiences. By becoming free of this conditioning, the patient was more oriented to the present and thus able to respond to sensations as they were actually experienced rather than to an image of pain that had grown more and more discomforting over time. Noting that pain is a composite phenomenon that has both a neurophysiological component (the pain sensation) and a psychological component (the pain affect), Stanislav Grof and Joan Halifax conclude that the primary influence of psychedelic therapy seems to be in modifying the psychological component.

Perhaps more significant than diminution of pain was a change of attitude toward death and dying among patients. After the psychedelic session, patients typically displayed a diminished fear of death and less anxiety about the life-threatening implications of the illness. According to Grof and Halifax, "Dying persons who had transcendental experiences developed a deep belief in the ultimate unity of all creation; they often experienced themselves as integral parts of it, including their disease and the often painful situations they were facing."[100]

Many patients exhibited a greater responsiveness to their families and their environment. Self-respect and morale were enhanced, and they showed greater appreciation of the subtleties of everyday life. The fact that such transcendental experiences were induced in randomly selected subjects was considered to

Now Let the Weeping Cease (Hymn)

Now let the weeping cease
Let no one mourn again
The love of God will bring you
   peace
There is no end

The Gospel at Colonus

be strong evidence that "matrices for such experiences exist in the unconscious as a normal constituent of the human personality."[101] (Although the general consensus among researchers was that there was enough positive evidence to justify continued research with LSD for therapeutic purposes such as pain relief, the "religious fervor of casual users and their calls for social revolution evoked a backlash that transformed LSD into a pariah substance and triggered laws that made its use in any context illegal.")[102]

As with the phenomena discussed in connection with near-death experiences, the psychedelic experience typically includes phenomena that are not scientifically explainable. Grof and Halifax point out that persons "unsophisticated in anthropology and mythology experience images, episodes, and even entire thematic sequences that bear a striking resemblance to the descriptions of the posthumous journey of the soul and the death-rebirth mysteries of various cultures."[103] As with near-death experiences, the result is usually a significantly altered outlook with respect to the meaning of life and death. The evidence accumulated through reports of near-death experiences, as well as psychedelic experiences, has led some researchers to the view that modern science should broaden its perspective on the nature of human consciousness. Stanislav Grof says, "Reality is always larger and more complex than the most elaborate and encompassing theory."[104]

Beliefs About Death: A Wall or a Door?

One writer comments, "Despite myths of an afterlife, the promises of sacred texts, and the hopes of the faithful, none of us really knows *what* continues, and if it does, *where* it goes or *how* it gets there."[105] In the last analysis, then, what shall we believe about personal immortality or the afterlife? Can we anticipate an ultimately fulfilling experience after death, as seems to be true from reports of near-death experiences? Or are such experiences merely psychological projections, wish-fulfilling fantasies that mask the terror of confronting one's own demise? Furthermore, what shall we say about various religious understandings? Do their concepts of the afterlife have some basis in reality? Or should we adopt a strictly scientific approach to such questions? Two basic philosophical views about death and the afterlife can be summarized as follows: Either death is a *wall* or it is a *door*.[106]

We can imagine many variations on these two positions regarding what happens at death. Indeed, the doctrines of the various religions and the explanations offered for paranormal experiences are just such variations. For example, stating a Christian perspective, we could say that death appears to be a wall, but at some time in the future—at the Resurrection—it turns out to have been a door. The Hindu concept of reincarnation would suggest that death is a door, not a wall. Buddhists might respond that death is both a door and a wall, and is neither. A standard psychological explanation of NDEs might support the view that death is a wall that is experienced as a door. Or perhaps the door and the wall are simply alternative ways of experiencing the same reality.

In the end, a statement made by the International Work Group on Death, Dying and Bereavement may be our best guide: "Dying is more than a biological occurrence. It is a human, social, and spiritual event, [but] too often the spiritual dimension of patients is neglected."[107] A close relationship between religion and health has existed since ancient times. Caregivers need to recognize and acknowledge the spiritual component of patient care. Appropriate resources should be offered to those who wish them. Each person's spiritual beliefs and preferences are to be respected.[108]

What we believe about death and the afterlife can influence the actions taken when we or others near death. If we have a materialist view, seeing death as a wall, we may insist that life-sustaining efforts be carried out to the end. Conversely, if we believe in continued existence after death, we may prefer to spend our final hours on earth in preparation for a transition into another mode of existence. Similarly, a bereaved person may find solace in his or her belief about what lies beyond death. The person who views death as the end may be reassured that the suffering of a loved one truly ends at death. Another person finds comfort in believing that the personality survives physical death. By understanding our own beliefs about death, we are able to "care more adequately for each other when death—wall or door—comes to those we love."[109]

Further Readings

Paul Badham and Linda Badham, eds. *Death and Immortality in the Religions of the World.* New York: Paragon House, 1987.

John Bowker. *The Meanings of Death.* New York: Cambridge University Press, 1991.

David Chidester. *Patterns of Transcendence: Religion, Death, and Dying.* 2nd ed. Belmont, Calif.: Wadsworth, 2002.

Jasper Griffin. *Homer on Life and Death.* Oxford: Clarendon Press, 1980.

Murray J. Harris. *Raised Immortal: Resurrection and Immortality in the New Testament.* Grand Rapids, Mich.: Eerdmans, 1985.

Christine Longaker. *Facing Death and Finding Hope: A Guide to the Emotional and Spiritual Care of the Dying.* New York: Doubleday, 1997.

Alister E. McGrath. *A Brief History of Heaven.* Malden, Mass.: Blackwell, 2003.

Alan F. Segal. *Life After Death: A History of the Afterlife in the Religions of the West.* New York: Doubleday, 2004.

J. I. Smith and Y. Haddad. *The Islamic Understanding of Death and Resurrection.* Albany: State University of New York Press, 1981.

Charles Taylor. *A Secular Age.* Cambridge, Mass.: Harvard University Press, 2007.

Richard P. Taylor. *Death and the Afterlife: A Cultural Encyclopedia.* Santa Barbara, Calif.: ABC-Clio, 2000.

Photojournalist W. Eugene Smith's children appear in his 1946 photograph, "The Walk to Paradise Garden," the first taken by Smith after two years of inactivity and numerous operations to make him sound again after multiple wounds received in the Pacific during World War II. Smith said he was determined that his first frame successfully "speak of a gentle moment of spirited purity in contrast to the depraved savagery I had raged against with my war photographs."

CHAPTER 15

The Path Ahead: Personal and Social Choices

Death is the ultimate challenge to human pretensions. "In the last analysis," says sociologist David Clark, "human societies are merely men and women banded together in the face of death."[1] Death may be devalued, even denied for a time, but it cannot be eluded. In telling "The Mortal King," a Chinese folk tale, Allan Chinen draws attention to the fact that the desire for immortality has its own pitfalls.[2] Surveying his realm one day, a king is struck by the awesome thought that someday he will die and lose it all. "I wish we could live forever!" the king exclaims. "That would be wonderful!" Encouraged by his friends, the king fantasizes how great it would be if they were never to grow old and die. Of all his companions, only one refrained from delighting in this prospect. Instead, he bowed to the king and explained, "If we all lived forever as you suggest, why, then, all the great heroes of history would still live among us; compared to them, we would be fit only to plow the fields or be clerks in the provinces."

In our complex relationship with death, we are both survivors and experiencers. In previous chapters we have seen that there are many different attitudes toward death and dying. Death can be seen as a threat or as a catalyst provoking greater awareness and creativity in life. Death may seem the ignominious end to even the best of human accomplishment, or it may be seen as a welcome respite from life's sufferings. Death holds many meanings.

One student in a death and dying class said, "Confronting death has put me in touch with life." Acknowledging the impact of death in our lives awakens us to the preciousness of life. This insight can lead to a greater appreciation of the relationships in one's life. Learning about death can also bring insights concerning the death of old notions of self, as one grows beyond limiting concepts of "who I am."

Death is inseparable from the whole of human experience. The study of death and dying touches on the past, the present, and the future. It takes account of individual acts as well as customs of entire societies. The study of death and dying leads naturally to the arena of political decision, and it ultimately brings us to choices of an emphatically personal nature. Death education is important in social relationships, as well as in the confrontation with mortality that comes in the most private, personal moments of solitude and introspection.

Think about your own relationship to death. What place does death have in your life? What kinds of meanings does death hold for you? Are death and dying compartmentalized in a category all their own, or are they woven into the fabric of your experience?

Death can be viewed as a burden or as a blessing. Its meaning changes as circumstances change and as our understanding evolves toward new recognitions of its place in our lives.

Jerry Soloway, UPI/Corbis-Bettmann Newsphotos

In this chapter we discuss some of the ways in which what we learn about death impinges on individual and social experience. Rather than providing answers, our aim is to stimulate inquiry, to raise questions, to speculate about the path ahead.

The Value of Exploring Death and Dying

Taking a course or reading a book about death and dying offers an opportunity to take death "out of the closet" and examine it from many perspectives. Possibly you are making new choices in your life as a result of your personal exploration of death. Reflecting on the study of death and dying, one student remarked, "The thought of death had always created a lot of fear; now I find that there's something very fascinating about exploring my own feelings about death and the way that society relates to death." Often, the study of death brings insights into past experiences in one's life. One woman said, "I see now what a big part denial and mutual pretense played in my family's experience of death; the subject of death has *really* been taboo." Another said, "I am surprised to find how many events in my own life carry the same kind of emotional impact as a death. Divorce, separation, illness, disappointment—all mean coping with grief, loneliness, fear, and sadness in much the same way as when dealing with a death."

As you think about the various topics covered in this book, what do you notice concerning your understanding of death? Has learning about death and dying expanded your perspective or altered your attitude toward death? Do the terms *death* and *dying* elicit the same thoughts and emotions as when you began your study?

"When I thought about my own death," a student remarked, "I slammed the door, thinking of all the things I still want to do in my lifetime. Now, I've become a bit more calm, a bit more balanced about it." Another said, "Before I got involved in studying death, I wasn't really down with it, especially my own death, even though I haven't had many personal encounters with death. Now I feel that facing my own death is not as difficult, really, as being a survivor of other people's deaths." For some, investigation of death and dying allows a more accurate perception of what one can do to protect or be responsible for another. A parent said, "I've learned something about letting go where my children are concerned. No matter how much you might wish it were otherwise, you can never shield your loved ones from everything."

Responding to this awareness, one student said, "I learned how important it is to appreciate people while you've got them." Becoming aware of death can focus attention on the importance in relationships of taking care of unfinished business, saying the things that need to be said, and not being anxious about those things that do not. As one student expressed it, her study of death and dying had impressed upon her a sense of "the precariousness of life."

Recognizing that the human situation is revealed not only in major changes—such as those brought about by death—but also in the less noticed changes experienced in daily life, one can choose to be attentive to the things

I attended your Dealing with Death and Dying class May 10 and 11. You excused me at 1:00, May 11, so that I could go to a function that I needed to attend. I agreed to write notes on an article on cancer to compensate for the class time that I'd miss.

At the same time I was driving home from the class, my Mother was admitted to a Midwestern hospital for internal bleeding due to her accelerated cancerous condition. I left the Bay Area soon after and arrived in Iowa to deal with the reality of death.

Comments on the article don't seem as important to me, now, as some other comments I'd like to make. They concern the necessity of dealing with death and dying.

Had it not been for your class, I would have had more severe problems dealing with all the things death causes us to deal with. The openness of the people in class helped me work through some of the pain I was experiencing as I knew that my Mother didn't have long to live. The class helped me during the time the mortician sat with us and helped us work out the business details, and it helped me through the Midwestern Protestant wake. I was helped as I remembered to make sure that we got what we wanted and were allowed to say our good-byes in ways we wanted. I was able to help my family think clearly about the needs they had so that after Mother was removed from us, we would not say "if only."

A student in a Death and Dying class

and people that are most highly valued. As Thomas Attig points out, coming to terms with our own finiteness and mortality can be understood as a grieving process.[3] Such self-mourning is really a lifelong process of coming to terms with impermanence, uncertainty, and vulnerability—qualities inherent in being mortal.

As more people willingly confront issues surrounding death and dying, and examine options for themselves, changes are occurring throughout society. Examples are the establishment of hospices and suicide intervention programs, as well as support groups that aid individuals and families in crisis. As death is subjected to less fearful scrutiny, there is movement—both individually and as a society—toward gaining knowledge that can be helpful in dealing with death intelligently and compassionately. Think about the personal and social implications of death and dying. Have your previous opinions on such issues as euthanasia, funerals and body disposition, and war, among others, been confirmed? Or have they changed as a result of your studies?

For some, the close examination of death brings insights that help dissipate or resolve long-held feelings of guilt or blame about a loved one's death. The encounter with death that comes through study can open up new and creative possibilities that result in an easier, more comfortable relationship with others and with life itself. The study of death and dying can help to put previously unsettling experiences into perspective.

The notions that may be present at the beginning of a personal exploration of death and dying are expressed in the following statement:

When I first began to recognize the seriousness of death and dying, I fled from it in fear, although I didn't realize what I was doing. Emotionally, it was harder than I had expected. But I learned that people do survive their losses, and I now know why they are called "survivors." I also learned a lot about myself, not all pleasant. A lot of my learning occurred amidst avoidance and trepidation. I thought about things that I had neglected for a long time . . . all my old concepts of death, shadowed in images of hells and old horror movies.

For one man who had felt frustrated, resentful, and guilty about his brother's death twenty years earlier, the study of death provided an opportunity to open up unexpressed and unresolved grief about a number of close family deaths. As the "stored tears" began to be expressed, he summed up the benefit of his exploration of death: "It feels so good to get rid of that ache."

For some, the study of death and dying brings benefits related to professional concerns. One nurse said: "When death occurs on the ward, people often think, 'Oh, well, you're a nurse; it shouldn't bother you.' But it does. . . . I really miss the patient; it's a real loss." A ward clerk in a hospital emergency room described the new and more helpful choices she could use in relating to survivors:

> My desk is in the same area with the survivors of an ER [emergency room] death. I used to feel a pain right in the pit of my stomach, wondering what to say to them. I thought I should be able to comfort them in some way, that I should somehow offer them words of wisdom. But now I don't feel that way. I've learned how important it is to simply listen, to be supportive just by being there, instead of trying to find some words that will magically make it all go away.

Others find the study of death and dying academically intriguing. The avenues of exploration into other cultures or into one's own society opened up through such study can be a rapid means of gaining insight into what is essential about a society's values and concepts. Learning about the meaning of death in feudal Japan, for example, provides the student of Japanese culture an appreciation that goes beyond the usual aesthetic or historic approach to cross-cultural understanding. Cultural attitudes toward death are reflected in a society's programs for the aged and its care of the dying. The willingness of a society to engage in activities that pose risks for the well-being of its citizens also reveals something of the social consensus with regard to the value of human life. Funeral customs reflect a society's attitudes toward death and intimate relationships. Investigating a society's relationship with death makes available a wealth of information to the person with an inquiring mind and an interest in discerning the larger patterns of belief and behavior.

New Directions in Thanatology

Thanatology is a diverse, expanding, and maturing field of study and practice. In this section, we take a brief tour of some tasks and topics that constitute what might be called new directions in thanatology. These include efforts to (1) narrow the gap between theorists and practitioners so that research findings are better integrated into practice, (2) clarify the goals of death education, and (3) gain a global perspective. The section concludes with an examination of one of the most important new directions: creating compassionate cities.

Bridging Research and Practice

Do counselors, therapists, and other health or medical professionals make use of the knowledge and insights derived from thanatological research? Or is there a "cultural split" between researchers and clinicians? In examining critical issues in thanatology two decades ago, Robert Kastenbaum remarked that there are few signs that practitioners have made much use of either research or theory in their work with patients or with the bereaved. It appears "that many practitioners in the area of terminal care and bereavement have neither an up-to-date mastery of thanatological research nor a secure grasp of the historical and theoretical dimensions." In his portrait of research, theory, and practice, Kastenbaum concludes that,

> at the worst, perhaps, we have sketched a picture of practitioners who fail to read a literature that wouldn't help them very much anyway. The academicians continue to tread their mills . . . with only each other to amuse, while the practitioners base their services on individual experiences and a grab-bag of unexamined assumptions and "facts" whose veridicality has seldom been tested, let alone established.[4]

Echoing such thoughts, Myra Bluebond-Langner observes that, "while the quantity of research has increased, what more do we actually know? Has progress in thanatology kept pace with publication? What differences have our efforts made in the care of dying patients and their families, and in our own responses to death and impending disasters?"[5]

As Robert Fulton wrote some years ago, we often see a tendency to fixate on nineteenth-century hydrostatic models of grief, which postulate a certain volume of grief that must be poured out.[6] In this view, grieving is conceived of as a step-by-step progression, rather than as a dynamic process of "unraveling the skein of grief." Since Fulton made these points, theorists and scholars have suggested alternatives to the linear, hydrostatic model of grief, but frequently these theories are not known by caregivers who assist the bereaved or terminally ill.

More recently, John Jordan observes that "theory is the bridge over which empirical findings can cross into the world of the practitioner," and he encourages researchers to "explain with more clarity and depth what their findings could mean for clinical practice."[7] To bridge the gap that separates researchers and practitioners, we need what David Balk refers to as a "scholarship of application," a dynamic exchange between theory and practice that makes "research a useful form of gaining knowledge."[8]

Clarifying the Goals of Death Education

Hannelore Wass notes that "less than a fifth of students in the health professions are offered a course on death; the rest typically are provided

During an annual cremation ceremony in Bali, young men carry a papier-mâché tiger containing the remains of a villager through the center of town to a temple outside the village, where the actual cremation takes place. On the way, they run, halt abruptly, shout and make noise, and turn the palanquin around and around to confuse the spirit so that it leaves the earthly realm and journeys to the afterworld.

death-related content in a few lectures."[9] Emergency medical technicians, police officers, firefighters, and military mortuary officers receive minimum or no preparation in thanatology despite the fact that they routinely work in situations that involve death. Thus, part of the mission of thanatology must be to expand its reach so that information can get to those on the front lines, as well as their clients and patients.

The personal dimension of death education is also important. We need to be alert to presuppositions that originate in a caregiver's own preferences rather than from informed study and appraisal. A caregiver who places a high value on resolving conflicts may unintentionally demand, expect, or wish that his or her clients or patients do the same. In striving to improve care of the dying and the bereaved, paternalism may replace sensitivity if answers are proposed before the necessary questions have been asked.

Death education is a relatively new field of study. As a clearer sense of continuity and common tradition continues to evolve, the curricula of death education and thanatology are being refined and new directions explored. There is also ongoing discussion about the goals of death education. The question of accountability in death education is difficult to address, partly because such education takes place in a variety of settings, often with differing methodologies and goals. Should death education aim to *alleviate* discomfort and anxiety about dying and death? If acceptance of death is thought to be "superior" to denial, that notion needs to be investigated and validated.[10] As with this example, further research is needed to address fundamental issues.

Ethnic groups and other minorities are underrepresented in the resource materials commonly used in death education. Although this situation has improved in recent years, many of the "lessons taught" are still predominantly based on studies of middle-class, white populations. Darrell Crase asks the rhetorical question "Black people do die, don't they?"[11] In a culturally diverse environment, this question applies to people from other ethnic backgrounds as well. Some of the most insightful research findings and theories in recent decades have resulted from scholars taking a broad cross-cultural view of dying, death, and bereavement.

The comprehensive concerns that are intrinsically part of death education are aptly summarized in a document formulated by the International Work Group on Death, Dying and Bereavement:

> Death, dying, and bereavement are fundamental and pervasive aspects of the human experience. Individuals and societies achieve fullness of living by understanding and appreciating these realities. The absence of such understanding and appreciation may result in unnecessary suffering, loss of dignity, alienation, and diminished quality of living. Therefore, education about death, dying, and bereavement, both formal and informal, is an essential component of the educational process at all levels.[12]

Gaining an International Perspective

As death education and thanatology continue to evolve, there are calls for a global perspective. Although personal experiences related to dying and

My Death

"Death is our eternal companion,"
Don Juan said with a most serious
air. "It is always to our left, at
an arm's length. . . . It has always been
watching you. It always will until
the day it taps you."

        Carlos Castenada

My death
looks exactly like me,
She lives to my left,
at exactly an arm's length.
She has my face, hair, hands;
she ages
as I grow older.

Sometimes, at night,
my death awakens me

or else appears in dreams
I did not write.
Sometimes a sudden wind
blows from nowhere,
& I look left
& see my death.
Alive, I write
with my right hand only.
When I am dead,
I shall write with my left.

But later I will have to write
through others.
I may appear
to future poets
as their deaths.

        Erica Jong

---

death are indeed central concerns, the global dimensions of death—disaster, war, terrorism, environmental catastrophe—are important in thanatology. Daniel Leviton and William Wendt offer a framework that focuses on the reality of death to help improve the quality of civilized life.[13] In this model, death education not only aids individuals in their personal confrontations with death, but also helps ameliorate the causes of large-scale deaths that are human-caused and unnecessary. The term *horrendous death* describes such confrontations with death, a term that Leviton and Wendt define as

> a form of premature death which is ugly, fashioned by man, without any trace of grace, totally unnecessary, and, as they say of pornography, lacking any redeeming social value. It is that death which is caused by war, homicide, holocaust, terrorism, starvation, and poisoning of the environment.

Allan Kellehear suggests that the ideas of compassion, the universality of death and loss, and "the integration and recognition of death as an experience greater than physical demise" provide an inclusive and practical way forward. In the public health arena, this is based on *universal* human experiences of suffering and well-being, not simply categories of illness, disease, or health states.[14] Kellehear says, "These widespread experiences of endings, and the losses that inevitably emerge in their wake, are the most important potential basis of our interpersonal and international connection with one another."[15] Such a focus could constitute what Kellehear calls a promising basis for a "third wave" of public health initiatives in the twenty-first century.

© Carol A. Foote

Culture and individual personality shape our attitudes toward death. What we understand of death and what meanings we ascribe to it become significant to the extent that we construct a meaningful relationship with the experience of death and dying in our lives. This grave marker expresses a memorialization that is consonant with the lifestyles of both the deceased and her survivors.

Creating Compassionate Cities

It is said that communities give individuals roots, a sense of place, and a location within the broader scheme of human affairs. As the present century progresses, scholars tell us that our "identities will be layered along a continuum from local to global." National boundaries will mean less and less as people begin to have enough in common to share a transnational identity. This identity "involves the ability to live ethnically and culturally in both the global and local spheres at the same time."[16]

This has important implications with respect to death and to the goal of *creating compassionate cities,* a term coined by Allan Kellehear to denote "a model of public health that encourages community participation in all types of end-of-life care."[17] He highlights two lessons from our past experience in this regard: First, care of the dying has been *normal and routine* for families and communities; and second, past patterns of community care have illustrated the importance of *community relationships* in that care. With our dependence on professional services, we have lost sight of these lessons. "Death knowledge is professional knowledge, not personal knowledge."[18] There is a need for community involvement and consideration of death as a fact of life.[19] Moreover, Kellehear calls attention to the fact that end-of-life care is more than palliative care.

> Every day people die in road traumas, suicides, and homicides, and disasters take people in hundreds and thousands at a time. Aside from death from old age, there are also tolls of death from the political and social plight of indigenous peoples all over the world. From civil wars to the negative health effects of dispossession, our current understandings about caring for those dying and experiencing loss have yet to be inclusive of these people and contexts.[20]

These are also relevant end-of-life care matters and experiences. Death is inevitable and loss is universal. Kellehear offers the following defining characteristics of a "compassionate city":[21]

- Meets the special needs of its aged, those living with life-threatening illness, and those living with loss.
- Has a strong commitment to social and cultural differences.
- Offers its inhabitants access to a wide variety of supportive experiences, interactions, and communication.
- Promotes and celebrates reconciliation with indigenous peoples and the memory of other important community losses.
- Has a recognition of and plans to accommodate those disadvantaged by the economy, including rural and remote populations, indigenous people and the homeless.
- Preserves and promotes a community's spiritual traditions and storytellers.

What is "new" about compassionate cities? Kellehear says, "The connection of death and loss to the wider problems of living together as communities in all our evolving, modern diversity is new. The linking of the idea of compassion to health, death and loss, and the reconnecting of death and loss to the broader experience of change and endings, is news for many."[22] Robert Goss and Dennis Klass note that human bonds based in shared pain "do not fit easily into the cultural narrative of consumer capitalism in which happiness is regarded as the normal human condition."[23] Thus, the ideal of

© Carol A. Foote

The contemplation of death and its meaning will determine how we and our children think about and behave toward death in the decades ahead.

creating compassionate cities remains a challenge for thanatology and public health.

Herman Feifel calls attention to the need to "integrate existing knowledge concerning death and grief into our communal and public institutions."[24] People who are involved in death education, counseling, and care must participate in the work of formulating public policies that impinge on those areas of concern. Acknowledging that the still-young field of thanatology (and the so-called death awareness movement) has many tasks facing it, Feifel says that it can already be credited with a number of significant contributions to our collective well-being:

> The [death] movement has been a major force in broadening our grasp of the phenomenology of illness, in helping humanize medical relationships and health care, and in advancing the rights of the dying. It is highpointing values that undergird the vitality of human response to catastrophe and loss. Furthermore, it is contributing to reconstituting the integrity of our splintered wholeness. More important, perhaps, it is sensitizing us to our common humanity, which is all too eroded in the present world. It may be somewhat hyperbolic, but I believe that how we regard death and how we treat the dying and survivors are prime indications of a civilization's intention and target.[25]

The Illusion of Order

The world is not an ordered place. It is a chaotic place and random events occur in this chaotic world all the time. We fool ourselves into thinking that the world is an ordered place. That's how we get up in morning and how we go to bed at night, because we are ordering the world in some fashion and it is just an illusion, an illusion that keeps us going. If we didn't pretend that's the way it is, we wouldn't be able to function. We created a nice little world that we work in; we sleep from night to morning and we eat three meals a day. We know about gravity, and we know about the elements, but in fact we don't know anything. The world is just a massive pile of molecules zipping around, knocking into each other. At any time, one of these random events can occur. Earthquakes and floods and other acts of God, being symbols of all that, that all our houses with all of their roofs can be blown off, airplanes could crash into apartment buildings, babies can be taken away from their mothers. A baby that you've waited six years to conceive can go completely wrong inside. It's very, very difficult to go back to an ordered, normal life after this because my illusion of order has been shattered.

Julia

In commenting on the message of palliative care put forward by Elisabeth Kübler-Ross, Dame Cicely Saunders, and Mother Teresa of Calcutta, Robert Fulton and Greg Owen note that this message is also about "essential religious and spiritual values that extend beyond the immediate goal of care for the dying."[26] Death awareness fosters "compassionate acts of service" that are founded on recognition of the identity and worth of each human being.

Death in the Future

During the twentieth century, better living conditions and treatments for infectious diseases enabled many people to live long enough to be old enough to suffer from cardiovascular disease, cancers, and other degenerative conditions. The discoveries, inventions, and applications of twenty-first-century medicine will continue to push death farther into the future for those able to access the newest treatments.[27] "Our understandings of what is *natural* about human life, including the ways we respond to illness, grow older, and die, are forever being remade."[28]

Imagine the social patterns of death and dying fifty years from now. Think about the issues discussed in previous chapters, and consider present realities and possibilities. What speculations can you make about how our relationship with death and dying will change by the middle years of the twenty-first century? Looking into the future, what do you expect will be the questions about death and dying that will demand attention from individuals and societies? Consider the effects of an older population. In the United States, it is estimated that the number of people age sixty-five and over will grow to nearly 64 million by the year 2025 and nearly 87 million by 2050.[29] Can we imagine that care of the dying will become "big business," as corporations expand their role as surrogate caregivers for the aged and dying?

Think about the kinds of rituals or ceremonies surrounding the dead decades from now. Writing about the rapid pace of social change among societies in the South Pacific, Ron Crocombe comments on the trend of reducing the time devoted to funerals, marriages, births, and other such occasions of community celebration.[30] Increasingly, they are being moved from day to night and weekday to weekend. "Most traditional social rituals took more time than can be spared today," he says, "both because there are many more things to do, and because each person is doing different things."[31] Although our values and judgments play a role in determining how we spend our time, such decisions are rarely made independently of social norms and practices. If our work schedule conflicts with a midweek funeral, we may be reluctant to insist on time off unless the deceased is a close relative. As notions about community rituals and the use of time change, what kinds of funeral practices and services might evolve in response to such changes?

Consider, too, how changing circumstances may affect traditional patterns for disposition of the dead. Will there be enough land to continue the

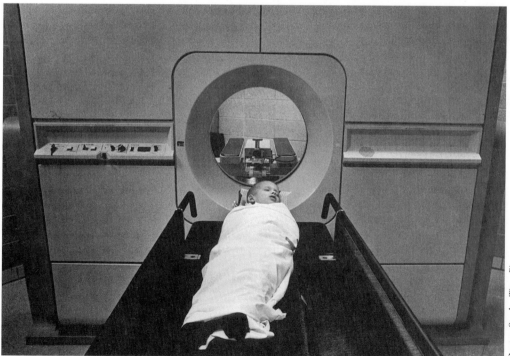

Burton Steele, *Times-Picayune*

Extrapolating from current medical technologies, we can foresee only faintly the questions and decisions about death and dying that children of the future will face.

practice of burials? Or might we see a substitution of high-rise cemeteries, cities of the dead towering above the landscape of the living? This is already happening in Japan, where burial space in large cities like Tokyo is at a premium. Current funeral practices are not likely to disappear altogether within the foreseeable future, but changes in methods of carrying out last rites will occur as people create new choices.

What types of social services for help in coping with the death of a loved one will be available in the years to come? Who could have foreseen the advent of specialized support and advocacy groups like Parents of Murdered Children and Mothers Against Drunk Driving? In recent years, innovative forms of social support—as well as resources for learning about death, dying, and bereavement—have become available on the Internet and World Wide Web.[32] What other developments in bereavement, grief, and mourning may take place in the coming years?

Recent decades have also seen increased emphasis on counseling or therapy following bereavement. In the future, might there be "grief clinics" available for emergencies? Would these clinics—much like present health institutions— send out reminders for individuals to come in for a bereavement checkup before the anniversary date of a significant death? Perhaps the time is not far off when some kind of professional assistance in coping with grief is the norm. Would this be a good thing, or is it something to be discouraged?

If life-threatening diseases such as cancer and heart disease become matters of routine prevention or cure in the future, what diseases will endanger our survival? Given the rapid pace of medical innovation, what change do you imagine will occur within even as short a time as the next decade? The prognosis for a given disease may change from very poor to exceptionally good within the span of a few years. At the same time, diseases previously unknown present new threats. As a case in point: Who could have foreseen the implications of AIDS? Yet it quickly assumed proportions comparable to the great plagues of the Middle Ages in terms of public fear and uncertainty. Will new diseases and threats cause similar distress in the future?

It is difficult to imagine a time when *no* disease or illness will be life-threatening. Yet we have lived through many technological advances that now make it possible to sustain life beyond any measure conceivable by earlier generations. Perhaps in the future "off-the-shelf" replaceable body parts will

---

 I was sitting by myself. The hotel had cleared. A little old lady came in, so I asked her to sit with me. And she told me her life. She had lived for twelve years in hotels. All she had was in this one little room. She had a daughter. She said her daughter wrote twice a week, but her daughter lived at a distance. She went into quite some detail, and I think it hit me then, harder than it ever had, that some day that might be me!

A student in a Death and Dying class

The Angel of Death

The Angel of Death is always with me—
the hard wild flowers of his teeth,
his body like cigar smoke
swaying through a small town jail.

He is the wind that scrapes through our months,
the train wheels grinding over our syllables.
He is the footstep continually pacing through our chests,
the small wound in the soul,
the meteor puncturing the atmosphere.
And sometimes he is merely a quiet between the start of an act
and its completion,
a silence so loud
it shakes you like a tree.

It is only then you look up from the wars,
from the kisses,
from the signing of the business agreements;
It is only then you observe the dimensions
housed in the air of each day,
each moment;

only then you hear the old caressing the cold rims of their sleep,
hear the middle-aged women in love with their pillows
weeping into the gray expanse of each dawn,
where young men, dozing in alleys,
envision their loneliness to be a beautiful girl
and do not know they are part of a young girl's dream,
as she does not know that she is the dream in the sleep
of middle-aged women and old men,
and that all are contained in a gray wind
that scrapes through our months.

sustain life when conventional methods prove futile. Organ substitution may take the place of organ transplantation. If it turns out that there is a "bionic" human in our future, what values should guide the use of such technologies, and who will decide? In Damon Knight's science fiction story, "Masks," a man who has suffered physically devastating injuries is repaired with functional artificial body parts.[33] But his mechanically sustained life causes him to question what constitutes a living human being.

Will medical scientists develop techniques for more accurately predicting the time of a person's death? This theme is explored in Clifford Simak's "Death Scene" and in Robert Heinlein's "Life-Line."[34] These stories suggest that the moment of one's death may be better left unknown. Although such explorations in speculative fiction are typically located in the future, in a setting different from our own, and often incorporate elements of fantasy, the

But soon we forget that the dead sleep in buried cities,
that our hearts contain them in ripe vaults,
We forget that beautiful women dry into parchment
and ball players collapse into ash;
that geography wrinkles and smoothes like the expressions on a face,
and that not even children
can pick the white fruit from the night sky.

And how *could* we laugh while looking at the face
that falls apart like wet tobacco?
How could we wake each morning
to hear the muffled gong beating inside us,
our mouths full of shadows, our rooms filled with a black dust?

Still,
it is humiliating to be born a bottle:
to be filled with air, emptied, filled again;
to be filled with water, emptied, filled again;
and, finally, to be filled with earth.

And yet I am glad that The Angel of Death is always with me:
his footsteps quicken my own,
his silence makes me speak,
his wind freshens the weather of my day.
And it is because of him
I no longer think
that with each beat
my heart
is a planet drowning from within
but an ocean filling for the first time.

Morton Marcus

themes investigated bear on present possibilities and on current dilemmas of ethical choice.

What changes are likely to occur in the health care system? What will be the quality of life—and of dying? In the story "Golden Acres," Kit Reed envisions a future in which the administrators of an institution for the aged make life-or-death decisions about the inmates in order to make room for new arrivals.[35] Golden Acres provides everything for its residents except the possibility of living out their lives in the ways they wish. Reed's story focuses on a resident who refuses to acquiesce in society's neglect of its aged members. As the protagonist describes it, Golden Acres is "a vast boneyard." Will that bleak description apply to the prospects facing the aged members of our own communities?

What about the threat of disaster? One scientist writes, "Comets are a real problem, and can do nearly as much damage as asteroids. . . . This is serious business, and the extent to which we all live on a knife-edge in relation to the devastation from these objects is very unsettling to those of us who keep track of these things."[36] He continues:

> On August 10, 1972, a famous daytime "fireball" skipped across the Grand Teton Mountains in Wyoming before returning harmlessly back to space over Canada. This object was estimated to be 200 yards across. If it had landed on one of thousands of towns or cities, it would have left a crater a half mile across. Needless to say, the inhabitants would have had absolutely no useful warning, and nowhere to escape.[37]

In learning from our encounters with dying and death that life is precious and precarious, we must also consider how the insights we've gained can be compassionately applied to the life of the planet as a whole. The poet Gary Snyder writes:

> The extinction of a species, each one a pilgrim of four billion years of evolution, is an irreversible loss. The ending of the lines of so many creatures with whom we have traveled this far is an occasion of profound sorrow and grief. Death can be accepted and to some degree transformed. But the loss of lineages and all their future young is not something to accept. It must be rigorously and intelligently resisted.[38]

Living with Death and Dying

As you review the varied perspectives covered in your study of death and dying, take a moment to assess the areas that seem particularly valuable to you. What insights did you gain by examining how death is seen in other cultures? How does your study of children's responses to death relate to your own experiences as a child or as an adult? What have you learned about your risk-taking behaviors? What choices would you now make regarding funeral ritual, terminal care, life-sustaining medical technologies? In sum, ask yourself, "What have I learned that can be helpful to me as a survivor of others' deaths—and in confronting my own death?" Have you become more comfortable in thinking about death and discussing it with others?

Recently, an advertisement in several high-fashion magazines used death imagery to showcase the desirable qualities of the product being promoted (see Figure 15-1). In "pushing the envelope" of advertising design, however, the manufacturer, ad agency, and others involved in the project received letters from disgruntled readers who found the use of death imagery "offensive and tasteless." Do you suppose this reaction might have been different if the letter writers were more comfortable with thinking about dying and death?

In considering the personal value derived from thinking about and exploring the meanings of death, notice how the study of death and dying engages both your mental faculties and your emotions. You may also notice that your exploration of death has a rippling effect, extending outward to your social milieu and relationships with others. Has a greater awareness of death had an impact on the quality of your relationships with family members and

Obsessively shoe obsessed

Figure *15-1 Death Imagery in Advertising Design*

friends or with the person down the street or at the neighborhood shop? Alfred Killilea says, "Rather than threatening to deprive life of all meaning, death deepens an appreciation of life and the capacity of every person to give life to others."[39]

Humanizing Death and Dying

Many people are encouraged by what appears to be increasing openness about death in society. There are signs that the circumstances surrounding death are being brought back into the personal control of the individuals and families who are closest to a particular death. Traditional customs and practices are being revived in new ways.

It is appropriate, however, to question whether this apparent openness toward death is somewhat illusory. When death becomes just another topic of casual (or sensational) discussion on television talk shows, does it reflect a kind of minimizing or devaluing of death? Is "openness" about death always to be applauded? Or does it sometimes reflect a nervous effort to achieve "death without regrets"? The urge to humanize death and dying, to accept death, is perhaps deserving of praise, but might it sometimes result in a more subtle form of denial? Death is not fully known when it is described in terms of rosy-colored projections and fantasies about the good death.

In a sense, no one is really able to "humanize" death. Death is already an intensely human experience. We can work to balance our fears with openness. We can try to understand the dynamics of grief, to make room for loss and change in our lives and in the lives of others. Death need not always be seen as something foreign to our nature, a foe to be fought to the bitter end.

While developing an easier familiarity with death, however, we should beware of becoming merely casual. Otherwise, we may find we have confronted only our *image* of death, not death itself. An increased casualness toward death is very evident in modern society. Consider, for example, the growing number of death notices that bear the announcement "No services are planned." Yet few people die without survivors who are affected by the loss. Is death a solitary or a communal event? Can I truly say that my death is "my own"? Or is

I say, "Why should a spirited mortal feel proud, when like a swift, fleet meteor or fast-flying cloud, man passes through life to his rest in the grave?" They've asked me, "How do I feel?" I told them that there's nothing to it; you do things the way they ought to be done. I don't see anything to be proud about. It's pretty difficult for a man to feel proud when knowing as he does the short space of time he's here and all paths, even those of our greatest glory, lead but to the grave. So it is very difficult to feel proud when Death says this. You're here today and gone sometimes today.

"A Very Long Conversation with James Van Der Zee at the Age of Ninety-One," in *The Harlem Book of the Dead* death an event whose significance ripples outward to touch the lives not only of friends and loved ones, but also the lives of casual acquaintances and even strangers in ways little understood?

Defining the Good Death

There is no single definition of what constitutes a *good* death. In ancient Greece, to die young, in the fullness of one's creative energies, was considered to be exceptional luck. In our society, death at a young age is considered a misfortune. The death of a young person just embarking on an independent life or of someone in the prime of life seems a great tragedy. "There is a widespread fantasy that one might reach 80 or 90 years in good health and die in one's sleep. But the epidemiological reality is rather different."[40]

The good death can be defined in many different ways. To an anthropologist interested in how our lives are celebrated in rites of passage, it might be something like the following: "Dying a good death is a ceremonially stylized way of exiting gracefully. By ritualized means, a grim necessity is transformed into a dignified and exemplary demise."[41] A religious concept of a good death, by contrast, might be defined as "one in which the person dies in a properly sanctified state."[42] How might you define a good death? Consider all of the factors—age, mode of death, surroundings, and so on—that would enter into your concept of a good death. Is your definition of a good death the same for yourself and for others? Some may question whether there can be any such thing as a good death. "Death is never good," they might say. "It can only cause pain and sadness."

Robert Kastenbaum has ennumerated some thoughts about what constitutes the good death, and we list them briefly here:[43]

1. People should be spared extreme physical, mental, and spiritual suffering at the end of their lives.
2. A good death should enact the highest values held by society. "Communal values are affirmed when people end their lives in a congruent manner."
3. The good death affirms our most significant personal relationships.

I've finally realised that my mother and father were right when they used to say, life is too short. At 20, 30, or 35, you don't understand. But it's so true. When you get to my age, 72, and look back, you realise that life has flown by. It's awe-inspiring.

I get the feeling I've only been around for a few weeks, that I've just arrived, and already I've got to leave. It's absurd. So tell me, why am I here? To continue the species, as they say? To reproduce, have children? That's wonderful, but it would be even better to be able to look after them, watch them for two or three hundred years. See what they're going to do, them, and their children, and my grandchildren's granchildren. Then life would be beautiful.

Marcello Mastroianni,
"A Last Interview with the Legendary Actor"

TABLE 15-1   *Components of a Good Death*

Pain and symptom management. Minimizing the likelihood of dying in pain or suffering "breakthrough pain" by providing adequate analgesia and other forms of pain relief.

Clear decision making. Empowering the dying person by striving for clear communication between the patient, his or her family, and the medical team. Discussing vital end-of-life decisions before crisis occurs and emotional reserves are low.

Preparation for death. Knowing what to expect during the end-stage of illness relative to the physical and psychosocial changes likely to occur as death approaches. Planning for actions to be taken following death. Exploring one's own feelings about death.

Completion. Acknowledging the importance of spirituality and other avenues of meaning-making, including life review, resolving conflicts, spending time with family and friends, enacting significant cultural rituals, and saying goodbye.

Contributing to others. Sharing meaningful aspects of oneself through tangible or intangible gifts, such as gifts of time, concern for others, and understanding gained through personal reflection.

Affirmation of the whole person. Seeing the dying person not as a "disease," but in the context of his or her life, values, and preferences.

Source: Adapted from Karen E. Steinhauser and others, "In Search of a Good Death: Observations of Patients, Families, and Providers," *Annals of Internal Medicine* 132, no. 10 (2002), pp. 825–832.

4. The good death is transfiguring. "One experiences an epiphany—a profound sense of beauty, love, or understanding. . . . The moment of death becomes the peak experience of life."

5. The good death is simply the final phase of the good life. "People should die as they have lived. . . . Why try to reshape a person's life at the last moment?"

6. The good death is coherent. "It is a story, a drama that makes sense, that satisfies our need for closure."

Another effort at defining the components of a good death is shown in Table 15-1. Notice that this definition, which was published in a medical journal, focuses as much on the *caregiver's* tasks in making a good death possible as on the tasks of the dying person himself or herself. Compare this list with Kastenbaum's description. Would combining these lists create a more complete or comprehensive definition?

An alternative way of defining a good death has been offered by Stu Farber and his colleagues. They propose the term "a respectful death," described as "a nonjudgmental relationship between parties." It is "a process of respectful exploration of the goals and values of patients and families at the end of life rather than a prescription for successfully achieving 'a good death.'"[44] Like the components given in Table 15-1, the concept of a respectful death emphasizes the mutuality of caregivers and patients.

Another way to think about the definition of a good death is to construct it in terms of an *appropriate* death. What makes some deaths seem more appropriate than others? Our answers are influenced by cultural values and by social context. Avery Weisman describes some of the elements that comprise the definition of appropriate death in contemporary societies.[45]

First, an appropriate death is relatively pain free; suffering is kept to a minimum. The social and emotional needs of the dying person are met to the fullest extent possible. There is no impoverishment of crucial human resources. Within the limits imposed by disabilities, the dying person is free to operate effectively as an individual and to enjoy mobility and independence. In addition, the dying person is able to recognize and resolve, as far as possible, any residual personal and social conflicts. The person is allowed to satisfy his or her wishes in ways that are consistent with the situation and with his or her self-identity and self-esteem.

As death approaches, the dying person is allowed to freely choose to relinquish control over various aspects of his or her life, turning over control to people in whom confidence and trust have been placed. The dying person also may choose to seek out or to relinquish relationships with significant others. In other words, the person chooses a comfortable level of social interaction.

Weisman said that to achieve an appropriate death we must first rid ourselves of the notion that death is *never* appropriate. Such a belief acts as a self-fulfilling prophecy. It stops us from creating the possibility of a more appropriate death.

For an appropriate death to become possible, the dying person must be protected from needless, dehumanizing, and demeaning procedures. The person's preferences about pain control and consciousness, and about the extent of solitude or gregarious interaction desired, should be respected. "An appropriate death," Weisman says, "is a death that someone might choose for himself—had he a choice."

Finally, we turn to the criteria for a good death suggested by Edwin Shneidman, a respected thanatologist and suicidologist. (See Table 15-2.) Shneidman's ideas about the good death represent the fruits of thoughtful contemplation, reflecting back on a life well lived. It is clearly focused on the dying person, though it acknowledges a continuity that includes family and younger generations. The good death, in this sense, involves more than just a civilized deathbed scene; it encompasses the dying person's "post-self," the self left behind in memory and the community. Shneidman says, "Have your dying be a courtly death, among the best things that you ever did."[46]

The death of Charles Lindbergh exemplifies many of the features of a good or appropriate death.[47] Lindbergh was diagnosed as having lymphoma. Until he died two years later, he continued living an active life, traveling and promoting the cause of conservation. When chemotherapy became ineffective, Lindbergh made arrangements for eventual burial on his beloved island of Maui. As his condition grew worse, he was hospitalized for several months, but the best efforts of his physicians could not alter the consequences or course of the disease. Lindbergh then asked that a cabin on Maui be obtained, and he was flown "home to Maui," where, with two nurses, his physician, and his family, he spent the last eight days of his life in the environment he loved.

T A B L E   15-2   *Ten Criteria for a Good Death*

Natural. Rather than accident, suicide, or homicide.
Mature. Elderly, near the pinnacle of mental functioning but old enough to have experienced and savored life.
Expected. Neither sudden nor unexpected; some warning of impending death.
Honorable. A positive obituary filled with honorifics (conveying honor).
Prepared. Plans made for the legalities surrounding death, such as funeral arrangements, wills, and trusts.
Accepted. "Willing the obligatory"; gracefully accepting the inevitable.
Civilized. Loved ones present; the dying scene enlivened by fresh flowers, beautiful pictures, and cherished music.
Generative. To have passed down the "wisdom of the tribe" to younger generations; to have shared memories and histories.
Rueful. To experience the contemplative emotions of sadness and regret without collapse; to die with some projects left undone; to "teach the paradigm that no life is completely complete."
Peaceable. The dying scene be filled with amicability and love and with relief from physical pain.

Source: Adapted from Edwin Shneidman, "Criteria for a Good Death," *Suicide and Life-Threatening Behavior* 37, no. 3 (2007): 245–247.

During these last days, Lindbergh gave instructions for the construction of his grave and conduct of his funeral, requesting that people attend in their work clothes. As Dr. Milton Howell, one of Lindbergh's physicians, describes this period, "There was time for reminiscing, time for discussion, and time for laughter."

Finally, Lindbergh lapsed into a coma and died twelve hours later. In accordance with his wishes, there had been no medical heroics. Dr. Howell says: "Death was another event in his life, as natural as his birth had been in Minnesota more than seventy-two years before."

Postscript and Farewell

Death education sometimes has immediate, practical consequences. At the conclusion of a course on death and dying, a student said, "It has helped me and my family deal with my mother's serious illness." For others, the practical application may be less immediate. Yet, as one student said, "I've gained a lot of useful information which may not be applicable to my life right now, but I know now that information and help is available and I didn't know that before."

Many people who complete a course in death and dying find that their explorations have consequences for their life that had not been foreseen when they first signed up for the course. One student said, "To me, this study has focused on more than just death and dying; it has dealt with ideas and with living, like a class on philosophy." Another student expressed the value

EASY STREET

HARM'S WAY

MANKOFF

of her death explorations as having "expanded my faith in the resilience of the human spirit." After describing how several individuals faced the prospect of dying, Sandra Bertman concluded that a common thread was the sense of "connectedness, affinity with all mankind: past, present, alive, dead."[48] After becoming more aware of the meanings of death, dying, and bereavement through their studies, some people choose to affirm this sense of connectedness by writing an *ethical will,* a sort of "nonmaterial bequest," or gift, that serves to document and pass on to relatives and even future generations one's personal values, life's lessons, beliefs, blessings, and inspirational advice.[49]

The study of death and dying includes components of information and data, but it also embraces a wisdom that arises out of the human encounter with death. This wisdom involves "a different kind of knowing, an integrative approach that refuses to look aside from the real human situation of uncertainty and ultimate death."[50] To be sure, death education does pertain to practical aspects of the individual and psychosocial encounter with death. But it offers more than that. Awareness of death and dying brings an added dimension to the moment-to-moment experience of living. It brings us into the present and serves as a reminder of the precious precariousness of life and the value of compassion through the ordinary as well as extraordinary circumstances of human experience.

Further Readings

Vincent Barry. *Philosophical Thinking About Death and Dying.* Belmont, Calif.: Wadsworth, 2007.

Daniel Callahan. *The Troubled Dream of Life: Living with Mortality.* New York: Simon & Schuster, 1993.

Lynne Ann DeSpelder and Albert Lee Strickland, eds. *The Path Ahead: Readings in Death and Dying.* Mountain View, Calif.: Mayfield, 1995.

Christopher A. Dustin and Joanna E. Ziegler. *Practicing Mortality: Art, Philosophy, and Contemplative Seeing.* New York: Palgrave Macmillan, 2005.

Allan Kellehear. *Compassionate Cities: Public Health and End-of-Life Care.* New York: Routledge, 2005.

J. Krishnamurti. *On Living and Dying.* San Francisco: HarperCollins, 1992.

Stephen Strack, ed. *Death and the Quest for Meaning: Essays in Honor of Herman Feifel.* Northvale, N.J.: Jason Aronson, 1997.

Studs Terkel. *Will the Circle Be Unbroken? Reflections on Death, Rebirth, and Hunger for a Faith.* New York: New Press, 2001.

Irvin D. Yalom. "Life, Death, and Anxiety." In *Existential Psychotherapy* (Chapter 2). New York: Basic Books, 1980.

E P I L O G U E

It's late. I wonder what Death will look like? A drooling ogre? Perhaps an unblinking skull, the Grim Reaper? A veiled mistress with beckoning arms? The standard forms. Or maybe Death will be a polished young man in a three-piece suit, all smiles and sincerity and confidence. What a disappointment that would be. No, I prefer the scythe— no ambiguity, no surrender . . . no dickering. What's that? . . . I hear him. He's here.

"May I come in?"

I nod. It's the young man who left me two days ago to knock on the doors of his neighbors' homes. "Well . . , ?" My breath is shorter than I thought.

He smiles, looks down at this hands, then at me. "Well, I did as you said. It didn't take long before I realized that I wasn't going to find a household that hadn't been touched by death."

"How many did you go to?"

He covers his mouth with his hand a moment, trying to hide his pride, I guess. "All of them."

"All?"

"Every house . . . I'm very stubborn."

We both smile. My wheezing is worse, and he notices. He shows his concern, and I can see that he understands what is happening.

"You're dying, aren't you, old man?"

I close my eyes in answer. When I open them again, he is at my side.

"Is there someone I should get for you? Your family?"

"Gone."

"Some friend?"

"Gone. All gone . . . except for you." The young man nods, then pulls his chair over next to my own. He takes my hand. I rest a moment. "There is something you must do for me," I wheeze. "When I'm dead, burn this house and everything in it, including me."

"Leave nothing behind?"

"This is only a filthy old shack. I'm leaving behind the only thing that anyone really can leave behind . . . the difference I've made in the lives of the people I've met." I squeeze his hand as best I can. He squeezes back. "Oh . . . and this." I try to lift the book in my lap—my book. He sees me struggling, and picks it up for me. "You take this. It's yours." His eyes widen.

"But I don't deserve—"

"There isn't time for that now!" He nods, and lays the book on his lap. Good, that's done. Moments pass. It gets quieter. . . . I must close my eyes. I witness again the glory of ten thousand mornings, ten thousand afternoons, ten thousand nights . . . then they, too, fade. All that's left is the sound of our breathing, and the wind. Time slows. Time changes. Where is the scythe? The young man's hand leaves mine and I hear his footsteps recede . . . stop . . . return. He sits down and I feel his hand on mine. He opens my fingers and lays something cool and light in my palm, all lace and limbs . . . the ballerina.

Now I can go.

David Gordon

CHAPTER *1*

1. See Philip A. Mellor and Chris Shilling, "Modernity, Self-Identity and the Sequestration of Death," *Sociology: The Journal of the British Sociological Association* 27, no. 3 (1993): 411–431; and Tony Walter, "Modern Death: Taboo or Not Taboo?" *Sociology* 25 (May 1991): 293–310.

2. Octavio Paz, *The Labyrinth of Solitude: Life and Thought in Mexico* (New York: Grove Press, 1961), p. 60.

3. See Bill Bytheway and Julia Johnson, "Valuing Lives? Obituaries and the Life Course," *Mortality* 1, no. 2 (1996): 219–234; Alan Marks and Tommy Piggee, "Obituary Analysis and Describing a Life Lived: The Impact of Race, Gender, Age, and Economic Status," *Omega: Journal of Death and Dying* 38, no. 1 (1998): 37–57; and Karol K. Maybury, "Invisible Lives: Women, Men, and Obituaries," *Omega: Journal of Death and Dying* 32, no. 1 (1995–1996): 27–37.

4. Robert Kastenbaum, *Death, Society, and Human Experience* (St. Louis: Mosby, 1977), p. 93.

5. Marilyn Johnson, *The Dead Beat: Lost Souls, Lucky Stiffs, and the Perverse Pleasures of Obituaries* (New York: HarperCollins, 2006), pp. 91, 106, 117, 223.

6. Jack Lule, "News Strategies and the Death of Huey Newton," in *The Path Ahead: Readings in Death and Dying*, ed. Lynne Ann DeSpelder and Albert Lee Strickland (Mountain View, Calif.: Mayfield, 1995), pp. 33–40.

7. "Why Do They React? Readers Assail Publication of Funeral, Accident Photos," *News Photographer* 36, no. 3 (March 1981): 20–23. See also, in the same issue, John L. Huffman, "Putting Grief in Perspective," pp. 21–22.

8. Robert M. Sapolsky, "On Human Nature: Primate Peekaboo," *The Sciences* 35, no. 2 (March–April 1995): 18.

9. See Lynne Ann DeSpelder, "September 11, 2001 and the Internet," *Mortality* 8, no. 1 (2003): 88–89.

10. Robert Fulton and Greg Owen, "Death and Society in Twentieth Century America," *Omega: Journal of Death and Dying* 18, no. 4 (1987–1988): 379–395.

11. *National Geographic* 210, no. 2 (August 2006), p. 21.

12. George Gerbner, "Death in Prime Time: Notes on the Symbolic Functions of Dying in the Mass Media," *Annals of the American Academy of Political and Social Science* 447 (January 1980): 64–70; see also George Gerbner and others, "Television's Mean World: Violence Profile Nos. 14–15," Annenberg School of Communications, University of Pennsylvania (September 1986).

13. Charles R. Berger, "Making It Worse than It Is: Quantitative Depictions of Threatening Trends in the News," *Journal of Communication* 51, no. 4 (2001): 655–677.

14. See David L. Altheide and R. Sam Michalowski, "Fear in the News: A Discourse of Control," *Sociological Quarterly* 40, no. 3 (1999): 475–503.

15. "Utilization of Selected Media," *Statistical Abstract of the United States: 2007,* 126th ed. (Washington, D.C.: Government Printing Office, 2006), p. 710.

16. Frederic B. Tate, "Impoverishment of Death Symbolism: The Negative Consequences," *Death Studies* 13, no. 3 (1989): 305–317.

17. Carolyn Marvin, "On Violence in Media," *Journal of Communication* 50, no. 1 (2000): 142–149.

18. Dolf Zillmann, "The Psychology of the Appeal of Portrayals of Violence," in *Why We Watch: The Attractions of Violent Entertainment,* ed. J. H. Goldstein (New York: Oxford University Press, 1998), pp. 179–211.

19. George Comstock and Victor C. Strasburger, "Media Violence: Q & A," *Adolescent Medicine* 4, no. 3 (October 1993): 495–509.

20. Quoted in Laura Winters, "An Italian Satirist Takes a Very Serious Turn," *New York Times,* January 27, 2002. The film won top prize, the Palme d'Or, at the Cannes International Film Festival.

21. Glenn Whipp, "Grief and Hope Merge in 'The Son's Room,'" *Los Angeles Daily News,* www.dailynews.com/socal/film/review/0102/25/mov04.asp (accessed April 16, 2002).

22. Colin McGinn, *The Power of Movies: How Screen and Mind Interact* (New York: Pantheon, 2005), p. 14.

23. Hannelore Wass, "A Perspective on the Current State of Death Education," *Death Studies* 28, no. 4 (2004): 289–308.

24. Bill Bryson, *The Mother Tongue: English and How It Got That Way* (New York: Perennial, 2001), p. 189.

25. Marsha McGee, "Faith, Fantasy, and Flowers: A Content Analysis of the American Sympathy Card," *Omega: Journal of Death and Dying* 11, no. 1 (1980–1981): 27, 29.

26. Lorraine Hedtke and John Winslade, "The Use of the Subjunctive in Re-Membering Conversations With Those Who Are Grieving," *Omega: Journal of Death and Dying* 50, no. 3 (2004): 197–215.

27. Alynn Day Harvey, "Evidence of a Tense Shift in Personal Experience Narratives," *Empirical Studies of the Arts* 4, no. 2 (1986): 151–162.

28. See Richard A. Pacholski, "Death Themes in Music: Resources and Research Opportunities for Death Educators," *Death Studies* 10, no. 3 (1986): 239–263.

29. Bruce L. Plopper and M. Ernest Ness, "Death as Portrayed to Adolescents Through Top 40 Rock and Roll Music," *Adolescence* 28, no. 112 (Winter 1993): 793–807.

30. John Thornburg, "From Rubble to Hope: Texts and Times after September 11, 2001," *The Hymn* 53, no. 3 (July 2002): 18.

31. Elijah Wald, *Narcocorrido: A Journey into the Music of Drugs, Guns, and Guerrillas* (New York: HarperCollins, 2002).

32. Edward Hirsch, *How to Read a Poem* (San Diego: Harvest, 1999), p. 271.

33. G. Chew and T. J. Mathiesen, "Thrēnos," *The New Grove Dictionary of Music Online,* www.grovemusic.com (accessed February 20, 2003).

34. See Michael Herzfeld, "In Defiance of Destiny: The Management of Time and Gender at a Cretan Funeral," *American Ethnologist* 20, no. 2 (1993): 241–255.

35. De Martino is discussed in James S. Amelang, "Mourning Becomes Eclectic: Ritual Lament and the Problem of Continuity," *Past & Present*, no. 187 (2005): 3–31. See also Ernesto De Martino, *Morte e Pianto Rituale nel Mondo Antico: Dal Lamento al Pianto di Maria* [Death and Ritual Mourning in the Ancient World: From Pagan Lament to the Mourning of Mary] (Turin: Einaudi, 1958).

36. Amelang, "Mourning Becomes Eclectic," p. 10.

37. Gail Holst-Warhaft, *The Cue for Passion: Grief and Its Political Uses* (Cambridge, Mass.: Harvard University Press, 2000), p. 200. For this lament, see also Loring M. Danforth, *The Death Ritual of Rural Greece* (Princeton, N.J.: Princeton University Press, 1982), p. 143.

38. George S. Kanahele, ed., *Hawaiian Music and Musicians* (Honolulu: University Press of Hawaii, 1979), pp. 53, 56.

39. Marguerite K. Ashford, Bishop Museum, Honolulu, personal communication.

40. Albert Lee Strickland, "The Healing Power of Music in Bereavement," *The Forum: Association for Death Education and Counseling* 29, no. 2 (2003): 4–5.

41. See Terrence Des Pres, *The Survivor: An Anatomy of Life in the Death Camps* (New York: Oxford University Press, 1976); Lawrence L. Langer, *Versions of Survival: The Holocaust and the Human Spirit* (Albany: State University of New York Press, 1982), *Holocaust Testimonies: The Ruins of Memory* (New Haven, Conn.: Yale University Press, 1991), and, edited by Langer, *Art from the Ashes: A Holocaust Anthology* (New York: Oxford University Press, 1995); and Alvin H. Rosenfeld, *A Double Dying: Reflections on Holocaust Literature* (Bloomington: Indiana University Press, 1980).

42. Lawrence Langer, *The Age of Atrocity: Death in Modern Literature* (Boston: Beacon Press, 1978).

43. Frederick J. Hoffman, *The Mortal No: Death and the Modern Imagination* (Princeton, N.J.: Princeton University Press, 1964).

44. William Ruehlmann, *Saint with a Gun: The Unlawful American Private Eye* (New York: New York University Press, 1984), p. 9.

45. Jahan Ramazani, *Poetry of Mourning: The Modern Elegy from Hardy to Heaney* (Chicago: University of Chicago Press, 1994), pp. 1, 361.

46. Hirsch, *How to Read a Poem*, p. 80.

47. William M. Lamers, Jr., "The Little Sounds of Grief: Poetry and Grief" (paper presented at the 21st International Death, Grief, and Bereavement Conference, University of Wisconsin, LaCrosse, May 28, 2003).

48. Ted Bowman, "Using Literary Resources in Bereavement Work: Evoking Words for Grief," *The Forum: Association for Death Education and Counseling* 29, no. 2 (2003): 8–9.

49. Elizabeth D. Samet, "Teaching Poetry to Soldiers in a Post-Heroic Age," *Armed Forces & Society* 29, no. 1 (2002): 109–127.

50. William Cooney, "The Death Poetry of Emily Dickinson," *Omega: Journal of Death and Dying* 37, no. 3 (1998): 241–249.

51. Kirk Varnedoe, "Dreams of a Summer Night," *Portfolio* (November–December 1982), p. 93.

52. See Richard A. Pacholski, "Death Themes in the Visual Arts: Resources and Research Opportunities for Death Educators," *Death Studies* 10, no. 1 (1986): 59–74.

53. Fritz Eichenberg, *Dance of Death: A Graphic Commentary on the Danse Macabre Through the Centuries* (New York: Abbeville, 1983).

54. Suse Lowenstein, quoted in Ann F. de Jong Hodgson, "Interviews and Issues: Dark Elegy," *Illness, Crises and Loss* 4, nos. 3–4 (1995): 18–38; quote p. 21. The sculpture is located in Livingston, New Jersey.

55. See Martha V. Pike and Janice Gray Armstrong, *A Time to Mourn: Expressions of Grief in Nineteenth Century America* (Stony Brook, N.Y.: The Museums at Stony Brook, 1980); and Anita Schorsch, *Mourning Becomes America: Mourning Art in the New Nation* (Philadelphia: Main Street Press, 1976).

56. Cindy Ruskin, *The Quilt: Stories from the Names Project* (New York: Pocket Books, 1988).

57. Robert E. Goss and Dennis Klass, *Dead But Not Lost: Grief Narrative in Religious Traditions* (Walnut Creek, Calif.: AltaMira, 2005), p. 276.

58. Maxine Borowsky Junge, "Mourning, Memory and Life Itself: The AIDS Quilt and the Vietnam Veterans' Memorial Wall," *Arts in Psychotherapy* 26, no. 3 (1999): 195–203. See also Michael Franklin, "AIDS Iconography and Cultural Transformation: Visual and Artistic Responses to the AIDS Crisis," *The Arts in Psychotherapy* 20, no. 4 (1993): 299–316. For a minority view regarding the Quilt, see Daniel Harris, "Making Kitsch from AIDS," *Harper's Magazine* (July 1994), pp. 55–60.

59. Holst-Warhaft, *The Cue for Passion,* p. 189.

60. See Jose Cardenas, "Sympathy Crafted by Hand," *Los Angeles Times* (May 4, 2004), pp. A1, A18; and Michael M. Phillips, "Quilters' Busy Hands Can't Quite Keep Up with Deaths in Iraq," *Wall Street Journal* (August 30, 2005), pp. A1, A4.

61. Quoted in Cardenas, "Sympathy Crafted by Hand."

62. International Work Group on Death, Dying, and Bereavement, "The Arts and Humanities in Health Care and Education," *Death Studies* 24, no. 5 (2000): 365–375; quote p. 366.

63. See Louis A. Gamino, "A Study in Grief: The Life and Art of Käthe Kollwitz," in *Grief and the Healing Arts: Creativity as Therapy,* ed. Sandra L. Bertman (Amityville, N.Y.: Baywood, 1999), pp. 277–287.

64. Sandra L. Bertman, "Volts of Connection: The Arts as Shock Therapy," *Grief Matters: The Australian Journal of Grief and Bereavement* 3, no. 3 (2000): 51–53; see also, by Bertman, *Facing Death: Images, Insights, and Interventions* (Philadelphia: Taylor & Francis, 1991).

65. See James A. Thorson, "Did You Ever See a Hearse Go By? Some Thoughts on Gallows Humor," *Journal of American Culture* 16, no. 2 (1993): 17–24.

66. Mary N. Hall, "Laughing as We Go" (paper presented at the annual meeting of the Forum for Death Education and Counseling, Philadelphia, April 1985); see also Mary N. Hall and Paula T. Rappe, "Humor and Critical Incident Stress," in *The Path Ahead,* ed. DeSpelder and Strickland, pp. 289–294.

67. John C. Meyer, "Humor as a Double-Edged Sword: Four Functions of Humor in Communication," *Communication Theory* 10, no. 3 (2000): 310–331; example from p. 321.

68. Linda Francis, Kathleen Monahan, and Candyce Berger, "A Laughing Matter? The Uses of Humor in Medical Institutions," *Motivation and Emotion* 23, no. 2 (1999): 155–174. See also Fabio Sala, Edward Krupat, and Debra Roter, "Satisfaction and the Use of Humor by Physicians and Patients," *Psychology and Health* 17, no. 3 (2002): 269–280.

69. Vera M. Robinson, *Humor and the Health Professions: The Therapeutic Use of Humor in Health Care,* 2nd ed. (Thorofare, N.J.: Slack, 1991), pp. 50, 53.

70. Linda D. Henman, "Humor as a Coping Mechanism: Lessons from POWs," *Humor: International Journal of Humor Research* 14, no. 1 (2001): 83–94; quote p. 86.

71. Patrick Vernon Dean, "Is Death Education a 'Nasty Little Secret'? A Call to Break the Alleged Silence," in *The Path Ahead,* ed. DeSpelder and Strickland, pp. 323–326.

72. Vanderlyn R. Pine, "A Socio-Historical Portrait of Death Education," *Death Education* 1, no. 1 (1977): 57–84; see also, by Pine, "The Age of Maturity for Death Education: A Socio-Historical Portrait of the Era 1976–1985," *Death Studies* 10, no. 3 (1986): 209–231; and Dan Leviton, "The Scope of Death Education," *Death Education* 1, no. 1 (1977): 41–56.

73. Darrell Crase, "Death Education: Its Diversity and Multidisciplinary Focus," *Death Studies* 13, no. 1 (1989): 25–29.

74. Thomas Attig, "Person-Centered Death Education," *Death Studies* 16, no. 4 (1992): 357–370.

75. See Tracy L. Smith and Bruce J. Walz, "Death Education in Paramedic Programs: A Nationwide Assessment," *Death Studies* 19, no. 3 (1995): 256–267; and Duane Weeks, "Death Education for Aspiring Physicians, Teachers, and Funeral Directors," *Death Studies* 13, no. 1 (1989): 17–24.

76. See Darrell Crase and Dan Leviton, "Forum for Death Education and Counseling: Its History, Impact, and Future," *Death Studies* 11, no. 5 (1987): 345–359; and Judith M. Stillion, "Association for Death Education and Counseling: An Organization for Our Times and for Our Future," *Death Studies* 13, no. 2 (1989): 191–201.

77. Herman Feifel, "The Thanatological Movement: Respice, Adspice, Prospice," *Loss, Grief, and Care* 6, no. 1 (1992): 5–16; and Hannelore Wass, "A Perspective on the Current State of Death Education," *Death Studies* 28, no. 4 (2004): 289–308. The symposium was titled "The Concept of Death and Its Relation to Behavior."

78. Herman Feifel, "Psychology and Death: Meaningful Rediscovery," in *The Path Ahead*, ed. DeSpelder and Strickland, pp. 19–28.

79. Gorer's essay was originally published in the journal *Encounter* in 1955; it was later reprinted in his 1965 book, *Death, Grief, and Mourning in Contemporary Britain*. For an account of the essay's influence, see Ian Andrews, "Pornography of Death," in *Encyclopedia of Death and Dying*, ed. Glennys Howarth and Oliver Leaman (New York: Routledge, 2001), pp. 361–362.

80. Lindsay Prior, *The Social Organization of Death* (London: Macmillan, 1989), esp. pp. 4–12. See also Neil Small, "Theories of Grief: A Critical Review," in *Grief, Mourning, and Death Ritual*, ed. Jenny Hockey, Jeanne Katz, and Neil Small (Buckingham, U.K.: Open University Press, 2001), pp. 19–48, esp. pp. 21–24.

81. Robert Kastenbaum, "Omega: Pre-History of a Journal," *Omega: Journal of Death and Dying* 48, no. 1 (2003): 69–84.

82. See John E. Fryer, "The Goose," *Illness, Crisis, and Loss* (January 2003): 65–69. See also International Work Group on Death, Dying, and Bereavement, *Statements on Death, Dying, and Bereavement* (London, Ont.: IWG, 1994).

83. See www.deathreference.com/index.html.

84. The first of these was *Encyclopedia of Death*, edited by Robert Kastenbaum and Beatrice Kastenbaum (Phoenix: Oryx Press, 1989); see also Glennys Howarth and Oliver Leaman, eds., *Encyclopedia of Death and Dying* (London and New York: Routledge, 2001); Robert Kastenbaum, ed., *Macmillan Encyclopedia of Death and Dying* (New York: Macmillan, 2003); and Clifton D. Bryant, ed., *Handbook of Death and Dying* (Thousand Oaks, Calif.: Sage, 2003).

85. See entry "United States," by Lynne Ann DeSpelder and Albert Lee Strickland, in *Encyclopedia of Death and Dying*, ed. Howarth and Leaman, pp. 460–463.

86. Hannelore Wass, "Visions in Death Education," in *The Path Ahead*, ed. DeSpelder and Strickland, pp. 327–334.

87. Anna Mathie, "Tolkien and the Gift of Mortality," *First Things* (November 2003), pp. 10–12.

88. Tom Arcaro and Ted Cox, "Human Existence as a Waltz of Eros and Thanatos," *Humanity & Society* 12, no. 1 (1988): 75–94.

89. Francesco Campione, *Manifesto della Tanatologia* [Manifesto of Thanatology] (Bologna: CLUEB, 2005).

90. Robert Kastenbaum, "Reconstructing Death in Postmodern Society," in *The Path Ahead*, ed. DeSpelder and Strickland, p. 8.

91. Robert Kastenbaum, "Death Writ Large," *Death Studies* 28, no. 4 (2004): 375–392; quote p. 390.

92. Herman Feifel, "The Thanatological Movement: Respice, Adspice, Prospice," *Loss, Grief, and Care* 6, no. 1 (1992): 5–16, esp. pp. 11–12.

93. Calvin Conzelus Moore and John B. Williamson, "The Universal Fear of Death and

the Cultural Response," in *Handbook of Death and Dying,* ed. Clifton D. Bryant (Thousand Oaks, Calif.: Sage, 2003), pp. 3–13.

94. Bert Hayslip, Jr., "Death Denial: Hiding and Camouflaging Death," in *Handbook of Death and Dying,* ed. Bryant, pp. 34–42; quote p. 35.

95. Hayslip, "Death Denial," p. 35.

96. Lindsay Prior, "Actuarial Visions of Death: Life, Death, Chance in the Modern World," in *The Changing Face of Death: Historical Accounts of Death and Disposal,* ed. Peter C. Jupp and Glennys Howarth (New York: St. Martin's, 1997), p. 189.

97. Avery Weisman, *The Realization of Death* (New York: Jason Aronson, 1974), p. 5.

98. Talcott Parsons, "Death in American Society: A Brief Working Paper," *American Behavioral Scientist* 6, no. 9 (1963): 61–65.

99. See Robert A. Neimeyer and David Van Brunt, "Death Anxiety," in *Dying: Facing the Facts,* 3rd ed., ed. Hannelore Wass and Robert A. Neimeyer (Washington, D.C.: Taylor & Francis, 1995), pp. 49–88.

100. Robert A. Neimeyer, Richard P. Moser, and Joachim Wittkowski, "Assessing Attitudes Toward Dying and Death: Psychometric Considerations," *Omega: Journal of Death and Dying* 47, no. 1 (2003): 45–76; quote pp. 46–47.

101. Robert A. Neimeyer, "Death Anxiety Research: The State of the Art" (paper presented at the annual meeting of the Association for Death Education and Counseling, Duluth, Minnesota, April 1991). See also *Death Anxiety Handbook: Research, Instrumentation, and Application,* ed. Robert A. Neimeyer (Washington, D.C.: Taylor & Francis, 1993); and Adrian Tomer, "Death Anxiety in Adult Life: Theoretical Perspectives," *Death Studies* 16, no. 6 (1992): 475–506.

102. Robert Kastenbaum, "Theory, Research, and Application: Some Critical Issues for Thanatology," *Omega: Journal of Death and Dying* 18, no. 4 (1987–1988): 397–410.

103. Herman Feifel, "Psychology and Death: Meaningful Rediscovery," in *The Path Ahead,* ed. DeSpelder and Strickland, pp. 19–28.

104. Becker's interview with Sam Keen was published in *Psychology Today.* See Daniel Liechty, "The Denial of Death Revisited," *Death Studies* 23, no. 8 (1999): 757–760; and "Reaction to Mortality: An Interdisciplinary Organizing Principle for the Human Sciences," *Zygon: Journal of Religion and Science* 33, no. 1 (1998): 45–58.

105. Maxine Sheets-Johnstone, "Size, Power, Death: Constituents in the Making of Human Morality," *Journal of Consciousness Studies* 9, no. 2 (2002): 49–67.

106. Jeff Greenberg, Sheldon Solomon, and Tom Pyszczynski, "Terror Management Theory of Self-Eseteem and Cultural Worldviews: Empirical Assessment and Conceptual Refinements," *Advances in Experimental Social Psychology* 29 (1997): 61–139; quote p. 100. See also, by Solomon, Greenberg, and Pyszczynski, "Tales from the Crypt: On the Role of Death in Life," *Zygon: Journal of Religion and Science* 33, no. 1 (1998): 9–43.

107. *Stanford Report,* June 14, 2005.

108. Ray S. Anderson, *Theology, Death, and Dying* (New York: Basil Blackwell, 1986), p. 10.

109. See James K. Crissman, *Death and Dying in Central Appalachia: Changing Attitudes and Practices* (Urbana: University of Illinois Press, 1994); and James J. Farrell, *Inventing the American Way of Death, 1830–1920* (Philadelphia: Temple University Press, 1980).

110. U.S. Census Bureau, "Expectation of Life at Birth," *Historical Statistics of the United States, Colonial Times to 1970* (Washington, D.C.: Government Printing Office), p. 55; and *Statistical Abstract of the United States: 2007,* 126th ed. (Washington, D.C.: Government Printing Office, 2006), p. 75. All statistics reflect the latest available data at the time this book was published.

111. Elizabeth Arias, "United States Life Tables, 2003," *National Vital Statistics Reports* 54, no. 14 (Hyattsville, Md.: National Center for Health Statistics, 2006), p. 4.

112. "Expectation of Life at Birth," *Statistical Abstract of the United States: 2007,* 126th ed.

(Washington, D.C.: Government Printing Office, 2006), p. 75.

113. "Births and Birth Rates" and "Deaths by Age and Selected Causes," *Statistical Abstract of the United States, 2007*, pp. 64, 85.

114. "Deaths by Age and Selected Causes," *Statistical Abstract of the United States: 2007*, p. 85.

115. "Deaths and Death Rates," *Historical Statistics of the United States*, p. 59; and *Statistical Abstract of the United States: 2007*, p. 78.

116. Jennie Benford, "Victorian Mourning at the Frick," *The Forum: Newsletter of the Association for Death Education and Counseling* 22, no. 1 (January–February 1996): 7–8.

117. "Deaths and Death Rates by Leading Causes of Death," *Statistical Abstract of the United States, 2007*, p. 86.

118. S. Jay Olshansky and A. Brian Ault, "The Fourth Stage of the Epidemiologic Transition: The Age of Delayed Degenerative Diseases," *Milbank Quarterly* 64, no. 3 (1986): 355–391.

119. "Annual Estimates of the Population by Age," *Historical Statistics of the United States*, p. 10; and "Resident Population by Age," *Statistical Abstract of the United States: 2007*, p. 12.

120. "Resident Population by Age: 1900 to 1997," *Statistical Abstract of the United States: 1999*, p. 869; and "Deaths and Death Rates by Leading Causes of Death and Age," *Statistical Abstract of the United States: 2007*, p. 86.

121. "Mobility Status of the Population," *Statistical Abstract of the United States: 2007*, p. 37.

122. Tony Walter, "A Death in Our Street," *Health & Place* 5 (1999): 119–124.

123. Robert E. Kavanaugh, *Facing Death* (Los Angeles: Nash, 1972).

124. David E. Stannard, *The Puritan Way of Death: A Study in Religion, Culture, and Social Change* (New York: Oxford University Press, 1977).

125. John Hostetler, *Amish Society*, 4th ed. (Baltimore: Johns Hopkins University Press, 1993), p. 206.

126. Kathleen B. Bryer, "The Amish Way of Death: A Study of Family Support Systems,"

American Psychologist 34, no. 3 (March 1979): 255–261.

127. Information from exhibit brochure and stories in the *Los Angeles Times* by Diane Haithman (January 22, 2005), p. E1, and Tonya Alanez (January 24, 2005), p. B1.

128. Paul Duro and others, "Postmodernism," in *Key Ideas in Human Thought*, ed. Kenneth McLeish (New York: Facts on File, 1993), pp. 584–585. See also William Simon, C. Allen Haney, and Russell Buenteo, "The Postmodernization of Death and Dying," *Symbolic Interaction* 16, no. 4 (1993): 411–426.

129. Ulrich Beck, "The Cosmopolitan Society and Its Enemies," *Theory, Culture & Society* 19, nos. 1–2 (2002): 17–44; quote p. 17.

130. Anthony Giddens, *Runaway World: How Globalization Is Reshaping Our Lives* (New York: Routledge, 2000), p. 23.

131. Daniel Levy and Natan Sznaider, "Memory Unbound: The Holocaust and the Formation of Cosmopolitan Memory," *European Journal of Social Theory* 51, no. 1 (2002): 87–106.

132. Glennys Howarth, "Dismantling the Boundaries Between Life and Death," *Mortality* 5, no. 2 (2000): 127–138; quote p. 135.

133. Marina Sozzi, "The Myth of Natural Death" (paper presented at the meeting of the International Association of Thanatology and Suicidology, Bologna, June 2005).

134. Daniel Callahan, "Frustrated Mastery: The Cultural Context of Death in America—Caring for Patients at the End of Life," *Western Journal of Medicine* 163, no. 3 (1995): 226–230.

135. Andrew S. Ziner, Department of Sociology, University of North Dakota, personal communication, May 1994.

136. See Nancy J. Moules, "Postmodernism and the Sacred: Reclaiming Connection in Our Greater-than-Human Worlds," *Journal of Marital and Family Therapy* 26, no. 2 (2000): 229–240.

137. Victor Davis Hanson and John Heath, *Who Killed Homer? The Demise of Classical Education and the Recovery of Greek Wisdom* (San Francisco: Encounter Books, 2001), pp. 203–204.

CHAPTER 2

1. Mark W. Speece and Sandor B. Brent, "The Development of Children's Understanding of Death," in *Handbook of Childhood Death and Bereavement,* ed. Charles A. Corr and Donna M. Corr (New York: Springer, 1996), pp. 29–50.

2. Brenda L. Kenyon, "Current Research in Children's Conceptions of Death: A Critical Review," *Omega: Journal of Death and Dying* 43, no. 1 (2001): 63–91; Mark W. Speece and Sandor B. Brent, "Children's Understanding of Death: A Review of Three Components of a Death Concept," *Child Development* 55, no. 5 (October 1984): 1671–1686; and Speece and Brent, "The Acquisition of a Mature Understanding of Three Components of the Concept of Death," *Death Studies* 16, no. 3 (1992): 211–229.

3. See Sandor B. Brent and Mark W. Speece, "'Adult' Conceptualization of Irreversibility: Implications for the Development of the Concept of Death," *Death Studies* 17, no. 3 (1993): 203–224.

4. Virginia Slaughter, "Young Children's Understanding of Death," *Australian Psychologist* 40, no. 3 (2005): 179–186; and Virginia Slaughter and Michelle Lyons, "Learning About Life and Death in Early Childhood," *Cognitive Psychology* 46, no. 1 (2003): 1–30. See also Susan Carey, *Conceptual Change in Childhood* (Cambridge, Mass.: MIT Press, 1985); and, also by Carey, "On the Origin of Causal Understanding," in *Causal Cognition: A Multidisciplinary Debate,* ed. D. Sperber, D. Premack, and A. Premack (New York: Oxford University Press, 1995).

5. Kenyon, "Current Research in Children's Conceptions of Death," p. 87.

6. Gerald Handel, Spencer Cahill, and Frederick Elkin, *Children and Society: The Sociology of Children and Childhood Socialization* (Los Angeles: Roxbury, 2007), p. 23.

7. Ross D. Parke, Peter A. Ornstein, John J. Rieser, and Carolyn Zahn-Waxler, "The Past as Prologue: An Overview of a Century of Developmental Psychology," in *A Century of Developmental Psychology,* ed. Parke et al. (Washington, D.C.:

American Psychological Association, 1994), p. 12.

8. John H. Flavell, "Cognitive Development: Past, Present, and Future," in *Childhood Cognitive Development: The Essential Readings,* ed. Kang Lee (Oxford: Blackwell, 2000), pp. 8–29.

9. Kang Lee, "Scientific Reasoning: Introduction," in *Childhood Cognitive Development: The Essential Readings,* ed. Lee (Oxford: Blackwell, 2000), pp. 265–266.

10. Paul Schilder and David Wechsler, "The Attitudes of Children Toward Death," *Journal of Genetic Psychology* 45 (1934): 406–451.

11. Sylvia Anthony, *The Discovery of Death in Childhood and After* (New York: Basic Books, 1972), revised edition of *The Child's Discovery of Death: A Study in Child Psychology* (London: Kegan Paul, 1940).

12. Maria H. Nagy, "The Child's Theories Concerning Death," *Journal of Genetic Psychology* 73 (1948): 3–27.

13. Slaughter, "Young Children's Understanding of Death."

14. Susan A. Gelman and John E. Opfer, "Development of the Animate-Inanimate Distinction," in *Blackwell Handbook of Childhood Cognitive Development,* ed. Usha Goswami (Oxford: Blackwell, 2004), pp. 151–166.

15. Thomas S. Weisner, "Ecocultural Understanding of Children's Developmental Pathways," *Human Development* 45, no. 4 (2002): 275–281; quote p. 276.

16. Erik Erikson, *Childhood and Society* (New York: Norton, 1950).

17. Jean Piaget, *The Child and Reality: Problems of Genetic Psychology,* trans. Arnold Rosin (New York: Grossman, 1973), and *The Child's Conception of the World* (London: Routledge & Kegan Paul, 1929). See also Mary Ann Spencer Pulaski, *Understanding Piaget: An Introduction to Children's Cognitive Development* (New York: Harper & Row, 1980).

18. From a conversation with Jean Piaget in Richard I. Evans, *The Making of Psychology: Discussions with Creative Contributors* (New York: Knopf, 1976), p. 46.

19. Robert Kastenbaum, *On Our Way: The Final Passage Through Life and Death* (Berkeley: University of California Press, 2004), p. 367.

20. Gerald P. Koocher, "Childhood, Death, and Cognitive Development," *Developmental Psychology* 9, no. 3 (1973): 369–375; "Talking with Children About Death," *American Journal of Orthopsychiatry* 44, no. 3 (April 1974): 404–411; and "Conversations with Children About Death," *Journal of Clinical Child Psychology* (Summer 1974): 19–21.

21. Helen L. Swain, "Childhood Views of Death," *Death Education* 2, no. 4 (1979): 341–358.

22. Lloyd D. Noppe and Illene C. Noppe, "Dialectical Themes in Adolescent Conceptions of Death," *Journal of Adolescent Research* 6, no. 1 (1991): 28–42; see also Noppe and Noppe, "Adolescent Experiences with Death: Letting Go of Immortality," *Journal of Mental Health Counseling* 26, no. 2 (2004): 146–167.

23. Jeffrey Jensen Arnett, "Emerging Adulthood: A Theory of Development from the Late Teens Through the Twenties," *American Psychologist* 55, no. 5 (2000): 469–480; quote p. 475.

24. Norman Goodman, *Introduction to Sociology* (New York: HarperCollins, 1992), p. 42.

25. Gordon Marshall, ed., *The Concise Oxford Dictionary of Sociology* (New York: Oxford University Press, 1994), p. 104. See also Don Brenneis, "Some Cases for Culture," *Human Development* 45, no. 4 (2002): 264–269; and Frederick Erickson, "Culture and Human Development," *Human Development* 45, no. 4 (2002): 299–306.

26. Hannelore Wass, "Death Education for Children," in *Dying, Death, and Bereavement: A Challenge for Living*, 2nd ed., ed. Inge Corless, Barbara B. Germino, and Mary A. Pittman (New York: Springer, 2003), pp. 25–41; quote p. 27.

27. Goodman, *Introduction to Sociology*, pp. 84–85.

28. Mark A. Mesler, "Negotiating Life for the Dying: Hospice and the Strategy of Tactical Socialization," *Death Studies* 19, no. 3 (1995): 235–255.

29. Kathleen R. Gilbert and Colleen I. Murray, "The Family, Larger Systems, and Death Education," in *Handbook of Thanatology*, ed. David Balk (Northbrook, Ill.: Association for Death Education and Counseling, 2007), pp. 345–353.

30. Iona Opie and Peter Opie, *The Lore and Language of Schoolchildren* (Oxford: Clarendon, 1959), p. 1.

31. Iona Opie and Peter Opie, *Children's Games in Street and Playground* (Oxford: Clarendon, 1969), pp. 62, 75.

32. Martha Wolfenstein and Gilbert Kliman, eds., *Children and the Death of a President: Multi-Disciplinary Studies* (Garden City, N.Y.: Anchor Press/Doubleday, 1965), esp. pp. 217–239.

33. See Maria Tatar, ed., *The Annotated Classic Fairy Tales* (New York: Norton, 2002).

34. Terri Windling, "On Tolkien and Fairy-Tales," in *Meditations on Middle-Earth*, ed. Karen Haber (New York: St. Martin's, 2001), pp. 215–229; quote p. 227.

35. Elizabeth P. Lamers, "Children, Death, and Fairy Tales," *Omega: Journal of Death and Dying* 31, no. 2 (1995): 151–167.

36. Carolyn Marvin, "On Violence in Media," *Journal of Communication* 50, no. 1 (2000): 142–149.

37. See Catherine Orenstein, *Little Red Riding Hood Uncloaked: Sex, Morality, and the Evolution of a Fairy Tale* (New York: Basic Books, 2002).

38. See, for example, Eve Morel, ed., *Fairy Tales and Fables* (New York: Grosset & Dunlap, 1970), pp. 11–13.

39. Ed Young, trans., *Lon Po Po: A Red-Riding Hood Story from China* (New York: Philomel Books, 1989).

40. Kalle Achte and others, "Themes of Death and Violence in Lullabies of Different Countries," *Omega: Journal of Death and Dying* 20, no. 3 (1989–1990): 193–204.

41. Sandra L. Bertman, "Death Education in the Face of a Taboo," in *Concerning Death: A Practical Guide for the Living*, ed. Earl A. Grollman (Boston: Beacon Press, 1974), p. 334.

42. Reported by Richard Lonetto, *Children's Conceptions of Death* (New York: Springer, 1980), p. 9.

43. Robert A. Emmons, "Religion in the Psychology of Personality: An Introduction," *Journal of Personality* 67, no. 6 (1999): 873–888. See also Alfred Kracher, "The Study of Religion: Conversation Point for Theology and Science," *Zygon: Journal of Religion and Science* 35, no. 4 (2000): 827–848.

44. Davina A. Allen and others, "Religion," in *Key Ideas in Human Thought*, ed. Kenneth McLeish (New York: Facts on File, 1993), pp. 626–627.

45. Phil Zuckerman, "The Sociology of Religion of W. E. B. Du Bois," *Sociology of Religion* 63, no. 2 (2002): 239–253.

46. Karolynn Siegel, Stanley J. Anderman, and Eric W. Schrimshaw, "Religion and Coping with Health-Related Stress," *Psychology and Health* 16 (2001): 631–653.

47. Lucy Bregman, "The Roles of Religions in the Death Awareness Movement," *The Forum* 32, no. 2 (2006): 4–5; quote p. 4.

48. Vernon Reynolds and Ralph Tanner, *The Social Ecology of Religion* (New York: Oxford University Press, 1995), p. 211.

49. Ruth A. Tanyi, "Towards Clarification of the Meaning of Spirituality," *Journal of Advanced Nursing* 39, no. 5 (2002): 500–509; quote p. 506.

50. Ralph L. Piedmont, "Does Spirituality Represent the Sixth Factor of Personality? Spiritual Transcendence and the Five-Factor Model," *Journal of Personality* 67, no. 6 (1999): 987–1013; quotes pp. 988–989.

51. Goodman, *Introduction to Sociology*, p. 215.

52. Michael E. McCullough and others, "Religious Involvement and Mortality: A Meta-Analytic Review," *Health Psychology* 19, no. 3 (2000): 211–222.

53. Justin L. Barrett, "Exploring the Natural Foundations of Religion," *Trends in Cognitive Sciences* 4, no. 1 (2000): 29–34.

54. Andrew J. Weaver and others, "Research on Religious Variables in Five Major Adolescent Research Journals: 1992 to 1996," *Journal of Nervous and Mental Disease* 188, no. 1 (2000): 36–44.

55. Lynne Ann DeSpelder and Albert Lee Strickland, "Using Life Experiences as a Way of Helping Children Understand Death," in *Beyond the Innocence of Childhood: Factors Influencing Children and Adolescents' Perceptions and Attitudes Toward Death*, ed. David W. Adams and Eleanor J. Deveau (Amityville, N.Y.: Baywood, 1995), pp. 45–54.

56. Lynne Ann DeSpelder and Nathalie Prettyman, *A Guidebook for Teaching Family Living* (Boston: Allyn & Bacon, 1980), pp. 130–134.

57. See Mary Anne Sedney, "Children's Grief Narratives in Popular Films," *Omega: Journal of Death and Dying* 39, no. 4 (1999): 315–324.

58. See, for example, Roger Rosenblatt, *Children of War* (New York: Anchor/Doubleday, 1983); Claudine Vegh, *I Didn't Say Goodbye: Interviews with the Children of the Holocaust* (New York: Dutton, 1985); and Robert Westall, *Children of the Blitz: Memories of Wartime Childhood* (New York: Viking, 1986).

59. *Newsweek*, May 5, 1980.

60. James Garbarino, "Challenges We Face in Understanding Children and War: A Personal Essay," in *The Path Ahead: Readings in Death and Dying*, ed. Lynne Ann DeSpelder and Albert Lee Strickland (Mountain View, Calif.: Mayfield, 1995), pp. 169–174; quote p. 169.

61. Zlata Filipovic, "Zlata's Diary: A Child's Life in Sarajevo," in *The Path Ahead*, ed. DeSpelder and Strickland, pp. 175–178; quote p. 178.

62. Ice T, "The Killing Fields," in *The Path Ahead*, ed. DeSpelder and Strickland, pp. 179–181.

63. Ronald Keith Barrett and Lynne Ann DeSpelder, "Ways People Die: The Influence of Environment on a Child's View of Death"

(paper presented at the annual meeting of the Association for Death Education and Counseling, Washington, D.C., June 26, 1997).

64. Albert Bandura, "Exploration of Fortuitous Determinants of Life Paths," *Psychological Inquiry* 9, no. 2 (1998): 95–115.

65. Nancy Scheper-Hughes, "Death Without Weeping: The Violence of Everyday Life in Brazil," in *The Path Ahead*, ed. DeSpelder and Strickland, pp. 41–58.

66. Kathy Charmaz, "Conceptual Approaches to the Study of Death," *Death and Identity*, 3rd ed., ed. Robert Fulton and Robert Bendiksen (Philadelphia: Charles Press, 1993), pp. 44–45.

67. Robert Blauner, "Death and Social Structure," in *Death and Identity*, rev. ed., ed. Robert Fulton (Bowie, Md.: Charles Press, 1976), pp. 35–59.

68. Robert Bendiksen, "The Sociology of Death," in *Death and Identity*, rev. ed., ed. Fulton, pp. 59–81.

69. Davina A. Allen, "Social Construction of Reality," in *Key Ideas in Human Thought*, ed. McLeish, pp. 725–726.

70. Robert Fulton and Robert Bendiksen, "Introduction," in *Death and Identity*, 3rd ed., ed. Fulton and Bendiksen, p. 7.

71. Myra Bluebond-Langner, *The Private Worlds of Dying Children* (Princeton, N.J.: Princeton University Press, 1978), p. 5.

72. Joseph M. Kaufert and John D. O'Neil, "Cultural Mediation of Dying and Grieving Among Native Canadian Patients in Urban Hospitals," in *The Path Ahead*, ed. DeSpelder and Strickland, pp. 59–74.

73. Goodman, *Introduction to Sociology*, p. 93.

74. Kenneth J. Gergen, "The Social Constructionist Movement in Modern Psychology," *American Psychologist* 40 (1985): 266–275.

75. Fiona J. Hibberd, *Unfolding Social Constructionism* (New York: Springer, 2005), p. xi.

76. Fulton and Bendiksen, "Introduction," p. 7.

77. Wolfgang Stroebe and Margaret Stroebe, "Is Grief Universal? Cultural Variations in the Emotional Reaction to Loss," in *Death and Identity*, 3rd ed., ed. Fulton and Bendiksen, p. 181.

78. Greg Owen, Robert Fulton, and Eric Marcusen, "Death at a Distance: A Study of Family Bereavement," in *Death and Identity*, 3rd ed., ed. Fulton and Bendiksen, p. 241.

79. Stroebe and Stroebe, "Is Grief Universal?" p. 197.

80. Christopher L. Hayes and Richard A. Kalish, "Death-Related Experiences and Funerary Practices of the Hmong Refugee in the United States," in *The Path Ahead*, ed. DeSpelder and Strickland, pp. 75–79.

81. Gerdien Jonker, "The Knife's Edge: Muslim Burial in the Diaspora," *Mortality* 1, no. 1 (1996): 27–43.

82. Pittu Laungani, "Death and Bereavement in India and England: A Comparative Analysis," *Mortality* 1, no. 2 (1996): 191–212.

83. Jeffrey Jensen Arnett, "The Psychology of Globalization," *American Psychologist* 57, no. 10 (2002): 774–783.

84. Arnett, "Psychology of Globalization," p. 782. See also Mary Buchholtz, "Youth and Cultural Practice," *Annual Review of Anthropology* 31 (2002): 525–552.

85. Ronald L. Akers, *Deviant Behavior: A Social Learning Approach*, 3rd ed. (Belmont, Calif.: Wadsworth, 1985), p. 57.

86. Ibid., p. 5.

87. Sandor B. Brent and Mark W. Speece, "'Adult' Conceptualization of Irreversibility: Implications for the Development of the Concept of Death," *Death Studies* 17, no. 3 (1993): 203–224.

88. Sandor B. Brent and others, "The Development of the Concept of Death Among Chinese and U.S. Children 3–17 Years of Age: From Binary to 'Fuzzy' Concepts?" *Omega: Journal of Death and Dying* 33, no. 1 (1996): 67–83. See also Shu Ching Yang and Shih-Fen Chen, "A Phenomenographic Approach to the Meaning

of Death: A Chinese Perspective," *Death Studies* 26, no. 2 (2002): 143–175.

89. David W. Plath, "Resistance at Forty-Eight: Old-Age Brinksmanship and Japanese Life Course Pathways," in *Aging and Life Course Transitions: An Interdisciplinary Perspective,* ed. Tamara K. Hareven and Kathleen J. Adams (New York: Guilford Press, 1982), pp. 109–125.

90. Martin Sokefeld, "Debating Self, Identity, and Culture in Anthropology," *Current Anthropology* 40, no. 4 (1999): 417–447.

91. Linda M. Hunt, "Beyond Cultural Competence: Applying Humility to Clinical Settings," *The Park Ridge Center Bulletin* (November–December 2001): 3–4.

CHAPTER 3

1. See Ernest Becker, *The Denial of Death* (New York: Free Press, 1973).

2. Charles Waddell and Beverly McNamara, "The Stereotypical Fallacy: A Comparison of Anglo and Chinese Australians' Thoughts About Facing Death," *Mortality* 2, no. 2 (1997): 149–161.

3. Richard A. Kalish and David K. Reynolds, *Death and Ethnicity: A Psychocultural Study* (Los Angeles: Ethel Percy Andrus Gerontological Center, University of Southern California, 1976).

4. Jeanne L. Tsai, Yu-Wen Ying, and Peter A. Lee, "The Meaning of 'Being Chinese' and 'Being American': Variation Among Chinese American Young Adults," *Journal of Cross-Cultural Psychology* 31, no. 3 (2000): 302–332.

5. Steven Mithen, *The Singing Neanderthals: The Origins of Music, Language, Mind and Body* (Cambridge, Mass.: Harvard University Press, 2006), p. 218.

6. See, for example, Ben Harder, "Evolving in Their Graves: Early Burials Hold Clues to Human Origins," *Science News* 160 (December 15, 2001): 380–381. On the origin of "religious feeling" in funeral practices, see Ina Wunn, "Beginning of Religion," *Numen: International Review for the History of Religions* 47, no. 4 (2000): 417–452.

7. The use of blood-red oxide to decorate corpses is possibly the earliest widespread funeral custom. Red ochre was mined in Africa by the earliest *Homo sapiens sapiens;* it appeared in Europe in Neanderthal funeral practices and was used in burials throughout Europe, Africa, Asia, Australia, and the Americas. If we imagine the earth as a living organism, hematite is analogous to the blood of Mother Earth.

8. Mike Parker Pearson, *The Archaeology of Death and Burial* (College Station: Texas A&M University Press, 2000), p. 3.

9. Giambattista Vico, *The First New Science,* ed. and trans. Leon Pompa (Cambridge: Cambridge University Press, 2002), p. 263.

10. Joseph Campbell, "Mythological Themes in Creative Literature and Art," in *Myths, Dreams, and Religion,* ed. Joseph Campbell (Dallas, Tex.: Spring Publications, 1970, 1988), pp. 138–175; see also, by Campbell, *Historical Atlas of World Mythology,* 5 vols. (New York: Harper & Row, 1988, 1989).

11. See Hans Abrahamson, *The Origin of Death: Studies in African Mythology* (New York: Arno Press, 1977); and Jacques Choron, *Death and Western Thought* (New York: Macmillan, 1963).

12. Anita J. Glaze, *Art and Death in a Senufo Village* (Bloomington: Indiana University Press, 1981), pp. 150–151.

13. See Ndolamb Ngokwey, "Pluralistic Etiological Systems in Their Social Context: A Brazilian Case Study," *Social Science & Medicine* 26, no. 8 (1988): 793–802; and Paul Katz and Faris R. Kirkland, "Traditional Thought and Modern Western Surgery," *Social Science & Medicine* 26, no. 12 (1988): 1175–1181.

14. Ninian Smart, *The Long Search* (Boston: Little, Brown, 1977), p. 231.

15. Carol Warren, "Disrupted Death Ceremonies: Popular Culture and the Ethnography of Bali," *Oceania* 64, no. 1 (September 1993): 36–56.

16. See Neville Drury, *The Elements of Shamanism* (Dorset, U.K.: Element Books, 1989); David Riches, "Shamanism: The Key to Religion," *Journal of the Royal Anthropological Institute* 29, no. 2 (1994): 381–405; and Lyle B. Steadman and Craig T. Palmer, "Visiting Dead Ancestors: Shamans as Interpreters of Religious Traditions," *Zygon: Journal of Religion and Science* 29, no. 2 (1994): 173–189.

17. Kenneth McLeish, "Necromancy," in *Key Ideas in Human Thought*, ed. McLeish (New York: Facts on File, 1993), pp. 508–509.

18. "Aborigine Painter Dies in Australia," *Associated Press Online*, June 22, 2002.

19. J. Peter Brosius, "Father Dead, Mother Dead: Bereavement and Fictive Death in Penan Geng Society," *Omega: Journal of Death and Dying* 32, no. 3 (1995–1996): 197–226.

20. T. H. Gaster, in James Frazer, *The New Golden Bough* (New York: New American Library, 1964), p. 241.

21. E. S. Craighill Handy and Mary Kawena Pukui, *The Polynesian Family System in Ka-'u, Hawai'i* (Rutland, Vt.: Charles E. Tuttle, 1972), pp. 98–101.

22. Important studies include Philippe Ariès, *Western Attitudes Toward Death: From the Middle Ages to the Present* (Baltimore: Johns Hopkins University Press, 1974), *The Hour of Our Death* (New York: Knopf, 1981), and *Images of Man and Death* (Cambridge, Mass.: Harvard University Press, 1985); Paul Binsky, *Medieval Death: Ritual and Representation* (London: British Museum Press, 1996); T. S. R. Boase, *Death in the Middle Ages: Mortality, Judgment and Remembrance* (New York: McGraw-Hill, 1972); Jacques Choron, *Death and Western Thought* (New York: Macmillan, 1963); Patrick J. Geary, *Living with the Dead in the Middle Ages* (Ithaca, N.Y.: Cornell University Press, 1994); Ian Gentles, "Funeral Customs in Historical Context," *Journal of Palliative Care* 4, no. 3 (1988): 16–20; and Frederick S. Paxton, *Christianizing Death: The Creation of a Ritual Process in Early Medieval Europe* (New York: Cornell University Press, 1990). Except where otherwise noted, quoted material is from Ariès's.

23. Nigel Llewelyn, *The Art of Death: Visual Culture in the English Death Ritual, c. 1500– c. 1800* (London: Reaktion Books, 1991), p. 27.

24. See Elisabeth Darby and Nicola Smith, *The Cult of the Prince Consort* (New Haven, Conn.: Yale University Press, 1983); Patricia Jalland, *Death in the Victorian Family* (New York: Oxford University Press, 1996); and John Morley, *Death, Heaven, and the Victorians* (Pittsburgh: University of Pittsburgh Press, 1971).

25. See, for example, Philip A. Mellor and Chris Schilling, "Modernity, Self-Identity, and the Sequestration of Death," *Sociology* 27, no. 3 (August 1993): 411–431; and Charles O. Jackson, "Death Shall Have No Dominion: The Passing of the World of the Dead in America," in *Death and Dying: Views from Many Cultures,* ed. Richard A. Kalish (New York: Baywood, 1980), pp. 47–55.

26. Elizabeth A. Hallam, "Turning the Hourglass: Gender Relations at the Deathbed in Early Modern Canterbury," *Mortality* 1, no. 1 (1996): 61–82; quote p. 78.

27. Valerie M. Hope, "Constructing Roman Identity: Funerary Monuments and Social Structure in the Roman World," *Mortality* 2, no. 2 (1997): 103–121.

28. See Peter Brown, *The Cult of the Saints: Its Rise and Function in Latin Christianity* (Chicago: University of Chicago Press, 1981); and Geary, *Living with the Dead in the Middle Ages.*

29. Rob Kay, *Santa Cruz Sentinel*, March 20, 1983. See also "Empire of the Dead," *Smithsonian* (April 2000).

30. Richard A. Etlin, *The Architecture of Death: The Transformation of the Cemetery in Eighteenth-Century Paris* (Cambridge, Mass.: MIT Press, 1984).

31. Kenneth T. Jackson and Camilo José Vergara, *Silent Cities: The Evolution of the American Cemetery* (New York: Princeton Architectural Press, 1989), pp. 22–23.

32. See Diana Williams Combs, *Early Gravestone Art in Georgia and South Carolina* (Athens: University of Georgia Press, 1986); James J. Farrell, *Inventing the American Way of Death, 1830–1920* (Philadelphia: Temple University Press, 1980), and "The Dying of Death: Historical Perspectives," *Death Education* 6, no. 2 (1982): 105–123; Gordon E. Geddes, *Welcome Joy: Death in Puritan New England* (Ann Arbor: UMI Research Press, 1981); David E. Stannard, *The Puritan Way of Death: A Study in Religion, Culture, and Social Change* (New York: Oxford University Press, 1977), and "Calm Dwellings: The Brief, Sentimental Age of the Rural Cemetery," *American Heritage* 30, no. 5 (August–September 1979): 42–55, and, edited by Stannard, *Death in America* (Philadelphia: University of Pennsylvania Press, 1975); Michael Vovelle, "A Century and One-Half of American Epitaphs: Toward the Study of Collective Attitudes About Death," *Comparative Studies in Society and History* 22, no. 4 (October 1980): 534–547.

33. Ray S. Anderson, *Theology, Death and Dying* (New York: Basil Blackwood, 1986), pp. 105–107.

34. Glennys Howarth, "Grieving in Public," in *Grief, Mourning, and Death Ritual*, ed. Jenny Hockey, Jeanne Katz, and Neil Small (Buckingham, U.K.: Open University Press, 2001), pp. 247–255; quote p. 247.

35. James Stevens Curl, *A Celebration of Death: An Introduction to Some of the Buildings, Monuments, and Settings of Funerary Architecture in the Western European Tradition* (New York: Charles Scribner's Sons, 1980), p. 367.

36. See, for example, John Cohen, "Death and the Danse Macabre," *History Today* (August 1982): 35–40; and Fritz Eichenberg, *Dance of Death: A Graphic Commentary on the Danse Macabre Through the Centuries* (New York: Abbeville, 1983).

37. See, for example, Norman F. Cantor, *In the Wake of the Plague: The Black Death and the World It Made* (New York: Free Press, 2001); and Colin Platt, *King Death: The Black Death and Its Aftermath in Late-Medieval England* (London: University College of London Press, 1996).

38. See Georges Bataille, *Death and Sensuality: A Study of Eroticism and the Taboo* (New York: Walker, 1962).

39. Frank Gonzalez-Crussi, "Anatomy and Old Lace: An Eighteenth-Century Attitude Toward Death," *The Sciences* (January–February 1988): 48–49; quote p. 48.

40. Robert Fulton, "Death, Society, and the Quest for Immortality," in *Death and the Quest for Meaning: Essays in Honor of Herman Feifel*, ed. Stephen Strack (Northvale, N.J.: Jason Aronson, 1997), pp. 329–344; quote p. 329.

41. Neil Small, "Theories of Grief: A Critical Review," in *Grief, Mourning and Death Ritual*, ed. Jenny Hockey, Jeanne Katz, and Neil Small (Buckingham, U.K.: Open University Press, 2001), pp. 19–48; quote p. 40.

42. Important works on the anthropology of death include Maurice Bloch and Jonathan Perry, eds., *Death and the Regeneration of Life* (New York: Cambridge University Press, 1982); Loring M. Danforth, *The Death Rituals of Rural Greece* (Princeton, N.J.: Princeton University Press, 1982); Richard Huntington and Peter Metcalf, *Celebrations of Death: The Anthropology of Mortuary Ritual* (New York: Cambridge University Press, 1979); and Johannes Fabian, "How Others Die: Reflections on the Anthropology of Death," *Social Research* 39 (1972): 543–567.

43. Charles Wilkinson, *Blood Struggle: The Rise of Modern Indian Nations* (New York: Norton, 2005), p. 353. See also Nicholas C. Peroff and Danial R. Wildcat, "Who Is an American Indian?" *Social Science Journal* 39, no. 3 (2002): 349–361.

44. See Donald Bahr, "Bad News: The Predicament of Native American Mythology," *Ethnohistory* 48, no. 4 (2001): 587–612; and Carl Waldman, *Atlas of the North American Indian* (New York: Facts on File, 1985).

45. Quoted in Vine Deloria, Jr., *God Is Red* (New York: Dell, 1973), pp. 176–177. See also Frank Waters, "Two Views of Nature: White and

Indian," *The South Dakota Review,* May 1964, pp. 28–29.

46. Clara Sue Kidwell and Alan Velie, *Native American Studies* (Lincoln: University of Nebraska Press, 2005), pp. 11, 21.

47. Louise B. Halfe, "The Circle: Death and Dying from a Native Perspective," *Journal of Palliative Care* 5, no. 1 (1989): 37–41. See also Paul Radin, *The Road of Life and Death: A Ritual Drama of the American Indians* (Princeton, N.J.: Princeton University Press, 1973).

48. Stephen Levine, *A Year to Live: How to Live This Year as If It Were Your Last* (New York: Bell Tower, 1997), p. 154.

49. Richard J. Preston and Sarah C. Preston, "Death and Grieving Among Northern Forest Hunters: An East Cree Example," in *Coping with the Final Tragedy: Cultural Variation in Dying and Grieving,* ed. David R. Counts and Dorothy A. Counts (Amityville, N.Y.: Baywood, 1991), pp. 135–155.

50. Jamake Highwater, *The Primal Mind: Vision and Reality in Indian America* (New York: Harper & Row, 1981), p. 165.

51. Åke Hultkrantz, *Native Religions of North America: The Power of Visions and Fertility* (New York: Harper & Row, 1987); see also, by Hultkrantz, *The Religions of the American Indians* (Berkeley: University of California Press, 1979), *The Study of American Indian Religions* (New York: Crossroad, 1983), and *Shamanic Healing and Ritual Drama: Health and Medicine in Native North American Religious Tradition* (New York: Crossroad, 1992).

52. Malcolm Margolin, *The Ohlone Way: Indian Life in the San Francisco Monterey Bay Area* (Berkeley, Calif.: Heyday Books, 1978), pp. 145–149.

53. John Witthoft, "Cherokee Beliefs Concerning Death," *Journal of Cherokee Studies* 8, no. 2 (Fall 1983): 68–72.

54. Robson Bonnichsen and Alan L. Schneider, "Battle of the Bones," *The Sciences* 40, no. 4 (2000): 40–46. See also "Human Remains: Contemporary Issues," in *Death Studies* 14, no. 6 (1990), ed. Glen W. Davidson and Larry W. Zimmerman.

55. Gerry R. Cox, "Native American Spirituality, Illness, Dying, and Death" (paper presented at the annual meeting of the Midwest Sociological Society, Chicago, 1995); see also his "The Native American Way of Death," in *Handbook of Death and Dying,* ed. Clifton D. Bryant (Thousand Oaks, Calif.: Sage, 2003), pp. 631–639; and Gerry R. Cox and Ronald J. Fundis, "Native American Burial Practices," in *Personal Care in an Impersonal World: A Multidimensional Look at Bereavement,* ed. John D. Morgan (Amityville, N.Y.: Baywood, 1993), pp. 191–203.

56. David G. Mandelbaum, "Social Uses of Funeral Rites," in *The Meaning of Death,* ed. Herman Feifel (New York: McGraw-Hill, 1959), pp. 189–217.

57. Quoted in Joseph Epes Brown, *The Spiritual Legacy of the American Indian* (Bloomington, Ind.: World Wisdom, 2007), p. 93.

58. Meyer Fortes, "An Introductory Commentary," in *Ancestors,* ed. William Newell (The Hague: Mouton, 1976), p. 5.

59. Noel Q. King, *Religions of Africa: A Pilgrimage into Traditional Religions* (New York: Harper & Row, 1970), pp. 13–14; see also, by King, *Christian and Muslim in Africa* (New York: Harper & Row, 1971), p. 95.

60. King, *Religions of Africa,* p. 68. See also Sjaak Van Der Geest, "'I Want to Go!' How Older People in Ghana Look Forward to Death," *Ageing and Society* 22 (2002): 7–28.

61. Kofi Asare Opoku, "African Perspectives on Death and Dying," in *Perspectives on Death and Dying: Cross-Cultural and Multidisciplinary Views,* ed. Arthur Berger and others (Philadelphia: Charles Press, 1989), pp. 14–23.

62. Francis Bebey, *African Music: A People's Art* (Brooklyn, N.Y.: Lawrence Hill, 1975), p. 126.

63. Kwasi Wiredu, "Death and the Afterlife in African Culture," in *Perspectives on Death and Dying,* ed. Berger and others, pp. 24–37.

64. John E. Reinhardt, *Life . . . Afterlife: African Funerary Sculpture* (Washington, D.C.: National Museum of African Art, 1982). On African religious thought, see John S. Mbiti, *African Religions and Philosophy* (Garden City, N.Y.: Anchor/Doubleday, 1970); see also Dominique Zahan, *The Religion, Spirituality, and Thought of Traditional Africa* (Chicago: University of Chicago Press, 1979).

65. From a story by Robert Dvorchak, *Los Angeles Times,* July 8, 1990.

66. Jack Goody, *Death, Property, and the Ancestors: A Study of the Mortuary Customs of the LoDagaa of West Africa* (Stanford, Calif.: Stanford University Press, 1962).

67. Olatunde Bayo Lawuyi, "Obituary and Ancestral Worship: Analysis of a Contemporary Cultural Form in Nigeria," *Sociological Analysis* 48, no. 4 (1988): 372–379. See also Kemi Adamolekun, "Survivors' Motives for Extravagant Funerals Among the Yorubas of Western Nigeria," *Death Studies* 25, no. 7 (2001): 609–619; and A. Odasuo Alali, "Management of Death and Grief in Obituary and in Memoriam Pages of Nigerian Newspapers," *Psychological Reports* 73 (1993): 835–842.

68. Mary Abrums, "Death and Meaning in a Storefront Church," *Public Health Nursing* 17, no. 2 (2000): 132–142. See also Sharon Hines Smith, "'Fret No More My Child . . . for I'm All Over Heaven All Day': Religious Beliefs in the Bereavement of African American, Middle-Aged Daughters Coping with the Death of an Elderly Mother," *Death Studies* 26, no. 4 (2002): 309–323.

69. Miguel De La Torre, *Santería: The Beliefs and Rituals of a Growing Religion in America* (Grand Rapids, Mich.: Eerdmans, 2004).

70. Stefania Capone, "Gods on the Net: The Rise of Religions of African Origin in the United States," *Homme,* no. 151 (1999): 47–74.

71. Miguel León-Portilla, "Those Made Worthy by Divine Sacrifice: The Faith of Ancient Mexico," in *South and Meso-American Native Spirituality: From the Cult of the Feathered Serpent to the Theology of Liberation,* ed. Gary H. Gossen (New York: Crossroad, 1993), pp. 41–64. See also, in the same volume, Louise M. Burkhart, "The Cult of the Virgin of Guadalupe in Mexico," pp. 198–227.

72. Rafael Jesús González, *El Corazón de la Muerte: Altars and Offerings for Days of the Dead* (Berkeley, Calif.: Heyday Books, 2005), p. 22. See also Barbara Brodman, *The Mexican Cult of Death in Myth and Literature* (Gainesville: University of Florida Press, 1976); Patricia Fernández Kelly, "Death in Mexican Folk Culture," *American Quarterly* 26, no. 5 (December 1974): 516–535; Joan Moore, "The Death Culture of Mexico and Mexican Americans," in *Death and Dying: Views from Many Cultures,* ed. Kalish, pp. 72–91; Patricia Osuna and David K. Reynolds, "A Funeral in Mexico: Description and Analysis," *Omega: Journal of Death and Dying* 1, no. 3 (1970): 249–269.

73. Luis Cardoza y Arogón, quoted in Claudio Lomnitz, *Death and the Idea of Mexico* (Cambridge, Mass.: MIT Press, 2005), p. 23.

74. Quoted in González, *El Corazón de la Muerte,* p. 26.

75. León-Portilla, "Those Made Worthy," p. 56.

76. Octavio Paz, *The Labyrinth of Solitude: Life and Thought in Mexico* (New York: Grove Press, 1961), p. 54.

77. See, for example, Robert Childs and Patricia B. Altman, *Vive tu Recuerdo: Living Traditions of the Mexican Days of the Dead* (Los Angeles: Museum of Cultural History, UCLA, 1982); Judith Strupp Green, "The Days of the Dead in Oaxaca, Mexico: An Historical Inquiry," in *Death and Dying: Views from Many Cultures,* ed. Kalish, pp. 56–71; and John Greenleigh and Rosalind Rosoff Beimler, *The Days of the Dead: Mexico's Festival of Communion with the Departed* (San Francisco: HarperCollins, 1991).

78. Glenn Whitney, "Mexico's Day of the Dead Is Actually Very Lively," United Press International story in the *Honolulu Star-Bulletin & Advertiser,* November 1, 1987.

79. Jorge Valadez, "Pre-Columbian and Modern Philosophical Perspectives in Latin America," in *From Africa to Zen: An Invitation to World Philosophy,* ed. Robert C. Solomon and Kathleen M. Higgins (Lanham, Md.: Rowman and Littlefield, 1993), pp. 81–124; quote p. 107. According to Valadez, this "purity of the heart" is especially true of children under the age of four.

80. Quoted in Whitney, "Mexico's Day of the Dead."

81. Paz, *Labyrinth of Solitude.*

82. Valadez, "Pre-Columbian and Modern Philosophical Perspectives in Latin America," p. 107.

83. Davíd Carrasco, "Religions of Mesoamerica: Cosmovision and Ceremonial Centers," in *Religious Traditions of the World,* ed. H. Byron Earhart (San Francisco: Harper-Collins, 1992), pp. 232–233.

84. See, for example: H. Byron Earhart, "Religions of Japan: Many Traditions Within One Sacred Way," in *Religious Traditions of the World,* ed. Earhart (San Francisco: HarperCollins, 1992); Dennis Klass, "Ancestor Worship in Japan: Dependence and the Resolution of Grief," *Omega: Journal of Death and Dying* 33, no. 4 (1996): 279–302; Hajime Nakamura, *Ways of Thinking of Eastern Peoples: India, China, Tibet, Japan,* trans. and ed. Philip P. Wiener (Honolulu: University of Hawaii Press, 1964); Sokyo Ono, *Shinto: The Kami Way* (Rutland, Vt.: Charles E. Tuttle, 1962); Daniel L. Overmyer, "Religions of China: The World as a Living System," in *Religious Traditions of the World,* ed. Earhart; Ian Reader, *Religion in Contemporary Japan* (Honolulu: University of Hawaii Press, 1991); Robert J. Smith, *Ancestor Worship in Contemporary Japan* (Stanford, Calif.: Stanford University Press, 1974); Yamaori Tetsuo, "The Metamorphosis of Ancestors," *Japan Quarterly* 33, no. 1 (January–March 1986): 50–53; and James L. Watson and Evelyn S. Rawski, eds., *Death Ritual in Late Imperial and Modern China* (Berkeley: University of California Press, 1988).

85. Inge Rösch-Rhomberg, "Hierarchical Opposition and the Concept of *um-yang (yin-yang)*: A Reevaluation of Values in the Light of the Symbolism of Korean Rituals for the Dead," *Anthropos* 89 (1994): 471–491.

86. Roberta Halporn, *Gods, Ghosts, and Ancestors: The Ching Ming Festival in America* (Brooklyn, N.Y.: Center for Thanatological Research and Education, 1994), and "Chinese Americans in Loss and Grief," *The Forum: Newsletter of the Association for Death Education and Counseling* 17, no. 6 (November–December 1992): 1, 16–20. See also Linda Sun Crowder, "Mortuary Practices in San Francisco China-town," *Chinese America: History and Perspectives* 13 (1999): 33–46.

87. See, for example, Barry Cunliffe, *The Ancient Celts* (New York: Oxford University Press, 1997); Hilda Ellis Davidson, *Myths and Symbols in Pagan Europe: Early Scandinavian and Celtic Religions* (Manchester, U.K.: Manchester University Press, 1988), and *The Lost Beliefs of Northern Europe* (London: Routledge, 1993); Peter Berresford Ellis, *The Celtic Empire: The First Millennium of Celtic History 1,000 BC–AD 51* (New York: Carroll & Graf, 2001); Ronald Hutton, *The Pagan Religions of the Ancient British Isles: Their Nature and Legacy* (Malden, Mass.: Blackwell, 1991); Prudence Jones and Nigel Pennick, *A History of Pagan Europe* (London: Routledge, 1995); J. A. MacCulloch, *The Celtic and Scandinavian Religions* (London: Hutchinson's University Library, 1948); Sabatino Moscati, ed., *The Celts* (New York: Rizzoli, 1991); Dáithé Ó'Hógáin, *The Celts: A History* (Cork: Boydell, 2020); and Ward Rutherford, *Celtic Mythology* (London: Thorsons, 1995).

88. John Sharkey, *Celtic Mysteries: The Ancient Religion* (New York: Thames & Hudson, 1975), p. 10.

89. Sandra M. Gilbert, *Death's Door: Modern Dying and the Ways We Grieve* (New York: Norton, 2006), p. 1.

90. See, for example, Nora K. Chadwick, *The Druids* (Cardiff: University of Wales Press,

1966); Paul R. Lonigan, *The Druids: Priests of the Ancient Celts* (Westport, Conn.: Greenwood, 1996).

91. Elizabeth Kantor, *The Politically Incorrect Guide to English and American Literature* (Washington, D.C.: Regnery, 2006), p. 15.

92. Philip V. Bohlman, *World Music: A Very Short Introduction* (New York: Oxford University Press, 2002), p. 80.

93. Eleanor C. Nordyke, *The Peopling of Hawai'i*, 2nd ed. (Honolulu: University of Hawaii Press, 1989), p. 1.

94. Patrick Vinton Kirch, *Feathered Gods and Fishhooks: An Introduction to Hawaiian Archeology and Prehistory* (Honolulu: University of Hawaii Press, 1985), p. 298.

95. Jonathan Y. Okamura, "Why There Are No Asian Americans in Hawai'i: The Continuing Significance of Local Identity," *Social Process in Hawaii* 35 (1994): 161–178.

96. Colette Browne, a specialist in aging at the University of Hawaii School of Social Work, quoted in John Griffin, "If You Have to Grow Old, Hawaii's a Good Place for It," *Honolulu Star-Bulletin & Advertiser*, July 23, 1989.

97. See Benjamin B. C. Young, "The Hawaiians," in *People and Cultures of Hawaii: A Psychocultural Profile*, ed. John F. McDermott, Jr., Wen-Shing Tseng, and Thomas W. Maretzki (Honolulu: John A. Burns School of Medicine and University of Hawaii Press, 1980), pp. 5–24.

98. Mary Kawena Pukui, E. W. Haertig, and Catherine A. Lee, *Nana I Ke Kumu (Look to the Source)*, 2 vols. (Honolulu: Hui Hanai; Queen Lili'uokalani Children's Center, 1972). A study conducted in the 1930s found families still tracing their lineage from ancestors who were viewed as spiritual guardians of their descendants and who often interceded in very practical ways. See E. S. Craighill Handy and Mary Kawena Pukui, *The Polynesian Family System in Ka-'u, Hawai'i* (Rutland, Vt.: Charles E. Tuttle, 1972).

99. George Hu'eu Sanford Kanahele, *Ku Kanaka, Stand Tall: A Search for Hawaiian Values* (Honolulu: University of Hawaii Press, 1986),

p. 182. On the soul after death and realms of the spirits of the dead, see also Donald D. Kilolani Mitchell, *Resource Units in Hawaiian Culture* (Honolulu: Kamehameha Schools Press, 1982), pp. 84–86.

100. Bob Krauss, "Wails and Prayers for Missing Bones," *Honolulu Advertiser*, March 6, 1994, p. A1.

101. Nordyke, *The Peopling of Hawai'i*, p. 52; see also Walter F. Char and others, "The Chinese," in *People and Cultures of Hawaii*, ed. McDermott, Tseng, and Maretzki, pp. 53–72.

102. This discussion of contemporary Chinese funeral customs in Hawaii is based on interviews by the authors with Anna Ordenstein and Ken Ordenstein who, along with their Chinese-Hawaiian-Jewish-Portuguese forebears, have provided funeral services to residents of Hawaii over the course of five generations. We are grateful for their assistance.

103. Terence Rogers and Satoru Izutsu, "The Japanese," in *People and Cultures of Hawaii*, ed. McDermott, Tseng, and Maretzki, pp. 73–99; see esp. pp. 87ff.

104. John F. McDermott, Jr., "Toward an Interethnic Society," in *People and Cultures of Hawaii*, ed. McDermott, Tseng, and Maretzki, p. 231; see also Wayne S. Wooden, *What Price Paradise? Changing Social Patterns in Hawaii* (Washington, D.C.: University Press of America, 1981).

105. McDermott, "Toward an Interethnic Society," pp. 229–230; see also Elvi Whittaker, *The Mainland Haole: The White Experience in Hawaii* (New York: Columbia University Press, 1986).

106. Mary Kawena Pukui and Samuel H. Elbert, *Hawaiian Dictionary*, rev. ed. (Honolulu: University of Hawaii Press, 1986), p. 34.

107. Paul Spickard, quoted in Susan Yim, "Hapa in Hawai'i," *Honolulu* (December 1994), pp. 44–47, 90, 92.

108. McDermott, "Toward an Interethnic Society," p. 231.

109. Goodman, *Introduction to Sociology*, p. 37.

110. David H. Olson and John DeFrain, *Marriage and Family: Diversity and Strengths* (Mountain View, Calif.: Mayfield, 1994), p. 37.

111. Madhavi Sunder, "Cultural Dissent," *Stanford Law Review* 54, no. 3 (2001): 495–567; see esp. pp. 497–498.

112. See M. Eisenbruch, "Cross-Cultural Aspects of Bereavement: Ethnic and Cultural Variations in the Development of Bereavement Practices," *Culture, Medicine, and Psychiatry* 8 (1984): 315–347; and Jimy M. Sanders, "Ethnic Boundaries and Identity in Plural Societies," *Annual Review of Sociology* 28 (2002): 327–357.

113. Ronald Keith Barrett, "Contemporary African-American Funeral Rites and Traditions," in *The Path Ahead,* ed. DeSpelder and Strickland, pp. 80–92; and "Psychocultural Influences on African-American Attitudes Toward Death, Dying, and Funeral Rites," in *Personal Care in an Impersonal World: A Multidimensional Look at Bereavement,* ed. John D. Morgan (Amityville, N.Y.: Baywood, 1995), pp. 213–230.

114. David R. Roediger, "And Die in Dixie: Funerals, Death & Heaven in the Slave Community, 1700–1865," *The Massachusetts Review* 22, no. 1 (Spring 1981): 163–183.

115. Alvin O. Korte, "*Despedidas* as Reflections of Death in Hispanic New Mexico," *Omega: Journal of Death and Dying* 32, no. 4 (1995–1996): 245–267.

116. See Philip A. Mellor, "Death in High Modernity: The Contemporary Presence and Absence of Death," in *The Sociology of Death,* ed. Clark, pp. 11–30 (esp. pp. 12–13, 18–19); and, in the same volume, Jane Littlewood, "The Denial of Death and Rites of Passage in Contemporary Societies," pp. 69–84; see also Philip A. Mellor and Chris Schilling, "Modernity, Self-Identity and the Sequestration of Death," *Sociology* 27, no. 3 (1993): 411–431.

117. Johannes Fabian, "How Others Die: Reflections on the Anthropology of Death," *Social Research* 39 (1972): 543–567.

118. Ronald L. Grimes, *Deeply into the Bone: Re-Inventing Rites of Passage* (Berkeley: University of California Press, 2000), p. 254.

119. Robert Pogue Harrison, *The Dominion of the Dead* (Chicago: University of Chicago Press, 2003), p. 70.

CHAPTER 4

1. Robert Kastenbaum, "Death System," in *Encyclopedia of Death,* ed. Robert Kastenbaum and Beatrice Kastenbaum (Phoenix, Ariz.: Oryx Press, 1989), pp. 90–93; and Kenneth J. Doka, "Death System," in *Macmillan Encyclopedia of Death and Dying,* ed. Robert Kastenbaum (New York: Macmillan, 2003), pp. 222–223.

2. Stephen Flynn, *The Edge of Disaster: Rebuilding a Resilient Nation* (New York: Random House, 2007), pp. xxi–xxxi.

3. Charles Perrow, *Normal Accidents: Living with High-Risk Technology* (New York: Basic Books, 1984).

4. Malcolm Gladwell, "Blowup," *New Yorker,* January 22, 1996, pp. 32–36.

5. Robert I. Tilling, U.S. Geological Survey, *Eruptions of Mount St. Helens: Past, Present, and Future* (Washington, D.C.: Government Printing Office, n.d.).

6. See Gerard Fryer, "The Most Dangerous Wave," *The Sciences* 35, no. 4 (July–August 1995): 38–43.

7. Philip Sarre, "Natural Hazards," in *Key Ideas in Human Thought,* ed. Kenneth McLeish (New York: Facts on File, 1993), pp. 502–504.

8. Neil Thompson, "The Ontology of Disaster," *Death Studies* 19, no. 5 (1995): 501–510. See also International Work Group on Death, Dying, and Bereavement, "Assumptions and Principles About Psychosocial Aspects of Disasters," *Death Studies* 26, no. 6 (2002): 449–462.

9. See James W. Pennebaker and Kent D. Harber, "A Social Stage Model of Collective Coping: The Loma Prieta Earthquake and the Persian Gulf War," *Journal of Social Issues* 49, no. 4 (1993): 125–145; and Kathleen M. Wright and others, "The Shared Experience of Catastrophe: An Expanded Classification of the Disaster Community," *American Journal of Orthopsychiatry* 60, no. 1 (1990): 35–42.

10. Brobson Lutz, M.D., quoted in Christopher Cooper and Robert Block, *Disaster: Hurricane Katrina and the Failure of Homeland Security* (New York: Times Books, 2006), p. 256.

11. Gail Walker, "Crisis-Care in Critical Incident Debriefing," *Death Studies* 14, no. 2 (1990): 121–133. See also Fran H. Norris and others, "60,000 Disaster Victims Speak: Part I, An Empirical Review of the Empirical Literature, 1981–2001," *Psychiatry* 65, no. 3 (2002): 207–239; and "60,000 Disaster Victims Speak: Part II, Summary and Implications of the Disaster Mental Health Research," *Psychiatry* 65, no. 3 (2002): 240–260.

12. Beverly McLeod, "In the Wake of Disaster," *Psychology Today,* October 1984, pp. 54–57.

13. U.S. Senate, Committee on Homeland Security and Governmental Affairs, *Hurricane Katrina: A Nation Still Unprepared* (Washington, D.C.: Government Printing Office, 2006), p. 21.

14. U.S. Senate, *Hurricane Katrina,* p. 2.

15. Cain Burdeau, "Army Corps: Levees Disjointed, Outdated" and "Corps Takes Blame for New Orleans Flooding," both *Associated Press Online,* June 1, 2006.

16. U.S. Senate, *Hurricane Katrina,* p. 4.

17. Michael Eric Dyson, *Come Hell or High Water: Hurricane Katrina and the Color of Disaster* (New York: Basic Civitas, 2006), p. 52.

18. Nicholas Lemann, "In the Ruins," *The New Yorker,* September 12, 2005, pp. 33–36; quote p. 34.

19. U.S. Senate, *Hurricane Katrina,* p. 3.

20. Flynn, *The Edge of Disaster,* pp. 50–51.

21. Henry Lundsgaarde, *Murder in Space City: A Cultural Analysis of Houston Homicide Patterns* (New York: Oxford University Press, 1977).

22. Hugo Adam Bedau, "An Abolitionist's Survey of the Death Penalty in America," in *Debating the Death Penalty: Should America Have Capital Punishment?* ed. Hugo Bedau and Paul Cassell (New York: Oxford University Press, 2004), pp. 26–27.

23. Ted Rohrlich and Fredric N. Tulsky, "Not All L.A. Murder Cases Are Equal," *Los Angeles Times,* December 3, 1995, pp. A1, A14–A15.

24. See N. Prabha Unnithan, "The Processing of Homicide Cases with Child Victims: Systemic and Situational Contingencies," *Journal of Criminal Justice* 22, no. 1 (1994): 41–50, and "Children as Victims of Homicide: Making Claims, Formulating Categories, and Constructing Social Problems," *Deviant Behavior* 15, no. 1 (1994): 63–83.

25. Quoted in Robert Kastenbaum and Ruth Aisenberg, *The Psychology of Death* (New York: Springer, 1972), pp. 269ff (italics in original).

26. Roman Espejo, ed., *Does Capital Punishment Deter Crime?* (Farmington Hills, Mich.: Greenhaven, 2003), p. 7.

27. "Movement of Prisoners Under Sentence of Death," *Statistical Abstract of the United States: 2008,* 127th ed. (Washington, D.C.: Government Printing Office, 2007), p. 213.

28. See Stanley Rothman and Stephen Powers, "Execution by Quota?" *The Public Interest* 116 (1994): 3–17.

29. Herb Haines, "Flawed Executions, the Anti-Death Penalty Movement, and the Politics of Capital Punishment," *Social Problems* 39, no. 2 (1992): 125–138.

30. Glenn M. Vernon, *Sociology of Death: An Analysis of Death-Related Behavior* (New York: Ronald Press, 1970). See also Dennis J. Stevens, "The Death Sentence and Inmate Attitudes," *Crime & Delinquency* 38, no. 2 (1992): 272–279.

31. Hugo A. Bedau, "Capital Punishment," *Academic American Encyclopedia Online Edition,* March 1991.

32. Kastenbaum and Aisenberg, *Psychology of Death,* pp. 95–96, 284–285.

33. Linda R. Monk, *The Words We Live By: Your Annotated Constitution* (New York: Stonesong, 2003), p. 187. On the risk of innocent deaths occurring in the operation of the death penalty, see James S. Liebman, "Rates of Reversible Error and the Risk of Wrongful Execution," *Judicature* 86, no. 2 (2002): 78–82; and Abraham L. Halpern and Alfred M. Freedman, "Participation by Physicians in Legal Executions

in the USA: An Update," *Current Opinion in Psychiatry* 15, no. 6 (2002): 605–609, esp. p. 608.

34. Lundsgaarde, *Murder in Space City,* p. 146.

35. Douglas N. Walton, *On Defining Death: An Analytic Study of the Concept of Death in Philosophy and Medical Ethics* (Montreal: McGill-Queen's University Press, 1979).

36. Ronald E. Cranford, "The Persistent Vegetative State: The Medical Reality," in *Medical Ethics: Applying Theories and Principles to the Patient Encounter,* ed. Matt Weinberg (Amherst, N.Y.: Prometheus, 2001), pp. 111–120.

37. William R. Clark, *Sex and the Origins of Death* (New York: Oxford University Press, 1996), p. 171.

38. Robert M. Veatch, *Death, Dying, and the Biological Revolution: Our Last Quest for Responsibility,* rev. ed. (New Haven, Conn.: Yale University Press, 1989); see also, by Veatch, *A Theory of Medical Ethics* (New York: Basic Books, 1981).

39. Duncan MacDougall, "Hypothesis Concerning Soul Substance Together with Experimental Evidence of the Existence of Such Substance," *Journal of the American Society for Psychical Research* 1, no. 5 (May 1907): 237–244.

40. Jay F. Rosenberg, *Thinking Clearly About Death* (Englewood Cliffs, N.J.: Prentice-Hall, 1983), p. 106.

41. "A Definition of Irreversible Coma: Report of the Ad Hoc Committee of the Harvard Medical School to Examine the Definition of Brain Death," *Journal of the American Medical Association* 205, no. 6 (August 5, 1968): 337–340.

42. See James L. Bernat, "The Biophilosophical Basis of Whole-Brain Death," *Social Philosophy & Policy* 19, no. 2 (2002): 324–342; Gary Greenberg, "As Good as Dead: Is There Really Such a Thing as Brain Death?" *New Yorker,* August 13, 2001, pp. 36–41; K. G. Karakatsanis and J. N. Tsanakas, "A Critique on the Concept of 'Brain Death,'" *Issues in Law and Medicine* 18, no. 2 (2002): 127–141; R. D. Truog, "Is It Time to Abandon Brain Death?" *Hastings Center Report* 27, no. 1 (1997): 29–37; and Robert M. Veatch, "The Impending Collapse of the Whole-Brain

Definition of Death," *Hastings Center Report* 23, no. 4 (1993): 18–24.

43. Karen G. Gervais, "Advancing the Definition of Death: A Philosophical Essay," *Medical Humanities Review* 3 (July 1989): 7–19; and, by Gervais, *Redefining Death* (New Haven, Conn.: Yale University Press, 1986). See also John P. Lizza, "Persons and Death: What's Metaphysically Wrong with Our Current Statutory Definition of Death?" *Journal of Medicine and Philosophy* 18 (1993): 351–374.

44. Robert M. Veatch, "What Counts as Basic Health Care? Private Values and Public Policy," *Hastings Center Report* 24, no. 3 (1994): 20–21.

45. President's Commission for the Study of Ethical Problems in Medicine and Biomedical and Behavioral Research, *Defining Death: A Report on the Medical, Legal and Ethical Issues in the Determination of Death* (Washington, D.C.: Government Printing Office, 1981), p. 45.

46. Alexander M. Capron and Leon R. Kass, "A Statutory Definition of the Standards for Determining Human Death: An Appraisal and a Proposal," *University of Pennsylvania Law Review* 121 (1972): 87–118.

47. President's Commission, *Defining Death.*

48. Albert R. Jonsen, *The Birth of Bioethics* (New York: Oxford University Press, 1998), pp. 238–244.

49. Susan Jeffrey, "Brain Death Guidelines Vary Widely at Top US Neurological Hospitals," *Medscape Medical News,* www.medscape.com (accessed November 5, 2007).

50. Mark H. Beers and Robert Berkow, eds., *The Merck Manual of Diagnosis and Therapy,* 17th ed. (Whitehouse Station, N.J.: Merck Research Laboratories, 1999), p. 1067. For a brief overview of current issues in organ donation and transplantation, see Margaret Lock, "Human Body Parts as Therapeutic Tools: Contradictory Discourses and Transformed Subjectivities," *Qualitative Health Research* 12, no. 10 (2002): 1406–1418.

51. Leonard L. Bailey, "Organ Transplantation: A Paradigm of Medical Progress," *Hastings*

Center Report (January–February 1990): 24–28; see also Susan L. Smith, "Progress in Clinical Organ Transplantation," www.medscape.com/medscape/transplantation/journal/2000/v01.n02/mt0406.smit-01.html (accessed September 4, 2000).

52. See Health Resources and Services Administration, "Organ Donation," http://organdonor.gov (accessed September 9, 2000).

53. Amy Dockser Marcus, "Extreme Transplants," *Wall Street Journal,* May 6, 2003, pp. D1, D8. See also Charles J. Dougherty, "Our Bodies, Our Families: The Family's Role in Organ Donation," *Second Opinion* 19, no. 2 (October 1993): 59–67; and Lesley A. Sharp, "Commodified Kin: Death, Mourning, and Competing Claims on the Bodies of Organ Donors in the United States," *American Anthropologist* 103, no. 1 (2001): 112–133.

54. United Network for Organ Sharing, "Organ Transplantation and Donation Facts at a Glance," www.unos.org/inTheNews/factSheets.asp (accessed July 1, 2003).

55. Margaret Robbins, "The Donation of Organs for Transplantation: The Donor Families," in *Contemporary Issues in the Sociology of Death, Dying, and Disposal,* ed. Glennys Howarth and Peter C. Jupp (New York: St. Martin's, 1996), pp. 179–192.

56. See Julia D. Mahoney, "The Market for Human Tissue," *Virginia Law Review* 86, no. 2 (2000): 163–223; Nancy Scheper-Hughes, "The Global Traffic in Human Organs," *Current Anthropology* 41, no. 2 (2000): 191–224; and Laura A. Siminoff and Mary Beth Mercer, "Public Policy, Public Opinion, and Consent for Organ Donation," *Cambridge Quarterly of Healthcare Ethics* 10, no. 4 (2001): 377–386.

57. Courtney S. Campbell, "The Selling of Organs, the Sharing of Self," *Second Opinion* 19, no. 2 (October 1993): 69–79. See also A. H. Barnett and David L. Kaserman, "The Shortage of Organs for Transplantation: Exploring the Alternatives," *Issues in Law and Medicine* 9, no. 2 (1993): 117–137; and Frank Th. de Charro,

Hans E. M. Akveld, and Dick J. Hessing, "Systems of Donor Transfer," *Health Policy* 25 (1993): 199–212.

58. See Robert P. Lanza, David K. C. Cooper, and William L. Chick, "Xenotransplantation," *Scientific American* 277, no. 1 (July 1997): 54–59; and Jeffrey L. Platt, "Xenotransplantation," *Science & Medicine* 3, no. 4 (July–August 1996): 62–71.

59. See Lindsay Prior, *The Social Organisation of Death* (London: Macmillan, 1989), p. 12. On the way in which a unique set of social and religious conditions facilitated acceptance of brain death and organ transplantation in the United States during the late 1960s, see William R. LaFleur, "From Agape to Organs: Religious Differences Between Japan and America in Judging the Ethics of the Transplant," *Zygon: Journal of Religion and Science* 37, no. 3 (2002): 623–642. For a brief survey of different religious perspectives, see Laurence J. O'Connell, "The Religious and Spiritual Perspective Toward Human Organ Donation and Transplantation," in *The Ethics of Organ Transplantation,* ed. Wayne Shelton and John Balint (New York: JAI Press, 2001), pp. 277–292.

60. This case study draws primarily on the following sources: Albert R. Jonsen, "Ethical Issues in Organ Transplantation," in *Medical Ethics,* 2nd ed., ed. Robert M. Veatch (Boston: Jones & Bartlett, 1997), pp. 239–274; Rihito Kimura, "Organ Transplantation and Brain-Death in Japan: Cultural, Legal, and Bioethical Background," *Annals of Transplantation* 3, no. 3 (1998): 5–58; Masahiro Morioka, "Bioethics and Japanese Culture: Brain Death, Patients' Rights, and Cultural Factors," *Eubios Journal of Asian and International Bioethics* 5 (1995): 87–90; Emiko Ohnuki-Tierney, "Brain Death and Organ Transplantation: Cultural Bases of Medical Technology," *Current Anthropology* 35, no. 3 (1994): 233–254; and Mona Newsome Wicks, "Brain Death and Transplantation: The Japanese," www.medscape.com/medscape/transplantation/

journal/2000/v01/mt0425.wick.htm (accessed September 4, 2000).

61. Darryl Macer, "Bioethics in and from Asia," *Journal of Medical Ethics* 25 (1999): 293–295.

62. Edwin S. Shneidman, *Deaths of Man* (New York: Quadrangle Books, 1973), pp. 121–130.

63. James K. Crissman and Mary A. Crissman, "Notifications of Death," in *Macmillan Encyclopedia of Death and Dying,* ed. Robert Kastenbaum (New York: Macmillan, 2003), p. 620.

64. R. Moroni Leash, *Death Notification: A Practical Guide to the Process* (Hinesburg, Vt.: Upper Access, 1994), p. 25. See also Janice H. Lord on behalf of MADD [Mothers Against Drunk Driving], *Breaking the Bad News with Concern for the Professional and Compassion for the Survivor* (Washington, D.C.: U.S. Department of Justice, n.d.); C. A. J. McLauchlan, "Handling Distressed Relatives and Breaking Bad News," *British Medical Journal* 301 (November 17, 1990): 1145–1149; and Alan E. Stewart, "Complicated Bereavement and Posttraumatic Stress Disorder Following Fatal Car Crashes: Recommendations for Death Notification Practice," *Death Studies* 23 (1999): 289–321.

65. Roger Ray, "Death Notification: A Dreaded Duty," *The Orlando Sentinel,* March 21, 2005.

66. Julian Guthrie, "The Saddest Duty: Informing Families of Loss," *San Francisco Chronicle,* April 6, 2003, p. W1.

67. "Deaths: Preliminary Data for 2004," *National Vital Statistics Reports* 54, no. 19 (2006): 18–19.

68. Leash, *Death Notification,* p. 48.

69. Leash, *Death Notification,* p. 52.

70. In addition to Leash, *Death Notification,* recommended resources include Kenneth V. Iserson, *Grave Words: Notifying Survivors About Sudden, Unexpected Deaths* (Tucson, Ariz.: Galen Press, 1999); and Alan Stewart and Janice Harris Lord, "The Death Notification Process,"

in *Handbook of Death & Dying,* ed. Clifton D. Bryant (Thousand Oaks, Calif.: Sage, 2003), pp. 513–522.

71. Brad Randall, *Death Investigation: The Basics* (Tucson, Ariz.: Galen, 1997), p. 1. For a popular account of the functioning of a big-city coroner's office, see Tony Blanche and Brad Schreiber, *Death in Paradise: An Illustrated History of the Los Angeles County Department of Coroner* (Los Angeles: General Publishing Group, 1998).

72. On "culture conflicts" regarding dead bodies, especially religious objections to autopsies, see Alison Dundes Renteln, "The Rights of the Dead: Autopsies and Corpse Mismanagement in Multicultural Societies," *South Atlantic Quarterly* 100, no. 4 (2001): 1005–1027.

73. Jon Yoshishige, "Searching for Answers: Lab Identifies Remains of Soldiers, Civilians," *Honolulu Advertiser,* August 8, 1993, pp. A1, A2.

74. Joseph B. Verrengia, "Remains of *Columbia* Crew Recovered," *Associated Press Online,* February 2, 2003.

75. John D. Lantos, *Do We Still Need Doctors?* (New York: Routledge, 1997), pp. 129–130.

76. Robert Kastenbaum, *Death, Society, and Human Experience,* 7th ed. (Needham Heights, Mass.: Allyn & Bacon, 2001), p. 62.

CHAPTER 5

1. Richard A. Deyo, "Cascade Effects of Medical Technology," *Annual Review of Public Health* 23 (2002): 23–44; quote p. 29.

2. James C. Robinson, "The Changing Boundaries of the American Hospital," *The Milbank Quarterly* 72, no. 2 (1994): 259–275.

3. V. David Schwantes, "Hospital Resource Allocation: The Real Story," *Hospitals & Health Networks* 68, no. 11 (June 5, 1994): 80.

4. Vanessa M. P. Johnson, Joan M. Teno, Meg Bourbonniere, and Vincent Mor, "Palliative Care Needs of Cancer Patients in U.S. Nursing Homes," *Journal of Palliative Medicine* 8, no. 2 (2005): 273–279.

5. Charles E. Rosenberg, "Institutionalized Ambiguity: Conflict and Continuity in the American Hospital," *Second Opinion* 12 (November 1989): 63–73; see also, by Rosenberg, *The Care of Strangers: The Rise of America's Hospital System* (New York: Basic Books, 1987).

6. Joshua Hauser and John Lantos, "Stories of Caring and Connection," *Hastings Center Report* 30, no. 2 (2000): 44–47.

7. See Margaretta K. Bowers and others, *Counseling the Dying* (New York: Thomas Nelson, 1964).

8. "National Health Expenditures," *Health, United States: 2002* (Hyattsville, Md.: National Center for Health Statistics, 2002), p. 9.

9. Alastair Gray, "International Patterns of Health Care, 1960 to the 1990s," in *Caring for Health: History and Diversity,* ed. Charles Webster, Health and Disease Series, Book 6 (Buckingham, U.K.: Open University Press, 1994), p. 174. See also Thomas S. Bodenheimer and Kevin Grumbach, *Understanding Health Policy: A Clinical Approach,* 3rd ed. (New York: Lange Medical Books, 2002).

10. Larry R. Churchill, "The United States Health Care System Under Managed Care: How the Commodification of Health Care Distorts Ethics and Threatens Equity," *Health Care Analysis* 7, no. 4 (1999): 393–411.

11. D. Lupton, "Consumerism, Reflexivity, and the Medical Encounter," *Social Science & Medicine* 45, no. 3 (1997): 373–381.

12. Howard M. Spiro, "If It Ain't Broke," *Science & Medicine* 3, no. 6 (November–December 1996): 4–5.

13. Clive F. Seale, "Changing Patterns of Death and Dying," *Social Science & Medicine* 51 (2000): 917–930.

14. Donna M. Wilson, "End-of-Life Care Preferences of Canadian Senior Citizens with Caregiving Experience," *Journal of Advanced Nursing* 31, no. 6 (2000): 1416–1421.

15. Daniel P. Sulmasy, "Physicians, Cost Control, and Ethics," *Annals of Internal Medicine* 116, no. 11 (June 1, 1992): 920–926.

16. Daniel Callahan, "The Limits of Medical Progress: A Principle of Symmetry," in *The Path Ahead: Readings in Death and Dying,* ed. Lynne Ann DeSpelder and Albert Lee Strickland (Mountain View, Calif.: Mayfield, 1995), pp. 103–105; quote p. 104. See also, by Callahan, *What Kind of Life: The Limits of Medical Progress* (New York: Simon & Schuster, 1990).

17. Michael D. Fetters and Howard Brody, "The Epidemiology of Bioethics," *Journal of Clinical Ethics* 10, no. 2 (1999): 107–115.

18. C. D. Bessinger, "Doctoring: The Philosophic Milieu," *Southern Medical Journal* 81, no. 12 (1988): 1558–1562. See also William Campbell Felch, *The Secret(s) of Good Patient Care: Thoughts on Medicine in the 21st Century* (Westport, Conn.: Praeger, 1996); and Edmund D. Pellegrino and David C. Thomasma, *A Philosophical Basis for Medical Practice: Towards a Philosophy and Ethic of the Healing Professions* (New York: Oxford University Press, 1981).

19. See J. Balint and W. Shelton, "Regaining the Initiative: Forging a New Model of the Patient-Physician Relationship," *Journal of the American Medical Association* 275, no. 11 (1996): 887–891; Dan W. Brock, "The Ideal of Shared Decision Making Between Physicians and Patients," *Kennedy Institute of Ethics Journal* (March 1991): 28–47; Christine K. Cassel, "The Patient-Physician Covenant: An Affirmation of Asklepios," *Annals of Internal Medicine* 124 (1996): 604–606; and C. Charles, A. Gafni, and T. Whelan, "Shared Decision-Making in the Medical Encounter: What Does It Mean? (Or, It Takes At Least Two to Tango)," *Social Science & Medicine* 44, no. 5 (1997): 681–692.

20. Stanley Joel Reiser, "The Era of the Patient: Using the Experience of Illness in Shaping the Missions of Health Care," in *The Path Ahead,* ed. DeSpelder and Strickland, pp. 106–115.

21. Joan L. Bottorff and others, "Facilitating Day-to-Day Decision Making in Palliative Care," *Cancer Nursing* 23, no. 2 (2000): 141–150.

22. Arthur W. Frank, "The Painter and the Cameraman: Boundaries in Clinical Relation-

ships," *Theoretical Medicine* 23 (2002): 219–232; quote p. 231.

23. See, for example, Dieter Birnbacher, "Predictive Medicine: The Right to Know and the Right Not to Know," *Acta Analytica: Philosophy and Psychology* 16 (2001): 35–47; Todd S. Elwyn, Michael D. Fetters, Hiroki Sasaki, and Tsukada Tsuda, "Responsibility and Cancer Disclosure in Japan," *Social Science & Medicine* 54, no. 2 (2002): 281–293; and Stan A. Kaplowitz, Shelly Campo, and Wai Tat Chiu, "Cancer Patients' Desires for Communication of Prognosis Information," *Health Communication* 14, no. 2 (2002): 221–241.

24. See, for example, Mei-che Samantha Pang, "Protective Truthfulness: The Chinese Way of Safeguarding Patients in Informed Treatment Decisions," *Journal of Medical Ethics* 25, no. 3 (1999): 247–253.

25. Michal Rassin, Orna Levy, Tirza Schwartz, and Dina Silner, "Caregivers' Role in Breaking Bad News: Patients, Doctors, and Nurses' Points of View," *Cancer Nursing* 29, no. 4 (2006): 302–308.

26. Karen Lutfey and Douglas W. Maynard, "Bad News in Oncology: How Physician and Patient Talk About Death and Dying Without Using Those Words," *Social Psychology Quarterly* 61, no. 4 (1998): 321–341. See also Abraham Rudnick, "Informed Consent to Breaking Bad News," *Nursing Ethics* 9, no. 1 (2002): 61–66.

27. Geoffrey H. Gordon, Sandra K. Joos, and Jennifer Byrne, "Physician Expressions of Uncertainty During Patient Encounters," *Patient Education and Counseling* 40, no. 1 (2000): 59–65. See also Chalmers C. Clark, "Trust in Medicine," *Journal of Medicine and Philosophy* 27, no. 1 (2002): 11–29; Susan Dorr Goold, "Trust and the Ethics of Health Care Institutions," *Hastings Center Report* 31, no. 6 (2001): 26–33; and W. A. Rogers, "Is There a Moral Duty for Doctors to Trust Patients?" *Journal of Medical Ethics* 28, no. 2 (2002): 77–80.

28. Pär Salander, "Bad News from the Patient's Perspective: An Analysis of the Written Narratives of Newly Diagnosed Cancer Patients," *Social Science & Medicine* 55 (2002): 721–732.

29. Thomas J. Smith, "Tell It Like It Is," *Journal of Clinical Oncology* 18, no. 19 (2000): 3441–3445.

30. For a model of such discussion, see Ernest Rosenbaum, "Oncology/Hematology and Psychosocial Support of the Cancer Patient," in *Psychosocial Care of the Dying Patient*, ed. Charles A. Garfield (New York: McGraw-Hill, 1978), pp. 169–184.

31. Virginia Teas Gill, "Doing Attributions in Medical Interaction: Patients' Explanations for Illness and Doctors' Responses," *Social Psychology Quarterly* 61, no. 4 (1998): 342–360.

32. Candace West, *Routine Complications: Troubles with Talk Between Doctors and Patients* (Bloomington: Indiana University Press, 1984).

33. Sandra L. Bertman, Michael D. Wertheimer, and H. Brownell Wheeler, "Humanities in Surgery, a Life-Threatening Situation: Communicating the Diagnosis," *Death Studies* 10, no. 5 (1986): 431–439.

34. Richard S. Sandor, "On Death and Coding," in *The Path Ahead*, ed. DeSpelder and Strickland, pp. 144–147.

35. Eugene A. Stead, Jr., *A Way of Thinking: A Primer on the Art of Being a Doctor* (Durham, N.C.: Carolina Academic Press, 1995), p. 126. See also Susan E. Hickman, "Improving Communication Near the End of Life," *American Behavioral Scientist* 46, no. 2 (2002): 252–267.

36. Albert Lee Strickland and Lynne Ann DeSpelder, "Communicating About Death and Dying," in *Dying, Death, and Bereavement: A Challenge for Living*, 2nd ed., ed. Inge Corless, Barbara B. Germino, and Mary A. Pittman (New York: Springer, 2003), pp. 7–24.

37. S. M. Johnson and M. E. Kurtz, "Name Usage in Clinical Practice: Ethnic and Gender Disparities," *Humane Medicine* 11, no. 3 (1995): 106–109. See also Felicity Goodyear-Smith and Stephen Buetow, "Power Issues in the Doctor-Patient Relationship," *Health Care Analysis* 9, no. 4 (2001): 449–462; and Robert M. Veatch,

"White Coat Ceremonies: A Second Opinion," *Journal of Medical Ethics* 28, no. 1 (2002): 5–9.

38. Jeanne Quint Benoliel, "Health Care Providers and Dying Patients: Critical Issues in Terminal Care," *Omega: Journal of Death and Dying* 18, no. 4 (1987–1988): 341–363; quote p. 345.

39. Mary Sawyers, "What to Say When Treatment Fails," *Oncology Issues* 17, no. 3 (2002): 44–45.

40. "Tapping Human Potential: An Interview with Norman Cousins," *Second Opinion* 14 (July 1990): 57–71.

41. See Balfour Mount, "Whole Person Care: Beyond Psychosocial and Physical Needs," *American Journal of Hospice and Palliative Care* 10, no. 1 (January–February 1993): 28–37.

42. Marilee Ivars Donovan and Sandra Girton Pierce, *Cancer Care Nursing* (New York: Appleton-Century-Crofts, 1976), p. 32.

43. Betty Davies and others, *Fading Away: The Experience of Transition in Families with - Terminal Illness* (Amityville, N.Y.: Baywood, 1996).

44. Elisabeth Kübler-Ross, *On Death and Dying* (New York: Macmillan, 1969), p. 249. For a biographical account of Kübler-Ross's experiences, see Elisabeth Kübler-Ross, *The Wheel of Life: A Memoir of Living and Dying* (New York: Scribner, 1997).

45. Balfour M. Mount, "Keeping the Mission," in *The Path Ahead*, ed. DeSpelder and Strickland, pp. 125–132; quote p. 125.

46. *NHPCO Facts and Figures—2005 Findings,* www.nhpco.org (accessed November 11, 2007).

47. Stephen R. Connor, Joan Teno, Carol Spench, and Neal Smith, "Family Evaluation of Hospice Care," *Journal of Pain and Symptom Management* 30, no. 1 (2005): 9–17.

48. David S. Greer, Vincent Mor, and Robert Kastenbaum, "Concepts, Questions, and Research Priorities," in *The Hospice Experiment,* ed. Vincent Mor, David S. Greer, and Robert Kastenbaum (Baltimore: Johns Hopkins University Press, 1988), p. 249.

49. S. Kay Toombs, "Chronic Illness and the Goals of Medicine," *Second Opinion* 21, no. 1 (July 1995): 11–19.

50. Inge B. Corless, "Dying Well: Symptom Control Within Hospice Care," in *Annual Review of Nursing Research* 12, eds. J. J. Fitzpatrick and J. S. Stevenson (New York: Springer, 1994), pp. 125–146.

51. See Rien M. J. P. A. Janssens, Zbigniew Zylicz, and Henk A. M. J. Ten Have, "Articulating the Concept of Palliative Care: Philosophical and Theological Perspectives," *Journal of Palliative Care* 15, no. 2 (1999): 38–44; and Allan Kellehear, "Spirituality and Palliative Care: A Model of Needs," *Palliative Medicine* 14 (2000): 149–155.

52. Inge B. Corless, "Settings for Terminal Care," *Omega: Journal of Death and Dying* 18, no. 4 (1987–1988): 319–340.

53. See, for example, Neil Small, "Social Work and Palliative Care," *British Journal of Social Work* 31 (2001): 961–971; and Avery D. Weisman, "Appropriate Death and the Hospice Program," *Hospice Journal* 4, no. 1 (1988): 65–77.

54. Ira Byock, "Palliative Care," in *On Our Own Terms: Moyers on Dying,* ed. Public Affairs Television (New York: WNET, 2000), pp. 10–11. See also, by Byock, "End-of-Life Care: A Public Health Crisis and an Opportunity for Managed Care," *American Journal of Managed Care* 7, no. 12 (2001): 1123–1132.

55. See William E. Phipps, "The Origin of Hospices/Hospitals," *Death Studies* 12, no. 2 (1988): 91–99; Susan Lynn Sloan, "The Hospice Movement: A Study in the Diffusion of Innovative Palliative Care," *American Journal of Hospice and Palliative Care* (May–June 1992): 24–31; and Sandol Stoddard, "Hospice in the United States: An Overview," *Journal of Palliative Care* 5, no. 3 (1989): 10–19.

56. James Luther Adams, "Palliative Care in the Light of Early Christian Concepts," *Journal of Palliative Care* 5, no. 3 (1989): 5–8.

57. See Thelma Ingles, "St. Christopher's Hospice," in *A Hospice Handbook: A New Way to*

Care for the Dying, ed. Michael P. Hamilton and Helen F. Reid (Grand Rapids, Mich.: Eerdmans, 1980), pp. 45–56. See also Cicely Saunders, "The Evolution of Palliative Care," *Patient Education and Counseling* 41, no. 1 (2000): 7–13.

58. Cicely Saunders, personal communication.

59. Quoted in Constance Holden, "Hospices for the Dying, Relief from Pain and Fear," in *Hospice Handbook*, ed. Hamilton and Reid, p. 61.

60. International Work Group on Death, Dying, and Bereavement, *Statements on Death, Dying, and Bereavement* (London, Ont.: IWG, 1994).

61. William M. Lamers, Jr., "Hospice: Enhancing the Quality of Life," in *The Path Ahead*, ed. DeSpelder and Strickland, pp. 116–124.

62. Robert Berkow, ed., *The Merck Manual of Diagnosis and Therapy*, 16th ed. (Rahway, N.J.: Merck Research Laboratories, 1992), p. 2571.

63. See F. Ackerman, "Goldilocks and Mrs. Ilych: A Critical Look at the 'Philosophy of Hospice,'" *Cambridge Quarterly of Healthcare Ethics* 6, no. 3 (1997): 314–324.

64. See Katherine Froggatt, "Rites of Passage and the Hospice Culture," *Mortality* 2, no. 2 (1997): 123–136.

65. R. Sean Morrison, Catherine Maroney-Galin, Peter D. Kravolec, and Diane E. Meier, "The Growth of Palliative Care Programs in United States Hospitals," *Journal of Palliative Medicine* 8, no. 6 (2005): 1127–1134.

66. Clive F. Seale, "What Happens in Hospices: A Review of Research Evidence," *Social Science & Medicine* 28, no. 6 (1989): 551–559.

67. Richard Smith, "A Good Death," *British Medical Journal* 320 (January 15, 2000): 129–130; quote p. 129.

68. For a recent, comprehensive report compiled by the National Hospice Work Group, see Bruce Jennings, True Ryndes, Carol D'Onofrio, and Mary Ann Baily, *Access to Hospice Care: Expanding Boundaries, Overcoming Barriers: Hastings Center Report Special Supplement* 33, no. 2 (2003): S3–S59.

69. Debbie Ward, "Women and the Work of Caring," *Second Opinion* 19, no. 2 (October 1993): 11–25.

70. Paul Glare and others, "A Systematic Review of Physicians' Survival Predictions in Terminally Ill Cancer Patients," *British Medical Journal* 327 (July 26, 2003): 195–198.

71. See Pamela J. Miller and Paula B. Mike, "The Medicare Hospice Benefit: Ten Years of Federal Policy for the Terminally Ill," *Death Studies* 19, no. 6 (1995): 531–542.

72. Lucette Lagnado, "Medicare Head Tackles Criticism on Hospice Care," *Wall Street Journal*, September 15, 2000, pp. B1, B4; and Nancy-Ann Min DeParle, Administrator, Health Care Financing Administration, "Letter to Medicare Hospices," September 12, 2000.

73. *NHPCO Facts and Figures—2005 Findings.*

74. Ronald K. Barrett, "Blacks, Death, Dying, and Funerals: Things You've Wondered About but Thought It Politically Incorrect to Ask" (keynote presentation, King's College 15th International Conference on Death & Bereavement, London, Ontario, May 12, 1997).

75. See, for example, Harold P. Freeman and Richard Payne, "Racial Injustice in Health Care," *New England Journal of Medicine* 342, no. 14 (April 6, 2000): 1045–1047; and Harold P. Freeman, Richard Payne, and Louis W. Sullivan, "Racial Injustice in Health Care: How Should It Be Addressed?" *Medical Crossfire* 2, no. 8 (2000): 31–33.

76. Sandol Stoddard, quoted in Susan Lynn Sloan, "The Hospice Movement: A Study in the Diffusion of Innovative Palliative Care," *American Journal of Hospice and Palliative Care* (May–June 1992): 24–31.

77. Richard Payne, "At the End of Life, Color Still Divides," *Washington Post*, February 15, 2000. See also Leslie J. Blackhall and others, "Ethnicity and Attitudes Towards Life Sustaining Technology," *Social Science & Medicine* 48, no. 12 (1999): 1779–1789; Eric L. Krakauer, Christopher Crenner, and Ken Fox, "Barriers to Optimum End-of-Life Care for Minority

Patients," *Journal of the American Geriatrics Society* 50, no. 1 (2002): 182–190; Eric W. Mebane and others, "The Influence of Physician Race, Age, and Gender on Physician Attitudes Toward Advance Care Directives and Preferences for End-of-Life Decision-Making," *Journal of the American Geriatrics Society* 47, no. 5 (1999): 579–591; Dona J. Reese and others, "Hospice Access and Use by African Americans: Addressing Cultural and Institutional Barriers," *Social Work* 44, no. 6 (1999): 549–559; and "Palliative Care in African-American Communities" (whole issue), *Innovations in End-of-Life Care: An International Online Journal* 3, no. 5 (September–October 2001), www.2.edu.org/lastacts/crntisue.asp (accessed September 25, 2001).

78. Carole A. Winston, Paula Leshner, Jennifer Kramer, and Gillian Allen, "Overcoming Barriers to Access and Utilization of Hospice and Palliative Care Services in African-American Communities," *Omega: Journal of Death and Dying* 50, no. 2 (2004–2005): 151–163; quote p. 161.

79. Stephen R. Connor, Martha Tecca, Judi LundPerson, and Joan Teno, "Measuring Hospice Care," *Journal of Pain and Symptom Management* 28, no. 4 (2004): 316–328; quote p. 325.

80. Inge B. Corless, "Hospice and Hope: An Incompatible Duo," *American Journal of Hospice and Palliative Care* (May–June 1992): 10–12.

81. See Nicky James and David Field, "The Routinization of Hospice: Charisma and Bureaucratization," *Social Science & Medicine* 34, no. 12 (1992): 1363–1375.

82. Inge B. Corless, "Settings for Terminal Care," *Omega: Journal of Death and Dying* 18, no. 4 (1987–1988): 319–340; quote p. 331.

83. See Betty Ferrell, Rose Virani, Marcia Grant, and Tami Borneman, "Analysis of Content Regarding Death and Bereavement in Nursing Texts," *Psycho-Oncology* 8, no. 6 (1999): 500–510; and Betty Ferrell, Rose Virani, Marcia Grant, and Gloria Juarez, "Analysis of Palliative Care Content in Nursing Textbooks," *Journal of Palliative Care* 16, no. 1 (2000): 39–47.

84. William M. Lamers, Jr., "How Patient Deaths Affect Health Professionals: A Plea for More Open Communication," *Journal of Pharmaceutical Care in Pain & Symptom Control* 5, no. 3 (1997): 59–71.

85. William M. Lamers, Jr., "Hospice Care and Its Effect on the Grieving Process," in *Living with Grief When Illness Is Prolonged*, ed. Kenneth J. Doka and Joyce Davidson (Washington, D.C.: Hospice Foundation of America, 1997), pp. 67–82. See also, by Lamers, "Defining Hospice and Palliative Care: Some Further Thoughts," *Journal of Pain & Palliative Care Pharmacotherapy* 16, no. 3 (2002): 65–71; and Inge B. Corless, "Palliative Care: One Does Not Need to Be Terminally Ill," in *The Nursing Profession and Beyond*, ed. Norma L. Chasha (Thousand Oaks, Calif.: Sage, 2001), pp. 561–573.

86. Nicholas A. Christakis and Theodore J. Iwashyna, "Impact of Individual and Market Factors on the Timing of Initiation of Hospice Terminal Care," *Medical Care* 38, no. 5 (2000): 528–541.

87. Pam Brown, Betty Davies, and Nola Martens, "Families in Supportive Care—Part II: Palliative Care at Home: A Viable Care Setting," *Journal of Palliative Care* 6, no. 3 (1990): 21–27.

88. Tony Chapman, "There's No Place Like Home," *Theory, Culture & Society* 18, no. 6 (2001): 135–146; quote p. 144.

89. Allan Kellehear, "Health-Promoting Palliative Care: Developing a Social Model for Practice," *Mortality* 4, no. 1 (1999): 75–82; quote p. 77.

90. Information provided by Frank Ostaseski, director of Zen Hospice Project, and based on the Project's "Mission Statement" and "At a Glance" fact sheet.

91. Frank Ostaseski, "Stories of Lives Lived and Now Ending," *Inquiring Mind: A Journal of the Vipassana Community* 10, no. 2 (Spring 1994): 14–16.

92. Jon Hendricks and C. Davis Hendricks, *Aging in Mass Society: Myths and Realities* (Cambridge, Mass.: Winthrop, 1977), pp. 284–285.

93. Hendricks and Hendricks, *Aging in Mass Society*, p. 282. See also Colleen L. Johnson and Leslie A. Grant, *The Nursing Home in Ameri-*

can Society (Baltimore: Johns Hopkins University Press, 1985).

94. See, for example, Colette Brown and Roberta Onzuka-Anderson, eds., *Our Aging Parents: A Practical Guide to Eldercare* (Honolulu: University of Hawaii Press, 1985); and Marty Richards, et al., *Choosing a Nursing Home: A Guidebook for Families* (Seattle: University of Washington Press, 1985).

95. See Muriel R. Gillick, "Do We Need to Create Geriatric Hospitals?" *Journal of the American Geriatrics Society* 50, no. 1 (2002): 174–177.

96. "Deaths and Death Rates by Selected Causes," *Statistical Abstract of the United States: 2007,* 126th ed. (Washington, D.C.: Government Printing Office, 2006), p. 84.

97. Seth B. Golbey, "Critical Cares: Life-Saving Aeromedical Helicopter Services," *AOPA Pilot* 30, no. 4 (April 1987): 39–46, and, also by Golbey, "Dust Off," pp. 46–48. See also Mickey Eisenberg, *Life in the Balance: Emergency Medicine and the Quest to Reverse Sudden Death* (New York: Oxford University Press, 1997).

98. Michael Nurok, "The Death of a Princess and the Formulation of Medical Competence," *Social Science & Medicine* 53 (2001): 1427–1438; quote p. 1436. See also Thomas A. Sancton, "Death of a Princess: Did Princess Diana Have to Die? A Study in French Emergency Medicine," *Internet Journal of Rescue and Disaster Medicine* 1, no. 2 (2000).

99. See Dale G. Larson, *The Helper's Journey: Working with People Facing Grief, Loss, and Life-Threatening Illness* (Champaign, Ill.: Research Press, 1993); and Danai Papadatou, "A Proposed Model of Health Professionals' Grieving Process," *Omega: Journal of Death and Dying* 41, no. 1 (2000): 59–77.

100. See, for example, John D. Sugimoto and Kevin Ann Oltjenbruns, "The Environment of Death and Its Influence on Police Officers in the United States," *Omega: Journal of Death and Dying* 43, no. 2 (2001): 145–155; and Laurence Miller, "Tough Guys: Psychotherapeutic Strategies with Law Enforcement and Emergency Services Personnel," in *Stress Management in Law Enforcement,* ed. Leonard Territo and James D. Sewell (Durham, N.C.: Carolina Academic Press, 1999), pp. 317–332.

101. Morag B. Harris, Mustafa Baloğlu, and James R. Stacks, "Mental Health of Trauma-Exposed Firefighters and Critical Incident Stress Debriefing," *Journal of Loss and Trauma* 7 (2002): 223–238.

102. Donald M. Sledz, "Nursing an Old Wound in Medicine," *Wall Street Journal,* February 6, 1997, p. A14.

103. See Patricia Boston, Anna Towers, and David Barnard, "Embracing Vulnerability: Risk and Empathy in Palliative Care," *Journal of Palliative Care* 17, no. 4 (2001): 248–253; Danai Papadatou, Irene Papazoglou, Dimitra Petraki, and Thalia Bellali, "Mutual Support Among Nurses Who Provide Care to Dying Children," *Illness, Crisis & Loss* 7, no. 1 (1999): 37–48; Rosanne M. Radziewicz, "Self-Care for the Caregiver," *Nursing Clinics of North America* 36, no. 4 (2001): 855–867; and Judi Webster and Linda J. Kristjanson, "'But Isn't It Depressing?': The Vitality of Palliative Care," *Journal of Palliative Care* 18, no. 1 (2002): 15–24.

104. Quoted by Marilyn Chase, "Tending to Patients with AIDS Teaches Valuable Lessons," *Wall Street Journal,* July 22, 1996, p. B1.

105. Jeanette Pickrel, "'Tell Me Your Story': Using Life Review in Counseling the Terminally Ill," *Death Studies* 13, no. 2 (1989): 127–135.

106. Tenshin Reb Anderson, quoted by Ostaseski, "Stories of Lives Lived and Now Ending," p. 29.

107. Janmarie Silvera, "Crossing the Border," in *The Path Ahead,* ed. DeSpelder and Strickland, pp. 301–302.

CHAPTER 6

1. See L. J. Blackhall and others, "Ethnicity and Attitudes Toward Patient Autonomy," *Journal of the American Medical Association* 274, no. 10 (1995): 820–825; and Larry O. Gostin, "Informed Consent, Cultural Sensitivity, and

Respect for Persons," *Death Studies* 17, no. 3 (1993): 844–845.

2. See Nancy S. Jecker, "The Role of Intimate Others in Medical Decision Making," *Gerontologist* (February 1990): 65–71.

3. Timothy E. Quill and Christine K. Cassel, "Nonabandonment: A Central Obligation for Physicians," *Annals of Internal Medicine* 122, no. 5 (1995): 368–374.

4. Alexander Morgan Capron, "The Burden of Decision," *Hastings Center Report* (May–June 1990): 36–41.

5. John D. Lantos, *Do We Still Need Doctors?* (New York: Routledge, 1997), pp. 47–48.

6. See Edmund D. Pellegrino and David C. Thomasma, *The Virtues in Medical Practice* (New York: Oxford University Press, 1993).

7. President's Commission for the Study of Ethical Problems in Medicine and Biomedical and Behavioral Research, *Making Health Care Decisions: The Ethical and Legal Implications of Informed Consent in the Patient–Practitioner Relationship,* vol. 1, *Report,* and vol. 3, *Studies on the Foundations of Informed Consent* (Washington, D.C.: Government Printing Office, 1982).

8. See Jon F. Merz, "On a Decision-Making Paradigm of Medical Informed Consent," *Journal of Legal Medicine* 14 (1993): 231–264.

9. R. B. Deber and others, "What Role Do Patients Wish to Play in Treatment Decision Making?" *Archives of Internal Medicine* 156, no. 13 (1996): 1414–1420; and R. F. Nease and W. B. Brooks, "Patient Desire for Information and Decision Making in Health Care Decisions: The Autonomy Preference Index and the Health Opinion Survey," *Journal of General Internal Medicine* 10, no. 11 (1995): 539–600.

10. Donald Oken, "What to Tell Cancer Patients: A Study of Medical Attitudes," *Journal of the American Medical Association* 175 (1961): 1120–1128.

11. D. H. Novack and others, "Changes in Physicians' Attitudes Toward Telling the Cancer Patient," *Journal of the American Medical Association* 241 (March 2, 1979): 897–900.

12. D. H. Novack and others, "Physicians' Attitudes Toward Using Deception to Resolve Difficult Ethical Problems," *Journal of the American Medical Association* 261 (May 26, 1989): 2980–2985.

13. Robert Berkow, ed., *The Merck Manual of Medical Information: Home Edition* (Whitehouse Station, N.J.: Merck Research Laboratories, 1997), p. 16.

14. *Steadman's Medical Dictionary,* 26th ed. (Baltimore: Williams & Wilkins, 1995), p. 1371.

15. David W. Towle, "Medical Ethics," *Academic American Encyclopedia* online (accessed March 1991). See also Walter A. Brown, "The Placebo Effect," *Scientific American* 278, no. 1 (January 1998): 90–95.

16. Margot L. White and John C. Fletcher, "The Story of Mr. and Mrs. Doe: 'You Can't Tell My Husband He's Dying; It Will Kill Him,'" in *The Path Ahead: Readings in Death and Dying,* ed. Lynne Ann DeSpelder and Albert Lee Strickland (Mountain View, Calif.: Mayfield, 1995), pp. 148–153.

17. The SUPPORT Principal Investigators, "A Controlled Trial to Improve Care for Seriously Ill Hospitalized Patients: The Study to Understand Prognoses and Preferences for Outcomes and Risks of Treatment (SUPPORT)," *Journal of the American Medical Association* 274, no. 20 (1995): 1591–1598. See also in *Journal of the American Geriatrics Society* 48, no. 5 (2000): Russell S. Phillips and others, "Findings from SUPPORT and HELP: An Introduction," pp. S1–S5; Neil S. Wenger and others, "Physician Understanding of Patient Resuscitation Preferences: Insights and Clinical Implications," pp. S44–S51; and Carol E. Golin and others, "A Prospective Study of Patient-Physician Communication About Resuscitation," pp. S52–S60.

18. See C. H. Braddock and others, "How Doctors and Patients Discuss Routine Clinical Decisions: Informed Decision Making in the Outpatient Setting," *Journal of General Internal Medicine* 12, no. 6 (1997): 339–345; and, in the same issue, S. J. Diem, "How and When Should

Physicians Discuss Clinical Decisions with Patients?" pp. 397–398; see also Jan C. Hoffman and others, "Patient Preferences for Communication with Physicians About End-of-Life Decisions," *Annals of Internal Medicine* 127, no. 1 (1997): 1–11.

19. See Jessica H. Muller, "Shades of Blue: The Negotiation of Limited Codes by Medical Residents," *Social Science & Medicine* 34, no. 8 (1992): 885–898; Ian N. Olver, Jaklin A. Eliott, and Jane Blake-Mortimer, "Cancer Patients' Perceptions of Do Not Resuscitate Orders," *Psycho-Oncology* 11, no. 3 (2002): 181–187; and Tom Tomlinson and Howard Brody, "Futility and the Ethics of Resuscitation," *Journal of the American Medical Association* 264 (September 12, 1990): 1276–1280.

20. Sharon R. Kaufman, *And a Time to Die: How American Hospitals Shape the End of Life* (New York: Scribner, 2005), p. 49.

21. See Yvonne K. Scherer and Michael H. Ackerman, "Ethical and Legal Controversies in Critical Care Nursing," in *Nursing Issues for the Nineties and Beyond,* ed. B. Bullough and V. L. Bullough (New York: Springer, 1994), pp. 122–138.

22. Howard Brody and others, "Withdrawing Intensive Life-Sustaining Treatment: Recommendations for Compassionate Clinical Management," *New England Journal of Medicine* 336, no. 9 (1997): 652–657.

23. S. J. Diem and J. D. Lantos, "Cardiopulmonary Resuscitation on Television: Miracles and Misinformation," *New England Journal of Medicine* 334, no. 24 (1996): 1578–1582.

24. A. Halevy and B. A. Brody, "A Multi-Institutional Collaborative Policy on Medical Futility," *Journal of the American Medical Association* 276, no. 7 (1996): 571–574. See also Andrew I. Batavia, "Disability Versus Futility in Rationing Health Care Services: Defining Medical Futility Based on Permanent Unconsciousness: PVS, Coma, and Anencephaly," *Behavioral Sciences and the Law* 20, no. 3 (2002): 219–233; and Donald Joralemon, "Reading Futility: Reflections on a Bioethical Concept," *Cambridge Quarterly of Healthcare Ethics* 11, no. 2 (2002): 127–133.

25. Berkow, ed., *Merck Manual of Medical Information: Home Edition,* p. 16.

26. President's Commission for the Study of Ethical Problems in Medicine and Biomedical and Behavioral Research, *Summing Up: Final Report on Studies of the Ethical and Legal Problems in Medicine and Biomedical and Behavioral Research* (Washington, D.C.: Government Printing Office, March 1983), p. 31. See also the companion volume, *Deciding to Forego Life-Sustaining Treatment: A Report on the Ethical, Medical, and Legal Issues in Treatment Decisions* (Washington, D.C.: Government Printing Office, March 1983).

27. Joseph Fletcher, "The Patient's Right to Die," in *Euthanasia and the Right to Die: The Case for Voluntary Euthanasia,* ed. A. B. Downing (London: Peter Owen, 1969), p. 30.

28. *In the Matter of Karen Quinlan: The Complete Legal Briefs, Court Proceedings and Decisions in the Superior Court of New Jersey* (1975) and *In the Matter of Karen Quinlan, Volume 2: The Complete Briefs, Oral Arguments, and Opinion in the New Jersey Supreme Court* (1976; Arlington, Va.: University Publications of America).

29. See Peter Allmark, "Death with Dignity," *Journal of Medical Ethics* 28, no. 4 (2002): 255–257.

30. "Medical Aspects of the Persistent Vegetative State," *New England Journal of Medicine* 331, no. 21 (1994): 1499–1508. In recent years, neurologists have been moving away from putting emphasis on "persistent," preferring to speak simply of a "vegetative state."

31. Background to the Cruzan case and arguments on both sides of the issue can be found in *Hastings Center Report* (January–February 1990): 38–50. See also Ron Hamel, "The Supreme Court's Decision in the *Cruzan* Case: A Synopsis," *Bulletin of the Park Ridge Center* (September 1990): 18, 20; and Thane Josef Messinger, "A Gentle and Easy Death: From

Ancient Greece to Beyond Cruzan Toward a Reasoned Legal Response to the Societal Dilemma of Euthanasia," *Denver University Law Review* 71, no. 1 (1993): 175–251.

32. Jon Eisenberg, *Using Terri: The Religious Right's Conspiracy to Take Away Our Rights* (San Francisco: HarperCollins, 2005), p. 160.

33. William Colby, *Unplugged: Reclaiming Our Right to Die in America* (New York: Amacom, 2006), p. 95.

34. J. T. Giacino and others, "The Minimally Conscious State: Definition and Diagnostic Criteria," *Neurology* 58 (2002): 349–353.

35. Ronald E. Cranford, "What Is a Minimally Conscious State?" *Western Journal of Medicine* 176 (2002): 129–130.

36. See Howard Brody, "Assisted Death: A Compassionate Response to a Medical Failure," *New England Journal of Medicine* 327 (November 5, 1992): 1384–1388; Eugenie Anne Gifford, "*Artes Moriendi:* Active Euthanasia and the Art of Dying," *UCLA Law Review* 40 (1993): 1545–1585; Albert R. Jonsen, "Living with Euthanasia: A Futuristic Scenario," *Journal of Medicine and Philosophy* 18 (1993): 241–251; Patricia A. King and Leslie E. Wolf, "Lessons for Physician-Assisted Suicide from the African-American Experience," in *Physician-Assisted Suicide: Expanding the Debate,* ed. Margaret P. Battin, Rosamond Rhodes, and Anita Silvers (New York: Routledge, 1998), pp. 91–112; and Timothy Quill, "Care of the Hopelessly Ill: Proposed Clinical Criteria for Physician-Assisted Suicide," *New England Journal of Medicine* 327 (November 5, 1992): 1380–1384.

37. See Choice in Dying, "Physician-Assisted Suicide: *Vacco v. Quill* and *Washington v. Glucksberg,*" www.choices.org/sctdec.htm (accessed September 9, 2000); John Dinan, "Rights and the Political Process: Physician Assisted Suicide in the Aftermath of *Washington v. Glucksberg,*" *Publius: The Journal of Federalism* 31, no. 4 (2001): 1–21; and James L. Werth, Jr., and Judith R. Gordon," Amicus Curiae Brief for the United States Supreme Court on Mental Health

Issues Associated with 'Physician-Assisted Suicide.'" *Journal of Counseling & Development* 80, no. 2 (2002): 160–172.

38. "Physician-Assisted Suicide Initiative Passes in Oregon," *Western Bioethics News,* no. 53 (January 1995): 2–3. See also Lori A. Roscoe and others, "A Comparison of Characteristics of Kevorkian Euthanasia Cases and Physician-Assisted Suicides in Oregon," *Gerontologist* 41, no. 4 (2001): 439–446.

39. Oregon Health Division, "Summary of Oregon's Death with Dignity Act—2006," http://oregon.gov/DHS/ph/pas/ar-index.shtml (accessed November 17, 2007); see also Christine Neylon O'Brien, Gerald A. Madek, and Gerald R. Ferrera, "Oregon's Guidelines for Physician-Assisted Suicide: A Legal and Ethical Analysis," *University of Pittsburgh Law Review* 61, no. 2 (2000): 329–365.

40. See Clare E. Kendall, "A Double Dose of Double Effect," *Journal of Medical Ethics* 26, no. 3 (2000): 204–205.

41. See J. A. Billings and S. D. Block, "Slow Euthanasia," *Journal of Palliative Care* 12, no. 4 (1996): 21–30; and Howard Brody, "Commentary on Billings and Block's 'Slow Euthanasia,'" in the same issue, pp. 38–41. See also P. Rousseau, "Terminal Sedation in the Care of Dying Patients," *Archives of Internal Medicine* 1556, no. 16 (1996): 1785–1786.

42. Richard Carelli, "Court: No Right to Assisted Suicide," *Associated Press Online,* June 26, 1997.

43. Ira Byock, "Dying: After the Court Ruling," *Wall Street Journal,* June 25, 1997, p. A14.

44. John A. Pridonoff, "Introduction," in *Hospice and Hemlock: Retaining Dignity, Integrity, and Self-Respect in End-of-Life Decisions,* ed. Michele A. Trepkowski (Eugene, Ore.: Hemlock Society, 1993).

45. See David Orentlicher, "The Alleged Distinction Between Euthanasia and the Withdrawal of Life-Sustaining Treatment: Conceptually Incoherent and Impossible to Maintain," *University of Illinois Law Review* (1998): 837–859.

46. Arthur S. Berger, *Dying & Death in Law & Medicine: A Forensic Primer for Health and Legal Professionals* (Westport, Conn.: Praeger, 1993), p. 48.

47. See Michael A. DeCesare, "Public Attitudes Toward Euthanasia and Suicide for Terminally Ill Persons: 1977 and 1996," *Social Biology* 47, nos. 3–4 (2000): 264–276.

48. "It's Over, Debbie," *Journal of the American Medical Association* 259 (January 8, 1988): 272.

49. See Raphael Cohen-Almagor, "Why the Netherlands?" *Journal of Law, Medicine & Ethics* 30, no. 1 (2002): 95–104, and "'Culture of Death' in the Netherlands: Dutch Perspectives," *Issues in Law & Medicine* 17, no. 2 (2001): 167–179; Herbert Hendin, "The Dutch Experience," *Issues in Law & Medicine* 17, no. 3 (2002): 223–246; and Herman H. van der Kloot Meijburg, "How Health Care Institutions in the Netherlands Approach Physician-Assisted Death," *Omega: Journal of Death and Dying* 32, no. 3 (1995–1996): 179–196.

50. David J. Roy, "Euthanasia—Taking a Stand," *Journal of Palliative Care* 6, no. 1 (1990): 3–5; and "Palliative Care and Euthanasia: A Continuing Need to Think Again," *Journal of Palliative Care* 18, no. 1 (2002): 3–5.

51. Dame Cicely Saunders, "A Response to Logue's 'Where Hospice Fails—The Limits of Palliative Care,'" *Omega: Journal of Death and Dying* 32, no. 1 (1995–1996): 1–5; quote p. 2.

52. Charles J. Dougherty, "The Common Good, Terminal Illness, and Euthanasia," in *The Path Ahead*, ed. DeSpelder and Strickland, pp. 154–164.

53. Thomas Attig, "Can We Talk? On the Elusiveness of Dialogue," *Death Studies* 19, no. 1 (1995): 1–19.

54. R. J. Connelly, "The Sentiment Argument for Artificial Feeding of the Dying," *Omega: Journal of Death and Dying* 20, no. 3 (1989–1990): 229–237. See also Germain Grisez and Kevin O'Rourke, "Should Nutrition and Hydration Be Provided to Permanently Unconscious and Other Mentally Disabled Persons?" *Issues in Law & Medicine* 5 (1989): 165–196; James J. McCartney and Jane Mary Trau, "Cessation of the Artificial Delivery of Food and Fluids: Defining Terminal Illness and Care," *Death Studies* 14, no. 5 (1990): 435–444; Steven H. Miles, "Nourishment and the Ethics of Lament," *Linacre Quarterly* 56 (August 1989): 64–69; and J. Slomka, "What Do Apple Pie and Motherhood Have to Do with Feeding Tubes and Caring for the Patient?" *Archives of Internal Medicine* 155, no. 12 (1995): 1258–1263.

55. Dena S. Davis, "Old and Thin," *Second Opinion* 15 (November 1990): 26–32; see also, in the same issue, Ronald M. Green, "Old and Thin: A Response," pp. 34–39. On Japanese attitudes toward withdrawing nutrition and hydration, see Emiko Konishi, Anne J. Davis, and Toshiaki Aiba, "The Ethics of Withdrawing Artificial Food and Fluid from Terminally Ill Patients: An End-of-Life Dilemma for Japanese Nurses and Families," *Nursing Ethics* 9, no. 1 (2002): 7–19.

56. Richard A. McCormick, "To Save or Let Die: The Dilemma of Modern Medicine," in *Ethical Issues in Death and Dying*, ed. Robert F. Weir (New York: Columbia University Press, 1977), pp. 173–184.

57. See, for example, Berit Støre Brinchmann, "Neonatal Medicine in Norway," *Journal of Clinical Ethics* 12, no. 3 (2001): 307–311; Peter A. Clark, "Medical Futility in Pediatrics: Is It Time for a Public Policy?" *Journal of Public Health Policy* 23, no. 1 (2002): 66–89; and John J. Paris, Jeffrey Ferranti, and Frank Reardon, "From the Johns Hopkins Baby to Baby Miller: What Have We Learned from Four Decades of Reflection on Neonatal Cases?" *Journal of Clinical Ethics* 12, no. 3 (2001): 207–214.

58. President's Commission for the Study of Ethical Problems in Medicine and Biomedical and Behavioral Research, *Deciding to Forego Life-Sustaining Treatment*, p. 7.

59. See Peter H. Ditto and others, "Advance Directives as Acts of Communication,"

Archives of Internal Medicine 161 (2001): 421–430; Angela Fagerlin and others, "Projection in Surrogate Decisions About Life-Sustaining Medical Treatments," *Health Psychology* 20, no. 3 (2001): 166–175; and Angela Fagerlin and others, "The Use of Advance Directives in End-of-Life Decision Making: Problems and Possibilities," *American Behavioral Scientist* 46, no. 2 (2002): 268–283.

60. Judi Lund Person, "Regulatory Issues in the Care of Dying," in *Dying, Death, and Bereavement,* 2nd ed., ed. Corless, Germino, and Pittman, p. 205.

61. President's Council on Bioethics, *Ethical Caregiving in Our Aging Society* (Washington, D.C.: Government Printing Office, 2005), p. 55.

62. Robert Berkow, ed., *The Merck Manual of Medical Information: Home Edition* (Whitehouse Station, N.J.: Merck Research Laboratories, 1997), p. 17.

63. See Linda L. Emanuel and others, "Advance Directives: Can Patients' Stated Treatment Choices Be Used to Infer Unstated Choices?" *Medical Care* 32, no. 2 (1994): 95–105; and Jim Stone, "Advance Directives, Autonomy, and Unintended Death," *Bioethics* 8, no. 3 (1994): 223–246.

64. The authors thank Senator John C. Danforth, sponsor of this measure, for providing information about its provisions. See also Elizabeth Leibold McCloskey, "The Patient Self-Determination Act," *Kennedy Institute of Ethics Journal* 1, no. 2 (1991): 163–169.

65. Zelda Foster, "The Struggle to End My Father's Life," in *Dying, Death, and Bereavement,* 2nd ed., ed. Corless, Germino, and Pittman, pp. 79–85. See also Renée Semonin Holleran, "When Is Dead, Dead? The Ethics of Resuscitation in Emergency Care," *Nursing Clinics of North America* 37, no. 1 (2002): 11–18.

66. See Kenneth J. Doka, "The Monkey's Paw: The Role of Inheritance in the Resolution of Grief," *Death Studies* 16, no. 1 (1992): 45–58. For a cross-cultural comparison of inheritance practices, see Misa Izuhara, "Care and Inheritance: Japanese and English Perspectives on the 'Generational Contract,'" *Ageing and Society* 22 (2002): 61–77.

67. Barton E. Bernstein, "Lawyer and Counselor as an Interdisciplinary Team: Interfacing for the Terminally Ill," *Death Education* 1, no. 3 (Fall 1977): 277–291; "Lawyer and Therapist as an Interdisciplinary Team: Serving the Terminally Ill," *Death Education* 3, no. 1 (Spring 1979): 11–19; and "Lawyer and Therapist as an Interdisciplinary Team: Serving the Survivors," *Death Education* 4, no. 2 (Summer 1980): 179–188.

68. See Carole Shammas, Marylynn Salmon, and Michel Dahlin, *Inheritance in America from Colonial Times to the Present* (New Brunswick, N.J.: Rutgers University Press, 1987).

69. See Joseph M. Belth, *Life Insurance: A Consumer's Handbook,* 2nd ed. (Bloomington: Indiana University Press, 1985).

70. Leon R. Kass, "Practicing Ethics: Where's the Action?" *Hastings Center Report* (January–February 1990): 5–12.

71. Alexander Morgan Capron, "Why Law and the Life Sciences?" *Hastings Center Report* 24, no. 3 (1994): 42–44.

CHAPTER 7

1. Cassandra Lorius, "Taboo," in *Key Ideas in Human Thought,* ed. Kenneth McLeish (New York: Facts on File, 1993), p. 731.

2. S. Kay Toombs, "Chronic Illness and the Goals of Medicine," *Second Opinion* 21, no. 1 (July 1995): 11–19. See also Charles E. Rosenberg, "The Tyranny of Diagnosis: Specific Entities and Individual Experience," *Milbank Quarterly* 80, no. 2 (2002): 237–260.

3. Betsy L. Fife, "The Conceptualization of Meaning in Illness," *Social Science & Medicine* 38, no. 2 (1994): 309–316.

4. Peter Conrad, "Wellness as Virtue: Morality and the Pursuit of Health," *Culture, Medicine, and Psychiatry* 18 (1994): 385–401.

5. See Margaret I. Fitch, Terry Bunston, and Mary Elliot, "When Mom's Sick: Changes in a Mother's Role and in the Family After Her Diagnosis of Cancer," *Cancer Nursing* 22, no. 1 (1999): 58–63; and G. P. Sholevar and R. Perkel, "Family Systems Intervention and Physical Illness," *General Hospital Psychiatry* 12 (1990): 363–372.

6. See Charles A. Garfield, *Stress and Survival: The Emotional Realities of Life-Threatening Illness* (St. Louis: Mosby, 1979).

7. Arthur Kleinman, *The Illness Narratives: Suffering, Healing, and the Human Condition* (New York: Basic Books, 1988), pp. 3–6.

8. Carl May, "Disclosure of Terminal Prognosis in a General Hospital: The Nurse's View," *Journal of Advanced Nursing* 18 (1993): 1362–1368.

9. Arthur W. Frank, "The Pedagogy of Suffering: Moral Dimensions of Psychological Therapy and Research with the Ill," *Theory & Psychology* 2, no. 4 (1992): 467–485.

10. See Kevin P. Kaut, "Religion, Spirituality, and Existentialism Near the End of Life: Implications for Assessment and Application," *American Behavioral Scientist* 46, no. 2 (2002): 220–234.

11. Barney G. Glaser and Anselm L. Strauss, *Awareness of Dying* (Chicago: Aldine, 1965).

12. E. Mansell Pattison, *The Experience of Dying* (Englewood Cliffs, N.J.: Prentice-Hall, 1977); and "The Living-Dying Process," in *Psychological Care of the Dying,* ed. Charles Garfield (New York: McGraw-Hill, 1978), pp. 163–168. See also Karin L. Olson and others, "Linking Trajectories of Illness and Dying," *Omega: Journal of Death and Dying* 42, no. 4 (2001): 293–308.

13. Avery D. Weisman, *On Dying and Denying: A Psychiatric Study of Terminality* (New York: Behavioral Publications, 1972).

14. Elisabeth Kübler-Ross, *On Death and Dying* (New York: Macmillan, 1969).

15. Harold Brodkey, "To My Readers," in *The Path Ahead: Readings in Death and Dying,* ed. Lynne Ann DeSpelder and Albert Lee Strickland (Mountain View, Calif.: Mayfield, 1995), pp. 295–300; quote p. 298. See also Robert Connelly, "Living with Death: The Meaning of Acceptance," *Journal of Humanistic Psychology* 43, no. 1 (2003): 45–63.

16. Edwin S. Shneidman, *Lives and Deaths: Selections from the Works of Edwin S. Shneidman,* ed. Antoon A. Leenaars (Philadelphia: Brunner-Mazel, 1999), p. 260.

17. Herman Feifel, "Psychology and Death: Meaningful Rediscovery," in *The Path Ahead,* ed. DeSpelder and Strickland, pp. 19–28; quote p. 23.

18. Tone Rustøen and Ingela Wiklund, "Hope in Newly Diagnosed Patients with Cancer," *Cancer Nursing* 23, no. 3 (2000): 214–219. See also Jaklin Eliott and Ian Olver, "The Discursive Properties of 'Hope': A Qualitative Analysis of Cancer Patients' Speech," *Qualitative Health Research* 12, no. 2 (2002): 173–193.

19. Charles A. Corr, "A Task-Based Approach to Coping with Dying," *Omega: Journal of Death and Dying* 24, no. 2 (1991–1992): 81–94. See also, by Corr, "Coping with Dying: Lessons That We Should and Should Not Learn from the Work of Elisabeth Kübler-Ross," *Death Studies* 17, no. 1 (1993): 69–83.

20. Kenneth J. Doka, "Coping with Life-Threatening Illness: A Task Model," *Omega: Journal of Death and Dying* 32, no. 2 (1995–1996): 111–122. See also Charles A. Corr and Kenneth J. Doka, "Current Models of Death, Dying, and Bereavement," *Critical Care Nursing Clinics of North America* 6, no. 3 (1994): 545–552; and by Doka, *Living with Life-Threatening Illness: A Guide for Patients, Their Families, and Caregivers* (New York: Lexington, 1993).

21. Avery D. Weisman, *The Coping Capacity: On the Nature of Being Mortal* (New York: Human Sciences Press, 1986).

22. Weisman, *On Dying and Denying.* See also, by Weisman, *Coping with Cancer* (New York: McGraw-Hill, 1979); and "Thanatology," in *Comprehensive Textbook of Psychiatry,* ed. O. Kaplan (Baltimore: Williams & Wilkins, 1980).

23. Susan Folkman and Steven Greer, "Promoting Psychological Well-Being in the Face of Serious Illness: When Theory, Research and Practice Inform Each Other," *Psycho-Oncology* 9, no. 1 (2000): 11–19.

24. Therese A. Rando, *Grief, Dying, and Death: Clinical Interventions for Caregivers* (Lexington, Mass.: Lexington, 1993).

25. See Phoebe Cramer, "Coping and Defense Mechanisms: What's the Difference?" *Journal of Personality* 66, no. 6 (1998): 919–946; and "Defense Mechanisms in Psychology Today: Further Processes for Adaptation," *American Psychologist* 55, no. 6 (2000): 637–646.

26. Russell Noyes, Jr., and others, "Illness Fears in the General Population," *Psychosomatic Medicine* 62, no. 3 (2000): 318–325.

27. See Susan Folkman, "Positive Psychological States and Coping with Severe Stress," *Social Science & Medicine* 45, no. 8 (1997): 1207–1221; and Susan Folkman and Judith Tedlie Moskowitz, "Positive Affect and the Other Side of Coping," *American Psychologist* 55, no. 6 (2000): 647–654.

28. Mark R. Somerfield and Robert R. McCrae, "Stress and Coping Research: Methodological Challenges, Theoretical Advances, and Clinical Applications," *American Psychologist* 55, no. 6 (2000): 620–625.

29. Richard S. Lazarus, "Toward Better Research on Stress and Coping," *American Psychologist* 55, no. 6 (2000): 665–673.

30. Folkman and Greer, "Promoting Psychological Well-Being in the Face of Serious Illness."

31. Betsy L. Fife, "The Measurement of Meaning in Illness," *Social Science & Medicine* 40, no. 8 (1995): 1021–1028.

32. See Judith A. Skala and Kenneth E. Freedland, "Death Takes a Raincheck," *Psychosomatic Medicine* 66 (2004): 382–386; and Debra Wood, "Postponing Death: How Strong Is the Will to Live?" www.healthgate.com (accessed August 2000).

33. Mary-Jo Del Vecchio Good and others, "Oncology and Narrative Time," *Social Science & Medicine* 38, no. 6 (1994): 855–862.

34. Robert L. Wrenn, Dan Levinson, and Danai Papadatou, *End of Life Decisions: Guidelines for the Health Care Provider* (Tucson: University of Arizona Health Sciences Center, 1996), p. 20.

35. Orville Kelly, "Making Today Count," in *Death and Dying: Theory/Research/Practice,* ed. Larry A. Bugen (Dubuque, Iowa: William C. Brown, 1979), pp. 277–283; see also, by Kelly, *Until Tomorrow Comes* (New York: Everest House, 1979).

36. Paolo Venies, "Definition and Classification of Cancer: Monothetic or Polythetic?" *Theoretical Medicine* 14 (1993): 249–256.

37. Linda J. Kristjanson and Terri Ashcroft, "The Family's Cancer Journey: A Literature Review," *Cancer Nursing* 17, no. 1 (1994): 1–17.

38. Robert Berkow, ed., *The Merck Manual of Diagnosis and Therapy,* 16th ed. (Rahway, N.J.: Merck Research Laboratories, 1992), p. 1275.

39. See Lesley F. Degner, "Treatment Decision Making," in *A Challenge for Living: Dying, Death, and Bereavement,* ed. Inge B. Corless, Barbara B. Germino, and Mary A. Pittman (Boston: Jones & Bartlett, 1995), pp. 3–16.

40. Berkow, ed., *Merck Manual of Diagnosis and Therapy,* 16th ed., p. 1275.

41. Laurence McCahill and Betty Ferrell, "Palliative Surgery for Cancer Pain," *Western Journal of Medicine* 176, no. 2 (2002): 107–110.

42. See Berkow, ed., *Merck Manual of Diagnosis and Therapy,* 16th ed., pp. 1276–1277; and *Merck Manual: Home Edition,* p. 801; and R. A. Hope and others, *Oxford Handbook of Clinical Medicine,* 3rd ed. (New York: Oxford University Press, 1994), p. 768.

43. See Berkow, ed., *Merck Manual of Diagnosis and Therapy,* 16th ed., pp. 55, 1277, 1287; and *Merck Manual: Home Edition,* pp. 799, 802; and Hope and others, *Oxford Handbook of Clinical Medicine,* p. 768.

44. See *Alternative Medicine: Expanding Medical Horizons, A Report to the National Institutes of Health on Alternative Medical Systems and Practices in the United States* (Bethesda, Md.: National Institutes of Health, 1992). See also Arthur Kleinman, *Patients and Healers in the Context of Culture*

(Berkeley: University of California Press, 1980); and Mary Jane Ott, "Complementary and Alternative Therapies in Cancer Symptom Management," *Cancer Practice* 10, no. 3 (2002): 162–166.

45. See Josep M. Comelles, "The Role of Local Knowledge in Medical Practice: A Trans-Historical Perspective," *Culture, Medicine and Psychiatry* 24, no. 1 (2000): 41–75.

46. Quoted in Anne Fadiman, *The Spirit Catches You and You Fall Down: A Hmong Child, Her American Doctors, and the Collision of Two Cultures* (New York: Farrar, Straus and Giroux, 1997), p. 261.

47. Lori Arviso Alvord and Elizabeth Cohen Van Pelt, *The Scalpel and the Silver Bear* (New York: Bantam, 1999).

48. Robert T. Trotter II and Juan Antonio Chavira, *Curanderismo: Mexican-American Folk Healing,* 2nd ed. (Athens: University of Georgia Press, 1997).

49. Kaja Finkler, "Sacred Healing and Biomedicine Compared," *Medical Anthropology Quarterly* 8, no. 2 (June 1994): 178–197.

50. Berkow, ed., *Merck Manual of Diagnosis and Therapy,* 16th ed., pp. 2593–2596.

51. Berkow, ed., *Merck Manual of Diagnosis and Therapy,* 16th ed., p. 1263.

52. Lawrence J. Schneiderman, "Alternative Medicine or Alternatives to Medicine? A Physician's Perspective," *Cambridge Quarterly of Healthcare Ethics* 9, no. 1 (2000): 83–97.

53. David K. Reynolds, *A Thousand Waves: A Sensible Life Style for Sensitive People* (New York: Quill/Morrow, 1990).

54. Anson Shupe and Jeffrey K. Hadden, "Symbolic Healing," *Second Opinion* 12 (November 1989): 74–97.

55. Barrie R. Cassileth, "Complementary Therapy," *Science & Medicine* 3, no. 6 (November–December 1996): 8–9.

56. Doris M. Schoenhoff, *The Barefoot Expert: The Interface of Computerized Knowledge Systems and Indigenous Knowledge Systems* (Westport, Conn.: Greenwood, 1993), pp. 13–14.

57. Desmond Manderson, "Formalism and Narrative in Law and Medicine: The Debate over Medical Marijuana Use," *Journal of Drug Issues* 29, no. 1 (1999): 121–133.

58. Stanley J. Watson, John A. Benson, Jr., and Janet E. Joy, "Marijuana and Medicine: Assessing the Science Base," *Archives of General Psychiatry* 57 (2000): 547–552. See also Linda R. Gowing, Robert L. Ali, Paul Christie, and Jason M. White, "Therapeutic Use of Cannabis: Clarifying the Debate," *Drug and Alcohol Review* 17 (1998): 445–452; and Franjo Grotenhermen, "The Medical Use of Cannabis in Germany," *Journal of Drug Issues* 32, no. 2 (2002): 607–633.

59. "Tapping Human Potential: An Interview with Norman Cousins," *Second Opinion* 14 (July 1990): 57–71. See also Norman Cousins, *Anatomy of an Illness as Perceived by the Patient: Reflections on Healing and Regeneration* (New York: Norton, 1979).

60. Marcia K. Merboth and Susan Barnason, "Managing Pain: The Fifth Vital Sign," *Nursing Clinics of North America* 35, no. 2 (2000): 375–383. See also Marni Jackson, *Pain: The Fifth Vital Sign* (New York: Crown, 2002).

61. Paul J. Weithman, "Of Assisted Suicide and 'The Philosophers' Brief,'" *Ethics* 109, no. 3 (1999): 548–578.

62. Alison Twycross, "Education About Pain: A Neglected Area?" *Nurse Education Today* 20, no. 3 (2000): 244–253. See also, by Twycross, "Educating Nurses About Pain Management: The Way Forward," *Journal of Clinical Nursing* 11, no. 6 (2002): 705–714.

63. Berkow, ed., *Merck Manual of Diagnosis and Therapy,* 16th ed., p. 1409.

64. *Dorland's Illustrated Medical Dictionary,* 26th ed. (Philadelphia: Saunders, 1985), p. 954.

65. Linda C. Garro, "Culture, Pain and Cancer," *Journal of Palliative Care* 6, no. 3 (1990): 34–44. See also David B. Morris, *The Culture of Pain* (Berkeley: University of California Press, 1991).

66. Berkow, ed., *Merck Manual of Diagnosis and Therapy,* 16th ed., pp. 1409, 1412. See also Fredrica A. Preston, Siew Tzuh Tang, and Ruth McCorkle, "Symptom Management for the Terminally Ill," in *Dying, Death, and Bereavement:*

A Challenge for Living, 2nd ed., ed. Inge Corless, Barbara B. Germino, and Mary A. Pittman (New York: Springer, 2003), pp. 145–180.

67. See Ada Jacox and others, *Management of Cancer Pain, Clinical Practice Guideline* No. 9, (Rockville, Md.: Agency for Health Care Policy and Research, 1994).

68. See Betty Rolling Ferrell, ed., "Issues in Cancer Pain Management: Models of Success," *Cancer Practice* 10, Supplement 1 (2002): whole issue.

69. See Karen L. Schumacher and others, "Pain Management Autobiographies and Reluctance to Use Opioids for Cancer Pain Management," *Cancer Nursing* 25, no. 2 (2002): 125–133; and James L. Werth, Jr., "Reinterpreting the Controlled Substances Act: Predictions for the Effect on Pain Relief," *Behavioral Sciences and the Law* 20, no. 3 (2002): 287–305.

70. Michael de Ridder, "Heroin: New Facts About an Old Myth," *Journal of Psychoactive Drugs* 26, no. 1 (1994): 65–68. See also Rita Carter, "Give a Drug a Bad Name . . . ," *New Scientist* 150 (April 6, 1996): 14–15.

71. Judith A. Paice and Michelle M. Buck, "Intraspinal Devices for Pain Management," *Nursing Clinics of North America* 28, no. 4 (1993): 921–935.

72. Mary K. Sheehan, Philip G. Janicak, and Sheila Dowd, "The Role of Psychopharmacotherapy in the Dying Patient," *Psychiatric Annals* 24, no. 2 (1994): 98–103.

73. See David Clark, "'Total Pain': Disciplinary Power and the Body in the Work of Cicely Saunders, 1958–1967," *Social Science & Medicine* 49 (1999): 727–736.

74. Robert Kastenbaum and Claude Normand, "Deathbed Scenes as Imagined by the Young and Experienced by the Old," *Death Studies* 14, no. 3 (1990): 201–217.

75. Barney G. Glaser and Anselm L. Strauss, *Time for Dying* (Chicago: Aldine, 1968). See also E. Mansell Pattison, *The Experience of Dying* (Englewood Cliffs, N.J.: Prentice-Hall, 1977).

76. Inge B. Corless, "Dying Well: Symptom Control Within Hospice Care," in *Annual Review of Nursing Research,* vol. 12, ed. J. J. Fitzpatrick and J. S. Stevenson (New York: Springer, 1994), pp. 125–146.

77. Berkow, ed., *Merck Manual: Home Edition,* pp. 18–20.

78. Eric J. Cassell, "Dying in a Technological Society," in *Death Inside Out: The Hastings Center Report,* ed. Peter Steinfels and Robert M. Veatch (New York: Harper & Row, 1974), pp. 43–48; see also, by Cassell, *The Nature of Suffering and the Goals of Medicine* (New York: Oxford University Press, 1991); Glaser and Strauss, *Awareness of Dying;* and David Sudnow, *Passing On: The Social Organization of Dying* (Englewood Cliffs, N.J.: Prentice-Hall, 1967).

79. Arthur W. Frank, "The Pedagogy of Suffering: Moral Dimensions of Psychological Therapy and Research with the Ill," *Theory & Psychology* 2, no. 4 (1992): 467–485. See also, by Frank, "What Kind of Phoenix? Illness and Self-Knowledge," *Second Opinion* 18, no. 2 (October 1992): 31–41.

80. Marjorie Kagawa-Singer, "Redefining Health: Living with Cancer," *Social Science & Medicine* 37, no. 3 (1993): 295–304.

81. Talcott Parsons, *The Social System* (New York: Free Press, 1951). See also Russell Noyes, Jr., and John Clancy, "The Dying Role: Its Relevance to Improved Patient Care," *Psychiatry* 40 (February 1977): 41–47.

82. Robert J. Baugher and others, "A Comparison of Terminally Ill Persons at Various Time Periods to Death," *Omega: Journal of Death and Dying* 20, no. 2 (1989–1990): 103–155.

83. Allan Kellehear and Terry Lewin, "Farewells by the Dying: A Sociological Study," *Omega: Journal of Death and Dying* 19, no. 4 (1988–1989): 275–292.

84. Roderick Cosh, "Spiritual Care of the Dying," in *A Challenge for Living,* ed. Corless, Germino, and Pittman, pp. 131–143.

85. Ibid., p. 136.

86. Makoto Ueda, *Modern Japanese Writers and the Nature of Literature* (Stanford, Calif.: Stanford University Press, 1976), p. 193.

CHAPTER 8

1. See Lynne Ann DeSpelder and Albert Lee Strickland, "Ceremonies," in *Encyclopedia of Death and Dying,* ed. Glennys Howarth and Oliver Leaman (New York: Routledge, 2001), pp. 84–85.

2. Mike Parker Pearson, *The Archaeology of Death and Burial* (College Station: Texas A&M University Press, 2000), p. 194.

3. This account is based on the following sources: "Coffins and Sarcophagi," exhibition notes, Metropolitan Museum of Art, New York; Henri Frankfort, *Ancient Egyptian Religion: An Interpretation* (New York: Harper & Row, 1948, 1961); Manfred Lurker, *The Gods and Symbols of Ancient Egypt* (New York: Thames & Hudson, 1980); and Barbara Watterson, *The Gods of Ancient Egypt* (New York: Facts on File, 1984). See also Morris Bierbrier, *The Tomb-Builders of the Ancient Pharaohs* (New York: Scribner, 1982); John Romer, *Ancient Lives: Daily Life in Egypt of the Pharaohs* (New York: Holt, Rinehart & Winston, 1984); and A. J. Spencer, *Death in Ancient Egypt* (New York: Penguin, 1982).

4. Vanderlyn R. Pine, "Funerals: Life's Final Ceremony," in *A Challenge for Living: Dying, Death, and Bereavement,* ed. Inge B. Corless, Barbara B. Germino, and Mary A. Pittman (Boston: Jones & Bartlett, 1995), pp. 159–171. See also Jenny Hockey, "Encountering the 'Reality of Death' Through Professional Discourse: The Matter of Materiality," *Mortality* 1, no. 1 (1996): 45–60.

5. Thomas Lynch, *The Undertaking: Life Studies from the Dismal Trade* (New York: Norton, 1997), p. 21.

6. David Sudnow, *Passing On: The Social Organization of Dying* (Englewood Cliffs, N.J.: Prentice-Hall, 1967), pp. 153–168.

7. Ronald K. Barrett, "Contemporary African-American Funeral Rites and Traditions," in *The Path Ahead: Readings in Death and Dying,* ed. Lynne Ann DeSpelder and Albert Lee Strickland (Mountain View, Calif.: Mayfield, 1995), pp. 80–92; quote p. 88. See also by Barrett, "The Legacy of Traditional African-American Funeral Rites," *Thanos* 16 (October 1994): 18–20; "Affirming and Reclaiming African-American Funeral Rites," *The Director* 66, no. 11 (October 1994): 36–40; and "Psychocultural Influences on African American Attitudes Toward Death, Dying, and Funeral Rites," in *Personal Care in an Impersonal World,* ed. John Morgan (Amityville, N.Y.: Baywood, 1993), pp. 213–230. See also Elaine Nichols, ed., *The Last Miles of the Way: African-American Homegoing Traditions, 1890–Present* (Columbia: South Carolina State Museum, 1989).

8. See Ben H. Bagdikian, *The Information Machines: Their Impact on Men and the Media* (New York: Harper & Row, 1971), pp. 39, 59; and Bradley Greenberg, "Diffusion of News of the Kennedy Assassination," *Public Opinion Quarterly* 28, no. 2 (Summer 1964): 225–232.

9. J. Z. Young, *Programs of the Brain* (New York: Oxford University Press, 1978), p. 255.

10. Vernon Reynolds and Ralph Tanner, *The Social Ecology of Religion* (New York: Oxford University Press, 1995), p. 213.

11. John R. Elliott, "Funerary Artifacts in Contemporary America," *Death Studies* 14, no. 6 (1990): 601–612.

12. Federal Trade Commission, *Compliance Guidelines: Trade Regulation Rule on Funeral Industry Practices* (Washington, D.C., 1984).

13. See Robert W. Habenstein and William M. Lamers, *The History of American Funeral Directing* (Milwaukee: Bulfin Printers, 1962).

14. See Glennys Howarth, *Last Rites: The Work of the Modern Funeral Director* (Amityville, N.Y.: Baywood, 1996).

15. O. Duane Weeks and Catherine Johnson, "Developing a Successful Aftercare

Program," *The Director* 67, no. 12 (December 1995): 12–18.

16. LeRoy Bowman, *The American Funeral: A Study in Guilt, Extravagance, and Sublimity* (Washington, D.C.: Public Affairs Press, 1959).

17. Jessica Mitford, *The American Way of Death* (New York: Simon & Schuster, 1963), pp. 16–19.

18. D. van Vuure, "The Relatives Asked for a Duo-Committal for Their Parents," *Thanos* 22 (1996): 28–30.

19. Lynch, *The Undertaking,* p. 191.

20. National Funeral Directors Association, "NFDA Fact Sheets," www.nfda.org/ nfdafactsheets.php (accessed February 2, 2007).

21. "Other Services—Estimated Revenue," *Statistical Abstract of the United States: 2007,* 126th ed. (Washington, D.C.: Government Printing Office, 2006), p. 788.

22. Ronny E. Turner and Charles Edgley, "Death as Theatre: A Dramaturgical Analysis of the American Funeral," *Sociology and Social Research* 60, no. 4 (1976): 377–392. See also Liam Hyland and Janice M. Morse, "Orchestrating Comfort: The Role of Funeral Directors," *Death Studies* 19, no. 5 (1995): 453–474.

23. Kenneth V. Iserson, *Death to Dust: What Happens to Dead Bodies?* 2nd ed. (Tucson, Ariz.: Galen Press, 2001), p. 226; see also pp. 241–257 for a detailed description of embalming and other body-preparation procedures.

24. Edward C. Johnson and Melissa Johnson Williams, "Dr. Charles DeCosta Brown, Civil War Embalming Surgeon and the Masonic Order," *American Funeral Director* 120, no. 9 (September 1997): 74–78.

25. Vanderlyn Pine, "The Care of the Dead: A Historical Portrait," in *Death and Dying: Challenge and Change,* ed. Robert Fulton, Eric Markusen, Greg Owen, and Jane L. Scheiber (San Francisco: Boyd & Fraser, 1978), p. 276; see also, by Pine, *Caretaker of the Dead: The American Funeral Director* (New York: Irvington, 1985).

26. Briefly summarized, exceptions to this requirement occur when (1) state or local law requires embalming or (2) there are "exigent circumstances," such as (a) when a family member or other authorized person cannot be contacted despite diligent efforts, and (b) there is no reason to believe the family does not want embalming, and (c) after the body has been embalmed, the family is notified that no fee will be charged if they choose a funeral that does not require embalming.

27. *Thanos* 24 (1997): 9.

28. Reynolds and Tanner, *The Social Ecology of Religion,* p. 221.

29. Iserson, *Death to Dust,* p. 390.

30. See Niels Bonde and Arne Emil Christensen, "Dendrochronological Dating for the Viking Age Ship Burials at Oseberg, Gokstad, and Tune, Norway," *Antiquity* 67 (1993): 575–583.

31. See Bruce A. Iverson, "Bodies for Science," *Death Studies* 14, no. 6 (1990): 577–587; Robert D. Reece and Jesse H. Ziegler, "How a Medical School (Wright State University) Takes Leave of Human Remains," *Death Studies* 14, no. 6 (1990): 589–600; and Kathleen A. Schotzinger and Elizabeth Kirkley Best, "Closure and the Cadaver Experience: A Memorial Service for Deeded Bodies," *Omega: Journal of Death and Dying* 18, no. 3 (1987–1988): 217–227.

32. *Honolulu Star-Bulletin & Advertiser,* June 3, 1984.

33. See Hali J. Weiss, "In the Long Run: Staying Relevant Amidst Cultural Change," *Cemetery Management* (January 1995): 14–16; and, also by Weiss, "Dust to Dust: Transforming the American Cemetery," *Tikkun* 10, no. 5 (1996): 21–25.

34. Jack Goody and Cesare Poppi, "Flowers and Bones: Approaches to the Dead in Anglo-American and Italian Cemeteries," *Comparative Studies in Society and History* 36, no. 1 (1994): 146–175.

35. See Diane O. Bennett, "Bury Me in Second Class: Contested Symbols in a Greek Cemetery," *Anthropological Quarterly* 67, no. 3 (1994): 122–134.

36. Douglas Keister, "A Brief History of the Community Mausoleum," *American Cemetery* 69, no. 9 (September 1997): 20–21, 50–52.

37. See Stephen Prothero, *Purified By Fire: A History of Cremation in America* (Berkeley: University of California Press, 2001).

38. National Funeral Directors Association, "U.S. Cremation Statistics," www.nfda.org/nfdafactsheets.php (accessed November 19, 2007).

39. Sally Gribbin, "The Social Crisis Facing the Cremation Industry," *Cemetery Management* (January 1994), reprint.

40. Dan Morse, "Shirts for the Dead Are the New Rage in Some Inner Cities," *Wall Street Journal*, February 4, 1999, pp. A1, A16. For a related version of inner-city memorialization, see Martha Cooper and Joseph Sciorra, *R.I.P.: Memorial Wall Art* (New York: Henry Holt, 1994).

41. Cooper and Sciorra, *R.I.P.: Memorial Wall Art*.

42. Holly Everett, *Roadside Crosses in Contemporary Memorial Culture* (Denton: University of North Texas Press, 2002).

43. Brochure, Leif Technologies, 1997.

44. William Lamers, Sr., quoted in *Concerning Death: A Practical Guide for the Living*, ed. Earl Grollman (Boston: Beacon Press, 1974), and in *Successful Funeral Service Practice*, ed. Howard C. Raether (Englewood Cliffs, N.J.: Prentice-Hall, 1971).

45. See *Funeral Rites and Customs* (Dallas, Tex.: Professional Training Schools, 1991). See also Paul Irion, *A Manual and Guide for Those Who Conduct a Humanist Funeral Service* (Baltimore: Waverly Press, 1971), and "Changing Patterns of Ritual Response to Death," *Omega: Journal of Death and Dying* 22, no. 3 (1990–1991): 159–172; Edgar N. Jackson, *The Christian Funeral: Its Meaning, Its Purpose, and Its Modern Practice* (New York: Channel Press, 1966); and Ernest Morgan, *Dealing Creatively with Death: A Manual of Death Education and Simple Burial*, 11th ed. (Burnsville, N.C.: Celo Press, 1988).

46. See Lisa Takeuchi Cullen, *Remember Me: A Lively Tour of the New American Way of Death* (New York: HarperCollins, 2006); and Mark Harris, *Grave Matters: A Journey Through the Modern Funeral Industry to a Natural Way of Burial* (New York: Scribner, 2007).

47. See, for example, Andre Van Gemert, "The Digital Death," *Thanos* 21 (1996): 18–21; Lucette Lagnado, "Phone Eulogies, Cyber-mourners Make Funerals into Virtual Events," *Wall Street Journal*, August 21, 1996, p. B1.

48. Brochure, The Virtual Memorial Company, 1997.

49. William M. Lamers, Jr., "Funerals Are Good for People: M.D.'s Included," *Medical Economics* (June 23, 1969): 1–4.

50. Alan Wolfelt, "Understanding the Trend Toward Deritualization of the Funeral," *The Forum: Newsletter of the Association for Death Education and Counseling* 20, no. 6 (November–December 1994): 1, 15–17.

51. Sabine Bode and Fritz Roth, *Der Trauer Eine Heimat Geben: Für Einen Lebendigen Umgang mit dem Tod* [Giving Grief a Home] (Bergisch Gladbach, Ger.: Gustav Lübbe Verlag, 1998); and *Trauer hat Viele Farben* [Grief Has Many Colors] (Bergisch Gladbach, Ger.: Ehrenwirth, 2004).

52. E. S. Craighill Handy and Mary Kawena Pukui, *The Polynesian Family System in Ka-'u, Hawai'i* (Rutland, Vt.: Charles E. Tuttle, 1972), p. 157; and Mary Kawena Pukui, E. W. Haertig, and Catherine A. Lee, *Nana I Ke Kumu (Look to the Source)*, vol. 1 (Honolulu: Hui Hanai; Queen Lili'uokalani Children's Center, 1972), p. 139.

CHAPTER 9

1. Elaine M. Blinde and Terese M. Stratta, "The 'Sport Career Death' of College Athletes: Involuntary and Unanticipated Sports Exits," *Journal of Sport Behavior* 15, no. 1 (1994): 3–20.

2. Bob Krizek, "Goodbye Old Friend: A Son's Farewell to Comiskey Park," *Omega: Journal of Death and Dying* 25, no. 2 (1992): 87–93.

3. See Lynne Ann DeSpelder and Albert Lee Strickland, "Loss," in *Encyclopedia of Death and Dying*, ed. Glennys Howarth and Oliver Leaman (New York: Routledge, 2001), pp. 288–289.

4. Dennis Klass, "John Bowlby's Model of Grief and the Problem of Identification," *Omega: Journal of Death and Dying* 18, no. 1 (1987–1988): 13–32. See also William M. Lamers, Jr., "On the Psychology of Loss," in *Grief and the Healing Arts: Creativity as Therapy*, ed. Sandra L. Bertman (Amityville, N.Y.: Baywood, 1998), pp. 1–18.

5. Paul J. Robinson and Stephen Fleming, "Differentiating Grief and Depression," *Hospice Journal* 5, no. 1 (1989): 77–88; and "Depressotypic Cognitive Patterns in Major Depression and Conjugal Bereavement," *Omega: Journal of Death and Dying* 25, no. 4 (1992): 291–305.

6. Arthur S. Berger, "Quote the Raven: Bereavement and the Paranormal," *Omega: Journal of Death and Dying* 31, no. 1 (1995): 1–10; and, in the same issue, Torill Christine Lindstrøm, "Experiencing the Presence of the Dead: Discrepancies in 'The Sensing Experience' and Their Psychological Concomitants," pp. 11–21. See also Louis E. Lagrand, *After-Death Communication: Final Farewells* (New York: Llewellyn, 1997); and *Messages and Miracles: Extraordinary Experiences of the Bereaved* (New York: Llewellyn, 1999).

7. See Thomas A. Attig, *How We Grieve: Relearning the World* (New York: Oxford University Press, 1996); and Jeffrey Kauffman, ed., *Loss of the Assumptive World: A Theory of Traumatic Loss* (New York: Brunner-Routledge, 2002).

8. See, for example, Paul C. Rosenblatt, "Grief: The Social Context of Private Feelings," *Journal of Social Issues* 44, no. 3 (1988): 67–78.

9. Mary Caroline Crawford, *Social Life in Old New England* (Boston: Little, Brown, 1914), p. 461.

10. Terry Tafoya, "The Widow as Butterfly: Treatment of Grief/Depression Among the Sahaptin," unpublished paper.

11. See Vernon Reynolds and Ralph Tanner, *The Social Ecology of Religion* (New York: Oxford University Press, 1995), p. 214.

12. Philippe Ariès, "The Reversal of Death: Changes in Attitudes Toward Death in Western Societies," in *Death in America*, ed. David E. Stannard (Philadelphia: University of Pennsylvania Press, 1975), pp. 134–158.

13. See Robert M. Sapolsky, "The Solace of Patterns," *The Sciences* 34, no. 6 (November–December 1994): 14–16.

14. Sigmund Freud, "Mourning and Melancholia," *Collected Papers*, vol. 4 (New York: Basic Books, 1959), pp. 152–170. Originally published in 1917. See also Lorraine Siggins, "Mourning: A Critical Survey of the Literature," *International Journal of Psycho-Analysis* 47 (1966): 14–25.

15. Therese A. Rando, "Grief and Mourning: Accommodating to Loss," in *Dying: Facing the Facts*, 3rd ed., ed. Hannelore Wass and Robert A. Neimeyer (Washington, D.C.: Taylor & Francis, 1995), pp. 211–241; quote p. 212.

16. See John Bowlby's three-volume work, *Attachment and Loss* (New York: Basic Books): vol. 1, *Attachment* (1969); vol. 2, *Separation: Anxiety and Anger* (1973); and vol. 3, *Loss: Sadness and Depression* (1982); and *The Making and Breaking of Affectional Bonds* (London: Tavistock, 1979). See also Dale Vincent Hardt, "An Investigation of the Stages of Bereavement," *Omega: Journal of Death and Dying* 9, no. 3 (1978–1979): 279–285; and Klass, "John Bowlby's Model of Grief and the Problem of Identification."

17. Erich Lindemann, "The Symptomatology and Management of Acute Grief," *American Journal of Psychiatry* 101 (1944): 141–148.

18. Colin Murray Parkes, "Research: Bereavement," *Omega: Journal of Death and Dying* 18, no. 4 (1987–1988): 365–377; quote p. 366.

19. See Dennis Klass, "Developing a Cross-Cultural Model of Grief: The State of the Field," *Omega: Journal of Death and Dying* 39, no. 3 (1999): 153–178.

20. Margaret Stroebe, "Coping with Bereavement: A Review of the Grief Work Hypothesis," *Omega: Journal of Death and Dying* 26, no. 1 (1992–1993): 19–42.

21. See George A. Bonanno, ed., "New Directions in Bereavement Research and Theory (special issue)," *American Behavioral Scientist* 44, no. 3 (2001); Torill Christine Lindstrøm, "'It Ain't Necessarily So': Challenging Mainstream Thinking About Bereavement," *Family & Community Health* 25, no. 1 (2002): 11–21; R. J. Russac, Nina S. Steighner, and Angela I. Canto, "Grief Work Versus Continuing Bonds: A Call for Paradigm Integration or Replacement?" *Death Studies* 26, no. 6 (2002): 463–478; and Margaret Stroebe and others, "Does Disclosure of Emotions Facilitate Recovery from Bereavement? Evidence from Two Prospective Studies," *Journal of Consulting and Clinical Psychology* 70, no. 1 (2002): 169–178.

22. Personal communication.

23. J. William Worden, *Grief Counseling and Grief Therapy: A Handbook for the Mental Health Practitioner,* 3rd ed. (New York: Springer, 2002), esp. pp. 27–37.

24. Therese A. Rando, *Treatment of Complicated Mourning* (Champaign, Ill.: Research Press, 1993).

25. Phyllis R. Silverman, "Social Support and Mutual Help for the Bereaved," in *Dying, Death, and Bereavement: A Challenge for Living,* 2nd ed., ed. Inge Corless, Barbara B. Germino, and Mary A. Pittman (New York: Springer, 2003), pp. 247–265.

26. Margaret Stroebe, Mary M. Gergen, Kenneth J. Gergen, and Wolfgang Stroebe, "Broken Hearts or Broken Bonds: Love and Death in Historical Perspective," in *The Path Ahead: Readings in Death and Dying,* ed. Lynne Ann DeSpelder and Albert Lee Strickland (Mountain View, Calif.: Mayfield, 1995), pp. 231–241.

27. See Dennis Klass and Robert Goss, "Spiritual Bonds to the Dead in Cross-Cultural and Historical Perspective: Comparative Religion and Modern Grief," *Death Studies* 23, no. 6 (1999): 547–567.

28. Sandra L. Bertman, "Communicating with the Dead: An Ongoing Experience as Expressed in Art, Literature, and Song," in *Between Life and Death,* ed. Robert J. Kastenbaum (New York: Springer, 1979), pp. 124–155.

29. See Simon Shimson Rubin, "Psychodynamic Therapy with the Bereaved: Listening for Conflict, Relationship, and Transference," *Omega: Journal of Death and Dying* 39, no. 2 (1999): 83–98.

30. Dennis Klass, "Solace and Immortality: Bereaved Parents' Continuing Bond with Their Children," in *The Path Ahead,* ed. DeSpelder and Strickland, pp. 246–259.

31. Dennis Klass, "The Inner Representation of the Dead Child and the Worldviews of Bereaved Parents," *Omega: Journal of Death and Dying* 26, no. 4 (1992–1993): 255–272.

32. Phyllis R. Silverman, Steven Nickman, and J. William Worden, "Detachment Revisited: The Child's Reconstruction of a Dead Parent," in *The Path Ahead,* ed. DeSpelder and Strickland, pp. 260–270.

33. David E. Balk and Nancy S. Hogan, "Religion, Spirituality, and Bereaved Adolescents," in *Loss, Threat to Life, and Bereavement: The Child's Perspective,* ed. David W. Adams and Ellie J. Deveau (Amityville, N.Y.: Baywood, in press). See also Nancy Hogan and Lydia DeSantis, "Adolescent Sibling Bereavement: An Ongoing Attachment," *Qualitative Health Research* 2 (1992): 159–177.

34. Rando, *Treatment of Complicated Mourning,* p. 53.

35. Lyn H. Lofland, "Loss and Human Connection: An Exploration into the Nature of the Social Bond," in *Personality, Roles, and Social Behavior,* ed. William Ickes and Eric S. Knowles (New York: Springer-Verlag, 1982), pp. 219–242.

36. John D. Kelly, "Grief: Re-forming Life's Story," in *The Path Ahead,* ed. DeSpelder and Strickland, pp. 242–245.

37. Jerome Bruner, "The Narrative Construction of Reality," *Critical Inquiry* 18 (1991): 1–21; quote p. 4.

38. Carolyn Ellis, "'There Are Survivors': Telling a Story of Sudden Death," *Sociological Quarterly* 34, no. 4 (1993): 711–730.

39. Mary Anne Sedney, John E. Baker, and Esther Gross, "'The Story' of a Death: Therapeutic Considerations with Bereaved Families," *Journal of Marital and Family Therapy* 20, no. 3 (1994): 287–296. See also Jack J. Bauer and George A. Bonanno, "Continuity amid Discontinuity: Bridging One's Past and Present in Stories of Conjugal Bereavement," *Narrative Inquiry* 11, no. 1 (2001): 123–158; Kathleen R. Gilbert, "Taking a Narrative Approach to Grief Research: Finding Meaning in Stories," *Death Studies* 26, no. 3 (2002): 223–239; and Brian Schiff, Chaim Noy, and Bertram J. Cohler, "Collected Stories in the Life Narratives of Holocaust Survivors," *Narrative Inquiry* 11, no. 1 (2001): 159–193.

40. Jane Harper Chelf, and others, "Storytelling: A Strategy for Living and Coping with Cancer," *Cancer Nursing* 23, no. 1 (2000): 1–5.

41. Tony Walter, "A New Model of Grief: Bereavement and Biography," *Mortality* 1, no. 1 (1996): 7–25; quote p. 13. See also James A. Thorson, "Qualitative Thanatology," *Mortality* 1, no. 2 (1996): 177–190.

42. Stephen J. Fleming and Paul J. Robinson, "The Application of Cognitive Therapy to the Bereaved," in *The Challenge of Cognitive Therapy: Applications to Nontraditional Populations,* ed. T. M. Vallis, J. L. Howes, and P. C. Miller (New York: Plenum Press, 1991), pp. 135–158.

43. See George A. Bonanno, Anthony Papa, and Kathleen O'Neill, "Loss and Human Resilience," *Applied & Preventive Psychology* 10, no. 3 (2001): 193–206; Louis A. Gamino, Nancy S. Hogan, and Kenneth W. Sewell, "Feeling the Absence: A Content Analysis from the Scott and White Grief Study," *Death Studies* 26, no. 10 (2002): 793–813; Judith A. Murray, "Loss as a Universal Concept: A Review of the Literature to Identify Common Aspects of Loss in Diverse Situations," *Journal of Loss and Trauma* 6, no. 3 (2001): 219–241; Robert A. Neimeyer, "Reauthoring Life Narratives: Grief Therapy as Meaning Reconstruction," *Israel Journal of Psychiatry and Related Sciences* 38, nos. 3–4 (2001): 171–183; and Robert A. Neimeyer, Holly G.

Prigerson, and Betty Davies, "Mourning and Meaning," *American Behavioral Scientist* 46, no. 2 (2002): 235–251.

44. Paul C. Rosenblatt, *Parent Grief: Narratives of Loss and Relationship* (Philadelphia: Brunner/Mazel, 2000), p. 11.

45. Nancy L. Moos, "An Integrative Model of Grief," *Death Studies* 19, no. 4 (1995): 337–364; quote p. 337.

46. David W. Kissane and Sidney Bloch, "Family Grief," *British Journal of Psychiatry* 164 (1994): 728–740.

47. Terry L. Martin and Kenneth J. Doka, *Men Don't Cry . . . Women Do: Transcending Gender Stereotypes of Grief* (Philadelphia: Brunner/Mazel, 2000); see also, by Martin and Doka, "Revisiting Masculine Grief," in *Living with Grief: Who We Are, How We Grieve,* ed. Kenneth J. Doka and Joyce D. Davidson (Washington, D.C.: Hospice Foundation of America, 1998), pp. 133–142; and Judith M. Stillion and Susan B. Noviello, "Living and Dying in Different Worlds: Gender Differences in Violent Death and Grief," *Illness, Crisis & Loss* 9, no. 3 (2001): 247–259.

48. Margaret Stroebe and Henk Schut, "The Dual Process Model of Coping with Bereavement" (paper presented at the Meeting of the International Work Group on Death, Dying, and Bereavement, Oxford England, June 1995).

49. Colin Murray Parkes, "Bereavement in Adult Life," *British Medical Journal* 316 (1998): 856–859; and "Facing Loss," *British Medical Journal* 316 (1998): 1521–1524. See also, by Parkes, "Bereavement Dissected: A Reexamination of the Basic Components Influencing the Reaction to Loss," *Israel Journal of Psychiatry and Related Sciences* 38, nos. 3–4 (2001): 150–156; and "Grief: Lessons from the Past, Visions for the Future," *Death Studies* 26, no. 5 (2002): 367–385.

50. Fleming and Robinson, "The Application of Cognitive Therapy to the Bereaved," pp. 135–158. See also Ruth Malkinson, "Cognitive-Behavioral Therapy of Grief: A Review and Application," *Research on Social Work Practice* 11, no. 6 (2001): 671–698.

51. Sandra L. Bertman, Helen K. Sumpter, and Harry L. Green, "Bereavement and Grief," in *Introduction to Clinical Medicine,* ed. Harry L. Green (Philadelphia: B. C. Decker, 1991), p. 682.

52. See Liam Hyland and Janice M. Morse, "Orchestrating Comfort: The Role of Funeral Directors," *Death Studies* 19, no. 5 (1995): 453–474.

53. Bertman, Sumpter, and Green, "Bereavement and Grief," p. 682.

54. See Beverly Raphael and Christine Minkov, "Abnormal Grief," *Current Opinion in Psychiatry* 12, no. 1 (1999): 99–102.

55. Sarah Brabant, "Old Pain or New Pain: A Social Psychological Approach to Recurrent Grief," *Omega: Journal of Death and Dying* 20, no. 4 (1989–1990): 273–279.

56. M. A. Bull, S. Clark, and K. Duszynski, "Lessons from a Community's Response to the Death of Diana, Princess of Wales," *Omega: Journal of Death and Dying* 46, no. 1 (2002): 35–49.

57. Ira O. Glick, Robert S. Weiss, and Colin Murray Parkes, *The First Year of Bereavement* (New York: Wiley, 1974), p. viii; see also Colin Murray Parkes and Robert S. Weiss, *Recovery from Bereavement* (New York: Basic Books, 1983); and Robert S. Weiss, "Loss and Recovery," *Journal of Social Issues* 44, no. 3 (1988): 37–52.

58. Therese A. Rando, *The Treatment of Complicated Mourning* (Champaign, Ill.: Research Press, 1993).

59. See Kjell Kallenberg and Björn Söderfeldt, "Three Years Later: Grief, View of Life, and a Personal Crisis After Death of a Family Member," *Journal of Palliative Care* 8, no. 4 (1992): 13–19; and Hans Stifoss-Hanssen and Kjell Kallenberg, *Existential Questions and Answers: Research Frontlines and Challenges* (Stockholm: Swedish Council for Planning and Coordination of Research, 1996), p. 54.

60. Therese A. Rando, "The Increasing Prevalence of Complicated Mourning: The Onslaught Is Just Beginning," *Omega: Journal of Death and Dying* 26, no. 1 (1992–1993): 43–59.

61. Holly G. Prigerson and Selby C. Jacobs, "Traumatic Grief as a Distinct Disorder: A Rationale, Consensus Criteria, and a Preliminary Empirical Test," in *Handbook of Bereavement Research: Consequences, Coping and Care,* ed. Margaret S. Stroebe, Robert O. Hansson, Wolfgang Stroebe, and Henk Schut (Washington, D.C.: American Psychological Association, 2001), pp. 613–637.

62. Prigerson and Jacobs, "Traumatic Grief as a Distinct Disorder," pp. 623, 625.

63. See Brian P. Enright and Samuel J. Marwit, "Reliability of Diagnosing Complicated Grief: A Closer Look," *Journal of Clinical Psychology* 58, no. 7 (2002): 747–757; Margaret Stroebe, Henk Schut, and Catrin Finkenauer, "The Traumatization of Grief? A Conceptual Framework for Understanding the Trauma-Bereavement Interface," *Israel Journal of Psychiatry and Related Sciences* 38, nos. 3–4 (2001): 185–201; and Margaret Stroebe and others, "On the Classification and Diagnosis of Pathological Grief," *Clinical Psychology Review* 20, no. 1 (2000): 57–75.

64. Phyllis R. Silverman, "Dying and Bereavement in Historical Perspective," in *Living with Dying: A Handbook for End-of-Life Care Practitioners,* ed. Joan Berzoff and Phyllis R. Silverman (New York: Columbia University Press, 2004), pp. 128–149; quote p. 144.

65. Silverman, "Dying and Bereavement in Historical Perspective," pp. 144–145.

66. See Jerome F. Fredrick, "Grief as a Disease Process," *Omega: Journal of Death and Dying* 7, no. 4 (1976–1977): 297–305; and Edgar N. Jackson, "The Physiology of Crisis," in his *Coping with the Crises of Your Life* (New York: Hawthorne Books, 1974), pp. 48–55.

67. Quoted in Jerry E. Bishop, "Secrets of the Heart: Can It Be 'Broken'?" *Wall Street Journal,* February 14, 1994, pp. B1, B5.

68. Margaret S. Stroebe, "The Broken Heart Phenomenon: An Examination of the Mortality of Bereavement," *Journal of Community & Applied Social Psychology* 4 (1994): 47–61.

69. Hans Selye, *The Stress of Life,* rev. ed. (New York: McGraw-Hill, 1976).

70. W. D. Rees and S. G. Lutkins, "The Mortality of Bereavement," *British Medical Journal* 4 (1967): 13–16.

71. Arthur C. Carr and Bernard Schoenberg, "Object-Loss and Somatic Symptom Formation," in *Loss and Grief: Psychological Management in Medical Practice,* ed. Bernard Schoenberg and others (New York: Columbia University Press, 1970), pp. 36–47.

72. See Nicholas R. Hall and Allan L. Goldstein, "Thinking Well: The Chemical Links Between Emotions and Health," *The Sciences* 26, no. 2 (March–April 1986): 34–40.

73. For a review of these studies, see Colin Murray Parkes, "Research: Bereavement," *Omega: Journal of Death and Dying* 18, no. 4 (1987–1988): 365–377.

74. George L. Engel, "Sudden and Rapid Death During Psychological Stress," *Annals of Internal Medicine* 74 (1971); see also, by Engel, "Emotional Stress and Sudden Death," *Psychology Today,* November 1977.

75. Colin Murray Parkes, "The Broken Heart," in his *Bereavement: Studies of Grief in Adult Life,* 3rd ed. (Philadelphia: Routledge, 2001), pp. 14–30; quote p. 17.

76. Edgar N. Jackson, *Understanding Grief: Its Roots, Dynamics, and Treatment* (Nashville: Abingdon Press, 1957), p. 27; see also, by Jackson, *The Many Faces of Grief* (Nashville: Abingdon Press, 1977). In an interview with the authors, Dr. Jackson described how the death of his young son became the impetus for his studies of grief. In effect, his studies of grief were in part a mechanism for coping with, understanding, and coming to terms with the loss. This is an example of how an individual survivor's value system shapes the means of coping with a loss.

77. Karen S. Pfost, Michael J. Stevens, and Anne B. Wessels, "Relationship of Purpose in Life to Grief Experiences in Response to the Death of a Significant Other," *Death Studies* 13, no. 4 (1989): 371–378.

78. See Paul C. Rosenblatt, "Grief: The Social Context of Private Feelings," *Journal of Social Issues* 44, no. 3 (1988): 67–78. See also Richard A. Kalish and David K. Reynolds, *Death and Ethnicity: A Psychocultural Study* (Los Angeles: Ethel Percy Andrus Gerontology Center, University of Southern California, 1976).

79. Unni Wikan, "Bereavement and Loss in Two Muslim Communities: Egypt and Bali Compared," *Social Science & Medicine* 27, no. 5 (1988): 451–460.

80. Fred Sklar and Shirley F. Hartley, "Close Friends as Survivors: Bereavement Patterns in a 'Hidden' Population," *Omega: Journal of Death and Dying* 21, no. 2 (1990): 103–112.

81. See entry "Grief, Vicarious," by Lynne Ann DeSpelder and Albert Lee Strickland, in *Encyclopedia of Death and Dying,* ed. Howarth and Leaman, pp. 225–226.

82. Larry A. Bugen, "Human Grief: A Model for Prediction and Intervention," *American Journal of Orthopsychiatry* 47, no. 2 (1977): 196–206. See also Sherry L. Chenell and Shirley A. Murphy, "Beliefs of Preventability of Death Among the Disaster Bereaved," *Western Journal of Nursing Research* 14, no. 5 (1992): 576–594; and Charles A. Guarnaccia, Bert Hayslip, and Lisa Pinkenburg Landry, "Influence of Perceived Preventability of the Death and Emotional Closeness to the Deceased: A Test of Bugen's Model," *Omega: Journal of Death and Dying* 39, no. 4 (1999): 261–276.

83. Robert J. Smith, John H. Lingle, and Timothy C. Brock, "Reactions to Death as a Function of Perceived Similarity to the Deceased," *Omega: Journal of Death and Dying* 9, no. 2 (1978–1979): 125–138.

84. See Robert L. Fulton, "Death, Grief, and Social Recuperation," *Omega: Journal of Death and Dying* 1, no. 1 (1970): 23–28; and Bruce J. Horacek, "A Heuristic Model of Grieving After High-Grief Death," *Death Studies* 19, no. 1 (1995): 21–31. See also Ruth Malkinson, Simon Shimson Rubin, and Eliezer Witzsum, eds., *Traumatic and Nontraumatic Loss and Bereavement: Clinical Theory and Practice* (Madison, Conn.: Psychosocial Press, 2000).

85. Richard M. Leliaert, "Spiritual Side of 'Good Grief': What Happened to Holy Saturday?" *Death Studies* 13, no. 2 (1989): 103–117; quote p. 103.

86. Arlene Sheskin and Samuel E. Wallace, "Differing Bereavements: Suicide, Natural, and Accidental Death," *Omega: Journal of Death and Dying* 7, no. 3 (1976): 229–242. In addition to differing modes of death, some losses are characterized as "ambiguous" because they are somehow incomplete or uncertain. Examples include losses where the body is present but the mind is absent (such as Alzheimer's disease, chronic mental illness, head trauma, addictions), as well as those where the body is absent but the person is psychologically present in the lives of family members and friends (such as military personnel missing in action, missing children, hostages). For more on this topic, see Pauline Boss, *Ambiguous Loss: Learning to Live with Unresolved Grief* (Cambridge, Mass.: Harvard University Press, 1999).

87. Therese A. Rando, *Loss and Anticipatory Grief* (Lexington, Mass.: Lexington, 1986), p. 24.

88. See Bernard Schoenberg, Arthur C. Carr, Austin H. Kutscher, David Peretz, and Ivan K. Goldberg, eds., *Anticipatory Grief* (New York: Columbia University Press, 1974), p. 4.

89. Sylvia Sherwood, Robert Kastenbaum, John N. Morris, and Susan M. Wright, "The First Months of Bereavement," in *The Hospice Experiment*, ed. Vincent Mor, David S. Greer, and Robert Kastenbaum (Baltimore: Johns Hopkins University Press, 1988), p. 150.

90. Yvonne K. Ameche, "A Story of Loss and Survivorship," *Death Studies* 14, no. 2 (1990): 185–198.

91. Robert G. Dunn and Donna Morrish-Vidners, "The Psychological and Social Experience of Suicide Survivors," *Omega: Journal of Death and Dying* 18, no. 3 (1987–1988): 175–215; David E. Ness and Cynthia R. Pfeffer, "Sequelae of Bereavement Resulting from Suicide," *American Journal of Psychiatry* 147 (1990): 279–285; Lillian M. Range and Nathan M. Niss, "Long-Term Bereavement from Suicide, Homicide,

Accidents, and Natural Deaths," *Death Studies* 14, no. 5 (1990): 423–433; and Jan Van der Wal, "The Aftermath of Suicide: A Review of Empirical Evidence," *Omega: Journal of Death and Dying* 20, no. 2 (1989–1990): 149–171.

92. Carol J. Van Dongen, "Social Context of Postsuicide Bereavement," *Death Studies* 17, no. 2 (1993): 125–141; quote p. 130.

93. See Charles P. McDowell, Joseph M. Rothberg, and Ronald J. Koshes, "Witnessed Suicides," *Suicide and Life-Threatening Behavior* 24, no. 3 (1994): 213–223.

94. Francoise M. Reynolds and Peter Cimbolic, "Attitudes Toward Suicide Survivors as a Function of Survivors' Relationship to the Victim," *Omega: Journal of Death and Dying* 19, no. 2 (1988–1989): 125–133.

95. Gordon Thornton, Katherine D. Whittemore, and Donald U. Robertson, "Evaluation of People Bereaved by Suicide," *Death Studies* 13 (1989): 119–126.

96. Lula M. Redmond, *Surviving When Someone You Love Was Murdered: A Professional's Guide to Group Therapy for Families and Friends of Murder Victims* (Clearwater, Fla.: Psychological Consultation and Education Services, 1989), pp. 38–39, 46–49, 52–53; quote p. 38.

97. James D. Sewell, "The Stress of Homicide Investigations," *Death Studies* 18, no. 6 (1994): 565–582.

98. See June S. Church, "The Buffalo Creek Disaster: Extent and Range of Emotional and Behavioral Problems," *Omega: Journal of Death and Dying* 5, no. 1 (1974): 61–63.

99. Terrence Des Pres, *The Survivor* (New York: Oxford University Press, 1976; Pocket Books, 1977); and Lawrence L. Langer, *Versions of Survival: The Holocaust and the Human Spirit* (Albany: State University of New York Press, 1982). See also Robert Jay Lifton, *Death in Life: Survivors of Hiroshima* (New York: Simon & Schuster, 1967).

100. See entry on survivors' grief, by Lynne Ann DeSpelder and Albert Lee Strickland, in *Encyclopedia of Death and Dying*, ed. Howarth and Leaman, pp. 221–223.

101. Terry Tafoya, "Coyote, Chaos, and Crisis: Counseling the Native American Male," unpublished paper. See also David E. Stannard, *American Holocaust: Columbus and the Conquest of the New World* (New York: Oxford University Press, 1992).

102. See J. William Worden, "Grieving a Loss from AIDS," *Hospice Journal* 7 (1991): 143–150.

103. Ruben Schindler, "Mourning and Bereavement Among Jewish Religious Families: A Time for Reflection and Recovery," *Omega: Journal of Death and Dying* 33, no. 2 (1996): 121–129.

104. Kenneth J. Doka, "Disenfranchised Grief," in *The Path Ahead,* ed. DeSpelder and Strickland, pp. 271–275; and, edited by Doka, *Disenfranchised Grief: Recognizing Hidden Sorrow* (Lexington, Mass.: Lexington, 1989). See also Charles A. Corr, "Enhancing the Concept of Disenfranchised Grief," *Omega: Journal of Death and Dying* 38, no. 1 (1998): 1–20.

105. Darlene A. Kloeppel and Sheila Hollins, "Double Handicap: Mental Retardation and Death in the Family," *Death Studies* 13, no. 1 (1989): 31–38.

106. Kemi Adamolekun, "In-Laws' Behavior as a Social Factor in Subsequent Temporary Upsurges of Grief in Western Nigeria," *Omega: Journal of Death and Dying* 31, no. 1 (1995): 23–34. See also M. A. Sossou, "Widowhood Practices in West Africa: The Silent Victims," *International Journal of Social Welfare* 11, no. 3 (2002): 201–209.

107. J. William Worden, *Grief Counseling and Grief Therapy: A Handbook for the Mental Health Practitioner,* 3rd ed. (New York: Springer, 2002), esp. pp. 51, 101.

108. John R. Jordan and Robert A. Neimeyer, "Does Grief Counseling Work?" *Death Studies* 27 (2003): 765–786; quote p. 781.

109. Dale G. Larson and William T. Hoyt, "What Has Become of Grief Counseling? An Evaluation of the Empirical Foundations of the New Pessimism," *Professional Psychology: Research and Practice* 38, no. 4 (2007): 347–355; quote p. 354.

110. Silverman, "Dying and Bereavement in Historical Perspective," p. 145.

111. See Bob Baugher and Darcie Sims, *The Crying Handbook* (Newcastle, Wash.: Baugher, 2007).

112. Glenn M. Vernon, *Sociology of Death: An Analysis of Death-Related Behavior* (New York: Ronald Press, 1970), p. 159.

113. Mary Kawena Pukui, E. W. Haertig, and Catherine A. Lee, *Nana I Ke Kumu (Look to the Source),* vol. 1 (Honolulu: Hui Hanai; Queen Lili'uokalani Children's Center, 1972), pp. 135–136, 141.

114. Nissan Rubin, "Social Networks and Mourning: A Comparative Approach," *Omega: Journal of Death and Dying* 21, no. 2 (1990): 113–127. See also Jason Castle, "Grief Rituals: Aspects That Facilitate Adjustment to Bereavement," *Journal of Loss & Trauma* 8, no. 1 (2003): 41–71.

115. For more information, contact T.A.P.S., 2001 S Street NW, Suite 300, Washington, DC 20009; (800) 959–8277.

116. Stephen J. Fleming and Leslie Balmer, "Bereaved Families of Ontario: A Mutual-Help Model for Families Experiencing Death," in *The Path Ahead,* ed. DeSpelder and Strickland, pp. 281–288; quote p. 288.

117. Giorgio Di Mola, Marcello Tamburini, and Claude Fusco, "The Role of Volunteers in Alleviating Grief," *Journal of Palliative Care* 6, no. 1 (1990): 6–10.

118. Onno van der Hart, *Coping with Loss: The Therapeutic Use of Leave-Taking Ritual* (New York: Irvington, 1988); and, also by van der Hart, "An Imaginary Leave-Taking Ritual in Mourning Therapy: A Brief Communication," *The International Journal of Clinical and Experimental Hypnosis* 36, no. 2 (1988): 63–69.

119. Nancy C. Reeves and Frederic J. Boersma, "The Therapeutic Use of Ritual in Maladaptive Grieving," *Omega: Journal of Death and Dying* 20, no. 4 (1989–1990): 281–291.

120. Vamik Volkan and C. R. Showalter, "Known Object Loss, Disturbance in Reality

Testing, and 'Re-grief' Work as a Method of Brief Psychotherapy," *Psychiatric Quarterly* 42 (1968): 358–374; and Vamik Volkan, "A Study of a Patient's 'Re-grief' Work," *Psychiatric Quarterly* 45 (1971): 255–273.

121. John Schneider, *Stress, Loss, and Grief: Understanding Their Origins and Growth Potential* (Baltimore: University Park Press, 1984), pp. 66–76.

122. Lawrence G. Calhoun and Richard G. Tedeschi, "Positive Aspects of Critical Life Problems: Recollections of Grief," *Omega: Journal of Death and Dying* 20, no. 4 (1989–1990): 265–272.

123. Georges Bataille, "Sacrifice, the Festival, and the Principles of the Sacred World," *Theory of Religion*, trans. Robert Hurley (New York: Zone Books, 1992), p. 48.

124. Julie Fritsch with Sherokee Ilse, *The Anguish of Loss* (Maple Plain, Minn.: Wintergreen Press, 1988).

125. Glennys Howarth, "Dismantling the Boundaries Between Life and Death," *Mortality* 5, no. 2 (2000): 127–138.

CHAPTER 10

1. Adah Maurer, "Maturation of Concepts of Death," *British Journal of Medicine and Psychology* 39 (1966): 35–41.

2. Mark W. Speece, "Very Young Children's Experiences with and Reactions to Death" (master's thesis, Wayne State University, 1983).

3. Sandor B. Brent, "Puns, Metaphors, and Misunderstandings in a Two-Year-Old's Conception of Death," *Omega: Journal of Death and Dying* 8, no. 4 (1977–1978): 285–293. The son, who is now an adult, has no recollection of this death-related experience. Dr. Brent believes that this indicates a successfully managed event. (Personal communication.)

4. William G. Bartholome, "Care of the Dying Child: The Demands of Ethics," in *The Path Ahead: Readings in Death and Dying*, ed. Lynne Ann DeSpelder and Albert Lee Strickland (Mountain View, Calif.: Mayfield, 1995), pp. 133–143. See also Judith M. Stillion and Danai Papadatou, "Suffer the Children: An Examination of Psychosocial Issues in Children and Adolescents with Terminal Illness," *American Behavioral Scientist* 46, no. 2 (2002): 299–315.

5. Myra Bluebond-Langner, *The Private Worlds of Dying Children* (Princeton, N.J.: Princeton University Press, 1978).

6. Marilyn J. Field and Richard E. Behrman, eds., *When Children Die: Improving Palliative and End-of-Life Care for Children and Their Families* (Washington, D.C.: National Academies Press, 2002), p. 323.

7. Betty Davies, and others, "Addressing Spirituality in Pediatric Hospice and Palliative Care," *Journal of Palliative Care* 18, no. 1 (2002): 59–67.

8. Field and Behrman, eds., *When Children Die*, p. 3.

9. See Maurice Levy and others, "Home-Based Palliative Care for Children—Part 1: The Institution of a Program," *Journal of Palliative Care* 6, no. 1 (1990): 11–15; Ciaran M. Duffy and others, "Home-Based Palliative Care for Children—Part 2: The Benefits of an Established Program," *Journal of Palliative Care* 6, no. 2 (1990): 8–14; D. F. Dufour, "Home or Hospital Care for the Child with End-Stage Cancer: Effects on the Family," *Issues in Comprehensive Pediatric Nursing* 12 (1989): 371–383; Ida M. Martinson, "Impact of Childhood Cancer on Families at Home," in *Key Aspects of Caring for the Chronically Ill: Hospital and Home*, ed. Sandra G. Funk and others (New York: Springer, 1993), pp. 312–319; Ida M. Martinson, ed., *Home Care for the Dying Child: Professional and Family Perspectives* (Norwalk, Conn.: Appleton-Century-Crofts, 1976); Ida M. Martinson and others, "Home Care for Children Dying of Cancer," *Pediatrics* 62 (1978): 106–113; and D. Gay Moldow, Ida M. Martinson, and Arthur Kohrman, *Home Care for Seriously Ill Children: A Manual for Parents* (Alexandria, Va.: Children's Hospice of Virginia, 1984).

10. "Children's Hospice: An Omega Interview [by Robert Kastenbaum] with Ida M.

Martinson," *Omega: Journal of Death and Dying* 31, no. 4 (1995): 253–261.

11. Betty Davies and others, "Living in the Dragon's Shadow: Father's Experiences of a Child's Life-Limiting Illness," *Death Studies 28* (2004): 111–135.

12. Thesi Bergmann and Anna Freud, *Children in the Hospital* (New York: International Universities Press, 1965), pp. 27–28.

13. Donna Juenker, "Child's Perception of His Illness," in *Nursing Care of the Child with Long-Term Illness,* 2nd ed., ed. Shirley Steele (New York: Appleton-Century-Crofts, 1977), p. 177. See also Jo-Eileen Gyulay, *The Dying Child* (New York: McGraw-Hill, 1978).

14. Marilyn Hockenberry-Eaton, Virginia Kemp, and Coleen Dilorio, "Cancer Stressors and Protective Factors: Predictors of Stress Experienced During Treatment for Childhood Cancer," *Research in Nursing and Health* 17 (1994): 351–361.

15. See John E. Baker, Mary Anne Sedney, and Esther Gross, "Psychological Tasks for Bereaved Children," *American Journal of Orthopsychiatry* 62, no. 1 (1992): 105–116; Cathy Krown Buirski and Peter Buirski, "The Therapeutic Mobilization of Mourning in a Young Child," *Bulletin of the Menninger Clinic* 58, no. 3 (1994): 339–354; and Stephen Fleming, "Children's Grief: Individual and Family Dynamics," in *Hospice Approaches to Care,* ed. Charles Corr and Donna Corr (New York: Springer, 1985), pp. 197–218.

16. See Linda Goldman, *Breaking the Silence: A Guide to Helping Children with Complicated Grief—Suicide, Homicide, AIDS, Violence, and Abuse,* 2nd ed. (New York: Brunner-Routledge, 2001); and, also by Goldman, *Life & Loss,* 2nd ed. (Philadelphia: Taylor & Francis, 1999).

17. Kelly A. McCutcheon and Stephen J. Fleming, "Grief Resulting from Euthanasia and Natural Death of Companion Animals," *Omega: Journal of Death and Dying* 44, no. 2 (2001–2002): 169–188.

18. Ute Carson, "A Child Loses a Pet," *Death Education* 3 (1980): 399–404.

19. McCutcheon and Fleming, "Grief Resulting from Euthanasia and Natural Death of Companion Animals."

20. Jane Brody, "When Your Pet Dies," *Honolulu Star-Bulletin & Advertiser,* December 8, 1985.

21. See John Archer and Gillian Winchester, "Bereavement Following the Death of a Pet," *British Journal of Psychology* 85 (1994): 259–271; Gerald H. Gosse and Michael J. Barnes, "Human Grief Resulting from the Death of a Pet," *Anthrozoös* 7, no. 2 (1994): 103–112; and Morris A. Wessel, "Loss of a Pet," in *A Challenge for Living: Dying, Death, and Bereavement,* 2nd ed., ed. Inge B. Corless, Barbara B. Germino, and Mary A. Pittman (New York: Springer, 2003), pp. 303, 305.

22. Allan Kellehear and Jan Fook, "Lassie Come Home: A Study of 'Lost Pet' Notices," *Omega: Journal of Death and Dying* 34, no. 3 (1996–1997): 191–202; quote p. 192.

23. McCutcheon and Fleming, "Grief Resulting from Euthanasia and Natural Death of Companion Animals."

24. See William J. Kay, ed., *Pet Loss and Human Bereavement* (Ames: Iowa State University Press, 1995); Lynn A. Planchon, Donald I. Templer, Shelley Stokes, and Jacqueline Keller, "Death of a Companion Cat or Dog and Human Bereavement: Psychosocial Variables," *Society & Animals* 10, no. 1 (2002): 93–105; and Wallace Sife, *The Loss of a Pet,* rev. ed. (New York: Howell, 1998).

25. Avery D. Weisman, "Bereavement and Companion Animals," in *The Path Ahead,* ed. DeSpelder and Strickland, pp. 276–280; quote p. 280.

26. Classic studies include Erna Furman, *A Child's Parent Dies: Studies in Childhood Bereavement* (New Haven, Conn.: Yale University Press, 1974); and Robert A. Furman, "The Child's Reaction to Death in the Family," in *Loss and Grief: Psychological Management in Medical Practice,* ed. Bernard Schoenberg et al. (New York: Columbia University Press, 1970), pp. 70–86. See also Min-Tao Hsu, David L. Kahn, and Chun-Man

Huang, "No More the Same: The Lives of Adolescents in Taiwan Who Have Lost Fathers," *Family & Community Health* 25, no. 1 (2002): 43–56; Heather L. Servaty and Bert Hayslip, "Adjustment to Loss Among Adolescents," *Omega: Journal of Death and Dying* 43, no. 4 (2001): 311–330; and entry on death of parents, by Lynne Ann DeSpelder and Albert Lee Strickland, in *Encyclopedia of Death and Dying*, ed. Glennys Howarth and Oliver Leaman (New York: Routledge, 2001), pp. 346–347.

27. Phyllis R. Silverman, Steven Nickman, and J. William Worden, "Detachment Revisited: The Child's Reconstruction of a Dead Parent," in *The Path Ahead*, ed. DeSpelder and Strickland, pp. 260–270. See also Phyllis R. Silverman and J. William Worden, "Children's Reactions in the Early Months After the Death of a Parent," *American Journal of Orthopsychiatry* 62, no. 1 (January 1992): 93–104; and J. William Worden and Phyllis R. Silverman, "Parental Death and the Adjustment of School-Age Children," *Omega: Journal of Death and Dying* 32, no. 2 (1996): 91–102.

28. See Gregg M. Furth, *The Secret World of Drawings: Healing Through Art* (Boston: Sigo Press, 1988); and Maare E. Tamm and Anna Granqvist, "The Meaning of Death for Children and Adolescents: A Phenomenographic Study of Drawings," *Death Studies* 19, no. 3 (1995): 203–222.

29. Barbara Betker McIntyre, "Art Therapy with Bereaved Youth," *Journal of Palliative Care* 6, no. 1 (1990): 16–23.

30. Betty Davies, "The Study of Sibling Bereavement: An Historical Perspective," in *Dying, Death, and Bereavement*, 2nd ed., ed. Corless, Germino, and Pittman, pp. 287–302. See also Darlene E. McCown and Betty Davies, "Patterns of Grief in Young Children Following the Death of a Sibling," *Death Studies* 19, no. 1 (1995): 41–53.

31. David E. Balk, "Sibling Death, Adolescent Bereavement, and Religion," *Death Studies* 15, no. 1 (1991): 1–20.

32. Nancy Hogan and Lydia DeSantis, "Adolescent Sibling Bereavement: An Ongoing Attachment," *Qualitative Health Research* 2, no. 2 (1992): 159–177. See also Nancy S. Hogan and David E. Balk, "Adolescent Reactions to Sibling Death: Perceptions of Mothers, Fathers, and Teenagers," *Nursing Research* 39, no. 2 (1990): 103–106; and Nancy S. Hogan and Daryl B. Greenfield, "Adolescent Sibling Bereavement: Symptomatology in a Large Community Sample," *Journal of Adolescent Research* 6, no. 1 (1991): 97–112.

33. Nancy S. Hogan and Lydia DeSantis, "Things That Help and Hinder Adolescent Sibling Bereavement," *Western Journal of Nursing Research* 16, no. 2 (1994): 132–153.

34. Guidebooks for adults and children are available on a range of topics. Access www.dougy.org for information about these publications.

35. Dana Cable, Laurel Cucchi, Faye Lopez, and Terry Martin, "Camp Jamie," *American Journal of Hospice and Palliative Care* 9, no. 5 (1992): 18–21.

36. *HUGS Fact Sheet*. For more information, contact HUGS (Help, Understanding, and Group Support for Hawaii's Seriously Ill Children and Their Families), 3636 Kilauea Avenue, Honolulu, HI 96816; (808) 732-4846; www.hugslove.org.

37. Lori S. Wiener and others, "National Telephone Support Groups: A New Avenue Toward Psychosocial Support for HIV-Infected Children and Their Families," *Social Work with Groups* 16, no. 3 (1993): 55–71.

38. For an example of one such electronic network, see the following articles published in *Children's Health Care* 31, no. 1 (2002): Haven B. Battles and Lori S. Wiener, "STARBRIGHT World: Effects of an Electronic Network on the Social Environment of Children with Life-Threatening Illnesses," pp. 47–68; Ruth T. Brokstein, Susan O. Cohen, and Gary A. Walco, "STARBRIGHT World and Psychological Adjustment in Children with Cancer: A Clinical Series," pp. 29–45; and Ann Hazzard, Marianne Celano, Marietta Collins, and Yana Markov, "Effects of STARBRIGHT World on Knowledge,

Social Support, and Coping in Hospitalized Children with Sickle Cell Disease and Asthma," pp. 69–86.

39. Sunshine Foundation, 1041 Mill Creek Drive, Feasterville, PA 19052; (215) 396-4770 or (800) 767-1976, www.sunshinefoundation.org; Starlight Children's Foundation International, 5900 Wilshire Blvd., Suite 2530, Los Angeles, CA 90036; (323) 634-0080; www.starlight.org.

40. See Myra Bluebond-Langner, *In the Shadow of Illness: Parents and Siblings of the Chronically Ill Child* (Princeton, N.J.: Princeton University Press, 1996); and "Worlds of Dying Children and Their Well Siblings," *Death Studies* 13, no. 1 (1989): 1–16. See also Linda K. Birenbaum and others, "The Response of Children to the Dying and Death of a Sibling," *Omega: Journal of Death and Dying* 20, no. 3 (1989–1990): 213–228; John Graham-Pole, Hannelore Wass, Sheila Eyberg, and Luis Chu, "Communicating with Dying Children and Their Siblings: A Retrospective Analysis," *Death Studies* 13, no. 5 (1989): 465–483; and T. Havermans and C. Eiser, "Siblings of a Child with Cancer," *Child: Care, Health, and Development* 20 (1994): 309–322.

41. Joanna H. Fanos and Lori Wiener, "Tomorrow's Survivors: Siblings of Human Immunodeficiency Virus-Infected Children," *Developmental and Behavioral Pediatrics* 15, no. 3 (June 1994, Supplement): S43–S48. See also Anne Hunsaker Hawkins, *A Small, Good Thing: Stories of Children with HIV and Those Who Care for Them* (New York: Norton, 2000).

42. This and the following anecdote from Gyulay, *The Dying Child*, pp. 17–18.

43. See Mary A. Fristad and others, "The Role of Ritual in Children's Bereavement," *Omega: Journal of Death and Dying* 42, no. 4 (2001): 321–339; and Phyllis R. Silverman and J. William Worden, "Children's Understanding of Funeral Ritual," *Omega: Journal of Death and Dying* 25, no. 4 (1992): 319–331.

44. Carol F. Berns, "Bibliotherapy: The Use of Literature in Working with Bereaved Children," *Omega: Journal of Death and Dying* 48,

no. 4 (2004): 321–336. See also Elizabeth P. Lamers, "Helping Children During Bereavement," in *Dying, Death, and Bereavement,* 2nd ed., ed. Corless, Germino, and Pittman, pp. 267–286.

45. Erik Erikson, *Childhood and Society* (New York: Norton, 1950), p. 233.

CHAPTER 11

1. Charles W. Brice, "Mourning Throughout the Life Cycle," *American Journal of Psychoanalysis* 42, no. 4 (1982): 320–321.

2. Michele A. Paludi, ed., *Human Development in Multicultural Contexts* (Upper Saddle River, N.J.: Prentice-Hall, 2002), p. 190.

3. Erik H. Erikson, *The Life Cycle Completed: A Review* (New York: Norton, 1982), p. 67. See also Christina Röcke and Katie E. Cherry, "Death at the End of the 20th Century: Individual Processes and Developmental Tasks in Old Age," *International Journal of Aging and Human Development* 54, no. 4 (2002): 315–333.

4. Laura S. Smart, "Parental Bereavement in Anglo American History," *Omega: Journal of Death and Dying* 28, no. 1 (1993–1994): 49–61.

5. See Mildred J. Braun and Dale H. Berg, "Meaning Reconstruction in the Experience of Parental Bereavement," *Death Studies* 18, no. 2 (1994): 105–129; Brian DeVries, Rose Dalla Lana, and Vilma T. Falck, "Parental Bereavement over the Life Course: A Theoretical Intersection and Empirical Review," *Omega: Journal of Death and Dying* 29, no. 1 (1994): 47–69; Harriett Sarnoff Schiff, *The Bereaved Parent* (New York: Crown, 1977); and Kay Talbot, *What Forever Means After the Death of a Child: Transcending the Trauma, Living with the Loss* (New York: Brunner-Routledge, 2002).

6. Exhibition note, "Native Peoples," Glenbow Museum, Calgary, Alberta, Canada.

7. Dennis Klass, "Solace and Immortality: Bereaved Parents' Continuing Bond with Their Children," in *The Path Ahead: Readings in Death and Dying,* ed. Lynne Ann DeSpelder and Albert Lee Strickland (Mountain View, Calif.: Mayfield,

1995), pp. 246–259; and *The Spiritual Lives of Bereaved Parents* (Philadelphia: Brunner/Mazel, 1999).

8. Laura S. Smart, "The Marital Helping Relationship Following Pregnancy Loss and Infant Death," *Journal of Family Issues* 13, no. 1 (1992): 81–98.

9. Dennis Klass, *Parental Grief: Solace and Resolution* (New York: Springer, 1988).

10. Kathleen R. Gilbert, "Interactive Grief and Coping in the Marital Dyad," *Death Studies* 13, no. 6 (1989): 605–626. See also Kathleen R. Gilbert and Laura S. Smart, *Coping with Infant or Fetal Loss: The Couple's Healing Process* (New York: Brunner/Mazel, 1992).

11. See Cynthia Bach-Hughes and Judith Page-Lieberman, "Fathers Experiencing a Perinatal Loss," *Death Studies* 13, no. 6 (1989): 537–556; Judy Rollins Bohannon, "Grief Responses of Spouses Following the Death of a Child: A Longitudinal Study," *Omega: Journal of Death and Dying* 22, no. 2 (1990–1991): 109–121; Nancy Feeley and Laurie N. Gottlieb, "Parents' Coping and Communication Following Their Infant's Death," *Omega: Journal of Death and Dying* 19, no. 1 (1988–1989): 51–67; and Reiko Schwab, "Paternal and Maternal Coping with the Death of a Child," *Death Studies* 14, no. 5 (1990): 407–422.

12. "Fetal and Infant Deaths," *Statistical Abstract of the United States: 1999,* 119th ed. (Washington, D.C.: Government Printing Office, 1999), p. 97.

13. *Dorland's Illustrated Medical Dictionary,* 26th ed. (Philadelphia: Saunders, 1985), p. 828.

14. Wendy Simonds and Barbara Katz Rothman, *Centuries of Solace: Expressions of Maternal Grief in Popular Literature* (Philadelphia: Temple University Press, 1992), p. 252.

15. *Dorland's Illustrated Medical Dictionary,* pp. 664, 1251.

16. Leverett Millen and Samuel Roll, "Solomon's Mothers: A Special Case of Pathological Bereavement," *American Journal of Orthopsychiatry* 55, no. 3 (1985): 411–418.

17. See Phyllis R. Silverman, Lee Campbell, Patricia Patti, and Carolyn Briggs Style, "Reunions Between Adoptees and Birth Parents: The Birth Parents' Experience," *Social Work* 33, no. 6 (1988): 523–528; and, by Silverman, Patti, and Campbell, "Reunions Between Adoptees and Birth Parents: The Adoptive Parents' View," *Social Work* 39, no. 5 (1994): 542–548. On the loss experiences of foster parents, see Susan B. Edelstein, Dorli Burge, and Jill Waterman, "Helping Foster Parents Cope with Separation, Loss, and Grief," *Child Welfare* 80, no. 1 (2001): 5–25.

18. Glen W. Davidson, "Death of a Wished-for Child: A Case Study," *Death Education* 1, no. 3 (1977): 265–275. See also Susan Roos, *Chronic Sorrow: A Living Loss* (New York: Brunner-Routledge, 2002).

19. Judith A. Savage, *Mourning Unlived Lives: A Psychological Study of Childbearing Loss* (Wilmette, Ill.: Chiron, 1989).

20. Ibid., p. xiii.

21. Irwin J. Weinfeld, "An Expanded Perinatal Bereavement Support Committee: A Community-Wide Resource," *Death Studies* 14, no. 3 (1990): 241–252.

22. Irving G. Leon, "Perinatal Loss: Choreographing Grief on the Obstetric Unit," *American Journal of Orthopsychiatry* 62, no. 1 (1992): 7–8.

23. Larry G. Peppers, "Grief and Elective Abortion: Breaking the Emotional Bond?" *Omega: Journal of Death and Dying* 18, no. 1 (1987–1988): 1–12.

24. Simonds and Rothman, *Centuries of Solace*, p. 259.

25. See William R. LaFleur, *Liquid Life: Abortion and Buddhism in Japan* (Princeton, N.J.: Princeton University Press, 1992). See also Dennis Klass and Amy Olwen Heath, "Grief and Abortion: *Mizuko Kuyo,* the Japanese Ritual Resolution," *Omega: Journal of Death and Dying* 34, no. 1 (1996–1997): 1–14; and Takada Yoshihito and James M. Vardaman, Jr., *Talking About Buddhism* (Tokyo: Kodansha, 1997), pp. 183–185.

26. Kenneth J. Doka, "Disenfranchised Grief" (paper presented at the annual meeting of the Association for Death Education and Counseling, Atlanta, Spring 1986); and, edited by Doka, *Disenfranchised Grief—Recognizing Hidden Sorrow* (Lexington, Mass.: Lexington, 1989). See also Charles A. Corr, "Enhancing the Concept of Disenfranchised Grief," *Omega: Journal of Death and Dying* 38, no. 1 (1998): 1–20.

27. John DeFrain and others, "The Psychological Effects of a Stillbirth on Surviving Family Members," *Omega: Journal of Death and Dying* 22, no. 2 (1990–1991): 81–108; see also John DeFrain, "Learning About Grief from Normal Families: SIDS, Stillbirth, and Miscarriage," *Journal of Marital and Family Therapy* 17, no. 3 (1991): 215–232.

28. Jay Ruby, "Portraying the Dead," *Omega: Journal of Death and Dying* 19, no. 1 (1988–1989): 1–20; and Joy Johnson and S. Marvin Johnson, with James H. Cunningham and Irwin J. Weinfeld, *A Most Important Picture: A Very Tender Manual for Taking Pictures of Stillborn Babies and Infants Who Die* (Omaha: Centering Corp., 1985).

29. DeFrain and others, "Psychological Effects of a Stillbirth," p. 87.

30. Mark H. Beers and others, eds., *The Merck Manual of Diagnosis and Therapy,* 18th ed. (Whitehouse Station, N.J.: Merck Research Laboratories, 2006), pp. 2402–2403.

31. Beverly Raphael, *The Anatomy of Bereavement* (New York: Basic Books, 1983), p. 229.

32. "Deaths and Death Rates by Leading Cause of Death and Age: 2003," *Statistical Abstract of the United States: 2007,* 126th ed. (Washington, D.C.: Government Printing Office, 2006), p. 86.

33. Committee on Trauma Research, National Research Council, *Injury in America: A Continuing Public Health Problem* (Washington, D.C.: National Academy Press, 1985).

34. Jerome L. Schulman, *Coping with Tragedy: Successfully Facing the Problem of a Seriously Ill Child* (Chicago: Follett, 1976), p. 335. See also Marilyn McCubbin and others, "Family Resiliency in Childhood Cancer," *Family Relations* 51, no. 2 (2002): 103–111.

35. Kay Talbot, "Mothers Now Childless: Survival After the Death of an Only Child," *Omega: Journal of Death and Dying* 34, no. 3 (1996–1997): 177–189. See also, by Talbot, *What Forever Means After the Death of a Child: Transcending the Trauma, Living with the Loss* (New York: Brunner-Routledge, 2002).

36. Gordon Riches and Pam Dawson, "Communities of Feeling: The Culture of Bereaved Parents," *Mortality* 1, no. 2 (1996): 143–161.

37. See entry on death of parents, by Lynne Ann DeSpelder and Albert Lee Strickland, in *Encyclopedia of Death and Dying,* ed. Glennys Howarth and Oliver Leaman (New York: Routledge, 2001), pp. 346–347.

38. Joan Delahanty Douglas, "Patterns of Change Following Parent Death in Midlife Adults," *Omega: Journal of Death and Dying* 22, no. 2 (1990–1991): 123–137.

39. Marion Osterweis, Fredric Solomon, and Morris Green, eds., *Bereavement: Reactions, Consequences, and Care* (Washington, D.C.: National Academy Press, 1984), p. 85; see also Andrew E. Scharlach and Karen I. Fredriksen, "Reactions to the Death of a Parent During Midlife," *Omega: Journal of Death and Dying* 27, no. 4 (1993): 307–319.

40. Miriam S. Moss, Sidney Z. Moss, Robert Rubinstein, and Nancy Resch, "Impact of Elderly Mother's Death on Middle Aged Daughters," *International Journal of Aging and Human Development* 37, no. 1 (1992–1993): 1–22; see also Jennifer Klapper, Sidney Moss, Miriam Moss, and Robert L. Rubinstein, "The Social Context of Grief Among Adult Daughters Who Have Lost a Parent," *Journal of Aging Studies* 8, no. 1 (1994): 29–43; and Sidney Z. Moss, Robert L. Rubinstein, and Miriam S. Moss, "Middle-Aged Son's Reactions to Father's Death," *Omega: Journal of Death and Dying* 34, no. 4 (1996–1997): 259–277.

41. See Harold Ivan Smith, *Grieving the Death of a Mother* (Minneapolis: Augsburg, 2003).

42. Debra Umberson and Meichu D. Chen, "Effects of a Parent's Death on Adult Children: Relationship Salience and Reaction to Loss," *American Sociological Review* 59, no. 1 (1994): 152–168.

43. Raphael, *Anatomy of Bereavement*, p. 177.

44. Savine Gross Weizman and Phyllis Kamm, *About Mourning: Support and Guidance for the Bereaved* (New York: Human Sciences, 1985), p. 130; see also Jill Truman, *Letter to My Husband: Notes About Mourning and Recovery* (New York: Viking Penguin, 1987).

45. See Kate Mary Bennett, "Widowhood in Elderly Women: The Medium- and Long-Term Effects on Mental and Physical Health," *Mortality* 2, no. 2 (1997): 137–148; Paula J. Clayton, "The Sequelae and Non-Sequelae of Conjugal Bereavement," *American Journal of Psychiatry* 136 (1979): 1530–1543; Ira O. Glick, Robert S. Weiss, and Colin Murray Parkes, *The First Year of Bereavement* (New York: Wiley, 1974), and its follow-up by Colin Murray Parkes and Robert S. Weiss, *Recovery from Bereavement* (New York: Basic Books, 1983); Herbert H. Hyman, *Of Time and Widowhood: Nationwide Studies of Enduring Effects* (Durham, N.C.: Duke University Press, 1983); Colin Murray Parkes, *Bereavement: Studies of Grief in Adult Life*, 3rd ed. (Philadelphia: Routledge, 2001).

46. Sara Wilcox and others, "The Effects of Widowhood on Physical and Mental Health, Health Behaviors, and Health Outcomes: The Women's Health Initiative," *Health Psychology* 22, no. 5 (2003): 1–10.

47. Judith M. Stillion, *Death and the Sexes: An Examination of Differential Longevity, Attitudes, Behaviors, and Coping Skills* (Washington, D.C.: Hemisphere, 1985). See also Luann M. Daggett, "Living with Loss: Middle-Aged Men Face Spousal Bereavement," *Qualitative Health Research* 12, no. 5 (2002): 625–639; Geraldine P. Mineau, Ken R. Smith, and Lee L. Bean, "Historical Trends of Survival Among Widows and Widowers," *Social Science & Medicine* 54, no. 2 (2002): 245–254; and John M. O'Brien, Linda M. Forrest, and Ann E. Austin, "Death of a Partner: Perspectives of Heterosexual and Gay Men," *Journal of Health Psychology* 7, no. 3 (2002): 317–328.

48. See Ian Patterson and Gaylene Carpenter, "Participation in Leisure Activities After the Death of a Spouse," *Leisure Sciences* 16 (1994): 105–117; and Rebecca L. Utz, Deborah Carr, Randolph Nesse, and Camille B. Wortman, "The Effect of Widowhood on Older Adults' Social Participation: An Evaluation of Activity, Disengagement, and Continuity Theories," *Gerontologist* 42, no. 4 (2002): 522–533.

49. David M. Bass and others, "Losing an Aged Relative: Perceptual Differences Between Spouses and Adult Children," *Omega: Journal of Death and Dying* 21, no. 1 (1990): 21–40. See also Karen L. Fingerman, "A Distant Closeness: Intimacy Between Parents and Their Children in Later Life," *Generations: Journal of the American Society on Aging* 25, no. 2 (2001): 26–33.

50. See Phyllis R. Silverman, *Widow to Widow: How the Bereaved Help One Another,* 2nd ed. (New York: Brunner-Routledge, 2004); and, also by Silverman, "Widowhood as the Next Stage in the Life Cycle," in *Widows: North America,* ed. Helena Z. Lopata (Durham, N.C.: Duke University Press, 1987); and "The Widow-to-Widow Program: An Experiment in Preventive Intervention," *Mental Hygiene* 53, no. 3 (1969), a landmark report by Silverman on her work at Harvard Medical School's Laboratory of Community Psychiatry. See also Helena Z. Lopata, *Widowhood in an American City* (Cambridge, Mass.: Schenkman, 1973), *Women as Widows: Support Systems* (New York: Elsevier, 1979), and *Current Widowhood: Myths and Realities* (Thousand Oaks, Calif.: Sage, 1996).

51. Harold Ivan Smith, *Friendgrief: An Absence Called Presence* (Amityville, N.Y.: Baywood, 2000).

52. See Sarah Greenberg and others, "Friendship Across the Life Cycle: A Support Group for Older Women," *Journal of Gerontological*

Social Work 32, no. 4 (1999): 7–23. See also Rosemary Blieszner, "'She'll Be on My Heart': Intimacy Among Friends," *Generations: Journal of The American Society on Aging* 25, no. 2 (2001): 48–54.

53. See Stanley Brandes, *Forty: The Age and the Symbol* (Nashville: University of Tennessee Press, 1985).

54. Bernice L. Neugarten, "Growing as Long as We Live," *Second Opinion* 15 (November 1990): 42–51.

55. Robert M. Sapolsky and Caleb E. Finch, "On Growing Old," *The Sciences* 31 (March–April 1991): 30–38.

56. R. A. Hope and others, *Oxford Handbook of Clinical Medicine,* 3rd ed. (Oxford: Oxford University Press, 1994), p. 64.

57. James F. Fries, Lawrence W. Green, and Sol Levine, "Health Promotion and the Compression of Morbidity," *Lancet* (March 4, 1989): 481–483; see also, by Fries, "The Compression of Morbidity," *Milbank Memorial Fund Quarterly* 61 (1983): 397–419.

58. Iris Chi and James Lubben, "The California Preventive Health Care for the Aging Program: Differences Between the Younger Old and the Oldest Old," *Health Promotion International* 9, no. 3 (1994): 169–176; see also, by Chi and Lubben, "Patterns of Aging: A Special Report," *Science* 273 (July 5, 1996): 41–79; and Mark Snyder and Peter K. Miene, "Stereotyping of the Elderly: A Functional Approach," *British Journal of Social Psychology* 33 (1994): 63–82.

59. Neugarten, "Growing as Long as We Live."

60. Sandra L. Bertman, "Aging Grace: Treatment of the Aged in the Arts," *Death Studies* 13, no. 6 (1989): 517–535. See also Pamela T. Amoss and Steven Harrell, eds., *Other Ways of Growing Old: Anthropological Perspectives* (Palo Alto, Calif.: Stanford University Press, 1981); and M. Powell Lawton, Miriam Moss, and Allen Glicksman, "The Quality of the Last Year of Life of Older Persons," *Milbank Quarterly* 68 (1990): 1–28.

61. Daniel Callahan, "Can Old Age Be Given a Public Meaning?" *Second Opinion* 15 (November 1990): 12–23.

62. Jane W. Peterson, "Age of Wisdom: Elderly Black Women in Family and Church," in *The Cultural Context of Aging: Worldwide Perspectives,* ed. Jay Sokolovsky (New York: Bergin & Garvey, 1990), pp. 213–227.

63. See, for example, Cesare Marino, "Honor the Elders: Symbolic Associations with Old Age in Traditional Eastern Cherokee Culture," *Journal of Cherokee Studies* 13 (1988): 3–18.

64. Jay F. Rosenberg, *Thinking Clearly About Death* (Englewood Cliffs, N.J.: Prentice-Hall, 1983), p. 208.

65. Rosenberg, *Thinking Clearly About Death,* pp. 211–212.

66. Robert N. Butler, *Why Survive? Being Old in America* (New York: Harper & Row, 1975), p. 421.

67. Butler, *Why Survive?* p. 422. See also Robert Kastenbaum, "Exit and Existence: Society's Unwritten Script for Old Age and Death," in *Aging, Death, and the Completion of Being,* ed. David D. Van Tassel (Philadelphia: University of Pennsylvania Press, 1979), pp. 69–94.

CHAPTER 12

1. Judith M. Stillion, "Premature Exits: Understanding Suicide," in *The Path Ahead: Readings in Death and Dying,* ed. Lynne Ann DeSpelder and Albert Lee Strickland (Mountain View, Calif.: Mayfield, 1995), pp. 182–197; quote p. 182.

2. Kay Redfield Jamison, *Night Falls Fast: Understanding Suicide* (New York: Knopf, 1999), p. 292.

3. "Deaths and Death Rates by Selected Causes," *Statistical Abstract of the United States: 2007,* 126th ed. (Washington, D.C.: Government Printing Office, 2006), p. 84.

4. Mark H. Beers and others, eds., *The Merck Manual of Diagnosis and Therapy,* (White-

house Station, N.J.: Merck Research Laboratories, 2006), p. 1741.

5. Edwin S. Shneidman, *Comprehending Suicide: Landmarks in 20th Century Suicidology* (Washington, D.C.: American Psychological Association, 2001), p. 154.

6. Jamison, *Night Falls Fast,* p. 291.

7. Glen Evans and Norman L. Farberow, *The Encyclopedia of Suicide* (New York: Facts on File, 1988), p. 268.

8. See Robert J. Homant and Daniel B. Kennedy, "Suicide by Police: A Proposed Typology of Law Enforcement Officer-Assisted Suicide," *Policing: An International Journal of Police Strategies & Management* 23, no. 3 (2000): 339–355; and Vivian B. Lord, "Law Enforcement-Assisted Suicide," *Criminal Justice and Behavior* 27, no. 3 (2000): 401–419.

9. Katherine Van Wormer and Chuk Odiah, "The Psychology of the Suicide-Murder and the Death Penalty," *Journal of Criminal Justice* 27, no. 4 (1999): 361–370.

10. Edwin S. Shneidman, "Suicide," in *Death: Current Perspectives,* 2nd ed., ed. Shneidman (Mountain View, Calif.: Mayfield, 1980), p. 432.

11. James R. P. Ogloff and Randy K. Otto, "Psychological Autopsy: Clinical and Legal Perspectives," *Saint Louis University Law Journal* 37, no. 3 (Spring 1993): 607–646. See also Edwin S. Shneidman, *Clues to Suicide* (New York: McGraw-Hill, 1957); and, by Avery D. Weisman, *The Psychological Autopsy* (New York: Human Sciences Press, 1968) and *The Realization of Death: A Guide for the Psychological Autopsy* (Northvale, N.J.: Aronson, 1974).

12. For an example of the data-gathering approach used in psychological autopsies, see Tracy L. Cross, Karyn Gust-Brey, and P. Bonny Ball, "A Psychological Autopsy of the Suicide of an Academically Gifted Student: Researchers' and Parents' Perspectives," *Gifted Child Quarterly* 46, no. 4 (2002): 247–264.

13. Thomas J. Young, "Procedures and Problems in Conducting a Psychological Au-topsy," *International Journal of Offender Therapy and Comparative Criminology* 36, no. 1 (Spring 1992): 43–52.

14. See Norman Poythress and others, "APA's Expert Panel in the Congressional Review of the USS 'Iowa' Incident," *American Psychologist* 48, no. 1 (January 1993): 8–15; Randy K. Otto and others, "An Empirical Study of the Reports of APA's Peer Review Panel in the Congressional Review of the U.S.S. IOWA Incident," *Journal of Personality Assessment* 61, no. 3 (December 1993): 425–442; Ogloff and Otto, "Psychological Autopsy: Clinical and Legal Perspectives"; and Charles C. Thompson II, *A Glimpse of Hell: The Explosion on the USS Iowa and Its Cover-Up* (New York: Norton, 1999).

15. Quoted material from Poythress and others, "APA's Expert Panel."

16. See David A. Brent, "The Psychological Autopsy: Methodological Considerations for the Study of Adolescent Suicide," *Suicide and Life-Threatening Behavior* 19 (Spring 1989): 43–57; and Mohammad Shafi and others, "Psychological Autopsy of Completed Suicide in Children and Adolescents," *American Journal of Psychiatry* 142 (1985): 1061–1064.

17. Emile Durkheim, *Suicide: A Study in Sociology* (New York: Free Press, 1951).

18. Thomas Joiner, *Why People Die by Suicide* (Cambridge, Mass.: Harvard University Press, 2005), p. 34.

19. Norman Farberow, "The History of Suicide," in Evans and Farberow, *Encyclopedia of Suicide,* p. viii.

20. Jack Seward, *Hara-Kiri: Japanese Ritual Suicide* (Rutland, Vt.: Charles E. Tuttle, 1968). See also Robert Jay Lifton, Shuichi Kato, and Michael R. Reich, *Six Lives, Six Deaths: Portraits from Modern Japan* (New Haven, Conn.: Yale University Press, 1979).

21. See Charles R. Chandler and Yung-Mei Tsai, "Suicide in Japan and the West: Evidence for Durkheim's Theory," *International Journal of Comparative Sociology* 34, nos. 3–4 (1993): 244–259; and Jerome Young, "Morals, Suicide,

and Psychiatry: A View from Japan," *Bioethics* 16, no. 5 (2002): 412–424.

22. See Catherine Weinberger-Thomas, *Ashes of Immortality: Widow-Burning in India* (Chicago: University of Chicago Press, 1999).

23. Jeffrey W. Riemer, "Durkheim's 'Heroic Suicide' in Military Combat," *Armed Forces & Society* 25, no. 1 (1998): 103–120. See also Albert Axell, "The Kamikaze Mindset," *History Today* 52, no. 9 (2002): 3–4.

24. See David Chidester, *Salvation and Suicide: An Interpretation of Jim Jones, the Peoples Temple, and Jonestown* (Bloomington: Indiana University Press, 1988); Jose I. Lasaga, "Death in Jonestown: Techniques of Political Control by a Paranoid Leader," *Suicide and Life-Threatening Behavior* 10, no. 4 (1980): 210–213; and Richard H. Seiden, "Reverend Jones on Suicide," *Suicide and Life-Threatening Behavior* 9, no. 2 (1979): 116–119. For a brief overview of mass suicide, see Iginia Mancinelli, Anna Comparelli, Paolo Girardi, and Roberto Tatarelli, "Mass Suicide: Historical and Psychodynamic Considerations," *Suicide and Life-Threatening Behavior* 32, no. 1 (2002): 91–100.

25. Andrew Selsky and Jennifer Loven, "3 Gitmo Inmates Hanged Themselves," *Associated Press Online* (accessed June 10, 2006).

26. See Herbert Hendin, "The Psychodynamics of Suicide," *International Review of Psychiatry* 4 (1992): 157–167.

27. Edwin S. Shneidman, "Suicide," Encyclopedia Britannica, vol. 21 (Chicago: William Benton, 1973), p. 385; reprinted in *Lives and Deaths: Selections from the Works of Edwin S. Shneidman,* ed. Antoon A. Leenaars (Philadelphia: Brunner-Mazel, 1999), p. 184.

28. Erwin Stengel, "A Matter of Communication," in *On the Nature of Suicide,* ed. Edwin S. Shneidman (San Francisco: Jossey-Bass, 1969), pp. 78–79.

29. Edwin S. Shneidman, "Suicide as Psychache," *Journal of Nervous and Mental Disease* 181, no. 3 (1993): 147–149, and "Some Controversies in Suicidology: Toward a Mentalistic Disci-

pline," *Suicide and Life-Threatening Behavior* 23, no. 4 (1993): 292–298.

30. Shneidman, *Comprehending Suicide,* p. 200.

31. Shneidman, *Comprehending Suicide,* pp. 202–203.

32. J. John Mann and others, "The Neurobiology of Suicide Risk: A Review for the Clinician," *Journal of Clinical Psychiatry* 60, Supplement 2 (1999): 7–11. See also Alec Roy, "Recent Biologic Studies on Suicide," *Suicide and Life-Threatening Behavior* 24, no. 1 (1994): 10–14; and Andrew Edmund Slaby, "Psychopharmacotherapy of Suicide," *Death Studies* 18, no. 5 (1994): 483–495.

33. Roy F. Baumeister, "Suicide as Escape from Self," *Psychological Review* 97 (1990): 90–113.

34. Evans and Farberow, *Encyclopedia of Suicide,* p. 21.

35. Ronald W. Maris, *Pathways to Suicide: A Survey of Self-Destructive Behaviors* (Baltimore: Johns Hopkins University Press, 1981), and *Understanding and Preventing Suicide* (New York: Guilford Press, 1988). On the ambiguity concerning the degree of self-harm intended in suicide attempts, see Barry M. Wagner, Steven A. Wong, and David A. Jobes, "Mental Health Professionals' Determinations of Adolescent Suicide Attempts," *Suicide and Life-Threatening Behavior* 32, no. 3 (2002): 284–300.

36. Judith M. Stillion, Eugene E. McDowell, and Jacque H. May, *Suicide Across the Life Span: Premature Exits* (New York: Hemisphere, 1989), p. 69. See also Silvia Sara Canetto, "She Died for Love and He for Glory: Gender Myths of Suicidal Behavior," *Omega: Journal of Death and Dying* 26, no. 1 (1992–1993): 1–17, and "Gender and Suicidal Behavior: Theories and Evidence," in *Review of Suicidology 1997,* ed. Ronald W. Maris, Morton M. Silverman, and Silvia Sara Canetto (New York: Guilford Press, 1997), pp. 138–167.

37. Edwin S. Shneidman, *Deaths of Man* (New York: Quadrangle Books, 1973), pp. 81–90.

38. Philip A. May and Nancy Westlake Van Winkle, "Durkheim's Suicide Theory and Its Applicability to Contemporary American Indians and Alaska Natives," in *Emile Durkheim: Le Suicide 100 Years Later,* ed. David Lester (Philadelphia: Charles Press, 1994).

39. Kathleen Erwin, "Interpreting the Evidence: Competing Paradigms and the Emergence of Lesbian and Gay Suicide as a 'Social Fact,'" in *The Path Ahead,* ed. DeSpelder and Strickland, pp. 211–220.

40. Kevin E. Early and Ronald L. Akers, "'It's a White Thing'—An Exploration of Beliefs About Suicide in the African-American Community," in *The Path Ahead,* ed. DeSpelder and Strickland, pp. 198–210. See also Kevin E. Early, *Religion and Suicide in the African-American Community* (Westport, Conn.: Greenwood, 1992).

41. Richard H. Seiden and Raymond P. Freitas, "Shifting Patterns of Deadly Violence," *Suicide and Life-Threatening Behavior* 10, no. 4 (Winter 1980): 209.

42. Brian Barry, "Suicide: The Ultimate Escape," *Death Studies* 13, no. 2 (1989): 185–190; quote p. 188.

43. Quoted in Alfred Alvarez, *The Savage God: A Study of Suicide* (New York: Random House, 1971).

44. See, for example, Herbert Hendin, "The Suicide of Anne Sexton," *Suicide and Life-Threatening Behavior* 23, no. 3 (1993): 257–262.

45. D. E. Ness and C. R. Pfeffer, "Sequelae of Bereavement Resulting from Suicide," *American Journal of Psychiatry* 147 (March 1990): 279–285.

46. Donald H. Rubinstein, "Epidemic Suicide Among Micronesian Adolescents," *Social Science & Medicine* 17 (1983): 657–665, and "Suicide in Micronesia," in *Culture, Youth and Suicide in the Pacific: Papers from an East-West Center Conference,* ed. Francis X. Hezel, Donald H. Rubinstein, and Geoffrey M. White (Honolulu: Pacific Islands Study Program, University of Hawaii, 1985), pp. 88–111.

47. Cynthia R. Pfeffer and others, "Suicidal Children Grow Up: Suicidal Episodes and Effects of Treatment During Follow-Up," *Journal of the American Academy of Child and Adolescent Psychiatry* 33, no. 2 (1994): 225–230.

48. See Brian L. Mishara, "Conceptions of Death and Suicide in Children Ages 6–12 and Their Implications for Suicide Prevention," *Suicide and Life-Threatening Behavior* 29, no. 2 (1999): 105–118.

49. C. J. Lennings, "A Cognitive Understanding of Adolescent Suicide," *Genetic, Social, and General Psychology Monographs* 120, no. 3 (1994): 289–307.

50. "Deaths and Death Rates by Leading Causes of Death and Age," *Statistical Abstract of the United States: 2007,* p. 86.

51. David A. Brent and others, "Stressful Life Events: Psychopathology and Adolescent Suicide: A Case Control Study," *Suicide and Life-Threatening Behavior* 23, no. 3 (1993): 179–187, and "Personality Disorder, Personality Traits, Impulsive Violence, and Completed Suicide in Adolescents," *Journal of the American Academy of Child and Adolescent Psychiatry* 33, no. 8 (1994): 1080–1086. See also Stephen Briggs, "Working with the Risk of Suicide in Young People," *Journal of Social Work Practice* 16, no. 2 (2002): 135–148.

52. Herbert Hendin, "Psychodynamics of Suicide, with Particular Reference to the Young," *American Journal of Psychiatry* 148, no. 9 (1991): 1150–1158.

53. Paulina F. Kernberg, "Psychological Interventions for the Suicidal Adolescent," *American Journal of Psychotherapy* 48, no. 1 (1994): 52–63.

54. Lennings, "A Cognitive Understanding of Adolescent Suicide."

55. See M. S. Gould, S. Wallenstein, and L. Davidson, "Suicide Clusters: A Critical Review," *Suicide and Life-Threatening Behavior* 19 (Spring 1989): 17–29; and James A. Mercy and others, "Is Suicide Contagious? A Study of the Relation Between Exposure to the Suicidal Behavior of

Others and Nearly Lethal Suicide Attempts," *American Journal of Epidemiology* 154, no. 2 (2001): 120–127.

56. See R. Milin and A. Turgay, "Adolescent Couple Suicide: Literature Review," *Canadian Journal of Psychiatry* 35 (March 1990): 183–186. Examples cited by Evans and Farberow, *Encyclopedia of Suicide*, pp. 26–27, 72, 254.

57. Bruce L. Danto, Mark L. Taff, and Lauren R. Boglioli, "Graveside Deaths," *Omega: Journal of Death and Dying* 33, no. 4 (1996): 265–278.

58. Jason B. Luoma and Jane L. Pearson, "Suicide and Marital Status in the United States, 1991–1996: Is Widowhood a Risk Factor?" *American Journal of Public Health* 92, no. 9 (2002): 1518–1522.

59. Benjamin N. Shain and the Committee on Adolescence, "Suicide and Suicide Attempts in Adolescents," *Pediatrics* 120 (2007): 669–676.

60. James Janik and Howard M. Kravitz, "Linking Work and Domestic Problems," *Suicide and Life-Threatening Behavior* 24, no. 3 (1994): 267–274.

61. Y. Conwell and J. L. Pearson, "Suicidal Behaviors in Older Adults," *American Journal of Geriatric Psychiatry* 10, no. 4 (2002): 359–361; and, in the same issue, C. L. Turvey and others, "Risk Factors for Late-Life Suicide: A Prospective, Community-Based Study," pp. 398–406.

62. Susanne S. Carney and others, "Suicide over 60: The San Diego Study," *Journal of the American Geriatrics Society* 42 (1994): 174–180.

63. J. Conrad Glass, Jr., and Susan E. Reed, "To Live or Die: A Look at Elderly Suicide," *Educational Gerontology* 19 (1993): 767–778.

64. Stillion, McDowell, and May, *Suicide Across the Life Span*, pp. 180–181.

65. Antoon A. Leenaars and David Lester, "The Significance of the Method Chosen for Suicide in Understanding the Psychodynamics of the Suicidal Individual," *Omega: Journal of Death and Dying* 19, no. 4 (1988–1989): 311–314.

66. Edwin S. Shneidman, "Self-Destruction: Suicide Notes and Tragic Lives," in *Death: Current Perspectives*, 2nd ed., ed. Shneidman,

p. 467; and, by Shneidman, "A Bibliography of Suicide Notes: 1856–1979," in *Suicide and Life-Threatening Behavior* 9, no. 1 (Spring 1979): 57–59.

67. Stephen T. Black, "Comparing Genuine and Simulated Suicide Notes: A New Perspective," *Journal of Consulting and Clinical Psychology* 61, no. 4 (1993): 699–702.

68. Shneidman, *Comprehending Suicide*, pp. 167, 170.

69. Evans and Farberow, *Encyclopedia of Suicide*, p. 187.

70. Stillion, McDowell, and May, *Suicide Across the Life Span*, p. 13.

71. C. James Frankish, "Crisis Centers and Their Role in Treatment: Suicide Prevention Versus Health Promotion," *Death Studies* 18, no. 4 (1994): 327–339.

72. See Diego De Leo, "Why Are We Not Getting Any Closer to Preventing Suicide?" *British Journal of Psychiatry* 181 (2002): 372–374; and David Lester, "Challenges in Preventing Suicide," *Death Studies* 18, no. 6 (1994): 623–639.

73. Stillion, McDowell, and May, *Suicide Across the Life Span*, p. 194.

74. Stanley Beardy and Margaret Beardy, "Healing Native Communities Through 'Helping Hands'" (paper presented at the annual meeting of the Association for Death Education and Counseling, Duluth, Minnesota, April 1991).

75. Patrick W. O'Carroll, Morton M. Silverman, and Alan L. Berman, "Community Suicide Prevention: The Effectiveness of Bridge Barriers," *Suicide and Life-Threatening Behavior* 24, no. 1 (Spring 1994): 89–99.

76. Antoon A. Leenaars, "Crisis Intervention with Highly Lethal Suicidal People," *Death Studies* 18, no. 4 (1994): 341–360.

77. Shneidman, *Comprehending Suicide*, p. 203.

78. See Alison Wertheimer, *A Special Scar: The Experiences of People Bereaved by Suicide*, 2nd ed. (Philadelphia: Brunner-Routledge, 2001).

79. See Charles P. McDowell, Joseph M. Rothberg, and Ronald J. Koshes, "Witnessed Suicides," *Suicide and Life-Threatening Behavior* 24, no, 3 (1994): 213–223.

80. Richard Farmer, Ian O'Donnell, and Troy Tranah, "Suicide on the London Underground System," *International Journal of Epidemiology* 20, no. 3 (1991): 707–711; I. O'Donnell and R. D. T. Farmer, "Suicidal Acts on Metro Systems: An International Perspective," *Acta Psychiatrica Scandinavica* 86 (1992): 60–63; and A. Schmidtke, "Suicidal Behavior on Railways in the FRG," *Social Science & Medicine* 38, no. 3 (1994): 419–426.

81. Richard Farmer and others, "Railway Suicide: The Psychological Effects on Drivers," *Psychological Medicine* 22 (1992): 407–414; and T. Tranah and R. D. T. Farmer, "Psychological Reactions of Drivers to Railway Suicide," *Social Science & Medicine* 38, no. 3 (1994): 459–469.

82. Evans and Farberow, *Encyclopedia of Suicide,* pp. 58–59, 63.

83. Jack D. Douglas, *The Social Meanings of Suicide* (Princeton, N.J.: Princeton University Press, 1967), pp. 324ff.

84. A. C. Grayling, *Life, Sex, and Ideas: The Good Life Without God* (New York: Oxford University Press, 2003), p. 163.

85. Stillion, McDowell, and May, *Suicide Across the Life Span,* p. 24.

CHAPTER 13

1. From *Letters of E. B. White,* collected and edited by Dorothy Lobrano Guth (New York: Harper & Row, 1976), p. 558.

2. Anthony Giddens, *Runaway World: How Globalization Is Reshaping Our Lives* (New York: Routledge, 2000), p. 52.

3. See Harvey M. Sapolsky, "The Politics of Risk," *Daedalus: Journal of the American Academy of Arts and Sciences* 119 (Fall 1990): 83–96.

4. Giddens, *Runaway World,* p. 40.

5. Kevin Young, "Violence, Risk, and Liability in Male Sports Culture," *Sociology of Sport Journal* 10 (1993): 373–396.

6. Kawahito Hiroshi, "Death and the Corporate Warrior," *Japan Quarterly* 38 (April–June 1991): 149–157.

7. Reinhold Messner, quoted in Caroline Alexander, "Greatest Mountaineer," *National Geographic* 210, no. 5 (November 2006): 44.

8. James A. Thorson and F. C. Powell, "To Laugh in the Face of Death: The Games That Lethal People Play," *Omega: Journal of Death and Dying* 21, no. 3 (1990): 225–239.

9. Kenneth J. Doka, Eric C. Schwartz, and Catherine Schwarz, "Risky Business: Observations on the Nature of Death in Hazardous Sports," *Omega: Journal of Death and Dying* 21, no. 3 (1990): 215–223.

10. Robert Kastenbaum and Ruth Aisenberg, *The Psychology of Death: Concise Edition* (New York: Springer, 1976), p. 319. See also Alan E. Stewart and Janice Harris Lord, "Motor Vehicle Crash Versus Accident: A Change in Terminology Is Necessary," *Journal of Traumatic Stress* 15, no. 4 (2002): 333–335.

11. "Murder Victims by Age, Sex, and Race," *Statistical Abstract of the United States: 2007,* 126th ed. (Washington, D.C.: Government Printing Office, 2006), p. 194.

12. "Murder Victims—Circumstances and Weapons Used," *Statistical Abstract of the United States: 2007,* p. 194.

13. "'Vietnam Style' Triage Techniques Used to Treat Urban Assault Weapon Injuries," *Bulletin of the Park Ridge Center* (May 1989): 11–12.

14. See Ronald K. Barrett, "Urban Adolescent Homicidal Violence: An Emerging Public Health Concern," *Urban League Review* 16, no. 2 (1993): 67–75.

15. American Medical Association, Council on Scientific Affairs, "Firearms Injuries and Deaths: A Critical Public Health Issue," *Public Health Reports* 104 (1989): 111–120. See also Leland Ropp and others, "Death in the City: An American Childhood Tragedy," *Journal of the American Medical Association* 267, no. 21 (1992): 2905–2910.

16. Ice T, "The Killing Fields," in *The Path Ahead: Readings in Death and Dying,* ed. Lynne Ann DeSpelder and Albert Lee Strickland (Mountain View, Calif.: Mayfield, 1995), pp. 178–181.

17. Bruce L. Danto, Mark L. Taff, and Lauren R. Boglioli, "Graveside Deaths," *Omega: Journal of Death and Dying* 33, no. 4 (1996): 265–278.

18. Mitch Albom, "Random Shooting Paralyzes Football Player," *Detroit Free Press,* December 28, 1994, p. C1.

19. Quoted in Drew Leder, "Guns and Voices," *Second Opinion* 20, no. 2 (1994): 83–89.

20. Betsy McAlister Groves and others, "Silent Victims: Children Who Witness Violence," *Journal of the American Medical Association* 269, no. 2 (1993): 262–264.

21. Larry Cohen and Susan Swift, "A Public Health Approach to the Violence Epidemic in the United States," *Environment and Urbanization* 5, no. 2 (1993): 50–66. See also Mary R. Jackman, "Violence in Social Life," *Annual Review of Sociology* 28 (2002): 387–415.

22. Dana D. DeHart and John M. Mahoney, "The Serial Murderer's Motivations: An Interdisciplinary Review," *Omega: Journal of Death and Dying* 29, no. 1 (1994): 29–45.

23. Kastenbaum and Aisenberg, *Psychology of Death,* pp. 281–282.

24. Lula M. Redmond, *Surviving When Someone You Love Was Murdered: A Professional's Guide to Group Grief Therapy for Families and Friends of Murder Victims* (Clearwater, Fla.: Psychological Consultation and Education Services, 1989), p. 37.

25. Robert J. Sampson, Stephen W. Raudenbush, and Felton Earls, "Neighborhoods and Violent Crime: A Multilevel Study of Collective Efficacy," *Science* 277 (August 15, 1997): 918–923.

26. George B. Palermo and Douglas Simpson, "At the Roots of Violence: The Progressive Decline and Dissolution of the Family," *International Journal of Offender Therapy and Comparative*

Criminology 38, no. 2 (1994): 105–116. See also George B. Palermo and others, "Modes of Defensive Behavior in a Violent Society," *International Journal of Offender Therapy and Comparative Criminology* 37, no. 3 (1993): 251–261.

27. Cohen and Swift, "A Public Health Approach to the Violence Epidemic in the United States."

28. Arnold Toynbee, "Death in War," in *Death and Dying: Challenge and Change,* ed. Robert Fulton and others (Reading, Mass.: Addison-Wesley, 1978), p. 367.

29. Dalton Trumbo, *Johnny Got His Gun* (New York: Bantam Books, 1970), pp. 214, 224.

30. World Campaign for the Protection of Victims of War, International Red Cross and Red Crescent Movement. See also James Garbarino, "Challenges We Face in Understanding Children and War: A Personal Essay," in *The Path Ahead,* ed. DeSpelder and Strickland, pp. 169–174.

31. United Nations Population Fund, "Overview of Adolescent Life," *State of World Population 2003,* www.unfpa.org/swp/2003/english/ch1/index.htm (accessed October 10, 2003).

32. Christie W. Kiefer, "Militarism and World Health," *Social Science & Medicine* 34, no. 7 (1992): 719–724.

33. Sam Keen, *Faces of the Enemy: Reflections of the Hostile Imagination* (San Francisco: Harper & Row, 1986), p. 71.

34. Gil Elliot, "Agents of Death," in *Death: Current Perspectives,* ed. Edwin S. Shneidman, 3rd ed. (Mountain View, Calif.: Mayfield, 1984), pp. 422–440.

35. Tom D. Crouch, *Wings: A History of Aviation from Kites to the Space Age* (New York: Norton, 2003), p. 425.

36. Elliot, "Agents of Death," pp. 422–440.

37. Quoted in Shono Naomi, "Mute Reminders of Hiroshima's Atomic Bombing," *Japan Quarterly* (July–September 1993): 267–272. See also Robert Jay Lifton, "Psychological Effects of the Atomic Bomb in Hiroshima: The Theme of Death," in *The Threat of Impending Disaster:*

Contributions to the Psychology of Stress, ed. George H. Grosser, Henry Wechsler, and Milton Greenblatt (Cambridge, Mass.: MIT Press, 1964), pp. 152–193.

38. Robert Jay Lifton and Eric Olson, *Living and Dying* (New York: Praeger, 1974), p. 32.

39. Gail Holst-Warhaft, *The Cue for Passion: Grief and Its Political Uses* (Cambridge, Mass.: Harvard University Press, 2000), p. 174.

40. Glenn M. Vernon, *Sociology of Death: An Analysis of Death-Related Behavior* (New York: Ronald Press, 1970), p. 46.

41. Toynbee, "Death in War," p. 367.

42. Anthony Swofford, *Jarhead: A Marine's Chronicle of the Gulf War and Other Battles* (New York: Scribner, 2003), p. 7.

43. Joel Baruch, "Combat Death," in *Death: Current Perspectives,* ed. Edwin S. Shneidman (Palo Alto, Calif.: Mayfield, 1976), pp. 92–93.

44. Personal communication.

45. Quoted in Trish Wood, *What Was Asked of Us: An Oral History of the Iraq War by the Soldiers Who Fought It* (New York: Little, Brown, 2006), p. 127.

46. See Robert Jay Lifton, *Home from the War: Vietnam Veterans, Neither Victims Nor Executioners* (New York: Basic Books, 1985); and Harvey J. Schwartz, "Fear of the Dead: The Role of Social Ritual in Neutralizing Fantasies from Combat," in *Psychotherapy of the Combat Veteran,* ed. H. J. Schwartz (New York: SP Medical & Scientific Books, 1984), pp. 253–267.

47. Ervin Staub, *The Roots of Evil: The Origins of Genocide and Other Group Violence* (New York: Cambridge University Press, 1989).

48. Colin Murray Parkes, "Genocide in Rwanda: Personal Reflections," *Mortality* 1, no. 1 (1996): 95–110.

49. Theodore Nadelson, "Attachment to Killing," *Journal of the American Academy of Psychoanalysis* 20, no. 1 (1992): 130–141.

50. See Harold A. Widdison and Howard G. Salisbury, "The Delayed Stress Syndrome: A Pathological Delayed Grief Reaction?" *Omega: Journal of Death and Dying* 20, no. 4 (1989–1990): 293–306.

51. Quoted in Michael Browning, "Homer's 'Iliad' Has Lessons for Vietnam Nightmare," *Honolulu Advertiser,* February 12, 1995, pp. B1, B4. See also Jonathan Shay, *Achilles in Vietnam: Combat Trauma and the Undoing of Character* (New York: Atheneum, 1994).

52. Paul Recer, "A Different Johnny," Associated Press wire story, March 3, 1991.

53. The examples of "The Lost Patrol" and the "walking meditation" are from Maja Beckstrom, "Vietnam Vets Find Peace in Healing Ceremonies: Rituals Help End the War Within," *Utne Reader* (March–April 1991): 34–35.

54. From an account by Barbara Carton, Washington Park Service, in the *Honolulu Star-Bulletin & Advertiser,* August 11, 1985.

55. Marian Faye Novak, *Lonely Girls with Burning Eyes: A Wife Recalls Her Husband's Journey Home from Vietnam* (Boston: Little, Brown, 1991), p. 3.

56. Lee Woodruff and Bob Woodruff, *In an Instant: A Family's Journey of Love and Healing* (New York: Random house, 2007), p. 140.

57. Keen, *Faces of the Enemy,* pp. 10–14.

58. Debra Umberson and Kristin Henderson, "The Social Construction of Death in the Gulf War," *Omega: Journal of Death and Dying* 25, no. 1 (1992): 1–15.

59. Keen, *Faces of the Enemy,* pp. 180–181.

60. Ibid., p. 137.

61. Anonymous epigraph in Aref M. Al-Kattar, *Religion and Terrorism: An Interfaith Perspective* (Westport, Conn.: Praeger, 2003), p. 3.

62. See Philip Jenkins, *Images of Terror: What We Can and Can't Know About Terrorism* (New York: Aldine de Gruyter, 2003), p. 28; and Walter Laqueur, *No End to War: Terrorism in the Twenty-First Century* (New York: Continuum, 2003), p. 233.

63. See, for example, Caleb Carr, *The Lessons of Terror: A History of Warfare Against Civilians, Why It Has Always Failed and Why It Will Fail Again* (New York: Random House, 2002), pp. 7, 9, 12–14.

64. *Merriam-Webster's Collegiate Dictionary,* 11th ed. (Springfield, Mass.: Merriam-Webster, 2003), p. 1049.

65. Walter Laqueur, *The Age of Terrorism* (Boston: Little, Brown, 1987), p. 72.

66. Cindy C. Combs and Martin Slann, *Encyclopedia of Terrorism* (New York: Facts on File, 2002), pp. 208–211.

67. Tom Pyszczynski, Sheldon Solomon, and Jeff Greenberg, *In the Wake of 9/11: The Psychology of Terror* (Washington, D.C.: American Psychological Association, 2003), pp. 8, 16, 127.

68. On September 17, 1862, in the Battle of Antietam, 6000 soldiers were killed outright or mortally wounded, and another 16,000 were wounded and survived. At least 620,000 died during the course of the Civil War. See James M. McPherson, "The Lesson of Antietam," *The American Scholar* 71, no. 1 (2002): 64–65.

69. Nilüfer Göle, "Close Encounters, Islam, Modernity, and Violence," in *Understanding September 11,* ed. Craig Calhoun, Paul Price, and Ashley Timmer (New York: New Press, 2002), pp. 332–344. See also CBS News, *What We Saw: The Events of September 11 in Words, Pictures, and Video* (New York: Simon & Schuster, 2002).

70. Richard Bernstein and Staff of New York Times, *Out of the Blue: The Story of September 11, 2001, From Jihad to Ground Zero* (New York: Times Books, 2002), p. 3. See also Brian Doyle, "Leap," *The American Scholar* 71, no. 1 (2002): 69–70.

71. Cathy Trost and Alicia C. Shepard, *Running Toward Danger: Stories Behind the Breaking News of 9/11* (Lanham, Md.: Rowman & Littlefield, 2002), p. xiii.

72. Harold Dow, quoted in Trost and Shepard, *Running Toward Danger,* p. 247.

73. William Langewiesche, *American Ground: Unbuilding the World Trade Center* (New York: North Point, 2002), p. 45.

74. Lynne Ann DeSpelder, "September 11, 2001 and the Internet," *Mortality* 8, no. 1 (2003): 88–89.

75. Craig Calhoun, Paul Price, and Ashley Timmer, "Introduction," in Calhoun, Price, and

Timmer, *Understanding September 11,* p. 4. See also Shashi Tharoor, "The Global Century," *The American Scholar* 71, no. 1 (2002): 66–68.

76. See Marita Sturken, "Memorializing Absence," in Calhoun, Price, and Timmer, *Understanding September 11,* pp. 374–384, esp. 378–381.

77. Langewiesche, *American Ground,* p. 99.

78. Langewiesche, *American Ground,* pp. 69, 156.

79. Loolwa Khazzoom, "For Zaka Rescue Volunteers, Grisly Deaths Are a Part of Life," *Global News Service of the Jewish People,* September 29, 2003, www.jta.org (accessed October 9, 2003).

80. Michael Schudson, "What's Unusual About Covering Politics as Usual," in *Journalism After September 11,* ed. Barbie Zelizer and Stuart Allan (New York: Routledge, 2002), pp. 38–39; see also introduction by Zelizer and Allan, pp. 8–9.

81. The authors thank Professor Carla Sofka for providing information about the archival project at the New York State Museum to catalog and preserve many of the items created by children in response to September 11, 2001.

82. Philip Jenkins, *Images of Terror: What We Can and Can't Know About Terrorism* (New York: Aldine de Gruyter, 2003), pp. 82–83.

83. Combs and Slann, *Encyclopedia of Terrorism,* p. 166.

84. Bruce D. Berkowitz, *The New Face of War: How War Will Be Fought in the 21st Century* (New York: Free Press, 2003), pp. 16–17; see also Philip Bobbitt, *The Shield of Achilles: War, Peace, and the Course of History* (New York: Knopf, 2002), pp. 811, 821.

85. Mark Juergensmeyer, "Religious Terror and Global War," in Calhoun, Price, and Timmer, *Understanding September 11,* pp. 27–49; quote p. 29. See also Kelton Cobb, "Violent Faith," in *11 September: Religious Perspectives on the Causes and Consequences,* ed. Ian Markham and Ibrahim M. Abu-Rabi (Oxford: OneWorld, 2002), pp. 136–163; and Bruce Lincoln, *Holy*

Terrors: Thinking About Religion After September 11 (Chicago: University of Chicago Press, 2003).

86. Laqueur, *No End to War,* pp. 71, 91.

87. Aaron T. Beck, "Prisoners of Hate," *Behaviour Research and Therapy* 40, no. 3 (2002): 209–216, and *Prisoners of Hate: The Cognitive Basis of Anger, Hostility, and Violence* (New York: HarperCollins, 1999).

88. Pyszczynski, Solomon, and Greenberg, *In the Wake of 9/11,* p. 149.

89. Beck, "Prisoners of Hate," p. 216.

90. Tharoor, "Global Century," p. 68.

91. J. Travis, "New Drugs Beat Old Flu," *Science News* 162 (September 28, 2002): 196.

92. Travis, "New Drugs Beat Old Flu." See also Monica Schoch-Spana, "'Hospital's Full-Up': The 1918 Influenza Pandemic," *Public Health Reports* 116 (2001): 32–33.

93. Robert Kastenbaum, "Reconstructing Death in Postmodern Society," in *The Path Ahead,* ed. DeSpelder and Strickland, pp. 7–18.

94. Brandon F. Keele and others, "Chimpanzee Reservoirs of Pandemic and Nonpandemic HIV-1," *Science* 313, no. 5786 (July 28, 2006): 523–526.

95. Joint United Nations Programme on HIV/AIDS (UNAIDS), Press Office, "Global Facts and Figures, 2006"; and *AIDS Epidemic Update: Special Report on HIV/AIDS, December 2006.* www.unaids.org/2006_EpiUpdate_en.pdf (accessed February 1, 2007).

96. Edith M. Lederer, "More Than 2 Million Kids Have HIV," *Associated Press Online* (accessed May 27, 2006).

97. United Nations, "AIDS Orphans in sub-Saharan Africa: A Looming Threat to Future Generations," www.un.org/events/tenstories/print.asp?storyID=400 (accessed May 17, 2006).

98. Peter Piot, "AIDS: A Global Response," *Science* 272 (28 June 1996): 1855.

99. See Mary Catherine Bateson and Richard Goldsby, *Thinking AIDS: The Social Response to the Biological Threat* (Reading, Mass.: Addison-Wesley, 1988); Douglas Crimp, ed., *AIDS: Cultural Analysis, Cultural Activism* (Cambridge, Mass.: MIT Press, 1988); Eve K. Nichols, *Mobilizing Against AIDS,* rev. ed. (Cambridge, Mass.: Harvard University Press, 1989); and Randy Shilts, *And the Band Played On: Politics, People, and the AIDS Epidemic* (New York: Viking Penguin, 1988).

100. Malcolm D. Gibson, "AIDS and the African Press," *Media, Culture & Society* 16 (1994): 349–356.

101. Karen A. Bonuck, "AIDS and Families: Cultural, Psychosocial, and Functional Impacts," *Social Work in Health Care* 18, no. 2 (1993): 75–89.

102. Ronald Keith Barrett, "Elephant People: The Phenomena of Social Withdrawal and Self-Imposed Isolation of People Dying with AIDS," *AIDS Patient Care* (October 1995): 240–244.

103. "DMV Reverses AIDS Plate Denial," *Associated Press Online,* October 25, 1994.

104. Charles E. Rosenberg, "What Is an Epidemic? AIDS in Historical Perspective," in *The Path Ahead,* ed. DeSpelder and Strickland, pp. 29–32.

105. This description of the diagnosis and treatment of HIV and AIDS is drawn primarily from the following sources: Robert Berkow, ed., *The Merck Manual of Diagnosis and Therapy,* 16th ed. (Rahway, N.J.: Merck Research Laboratories, 1992), pp. 55, 77, 83, 86; Robert Berkow, ed., *The Merck Manual of Medical Information: Home Edition* (Whitehouse Station, N.J.: Merck Research Laboratories, 1997), pp. 926–932; and Virginia F. Sendor and Patrice M. O'Connor, *Hospice & Palliative Care: Questions and Answers* (Lanham, Md.: Scarecrow Press, 1997), pp. 46–47.

106. Quoted in Jon Cohen, "Advances Painted in Shades of Gray at a D.C. Conference," *Science* 275 (January 31, 1997): 615.

107. Margaret A. Chesney, "Health Psychology in the 21st Century: Acquired Immunodeficiency Syndrome as a Harbinger of Things to Come," *Health Psychology* 12, no. 4 (1993): 259–268.

108. See Laurie Garrett, *The Coming Plague: Newly Emerging Diseases in a World Out of Balance*

(New York: Farrar, Straus & Giroux, 1994). See also Berkow, ed., *The Merck Manual of Diagnosis and Therapy,* pp. 211–220.

109. Bernard Le Guenno, "Emerging Viruses," *Scientific American* (October 1995): 56–64.

110. See Gunjan Sinha and Burkhard Bilger, "Skeletons in the Attic: Has the Scourge of Athens Returned to Haunt Us?" *The Sciences* 36, no. 5 (September–October 1996): 11; and Matt Crenson, "Researcher: Plague Sparked Ebola," *Associated Press Online,* January 20, 1997.

111. Paul Recer, "Origin of 1918 Flu Pandemic Found," *Associated Press Online,* March 20, 1997.

112. William R. Clark, *Sex and the Origins of Death* (New York: Oxford University Press, 1996), p. 177.

113. Rodrick Wallace and Deborah Wallace, "Inner-City Disease and the Public Health of the Suburbs: The Sociogeographical Dispersion of Point-Source Infection," *Environment and Planning Abstracts* 25 (1993): 1707–1723; and "The Coming Crisis of Public Health in the Suburbs," *Milbank Quarterly* 71, no. 4 (1993): 543–564. See also Rodrick Wallace and others, "Will AIDS Be Contained Within U.S. Minority Urban Populations?" *Social Science & Medicine* 39, no. 8 (1994): 1051–1062.

114. Rodrick Wallace and John Pittman, "Recurrence of Contagious Urban Desertification and the Social Thanatology of New York City," *Environment and Planning Abstracts* 24 (June 1992): 1–6.

115. Wallace and Pittman, "Recurrence of Contagious Urban Desertification," p. 1.

116. Richard Rothenberg, "Chronicle of an Epidemic Foretold: A Response to the Wallaces," *Milbank Quarterly* 71, no. 4 (1993): 565–574.

117. Mitchell Duneier, *Slim's Table: Race, Respectability, and Masculinity* (Chicago: University of Chicago Press, 1992), p. 75.

118. Rachel Nowak, "WHO Calls for Action Against TB," *Science* 267 (March 24, 1995): 1763.

See also Stuart B. Levy, "The Challenge of Antibiotic Resistance," *Scientific American* 278, no. 3 (March 1998): 46–53.

119. Charles J. Hanley, "Malaria Stages Comeback," *Associated Press Online,* May 12, 1996.

120. Daniel Leviton, "Horrendous Death: Improving the Quality of Global Health," in *The Path Ahead,* ed. DeSpelder and Strickland, pp. 165–168; see also, edited by Leviton, *Horrendous Death, Health, and Well-Being* (New York: Hemisphere, 1991).

121. Daniel Leviton, "Horrendous Death," in *Death and the Quest for Meaning: Essays in Honor of Herman Feifel,* ed. Stephen Strack (Northvale, N.J.: Jason Aronson, 1997), pp. 301–327; quote p. 303.

122. Ibid., p. 309.

CHAPTER 14

1. Quoted in Jeffery L. Sheler, "Heaven in the Age of Reason," *U.S. News & World Report* 122, no. 12 (1997): 65–66; italics added.

2. Interview with Mikal Gilmore, *Rolling Stone,* December 22, 2001.

3. Bertrand Russell, *Unpopular Essays* (New York: Simon & Schuster, 1950), p. 141.

4. See "The Problem of Immortality," in Jacques Choron, *Death and Modern Man* (New York: Collier, 1964).

5. Geddes MacGregor, *Images of Afterlife: Beliefs from Antiquity to Modern Times* (New York: Paragon House, 1992), p. 209.

6. Mary Kawena Pukui, E. W. Haertig, and Catherine A. Lee, *Nana I Ke Kumu (Look to the Source),* vols. 1 and 2 (Honolulu: Hui Hanai; Queen Lili'uokalani Children's Center, 1972). See also E. S. Craighill Handy and Mary Kawena Pukui, *The Polynesian Family System in Ka-'u, Hawai'i* (Rutland, Vt.: Charles E. Tuttle, 1972).

7. Ray S. Anderson, *Theology, Death and Dying* (New York: Basil Blackwell, 1986), p. 38.

8. Ellen Levine, "Jewish Views and Customs on Death," in *Death and Bereavement Across Cul-*

tures, ed. Colin Murray Parkes, Pitti Laungani, and Bill Young (New York: Routledge, 1997), pp. 98–130.

9. Job 7:9, *The Jerusalem Bible.* See also Job 14:7–12.

10. Daniel 12:2, *The Jerusalem Bible.*

11. Stephen J. Vicchio, "Against Raising Hope of Raising the Dead: Contra Moody and Kübler-Ross," *Essence: Issues in the Study of Ageing, Dying and Death* 3, no. 2 (1979): 63.

12. See Lou H. Silberman in "Death in the Hebrew Bible and Apocalyptic Literature," in *Perspectives on Death,* ed. L. O. Mills (Nashville: Abingdon Press, 1969), pp. 13–32. The "Samuel" story is told in the first book of Samuel (28:3–25).

13. H. Wheeler Robinson, "Hebrew Psychology," in *The People and the Book,* ed. Arthur S. Peake (London: Oxford University Press, 1925), pp. 353–382.

14. See, for example, Leon Wieseltier, *Kaddish* (New York: Knopf, 1998).

15. Earl A. Grollman, "The Ritualistic and Theological Approach of the Jew," in *Explaining Death to Children,* ed. Grollman (Boston: Beacon Press, 1967), pp. 223–245; and Jonathan Boyarin, "Death and the *Minyan,*" *Cultural Anthropology* 9, no. 1 (1994): 3–22.

16. See C. Fred Alford, "Greek Tragedy and the Place of Death in Life: A Psychoanalytic Perspective," *Psychoanalysis and Contemporary Thought* 15, no. 2 (1992): 129–159.

17. Carol Zaleski, "In Defense of Immortality," *First Things* (August–September 2000): 36–42; quote p. 40.

18. William Barclay, *Introducing the Bible* (Nashville: Abingdon Press, 1972), p. 123.

19. Anderson, *Theology, Death and Dying,* p. 59.

20. Milton McC. Gatch, *Death: Meaning and Mortality in Christian Thought and Contemporary Culture* (New York: Seabury Press, 1969), p. 78.

21. Richard P. McBrien, *The HarperCollins Encyclopedia of Catholicism* (San Francisco: HarperCollins, 1995), p. 1070. See also Alan E. Bernstein, *The Formation of Hell: Death and Retribution in the Ancient and Early Christian Worlds* (Ithaca, N.Y.: Cornell University Press, 1993); Stephen Greenblatt, *Hamlet in Purgatory* (Princeton, N.J.: Princeton University Press, 2001); and Jacques Le Goff, *The Birth of Purgatory* (Chicago: University of Chicago Press, 1984).

22. Purgatory is not to be confused with *limbo,* "a place or state where unbaptized persons enjoy a natural happiness, though they remain excluded from the Beatific Vision." See McBrien, *The HarperCollins Encyclopedia of Catholicism,* p. 771.

23. Zaleski, "In Defense of Immortality," quote p. 41. See also Alister E. McGrath, "Last Things: The Christian Hope" (Chapter 18), in *Christian Theology: An Introduction,* 3rd ed. (Malden, Mass.: Blackwell, 2001), pp. 553–577.

24. Vicchio, "Against Raising Hope," p. 62. See also Gordon E. Geddes, *Welcome Joy: Death in Puritan New England* (Ann Arbor, Mich.: UMI Research Press, 1981); and David E. Stannard, *The Puritan Way of Death: A Study of Religion, Culture, and Social Change* (New York: Oxford University Press, 1977).

25. Constantine Callinicos, *Beyond the Grave: An Orthodox Theology of Eschatology,* trans. George Dimopoulos and Leslie Jerome Newville (Scranton, Penn.: Christian Orthodox Editions, 1969), p. 158. See also Stanley Samuel Harakas, *Health and Medicine in the Eastern Orthodox Tradition: Faith, Liturgy, and Wholeness* (New York: Crossroad, 1990), esp. pp. 151–159.

26. Peter C. Phan, *Responses to 101 Questions on Death and Eternal Life* (New York: Paulist Press, 1997), pp. 18, 129. See also Douglas Connelly, *Bible Prophecy for Blockheads: A User-Friendly Look at the End Times* (Grand Rapids, Mich.: Zondervan, 2002), pp. 164–166; and Regis Martin, *The Last Things: Death, Judgment, Heaven, Hell* (San Francisco: Ignatius, 1998), p. 118.

27. John L. Esposito, *Islam: The Straight Path* (New York: Oxford University Press, 1988), p. 22.

28. Frithjof Schuon, *Understanding Islam* (Baltimore: Penguin, 1972), p. 16.

29. Alfred T. Welch, "Death and Dying in the Qur'an," in *Religious Encounters with Death: Insights from the History and Anthropology of Religions,* ed. Frank E. Reynolds and Earle H. Waugh (University Park: Pennsylvania State University Press, 1977), p. 184. See also Shahzad Bashir, "Deciphering the Cosmos from Creation to Apocalypse: The Hurufiyya Movement and Medieval Islamic Esotericism," in *Imagining the End: Visions of Apocalypse from the Ancient Middle East to Modern America,* ed. Abbas Amanat and Magnus Bernhardsson (London: I. B. Tauris, 2002), pp. 168–184; and "Enshrining Divinity: The Death and Memorialization of Fazlallah Astarabadi in Hurufi Thought," *Muslim World* 90, nos. 3–4 (2000): 289–308.

30. Huston Smith, *The Religions of Man* (New York: New American Library, 1958), p. 215.

31. Esposito, *Islam: The Straight Path,* p. 35.

32. Welch, "Death and Dying in the Qur'an," p. 193.

33. D. S. Roberts, *Islam: A Concise Introduction* (San Francisco: Harper and Row, 1981), p. 128.

34. Ibid. See also Suzanne Evans, "The Scent of a Martyr," *Numen: International Review for the History of Religions* 49, no. 2 (2002): 193–211.

35. Abdul Latif Al Hoa, *Islam* (New York: Bookwright Press, 1987), p. 20.

36. Hend Yasien-Esmael and Simon Shimson Rubin, "The Meaning Structures of Muslim Bereavements in Israel: Religious Traditions, Mourning Practices, and Human Experience," *Death Studies* 29 (2005): 495–518.

37. Chuang Tzu, *Basic Writings,* trans. Burton Watson (New York: Columbia University Press, 1964), p. 76.

38. T. N. Madan, "Dying with Dignity," *Social Science & Medicine* 35, no. 4 (1992): 425–432.

39. *Bhagavad-Gita* II.27, trans. Swami Nikhilananda (New York: Ramakrishna-Vivekananda Center, 1952), p. 79.

40. Smith, *Religions of Man,* p. 34.

41. E. M. Jackson, "Moksha," in *Key Ideas in Human Thought,* ed. Kenneth McLeish (New York: Facts on File, 1993), pp. 482–483.

42. *Bhagavad-Gita* II.22, trans. Nikhilananda, p. 77.

43. J. Bruce Long, "Death as a Necessity and a Gift in Hindu Mythology," in *Religious Encounters with Death,* ed. Reynolds and Waugh, p. 92; see also pp. 73–96.

44. David R. Kinsley in "The 'Death That Conquers Death': Dying to the World in Medieval Hinduism," in *Religious Encounters with Death,* ed. Reynolds and Waugh, pp. 97–108. See also Pittu Laungani, "Death in a Hindu Family," in *Death and Bereavement Across Cultures,* pp. 52–72.

45. Philip Kapleau, *Zen: Dawn in the West* (Garden City, N.Y.: Anchor Press/Doubleday, 1979), p. 296. See also, edited by Kapleau, *The Wheel of Death: A Collection of Writings from Zen Buddhist and Other Sources on Death-Rebirth-Dying* (New York: Harper and Row, 1971), and *The Wheel of Life and Death: A Practical and Spiritual Guide* (New York: Doubleday, 1989).

46. "Awakening to the Bodhi-Mind (Hotsu Bodai-shin)," from the Shobo-Genzo, in *Zen Master Dōgen,* trans. Yuho Yokoi, p. 109.

47. Kapleau, *Zen: Dawn in the West,* pp. 67–68.

48. Ronald L. Grimes, *Deeply into the Bone: Re-Inventing Rites of Passage* (Berkeley: University of California Press, 2000), p. 225.

49. Grimes, *Deeply into the Bone,* p. 224.

50. "The Meaning of Practice-Enlightenment (Susho-gi)," in *Zen Master Dōgen: An Introduction with Selected Writings,* trans. Yuho Yokoi (New York/Tokyo: Weatherhill, 1976), p. 58.

51. "The Meaning of Practice-Enlightenment (Shusho-gi)," p. 58.

52. *The Zen Master Hakuin: Selected Writings,* trans. Philip B. Yampolsky (New York: Columbia University Press, 1971).

53. Kapleau, *Zen: Dawn in the West,* p. 69.

54. W. Y. Evans-Wentz, *The Tibetan Book of the Dead: or, the After-Death Experiences on the Bardo*

Plane, According to Lama Kazi Dawa-Samup's English Rendering (New York: Oxford University Press, 1960).

55. Quoted in Kapleau, *Zen: Dawn in the West,* p. 68.

56. Quoted in William R. Clark, *Sex and the Origins of Death* (New York: Oxford University Press, 1996), p. 159.

57. See Robert E. Goss and Dennis Klass, "Tibetan Buddhism and the Resolution of Grief: The Bardo-Thodol for the Dying and Grieving," *Death Studies* 21 (1997): 377–395.

58. Francesca Fremantle and Chögyam Trungpa, eds., *The Tibetan Book of the Dead: The Great Liberation Through Hearing in the Bardo, by Guru Rinpoche According to Karma Lingpa* (Boulder, Colo.: Shambhala, 1975).

59. Christopher Carr, "Death and Near-Death: A Comparison of Tibetan and Euro-American Experiences," *Journal of Transpersonal Psychology* 25, no. 1 (1993): 59–110. See also Uwe P. Gielen, "A Death on the Roof of the World," in *Death and Bereavement Across Cultures,* pp. 73–97.

60. Davina A. Allen, "Secularization," in *Key Ideas in Human Thought,* ed. McLeish, p. 668. See also James Turner, *Without God, Without Creed: The Origins of Unbelief in America* (Baltimore: Johns Hopkins University Press, 1985).

61. Colin Murray Parkes, "Conclusions II: Attachments and Losses in Cross-Cultural Perspective," in *Death and Bereavement Across Cultures,* pp. 233–243; quote p. 234.

62. E. M. Jackson and Kenneth McLeish, "Humanism," in *Key Ideas in Human Thought,* ed. McLeish, pp. 355–356.

63. Kenneth McLeish, "Existentialism," in *Key Ideas in Human Thought,* ed. McLeish, pp. 265–266; quote p. 265. See also William Barrett, *Irrational Man: A Study in Existential Philosophy* (New York: Doubleday, 1958), and *Death of the Soul: From Descartes to the Computer* (New York: Anchor/Doubleday, 1986).

64. See Robert J. Lifton, *The Future of Immortality and Other Essays for a Nuclear Age* (New York: Basic Books, 1987), and *The Broken Connection: On Death and the Continuity of Life* (New York: Basic Books, 1983; reprint, Washington, D.C.: American Psychiatric Press, 1996).

65. Sheler, "Heaven in the Age of Reason"; see also Jeffery L. Sheler, "Hell's Sober Comeback," *U.S. News & World Report,* March 25, 1991, pp. 56–57; and Daniel J. Klenow and Robert C. Bolin, "Belief in an Afterlife: A National Survey," *Omega: Journal of Death and Dying* 20, no. 1 (1989–1990): 63–74.

66. Andrew M. Greeley and Michael Hout, "Americans' Increasing Belief in Life After Death: Religious Competition and Acculturation," *American Sociological Review* 64, no. 6 (1999): 813–835.

67. David Lester and others, "What Is the Afterlife Like? Undergraduate Beliefs About the Afterlife," *Omega: Journal of Death and Dying* 44, no. 2 (2001–2002): 113–126.

68. Quoted in David Cockburn, "Simone Weil on Death," *Mortality* 2, no. 1 (1997): 63–72.

69. Carol Zaleski, *Otherworld Journeys: Accounts of Near-Death Experience in Medieval and Modern Times* (New York: Oxford University Press, 1987).

70. Paul Badham, "Religious and Near-Death Experience in Relation to Belief in a Future Life," *Mortality* 2, no. 1 (1997): 7–21.

71. Bruce Greyson, "Near-Death Experiences," in *Varieties of Anomalous Experience: Examining the Scientific Evidence,* ed. Etzel Cardeña, Steven Jay Lynn, and Stanley Krippner (Washington, D.C.: American Psychological Association, 2000), pp. 315–352; definition pp. 315–316.

72. Kenneth Ring, *Life at Death: A Scientific Investigation of the Near-Death Experience* (New York: Coward, McCann & Geoghegan, 1980), and *Heading Toward Omega: In Search of the Meaning of the Near-Death Experience* (New York: Morrow, 1984). See also Bruce Greyson, "Varieties of Near-Death Experience," *Psychiatry* 56 (1993): 390–399; and Raymond A. Moody, Jr., *Life After Life,* and its sequel, *Reflections on Life After Life* (various editions).

73. Bruce Greyson, "Reduced Death Threat in Near-Death Experiencers," in *Death Anxiety Handbook: Research, Instrumentation, and Application,* ed. Robert A. Neimeyer (Washington, D.C.: Taylor & Francis, 1994), pp. 169–179, esp. pp. 169, 177.

74. H. J. Irwin, *An Introduction to Parapsychology* (Jefferson, N.C.: McFarland, 1989), pp. 188–190.

75. William J. Serdahely, "The Near-Death Experience: Is the Presence Always the Higher Self?" *Omega: Journal of Death and Dying* 18, no. 2 (1987–1988): 129–134.

76. William J. Serdahely, "A Pediatric Near-Death Experience: Tunnel Variants," *Omega: Journal of Death and Dying* 20, no. 1 (1989–1990): 55–62. See also William J. Serdahely and Barbara A. Walker, "A Near-Death Experience at Birth," *Death Studies* 14, no. 2 (1990): 177–183.

77. See Bruce Greyson and Nancy Evans Bush, "Distressing Near-Death Experiences," *Psychiatry* 55 (February 1992): 95–110; and P. M. H. Atwater, "Is There a Hell? Surprising Observations About the Near-Death Experience," *Journal of Near-Death Studies* 10, no. 3 (Spring 1992): 149–160.

78. Brendan I. Koerner, "Is There Life After Death?" *U.S. News & World Report* 122, no. 12 (1997): 59–64.

79. Ian Stevenson, Emily W. Cook, Nicholas McClean-Rice, "Are Persons Reporting 'Near-Death Experiences' Really Near Death? A Study of Medical Records," *Omega: Journal of Death and Dying* 20, no. 1 (1989–1990): 45–54.

80. For an introduction to the main points of view, see Stephen J. Vicchio, "Near-Death Experiences: A Critical Review of the Literature and Some Questions for Further Study," *Essence: Issues in the Study of Ageing, Dying and Death* 5, no. 1 (1981): 77–89. See also James E. Alcock, "Psychology and Near-Death Experiences," *The Skeptical Inquirer* 3, no. 3 (Spring 1979): 25–41; Michael B. Sabom, *Recollections of Death: A Medical Investigation* (New York: Harper and Row, 1981); and Stephen J. Vicchio, "Near-Death Ex-

periences: Some Logical Problems and Questions for Further Study," *Anabiosis: The Journal of the International Association for Near-Death Studies* (1981): 66–87. The history of research into NDEs is traced in Stanislav Grof and Joan Halifax, *The Human Encounter with Death* (New York: E. P. Dutton, 1978), Chapter 7, "Consciousness and the Threshold of Death," pp. 131–157.

81. See Handy and Pukui, *The Polynesian Family System in Ka-'u, Hawai'i;* Donald D. Kilolani Mitchell, *Resource Units in Hawaiian Culture* (Honolulu: Kamehameha Schools Press, 1982); and Pukui, Haertig, and Lee, *Nana I Ke Kumu (Look to the Source),* vols. 1 and 2.

82. Pukui, Haertig, and Lee, *Nana I Ke Kumu (Look to the Source),* vol. 1, p. 40.

83. See Roy Kletti and Russell Noyes, Jr., "Mental States in Mortal Danger," which includes a translation of Oskar Pfister's 1930 paper commenting on Heim's observations, in *Essence: Issues in the Study of Ageing, Dying and Death* 5, no. 1 (1981): 5–20.

84. See Russell Noyes, Jr., "Dying and Mystical Consciousness," *Journal of Thanatology* I (1971): 25–41; Russell Noyes, Jr., and Roy Kletti, "Depersonalization in the Face of Life-Threatening Danger: An Interpretation," *Omega: Journal of Death and Dying* 7, no. 2 (1976): 103–114, and "Panoramic Memory: A Response to the Threat of Death," *Omega: Journal of Death and Dying* 8, no. 3 (1977): 181–194; Russell Noyes, Jr., "Near-Death Experiences: Their Interpretation and Significance," in *Between Life and Death,* ed. Robert Kastenbaum (New York: Springer, 1979), pp. 73–78; and Russell Noyes, Jr., "The Encounter with Life-Threatening Danger: Its Nature and Impact," *Essence: Issues in the Study of Ageing, Dying and Death* 5, no. 1 (1981): 21–32.

85. Karlis Osis and Erlendur Haraldsson, "Deathbed Observations of Physicians and Nurses: A Cross-Cultural Survey," in *The Signet Handbook of Parapsychology,* ed. Martin Ebon (New York: Signet/NAL, 1978); and, by Osis and Haraldsson, *At the Hour of Death* (New York: Avon Books, 1977). See also, by Haraldsson,

"Survey of Claimed Encounters with the Dead," *Omega: Journal of Death and Dying* 19, no. 2 (1988–1989): 103–113.

86. George Gallup, Jr., *Adventures in Immortality* (New York: McGraw-Hill, 1982). See also Sheler, "Heaven in the Age of Reason"; Greeley and Hout, "Americans' Increasing Belief in Life After Death"; and Klenow and Bolin, "Belief in an Afterlife: A National Survey."

87. Louis Appleby, *British Medical Journal* 298 (April 15, 1989): 976–977. See also Michael Potts, "Sensory Experiences in Near-Death Experiences and the Thomistic View of the Soul," *International Journal for Philosophy of Religion* 49, no. 2 (2001): 85–100.

88. Zaleski, *Otherworld Journeys,* p. 182.

89. Raymond A. Moody, Jr., "An Omega Interview [by Robert Kastenbaum]," *Omega: Journal of Death and Dying* 31, no. 2 (1995): 87–97.

90. From a conversation between Herman Feifel and John Morgan, "Humanity Has to Be the Model," *Death Studies* 10, no. 1 (1986): 1–9.

91. Robert Kastenbaum, "Happily Ever After," in *Between Life and Death,* ed. Kastenbaum, pp. 17, 19.

92. Charles A. Garfield, "The Dying Patient's Concern with 'Life After Death,'" in *Between Life and Death,* ed. Kastenbaum, pp. 52–57.

93. Kelly Bulkeley and Patricia Bulkley, *Dreaming Beyond Death: A Guide to Pre-Death Dreams and Visions* (Boston: Beacon Press, 2005), p. 12.

94. Marie-Louise von Franz, *On Death and Dreams: A Jungian Interpretation* (Boston: Shambhala, 1986), pp. viii–ix.

95. Ibid., p. 156.

96. Ibid., pp. 66–67.

97. Some evidence suggests that LSD may interfere with the transfer of oxygen on the enzymatic level. Anoxia, or diminished levels of oxygen in the bodily tissues, is also found in dying patients as well as in conjunction with certain yogic techniques involving breath control. Thus, anoxia may activate transpersonal matrices in the unconscious, giving rise to experiences associated with near-death experiences, certain yogic states, and LSD sessions. See Grof and Halifax, *The Human Encounter with Death,* pp. 183ff; and Thomas J. Riedlinger and June R. Riedlinger, "Psychedelic and Entactogenic Drugs in the Treatment of Depression," *Journal of Psychoactive Drugs* 26, no. 1 (1994): 41–55.

98. Stanislav Grof, *Realms of the Human Unconscious: Observations from LSD Research* (New York: E. P. Dutton, 1976). See also Robert B. Millman and Ann Bordwine Beeder, "The New Psychedelic Culture: LSD, Ecstasy, 'Rave' Parties, and the Grateful Dead," *Psychiatric Annals* 24, no. 3 (1994): 148–150; and Susanna Prepeliczay, "Socio-Cultural and Psychological Aspects of Contemporary LSD Use in Germany," *Journal of Drug Issues* 32, no. 2 (2002): 431–458.

99. See Stanislav Grof, *LSD Psychotherapy* (Pomona, Calif.: Hunter House, 1980), pp. 252ff; Grof and Halifax, *The Human Encounter with Death,* pp. 16ff; and Peter Stafford, *Psychedelics Encyclopedia* (Berkeley, Calif.: And/Or Press, 1977), pp. 23–39.

100. Grof and Halifax, *The Human Encounter with Death,* pp. 120–121.

101. Stanislav Grof and Christina Grof, *Beyond Death: The Gates of Consciousness* (New York: Thames & Hudson, 1980), p. 24.

102. David M. Wulff, "Mystical Experience," in *Varieties of Anomolous Experience: Examining the Scientific Evidence,* eds. Etzel Cardeña, Steven Jay Lynn, and Stanley Krippner (Washington, D.C.: American Psychological Association, 2000), pp. 397–440.

103. Stanislav Grof and Joan Halifax, "Psychedelics and the Experience of Dying," in *Life After Death,* ed. Arnold Toynbee and others (New York: McGraw-Hill, 1976), pp. 192–193.

104. Grof, *LSD Psychotherapy,* p. 294. See also, by Grof, *Psychology of the Future: Lessons from Modern Consciousness Research* (Albany: State University of New York, 2000).

105. Grimes, *Deeply into the Bone,* p. 237.

106. Herman Feifel, *The Meaning of Death* (New York: McGraw-Hill, 1959), p. xiv.

107. International Work Group on Death, Dying and Bereavement, "Assumptions and Principles of Spiritual Care," *Death Studies* 14, no. 1 (1990): 75–81.

108. See Thomas Attig, "Respecting the Spiritual Beliefs of the Dying and the Bereaved," in *Dying, Death, and Bereavement: A Challenge for Living,* 2nd ed., ed. Inge Corless, Barbara B. Germino, and Mary A. Pittman (New York: Springer, 2003), pp. 61–75.

109. Clyde M. Nabe, "'Seeing As': Death As Door or Wall," in *Priorities in Death Education and Counseling,* ed. Richard A. Pacholski and Charles A. Corr (Arlington, Va.: Forum for Death Education and Counseling, 1982), pp. 161–169.

CHAPTER 15

1. David Clark, ed., *The Sociology of Death: Theory, Culture, Practice* (Cambridge, Mass.: Blackwell, 1993), p. 3.

2. Allan B. Chinen, "The Mortal King," in *The Path Ahead: Readings in Death and Dying,* ed. Lynne Ann DeSpelder and Albert Lee Strickland (Mountain View, Calif.: Mayfield, 1995), pp. 335–336.

3. Thomas Attig, "Coping with Mortality: An Essay on Self-Mourning," in *The Path Ahead,* ed. DeSpelder and Strickland, pp. 337–341. See also Herman Feifel and Steven Strack, "Thanatologists View Death: A 15-Year Perspective," *Omega: Journal of Death and Dying* 43, no. 2 (2001): 97–111; and, in the same issue, Jeanne Quint Benoliel, "Commentary: Thanatologists View Death" (117–118).

4. Robert Kastenbaum, "Theory, Research, and Application: Some Critical Issues for Thanatology," *Omega: Journal of Death and Dying* 18, no. 4 (1987–1988): 397–410, quote p. 408.

5. Myra Bluebond-Langner, "Wither Thou Goest?" *Omega: Journal of Death and Dying* 18, no. 4 (1987–1988): 257–263. See also James A. Thorson, "Qualitative Thanatology," *Mortality* 1, no. 2 (1996).

6. Robert Fulton, "Unanticipated Grief" (paper presented at the annual meeting of the Forum for Death Education and Counseling, Philadelphia, April 12, 1985).

7. John R. Jordan, "Research That Matters: Bridging the Gap Between Research and Practice in Thanatology," *Death Studies* 24 (2000): 457–467; quote pp. 461, 463.

8. David E. Balk, "Scholarship, Students, and Practitioners: Bringing Scholarship into the Expectations of Practitioners," *Death Studies* 29 (2005): 123–144.

9. Hannelore Wass, "A Perspective on the Current State of Death Education," *Death Studies* 28 (2004): 289–308; quote p. 297.

10. J. Eugene Knott and Richard W. Prull, "Death Education: Accountable to Whom? For What?" *Omega: Journal of Death and Dying* 7, no. 2 (1976): 178; see also Joseph A. Durlak, "Changing Death Attitudes Through Death Education," in *Death Anxiety Handbook: Research, Instrumentation, and Application,* ed. Robert A. Neimeyer (Washington, D.C.: Taylor & Francis, 1993), pp. 243–259.

11. Darrell Crase, "Black People Do Die, Don't They?" *Death Studies* 11, no. 3 (1987): 221–228. The role of gender in shaping attitudes and behaviors relative to dying and death is similarly underrepresented; see, for example, Felicity Allen, "Where Are the Women in End-of-Life Research?" *Behaviour Change* 19, no. 1 (2002): 39–51.

12. International Work Group on Death, Dying and Bereavement, "A Statement of Assumptions and Principles Concerning Education About Death, Dying, and Bereavement," in *Statements on Death, Dying, and Bereavement* (London, Ont.: IWG, 1994). The three documents on death education prepared by this group were originally published in the following journals: *Death Studies* 16, no. 1 (1991): 59–65 (on education in general); *Omega: Journal of Death and Dying* 23, no. 3 (1991): 235–239 (on education for professionals in health care and human services); and *American Journal of Hospice and*

Palliative Care 7 (1991): 26–27 (on education for volunteers and nonprofessionals).

13. Daniel Leviton and William Wendt, "Death Education: Toward Individual and Global Well-Being," *Death Education* 7, no. 4 (1983): 369–384; and, edited by Leviton, *Horrendous Death, Health, and Well-Being* (New York: Hemisphere, 1991) and *Horrendous Death and Health: Toward Action* (New York: Hemisphere, 1991). See also Richard A. Pacholski, "Teaching Nuclear Holocaust, the Basic Thanatological Topic," *Death Studies* 13, no. 2 (1989): 175–183.

14. Allan Kellehear, *Compassionate Cities: Public Health and End-of-Life Care* (New York: Routledge, 2005), pp. 160–161.

15. Ibid., p. 162.

16. Helen Youngelson-Neal, Arthur G. Neal, and Jacob Fried, "Global and Local Culture in the 21st Century," *Journal of American and Comparative Cultures* 24, nos. 3–4 (Fall 2001): 31–36, esp. 33–35.

17. Kellehear, *Compassionate Cities,* p. x. The material in this section is drawn from this book unless otherwise noted.

18. Ronald L. Grimes, *Deeply into the Bone: Re-Inventing Rites of Passage* (Berkeley: University of California Press, 2000), p. 221.

19. Phyllis Silverman et al., "The 2004 Tucson IWG (International Work Group) Charter for the Normalization of Dying, Death, and Loss," *Omega: Journal of Death and Dying* 50 (2004–2005): 331–336, esp. p. 332.

20. Kellehear, *Compassionate Cities,* p. 16.

21. Ibid., p. 46.

22. Ibid., pp. 79–80.

23. Robert E. Goss and Dennis Klass, *Dead but Not Lost: Grief Narratives in Religious Traditions* (Walnut Creek, Calif.: AltaMira Press, 2005), p. 279.

24. Feifel, "Psychology and Death," p. 27.

25. Ibid., "Psychology and Death," p. 28.

26. Robert Fulton and Greg Owen, "Death and Society in Twentieth-Century America," *Omega: Journal of Death and Dying* 18, no. 4 (1987–1988): 390. On the many key contributions by women to both clinical and academic approaches in the field, see the special issue focusing on "Women in Thanatology," edited by Inge B. Corless, in *Illness, Crisis & Loss* 9, no. 1 (2001), which includes articles by Jeanne Quint Benoliel, David Clark (on Cicely Saunders), Thelma Bates, Zelda Foster, Catherine Sanders, Doris A. Howell, Ida M. Martinson, Sandra Bertman, Hannelore Wass, Phyllis R. Silverman, and Mary L. S. Vachon.

27. Sharon R. Kaufman, *And a Time to Die: How American Hospitals Shape the End of Life* (New York: Scribner, 2005), p. 323.

28. Ibid., p. 324.

29. "Resident Population by Sex and Age: 1980 to 2005" and "Resident Population Projections by Sex and Age: 2010 to 2050," *Statistical Abstract of the United States: 2007,* 126th ed. (Washington, D.C.: Government Printing Office, 2006), pp. 12, 13.

30. Ron Crocombe, *The South Pacific: An Introduction* (Auckland, New Zealand: Longman Paul, 1983).

31. Ibid., p. 73.

32. See Carla J. Sofka, "Social Support 'Internetworks,' Caskets for Sale, and More: Thanatology and the Information Superhighway," *Death Studies* 21, no. 6 (1997): 553–574.

33. Damon Knight, "Masks," in *A Pocketful of Stars,* ed. Knight (New York: Doubleday, 1971).

34. Clifford Simak, "Death Scene," in *The Worlds of Clifford Simak* (New York: Simon & Schuster, 1960); Robert A. Heinlein, "Life-Line," in *The Man Who Sold the Moon: Harriman and the Escape from the Earth to the Moon!* ed. Heinlein (New York: Shasta, 1950).

35. Kit Reed, "Golden Acres," in *Social Problems Through Science Fiction,* ed. John W. Miestead and others (New York: St. Martin's, 1975).

36. Sten Odenwald, *Back to the Astronomy Café* (Boulder, Colo.: Westview, 2003), p. 39.

37. Ibid., p. 88.

38. Gary Snyder, *The Practice of the Wild: Essays* (San Francisco: North Point Press, 1990), p. 176.

39. Alfred G. Killilea, "The Politics of Being Mortal," in *The Path Ahead,* ed. DeSpelder and Strickland, pp. 342–347. See also Gerry R. Cox, Robert A. Bendiksen, and Robert G. Stevenson, eds., *Making Sense of Death: Spiritual, Pastoral, and Personal Aspects of Death, Dying, and Bereavement* (Amityville, N.Y.: Baywood, 2003).

40. Allan Kellehear, *A Social History of Dying* (New York: Cambridge University Press, 2007), p. 232.

41. Grimes, *Deeply into the Bone,* p. 223.

42. Vernon Reynolds and Ralph Tanner, *The Social Ecology of Religion* (New York: Oxford University Press, 1995), p. 204. For an engaging account of how individuals sustained this concept of a good death despite distressing and unusual circumstances, see Drew Gilin Faust, "The Civil War Soldier and the Art of Dying," *Journal of Southern History* 67, no. 1 (2001): 3–38.

43. Robert Kastenbaum, *On Our Way: The Final Passage Through Life and Death* (Berkeley: University of California Press, 2004), pp. 131–135.

44. Stu Farber, Thomas Egnew, and Annalu Farber, "What is a Respectful Death?" in *Living with Dying: A Handbook for End-of-Life Care Practitioners,* eds. Joan Berzoff and Phyllis R. Silverman (New York: Columbia University Press, 2004), pp. 102–127; quote p. 103.

45. Avery Weisman, *On Dying and Denying: A Psychiatric Study of Terminality* (New York: Behavioral Publications, 1972), pp. 39–40; see also, by Weisman, *The Coping Capacity: On the Nature of Being Mortal* (New York: Human Sciences, 1984).

46. Edwin Shneidman, "Criteria for a Good Death," *Suicide and Life-Threatening Behavior* 37, no. 3 (2007): 245–247; quote p. 247.

47. This account of Lindbergh's death draws from various sources, including a description by Dr. Milton H. Howell, one of Lindbergh's physicians, reported by Ernest H. Rosenbaum, "The Doctor and the Cancer Patient," in *A Hospice Handbook,* ed. Michael P. Hamilton and Helen F. Reid (Grand Rapids, Mich.: Eerdmans, 1980), pp. 19–43.

48. Sandra L. Bertman, "Bearing the Unbearable: From Loss, the Gain," in *The Path Ahead,* ed. DeSpelder and Strickland, pp. 348–354.

49. See Barry K. Baines, *Ethical Wills: Putting Your Values on Paper* (New York: Perseus, 2002).

50. Doris M. Schoenhoff, *The Barefoot Expert: The Interface of Computerized Knowledge Systems and Indigenous Knowledge Systems* (Westport, Conn.: Greenwood, 1993), p. 100.

Credits and Sources

Prologue and Epilogue: Copyright © 1982 by David Gordon. Used by permission.

Page 17: "Buffalo Bill's" by E. E. Cummings reprinted from *Complete Poems: 1904–1962* by E. E. Cummings, edited by George J. Firmage. Copyright © 1923, 1951, 1991 by the Trustees for the E. E. Cummings Trust. Copyright © 1976 by George James Firmage. Reprinted by permission of Liveright Publishing Corporation and Grafton Books.

Page 25: Reprinted by permission of G. P. Putnam's Sons from *Cruel Shoes* by Steve Martin. Copyright © 1977, 1979 by Steve Martin.

Pages 32, 145, 187, 215, 253, 284, 323 & 549: The New Yorker Collection drawings from The Cartoon Bank. All Rights Reserved.

Page 35: From "Death in Cades Cove" by A. Crosby, in *Appalachia: When Yesterday Is Today,* ed. students at the University of Tennessee, Knoxville, 1965, pp. 1–3; quoted in *Death and Dying in Central Appalachia: Changing Attitudes and Practices* by James K. Crissman; University of Illinois Press, 1994.

Page 41: From the *Los Angeles Times* (December 21, 1990).

Page 42: "Grandmother, When Your Child Died," first published by the California State Poetry Society. Used by permission of Joan Neet George.

Pages 43, 139 & 281: Courtesy of Edward C. and Gail R. Johnson.

Pages 55, 306–307 & 369: Used with permission of Joe Allen, Brooks Allen, and Janice Laurent.

Page 59: From *The Interpretation of Dreams* by Sigmund Freud, trans. and ed. James Strachey; Basic Books, 1953.

Page 66: From *Journeys Through Bookland,* Vol. 1, ed. Charles H. Sylvester; Bellows-Reeve Company, Publishers, Chicago, 1922.

Page 67: "The Shroud" from *Grimms' Tales for Young and Old*, trans. Ralph Manheim. Reprinted by permission of Doubleday & Company, Inc.

Page 70: From *Trinity* by Leon Uris; Doubleday & Company, 1976.

Page 75 (bottom): Drawing by Dominic Horath created in Mrs. Bronwyn Luffman's classroom at Salesian Sisters School and provided by Linda DaValle. Reprinted by permission of Mary and Frank Horath.

Page 80: From *Winesburg, Ohio* by Sherwood Anderson; Viking Press, 1958.

Page 87: Illustration copyright © 1982 by Eric Mathes. Courtesy of Eric Mathes.

Page 87 (bottom): From *Death Customs* by E. Bendann; Knopf, 1930.

Page 88: "When Hare Heard of Death" excerpted from pp. 23–24 of *The Road of Life and Death: A Ritual Drama of the American Indians* by Paul Radin, Bollingen Series V. Copyright © 1945, renewed 1973, by Princeton University Press. Reprinted by permission of Princeton University Press and Doris Woodward Radin.

Page 89: Aesop's "Eros and Death" reworked by Steve Sanfield, from *Death: An Anthology of Ancient Texts, Songs, Prayers, and Stories,* ed. David Meltzer; North Point Press, 1984.

Page 92: From *Strange Facts About Death* by Webb Garrison. Copyright © 1978 by Webb Garrison. Used by permission of the publisher, Abingdon Press.

Page 103: Papago song by Juana Manwell. By permission of Smithsonian Institution Press from *Papago Music* by Frances Densmore. Bureau of American Ethnology Bulletin 90. Smithsonian Institution, Washington, D.C., 1929.

Page 103: Dakota song from *The Primal Mind: Vision and Reality in Indian America* by Jamake Highwater; Harper and Row, 1981.

Page 103: Warrior song (Omaha; Hethúska Society) from *The Omaha Tribe* by Alice Fletcher and Francis LaFlesche. Bureau of American Ethnology, 27th Report, Smithsonian Institution, 1911.

Page 106: Burial oration (Wintu) from "Wintu Ethnography" by Cora Du Bois, in *University of California Publications in American Archaeology and Ethnology* 36 (1935). Reprinted by permission of the University of California Press.

Page 110: From *Religions of Africa: A Pilgrimage into Traditional Religions* by Noel Q. King; Harper and Row, 1970.

Page 114: From *Chuang Tzu: Basic Writings,* trans. Burton Watson; Columbia University Press, 1964, p. 113.

Page 115: From *Japanese Death Poems,* comp. Yoel Hoffman; Charles E. Tuttle, Co., Inc., of Boston, Massachusetts and Tokyo, Japan, 1986. Reprinted by permission.

Page 118: From *The Four Seasons: Japanese Haiku Second Series,* trans. Peter Beilenson. Copyright © 1958 by The Peter Pauper Press.

Page 134: From *Murder in Space City: A Cultural Analysis of Houston Homicide Patterns* by Henry P. Lundsgaarde. Copyright © 1977 by Oxford University Press, Inc. Reprinted by permission.

Page 136: From *Custer Died for Your Sins: An Indian Manifesto* by Vine Deloria, Jr.; Macmillan, 1969.

Page 140: From *Care of the Dying* by Richard Lamerton; Technomic Publishing, 1976.

Page 144: From *Mystics, Magicians, and Medicine People: Tales of a Wanderer* by Doug Boyd. Copyright © 1989 by Doug Boyd. Reprinted by permission of Paragon House.

Page 147: Used by permission of Elizabeth Bradbury.

Page 169: From *Dying and Death: A Clinical Guide for Caregivers,* ed. David Barton. Copyright © 1977 by the Williams & Wilkins Company. Used with permission of the Williams & Wilkins Company and by courtesy of David Barton, M.D.

Page 171: From Ruth Walter and Brenda Gameau, "Australia: Its Land, Its People, Its Health Care System, and Unique Health Issues," *Social Work in Health Care* 18, nos. 3–4 (1993): 56–57.

Page 174: From *It's Not About the Bike: My Journey Back to Life* by Lance Armstrong; Putnam, 2000, p. 103.

Page 177: From the *Honolulu Star-Bulletin* (October 20, 1985).

Page 178: From "Medicine and the Question of Suffering" by Richard B. Gunderman, in *Second Opinion: Health, Faith, and Ethics* 14 (July 1990).

Page 182: Reprinted with permission of Simon & Schuster from *To Live Until We Say Good-Bye*, text by Elisabeth Kübler-Ross and photographs by Mal Warshaw. Copyright © 1978 by Ross Medical Associates, S.C., and Mal Warshaw. Photograph copyright © 1978 by Mal Warshaw.

Pages 189 & 400: From *You Don't Miss Your Water* by Cornelius Eady, © 1995 by Cornelius Eady; Henry Holt, 1995; first published in *Pequod*, no. 35 (1993), p. 114. Reprinted by permission of the author and Henry Holt and Co.

Pages 192 & 313: From *Passing On: The Social Organization of Dying* by David Sudnow; Prentice-Hall, 1967.

Page 196: From *A Gradual Awakening* by Stephen Levine. Copyright © 1979 by Stephen Levine. Reprinted by permission of Doubleday & Company, Inc.

Page 201: From "Tapping Human Potential" by Norman Cousins; *Second Opinion: Health, Faith, and Ethics* 14 (July 1990).

Page 210: Michael Schiavo with Michael Hirsh. *Terri: The Truth*. New York: Dutton, 2006, p. 321.

Page 225: From *You and Your Will* by Paul P. Ashley; New American Library, 1977.

Pages 229–230: Will of Tomas Antonio Yorba, trans. H. Noya [HM26653]. Reproduced by permission of The Huntington Library, San Marino, California.

Page 232: From *To a God Unknown* by John Steinbeck; R. O. Ballou, 1933.

Page 236 (top): From the *Honolulu Star-Bulletin & Advertiser* (August 26, 1990).

Page 236: From *News from Native California* 4 (August–October 1990).

Page 242: From "Of Dragons and Garden Peas: A Cancer Patient Talks to Doctors" by Alice Stewart Trillin; *New England Journal of Medicine* (March 19, 1981).

Page 243: From *Experiment Perilous* by Renée Fox; University of Pennsylvania Press, 1974.

Page 246: From "Scream of Consciousness" by Ruth Kramer Ziony; *Neworld* (1977).

Page 252: Used by permission of Joan J. Conn.

Pages 256–257: Adapted from *Living with Cancer* by Ernest H. Rosenbaum; The Mosby Medical Library series, The C. V. Mosby Company, St. Louis, 1982. Used with permission of the C. V. Mosby Company.

Page 261: From *There Is a Rainbow Behind Every Dark Cloud*, compiled by the Center for Attitudinal Healing; Celestial Arts, 1978. Used with permission of the Center for Attitudinal Healing.

Page 264: "But You Look So Good" from *No Pain, No Gain*. Reprinted by permission of Judith L. Ellsworth.

Page 266: From "Pain Management on Trial" by Maureen Cushing; *American Journal of Nursing* 7 (February 1992): 21–22.

Page 270: From *The Language of Cells: A Doctor and His Patients* by Spencer Nadler; Vintage, 2001, p. 16.

Page 279: From "Take Only As Directed" by Wayne Delk; *U.S. Gospel News* (September 1999). Reprinted by permission of the author.

Page 288: Used by permission of Edgar N. Jackson.

Pages 290 & 391: From *The Undertaking: Life Studies from the Dismal Trade* by Thomas Lynch; W. W. Norton, 1997, pp. 82–83, 51.

Page 291: Athenaeum of Philadelphia Collection.

Page 295: Michael Kubasak and William M. Lamers, Jr., *Traversing the Minefield—Best Practice: Reducing Risk in Funeral-Cremation Service* (Pasadena, Calif.: LMG Publishing, 2007), p. 233.

Page 296: From *The History of American Funeral Directing* by Robert W. Habenstein and William M. Lamers; Bulfin Printers, Milwaukee, 1962.

Pages 298–299: From *Working: People Talk About What They Do All Day and How They Feel About What They Do* by Studs Terkel. Copyright © 1972, 1974 by Studs Terkel. Reprinted by permission of Pantheon Books, a Division of Random House, Inc., and Wildwood House Ltd., London.

Page 304: From *The Papers of Benjamin Franklin*, Volume 1, ed. Leonard W. Labaree; Yale University Press, 1959.

Page 308: Courtesy of Fritz and Inge Roth, Pütz-Roth, Bergisch Gladbach, Germany.

Page 315: From *Living Your Dying* by Stanley Keleman; Random House, 1974.

Page 318 (left): From *Victorian Cemetery Art* by Edward V. Gillon, Jr.; Dover, 1972. Reproduced by permission of Edward V. Gillon, Jr.

Page 320: From *A Death in the Sanchez Family* by Oscar Lewis; Random House, 1969.

Page 331: From *Class: A View from Middle England* by Jilly Cooper; Methuen, 1979.

Page 333: From *Nana I Ke Kumu (Look to the Source)* by Mary Kawena Pukui et al.; Hui Hanai, Honolulu, 1972. Courtesy of Queen Lili'uokalani Children's Center, Lili'uokalani Trust.

Page 337: From *A Harvest Yet to Reap: A History of Prairie Women* by Linda Rasmussen et al.; Women's Press, Toronto, Ontario, 1976.

Page 338: From *Who Dies?* by Stephen Levine. Reprinted by permission of Doubleday & Company, Inc.

Page 345: Used by permission of The Centre for Living with Dying.

Page 348: "Anguish of Loss," "Sharing the Grief," and "Collapsing" from *The Anguish of Loss*, 2nd ed. Copyright © 1992 by Julie Fritsch and Sherokee Ilse. Photographs by Paul Schraub. Reprinted by permission of Wintergreen Press and Julie Fritsch.

Page 353: From "Death Education for Children and Youth" by Dan Leviton and Eileen C. Forman in *Journal of Clinical Child Psychology* (Summer 1974).

Page 361: From *The Accident* by Carol and Donald Carrick; Seabury, 1976.

Page 365: From *A Tropical Childhood and Other Poems* by Edward Lucie-Smith. Copyright © Oxford University Press, 1961. Reprinted by permission of Oxford University Press.

Page 366: Used with permission of Christine and Donovan Longaker.

Pages 371 & 415: *Never the Same: Coming to Terms with the Death of a Parent* by Donna Schuurman; St. Martin's Press, 2003.

Page 372: "Peanuts" reprinted by permission of United Features Syndicate, Inc.

Page 373: From *My Grandson Lew* by Charlotte Zolotow; Harper and Row, 1974.

Page 377: Caption to cartoon by E. H. Shepard, © Punch/Rothco. Reprinted by permission of Rothco Cartoons, Inc.

Pages 392 & 444: Used by permission of Maude Meehan.

Page 397: From "Psychological Aspects of Sudden Unexpected Death in Infants and Children" by Abraham B. Bergman; *Pediatric Clinics of North America* 21, no. 1 (February 1974).

Page 398: Transcribed by the authors from an inscription at the National Civil Rights Museum in Memphis, Tennessee.

Pages 404–405: Courtesy of Christine Longaker. All rights reserved.

Page 406: From *The Warming of Winter* by Maxine Dowd Jensen; Abingdon Press.

Page 407: From *Love and Profit: The Art of Caring Leadership* by James A. Autry; William Morrow, 1991. Reprinted by permission of HarperCollins Publishers, Inc.

Page 410: From *Chipping Bone: Collected Poems* by Maude Meehan; Embers Press, 1985. Courtesy of Maude Meehan.

Pages 420–421: Courtesy of Magaret Macro.

Page 423: From *The Goodbye Book* by Robert Ramsey and Randall Toye. Copyright © 1979 by Robert Ramsey. Reprinted by permission of Van Nostrand Reinhold Co.

Pages 424, 428, 431, 436, 443 & 447: Suicide notes courtesy of Edwin S. Shneidman.

Page 425: Edwin Arlington Robinson, "Richard Cory," in *The Children of the Night;* Charles Scribner's Sons, 1897. Copyright under the Berne Convention. Reprinted with the permission of Charles Scribner's Sons.

Page 427: Adapted from *Death, Society, and Human Experience,* 2nd ed., by Robert J. Kastenbaum; The C. V. Mosby Company, St. Louis, 1981. Used with permission of The C. V. Mosby Company and Robert J. Kastenbaum.

Page 430: Adapted from *Deaths of Man* by Edwin S. Shneidman; Quadrangle Books, 1973. Courtesy of Edwin S. Shneidman.

Page 438: From *The Savage God: A Study of Suicide* by A. Alvarez; Random House, 1972.

Page 441 "Resume" by Dorothy Parker, from *The Portable Dorothy Parker,* revised and enlarged edition, ed. Brendan Gill. Copyright 1926 by Dorothy Parker. Reprinted by permission of Viking Penguin, Inc., and from *The Collected Dorothy Parker* by permission of Gerald Duckworth, Ltd.

Page 448: From *A Hole in the World: An American Boyhood* by Richard Rhodes; Simon & Schuster, 1990.

Page 456: From "Groundfall" by William G. Higgins; *Sierra* (November–December 1979).

Page 460: From *American Blood* by John Nichols; Henry Holt, 1987.

Page 467: From *A Rumor of War* by Philip Caputo. Copyright © 1977 by Philip Caputo. Reprinted by permission of Holt, Rinehart and Winston, Publishers. Used by permission of Macmillan Press, Ltd., London and Basingstoke.

Page 469: Copyright © 1981 New York Times Company. Reprinted by permission. Courtesy of Harvey J. Schwartz, M.D.

Page 479: Courtesy of Carla Sofka, Ph.D., the New York State Museum History Collection, and the World Trade Center Relief Fund. Acquisition number 202.25.184 (cover). All rights reserved.

Page 481: From "The Flesh Made Word," in *Writing in an Era of Conflict: The National Book Week Lectures;* Library of Congress, 1990, p. 6.

Page 483: From "Back to a Future: One Man's AIDS Tale Shows How Quickly Epidemic Has Turned" by David Sanford; *Wall Street Journal* (November 8, 1996).

Page 488: From *Publishers Weekly* (October 25, 1985). Copyright © Bowker Magazine Group, Reed Publishing USA. Used by permission.

Page 495: Courtesy of Barbara J. Paul, Ph.D. All rights reserved.

Page 501: From "Go Down Death—a Funeral Sermon," in *God's Trombones* by James Weldon Johnson. Copyright 1927 by Viking Press, Inc. Copyright renewed 1955 by Grace Nail Johnson. Reprinted by Permission of Viking Penguin Inc.

Page 502: From *Religious Encounters with Death: Insights from the History and Anthropology of Religions,* ed. Frank E. Reynolds and Earle H. Waugh; Pennsylvania State University Press, 1977.

Page 503: From *Zen Mind, Beginner's Mind* by Shunryu Suzuki; 1970. Reprinted by permission of John Weatherhill, Inc.

Page 511: From *Selected Works of Miguel de Unamuno,* Bollingen Series LXXXV, Vol. 4: *The Tragic Sense of Life in Men and Nations,* trans. Anthony Kerrigan. Copyright © 1972 by Princeton University Press.

Page 512: Calvin and Hobbes © Watterson. Reprinted with permission of Universal Press Syndicate. All rights reserved.

Page 521: From *The Gospel at Colonus*. Music by Bob Telson, lyrics by Lee Breuer.

Page 533: From *At the Edge of the Body* by Erica Jong. Copyright © 1979 by Erica Mann Jong. Reprinted by permission of the poet.

Page 537: Quoted in Gay Becker, "Metaphors in Disrupted Lives: Infertility and Cultural Constructions of Continuity," *Medical Anthropology Quarterly* 8, no. 4 (1994): 383–410.

Pages 540–541: From *Big Winds, Glass Mornings, Shadows Cast by Stars: Poems 1972–80* by Morton Marcus; Jazz Press, Los Angeles, 1981. Copyright © by Morton Marcus. Used by permission of Morton Marcus.

Page 543: Reprinted by permission. Advertising agency: Robaire and Hogshead, Venice, Calif. Photography: Michael Ruppert Studios, Los Angeles, Calif.

Page 544: From *Harlem Book of the Dead* by James Van Der Zee; Morgan and Morgan, 1978.

Page 545: From "A Last Interview with the Legendary Actor" by Caroline Mangez; *Paris Match*. Published in *Hello!* No. 440 (11 January 1997), pp. 80–82.

Subject Index